A NATION OF IMMIGRANTS:
Women, Workers, and Communities in Canadian History, 1840s–1960s

This collection brings together a wide array of writings on Canadian immigrant history, including many highly regarded, influential essays. Though most of the chapters have been previously published, the editors have also commissioned original contributions on understudied topics in the field.

The readings highlight the social history of immigrants, their pre-migration traditions as well as migration strategies and Canadian experiences, their work and family worlds, and their political, cultural, and community lives. They explore the public display of ethno-religious rituals, race riots, and union protests; the quasi-private worlds of all-male boarding-houses and of female domestics toiling in isolated workplaces; and the intrusive power that government and even well-intentioned social reformers have wielded over immigrants deemed dangerous or otherwise in need of supervision.

Organized partly chronologically and largely by theme, the topical sections will offer students a glimpse into Canada's complex immigrant past. In order to facilitate classroom discussion, each section contains an introduction that contextualizes the readings and raises some questions for debate. *A Nation of Immigrants* will be useful both in specialized courses in Canadian immigration history and in courses on broader themes in Canadian history.

FRANCA IACOVETTA is a history professor at the University of Toronto. She is co-editor of *Gender Conflicts* and of two series, Themes in Canadian Social History and Studies in Gender and History. PAULA DRAPER, PhD, is a Toronto historian specializing in memory and the Holocaust. ROBERT VENTRESCA is a doctoral candidate in the Department of History at the University of Toronto.

EDITED BY FRANCA IACOVETTA, WITH
PAULA DRAPER AND ROBERT VENTRESCA

A Nation of Immigrants: Women, Workers, and Communities in Canadian History, 1840s–1960s

UNIVERSITY OF TORONTO PRESS
Toronto Buffalo London

© University of Toronto Press Incorporated 1998
Toronto Buffalo London

Printed in Canada

Reprinted 2002, 2007

ISBN 0-8020-0466-0 (cloth)
ISBN 0-8020-7482-0 (paper)

∞

Printed on acid-free paper

Canadian Cataloguing in Publication Data

Main entry under title:

A nation of immigrants : women, workers, and communities in Canadian
history, 1840s–1960s

ISBN 0-8020-0466-0 (bound)   ISBN 0-8020-7482-0 (pbk.)

1. Immigrants – Canada – History.   2. Multiculturalism – Canada.
I. Iacovetta, Franca, 1957– .   II. Draper, Paula Jean, 1953– .
III. Ventresca, Robert.

FC104.N38 1998   971   C97-931872-6
F1035.A1N38 1998

University of Toronto Press acknowledges the financial assistance to
its publishing program of the Canada Council for the Arts and the
Ontario Arts Council.

Contents

Preface

Immigrant History as Canadian History:
Perspectives on Class, Gender, Culture, and Conflict

Canadian historians have long been interested in issues related to immigration, immigration policy, and, more recently, multicultural politics. This is not surprising. After all, Canada, as many of us are fond of saying, is a nation of immigrants. Its history can be read in large part as the complex histories of succeeding waves of newcomers – women, men, and children – and the varied responses and developments that their arrival engendered. Canada's origins as a white settler society, it must be added, involved countless conflicts and negotiations between peoples of diverse racial and ethnic origins.[1] Few Canadians today would deny that Native-white relations and French-English relations, for example, remain subjects and issues critical to the ongoing process, and politics, of Canadian nation-building.

But while noting critical connections between immigration and nationalism, much earlier scholarship fundamentally ignored the immigrants themselves, or paid only perfunctory attention to their motives, strategies, and experiences. The newcomers' many and varied 'stories' were obscured or excluded by a meta-narrative of Canada that celebrated the 'story' of a country's rise from colony to nation. Unfortunately, the telling of that 'story' rarely examined the racial and gender biases that informed the process of nation-making, including the role played by immigration policy. Canadian nation-building was predicated upon the view that certain races were better suited for citizenship, and the history of Canada's immigration policy is revealing of the deplorable treatment of First Nations peoples, forced onto reserves to make way for white settlers, and of the constant vigilance taken by politicians and bureaucrats to exclude or restrict the admission of 'undesirables.' The case of South Asians, deemed racially inferior yet desired as a source of labour, illuminates the class, race, and gender components at play. Successive governments implemented a labour policy designed to recruit Asian men for low-paid, low-skilled jobs in industries considered important to domestic development. Though small numbers of South Asian women did come to Canada, prohibitions against them, like those against Chinese and Japanese women, actively discouraged the permanent settlement of entire families.[2]

During the past three decades, scholars trained in Canadian labour, family, women's, and immigrant/ethnic history, as well as race relations specialists from history and related disciplines, have produced a rich literature on immigrants and on the racial–ethnic dynamics that underscored such important historical developments and categories as class formation, industrial growth, women's work, reform movements, community, and politics. Often influenced by recent feminist and postcolonial scholarship on the processes of racialization, new and exciting research has also been undertaken on some of the more familiar themes in the field, including immigration admission policies, race and gender constructions of 'desirable' and 'undesirable' immigrants, and the relationship between nativism, racism, and nationalism.[3] While work on previously neglected or under-studied racial–ethnic individuals and groups should and does continue to take place, scholars have also begun to break out of the single-group or single-community approach characteristic of much historical writing about immigrants. Recent studies, for example, have dealt with the dynamics of multi-ethnic communities, the lives of immigrant women who did not reside within 'normal' family contexts, and immigrant and racial-minority women and men who came before the courts.[4]

With this book, we invite readers to consider Canada's remarkably diverse immigrants and their children, and the clashes and accommodations that have characterized relations between newcomers and hosts, between members of the dominant culture and the 'others.' Far from being relegated to the margins of Canadian history,[5] here the immigrants, particularly but not exclusively those from non-British backgrounds, occupy the centre stage. Many of the readings highlight the social history of immigrants, their pre-migration traditions, and their migration strategies and varied Canadian experiences; their work and family worlds; and their political, cultural, and community lives.

The authors explore the aggressively public display of ethno-religious rituals, race riots, and union protests, the quasi-private worlds of all-male boarding-houses and female domestics toiling in isolated workplaces, and the intrusive power that government and even well-intentioned social reformers wielded over immigrants deemed dangerous or otherwise in need of supervision. By the same token, the political dimensions of immigration and reception, including state surveillance of immigrants and the Canadianization efforts of social agencies and reformers, are not ignored. These topics are integral to the study of immigrant life and help us to see the complex class and power relations that shaped encounters between immigrants and Canadians.

This collection of essays examines immigrants and racial–ethnic relations in Canada from the mid-nineteenth century to the early post-1945 era. Organized partly chronologically and largely by theme, the topical sections offer students a glimpse into Canada's immigrant past and, we hope, encourage them to scrutinize the evidence and interpretations presented and to debate the still controversial issues surrounding immigration policy, reception, and Canadian-immigrant relations. We make no claim to be comprehensive with respect to the number of racial–ethnic groups or migration waves actually covered. Rather, our choices were guided by several criteria. First, the selected topics are meant to introduce students and non-specialists to a variety of approaches and methodologies in the field, the diversity of male and female experiences, the richness and complexity of immigrant working-class life, and the gendered and racialized character of immigration politics and policy. Readers will notice, for example, that several readings highlight women's and workers' lives and develop provocative analyses of how class, gender, and race/ethnicity have shaped both immigrant experiences and relations between immigrants and caretakers. Second, our selection was influenced by the analytical and thematic categories central to the study of immigrants in the Canadian past – namely, class, gender, culture, community, and conflict. Third, by choosing a wide variety of topics and perspectives in the field of immigrant and racial–ethnic history, we wanted to underscore the point that Canadian immigrant history is Canadian history.

We do not make that last claim lightly. We invite students to take up the challenge to rethink Canadian history from the vantage-point of the women and men who have so often occupied the disadvantaged position of 'foreigner,' 'dangerous foreigner,' 'other,' and 'hyphenated

Canadian.' And we ask that they do so fully aware of the fact that immigrant recruitment and settlement – as in the case of turn-of-the-century western Canada – often has been contingent on the displacement and subjugation of Canada's First Nations. We hope too that these readings will enable students to focus on important historical concepts through the lens of immigrant and minority lives. The essays dealing with immigrant women's work experiences and their participation in union campaigns and radical politics, for example, should act as a powerful reminder that the Canadian 'working woman' often wore a distinctly 'foreign' face. Similarly, the section on nineteenth-century African-American migration to Upper Canada suggests the diverse class, gender, and political backgrounds of the newcomers and highlights their varied settlement experiences. The articles dealing with work, militancy, and community politics should alert students to the fact that immigrant workers, though often dismissed by Canadian unionists and historians as strikebreakers or unreliable comrades, have contributed enormously to the rich history of radical culture and union-building in this country. Finally, the essays exploring the encounters between immigrants and reception activists offer some differing evaluations of the Canadian activists involved and highlight some of the ways in which immigrants sought to influence these relationships. We invite our readers to debate these and other questions and issues raised by the essays. In order to facilitate classroom discussion, each thematic section contains an introduction that situates the readings within a context and raises some questions for debate. We hope that this volume will be useful not only in specialized courses in Canadian immigration history but also in survey and social history courses on Canada.

We are pleased to report that in making choices for this volume we suffered from an embarrassment of riches. Space and financial limitations forced us to eliminate many fine essays. This is not to suggest, of course, that the history of Canada's immigrants is nearly complete. Indeed, we strongly encourage readers to ask tough questions about histories that have not yet been sufficiently explored and subjects that remain poorly studied. The continuing neglect of women in studies of immigrant community and political histories and the paucity of gendered analyses of immigrant family and community life are obvious and glaring absences, for example. In several instances, we commissioned our colleagues in the field to produce an original essay for this reader precisely because we felt it crucial to include material on certain understudied topics, such as the gendered identities of male sojourners. Still, our task of selection was made pleasantly difficult by the sheer volume, range, and quality of recent scholarship.

Many colleagues have contributed to this volume. We are especially grateful to those who wrote original pieces or waived their reprint fee in the interests of producing an affordable book. Laura Macleod, now of UBC Press, and Rob Ferguson of University of Toronto Press offered critical initial support, and Ian Radforth let us take advantage of his teaching and writing skills. At UTP, Gerry Hallowell provided ongoing support and offered cogent advice on how to turn an unwieldy (and massive) volume into a tightly structured reader, while Emily Andrew calmly and graciously took care of the final editorial and scheduling details. This volume has been too long in the making: we thank our contributors for their patience and hope that they will find it a useful teaching tool.

FRANCA IACOVETTA

NOTES

1 For a detailed review of the scholarly literature, see Franca Iacovetta, 'Manly Militants, Cohesive Communities, and Defiant Domestics: Writing about Immigrants in Canadian Historical Scholarship,' *Labour/Le Travail* 36 (Fall 1995); and *The Writing of Canadian Immigrant History* (Ottawa 1998).

2 For further discussion see, for example, Singh Bolaria and Peter Li, *Racial Oppression in Canada* 2d ed. (Toronto 1988); Hugh Johnston, *The Voyage of the Komagata Maru* (Vancouver 1989); Peter Li, *The Chinese in Canada* (Don Mills 1988); Roxanna Ng, 'Racism, Sexism and Nation-Building in Canada,' in Cameron Mcarthy and W. Critchlow, eds, *Race, Identity and Representation in Education* (New York 1993); Ena Dua, "The Hindu Woman's Question: Canadian Nation-Building and the Social Construction of Gender for South Asian-Canadian Women," (manuscript in review).

3 Influential theoretical works include Benedict Anderson, *Imagined Communities: Reflections on the Origin and Spread of Nationalism* (London 1991); Edward Said, *Orientalism* (New York 1978); and Gayatri Chakravorty Spivak, 'Subaltern Studies: Deconstructing Historiography,' in Donna Landry and Gerald McLean eds, *The Spivak Reader* (New York 1996). On Canada, see, for example, Karen Anderson, *Vancouver's Chinatown: Racial Discourses in Canada 1875–1980* (Montreal and Kingston 1991); Vic Satchewich, *Racism and the Incorporation of*

Foreign Labour: Farm Labour to Canada since 1945 (London 1991); the references cited in note 2; and the essays in Topic 5 of this volume.

4 For example, the essays by Carmela Patrias and Varpu Lindström in this volume; Marlene Epp, 'Women without Men: Post-World War Two Mennonite Women to Canada' (PhD thesis, University of Toronto 1996); Judith Fingard, *The Dark Side of Life in Victorian Halifax* (Porters Lake, NS, 1989); Karen Dubinsky and Franca Iacovetta, 'Murder, Womanly Virtue and Motherhood: The Case of Angelina Napolitano, 1911–22' *Canadian Historical Review* 72:4 (Dec. 1991); Constance Backhouse, 'White Female Help and Chinese-Canadian Employers: Race, Class, Gender, and Law in the Case of Yee Clun, 1924' *Canadian Ethnic Studies* 26:3 (1994)

5 Recent survey texts have also highlighted racial–ethnic diversity, including Margaret Conrad et al., *History of the Canadian Peoples* (Toronto 1993) and Alison Prentice et al., *Canadian Women: A History* (Toronto 1988; 1996).

A NATION OF IMMIGRANTS

TOPIC ONE
The Irish in Nineteenth-Century Canada: Class, Culture, and Conflict

The year 1847 looms large in the history of the Irish in Canada. In that year, over 100,000 Irish emigrants reached Canada's shores in search of refuge from the poverty, disease, and hunger caused by the Great Potato Famine. For many contemporaries, the famine-era migrants came to define the Irish presence in Canada – destitute, shiftless, diseased, and Catholic. In the eyes of many, these immigrants were the helpless victims of forces beyond their control, forced to choose between migration or death. They were individuals abruptly uprooted from their homeland and relegated to living in the overcrowded, unsanitary, violent urban ghettos of North America.

This image of the Irish immigrant lived past the mid-nineteenth century, making its way into historical accounts of North America's Irish. But is the image accurate? Recent scholarly studies suggest not entirely. Irish emigrants represented the single largest immigrant group in nineteenth-century Canada. Most of them came before the Great Potato Famine. Between 1825 and 1845, 450,000 Irish emigrants landed in British North America. Less than one-half of them were Catholic, and of the Protestant majority most were Anglican. The high cost and long duration of travelling to North America during the nineteenth century meant that emigration appealed mostly to those with sufficient resources to undertake the move. They came from the more economically secure commercial farming classes. They were individuals and members of families motivated not by poverty or hunger but by the fear that they stood to lose their economic status if they stayed in Ireland. Once in Canada, the majority of the Irish, Protestant or Catholic, settled in rural areas, taking up the work they knew best on some of the most productive agricultural land British North America had to offer.

Yet even this paints much too simple a picture of the Irish in Canada. As the readings suggest, religious, class and regional differences make it difficult to speak of a single, cohesive Irish-Canadian community in the nineteenth century. We cannot regard the Irish simply as British immigrants or 'English' Canadians whose integration into the host society was a foregone conclusion. They were often treated as a group, even as a race, apart.

Michael Cottrell's essay reveals an Irish Catholic community internally divided over the proper response to their marginal status in nineteenth-century Toronto – accommodation or protest – and a broader Irish community divided between Catholics and Protestants. Scott See finds similar divisions among the Irish in mid-nineteenth-century Saint John, with violent results. He describes the race riots that broke out between Protestant Orangemen and the Catholics. See also documents and seeks to account for the growing popularity of the Orange Order and anti-Irish views among Canadian-born New Brunswickers and non-Irish immigrants. As he observes, anti-Irish prejudice had many features but can be understood as a symbolic fight to protect Protestant jobs against job-hungry Irish Catholic famine victims in a time of economic hardship. It could also be profoundly racist in tone and character. Both essays end with the semblance of integration and order. In the case of Toronto's Irish Catholic immigrants, the St Patrick's Day parade served as a vehicle for internal cohesion and integration into the host society. In the case of Saint John, social peace came with the return of economic prosperity in the 1850s and the dramatic reduction in the number of Irish Catholic emigrants to the city after 1848.

How best do we characterize the Famine-era Irish? Did they occupy a position as a 'visible' minority in places like Saint John at mid-century? How important was their class position, or their poverty, in accounting for the cold reception they received? To date little has been written on Irish women, but how might anti-Irish activity and Orange-Green conflicts have affected men and women differently? Given the differential treatment accorded Irish Protestants and Irish Catholics by the host society and its institutions, is it fair to say that religion was akin to race and religious bigotry akin to racism in nineteenth-century Canada? How did the experiences of white, Anglo-Celtic, Irish immigrants differ from those of the 'unmeltable' ethnics of subsequent generations? In what ways were those experiences similar?

BIBLIOGRAPHY AND SUGGESTED READINGS

Akenson, Donald. *The Irish in Ontario: A Study in Rural History.* Toronto 1984.
Duncan, Kenneth. 'Irish Famine Immigration and the Social Structure of Canada West.' *Canadian Review of Sociology and Anthropology* (1965) 19–40.
Elliot, Bruce. *Irish Migrants in the Canadas: A New Approach.* Kingston 1988.
Houston, Cecil J., and William J. Smyth. *Irish Emigration and Canadian Settlement: Patterns, Links and Letters.* Toronto 1990.
– *The Sash Canada Wore: A Historical Geography of the Orange Order in Canada.* Toronto 1980.
Katz, Michael B. *The People of Hamilton, Canada West: Family and Class in a Mid-Nineteenth Century City.* Cambridge 1975.
Kealey, Gregory S. 'The Orange Order in Toronto: Religious Riot and the Working Class.' In Gregory S. Kealey and Peter Warrian, eds., *Essays in Canadian Working Class History.* Toronto 1976.
See, Scott. *Riots in New Brunswick: Orange Nativism and Social Violence in the 1840s.* Toronto 1993.

The Orange Order and Social Violence in Mid-Nineteenth Century Saint John

SCOTT W. SEE

In March 1839, the St. Patrick's, St. George's and St. Andrew's societies held a joint meeting in Saint John, New Brunswick. Delegates noted and condemned the Protestant-Catholic confrontations that appeared to be endemic in Boston and other unfortunate American cities. In a spirit of congeniality, they applauded themselves on the good fortune of living in a British colony free of such acrimonious religious strife. Generous toasts were proposed to young Queen Victoria, Lieutenant-Governor Sir John Harvey and, most effusively, to each other.[1] A short eight years later, after Saint John and neighbouring Portland had experienced a series of bloody riots involving Protestant Orangemen and Irish Catholics, those sentiments would be recalled with bitter irony. Sarcastic comparisons would then be drawn between Saint John and New Orleans, a tumultuous city with a reputation for collective violence.[2]

What happened to shatter the calm, and why would the toasts of 1839 turn out to be so farcical in the light of events during the 1840s? Why would Saint John and Portland, relatively stable communities that escaped major incidents of social violence prior to the 1840s, become ethno-religious battlegrounds involving natives and immigrants?[3] The growth of Irish Catholic immigration to Saint John and Portland before mid-century was accompanied by the expansion of the Orange Order as an institutionalized nativist response to those unwelcome settlers. Confrontations between the two groups began with relatively mild clashes in the late 1830s and culminated in the great riots of 1847 and 1849. The Ireland-based Orange Order, fueled originally by British garrison troops and Irish Protestant immigrants, attracted significant numbers of native New Brunswickers and non-Irish immigrants because of its anti-Catholic and racist appeal. By mid-century it functioned as a nativist organization whose purpose was to defend Protestantism and British institutions against Irish Catholic encroachment. The clashes in Saint John and Portland were not primarily the result of transplanted rivalries between Protestant and Catholic Irish immigrants, as was commonly believed by contemporaries and historians.[4] Rather they represented both a vehement rejection of certain immigrants because of cultural and religious differences, as well as a symbolic struggle to protect Protestant jobs against competitive Irish Catholic famine victims during a decade of severe economic hardship. Thus as Irish Catholic immigration burgeoned, so did the nativist Orange Order.

Saint John was New Brunswick's most populous city in the nineteenth century.[5] Settled by Loyalists in 1783 and incorporated two years later, it rapidly developed into the province's primary port for the export of staple timber goods and the import of manufactured products and foodstuffs. Lying in its northern shadow was the shipbuilding and mill town of Portland, now annexed into greater Saint John. The localities were connected by several roads, the busiest thoroughfare being a dilapidated bridge spanning an inlet on the harbour's northern extremity.[6] Both communities bustled in mid-century; along the narrow streets and wharves sailors rubbed shoulders with tradesmen, merchants, lawyers, mill workers and itinerant labourers. Moreover, both gained their economic focus almost entirely from New Brunswick's timber staple. Sawn lumber and deals were shipped to the British Isles from their wharves, while numerous sawmills and shipyards dotted their skylines.

In turn, the two communities received the bulk of New Brunswick's imports, including immigrants.[7]

Despite their industriousness, Saint John and Portland had fallen on hard times in the 1840s. Indeed all of New Brunswick suffered from the worst sustained downturn since the colony's inception.[8] Several factors accounted for this. First, the colony had enjoyed decades of timber trading privileges with Great Britain due to a combination of preference subsidies and high tariffs for foreign imports. But starting in 1842, England began to shift toward a policy of free trade in an attempt to curtail its soaring deficits. Subsequently it lowered or dropped its foreign tariffs and increased colonial duties. News of England's policy change created chaos in New Brunswick. Fears of the ramifications of such a move led to a decade of lost confidence among investors and merchants. Although New Brunswick would experience a slight recovery in 1844, due primarily to speculation that Great Britain's railroad fever would stimulate timber trade, the decade would be marked by high unemployment, rising commodity prices, commercial bankruptcies and legislative indebtedness.[9] Second, a worldwide glut of lumber and the overexploitation of New Brunswick's forests caused a severe export slump.[10] Later in the decade, moreover, hundreds of workers were displaced as the province's sawmills abandoned labour-intensive operations in favor of steam-driven machinery.[11] These factors combined to create a decade of commercial distress that crippled Saint John and Portland, especially in the years 1842–3 and 1845–9.

During this decade of financial hardship, these communities experienced dramatic changes in immigrant patterns. Prior to the 1840s, both were relatively homogeneous. Indeed New Brunswick in general consisted primarily of the descendants of Loyalists and pre-Revolutionary War New England settlers, plus a moderate number of immigrants from England, Scotland and Ireland. The only significant non-Protestants were the Acadians, who populated the northern and eastern shores and the north-western interior. Moreover, the immigrant flow throughout the 1830s was strikingly consistent; for example, 1832 and 1841 differed in raw totals by only twelve.[12] This fairly uniform influx brought an increasingly large proportion of Irish, a trend that would continue to mid-century.[13]

Prior to the 1840s the majority of these Irishmen came from the Protestant northern counties. Most were of Scots or English ancestry, reflecting the British colonization of Ireland. They were artisans and tenant farmers with modest savings who sought a better life within the British colonial system. Most importantly, they shared cultural and ideological views with the native New Brunswickers and other British emigrants they encountered. They adhered to Protestantism and supported the English constitutional and political domination of Ireland. Thus they made a relatively smooth transition to their new lives in New Brunswick.[14]

During the 1830s, however, emigrant patterns within Ireland shifted and thereby profoundly altered the demographic face of New Brunswick. The more skilled, financially-solvent Protestant Irishmen from northern counties began to be replaced by more destitute Catholics from Ireland's poorer southern and western regions. The percentage of Irish Catholics who emigrated to New Brunswick before 1840 was small, yet ever-increasing. The trickle became a flood as a tragic potato famine decimated Ireland's staple crop from 1845 to 1848.[15] New Brunswick's immigration rate would increase yearly by at least 150 per cent from 1843 until 1847, when the Irish famine tide finally crested. For the mid-1840s, the province would receive virtually all of its immigrants from the Catholic districts of Ireland. For example, of the 9,765 immigrants arriving in 1846, 99.4 per cent were from Ireland. Of these, 87 per cent landed in Saint John, clearly underscoring the city's role as the province's chief immigration port. The overwhelming majority were poor Catholic agricultural laborers.[16] New Brunswick in the 1840s, and particularly Saint John, was bombarded with thousands of non-Anglo-Saxon Protestants.

The influx of Irish Catholics dramatically altered the ethno-religious faces of Saint John and Portland. Although perhaps half of the incoming Irish used the ports as temporary shelters, earning enough at manual labour along the docks for the fare on a coastal vessel heading for the United States, thousands of the poor agrarian peasants remained.[17] By mid-century, more than one-third of the residents of Saint John and Portland were born in Ireland. More profoundly, Catholicism mushroomed. Roman Catholics were as large as any Protestant sect in Saint John by the mid-1840s; when the 1861 census appeared, the first to include religious data, both localities had populations almost 40 per cent Catholic. Since the Acadians, who were New Brunswick's only other substantial Catholic population, were practically nonexistent in the Saint John region during mid-century, Irishmen accounted almost entirely for the high Catholic population.[18]

The Irish Catholics settled primarily in two sections of Saint John and Portland. They clustered in overcrowded squalour in York Point, a district of northwestern Saint John bounded roughly by Union Street to the south, George's Street to the east, Portland Parish to the north and the bay to the west.[19] In Portland, they huddled in the busy wharf area on the harbour's northern shore. The two districts, connected by the 'Portland Bridge,' grew into twin ethno-religious ghettos during the 1840s.[20] They were so strongly identified with Irish Catholics that they would play host to virtually all of the major episodes of social violence between Orangemen and Irishmen during the decade.

The influx of thousands of Celtic Catholics into the Protestant Anglo-Saxon bastions of Saint John and Portland triggered a nativist response among the more entrenched residents. A useful paradigm for interpreting nativism was pioneered by John Higham, and while his model concerned American movements, it applies equally well for any nativist response. Higham's nativism was the 'intense opposition to an internal minority on the ground of its foreign ... connections,' or a 'defensive type of nationalism.' Though Higham cautioned that the word 'nativism,' of nineteenth-century derivation, has become pejorative, his definition provides a valuable intellectual foundation for analyzing people's reaction to immigrants.[21] In the context of the British colonial experience, nativists tended less to focus on place of birth than to draw inspiration from the virtues of Protestantism and British institutions.[22] From this perspective, the local response to incoming Irish Catholics may clearly be considered as a nativist response. Protestants who wanted to discourage Catholic settlement and block further immigration began to channel their energies into an institutionalized counter-offensive during the 1840s. As Saint John's *Loyalist and Conservative Advocate* explained:

the necessity ... for Protestant organization in this Province, arose not more from the many murderous attacks committed upon quiet and unoffending Protestants, by Catholic ruffians, than from the dreary prospect which the future presented. The facts were these: several thousands of immigrants were annually landing upon our shores; they were nearly all Catholics, nearly all ignorant and bigotted, nearly all paupers, many of them depraved ... What have we to expect but murder, rapine, and anarchy? Let us ask, then, should not Protestants unite? Should they not organize?[23]

The call to battle was dutifully answered by an organization with a history of responding to similar entreaties in Ireland and England – the Loyal Orange Order.

The Orange Order became the vanguard of nativism in mid-nineteenth century New Brunswick, yet the organization was neither new nor unique to the province. After a violent birth in Loughgall, Ireland in 1795, Orangeism quickly spread throughout Northern Ireland and England. As a fraternal body tracing its roots to a feuding tradition between Protestant and Catholic weavers and farmers, the Orange Order paid ideological homage to the British Crown and Protestantism. Group cohesion was provided by a system of secret rituals, an internal hierarchy of five 'degrees' and the public celebration of symbolic holidays such as July 12, the anniversary of the victory of the Prince of Orange (King William III) over Catholic King James II at the Battle of the Boyne in 1690. In the early nineteenth century the Orange Order was firmly entrenched in the British Isles, where its members fervently combated the growth of Jacobinism and Roman Catholicism.[24]

Given the ideological foundations of the Orange Order, it transferred well within the British Empire. British garrison troops who joined the organization while stationed in Ireland carried warrants for new lodges when they transferred to new posts. Irish Protestant immigrants who settled in England and British North America also brought Orange warrants as part of their 'cultural baggage.' By the early nineteenth century, British regulars in Halifax and Montreal were holding formal Orange meetings. Lodges mushroomed as they found support among Loyalists and the swelling ranks of Irish Protestant immigrants. In 1830 a Grand Orange Lodge, headquartered in Upper Canada, obtained permission from Ireland to issue lodge warrants for all of British North America except New Brunswick.[25]

New Brunswick's organized lodges, dating from the turn of the century, clearly reflected a similar pattern of garrison troop and Irish immigrant conveyance. The earliest known lodge, formed among soldiers of the 74th Regiment in Saint John, met regularly by 1818. Six years later they obtained an official Irish warrant.[26] After several abortive efforts to establish civilian lodges in the mid-1820s, Orangeism became rooted among Saint John's Irish Protestants in 1831. Initial growth was sluggish. Fifteen local, or 'primary' lodges existed by 1838, representing ten in Saint John and Portland. Membership tended to be small, with some lodges having only a handful of regular participants. Even the establishment of a provincial Grand Orange Lodge in 1837–8, under the mastership of James McNichol, failed to generate widespread growth and attract significant numbers. With the advent of the 1840s New Brunswick's Orange Lodges, particularly in Saint John and Portland, were

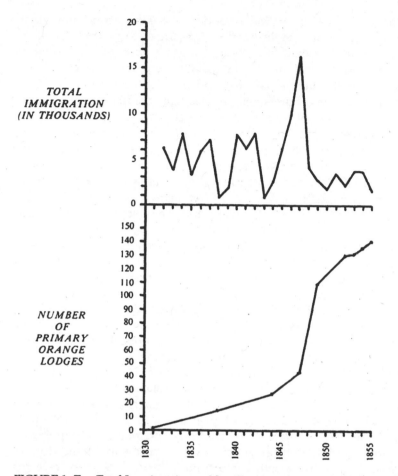

FIGURE 1: *Top*: Total Immigration to New Brunswick, 1832–1855 (in thousands of people); Source: Immigration Returns, New Brunswick Blue Books, 1832–55. Public Archives of Canada; 'Report on Trade and Navigation,' *Journal of the New Brunswick House of Assembly*, 1866. *Bottom*: Primary Orange Lodges in New Brunswick, 1832–1855; Source: *Minutes of the Grand Orange Lodge of New Brunswick*, 1846–55; Steele, *History of the Orange Lodges of New Brunswick*.

staffed primarily by small numbers of recent Irish Protestant immigrants and British troops.[27]

A catalyst appeared in the 1840s to spur growth in the fledgling organization. The rising tide of famine immigration brought concerned

Protestants to the organization's doorstep, seeking action and viable solutions to the Irish Catholic 'menace.' By the close of 1844, when the transition from Protestant to Catholic emigrant was well underway in Ireland, New Brunswick had 27 lodges. Of these, ten were less than a year old. As Irish Catholics arrived and filtered throughout the province, Orange Lodges burgeoned to lead the counter-offensive. But-tressed by a network of primary, county, district and provincial lodges, Orangeism swept up the St. John River Valley hard on the heels of the Catholic immigrants. Mid-century found 123 primary lodges across the province, representing a five year growth of 455 per cent.[28] Together with its smaller Nova Scotia affiliates, New Brunswick's Orange Order boasted an estimated 10,000 members. Yet despite its impressive expan-sion, the Orange Order's seat of power and membership base remained firmly rooted in Saint John and Portland.[29]

The traditional membership pools did not account for the explosive growth of Orangeism. Irish Protestant immigration dropped dramati-cally during the 1840s, becoming negligible by mid-century. Moreover, Britain reduced its garrison troops because of budgetary constraints. What, then, explained the Orange Order's meteoric rise? How did the organization broaden its attraction to ensure its survival? The answers were to be found in the Order's ideological appeal to native New Brunswickers and non-Irish Protestant immigrants.

Evidence of Orange membership in the 1840s clearly proved the ini-tiates came from various cultural groups and classes. While the organi-zation may have been rooted among British garrison troops and Irish Protestant settlers, it succeeded only because it found a willing supply of Loyalist and New England descendants and non-Irish immigrants who shared its philosophical tenets. In other words, to tell the story of Orangeism in mid-nineteenth century New Brunswick is to trace the growth of an indigenous social movement. At least half of all identified Orangemen in mid-century were born in New Brunswick. They came from all walks of life, including legislators, barristers, magistrates, doc-tors, ministers, farmers, artisans and unskilled labourers. Motivated primarily by locally-defined problems and prejudices, many New Brunswick natives and immigrants found the Orange Order both philo-sophically and socially attractive.[30]

In the Saint John region, some natives participated in Orange activi-ties when lodges first appeared in the early nineteenth century. Indeed, several of the nascent city lodges drew their membership exclusively from transplanted New Englanders and Loyalists from America's mid-

Atlantic and southern regions.[31] When the provincial Grand Orange Lodge organized in 1844, prestigious native Saint John residents were there. They included W.H. Needham, a justice of the peace, H. Boyd Kinnear, a lawyer, and Thomas W. Peters, Jr., a city official. Each would assume an Orange leadership role at some point in his career.[32] During the period of intensified social violence, from 1845–9, Saint John and Portland residents embraced the Orange Order because of its campaign to protect Protestantism and British hegemony against the bewildering and oftentimes frightening effects of Irish Catholic immigration.[33] For example, Portland's Wellington Lodge welcomed its largest initiate group since its inception in the meeting following the great Orange-Catholic riot of 12 July 1849.[34]

Membership lists also illuminated the Orange Order's effective appeal to native-born in Saint John and Portland. Data gleaned from official lodge returns, trial transcripts, Orange histories and newspapers yielded the names of 84 active Orange members in the late 1840s. When matched against the available 1851 manuscript census returns from Saint John County, they showed significant native involvement in Orangeism: 56 per cent were not Irish-born, including 43 per cent native and 13 per cent other Protestant immigrants.[35] Moreover, the entrenchment of Irish Protestants in the Orange Order was evident because 80 per cent of them had emigrated to New Brunswick prior to 1840. The occupational range already noted for provincial Orangemen was corroborated by the Saint John evidence, though a higher proportion of members could be classified as skilled or unskilled labourers. Finally, the portrait of Saint John Orangemen revealed a youthful organization: almost three-quarters of those traced were less than 40 years old in 1851.[36] Clearly, the Orange Order in Saint John and Portland in mid-century represented a mixture of native-born and Protestant immigrants.

The essential ideological glue of the Orange Order was unquestioning loyalty to the Crown and an emphatic rejection of Roman Catholicism. With these concepts codified in the initiation oaths, Orangeism guaranteed itself a philosophical continuum that transcended the divergent social appeals and emphases of individual primary lodges.[37] In New Brunswick, lodges exercised a great deal of independence. Several accepted only temperate men; others attracted members by offering burial insurance plans; still more touted their commitment to charitable endeavours.[38] New Brunswick's Orange Lodges had disparate social and functional appeals, and many men gathered under the symbolic Orange banner. Except in the rare case where evidence exists, individual motives for joining the organization are a matter for speculation. Nevertheless, the philosophies and goals of Orangemen may be justifiably construed from organizational rhetoric and collective behavior.

Orange rhetoric in the 1840s strikingly resembled the propaganda campaigns carried out by American and British nativists during the same period. New Brunswick Orangemen charted an elaborate counter-offensive to combat Irish Catholic immigration and permanent settlement. The organization's views were stated succinctly in two documents from the late 1840s. In a welcoming address to Lieutenant-Governor Edmund Head, Orangemen explained:

Our chief objects are the union of Protestants of the several denominations, to counteract the encroachments of all men, sects or parties, who may at any time attempt the subversion of the Constitution, or the severance of these Colonies from the British Empire; to bind Protestants to the strict observance of the Laws, and to strengthen the bonds of the local authorities, by the knowledge that there is ever a band of loyal men ready in case of emergency, to obey their commands, and assist them in the maintenance of order.[39]

Thomas Hill, the zealous Orange editor of the *Loyalist and Conservative Advocate*, was more direct in this appraisal of the fraternity:

Orangeism had its origins in the *necessity* of the case; it has spread in this Province, also from *necessity*, for had not the country been infested with gangs of lawless ruffians, whose numerous riots, and murderous deeds compelled Protestants to organize for mutual defence, Orangeism would have been scarcely known. And whenever the *Cause* shall disappear, Orangeism may retrograde.[40]

Underscored in the above quotations was the unique philosophical framework which Orangemen operated within: unquestioning loyalty, exclusive Protestantism and the threat to carry out their policies with vigilante force.

New Brunswick's Orangemen, in an effort to check the Irish Catholic invasion, fought a rhetorical battle on several fronts. The overarching goal was to maintain the colony as a Protestant and British bulwark against Catholicism. The Orange Order directly appealed to all Protestants who feared that the ethno-religious supremacy enjoyed by Anglo-Saxons would be permanently undermined or destroyed by the swelling numbers of Celtic Irishmen. Orangemen even advocated the repeal of legislation giving Catholics the franchise and the right to serve in the legislature.[41]

Anti-Catholic diatribes grew in part from a Papal conspiracy myth that enjoyed a North American vogue in the mid-nineteenth century.[42] New Brunswick's Orangemen claimed the famine immigration was but a skirmish in a global battle, masterminded in the Vatican, to expunge Protestantism from the earth. A Saint John editor who supported Orangeism warned that 'A great, perhaps a final, conflict is at hand between Protestant Truth and Popery leagued with Infidelity.'[43] Orangemen embarked on a propaganda campaign to educate Protestants about the Pope's despotic control over Catholics – in church, the home, the workplace and on the hustings. Only by removing the insidious network of priests, Orangemen argued, could papal control over the 'uncivilized minds' of the Irish Catholics in New Brunswick be broken.[44]

Another vital weapon in the Orangemen's arsenal rested upon the assumption that the Celtic Irish were inherently an unruly and violent race. The stereotype had a measure of truth. As a subjugated people under English rule, Irish Catholics often resorted to disruptive tactics to achieve their goals.[45] As poor Irish Catholics crowded into squalid quarters in York Point and Portland, Orangemen bandied stereotypes of the Celtic propensity for strong drink and villainy. After all, they argued, 'no one can deny that the lower orders of the Roman Catholic Irish are a quarrelsome, headstrong, turbulent, fierce, vindictive people.'[46] Petty crime did increase dramatically as Saint John and Portland absorbed thousands of the famine immigrants, but it is more plausible to suggest that factors such as overcrowding, poverty and hunger were more responsible for creating a crucible for crime than were cultural idiosyncrasies.[47] Tragically, Orangemen painted all Catholics with the same nativist brush. Though even the most scurrilous propagandists recognized that not all immigrants participated in this orgy of crime, they nevertheless called for Orange vigilantism in York Point and Portland. Moreover, they suggested dispersing the immigrants among loyal Protestants. The theory was that such a dilution would facilitate social control and the assimilation of those immigrants who chose to remain. For the Orangemen of mid-nineteenth century Saint John, every Celtic Irishman was a potential criminal.[48]

New Brunswick's Orange rhetoric was also laced with racism, mirroring the contemporary British philosophy of Anglo-Saxon superiority.[49] Ethnicity was mingled with class as Orangemen railed against the 'ignorant Mickie' hordes who formed a substandard 'class of people.' The destitution of famine immigrants as they disembarked in Saint John, and the squalor of their ghettos in York Point and Portland, appeared to corroborate Orange assertions of Celtic inferiority. Here was positive proof that the Protestant Anglo-Saxon must remain firmly in legislative and judicial control in order to assure the colony's peaceful survival.[50] The more zealous Orange propagandists, believing that assimilation was a bankrupt concept, called for the deportation of all Celtic Catholics. One might as well, they argued, 'attempt to change the colour of the Leopard's spots, or to "wash the Ethiope white," as to attempt to tame and civilize the wild, turbulent, irritable, savage, treacherous and hardened natives of the Cities and Mountains of Connaught and Munster.'[51] The editors of the *Loyalist and Conservative Advocate*, the *Weekly Chronicle* and the *Christian Visitor*, all either Orange members or openly sympathetic to the organization's policies, regularly exposed their readers to racist editorials, Irish jokes, and vignettes pointing out the sub-human proclivities of the Celtic immigrant. Through their efforts, the argument of Anglo-Saxon racial superiority fell convincingly upon the ears of native Protestants who feared the demise of peace, order and good government in New Brunswick.[52]

Yet another focal point for Orange propagandists was the tangible threat that the poor Irish Catholic immigrants represented a formidable and willing pool of cheap laborers.[53] The famine victims, thrust into the severely depressed economy of the 1840s, were greeted as pariahs by Saint John's working classes. The destitute Irish Catholics eagerly accepted the most demanding and lowest paying jobs, which in a healthy economic environment would be vacant. But during the 'hungry forties,' unemployed native laborers were forced to compete with the immigrants for these undesirable jobs.[54] In an attempt to combat the debilitating effects of immigrant competition, such as a general lowering of wage scales, Orangemen sounded the call for economic segregation. They suggested that Protestant merchants and employers should hire and do business only with coreligionists. By ostracizing Roman Catholic laborers, Orangemen hoped to persuade entrenched immigrants to leave and to discourage incoming Catholics from settling in the community.[55]

While Saint John's Orangemen fought a rigorous rhetorical battle, perhaps their most effective campaigns involved physical engagements with Irish Catholics. Indeed, collective social violence grew in direct proportion to the rising levels of famine immigration and Orange membership during the 1840s. In the aftermath of each confrontation,

Orangemen enjoyed even greater Protestant support from natives and immigrants alike. The number of local lodges and engorged memberships at mid-century were tributes to the Orange Order's successful appeal. The persuasive rhetorical campaigns may have won converts, but the bloody riots gave concerned Protestants tangible 'proof' of the Irish Catholics' uncivilized behavior.

The first clearly identifiable incident of collective violence between Orangemen and Catholics in Saint John occurred on 12 July 1837. Small Catholic crowds forced entry into two merchants' stores and attempted to burn them.[56] In later years such incendiarism was eclipsed by more traditional rioting. The spring of 1841 found Irish Catholics clashing with Orangemen in the streets of Saint John. At issue was an Orange commemorative arch erected to celebrate the visit of a dignitary.[57] Catholics reacted similarly the following year on 12 July, when a crowd of several hundred gathered outside a Saint John home flying the Union Jack festooned with orange ribbons. Their jeers and taunts brought Orange reinforcements from across the city; by evening a general riot prompted Mayor William Black to swear in 150 special constables. The all-Protestant volunteer squad arrested several Irish Catholics, most of whom were ultimately found guilty of rioting.[58] Although these early disturbances paled when compared to subsequent riots, they established important patterns that would be repeated throughout the decade. While Irish Catholics would be deservedly or incorrectly labelled the aggressors, the Orangemen would invariably be perceived as the defenders of Saint John's Protestant and Loyalist traditions. Moreover, an exclusively Protestant constabulary and judiciary would consistently arrest and convict only Irish Catholics for disturbing the peace.

The next three years, coinciding with the first substantial waves of Irish Catholic immigrants and the attendant surge of Orangeism, brought several important episodes of social violence. The Twelfth of July in 1843 witnessed clashes between religious crowds in Saint John and Portland, though an official Orange procession was not held.[59] A more serious incident occurred in March of the following year. Squire Manks, Worshipful Master of the recently established Wellington Orange Lodge, shot and mortally wounded a Catholic Irishman during a dispute at York Point. Angry residents poured into the streets and demanded revenge. Rather than being arrested, however, Manks was placed into protective custody and expeditiously exonerated by an examining board of city magistrates. The verdict was self-defence.[60] The year closed with sporadic riots from Christmas until after New Year's.

Crowds of up to 300 Irish Catholics roamed throughout York Point and Portland's wharf district, attacking Orangemen and their property. The Orangemen enthusiastically reciprocated. Two companies of British regulars finally succeeded in quashing the disturbances, but not before one Catholic had died and dozens more from both sides had received serious injuries. Although uninvolved residents bemoaned the apparent state of anarchy, the rioting was neither indiscriminate nor uncontrolled. Catholics and Orangemen carefully picked fights only with 'certain ... obnoxious individuals.'[61]

The tensions of the winter of 1844–5 culminated in a St. Patrick's Day riot that eclipsed all earlier Orange-Catholic conflicts in its violence. On 17 March 1845, Portland Orangemen fired without provocation upon a group of Catholic revellers. The incident touched off a wave of reprisals. By nightfall general rioting between Orangemen and Irish Catholics had spread throughout the wharf district and York Point. The fighting was most intense at the foot of Fort Howe Hill in Portland.[62] The rioters dispersed when British troops positioned an artillery piece near Portland's wharves. The ploy was at best symbolic, for the concentrated fighting abated in the evening when the well-armed Orangemen gained a measure of control over the streets. The riot killed at least one Catholic, although several bodies were probably secreted away from private burials. The tally of wounded was correspondingly high, with dozens of combatants being hurt seriously enough to warrant medical attention.[63] The examinations and trials in the riot's aftermath followed the patterns established in 1842. Although authorities arrested several Orangemen, including two suspected of murder, Saint John's all-Protestant Grand Jury preemptively threw out their bills before the cases could be brought to trial. Instead the jury returned bills for several Irish Catholic rioters, two of whom were ultimately found guilty and sentenced. The swift vindication of Orangemen by the Grand Jury, despite an abundance of damaging testimony, illustrated the reluctance of Protestant authorities to condemn Orange violence and their continuing propensity to convict only Irish Catholics.[64]

Saint John and Portland escaped collective social violence for the next two years, but the hiatus did nothing to diminish enmity or foster peaceful linkages between Orangemen and Irish Catholics. The latter abstained from public displays on the St. Patrick's Days of 1846 and 1847. Orangemen quietly observed July 12 in their lodges in 1845; the following year they took a steamer to Gagetown for a procession with their brethren from Queens, Kings and York Counties.[65] For 1847's Twelfth of July, when famine immigration was reaching its zenith, city

Orangemen invited neighbouring brethren and staged the largest procession since the organization's inception. On 14 July a Saint John newspaper trumpeted the now familiar requiem for the Orange holiday: 'Dreadful Riot! The Disaffected District [York Point] Again in Arms – Shots Fired – Several Persons Dreadfully Wounded – the Military Called Out.'[66] The two-year truce had yielded only larger numbers of Catholic immigrants and nativist Orangemen, and a more sophisticated network for the combatants in both groups to utilize in battle.

July 12 started quietly enough in 1847, but as Saint John's and Portland's Orangemen began to make their way to their lodges, crowds of wary Irish Catholics spilled into the streets. One of the larger Portland lodges, probably Wellington, entertained the amateur band from the local Mechanic's Institute. All of the band members were Orangemen. In the early evening, the group led a procession of Orangemen and onlookers through the streets of Portland, across the bridge, and into the heart of the Roman Catholic ghetto at York Point.[67] The tunes they played, like most Orange favourites, were clearly offensive to Irish Catholics.[68] At the foot of Dock Street, the crowd attacked the procession with sticks and bricks, smashing many of the band's instruments and forcing the revellers to flee back across the Portland Bridge. Gathering reinforcements and firearms from their lodges and homes, the undaunted Orangemen quickly returned to their enemy's stronghold.[69]

The Irish Catholic crowd, which by now had grown to several hundred, also made use of the respite and collected weapons in the event of a reappearance of the humiliated band members and Orangemen. The buttressed Orange legions did attempt to revive the procession and music when they reached York Point. A battle was inevitable. Volleys of shots from both parties shattered the summer air, leaving scores of wounded lying in the streets along the procession route. The melee continued throughout the evening, with most of the bloodshed occurring along Dock and Mill Streets and the bridge. At midnight detachments of the 33rd Regiment, dispatched at the mayor's request, converged upon York Point only to find the streets deserted. Rather than chance an engagement with the military, both sides ceased hostilities.[70] Aided by the darkness, the Irish Catholics escaped capture and returned to their homes. The constabulary failed to make any arrests after the riot, and the grand jury issued no warrants.[71]

Assessment of the riot's severity is hampered due to the secretive removal of the dead and wounded by both parties, particularly the Irish Catholics. Official tallies included only one Catholic killed and several seriously wounded, but everyone involved knew that many had died during the encounter.[72] The significance of the conflict, however, emerged unclouded in the following months. Both sides were organized, well-stocked with weapons and clearly prepared to kill for their beliefs. Catholics had gathered hours before the Orange procession had entered York Point; they were motivated by desire to 'defend' their 'territory.' Orangemen consciously provoked the enemy by twice marching in procession and playing obnoxious songs through the most Catholic district of Saint John. An undeniable linkage also emerged between the Orange Order and the Mechanic's Institute, which was symbolic of the nativist attraction that Orangeism had to the economically beleaguered Protestant workers facing stiff competition from famine immigrants. Finally, the riot underscored the Orange belief in vigilante justice. The procession's return to York Point represented a 'heroic' action to remove a dangerous Catholic 'mob' from Saint John's thoroughfares. According to Orange sympathizers, the anaemic state of the city's constabulary justified the vigilantism.[73] In retrospect, the riot of 1847 illuminated the entrenchment of social violence as a perennial method of interaction between Orangemen and Catholics.[74]

A year of bloody skirmishes was the riot's true legacy, for neither side had emerged with a clearcut victory on the Twelfth. A wave of assaults and murders swept Saint John and Portland during the weeks that followed; Orange and Catholic vengeance was the motive for all of them.[75] A sensational series of witness examinations after the murder of a suspected Orangeman in September brought religious antipathy to a fever pitch. Dozens of testimonials exposed paramilitary networks operated by militant Orangemen and Catholics. Personal revenge on a small scale appeared to be the favourite tactic of the weaker and outnumbered Catholics. Orangemen, enjoying the support of a Protestant majority, preferred a collective vigilantism whereby they dispensed extralegal justice while acting as an unofficial watchdog of the Irish lower orders.[76] By the year's end, it was apparent that the Orange-Catholic struggle had not diminished. Both sides habitually armed themselves if they ventured into unfriendly districts; each tried desperately to identify its most virulent enemies, and in many cases, both were prepared to kill for their causes.

The religious conflict of the 1840s peaked two years later in Saint John's worst riot of the nineteenth century. The city was quiet in 1848, much as it had been in 1846, because local Orangemen travelled to Fredericton to participate in a massive demonstration.[77] But as the Twelfth approached in 1849, Saint John's Orangemen advertised for the first time their plans for hosting provincial brethren and sponsoring an elaborate procession.[78] Motivated by vivid memories of the inconclusive 1847 conflict, Orangemen and Irish Catholics grimly prepared themselves for battle. On the eve of the holiday, Mayor Robert D. Wilmot met with local Orange officials and asked them to voluntarily abandon their plans to march. But the Orangemen, well-versed on their rights, rejected the suggestion because no provincial statute gave civilian officials the authority to ban public processions.[79] The march, they insisted, would proceed as planned.

With a measure of fatalism, Saint John prepared for the occasion. While Orangemen from Carleton, York, Kings and Queens Counties were boarding steamers and carriages for Saint John, Irish Catholics were buying arms and ammunition. Shopkeepers along Prince William Street, King Street and Market Square boarded their windows and decided to declare the day a business holiday.[80] Early on the morning of the Twelfth, hundreds of Orangemen from Saint John and Portland collected at Nethery's Hotel on Church Street and marched to a nearby wharf to greet the Carleton ferry. Among the disembarking brethren was Joseph Corum, the Senior Deputy Grand Master of the New Brunswick Grand Lodge. As the procession leader, Corum would have the honour of representing King William by riding a white horse. The Orangemen came heavily armed with pistols, muskets and sabres. After assuming a military file, they began the march to the Portland suburb of Indiantown where they would meet the steamer bringing reinforcements from the northern counties. Their planned route would take them through both Irish Catholic bastions – York Point and Portland's wharf district.[81]

Upon reaching York Point they encountered a large pine arch, symbolically green, which spanned the foot of Mill Street. Several hundred jeering Irish Catholics clustered near the arch's supporting poles; they implored the Orangemen to continue. Outnumbered for the moment, the Orangemen accepted the humiliation and dipped their banners as they passed under the arch. While a few stones were hurled at the Orangemen, and they responded with warning shots, no fighting broke out.[82] Without further incident, the procession reached Indiantown where it gratefully welcomed scores of reinforcements. Among the newcomers was another pivotal Orange leader. George Anderson, a Presbyterian grocer and primary lodge master, was a veteran of several disturbances in his home town of Fredericton. Anderson, bedecked with a sword that indicated his rank, assumed a position next to Corum at the column's head. The procession now numbered approximately 600 people. The men were heavily armed, the majority carrying muskets on shoulder straps. A few clutched axes that would be used to destroy the green bough when they returned to York Point. Finally, a wagon filled with weapons and supplies took up a station at the rear of the procession. As the Orangemen made their way back to York Point, Portland inhabitants observed that the procession resembled a confident army about to engage in battle.[83]

In the meantime, authorities attempted to alleviate the growing tensions with three separate plans, all of which would ultimately fail to prevent a conflict. Mayor Wilmot's first scheme was to defuse the powder keg by removing the pine arch and dispersing the Catholic crowd in York Point. Wilmot, accompanied by a magistrate and a constable, was physically rebuffed in this endeavour by a cohesive, territorially-minded crowd that chanted 'Stay off our ground!' He then dispatched Jacob Allan, the Portland police magistrate, to intercept the Orangemen before they reached York Point.[84] Allan asked Corum and Anderson to bypass the Catholic district by using the longer Valley Road on their approach to Saint John. After conferring with their followers, the leaders rejected Allan's suggestion. Their men had suffered humiliation during the morning's passage under the Catholic arch; now they insisted on 'Death or Victory.'[85] Wilmot borrowed the third and final plan from Saint John's history of dealing with riots. At his request, 60 British soldiers stationed themselves in Market Square to prevent general rioting. While the choice of location would do nothing to prevent a conflict, for Market Square lay to the south of York Point and the Orangemen would enter from the north over the Portland Bridge, it would serve to contain the battle to the Catholic ghetto. The detachment's failure to position itself between the advancing Orangemen and the offensive arch, when it had ample time to do so, raised questions about the sincerity of the authorities' attempts to prevent bloodshed.[86]

General rioting broke out along Mill Street before the procession arrived at the bough. The Catholic crowd now numbered approximately 500, and like the Orangemen, many had armed themselves with muskets. Reports of who fired the first shots varied, but roofers working on a Mill Street building agreed that Orangemmen opened fire after being met with a volley of stones and brickbats.[87] Several Catholics lay wounded or dying after the barrage, and then their guns answered the Orangemen's. A heated battle ensued. Men and women along Mill Street threw anything they could at the better-armed Orange contingent. Some engaged in fistfights with individuals that they were able to pull from the Orange ranks. Corum struggled to free himself after a handful of Irishmen grabbed his horse's tether. A dozen Catholics captured the wagon filled with arms and gave its driver a sound thrashing. Hundreds of shots were fired, and at least 12 combatants lost their lives. The Irish Catholics suffered most of the casualties. After several minutes of furious fighting, the Orangemen emerged from York Point. As they headed for the safety of the troops, their procession was still intact.[88]

The British garrison, after remaining stationary in Market Square throughout the heat of the battle, went into action as soon as the Orangemen left the Irish Catholic ghetto. Without firing a shot, the soldiers marched past the procession and positioned themselves on Dock Street to seal off the Catholic district. This manoeuvre effectively doused what remained of the conflict.[89] It also gave the Orangemen the opportunity to continue their procession unmolested, for any Catholics wishing to leave York Point in pursuit would have to contend first with the soldiers. The Orangemen, heady with their successful assault on the enemy's territory, proceeded through Market and King Squares and made a circle through the city's center. Only when they entered Market Square again, with the intention of parading through York Point for the third time, were the troops commanded to impede their progress. Being satisfied with their efforts, the Orangemen agreed to disband. With the Orange threat finally removed, the Irish Catholics waiting in York Point also dispersed. The great Saint John riot of 1849 was over.[90]

The riot's judicial aftermath followed patterns well-established by 1849, although there was one notable exception. At Lieutenant-Governor Edmund Head's insistence, the Saint John Grand Jury served warrants on Orange participants as well as the Catholics. This attempt at impartiality was severely undermined, however, by a prejudiced investigative team that included the prominent Orangeman W.H. Needham.[91] Ultimately, all but five of the bills against Orangemen, including those for Corum, Anderson and 18 others, were dropped before the defendants reached trial. The five Orangemen who actually stood in the dock were swiftly declared innocent by a jury that remained seated. Much to the prosecution's dismay, the jury ignored recent provincial legislation that clearly outlawed armed public processions.[92] For the Irish Catholics, on the other hand, the judicial pattern of the 1840s remained intact. Of the 24 implicated, six were tried on assault charges, one for attempted murder and four for unlawful assembly. Two were eventually found guilty, including the alleged 'ringleader' who led the defence of the green arch. John Haggerty, immigrant laborer and father

of three, would spend his sixty-third birthday in the provincial peniten-
tiary while serving his one-year sentence for assault.[93]

The 1849 riot signalled an end to collective social conflict between
Orangemen and Catholics, although small skirmishes would continue
for years.[94] Various factors brought about this extended truce, the most
important being the hegemony established by Orangemen in Saint John
and Portland. In a sense, Orangemen had won the battle of the 1840s. The
Irish Catholics' attempts to check the growth of Orangeism with counter-
demonstrations had failed. They undeniably suffered the most casualties
in the course of the riots. Moreover, a fusion between all levels of authority and the Orange Order had taken place. Orangemen, constables and
British soldiers had combined to contain every major disturbance within
the Irish Catholic ghettos of York Point and Portland. The Orange Order
became an acceptable accomplice for the maintenance of social control. A
double standard had clearly emerged: authorities found Orange vigilantism preferable to 'mob rule' by the Irish Catholic 'lower orders.'[95] During
the 1840s Orangemen served as constables, magistrates and legislative
representatives. Excepting one active magistrate in Saint John, the Irish
Catholics were excluded from power. This inequity profoundly shaped
law enforcement during the riots and trials. No Catholic would be
allowed to sit on juries; moreover, only Irish Catholics would be found
guilty of rioting offences. Even when Orangemen stood in the dock, such
as after the York Point riot of 1849, they were expeditiously exonerated.[96]
Ethnicity and religion targeted the Irish Catholics for suppression during
the 1840s; meanwhile Orangeism developed into an unofficial arm of
social control to protect the Protestant majority.

New Brunswick's improved economic environment after mid-century
contributed to the demise of collective conflict by alleviating some of the
fierce competition between immigrants and natives. The 'Hungry Forties' had indeed been more than a historical cliché to many colonists. A
sustained depression had brought scarcities of goods, food and services.
Natives had competed with Irish Catholic immigrants for limited jobs, a
factor that had contributed to the rapid growth of Orangeism. Economic
variables alone did not cause the Orange-Green riots, but they certainly
helped to account for a foundation of social tension.[97] As the province
successfully weathered the English transition to free trade in the 1850s,
investment capital increased and jobs became more available.[98] Thus
Orangemen found one of the key elements of their rhetorical campaign
against Irish Catholics undermined. Ultimately, fuller employment fostered better relations between Protestant and Catholic workers.

Another factor in the disappearance of perennial disturbances between Protestants and Catholics was the Orange Order's discontinuance of July 12 processions while it fought for provincial incorporation. Saint John and Portland Orangemen wisely decided not to risk any negative publicity that might accompany collective violence with Irish Catholics while the bill was being debated in the New Brunswick legislature. The process lasted 25 years, but eventually the trade-off of abstention for legitimacy proved fruitful.[99] Not until after the bill finally passed in 1875, in the midst of the emotional separate schools issue, would Orangemen again take to Saint John's streets to display their fervent brand of loyalty and Protestantism.[100]

Finally, a drastic reduction in the number of Irish Catholic immigrants after 1848 helped to subdue the nativist impulse. The tide of famine immigrants had dropped as precipitously as it had risen. Improving conditions in Ireland accounted for a general reduction in emigrants, especially from the poorer Catholic counties. In addition a discriminatory immigration policy, instituted at the behest of Lieutenant-Governors Sir William Colebrooke and Sir Edmund Head, curtailed Catholic immigration while it increased the number of more desirable Protestant settlers from the British Isles.[101] The results were striking: between 1851 and 1861 the percentages of Irish compared to the total immigrant population dropped dramatically in both Saint John and Portland. This decrease also reflected the continuing out-migration of transient Catholics to the 'Boston States' and to other British North American provinces.[102] Finally, it indicated the beginnings of a process of acculturation; the sons and daughters of Catholic and Protestant immigrants would be listed as New Brunswickers in the 1861 census. The 'soldiers' of the 1840s – both Orange and Green – would be supplanted by generations to whom the violent experiences of the 'Hungry Forties' would be historical anecdotes.

The Orange Order was New Brunswick's institutionalized nativist response to Irish Catholic immigration during the 1840s. Prior to this decade, the organization was a small and mostly invisible fraternal order dominated by Irish Protestant immigrants and British garrison troops. As Irish Catholic famine victims poured into Saint John and Portland during the 1840s, however, Protestant natives and non-Irish-born immigrants joined the Orange Order. Orangemen spearheaded a rhetorical campaign to combat the famine immigration, using anti-Catholic and racist propaganda to discourage the Irish from settling permanently in the city. Additionally, the Orange Order increasingly acted

as a paramilitary vigilante group that freely engaged in riots with belli-
cose Irish Catholics. The combination of nativist rhetoric and a mutual
willingness to engage in armed conflict provided a decade of collective
social violence that culminated in the tragic riot of 12 July 1849. Thus
Saint John and Portland, like several eastern seaboard cities in the
United States, experienced a strong nativist impulse and several
destructive episodes of social violence.

NOTES

This article is from *Acadiensis* 13 (1) (1983). Reprinted with permission.

1 *Weekly Chronicle* (Saint John), 22 March 1839.
2 *Morning News* (Saint John), 24 September 1847.
3 For this study, social violence is defined as 'assault upon an individual or his
  property solely or primarily because of his membership in a social category.'
  See Allen D. Grimshaw, 'Interpreting Collective Violence: An Argument for
  the Importance of Social Structure,' in James F. Short, Jr., and Marvin E. Wolf-
  gang, eds., *Collective Violence* (Chicago, 1972), pp. 12, 18–20.
4 Sir Edmund Head to Lord Grey, 15 July 1849, Colonial Office Series [CO] 188,
  Public Record Office [PRO], London; *Royal Gazette* (Fredericton), 19 September 1849; D.R. Jack, *Centennial Prize Essay on the History of the City and County
  of St. John* (Saint John, 1883), pp. 136–7; Reverend J.W. Millidge, 'Reminiscences of St. John from 1849 to 1860,' *New Brunswick Historical Society Collections*, Vol. IV (1919), pp. 8, 127.
5 Its mid-century population stood at 23,000, making one in every 8.5 New
  Brunswickers a Saint John resident. Portland, with 8,500 inhabitants, was
  roughly one-third the size of Saint John. See New Brunswick Census, 1851,
  Provincial Archives of New Brunswick [PANB].
6 Presentment of the Saint John Grand Jury, 27 October 1847, Minutes, Saint
  John General Sessions, PANB.
7 *Morning News*, 8, 11 September 1843; Abraham Gesner, *New Brunswick; with
  Notes for Emigrants* (London, 1847), pp. 122–4; Reverend W.C. Atkinson, *A
  Historical and Statistical Account of New Brunswick, B.N.A. with Advice to Emigrants* (Edinburgh, 1844), pp. 28–9, 36–7.
8 The 1840s was a particularly depressed decade, but as Graeme Wynn elo-
  quently pointed out, the colony was already a veteran of the 19th century
  boom and bust 'bandalore'; in 1819, 1825 and 1837, New Brunswick suffered
  trade depressions due to financial downturns and the erosion of speculation
  capital in Great Britain: *Timber Colony: A Historical Geography of Early Nineteenth Centruy New Brunswick* (Toronto, 1981), pp. 3–33, 43–53. See also P.D.

McClelland, 'The New Brunswick Economy in the Nineteenth Century,' *Journal of Economic History*, XXV (December 1965), pp. 686–90.

9 W.S. MacNutt, *New Brunswick, a History, 1784–1867* (Toronto, 1963), pp. 283–4, 296; MacNutt, 'New Brunswick's Age of Harmony: The Administration of Sir John Harvey,' *Canadian Historical Review*, XXXII (June 1951), pp. 123–4; D.G.G. Kerr, *Sir Edmund Head: The Scholarly Governor* (Toronto, 1954), pp. 39–54; Wynn, *Timber Colony*; pp. 43–4, 51–3.

10 *Colonial Advocate* (Saint John), 14 July 1845; MacNutt, *New Brunswick*, p. 285; Wynn, *Timber Colony*, pp. 51–3.

11 *New Brunswick Reporter* (Fredericton), 13 October 1848, 24 August 1849; *Morning News*, 28 May 1849; Wynn, *Timber Colony*, pp. 150–5; MacNutt, *New Brunswick*, p. 320.

12 Immigration Returns, New Brunswick Blue Books, 1832–50, Public Archives of Canada [PAC]; 'Report on Trade and Navigation,' *Journal of the House of Assembly of New Brunswick*, 1866.

13 Only in 1853, after the famine abated in Ireland, would English immigrants once again become the largest group. See New Brunswick Census, 1851; 'Report on Trade and Navigation,' *Journal of the House of Assembly of New Brunswick*, 1866; William F. Ganong, *A Monograph of the Origins of Settlements in the Province of New Brunswick* (Ottawa, 1904), pp. 90–120.

14 Cecil Woodham-Smith, *The Great Hunger; Ireland 1845–9* (London, 1962), pp. 206–9; Lawrence J. McCaffrey, *The Irish Diaspora in America* (Bloomington, Ind., 1976), pp. 59–62; William Forbes Adams, *Ireland and Irish Emigration to the New World* (New York, 1932); Donald Akenson, ed., *Canadian Papers in Rural History*, Vol. III (Gananoque, Ont., 1981), pp. 219–21.

15 Woodham-Smith, *Great Hunger*, pp. 29, 206–13; John I. Cooper, 'Irish Immigration and the Canadian Church Before the Middle of the Nineteenth Century,' *Journal of the Canadian Church Historical Society*, II (May 1955), pp. 13–4; Adams, *Ireland and Irish Emigration*; McCaffrey, *Irish Diaspora*, pp. 59–62; Oliver MacDonagh, 'Irish Emigration to the United States of America and the British Colonies During the Famine,' in R. Dudley Edwards and T. Desmond Williams, eds., *The Great Famine: Studies in Irish History 1845–52* (Dublin, 1956), pp. 332–9.

16 Immigration Returns, New Brunswick Blue Books, PAC; M.H. Perley's Report on 1846 Emigration, in William Colebrooke to Grey, 29 December 1846, CO 188.

17 Ibid.; *Royal Gazette*, 17 March, 7 July 1847; *Saint John Herald*, 12 November 1845; James Hannay, *History of New Brunswick* (Saint John, 1909), Vol. II, p. 70; MacDonagh, 'Irish Emigration,' pp. 368–73; Adams, *Ireland and Irish Emigration*, p. 234; Woodham-Smith, *Great Hunger*, pp. 209–10.

18 New Brunswick Census, 1851, 1861; *Morning News*, 8, 11 September 1843;

Alexander Monro, *New Brunswick; with a Brief Outline of Nova Scotia, and Prince Edward Island* (Halifax, 1855), p. 125; James S. Buckingham, *Canada, Nova Scotia, New Brunswick, and the Other British Provinces in North America* (London, 1843), pp. 409–10.

19 Kings Ward, which included all of York Point and was roughly equal in size to the other Saint John wards, had twice the population of any ward in the 1851 New Brunswick Census. For descriptions of York Point, see Grand Jury Reports, 16 December 1848, Minutes, Saint John General Sessions, PANB, and D.H. Waterbury, 'Retrospective Ramble Over Historic St. John,' *New Brunswick Historical Society Collections*, Vol. IV (1919), pp. 86–8.

20 Colebrooke to Grey, 28 January 1848, CO 188; Gesner, *New Brunswick*, p. 124.

21 John Higham, *Strangers in the Land: Patterns of American Nativism 1860–1925* (New Brunswick, N.J., 1955), pp. 3–4; Higham, 'Another Look at Nativism,' *Catholic Historical Review*, XLIV (July 1958), pp. 148–50.

22 For examples of Canadian nativist studies, see Howard Palmer, *Land of the Second Chance: A History of Ethnic Groups in Southern Alberta* (Lethbridge, 1972); Palmer, 'Nativism and Ethnic Tolerance in Alberta: 1920–1972,' PhD thesis, York University, 1974; Simon Evans, 'Spatial Bias in the Incidence of Nativism: Opposition to Hutterite Expansion in Alberta,' *Canadian Ethnic Studies*, Vol. VI, Nos. 1–2 (1974), pp. 1–16.

23 *Loyalist and Conservative Advocate* (Saint John), 13 August 1847. See also issues from 20, 27 August 1847.

24 For histories of the Orange Order, see Hereward Senior, *Orangeism in Ireland and Britain 1765–1836* (London, 1966), especially pp. 4–21, 194–206; Senior, 'The Early Orange Order 1795–1870,' in T. Desmond Williams, ed., *Secret Societies in Ireland* (Dublin, 1973); Peter Gibbon, 'The Origins of the Orange Order and the United Irishmen,' *Economy and Society*, I (1972), pp. 134–63.

25 Canadian Orange Order histories include Cecil Houston and W.J. Smyth, *The Sash Canada Wore: A Historical Geography of the Orange Order in Canada* (Toronto, 1980); Hereward Senior, *Orangeism: The Canadian Phase* (Toronto, 1972); Senior, 'The Genesis of Canadian Orangeism,' *Ontario History*, LX (June 1968), pp. 13–29.

26 James McNichol's report, *Loyal Orange Association Report, 1886*; (Toronto, 1886), *Sentinel*, 3 July 1930; J. Edward Steele, comp., *History and Directory of the Provincial Grand Orange Lodge and Primary Lodges of New Brunswick* (Saint John, 1934), p. 11.

27 Miscellaneous Orange documents, courtesy of Professor Peter Toner, University of New Brunswick at Saint John; James McNichol's report, *Loyal Orange Association Report*, 1886; Steele, *History of the Orange Lodges of New Brunswick*, pp. 11, 17–21; Houston and Smyth, *The Sash Canada Wore*, pp. 69–70.

28 Lodge returns, in *Minutes of the Grand Orange Lodge of New Brunswick* [various

publishers, 1846–53]; *Annual Reports of the Grand Orange Lodge of the Loyal Orange Association of B.N.A.* [various publishers, 1846–50]; *New Brunswick Reporter*, 10 May 1850; *Loyalist*, 8 June 1848; *Carleton Sentinel* (Woodstock), 15 July 1854; *Sentinel*, 3 July 1930; Steele, *History of the Orange Lodges of New Brunswick*, pp. 11–3, 37–9, 53–5, 59.

29 Because Nova Scotia's lodges, who received their warrants directly from New Brunswick, were only two years old in mid-century, the vast majority of the 10,000 members resided in New Brunswick. See 'Minutes of the Grand Orange Lodge of New Brunswick and Nova Scotia,' in *Weekly Chronicle*, 6 July 1849; Orange Order documents, Peter Toner; *Minutes of the Grand Orange Lodge of New Brunswick*, 1846–50; *Sentinel*, 3 July 1930.

30 Correspondence from John Earle in *Annual Report of the Grand Orange Lodge of the Loyal Orange Association of B.N.A.*, 1851; *New Brunswick Reporter*, 26 April 1850; Head to Grey, 7 September 1847, CO 188; *New Brunswick Courier* (Saint John), 25 July 1840; Steele, *History of the Orange Lodge of New Brunswick*, p. 11.

31 Houston and Smyth, *The Sash Canada Wore*, pp. 70–2; Steele, *History of the Orange Lodges of New Brunswick*, pp. 115–8.

32 'Minutes of the Organizational Meeting of the Grand Orange Lodge of New Brunswick, 1844,' in Steele, *History of the Orange Lodges of New Brunswick*, p. 11; New Brunswick Census, 1851.

33 James Brown letters to *New Brunswick Reporter*, 28 April, 5, 12 May 1848; *Morning News*, 18 July 1849; John Earle's correspondence, in *Annual Report of the Grand Orange Lodge of the Loyal Orange Association of B.N.A.*, 1851.

34 Minute book, Wellington orange Lodge, Portland, New Brunswick Museum [NBM], Saint John.

35 1851 manuscript census returns from Saint John County are incomplete. Returns from only four of the city's wards are extant: Kings, Dukes, Sydney Queens. Records from Portland Parish and Carleton are missing.

36 Returns for Saint John County, New Brunswick Manuscript Census, 1851, PANB; Orange documents, including dispensations and lodge returns, Peter Toner; *Minutes of the Grand Orange Lodge of New Brunswick*, 1846–55; Evidence, Saint John Riot Trials, Documents, New Brunswick Executive Council Records, PANB; New Brunswick Supreme Court Documents, PANB. The newspapers consulted were the *Loyalist*, *Weekly Chronicle* and *Morning News* for the 1840s, as well as the *Daily Sun* (Saint John), 13 July 1897, and Steele, *History of the Orange Lodges of New Brunswick*.

37 *Laws and Ordinances of the Orange Association of British North America* (Toronto, 1840), p. 11; *The Orange Question Treated by Sir Francis Hincks and the London 'Times'* (Montreal, 1877).

38 For example, Portland's Wellington Lodge attempted to combat negative

30   Scott W. See

publicity after a decade of social violence by declaring itself a 'benefit' organization in 1851. See Minute Book, Wellington Orange Lodge, NBM. See also
Rules and Regulations of the Orange Institution of British North America (Toronto,
1838), p. 5; Steele, *History of the Orange Lodges of New Brunswick.*

39 *Morning News*, 24 January 1849; *Headquarters* (Fredericton), 24 January 1849.
40 *Loyalist*, 1 October 1847.
41 *Minutes of the Grand Orange Lodge of New Brunswick*, 1852; Rev. Gilbert Spurr's
   address to Orangemen, in *Loyalist*, 15 October 1847; Head to Grey, 26 July
   1848, CO 188; *New Brunswick Reporter*, 26 October 1849; *Carleton Sentinel*,
   2 July 1850; *Weekly Chronicle*, 15 July 1842, 4 February 1848; *Christian Visitor*
   (Saint John), 8 March 1848; Steele, *History of the Orange Lodges of New Brunswick*, pp. 13–5, 21.
42 For discussions of the papal conspiracy theory in North America, see S.M.
   Lipset and Earl Raab, *The Politics of Unreason* (New York, 1970), pp. 47–59,
   David B. Davis, 'Some Themes of Counter-Subversion: An Analysis of Anti-
   Masonic, Anti-Catholic, and Anti-Mormon Literature,' *Mississippi Valley Historical Review*, XLVII (September 1960), pp. 205–7, Higham, *Strangers in the
   Land*, pp. 5–6.
43 *Church Witness* (Saint John), 21 September 1853.
44 *Minutes of the Grand Orange Lodge of New Brunswick*, 1846–55, particularly
   S.H. Gilbert's sermon in 1854; Grand Orange Lodge of New Brunswick's
   address to Queen Victoria, in Head to Grey, 28 April 1851, CO 188; *New
   Brunswick Reporter*, 9 April 1850; *Carleton Sentinel*, 16 July 1850; *New Brunswick Reporter*, 1 October 1847; *Weekly Chronicle*, 31 August 1849, 18 July 1851;
   Loyalist, 24 September 1847; *Church Witness*, 16 July, 13 August 1851, 6 July
   1853.
45 Adams, *Ireland and Irish Emigration*, pp. 363–4; Carl Wittke, *The Irish in America* (Baton Rouge, La., 1956), pp. 46–7; Kenneth Duncan, 'Irish Famine Immigration and the Social Structure of Canada West,' *Canadian Review of Sociology
   and Anthropology*, II (February 1965), pp. 33, 39.
46 *Loyalist*, 6 April 1848.
47 Alexander McHarg Diary, NBM; *Morning News*, 8 January, 8 December 1841,
   6 January, 14 June 1843, 5 January 1848; *Weekly Chronicle*, 5 January, 28 June
   1844, 26 November 1847; Queen vs. David Nice, New Brunswick Supreme
   Court Documents, PANB.
48 *Loyalist*, 30 March 1848; *New Brunswick Reporter*, 20 April 1850; *New Brunswick
   Assembly Debates*, 8 March 1850, PANB; *Morning News*, 24 January 1849; *Loyalist*, 16 July, 15, 28 October, 4 November 1847; *New Brunswick Reporter*,
   19 November 1847, 15 March 1850: *Morning News*, 11 August 1847.
49 For excellent studies of racism in the British Isle, see L.P. Curtis, Jr., *Anglo-*

Saxons and Celts: A Study of Anti-Irish Prejudice in Victorian England (Bridgeport, Conn., 1968), pp. 8–9, 24–6, and *Apes and Angels: The Irishman in Victorian Caricature* (Devon, England, 1971), passim.
50 *Weekly Chronicle*, 31 August, 28 September 1849; *Loyalist*, 24 September 1847.
51 *Loyalist*, 1 October, 11 November 1847.
52 *New Brunswick Reporter*, 10 May 1850; *Loyalist*, 16 July, 17 September, 15 October 1847; *Weekly Chronicle*, 29 July 1842.
53 The theme of competition between immigrant laborers and nativists in North America is explored in Oscar Handlin, *Boston's Immigrants* (Cambridge, Mass., 1959), pp. 180–7, Higham, *Strangers in the Land*, p. 57, Adams, *Ireland and Irish Emigration*, p. 353.
54 M.H. Perley's Report on 1846 Emigration, in Colebrooke to Grey, 29 December 1846, CO 188; *Royal Gazette*, 17 March, 7 July 1847; Wynn, *Timber Colony*, pp. 155–6; Kathryn Johnston, 'The History of St. John, 1837–1867: Civic and Economic,' Honours thesis, Mount Allison University, 1953, pp. 24–8.
55 *Loyalist*, 24 March 1845, 17 September, 28 October, 4 November, 9, 23 December 1847; *New Brunswick Reporter*, 10 September 1847; *New Brunswick Reporter*, 19 November 1847.
56 Joseph Brown to R.F. Hazen, 11 July 1837, R.F. Hazen Papers, NBM; *Weekly Chronicle*, 14 July 1837.
57 *New Brunswick Reporter*, 26 April, 10 May 1850.
58 *Morning News*, 13 July, 5 August 1842; *Weekly Chronicle*, 15 July, 12 August 1842; *New Brunswick Courier*, 16 July, 13, 27 August 1842; Minutes, Saint John General Sessions, 9, 10, 17 December 1842, 25 March 1843, PANB; *Sentinel*, 29 October 1891.
59 *New Brunswick Reporter*, 26 April 1850.
60 Mayor Lauchlan Donaldson to Alfred Reade, 8 March 1844, New Brunswick Supreme Court Documents, PANB; McHarg Diary; *Morning News*, 5 April 1844.
61 *Weekly Chronicle*, 3 January 1845; *Morning News*, 3 January 1845; *Headquarters*, 8 January 1845; McHarg Diary.
62 Donaldson to Reade, 29 March 1845, Saint John Grand Jury to Colebrooke, 27 March 1845. 'Riots and Disasters,' New Brunswick Executive Council Records [Executive Council Records], PANB; *Loyalist*, 24 March 1845; *Weekly Chronicle*, 21 March 1845.
63 Minutes, New Brunswick Executive Council, 7 April 1845, PANB; Report of Doctors Robert and William Bayard, 17 March 1845, 'Riots and Disasters,' Executive Council Records; McHarg Diary; *Weekly Chronicle*, 21 March 1845; *Morning News*, 19 March 1845; *Observer* (Saint John), 18 March 1845; *New Brunswick Reporter*, 21 March 1845; *New Brunswick Courier*, 22 March 1845; *Loyalist*, 24 March 1845.

64 Minutes, Saint John General Sessions, 20, 22, 26 March, 14 June 1845; Donaldson to Reade, 22 March 1845, 'Riots and Disasters,' Executive Council Records: *New Brunswick Courier*, 5 July 1845; *Saint John Herald*, 2 July 1845.

65 *Minutes of the Grand Orange Lodge of New Brunswick*, 1847; *Weekly Chronicle*, 17 July 1846.

66 *Morning News*, 14 July 1847.

67 Orange supporters tried to disassociate the Orange Order, the Mechanic's Institute Band and the crowd that followed the procession. *The Loyalist*, 16 July 1847, claimed that the band had nothing to do with the Orange procession, while Clarence Ward made the dubious assertion that the Orange entourage consisted of 'children.' See 'Old Times in St. John – 1847,' *Saint John Globe*, 1 April 1911, p. 8. Yet an article in the *Orange Sentinel*, 29 October 1891, proudly revealed that all the band members were Orangemen.

68 For examples of these songs, see *The Sentinel Orange and Patriotic Song Book* (Toronto, 1930?) and R. McBride, ed., *The Canadian Orange Ministrel for 1860, Contains Nine New and Original Songs, Mostly All of Them Showing Some Wrong that Affects the Order or the True Course of Protestant Loyalty to the British Crown* (London, 1860). Note particularly 'Croppies Lie Down,' a nineteenth-century favourite of Orangemen in Europe and North America.

69 *New Brunswick Courier*, 17 July 1847; *Morning News*, 14 July 1847; *Loyalist*, 16 July 1847; *Sentinel*, 29 October 1891; McHarg Diary.

70 *Morning News*, 14 July 1847; Colebrooke to Grey, 30 July 1847, Documents, Executive Council Records, PANB; McHarg Diary, *New Brunswick Courier*, 17 July 1847; *Loyalist*, 16 July 1847; Ward, 'Old Times in St. John – 1847.'

71 *New Brunswick Courier*, 7 August 1847.

72 Colebrooke to Grey, 30 July 1847, CO 188; *Morning New*, 14 July 1847.

73 *Loyalist*, 16 July 1847; Ward, 'Old Times in St. John – 1847.'

74 One newspaper referred to it as a 'civil war': *Morning News*, 14 July 1847.

75 *New Brunswick Courier*, 24 July 1847; *Morning News*, 14, 21, 23, 28 July 1847; *Loyalist*, 23 July 1847; *Weekly Chronicle*, 30 July 1847.

76 Queen vs. Dennis McGovern, 7–17 September 1847, New Brunswick Supreme Court Documents, PANB. Note especially the testimonies of Thomas Clark, James Clark, Ezekiel Downey and Edward McDermott. See also *Morning News*, 24 January 1848, *Weekly Chronicle*, 10 September 1847, *New Brunswick Courier*, 11 September 1847; *Loyalist*, 10 September 1847; *Morning News*, 8 September 1847.

77 *Weekly Chronicle*, 14 July 1848. Fredericton's Orangemen invited provincial brethren to celebrate the anniversary of their successful 1847 battle with Irish Catholics: *New Brunswick Reporter*, 10 May 1850.

78 *Weekly Chronicle*, 6 July 1849.

79 Head to Grey, 15 July 1849, CO 188. The question of the legality of public pro-cessions, especially armed ones, would become a hotly debated topic in the House of Assembly after the riot, yet no restrictive legislation would emerge from the debate.

80 Testimonies of Thomas Paddock and Francis Jones, 'Riots and Disasters,' Executive Council Records; *New Brunswick Reporter*, 13 July 1849; Head to Grey, 15 July 1849, CO 188.

81 *Morning News*, 13 July 1849; *New-Brunswicker* (Saint John), 14 July 1849; *New Brunswick Courier*, 14 July 1849; Testimonies of Francis Jones, George Noble, Jacob Allan, Charles Boyd, Squire Manks and George McKelvey, 'Riots and Disasters,' Executive Council Records; Head to Grey, 15 July 1849, CO 188.

82 Testimonies of Josiah Wetmore, Jeremiah McCarthy, George Nobel and Jacob Allan, 'Riots and Disasters,' Executive Council Records; Head to Grey, 15 July 1849, CO 188; *Sentinel*, 3 July 1930.

83 Testimonies of Jacob Allan, George Mason, Samuel Dalton, Samuel Gordon and Francis Jones, 'Riots and Disasters,' Executive Council Records; Head to Grey, 15 July 1849, CO 188; *Weekly Chronicle*, 13 July 1849; *New Brunswicker*, 14 July 1849; *Sentinel*, 3 July 1930.

84 Head to Grey, 15 July 1849, CO 188; Testimonies of James Gilbert, Henry Gil-bert, John Nixon, John Fitzpatrick, Joseph Wetmore and James Clark, 'Riots and Disasters,' Executive Council Records.

85 Testimonies of Jacob Allan, Francis Jones and Squire Manks, 'Riots and Disasters,' Executive Council Records; Head to Grey, 15 July 1849, CO 188; *Sentinel*, 29 October 1891, 3 July 1930.

86 Head to Grey, 17 July 1849, CO 188; Jacob Allan testimony, 'Riots and Disas-ters,' Executive Council Records; *Morning News*, 13 July 1849; *Temperance Tele-graph* (Saint John), 19 July 1849.

87 Testimonies of James McKenzie William Smith, Francis Wilson and Francis Jones, 'Riots and Disasters,' Executive Council Records; *Temperance Telegraph*, 19 July 1849; *Weekly Chronicle*, 13 July 1849; *Morning News*, 13 July 1849.

88 Testimonies of Squire Manks, James McKenzie, William Smith, Francis Wil-son and Jeremiah Smith, 'Riots and Disasters,' Executive Council Records; *Morning News*, 13 July 1849; *Christian Visitor*, 14 July 1849; *Weekly Chronicle*, 13 July 1849.

89 Head to Grey, 15 July 1849, CO 188; Charles Boyd testimony, 'Riots and Disasters,' Executive Council Records; *Morning News*, 13 July 1849; *New-Brunswicker*, 14 July 1849; *Weekly Chronicle*, 13 July 1849.

90 Testimonies of Charles Boyd and Jacob Allan, 'Riots and Disasters,' Execu-tive Council Records; *Morning News*, 13 July 1849; Head to Grey, 15 July 1849, CO 188.

91 Head to Grey, 15 July 1849, CO 188; *Morning News*, 23 July 1849; *New Brunswick Courier*, 21 July 1849.

92 William B. Kinnear to Head, extract, 6 September 1849, in Head to Grey, 7 September 1849, CO 188; Recognizances, July–September 1849, 'Riots and Disasters,' Executive Council Records; Documents, Saint John Justice Court, 1849, PANB; Inquests, 1849, New Brunswick Supreme Court Documents, PANB; 12 Victoria, c. 29, 1849, *New Brunswick Statutes*, 1849; *Morning News*, 30 July 1849; *New Brunswick Courier*, 21, 28 July 1849; *Temperance Telegraph*, 23 August 1849.

93 Documents, Saint John Justice Court, 1849; Kinnear to Head, extract, 6 September 1849, in Head to Grey, 7 September 1849, CO 188; John Haggerty petition to Head, September 1849, in Judicial Documents, Executive Council Records; *Weekly Chronicle*, 24 August 1849; *New Brunswick Courier*, 18, 25 August 1849.

94 *New Brunswick Courier*, 19 July 1851, 16, 23, 30 July 1853; *Weekly Chronicle*, 18 July 1851; *Morning News*, 15, 20 July 1853; *New Brunswick Reporter*, 15, 22 July 1853; *Freeman* (Saint John), 14 July 1855; McHarg Diary.

95 *Loyalist*, 30 March 1848; *New Brunswick Reporter*, 20 April 1850. Irish immigrants in the United States experienced a similar double standard: see Theodore M. Hammett, 'Two Mobs of Jacksonian Boston: Ideology and Interest,' *Journal of American History*, LXII (March 1976), pp. 866–7.

96 Documents, Saint John Justice Court, 1849; 'Riots and Disasters,' Executive Council Records.

97 W.W. Rostow explored the linkages between social unrest and economic downturns in *British Economy of the Nineteenth Century* (Oxford, 1948), pp. 123–5.

98 Wynn, *Timber Colony*, pp. 84–6, 166–7; MacNutt, *New Brunswick*, p. 329; James R. Rice, 'A History of Organized Labour in Saint John, New Brunswick, 1813–1890,' M.A. thesis, University of New Brunswick, 1968, pp. 33–4.

99 *Journal of the House of Assembly of New Brunswick*, 1850–1, 1853–4, 1857–60, 1867, 1872–5: 38 Victoria, c. 54, 1875, *Statutes of New Brunswick*, 1875.

100 Saint John's Orangemen sponsored a massive procession on the first Twelfth of July following the bill's assent. See *Freeman*, 13, 15, 18 July 1876; *Morning News*, 14, 17 July 1876.

101 Colebrooke to Grey, 30 July 1847, Head to Grey, 15 July 1849, CO 188; Colebrooke Correspondence, 1847, Head Correspondence, 1849, PANB.

102 New Brunswick Census, 1851, 1861; Immigration Returns, New Brunswick Blue Books, 1850–5, PAC; 'Report on Trade and Navigation,' in *Journal of the House of Assembly of New Brunswick*, 1866.

St. Patrick's Day Parades in Nineteenth-Century Toronto: A Study of Immigrant Adjustment and Elite Control

MICHAEL COTTRELL

Irish immigrants brought to nineteenth-century British North America a rich and diverse cultural heritage which continued to flourish in the areas they settled. A particular fondness for parades and processions was part of this inheritance and annual demonstrations commemorating the Battle of the Boyne and the feast of St. Patrick were soon common-place throughout the colonies. In the charged sectarian climate of Ireland, however, 'parades were at the very centre of the territorial ... political and economic struggle' and these connotations were also transplanted.[1] Especially in Toronto, where Catholic and Protestant Irish congregated in large numbers, parades frequently became the occasion of violent confrontation between Orange and Green.[2] But while the July 12 activities of the Orange Order figure prominently in Canadian historiography, little attention has been paid to St. Patrick's Day celebrations or their significance for Irish Catholic immigrants. This study seeks to redress this imbalance by tracing the evolution of St. Patrick's Day parades in nineteenth-century Toronto, beginning with a close examination of the 1863 celebration which was one of the largest and most impressive on record.

The tone was set the previous evening by the garrison drums beating 'St. Patrick's Day in the Morning' and this was followed by the Hibernian Benevolent Society band's late night promenade, 'discoursing some of the choicest [Irish] national airs.' Crowds began to gather at St. Paul's Church on King Street early the next morning and at ten o'clock, the procession began marching towards St. Michael's Cathedral. About two thousand strong, the assemblage was drawn largely from the 'humbler elements,' some of whom had reportedly journeyed to the city from surrounding districts. The Cathedral was 'filled to its utmost capacity' for the mass which was celebrated by Bishop John Joseph Lynch, assisted by over a dozen other Irish priests from the Toronto diocese.

The high point of the service was undoubtedly the sermon delivered by the Bishop on the exploits of the 'glorious saint,' concluding with an exposition on the providential mission of the Irish diaspora to spread Catholicism to the four corners of the world.[3]

Religious obligations having been fulfilled, the procession then reformed and paraded through the principal streets of the city. Led by the Hibernian band, whose repertoire seemed to consist of nostalgic and militant tunes in equal measure, the procession swelled even further as it slowly returned to St. Paul's Church. Here, a platform had been erected for the occasion and various notables, including the Bishop, members of the clergy, prominent Catholics and officers of various Irish organizations addressed the crowd. The obvious favourite, however, was Michael Murphy, president of the Hibernian Benevolent Society. Murphy's oration was received with 'loud cheers and applause,' especially when he denounced British government in Ireland as 'radically wrong' and compared it to the suffering of the Polish people under a 'powerful military despotism.' But he prophesied that Irish deliverance was at hand from an organization rapidly growing among her exiles. In Canada alone, he claimed, there were twenty thousand Irishmen ready to rally to the cause:

... three-fourths of the Catholic Irish of this country would offer themselves as an offering on the altar of freedom, to elevate their country and raise her again to her position in the list of nations. Nothing could resist the Irish pike when grasped by the sinewy arm of the Celt.[4]

Murphy then commended the Hibernians for keeping the spirit of Irish nationality alive in Canada, despite the opposition and hostility which this evoked from the host society. But he ended in a more conciliatory tone by expressing 'perfect satisfaction' with the laws of Canada because, here, the people 'were their own law-makers.'[5] When the speeches were over, the procession broke up into smaller parties and soirées which lasted late into the night. And 'thus passed away one of the most pleasant St. Patrick's Days we have ever spent in Toronto.'[6]

For those who participated, almost exclusively Catholic Irish immigrants, the St. Patrick's Day celebration was obviously an extremely important event. On a social level, it provided a holiday from work and an occasion to parade about the city dressed in their Sunday best. Those who lived outside the city could visit friends and relatives, shop at the large stores and partake of the excitement of city life for a day. This influx undoubtedly provided a welcomed boost for the many Irish cab-men, store-keepers and tavern-keepers who lived a normally precarious existence. For the pious, it was an occasion to worship, for the notables an opportunity to speechify and revel in a stature which rarely extended beyond that day. But the event also had a deeper significance, for it was, in essence, a communal demonstration, an annual and very public assertion of Irish Catholic presence and solidarity in Toronto. It was perhaps the one day in the year on which Irish Catholics could claim the city as their own and proudly publicize their distinctiveness on the main streets. The ritualistic nature of the celebrations – with parades, masses and speeches being constants – obviously played a vital role in re-kindling tribal memories and inculcating the collective consciousness necessary for reforging a group identity in a new environment. St. Patrick's Day parades were therefore central both to the emergence of Irish Catholic ethnicity in Toronto and to the communication of identity to the host society.[7]

The celebrations also reflected the interests and aspirations of those who assumed direct responsibility for organizing them. Since high visibility and prestige were the rewards, control of the event allowed different elements to establish supremacy within the Irish Catholic com-munity, to impose their stamp on the group's corporate image and thereby to decisively influence its relations with the larger society. Thus, the intermittent struggle both for control of the celebrations and over the form which they should take revealed a great deal about the experience of Irish Catholic immigrants as they adjusted to an unfamiliar and often hostile environment. Like most ethnic groups, the Irish oscillated between the extremes of separation and integration, persistence and assimilation; and the celebration of the feast of St. Patrick was central to the resolution of these internal tensions for Irish immigrants in Toronto.[8]

Yet, to the host society comprising largely Loyalist and British settlers, the event had a very different significance. An annual reminder of the existence of a substantial alien Irish presence, it also demonstrated the determination of these immigrants, once settled into the country, to pre-serve aspects of their traditional culture. More ominously, speeches such as that delivered by Michael Murphy in 1863 evidenced a continued Irish obsession with the problems of their homeland, and the frequent violence which accompanied the parades demonstrated that the impor-tation of these problems to British North America could prove extremely disruptive. Hence, the Canadian press was less than enthusi-astic in its coverage of the event, expressing the wish that such celebrations, and the Old World orientation which they represented, would shortly be abandoned.[9]

The establishment of the Toronto St. Patrick's Society in 1832 attested to the growing Irish presence in the city, and by 1861 Irish Catholic, constituted over one-quarter of the population. However, a sharp decrease in immigration and steady out-migration contributed to their decline as a percentage of the population thereafter.[10] Early St. Patrick's Day celebrations were usually low-key affairs – concerts, balls and soirées – which brought together the Irish elite to honour their patron saint and indulge their penchant for sentimental and self-congratulatory speeches.[11] Largely free from the sectarian biases so evident in the 1860s, they suggested a cordiality between early Catholic and Protestant immigrants. But while the St. Patrick's Society survived into the 1850s, the inclusive definition of Irish ethnicity which sustained it was undermined by the Famine immigration of the late 1840s. Since Catholics predominated among those who settled in Toronto, this influx shattered the virtual Protestant consensus which had previously existed, and the destitution of many of these Famine victims further contributed to a nativistic backlash from the host society.[12] This prejudice prompted Irish Protestants to dissociate themselves from the unpopular Catholic counterparts and instead to look to the Protestant, loyalist values of the Orange Order as the focus of their identity.[13] But since Catholics found themselves largely consigned to the lowest ranks of the occupational hierarchy and excluded from the emerging British Protestant colonial consensus, their response was to withdraw into an exclusive and essentially defensive form of ethnicity.[14] By the 1860s, the polarization of Irish immigrants along religious and cultural lines was complete and observers noted that the 'Irish constitute in some sort two peoples: the line of division being one of religion and ... one of race.'[15]

These changes were reflected in the way in which St. Patrick's Day was celebrated, as the 17 of March became increasingly identified with Irish Catholicism. Partly a response to rejection by the host society and dissociation of the Protestant Irish, this development was also encouraged by elements within the Irish Catholic community. After the Famine, the Roman Catholic Church created a network of social and religious institutions to assist the adjustment of Irish immigrants and reestablish clerical control over their lives.[16] After a few small-scale and generally disorganized parades in the late 1840s, the clergy soon enlisted St. Patrick in their campaign and by the early 1850s, the annual celebration revolved primarily around the Catholic Church. Organized

TABLE 1   Population of Toronto, 1848–1881

Date	Irish	Catholic	Total
1848	1,695	5,903	25,503
1851	11,305	7,940	30,775
1861	12,441	12,125	44,821
1871	10,336	11,881	56,092
1881	10,781	15,716	86,415

Source: Census of Canada, 1848–1881.

TABLE 2   Irish Catholic Occupational Profile, 1860

Unskilled	45.0%
Semi-skilled	13.5%
Skilled	12.1%
Clerical	2.8%
Business	16.7%
Professional	3.3%
Private means	6.6%

Source: B. Clarke, 'Piety, Nationalism and Fraternity: The Rise of Irish Catholic Voluntary Associations in Toronto, 1850–1895' (Ph.D. dissertation, University of Chicago, 1986), 33.

and led by Church-sponsored societies, processions to the Cathedral now became a regular feature and the clergy assumed a prominent role throughout.[17] But though the celebrations became larger and more public, the mass was clearly the focus of the event, and the sermons preached on these occasions had the effect both of strengthening the association between Irishness and Catholicism and of fostering a sense of ethno-religious particularism among Irish Catholic immigrants. The heroic figure St. Patrick provided an easy continuity between the Irish history of persecution and their current experience as unwelcomed exiles in a strange land, and served as a rallying symbol for Irish Catholics in the New World, as Father Synnott's exhortation of 1855 indicates:

Go on then, faithful, noble and generous children of St. Patrick, in your glorious career ... keep your eyes ever fixed on the faith of St. Patrick which shall ever be for you a fixed star by night and a pillar of light by day – forget not the examples and memorable deeds of your fathers – be faithful to the doctrines of your great apostle. A voice that speaks on the leaf of the shamrock – that speaks in the dismantled and ruined abbeys of lovely Erin – yea a voice that still speaks on the tombstones of your martyred fathers and in the homes of your exiled country-men – be faithful to the glorious legacy he has bequeathed to you.[18]

In the early 1850s, then, the Roman Catholic Church was instrumental in transforming St. Patrick's Day into an essentially religious event, to establish Catholicism as the primary identity of Irish immigrants and thereby strengthen clerical authority. For by encouraging Irish immigrants to see themselves first as Catholics and to hold themselves aloof from the Protestant majority, the clergy reinforced their claim to leadership and control. But the Catholic Church was unable to satisfy all the needs of Irish immigrants. Under the French-born Bishop Armand de Charbonnel, it was unable to express the cultural or political nationalism which these immigrants transported as baggage.[19] Moreover, the group's organizational infrastructure was so tightly controlled by the clergy that it frustrated the desire for leadership and initiative among the Irish Catholic laity, especially the small but ambitious middle class which began to emerge in the mid-1850s.[20]

Irish nationalism provided one of the few rationales for lay initiative independent of clergy, and it also served both as a catalyst and a vehicle for expressing the growing ethnic consciousness among Irish Catholics in Toronto.[21] Indicative of this was the establishment, in 1855, of the exclusively Catholic Young Men's St. Patrick's Association, an ethnic organization which sought to provide a social life for Irish immigrants, based on their traditional culture, and to secure their collective advancement in Toronto.[22] Animated by the Irish Catholic middle class, it quickly moved to put its stamp on what had become the group's leading communal event, and in the late 1850s, the new lay elite assumed responsibility for organizing the St. Patrick's Day celebrations.

Under their auspices, the event changed dramatically. Parades, which had previously been merely a prelude to the mass, now increased in size and colour to become major public demonstrations. In 1857, over one thousand people, their faces animated by 'a sacred patriotic fire,' marched behind four hundred members of the Young Men's St. Patrick's Association.[23] Religious hymns were replaced by popular tunes and secular emblems such as shamrocks, harps and wolfhounds were now more prominent than Catholic icons. As the clergy lost their previous stature in the extra-Cathedral festivities, the whole tone of these events also changed. Clerically-induced temperance gave way to alcoholic good cheer, and instead of the expressions of loyalty and three cheers for the Queen, which had previously characterized the proceedings, mildly anglophobic speeches were now heard.[24]

Alienated from the larger society by a growing 'No Popery' crusade which was expressed through the mainstream press and the hostile activities of the Orange Order, Irish Catholics in the late 1850s used St. Patrick's Day parades to assert their ethno-religious distinctiveness and protest their marginalized position within the city. But changes in the parade also reflected a shift in the internal dynamics of the group, as a struggle was clearly developing between the clergy and members of the laity for leadership and control of the Irish Catholic community. While the latter agreed that Catholicism defined the parameters of Irish ethnicity, they emphasized a secular and cultural dimension to this identity which went beyond the clergy's narrowly religious vision. These tensions were demonstrated by Bishop de Charbonnel's refusal, in 1856, to hold mass to coincide with the parade, but the events of St. Patrick's Day 1858 healed this rift, at least temporarily.[25]

The growth of the St. Patrick's Day population in the city, its increasing visibility and public assertiveness on occasions such as St. Patrick's Day were all seen as evidence of a growing menace by Upper Canadian Protestants already inflamed by the British Papal aggression crisis and the American Know-Nothing movement.[26] The parades, especially, were seen as unduly provocative by the Orange Order which had become the most popular vehicle for expressing militant Protestantism in Upper Canada.[27] This tension boiled over in 1858 when Orange attempts to disrupt the parade resulted in widespread violence during which one Catholic was fatally stabbed with a pitchfork.[28]

Coming at a time of growing self-confidence and rising expectations among the Catholic Irish population, this debacle was a sobering experience, for it demonstrated both the continued hostility of their traditional Orange enemies and the vulnerability which Catholics faced as a consequence of their minority position in Toronto. Moreover, the blatant partisanship of the police and judiciary indicated where the sympathies of the authorities lay, and served notice that the triumphalist behaviour involved in the parades was out of place in a community subscribing to a British and Protestant consensus.[29] As a result, both lay and clerical Irish leaders concluded that a lower public profile would have to be adopted if the acceptance, recognition and prosperity which they desired were to be achieved. This new spirit of conciliation and moderation was expressed most clearly by the decision to forgo public processions on St. Patrick's Day for an indefinite period. The suspension of the parades for the next three years followed a conscious decision of the Irish elite to relinquish their right to the streets in the interests of public harmony. Yet, while this moderation forwarded the desires of the clergy and middle class for an accommodation with the Canadian establishment, it did not meet acquiescence from all elements within the Irish Catholic community, and it was soon challenged by rumblings from below.

The murder of Matthew Sheedy by Orangemen on St. Patrick's Day 1858 was symptomatic of the growing hostility experienced by Irish Catholics in Toronto. Prejudice, harassment and attacks on Catholic priests and Church property all contributed to the growth of a siege mentality among Catholics. While this beleaguerment produced the above-mentioned conciliatory stance from the Irish elite, it also generated a more militant response in the form of the Hibernian Benevolent Society. Established after the 1858 debacle to protect Catholics from Orange aggression, the Hibernians invoked the traditional Irish peasant prerogative of self-defense in the face of the failure of the authorities to secure their rights or redress their grievances. But they soon rose above these Ribbonite roots and by the early 1860s had evolved into a full-fledged ethnic voluntary organization.[30] As well as rendering Toronto safer for Catholics, the Hibernians took over, from the Young Men's St. Patrick's Association, the tasks of generating an extensive social life and material benefits for its largely working-class male members. In keeping with the values of the latter, the organization also sought to inject a more aggressively nationalistic spirit into the Irish community to engender pride and self-confidence, thereby strengthening the demand for recognition and respect for the Irish in Toronto.[31]

One of their first steps in this direction was to reassert the Irish Catholic right to the streets of the city by resuming parades on St. Patrick's Day. Unlike the Young Men's St. Patrick's Association which had openly flouted the authority of the clergy, however, the Hibernians showed great deference to the new Bishop of Toronto, John Joseph Lynch. When the Hibernians sought clerical permission to revive the parades, in 1862, Lynch supported their decision despite strong opposition from 'the most respectable Catholic inhabitants of the city.' Led by members of the now-defunct Young Men's St. Patrick's Association, they argued that a resumption of public processions would inevitably provoke a confrontation with the Orangemen, and since Catholics would automatically be depicted as the aggressors, the good feelings which developed from their suspension would be lost. Lynch was thus implored to ban the parade or at the very least to 'hold mass at such an hour as not to suit the procession.'[32] But the Bishop chose to ignore their warnings and not only granted his approval, but addressed the parade from the steps of the cathedral and commended the Hibernians for their 'noble efforts on behalf of faith and fatherland.'[33]

This dispute over the resumption of the parades suggested an ongoing conflict within the Irish Catholic community about the appropriate response to their countries of origin and of adoption, and acute divisions on the strategy which would best secure them a comfortable niche in the latter. Upwardly mobile middle-class immigrants argued that the best route to success lay in winning the confidence of the host society by quietly discarding those aspects of their traditional culture which were found objectionable and by working through the political system to redress outstanding grievances. But the organized Irish working class, in the form of the Hibernians, rejected the timidity and abandonment of cultural distinctiveness which this policy entailed, and instead demanded a more vigorous assertion of the Irish Catholic presence in the city.[34] For symbolic effect, the St. Patrick's Day parade surpassed all else, since it represented both a commitment to the preservation of Irish culture and an insistence on the right to advertise this distinctiveness on the streets of Toronto.[35]

This conflict between strategies of accommodation and protest constitutes the typical dilemma faced by ethnic groups in a new environment and is frequently related to economic adjustment. Ironically, it was the Irish middle class which had first resorted to protest in the mid-1850s, only to retreat from ethnic militancy once it became obvious that this jeopardized its attainment of social acceptance and economic prosperity. Control of the parades had now changed hands and since this event provided one of the major opportunities for lay initiative, it seems that leadership of Irish-Catholic ethnicity in Toronto was passing from the moderate and accommodationist middle class to the militantly separatist lower class. The power and prestige of the Roman Catholic clergy were also demonstrated by this embroglio, however, for Bishop Lynch's moral code as adjudicator between the warring lay factions was clearly recognized. On this occasion, he sided with the Hibernians, primarily because their uncompromising nationalism reinforced the Church's attempt to foster religious particularism and strengthened the hierarchy's claim to communal leadership.[36] But the limits of this control would soon be tested and the alliance between clergy and nationalists severely strained in the process.

Unknown to Bishop Lynch, the Hibernians established contact with the revolutionary American Fenian Brotherhood in 1859, and the Hibernian president, Michael Murphy, became head-centre of the Fenian organization in the Toronto area. Although sworn Fenians were always a minority of the Hibernians' membership, the organization became more militant under their influence. The establishment in January 1863 of the weekly ethnic newspaper, the *Irish Canadian*, further evidenced their increasing sophistication, for this mouthpiece augmented their influence within the Irish-Catholic community and enabled the Fenians to articulate their concerns to the larger society. Under the editorship of Patrick Boyle, the *Irish Canadian* sought to 'link the past with the present, the old country with the new,' and propagated the simple message that religion, patriotism and support for the liberation of Ireland were all inseparably linked with the demand for Irish recognition and the achievement of prosperity, success and respect in their new environment.[37]

The prominence which the Hibernians established within the Irish Catholic community was demonstrated by their complete control of St. Patrick's Day celebrations in the early 1860s. As statements of Irish protest and radicalism, they surpassed all previous efforts. The years 1863 and 1864 saw the largest parades on record and in keeping with Hibernian membership; those who led and those who followed were increasingly drawn from the Irish Catholic lower class. A new militancy was apparent in the playing of martial tunes such as 'The Croppy Boy,' 'God Save Ireland' and 'The Rising of the Moon,' and changes in the route of the parade also suggested a spirit of confrontation previously lacking. These two parades covered a wider territory than ever before, and while this was obviously designed to assert their right to the entire city, the provocation involved in marching past so many Orange lodges could not have been lost on the organizers. Even more ominous was the proliferation of Fenian sunburst banners among the crowd and the open expressions of support for Fenianism which concluded both of these parades.[38]

Bordering on treason, Murphy's speeches incurred the wrath of the host society and also alienated many Irish Catholics who feared the new radicalism he represented. Led by Thomas D'Arcy McGee, moderates argued that the Fenian-sympathizing Hibernians would confirm the stereotype of Irish disloyalty held by the host society, inevitably prompting a violent reaction from the Orange Order. Even sympathetic Protestants would be alienated by this extremism, he suggested, and the resulting blacklash would obliterate all of the tangible gains made by Irish Catho-

lics since the bitter era of sectarian warfare in the 1850s.[39] The situation
was particularly embarrassing for the Catholic Church since Lynch's
presence alongside Murphy on the podium on both occasions gave rise
to allegations that the clergy sanctioned these treasonous sentiments. As
rumours of a Fenian invasion mounted, Bishop Lynch came under
increasing pressure to denounce the Hibernians and he finally bowed to
internal and external pressure. In August of 1865, he condemned the
Hibernians and called on all Catholics to quit the organization since
they had 'fallen away from Catholic principles.'[40]

Once again, a struggle for leadership and control of the Irish community was apparent, but the internal alliances had shifted since the early
1860s. Now the clergy were supported by the middle-class elite, as moderate Irish Catholics sought to rein in a working-class organization
whose radicalism threatened their interests. This clash, essentially one
between strategies of protest and accommodation, came to a head in
March 1866 amid rumours that the long-anticipated Fenian invasion
was to coincide with a huge St. Patrick's Day parade organized by the
Hibernians.[41] As tension within the city mounted in the preceding
weeks, Irish moderates sought to distance themselves from the Hibernians to reassure the Protestant majority that the latter's extremism was
not shared by all. Having supported and even encouraged the extrem-
ists, Bishop Lynch found himself at the centre of the storm, as moderates
appealed to him to control the Hibernians. 'Everything depends on Your
Lordship,' D'Arcy McGee warned the Bishop, and he insisted that the
future of the entire Irish Catholic community in Canada was at stake:
'The position of our Church and race in Canada for the next 25 years,
will be determined by the stand taken, during these next six weeks.'[42]

In this situation, Lynch clearly had no choice but to ban the parade,
which he did shortly thereafter by advising all Catholics to spend the
day either in Church or at home. By this point, however, the Hibernians
had moved beyond the control of the clergy. Having forgone the procession at the Bishop's insistence the previous year, they were less amenable on this occasion, and insisted on their right to take to the streets
regardless of the consequences. Clearly, the Hibernians were determined to push the strategy of protest and their strident assertion of ethnic persistence to its extreme. But they had by now left the bulk of Irish
Catholics behind in this respect. While a great many supported their call
for Irish liberation and fervently resented the domestic prejudice which
the Hibernians sought to counter, very few were willing to provoke the
wrath of the host society or flout the authority of their bishop to express

these sentiments. Thus, only the die-hard Hibernians turned out to march in the smallest parade in years, and the anti-climax was completed by the failure of the Fenian invasion to materialize.[43]

This caution was even more forcibly demonstrated when the Fenian raids finally occurred in June of 1866. For despite a widespread expression of sullen resentment, an overwhelming majority of Irish Canadians were induced to hold themselves aloof from the Irish American 'liberators' by a combination of clerical and lay pressure, instincts of self-preservation and the desire for acceptance in their new homeland.[44] The Fenian raids, nevertheless, cast a shadow of suspicion over the entire Irish community in Canada. The inevitable Protestant backlash produced what one individual described as a 'reign of terror,' confirming McGee's dire predictions of the consequences of flirting with treason.[45] In this hostile climate, Catholics naturally reverted to a low profile and there was no suggestion of holding a public celebration on St. Patrick's Day 1867.

Once boisterous and triumphant, the Hibernians found their influence and prestige within the Toronto Irish community greatly undermined, and the round-up of suspected Fenian sympathizers further decimated the radical leadership. Control of the organization now reverted to relative moderates, such as Patrick Boyle, editor of the *Irish Canadian*; and while he followed Murphy's old lead in some respects, marked changes soon became apparent. Nationalism had proven its effectiveness as a vehicle for mobilizing the ethnic consciousness of Irish Catholic immigrants and focusing their resentment against the marginalization they experienced in their new home. But unlike the American situation, where republican nationalism placed Irish immigrants within the ideological mainstream, in Canada these sentiments clearly isolated them from the larger British population.[46] As well as separating the Irish from their neighbours, it also had the effect of alienating Catholics from their Church, which was the only institution in Canada the Irish could claim as their own. To rehabilitate themselves, therefore, nationalist leaders had to reforge the link between nationalism and Catholicism; develop a variation of nationalism which integrated rather than isolated Irish Catholics from Canadian society; and make their message more relevant by addressing the material needs of Irish Catholic immigrants in Toronto and Ontario. As with many other shifts within the Irish community, these developments would be reflected in the way St. Patrick's Day was celebrated.

After the Fenian fiasco, the Hibernians reverted to their former deference towards the Catholic Church, and the first public sign of this rapprochement came in 1868 when Bishop Lynch approved a resumption of the St. Patrick's Day parades. Although four hundred Hibernians turned out to lead the procession, both the attendance and the tone were far cries from the massive demonstrations of the early 1860s. A subdued atmosphere pervaded the celebrations, and this was clearly reflected in the speech delivered by Patrick Boyle which focused on the plight of Fenian prisoners in Canadian jails, but avoided more contentious issues.[47] This uncharacteristic moderation of the Hibernians stood in sharp contrast to the obsession which the nationalist press began to exhibit in provincial and federal politics. Obviously a more practical and effective means of improving the position of the Irish than the Utopian promises of the Fenians, this new focus also facilitated a growing cordiality between nationalists and members of the middle class who were determined to transform Irish Catholics into an influential political pressure group in Ontario.[48] The politicization of Irish nationalism received public expression on St. Patrick's Day 1869 when John O'Donohoe, a former member of the Toronto corporation and veteran political activist, was invited to deliver the key-note speech to the procession from the steps of St. Michael's Cathedral.[49] Although he paid lip-service to the traditional nationalist shibboleths, O'Donohoe focussed primarily on the political situation and the social inferiority suffered by Irish Catholics because of their lack of political influence. In the Legislature of Ontario, he lamented, 'we find our body as completely excluded as if we formed no portion of the body politic,' and he insisted that the only means of improving their standing within the province was by putting aside their internal differences and demanding their rightful share of power and the spoils of office: 'Let us practice unanimity and in cordial co-operation form a united phalanx, determined to live in harmony with all men – but determined for our right.'[50]

A consensus clearly existed within the Irish community concerning its subordinate status in Ontario and on the efficacy of political activity as a means of overcoming it. With the new moderation of the nationalists paving the way for closer co-operation with the clergy and the lay elite, all were soon working together within the Catholic League, a political pressure group established in 1870 to forward the political interest of the province's Catholics.[51] The League soon became the focus of Irish organizational activities, and this new concern with politics was reflected in the prominence which these matters received in subsequent St. Patrick's Day celebrations. Long an occasion for reaffirming religious or nationalist solidarity, the parades in the early 1870s also became a vehicle for disseminating political propaganda – indicating once again the flexibility of Irish immigrants to adapt traditional cultural practices to the needs of a new environment.[52]

This concern with politics reflected a very important change in the celebration of St. Patrick's Day, a change which manifested a wider shift within the Irish Catholic community in Toronto. Rather than emphasizing religious or ethnic exclusivity and separatism as had been the practice in the past, both the sermons and the outdoor speeches now focussed on the need to carve out for Irish Catholics an acceptable place in Ontario society.[53] These new integrationist tendencies may be seen as by-products of the growing adjustment of Irish immigrants to Ontario and the increasing acceptance and respect which they were receiving from the host society.[54] Moreover, the success of the Catholic League in attracting attention to Irish grievances and securing the election of an increasing number of Irish candidates suggested that they were gradually coming to wield the power and influence they felt they deserved within the political structures of their adopted home.[55]

By the mid-1870s, therefore, the collective fortunes of Irish Catholics in Toronto had improved considerably, and these changes were reflected in the celebration of St. Patrick's Day. While it was still felt necessary to advertise their presence and distinctiveness by taking to the streets on the feast of their patron saint, the event differed radically from the boisterous nationalist demonstrations of the early 1860s. The Hibernians were still present, but they attracted nowhere near the numbers they previously commanded. Their once splendid banners were now dilapidated and the speeches in support of Home Rule and constitutional solutions to the Irish problem, while compatible with their presence in a self-governing colony, were a far cry from Michael Murphy's fiery harangues of an earlier time.[56] Increasingly anachronistic, the Hibernians no longer exercised a stranglehold over the celebrations, and they were forced to share the podium with organizations such as the Father Matthew Temperance Society, the Emerald Benevolent Association and the Sons of St. Patrick.[57] The values which the latter sought to impress both on their audience and on the host society – sobriety, temperance, self-help and thrift – in short, mid-Victorian respectability – represented the new collective identity of the Irish Catholic community.[58] Indeed, the primary function of St. Patrick's Day celebrations now seemed to be to put lingering stereotypes to rest by demonstrating that Irish Catholics were worthy of full citizenship and total acceptance from a host society that had once expressed reservations about their fitness.[59]

Distance and time were gradually weakening the attachment of Irish immigrants to the Old Country and militant nationalism was giving way to nostalgic sentimentality. Increasingly prosperous and secure both economically and socially, and with a new generation growing up for whom Ireland had very little relevance, Irish Torontonians were in fact becoming Canadianized.[60] On a personal level, it was no longer necessary to rely on the ethnic support group for survival, and collective self-respect no longer depended upon a constant assertion of distinctiveness. Their efforts, instead, were directed towards downplaying the differences between themselves and their neighbours and, in this, the St. Patrick's Day celebration was an obstacle rather than an asset. Commenting on the extremely poor turnout at the 1876 parade, Patrick Boyle suggested that the time had come to re-evaluate the annual celebrations. These demonstrations perpetuated the isolation of Irish Catholics, he concluded, for of all the ethnic groups in Canada, they alone insisted on 'placing before the public their persons and sentiments in a more or less ridiculous drapery.'[61] More important than the ridicule of their neighbours, however, was the fact that such displays were increasingly incompatible with their higher duty as citizens of Canada:

Their abandonment is demanded by many considerations of good citizenship. They serve to maintain in this land, to which we have all come for quiet rather than broil, the miserable dissension and violence of a past which the present generation has outlived and outgrown. As a duty to the concord of society, to peace and order, to industry and steadiness, to that perfect unity which proves strength to the State, those processions which are instances of bad citizenship in this country ... ought to be abandoned.[62]

With even the remnants of radical nationalism losing interest, the future of the event was obviously in doubt, and it came as no surprise that 1877 saw the last public St. Patrick's Day celebration in Toronto for over a century.[63]

While it lasted, the event was the most visible demonstration of Irishness in the city and, as such, provided an important continuity between the Old World and the New for Irish immigrants. The parades, however, can only be understood in the context of the needs of the Irish Catholic community in their new environment. The unfurling of the green banners on St. Patrick's Day asserted the Irish Catholic right to the streets and constituted both a 'ritualized demand for recognition and an affirmation of ethnic solidarity in a predominantly Protestant city.'[64] The parades thus allowed Irish immigrants to define their collective identity, to advertise their distinctiveness and, in the process, to demand corporate recognition for their presence. The two decades after the Famine were crucial to the first of these goals, as Catholicism and nationalism were established as the parameters of Irish ethnicity and served as the focus of the celebrations until the 1870s. Resolving the appropriate response to the host society was much more contentious, however, as evidenced by the struggle for control of the celebrations by different elements within the Irish community. Protest and accommodation were ultimately the alternatives offered by those vying for ethnic leadership, and by the mid-1870s, the issue had been resolved in favour of the latter. Thus, nationalism was largely discarded because of its fundamental incompatibility with the prevailing English-Canadian ideology, and religion became the primary identity for a group who increasingly defined themselves as English-speaking Catholic Canadians.

The abandonment of the parades in the mid-1870s may therefore be seen as a crucial indicator of Irish assimilation, but also points to an important relationship between ethnic persistence and structural integration. For as long as Irish Catholics found themselves outside the Canadian mainstream, elements within the group insisted on preserving and advertising their distinctiveness, especially on St. Patrick's Day. When the political and economic structures began to embrace them, and Irish Catholic were afforded the same social acceptance as other groups, however, the need for displaying such distinctiveness was no longer perceived to exist. Thus, public celebrations of St. Patrick's Day, which had once served the interest of Irish immigrants recently arrived in a strange environment, were abandoned when they became an impediment to the group's subsequent and natural desire to become Canadian

NOTES

This article is from *Histoire sociale–Social History* 25 (49) (1992). Reprinted with permission.

1 S.E. Baker, 'Orange and Green: Belfast, 1832–1912,' in H.J. Dyos and M. Wolff, eds., *The Victorian City: Images and Realities*, Vol. II (London and Boston: Routledge and Keegan Paul, 1973), 790; D.W. Miller, 'The Armagh Troubles,

1784–87,' in S. Clark and J.S. Donnelly, Jr., eds., *Irish Peasants: Violence and Political Unrest, 1780–1914* (Madison: University of Wisconsin Press, 1983), 174–176.

2 G.S. Kealey, 'The Orange Order in Toronto: Religious Riot and the Working Class,' in R. O'Driscoll and C. Reynolds, eds., *The Untold Story: The Irish in Canada* (Toronto: Celtic Arts of Canada, 1988), 841–847.

3 This report was taken from the *Irish Canadian*, 18 March 1863; the *Canadian Freeman*, 19 March 1863; and the *Globe*, 18 March 1863.

4 *Irish Canadian*, 18 March 1863.

5 Ibid.

6 *Canadian Freeman*, 19 March 1863.

7 St. Patrick's Day celebrations as an institution within the Irish diaspora have received surprisingly little attention. See C.J. Fahey, 'Reflections on the St. Patrick's Day Orations of John Ireland,' *Ethnicity*, Vol. II (1975), 244–257; O. MacDonagh, 'Irish Culture and Nationalism Translated: St. Patrick's Day, 1888 in Australia,' in O. MacDonagh, W.F. Mandle and P. Travers, eds., *Irish Culture and Nationalism, 1750–1950* (London: Macmillan, 1983), 69–82.

8 J. Higham, ed., *Ethnic Leadership in America* (Baltimore and London: The Johns Hopkins University Press, 1978), 1–18.

9 *Leader*, 18 March 1863; and *Globe*, 18 March 1863.

10 For a demographic profile of Irish Catholics in Toronto, see Table 1.

11 *Mirror*, 19 March 1841 and 24 March 1843.

12 G.J. Parr, 'The Welcome and the Wake: Attitudes in Canada West Toward the Irish Famine Migration,' *Ontario History*, Vol. LXVI (1974), 101–113; K. Duncan, 'Irish Famine Immigration and the Social Structure of Canada West,' *Canadian Review of Sociology and Anthropology*, Vol. II (1965), 19–40; D. Connor, 'The Irish Canadians: Image and Self-Image' (M.A. thesis, University of British Columbia, 1976), 50–92.

13 D.S. Shea, 'The Irish Immigrant Adjustment to Toronto: 1840–1860,' *Canadian Catholic Historical Association. Study Sessions* (1972), 55–56; C. Houston and W.J. Smyth, 'Transferred Loyalties: Orangeism in the United States and Canada,' *American Review of Canadian Studies*, Vol. XIV (1984), 193–211; G.S. Kealey, 'The Orange Order in Toronto: Religious Riot and the Working Class,' in G.S. Kealey and P. Warrian, eds., *Essays in Canadian Working Class History* (Toronto: McClelland and Stewart, 1976), 13–34.

14 For an occupational profile of Irish Catholics in Toronto, see Table 2.

15 *Leader*, 25 January 1862.

16 M.W. Nicolson, 'The Catholic Church and the Irish in Victorian Toronto' (Ph.D. dissertation, University of Guelph, 1981); idem, 'Irish Tridentine

Catholicism in Victorian Toronto: Vessel for Ethno-Religious Persistence,' *Canadian Catholic Historical Association. Study Sessions*, Vol. L (1983), 415–436; B.P. Clarke, 'Piety, Nationalism and Fraternity: The Rise of Irish Catholic Voluntary Associations in Toronto, 1850–1895' (Ph.D. dissertation, University of Chicago, 1986), Vol. I.

17 *Mirror*, 7 March 1851; 14 March 1852; and 11 March 1853.

18 *Mirror*, 23 March 1855.

19 For the complex relationship between Catholicism and nationalism in Irish culture, see L.J. McCaffrey, 'Irish Catholicism and Irish Nationalism: A Study in Cultural Identity,' *Church History*, Vol. XLII (1973), 524–534.

20 The best evidence for the existence of this middle class was the proliferation of advertisements for wholesale establishments and professional services in the Irish ethnic press. See the *Mirror* or *Canadian Freeman*, 1850s.

21 The emergence of lay voluntary organizations revolving around Irish nationalism is explored in detail in Clarke, 'Irish Voluntary Associations, Vol. II.'

22 *Mirror*, 30 November and 21 December 1855.

23 *Mirror*, 20 March 1857.

24 Ibid.

25 *Mirror*, 28 March 1856.

26 J.R. Miller, 'Bigotry in the North Atlantic Triangle: Irish, British and American Influences on Canadian Anti-Catholicism, 1850–1900,' *Studies in Religion*, Vol. XVI (1987), 289–301.

27 The power of the Order was perhaps best demonstrated by its virtual stranglehold on municipal politics for much of the nineteenth century. See G.S. Kealey, 'The Union of the Canadas,' in V.L. Russell, ed., *Forging a Consensus: Historic Essays on Toronto* (Toronto: University of Toronto Press, 1984), 41–86.

28 P. Toner, 'The Rise of Irish Nationalism in Canada' (Ph.D. dissertation, National University of Ireland, 1974), 27–35; Clarke, 'Irish Voluntary Associations,' 305–307.

29 *Globe*, 18 and 19 March 1858; *Leader*, 18 and 19 March 1858.

30 For an introduction to the Ribbonite tradition, see T. Garvin, 'Defenders, Ribbonmen and Others: Underground Political Networks in Pre-Famine Ireland,' *Past and Present*, Vol. LXXXXVI (1982), 133–155; and J. Lee, 'The Ribbonmen,' in T.D. Williams, ed., *Secret Societies in Ireland* (Dublin: Gill and Macmillan, 1973), 26–35.

31 Clarke, 'Irish Voluntary Associations,' esp. 289–329; G. Sheppard, 'God Save the Green: Fenianism and Fellowship in Victorian Ontario,' *Histoire Sociale– Social History*, Vol. XX (1987), 129–144.

32 Archives of the Archdiocese of Toronto (henceforth A.A.T.), Archbishop Lynch Papers, Rev. G.R. Northgraves to Lynch, 4 March 1865.
33 *Leader*, 18 March 1862 and *Canadian Freeman*, 20 March 1862.
34 Occupational profiles of Hibernian membership demonstrate it was 'predominantly a working-class organization.' Clarke, 'Irish Voluntary Associations,' 365–366.
35 *Canadian Freeman*, 20 March 1862; *Irish Canadian*, 18 March 1863 and 23 March 1864.
36 A.A.T., Lynch Papers, Bishop Lynch to Bishop Farrell, 12 August 1865 and Bishop Lynch to Archbishop T. Connolly, 1 February 1866.
37 *Irish Canadian*, 7 January 1863.
38 *Irish Canadian*, 18 March, 25 March 1863 and 23 March 1864; *Canadian Freeman*, 19 March 1863, 24 March and 31 March 1864; *Leader*, 18 March 1864.
39 *Canadian Freeman*, 31 March, 14 April and 21 April 1864.
40 A.A.T., Archbishop Lynch Papers, Bishop Lynch to Bishop Farrell, 12 August 1865, *Canadian Freeman*, 17 August 1865.
41 *Globe*, 9 March 1866.
42 A.A.T., Archbishop Lynch Papers, T.D. McGee to Bishop Lynch, 7 March 1866.
43 *Globe*, 18 March 1866; *Irish Canadian*, 21 March 1866.
44 W.S. Neidhardt, *Fenianism in North America* (Pennsylvania: Pennsylvania State University Press, 1975), 50–80.
45 National Archives of Canada, J.L.P. O'Hanley Papers, Vol. 1, J.L.P. O'Hanley to J. Hearn, 4 May 1868.
46 For the role of Irish nationalism in the integration of Irish immigrants into American society, see T.N. Brown, *Irish-American Nationalism, 1870–1890* (New York: J.P. Lippincott, 1966).
47 *Leader*, 18 March 1868 and *Irish Canadian*, 18 March 1868.
48 M. Cottrell, 'Irish Catholic Political Leadership in Toronto, 1855–1882: A Study of Ethnic Politics' (Ph.D. dissertation, University of Saskatchewan, 1988), 225–312.
49 For O'Donohoe's career, see M. Cottrell, 'John O'Donohoe and the Politics of Ethnicity in Ontario,' *Canadian Catholic Historical Association, Historical Papers*, forthcoming.
50 *Irish Canadian*, 24 March 1869.
51 M. Cottrell, 'Irish Political Leadership,' 225–312.
52 *Irish Canadian*, 23 March 1870, 20 March 1872, 19 March 1873 and 22 March 1876; *Canadian Freeman*, 23 March 1871.
53 *Irish Canadian*, 22 March 1871 and 18 March 1874.

54 M. McGowan, 'We Endure What We Cannot Cure: J.J. Lynch and Roman Catholic–Protestant Relations in Toronto, 1864–75. Frustrated Attempts at Peaceful Co-Existence,' *Canadian Society of Church History Papers*, Vol. XV (1984), 16–17.
55 M. Cottrell, 'Irish Political Leadership,' 313–454; D. Swainson, 'James O'Reilly and Catholic Politics,' *Historic Kingston*, Vol. XXI (1973), 11–21.
56 *Irish Canadian*, 20 March 1872 and 18 March 1874.
57 Ibid., 22 March 1876.
58 Clarke, 'Irish Voluntary Associations,' 433–438.
59 *Irish Canadian*, 22 March 1876 and 21 March 1877.
60 For the transformation of Toronto's Irish Catholics into an English-speaking Canadian Catholic community, see M. McGowan, 'We are All Canadians: A Social, Religious and Cultural Portrait of Toronto's English-Speaking Roman Catholics, 1890–1920' (Ph.D. dissertation, University of Toronto, 1988).
61 *Irish Canadian*, 5 April 1876.
62 Ibid., 5 April 1876.
63 Ibid., 20 March 1878.
64 Clarke, 'Irish Voluntary Associations,' 460.

TOPIC TWO
American Blacks in Nineteenth-Century Ontario: Challenging the Stereotypes

The legendary story of the Underground Railway is celebrated in a 'Heritage Minute,' one of a series of sixty-second docudramas broadcast regularly on television and designed to promote Canadian history. In it, a young black woman, a fugitive slave from the United States, anxiously awaits the arrival of her father, also an escaping slave who is being smuggled into Canada. At her side stands the calm and reassuring figure of a white Canadian woman abolitionist. Tensions mount when the black woman bursts out of the room in time to see the arrival of the carriage that was to carry her father safely to freedom. After some tense moments, 'Pa' emerges from his hiding place – a church pew atop the carriage – to embrace his relieved daughter and son. Seeking to assure the disoriented father that the journey to freedom was complete, one of his children cries: 'We're free! We're in Canada!'

The Underground Railway was a clandestine network of escape routes, personal contacts, and safe houses that facilitated the escape of slaves to places throughout the northern United States and Canada. The dramatization of the fugitive slaves and the white abolitionists is a striking illustration of the near-mythical place the Underground Railway holds in the history of Canada, and especially Ontario. The image of the white abolitionist guiding fugitive slaves from the clutches of American slave-owners to the freedom of British soil fits well with the commonly held assumption in Canada that our country is more tolerant than the United States. One could argue that this belief is not without some justification. In the 1830s, more than three decades before the end of slavery in the United States, Britain had abolished slavery throughout the empire. Since the 1790s, the colony of Upper Canada (later Ontario) had officially prohibited the recruitment of slave labour. Since the American

Revolution (1783–5), moreover, American blacks escaping slavery had looked to British North America as a place where they might enjoy basic civil rights. During the first half of the nineteenth century, especially in the decades before the U.S. Civil War (1860–5), Ontario (then Canada West) became the final terminus of the Underground Railway for thousands of American blacks. Men outnumbered women, but large numbers of families also arrived. Many of the newcomers settled in the southwestern part of the province, where some of them participated in experiments to build independent, all-Black, Christian, 'utopian' communities on frontier regions between Windsor and Toronto. In Ontario, American black abolitionists continued to wage their struggle against slavery south of the border.

Popular mythology, however, is often marked by omissions and errors. The dramatization described above, for example, falsely downplays the courageous role that African Americans, including ex-slaves like Harriet Tubman, played in maintaining the escape routes. For them, getting caught could mean re-enslavement. Also, many escaping slaves found alternative routes to freedom. The latest research also suggests that many black Americans who came to Ontario in this period, probably even a majority of them, were not slaves escaping the southern United States, but freed black men and women reacting to a deterioration in their civil rights.

What of the image of Canada as a more tolerant society? As the essays that follow reveal, this myth, too, must be analysed. Howard Law's essay suggests that the discrepancy between abolitionist ideals and ex-slaves' expectation, as well as white hostility to black communities, complicated the transition from slavery to freedom. His essay also probes the motives behind and the role of elites in the utopian experiments. What led abolitionists in Ontario to propose different strategies for adjustment? What were the main differences between a strategy of racial segregation and one of integration? Jason Silverman focuses on the black abolitionist Mary Ann Shadd Cary, educator, journalist, orator, and an advocate of black integration. What factors shaped her political activism? Did her disagreements with the segregationists hurt the cause of black settlement?

The essays by Law and Silverman challenge the notion of Canada as a haven for blacks. They also suggest that we should not view African American newcomers as a monolithic group, for this migration stream included ex-slaves, freed men and women, working-class people, farmers, and professionals. Michael Wayne's article alerts us to other popular misconceptions. Drawing on manuscript census data, he demonstrates, for example, that scholars have overestimated the number of these new-comers who actually returned to the United States during and after the Civil War. Why is it important to know precisely how many American blacks actually returned to the United States? What might it suggest about the nature of their experiences in Canada? How important was the guarantee to blacks of equality before the law in the face of perva-sive racism and sexism? Why did middle-class leaders like Shadd go back? Why did plenty of ordinary farmers and workers stay?

NOTE

1 Charles R. Bronfman Foundation, Heritage Minute, 'Underground Railway.'

BIBLIOGRAPHY AND SUGGESTED READINGS

Bristow, Peggy et al., eds. *We're Rooted Here They Can't Pull Us Up: Essays in Afri-can Canadian Women's History.* Toronto 1994.

Hill, Daniel. *The Blacks in Early Canada: The Freedom Seekers.* Agincourt, Ont. 1981.

Pease, William H., and Jane H. Pease. *Black Utopia: Negro Communal Experiments in America.* Madison 1963.

Ripley, C. Peter, et al., eds. *The Black Abolitionist Papers.* Vol. 2: *Canada, 1830–1865.* Chapel Hill 1986.

Silverman, Jason. *Unwelcome Guests: Canada West's Response to American Fugitive Slaves, 1880–1865.* Millwood, NY 1985.

Stouffer, Allen P. *The Light of Nature and the Law of God: Antislavery in Ontario, 1833–1877.* Montreal, 1992.

Winks, Robin. *The Blacks in Canada: A History.* Montreal 1971.

Yee, Shirley. 'Gender Ideology and Black Women: Community Builders in Ontario, 1850–1870.' *Canadian Historical Review* 75 (March 1994).

The Black Population of Canada West on the Eve of the American Civil War: A Reassessment Based on the Manuscript Census of 1861

MICHAEL WAYNE

There is a tour you can take through southwestern Ontario that stops at a number of historical sites associated with runaway slaves, including the home of Josiah Henson, once thought to be the model for Harriet Beecher Stowe's Uncle Tom. This tour, known as 'The Road to Freedom,' provides a good illustration of the extent to which fugitive slaves dominate popular perceptions of the history of blacks in nineteenth-century Ontario. So do the books that schoolchildren read about the exploits of the men and women of the Underground Railroad. So too do the stories that appear in newspapers each year during Black History Month recounting the trials and triumphs of slaves who made their way to Canada.

Scholars have raised doubts about the more extravagant claims made for the Underground Railroad and have brought an appropriately critical eye to the reminiscences of individual runaways.[1] Otherwise, however, they have presented a picture of the past that is largely in accord with the popular view. Indeed, it is the interpretation historians have offered of the demography of the period that provides the principal justification for placing the fugitive slave at the centre of nineteenth-century black history. That interpretation is built on four separate but related arguments: there were approximately 40,000 blacks in Canada West in 1860; an overwhelming majority of these 40,000 were runaway slaves and their children; the black population concentrated itself narrowly in a small number of communities along the western edge of Lake Ontario and in southwestern Ontario; and the great majority of blacks returned to the United States after the Civil War.[2]

It comes as a surprise, then, to discover that this interpretation is apparently wrong in all its particulars. The enumerators' schedules from the 1861 census for Canada West, hardly flawless but substantially more reliable than any other available source, suggest that historians have exaggerated the size of the black population in general, significantly overstated the proportion of that population who were fugitives from slavery, underestimated the degree to which blacks were dispersed throughout the province, and misrepresented the extent of return migration.

We can begin with the question of the number of blacks in the province before the war. The opinion of commentators varied at the time, with estimates ranging between 15,000 and 75,000. The historian who has done the most thorough survey of contemporary views, Robin Winks, argues that the most frequently quoted figure, 40,000, is probably reasonably accurate. As Winks acknowledges, however, it is difficult to know how seriously to take the impressionistic evidence. Most commentators had little upon which to base their estimates beyond personal observation, hearsay, and infrequent reports about blacks in local newspapers.[3] Furthermore, abolitionists, because they were determined to bring the horrors of slavery to the forefront of public consciousness, had reason to exaggerate the number of fugitives; so did the many white Canadians who were opposed to black immigration.

Because the census of 1861 provided for the collection of data on colour, in theory at least historians have always had the means to go beyond the speculation of contemporaries.[4] Until now, however, it has been assumed that the enumeration was so flawed as to make the data collected worthless.[5] The final report published by the Census Department indicated that there were only 11,223 blacks in Canada West.[6] Since that figure was almost 4,000 below even the lowest estimates made at the time, it seemed evident to historians that enumerators had neglected to record a significant proportion of the black population.

Examination of the original manuscript schedules, however, suggests that it was the clerks who transcribed the data who were at fault, not the enumerators. The census rolls include entries on 17,053 blacks, not the 11,000 quoted in the published report. The former figure falls within the low range of estimates made at the time. For example, Samuel Gridley Howe of the American Freedman's Inquiry Commission, described by Winks as 'on the whole a careful man,' claimed in 1863 that there were 15,000 to 20,000 blacks in the province.[7] There are also other more convincing reasons for accepting the results of the manuscript census. Instructions to enumerators regarding column 13 of the schedules, in which information on colour was to be recorded, stated: 'In this column mark a figure (1) after every *Colored* person's name, i.e. Negro or Negress. This was much neglected last Census and the number of colored persons was not ascertained.'[8] In other words, enumerators

TABLE 1 The Black Population of Designated Communities in Canada West as Recorded by Benjamin Drew in 1854 and in the Manuscript Census Schedules of 1861

	Drew	Census
St. Catharines	800	609
Toronto	1,000	987
Hamilton	274	476
Galt	40	31
London	350	370
Chatham	800	1,252
Windsor	250	533
Sandwich	100	95
Amherstburg	400–500	373
Colchester	450	937
Gosfield	78	101
Total	4,642	5,764

Sources: Canada West Manuscript Census Schedules, 1861, for Essex County, Kent County, Lincoln County, Waterloo County, City of Hamilton, City of London, City of Toronto; Drew, A North-Side View of Slavery, pp. 17–18, 94, 118, 136, 147, 234, 321, 341, 348, 367, 378.

were under express orders to secure an accurate count of blacks. Not that we should assume that they were invariably diligent in carrying out all their assigned duties. The Prescott County representative wrote his superiors asking how much information on blacks they wanted him to gather: 'It would be difficult in most cases to ascertain their Names Religion birth Place ages or any thing else ...'[9] Negligence in recording data on religion, age, or even names is not the same as leaving individuals off the rolls entirely, however, and there is little evidence to suggest that enumerators failed to take seriously their responsibility to provide Bureau officials with an accurate count.

The most compelling corroborating evidence is based on statistics. In 1854 the abolitionist Benjamin Drew came to Canada West to interview fugitive slaves. He accepted uncritically the claim by the Anti-Slavery Society that there were almost 30,000 blacks in Canada in 1852.[10] At the same time, in each community he visited he was able to ascertain through conversation with residents what was presumably a reasonably accurate figure on the size of the local black population. The figures he recorded for individual communities can be compared with the figures derived from the 1861 manuscript schedules. As Table 1 clearly indicates, the numbers that Drew reported – they total more than 1,000 fewer individuals than enumerators recorded seven years later – are far too low to support the estimate made by the Anti-Slavery Society. On

TABLE 2 The Black Population of Designated Communities in Canada West as Recorded by Samuel Gridley Howe in 1863 and in the Manuscript Census Schedules of 1861

	Howe	Census
St. Catharines	700	609
Hamilton	500+	476
Chatham	1,300	1,252
Toronto	934	987
Windsor	500	533
Total	3,934	3,857

Sources: Canada West Manuscript Census Schedules, 1861, for Essex County, Kent County, Lincoln County, City of Hamilton, City of Toronto; Howe, 'The Self-Freedmen of Canada West,' pp. 25, 101, 125.

the contrary, taking into account population growth over the last half of the decade through natural increase and especially immigration, they lend substantial support to the argument that the enumeration of 1861 should be regarded as reliable.

Further support comes from statistics collected by Samuel Gridley Howe during his investigation of the black population in 1863. As already indicated, Howe concluded that no more than 15,000 to 20,000 blacks were living in the province at that time, although he was aware that most contemporaries thought the true figure was much higher. In his report he cited presumably reliable estimates for the number of blacks in St. Catharines, Hamilton, Chatham, Toronto (provided by George Barber, Secretary of the Board of School Trustees), and Windsor (provided by Reverend A.R. Green, a black minister from the community). As Table 2 demonstrates, his estimates correspond closely to the figures based on the 1861 manuscript census.

All this does not mean that the number 17,053 should be taken as definitive. Numerous studies have indicated that there were substantial undercounts in the nineteenth-century American censuses – as much as 20 per cent in certain communities.[11] Canadian schedules are unlikely to be more reliable in this regard. Even if we assume that enumerators did miss fully one-fifth of the black population in Canada West, however, that would still leave a total of only about 20,500. Add another 2,000 or so for individuals passing as white – a phenomenon apparently fairly common in Toronto, although less so elsewhere – and we end up with a figure of maybe 22,500 or 23,000.[12] The conclusion seems inescapable: historians have significantly overestimated the black population of Canada West in 1860, probably by 75 per cent or more.

Once the figure for the black population is corrected downward, a second part of the standard interpretation has to be discarded: there was no mass migration of blacks back to the United States at the end of the Civil War. The claim that such a migration took place has always been based less on testimony by contemporaries than on statistical inference. The published census of 1871, considered a far more reliable source than the report produced a decade earlier, indicated that there were approximately 13,500 blacks in Canada West at that time.[13] If the correct figure for 1861 was 40,000, then fully two-thirds of the black population had left the province by the end of the decade, presumably emigrating, or returning, to the United States. Since in reality enumerators found about 17,000 blacks in 1861, it follows that only a minority left Canada West in the aftermath of the Civil War. If we assume that the 1871 census was no more or less likely to suffer from an undercount than the census a decade earlier, and if we conclude that the proportion of individuals passing as white remained roughly constant, then the black population of Canada West decreased by about 20 per cent during the period of 1861 to 1871. While this represents a substantial decline, it hardly amounts to an exodus. Apparently an overwhelming majority of blacks chose to remain in the province after the Civil War.

Although contemporaries differed widely over the size of the black population, there was unanimous agreement on another point: the great majority of blacks were fugitive slaves. The *First Report of the Anti-Slavery Society of Canada* noted in 1852 that 'nearly all the adults and many of the children have been fugitive slaves from the United States.'[14] In his autobiography, published in 1854, the fugitive Samuel Ringgold Ward observed, 'I do not believe that with the exception of the children born in Canada, there are 3,000 free-born coloured persons in the whole colony.'[15] When he travelled through Canada West seven years later the American abolitionist William Wells Brown was struck by the size of the fugitive population at each locality he visited. Of St. Catharines, he noted: 'Out of the eight hundred in St. Catharines, about seven hundred of them are fugitive slaves.' Of Chatham: 'The population here is made up entirely from the Slave States, with but a few exceptions.' Of Buxton: 'There are now nearly 600 persons in this settlement .... Most of these people were slaves in the South.' Of Windsor: 'a place of 2,500 inhabitants, 600 of whom are colored, and most of the latter class are fugitives from slavery.'[16]

Historians have always recognized that such estimates cannot be taken at face value. As already noted, it was in the interests of abolitionists to exaggerate the number of fugitives. As well, the prejudices of the times led most white Canadians to assume that any black person they encountered was a runaway slave.[17] But the main objection to contemporary estimates is simply that they are inconsistent with what we know about the incidence of successful flight by American blacks from slavery. No more than 1,000 or so slaves escaped during any given year, and of these the vast majority settled in the free states.[18] It is no doubt true that, following the passage of the restrictive Fugitive Slave Act of 1850, when life became much less secure for runaways in the North, the numbers continuing to Canada increased,[19] but it is unreasonable to assume that more than a small fraction took up residence outside the United States. Still, well aware of the problems with contemporary estimates, historians have without exception embraced the view that a significant majority of the blacks in Canada West before the Civil War were fugitive slaves and their children. Winks, for example, puts the figure at approximately 75 per cent.[20]

The manuscript census tells a different story. By 1861, of the total enumerated black population of over 17,000, approximately 9,800, or only about 57 per cent, were originally from the United States. Over 6,900, more than 40 per cent, were native-born Canadians (see Table 3). While most American blacks listed their birthplace in the schedules as 'United States,' a sizable number, 744, indicated the particular state in which they had been born. As Table 4 shows, the results confirm the popular impression that the great majority of blacks who came from the United States were natives of the slave states – over 70 per cent, in fact. Not all blacks from the South were fugitive slaves, however. Most had been born in either Maryland, Virginia, or Kentucky.[21] Over 150,000 free blacks lived in these three states in 1860. Free blacks represented 49.5 per cent of the black population in Maryland, 10.6 per cent in Virginia, and 4.5 per cent in Kentucky.[22] It was obviously far easier for a free person to get to Canada than it was for a slave, and conditions for free blacks were deteriorating rapidly in the 1850s. By the eve of the Civil War nearly every Southern state was considering legislation to relegate some or all of its free black population to slavery.[23] Even without any other evidence, it would be reasonable to assume that a significant proportion of the Southern blacks who came to Canada were free immigrants, not fugitive slaves.

As it happens, however, additional evidence is available. We can use the data on sex in the census schedules to make credible inferences about the percentage of the black population from the slave states that was free.

TABLE 3 Distribution of the Black Population of Canada West by Birthplace and Age, 1861

	Age				
	Unknown	Under 20	20 and over	Total	%
Africa	1	1	18	20	0.1
West Indies	–	1	43	44	0.3
British Isles	–	15	50	65	0.4
Maritime Provinces	–	2	8	10	0.0
Canada East	–	30	48	78	0.5
Canada West	21	5,765	1,120	6,906	40.5
United States	28	2,739	7,039	9,806	57.5
Other	–	0	7	7	0.0
Unknown	–	69	48	117	0.7
Total	50	8,622	8,381	17,053	100.0

Source: Canada West Manuscript Census Schedules, 1861.

As the statistics on blacks born in the Northern states make clear, it can be assumed that free men and women were more or less equally likely to relocate to Canada.[24] Historians agree that males made up a disproportionate number of the fugitives from slavery.[25] Men were more likely than women to have opportunities to travel beyond the plantation and to learn to read and write. Furthermore, women were less likely to be sold away from their children and as a result arguably had stronger emotional ties to family. The best estimates suggest that somewhere around 75 to 80 per cent of runaways were men. As Table 5 indicates, out of a total of 521 blacks in Canada West who indicated in the census schedules that they had been born in the slave states, 197 (or 38 per cent) were women and 324 (or 62 per cent) were men. If we assume that males would have made up 75 per cent of the fugitives from slavery, then simple algebra establishes that only 49 per cent of blacks from the Southern states were runaway slaves while 51 per cent were free.[26] This means that out of the total of approximately 9,800 blacks born in the United States, only 34 per cent were fugitives. Since American-born blacks represented only 57.5 per cent of all blacks in Canada West, slightly under 20 per cent of all the blacks in the province were fugitives.[27]

Of course, children made up a large proportion of the black population. As Table 3 indicates, a little over half the individuals recorded in the census were under 20 years of age. More to the point, at the time of the enumeration a substantial number of Canadian-born blacks, more

TABLE 4 Distribution of the Black Population of American Origin by State of Birth, 1861

Slave states	No.	Free states[a]	No.
D.C.	20	Massachusetts	4
Delaware	17	Vermont	8
Maryland	162	Connecticut	6
Virginia	169	'New England'	1
Kentucky	101	New York	75
Missouri	6	New Jersey	11
North Carolina	8	Pennsylvania	53
Tennessee	4	Ohio	28
South Carolina	7	Michigan	27
Georgia	7	Indiana	1
Alabama	2	Illinois	5
Louisiana	4	Kansas	1
'South States'	14	New Mexico	2
		Wisconsin	1
Total	521	Total	223
Proportion	70.0%	Proportion	30.0%

a) Kansas and New Mexico were territories, not states, at the time of the Canadian
    census. Under the terms of the doctrine of popular sovereignty applied to Kansas by
    the Kansas-Nebraska Act of 1854 and to New Mexico by the Compromise of 1850, it
    was up to the residents of the individual territories to decide for themselves whether
    they wanted to allow slavery. The issue was still unresolved in both jurisdictions at
    the outbreak of the Civil War. I have arbitrarily grouped both territories with the free
    states. The two individuals born in New Mexico and the one in Kansas were children
    of a tailor named George Washington and his wife, Frances, both of whom listed their
    birthplace as 'United States'. The family almost certainly was free.
Source: Canada West Manuscript Census Schedules, 1861.

than 4,500, were living with at least one parent who had either fled or
migrated to the province from the United States.[28] How many of these
American parents of Canadian-born children had escaped from slavery
is impossible to say, but there can be little reason to accept Robin
Winks's claim that fugitives and their sons and daughters represented
75 per cent of the black population. Somewhere between 30 and 40 per
cent would seem to be a much more reasonable estimate.

In the fall of 1861 William Wells Brown came to Canada West to promote the cause of Haitian emigration among blacks. He began his journey in Toronto, stopped for a time at Hamilton and St. Catharines,
turned west to London, and finally made his way to Chatham, Dresden,
Windsor, Amherstburg, Colchester, and the all-black Elgin settlement at
Buxton. His itinerary was much like the one the abolitionist Benjamin
Drew had followed in 1854 when he came to the province to interview

TABLE 5 Distribution of the American-Born Black Population by Sex, According to State of Birth, 1861

	Male	Female	Total
Slave states			
D.C.	9	11	20
Delaware	6	11	17
Maryland	98	64	162
Virginia	116	53	169
Kentucky	61	40	101
Missouri	4	2	6
North Carolina	5	3	8
Tennessee	3	1	4
South Carolina	4	3	7
Georgia	5	2	7
Alabama	1	1	2
Louisiana	3	1	4
'South States'	9	5	14
Total	324	197	521
Percentage	62.2%	37.8%	100.0%
Free states			
Massachusetts	1	3	4
Vermont	5	3	8
Connecticut	2	4	6
'New England'	1	0	1
New York	36	39	75
New Jersey	4	7	11
Pennsylvania	24	29	53
Ohio	16	12	28
Michigan	13	14	27
Indiana	1	0	1
Illinois	5	0	5
Kansas	0	1	1
New Mexico	2	0	2
Wisconsin	1	0	1
Total	111	112	223
Percentage	49.8%	50.2%	100.0%

Source: Canada West Manuscript Census Schedules, 1861.

fugitive slaves. Two years after Brown, Samuel Gridley Howe took a similar route when he travelled through the province gathering information for the Freedmen's Inquiry Commission.[29]

Brown, Drew, and Howe thought that they could take the measure of the black population by going to a limited number of centres where blacks had located in large numbers. Historians have, if anything, carried this reasoning even further by focusing on the handful of all-black communities that were established in the province. Winks reserves almost an entire chapter of his authoritative *The Blacks in Canada* for discussion of such communities. The Elgin settlement alone has been the subject of a book, several articles, and at least one doctoral dissertation.[30] Under the circumstances, it is scarcely surprising that many people appear to be under the impression that the great majority of blacks lived in separate enclaves in and around the Chatham area.

As the 1861 manuscript census reveals, however, the black population of Canada West was much more widely dispersed than anyone has ever imagined. Blacks appear in a total of 312 townships and city wards in the schedules, representing every county and city of the province and the Algoma district (see Appendix). Of course, they were much more heavily concentrated in some localities than others. By 1861 there were over 1,250 blacks in Chatham and over 1,300 in Raleigh township, where Elgin was located. Many whites in such commmunities claimed that they were being inundated by fugitive slaves, but it is important to go beyond the perspective of Canadian whites. Imagine, for instance, how things must have looked to an immigrant from Virginia. In his or her native state, 57 per cent of all blacks lived in counties in which blacks were in the majority. By contrast, the heaviest concentration of blacks in Canada West was in Raleigh township, where they represented only about one-third of the total population. In Virginia less than one per cent of all blacks lived in counties in which they constituted under 3 per cent of the population. In Canada almost 30 per cent of blacks lived in townships or city wards in which this was the case; over 12 per cent lived in communities where blacks were less than one per cent of the population.[31] As well, the concentration of blacks was substantially greater in Deep South states than it was in Virginia. To a fugitive slave who had escaped from Georgia or a free black who had emigrated from South Carolina, the contrast between his or her present and former surroundings must have been all that much more striking.

There are serious objections to treating the all-black settlements as windows into the black experience as a whole. Their fraction of the total black population was never significant. Furthermore, with the exception of Elgin, they were notoriously unsuccessful. No more than 150 to 200 individuals ever resided at Oro on Lake Simcoe or Wilberforce, the two earliest settlements, or at the Refugee Home Society, established in the 1850s outside Windsor. The population of Dawn near Dresden rose as high as 500 for a brief time in the early 1850s, but was never stable.[32] As for Elgin, William Wells Brown found about 600 people there in 1861.[33] That represented less than 3 per cent of the total black population of the province on the eve of the Civil War.

In sum, it appears that historians have overstated the importance of the all-black settlements and given far too little attention to the apparent willingness of blacks to settle in communities where they were outnumbered, often vastly so. A comparison is suggestive. The only immigrant group in the middle of the nineteenth century that was roughly comparable in size to the black population was the Germans.[34] About 35 per cent of German settlers took up residence in a single county, Waterloo. Under 28 per cent of all blacks lived in Kent, the county of heaviest black concentration.[35]

The pattern of settlement and the free origins of the majority of American immigrants suggest new directions for historical research into the black experience in Canada West. Before looking at what those directions may be, however, it would be useful to spend a moment considering some sources of bias in the existing impressionistic evidence. The issue of slavery dominated public debate in the United States during the 1850s, dividing the nation. There was no accompanying difference of opinion over race, however. With few exceptions whites from both sections subscribed to what George Fredrickson has called 'herrenvolk egalitarianism': a belief that black subservience was a precondition for white equality.[36] Almost all Northern states imposed substantial legal disabilities on blacks, which is why in the famous Dred Scott case Chief Justice Roger Taney felt justified in arguing that blacks had always been treated as if 'they had no rights which the white man was bound to respect,' and why several thousand blacks from the free states decided to emigrate.[37] This state of affairs – conflict over slavery but consensus over race – clearly influenced what was written at the time about blacks in Canada. There was great interest in runaway slaves – in the conditions they faced under slavery, the means by which they escaped, their adjustment to life in a free land.[38] By contrast, there was comparatively little attention paid to the background or experiences of free blacks. Indeed, as mentioned earlier, many whites seem to have assumed that any black they encountered was a runaway slave. Under the circumstances, it is scarcely surprising that fugitive slaves have come to play a disproportionately large role in both scholarly and popular histories of the period.

A second source of bias is directly related to the pattern of settlement. Where blacks concentrated in large numbers – and especially in areas where racial tensions were high – separate institutions emerged. The records of institutions can be a rich resource for historians. They are much more likely than the private papers of ordinary families to end up in archives and libraries, they frequently are clearly written and organized, and more often than not they contain a wealth of valuable information. There is a danger, however, that a scholar who relies heavily on such records may be inclined to exaggerate the extent to which members of a given institution are representative of other individuals of the same race, class, sex, or ethnicity. Historians of Ontario, like historians of the Northern states, have drawn extensively on documents from black churches, schools, and charitable organizations, along with surviving issues of black newspapers, to gain insight into nineteenth-century black life. Similarly, they have produced interpretations of the black experience that devote considerable attention to the development of separate institutions and take as their central theme the formation of a black 'community.'[39] But as the historical record makes quite clear, even in localities where blacks were heavily concentrated, many people decided against attending separate churches, objected in principle to separate schools, and chose not to subscribe to black newspapers (as the editors frequently complained). Those men and women who did make the decision to settle in towns such as Bowmanville or Sidney, where the number of black families was small, could hardly have done so in the expectation that they would be part of a separate black community or that their children and grandchildren – or they themselves, if they were single – would find black marriage partners. It is noteworthy that 385 black men listed in the census had white wives, mainly immigrant women from Europe or the British Isles. This represented approximately one out of every seven black married men, or almost one in five if we exclude those individuals from the United States who we can infer from the census were already married when they arrived in Canada.[40]

It is time, then, that historians gave serious attention to the men and women who chose to settle in localities where the black population was too small to sustain separate institutions or a separate culture. Obviously the lives of such people would have differed dramatically from the lives of blacks in, say, Chatham or St. Catharines. Perhaps so, too, did their assumptions about the meaning and significance of race. In addition, we need to know more about the free blacks who came to Canada West and about the blacks who were born in the province. The literature is not silent on these individuals, but at the moment we only have a slight understanding of how their experiences compared and contrasted to those of runaway slaves. Finally and most importantly, we need to know much more about how the different elements of the black population related to each other. A traveller passing through the townships or city wards where blacks resided in 1861 was liable to come across field hands escaped from cotton or tobacco plantations, artisans and clergymen from the Northern states, native-born farmers, labourers, and professionals, perhaps even one or two free blacks from the South who had themselves owned slaves.[41] At this point we really know very little about how men and women of such divergent backgrounds and, perhaps, material interests viewed each other. The truth is, we cannot even say with certainty that most blacks shared the assumption of both nineteenth-century whites and present-day historians that race mattered more than class, gender, religious affiliation, or nationality in defining who they were or in determining their place in Canadian society.

Whatever the direction of future research, it must take as its starting point an accurate picture of the demography of the period. Perhaps the most unfortunate consequence of the prevailing view is that it tends to perpetuate the nineteenth-century perception of blacks as outsiders. If most blacks were fugitives, if they lived by themselves in a limited number of communities near the border, and if the overwhelming majority returned to the United States after the Civil War, then clearly they were not truly part of the Canadian immigrant experience. Certainly one can find instances of American blacks who held what might be described as an 'exile mentality'.[42] They spoke with passion of their love for the United States and their dreams of returning home once the blight of slavery had been eliminated. More compelling, however, is the testimony of the many individuals, both slave and free, who saw Canada as a land of new possibilities. Listen to Alexander Hemsley, for example. Born a slave in Maryland, he escaped to Canada when he was in his thirties. After spending a short time in Toronto he moved to the St. Catharines area where, with another man, he acquired five acres of cleared land and started farming:

We were then making both ends meet. I then made up my mind that salt and potatoes in Canada were better than pound-cake and chickens in a state of suspense and anxiety in the United States. Now I am a regular Britisher. My American blood has been scourged out of me ...[43]

Finally, there is the testimony of the census itself. By 1861 blacks had made their way to all corners of Canada West and had become an integral part of the provincial economy. A great many – more than half – were from the United States. Contrary to popular opinion, however, they were mainly free blacks, not runaway slaves – immigrants not fugitives. In many respects Canada was unkind to both groups of Americans. Although entitled to equality before the law, they experienced persistent discrimination. Whites called them 'nigger' to their faces, and worse. Still, when the Civil War ended most chose to remain. Canada was not all they had hoped for, perhaps, but, despite what their white neighbours may have believed, it had become home. For the 40 per cent of the black population who had been born in the province, it had never been anything else.

APPENDIX Distribution of the Black Population of Canada West by Place of Residence, 1861

ALGOMA DISTRICT	12	DUNDAS (Continued)	
BRANT COUNTY (465)		Winchester	1
Brantford	58	DURHAM COUNTY (48)	
Town of Brantford	284	Bowmanville	10
Burford	73	Cavan	2
Onondaga	3	Clarke	6
Paris	18	Hope	4
South Dumfries	15	Newcastle	7
Tuscarora	14	Port Hope	19
BRUCE COUNTY (10)		ELGIN COUNTY (85)	
Arran	2	Bayham	8
Brant	2	Malahide	23
Kincardine	1	Southwold	11
Village of Kincardine	5	St. Thomas	40
CARLETON COUNTY (3)		Yarmouth	3
Fitzroy	1	ESSEX COUNTY (3,508)	
March	1	Amherstburg	373
Nepean	1	Anderdon	456
DUNDAS COUNTY (20)		Colchester	937
Matilda	1	East Sandwich	442
Morrisburgh	6	Gosfield	101
Williamsburgh	12	Maidstone	234

ESSEX (Continued)

Malden	275
Malden Asylum	9
Rochester	6
Town of Sandwich	95
West Sandwich	47
Windsor	533

FRONTENAC COUNTY (169)

Bedford	2
Hinchinbrooke	2
Kingston	21
Penitentiary	78
Pittsburgh	14
Portland	9
Portsmouth	10
Storrington	9
Wolfe Island	24

GLENGARRY COUNTY (43)

Charlottenburgh	13
Lancaster	30

GRENVILLE COUNTY (18)

Edwardsburg	5
Kemptville	1
Prescott	12

GREY COUNTY (379)

Artemesia	105
Bentinck	31
Collingwood	2
Derby	1
Egremont	4
Euphrasia	13
Glenelg	35
Holland	16
Melancthon	7
Normanby	45
Osprey	7
Owen Sound	86
St. Vincent	6

GREY (Continued)

Sullivan	16
Sydenham	5

HALDIMAND COUNTY (253)

Canboro	6
Dunn	5
Dunnville	62
Mouton	10
North Cayuga	118
Oneida	23
Seneca	27
Walpole	2

HALTON COUNTY (233)

Esquesing	11
Georgetown	3
Nassagaweya	51
Nelson	22
Oakville	37
Trafalgar	109

HASTINGS COUNTY (87)

Belleville	33
Hastings Road	5
Huntingdon	4
Madoc	1
Marmora	1
Rawdon	7
Sidney	13
Thurlow	4
Trenton	8
Tyendinaga	11

HURON COUNTY (92)

Ashfield	6
Biddulph	59
Colborne	1
Grey	12
Howick	1
Hullet	1
McGillivray	1

HURON (Continued)

McKillop	1
Stephen	8
Usborne	1
Wawanosh	1

KENT COUNTY (4,736)

Camden and Gore	669
Chatham	1,252
Chatham and Gore	737
Dover	209
East Tilbury	43
Harwich	457
Howard	51
Orford	8
Raleigh	1,310

LAMBTON COUNTY (133)

Brooke	2
Dawn	55
Euphemia	15
Moore	4
Plympton	3
Sarnia	4
Town of Sarnia	45
Warwick	5

LANARK COUNTY (12)

Burgess	6
Perth	4
Ramsey	2

LEEDS COUNTY (64)

Bastard	20
Brockville	9
Elizabethtown	27
Leeds	8

LENNOX COUNTY (29)

Adolphustown	1
Camden	4
Ernestown	8

LENNOX (Continued)

Fredericksburgh	2
Napanee	6
Richmond	7
Sheffield	1

LINCOLN COUNTY (911)

Caistor	8
Gainsborough	1
Grantham	96
Grimsby	33
Louth	17
Niagara	60
Town of Niagara	87
St. Catharines	609

MIDDLESEX COUNTY (319)

Caradoc	7
Delaware	6
East Williams	6
Ekfrid	15
Lobo	13
London	192
Metcalfe	8
Mosa	29
North Dorchester	24
Strathroy	8
West Nissouri	11

NORFOLK COUNTY (149)

Carlotteville	6
Town of Simcoe	48
Townsend	8
Walsingham	3
Windham	31
Woodhouse	53

NORTHUMBERLAND
COUNTY (129)

Alnwick	1
Village of Brighton	4
Cobourg	61

NORTHUMBERLAND
(Continued)

Colborne	3
Cramahe	3
Haldimand	23
Hamilton	24
Murray	9
Seymour	1

ONTARIO COUNTY (42)

East Whitby	8
Mara	1
Oshawa	8
Pickering	12
Reach	1
Scott	2
West Whitby	2
Town of Whitby	8

OXFORD COUNTY (552)

Blandford	7
Blenheim	19
Dereham	51
East Nissouri	1
East Oxford	20
East Zorra	25
Ingersoll	149
North Norwich	17
North Oxford	17
South Norwich	148
West Oxford	31
West Zorra	11
Woodstock	56

PEEL COUNTY (73)

Albion	1
Brampton	12
Caledon	6
Chinguacousy	17
Toronto	37

PERTH COUNTY (105)

Blanchard	11
Downie	1
Easthope	3
Ellice	6
Elma	7
Hibbert	2
Logan	1
Mitchell	3
Mornington	13
South Easthope	5
St. Mary's	14
Stratford	38
Wallace	1

PETERBOROUGH COUNTY (67)

Ashburnham	7
Asphodel	1
Ennismore	4
Minden	8
Monaghan	10
Otonabee	3
Peterborough	23
Smith	11

PRESCOTT COUNTY (2)

Longueuil	1
South Plantagenet	1

PRINCE EDWARD COUNTY (12)

Ameliasburgh	5
Hallowell	3
Picton	3
Sophiasburgh	1

RENFREW COUNTY (3)

Westneath	3

RUSSELL COUNTY (9)

Clarence	9

SIMCOE COUNTY (300)

Adjala	2

SIMCOE (Continued)

Barrie	54
Bradford	1
Collingwood	70
Essa	2
Flos	15
Innisfil	7
Mono	9
Mulmur	1
Nottawasaga	2
Orillia	9
Oro	97
Reformatory	7
Sunnidale	14
Tecumseth	2
Vespra	1
West Gwillimbury	7

STORMONT COUNTY (35)

Cornwall	17
Town of Cornwall	14
Osnabruck	4

VICTORIA COUNTY (3)

Lutterworth	1
Mariposa	2

WATERLOO COUNTY (123)

Berlin	9
Galt	31
North Dumfries	7
Preston	2
South Waterloo	5
Waterloo	1
Wellesley	41
Wilmot	7
Woolwich	20

WELLAND COUNTY (535)

Bertie	78
Chippawa	32
Clifton	26

WELLAND (Continued)

Crowland	1
Fort Erie	35
Humberstone	18
Jail	4
Pelham	13
Stamford	190
Thorold	61
Village of Thorold	39
Wainfleet	7
Willoughby	31

WELLINGTON COUNTY (410)

Amaranth	4
Arthur	1
Elora	9
Eramosa	8
Garafraxa	7
Guelph	7
Town of Guelph	39
Maryborough	14
Minto	1
Nichol	3
Peel	296
Pilkington	14
Puslinch	7

WENTWORTH COUNTY (364)

Ancaster	51
Barton	140
Beverley	13
Binbrook	4
Dundas	19
East Flamboro	31
Glanford	16
Saltfleet	27
West Flamboro	63

YORK COUNTY (482)

East Gwillimbury	40
Etobicoke	83
Holland Landing	5

YORK (Continued)	
King	41
Markham	10
North Gwillimbury	5
Scarborough	5
Vaughan	30
Whitchurch	1
York	224
Yorkville	38

CITY OF HAMILTON (476)	
St. Andrew Ward	111
St. George's Ward	86
St. Lawrence Ward	171
St. Mary's Ward	53
St. Patrick's Ward	55

CITY OF KINGSTON (162)	
Cataraqui Ward	23
Frontenac Ward	18
General Hospital	1
Ontario Ward	11

KINGSTON (Continued)	
Rideau Ward	32
St. Lawrence Ward	25
Sydenham Ward	12
Victoria Ward	40

CITY OF LONDON (370)	
Ward 1[a]	370

CITY OF OTTAWA (34)	
By Ward	19
Victoria Ward	2
Wellington Ward	13

CITY OF TORONTO (987)	
St. Andrew's Ward	116
St. David's Ward	22
St. George's Ward	21
St. James' Ward	86
St. John's Ward	539
St. Lawrence Ward	48
St. Patrick's Ward	155

a) The blacks of London were actually dispersed throughout the seven wards of the city, but confusion in the way in which the enumerators entered the data makes it appear as if they all lived in a single ward.
Source: Canada West Manuscript Census Schedules, 1861.

NOTES

This article is from *Histoire sociale–Social History* 28 (56) (1995). Reprinted with permission.

The author is indebted to Marnee Gamble, Shannon Lee, and Ken McLeod for assistance in compiling data from the manuscript census; to Harpreet Dhariwal and Yodit Seifu for computer programming; and to Ian Radforth, Franca Iacovetta, Arthur Silver, Allan Greer, Larry Powell, Richard Reid, Kris Inwood, Nancy Anderson, Joey Slinger, and Sandra Tychsen for their helpful comments.

1 See, for example, Larry Gara, *The Liberty Line: The Legend of the Underground*

Railroad (Lexington, Ky.: D.C. Heath, 1967); Robin Winks, *The Blacks in Canada: A History* (New Haven: Yale University Press, 1971), pp. 180–195, 240–244.

2 The most influential study is Winks, *The Blacks in Canada* (see especially pp. 233–240, Appendix). Other important works include C. Peter Ripley et al., eds., *The Black Abolitionist Papers: Volume II, Canada 1830–1865* (Chapel Hill: University of North Carolina Press, 1986); William H. Pease and Jane H. Pease, *Black Utopia: Negro Communal Experiments in America* (Madison, Wis.: State Historical Society, 1963); Jason Silverman, *Unwelcome Guests: American Fugitive Slaves in Canada, 1830–60* (Millwood, N.Y.: 1985). Two useful dissertations are Donald George Simpson, 'Negroes in Ontario from Early Times to 1870' (Ph.D. dissertation, University of Western Ontario, 1971); and Jonathan William Walton, 'Blacks in Buxton and Chatham, Ontario, 1830–1890: Did the 49th Parallel Make a Difference?' (Ph.D. dissertation, Princeton University, 1979).

3 Winks, *The Blacks in Canada*, pp. 233–240.

4 The instructions directed enumerators to 'mark a figure (1) after every *Colored* person's name, i.e. Negro or Negress ... If Mulatto, marked [*sic*] M after his or her name – thus, (1) M; and if Indian, mark "Ind."' For the purposes of this article I have treated both 'Negroes' and 'Mulattoes' as part of the black population since that is how they were viewed at the time. National Archives of Canada (hereafter NAC), RG31, 'Instructions to Enumerators,' Census Returns, Algoma District, 1861. For discussion of the problems involved in retrieving data on blacks from the census and in assessing the distinction drawn by enumerators between 'Negroes' and 'Mulattoes,' see Michael Wayne, 'Blacks in the Canada West Census of 1861,' paper delivered at the Conference on the Use of Census Manuscripts for Historical Research, Guelph, Ontario, March 5, 1993.

5 Winks, *The Blacks in Canada*, p. 492. Even contemporaries raised doubts about the enumeration. See, for example, John Langton, 'The Census of 1861,' *Transactions of the Literary and Historical Society of Quebec*, New Series, Part 2 (1864), pp. 105–124. Langton suggested that in certain instances the 'figures were cooked.' His investigation was confined to Lower Canada, however. Recently Bruce Curtis has demonstrated that the enumeration was carried out in a most careless and haphazard manner. Bruce Curtis, 'The Local Construction of Statistical Knowledge, or Mistaking the 1861 Census,' paper delivered at the Conference on the Use of Census Manuscripts for Historical Research, Guelph, Ontario, March 4, 1993.

6 *Census of the Canadas. 1860–1861. Personal Census. Vol. I* (Quebec, 1863), pp. 78–79. Curiously, the census of 1871, which included a recapitulation of previous census findings, reported the number of blacks in 1861 as 13,566.

Censuses of Canada. 1665 to 1871. Statistics of Canada. Vol. IV (Ottawa, 1876), p. 266.

7 National Archives (United States), RG94, Letters Received by the Adjutant General's Office, 1861–70, microcopy 619, roll 199, 'The Self-Freedmen of Canada West. Supplemental Report (A) of the American Freedmen's Inquiry Commission,' pp. 26–27; Winks, *The Blacks in Canada*, p. 489. The Commission was set up by Abraham Lincoln to help him formulate a set of policies for dealing with the emancipated slaves.

8 NAC, RG31, 'Instructions to Enumerators.'

9 NAC, RG17, vol. 2419, Charles Waters, Prescott County, February 2, 1861. I am indebted to Bruce Curtis for this reference.

10 Everyone recognized that the vast majority of these 30,000 lived in Canada West. Benjamin Drew, *A North-Side View of Slavery. The Refugee: Or the Narrative of Fugitive Slaves in Canada. Related by Themselves, With an Account of the History and Condition of the Colored Population of Upper Canada* (1856; New York: 1968), p. v. On the anti-slavery movement in Canada West, see Allen P. Stouffer, *The Light of Nature and the Law of God: Antislavery in Ontario 1833–1877* (Montreal and Kingston: McGill-Queen's University Press, 1992).

11 This problem is discussed in Richard Reid, 'A Preliminary Report on Black Underenumeration and the 1870 Census,' paper delivered at the Conference on the Use of Census Manuscripts for Historical Research, Guelph, Ontario, March 5, 1993. See also Richard H. Steckel, 'The Quality of Census Data for Historical Inquiry: A Research Agenda,' *Social Science History*, vol. 15 (1991), pp. 579–599; John B. Sharples and Ray M. Shortridge, 'Biased Underenumeration in Census Manuscripts: Methodological Implications,' *Journal of Urban History*, vol. 1 (1975), pp. 409–439; Peter R. Knights, 'Potholes in the Road of Improvement? Estimating Underenumeration by Longitudinal Tracing: U.S. Censuses, 1850–1880,' *Social Science History*, vol. 15 (1991), pp. 517–526; Peter R. Knights, *Yankee Destinies: The Lives of Ordinary Bostonians* (Chapel Hill: University of North Carolina Press, 1991), pp. 176–178. On the political implications of the enumeration of slaves and free blacks in the United States, see Margo J. Anderson, *The American Census: A Social History* (New Haven: Yale University Press, 1988), pp. 58–82.

12 William Wells Brown may have come up with the most accurate assessment. He wrote in the fall of 1861: 'The colored population of the Canadas have been largely over-rated. There are probably not more than 25,000 in both Provinces, and by far the greater number of these are in Canada West ...' Ripley et al., eds., *Black Abolitionist Papers: Volume II*, pp. 461, 463, 466.

13 Winks, *The Blacks in Canada*, pp. 233–234; *Censuses of Canada. 1608 to 1876. Statistics of Canada. Vol. V* (Ottawa, 1878), p. 20.

14 Quoted in Howe, 'The Self-Freedmen of Canada West,' pp. 26–27.

15 Samuel Ringgold Ward, *Autobiography of a Fugitive Negro: His Anti-Slavery Labours in the United States, Canada, and England* (London, 1855), p. 154.

16 Ripley et al., eds., *Black Abolitionist Papers: Volume II*, pp. 465, 470, 475, 477.

17 Winks, *The Blacks in Canada*, p. 234.

18 Eugene Genovese, *Roll, Jordan, Roll: The World the Slaves Made* (New York: Pantheon Books, 1974), p. 648; Winks, *The Blacks in Canada*, p. 235.

19 Fred Landon, 'The Negro Migration to Canada After the Passing of the Fugitive Slave Act,' *Journal of Negro History*, vol. 5 (1920), pp. 22–36. On the origins and consequences of the law itself, see Stanley W. Campbell, *The Slave Catchers: Enforcement of the Fugitive Slave Law, 1850–1860* (Chapel Hill: University of North Carolina Press, 1968). Under the act life became much less secure for free blacks as well.

20 Winks, *The Blacks in Canada*, p. 240.

21 This reflects in part the fact that it was easier for slaves in border states to escape than it was for slaves living in more distant regions. Early in the century the centre of the slave population lay much farther north and east than it did at the time of the Civil War, however. An undetermined proportion of the fugitive slaves who made their way to Canada West had been born in Maryland and Virginia but would have been taken or sold to the Deep South and presumably escaped from there. Kenneth Stamp, *The Peculiar Institution: Slavery in the Ante-Bellum South* (New York: Vintage Books, 1956), p. 118; Genovese, *Roll, Jordan, Roll*, p. 648.

22 Jos. C. G. Kennedy, *Preliminary Report on the Eighth Census. 1860* (Washington, D.C., 1862), pp. 261, 263, 286–289. For insight into the unique situation in Maryland, where slaves and free blacks were about equal in number, see Barbara Jeanne Fields, *Slavery and Freedom on the Middle Ground: Maryland During the Nineteenth Century* (New Haven: Yale University Press, 1985).

23 Ira Berlin, *Slaves Without Masters: The Free Negro in the Antebellum South* (New York: Oxford University Press, 1974), pp. 343–380; Michael Johnson and James Roark, *Black Masters: A Free Family of Color in the Old South* (New York: Norton, 1984), pp. 153–287.

24 The fact that roughly equal numbers of men and women reported being born in the free states suggests that virtually no fugitive slaves saw an advantage in claiming birth in the North. On the life of blacks in the free states before the Civil War, see James Oliver Horton, *Free People of Color: Inside the African American Community* (Washington, D.C.: Smithsonian Institution Press, 1993); Leonard P. Curry, *The Free Black in Urban America, 1800–1850: The Shadow of the Dream* (Chicago: University of Chicago Press, 1981); Leon Litwack, *North of Slavery: The Negro in the Free States, 1790–1860* (Chicago: University of

Chicago Press, 1961); Gary B. Nash, *Forging Freedom: The Formation of Philadelphia's Black Community, 1720–1840* (Cambridge, Mass.: Harvard University Press, 1988).

25 Deborah Gray White, *Ar'n't I a Woman? Female Slaves in the Plantation South* (New York: Norton, 1985), pp. 70–74; Genovese, *Roll, Jordan, Roll*, p. 648; Gerald W. Mullin, *Flight and Rebellion: Slave Resistance in Eighteenth-Century Virginia* (New York: Oxford University Press, 1972), p. 40.

26 Let x equal the number of females from the South who were fugitive slaves and y the number of females who were free. Then $x + y = 197$ (the total number of women indicating they had been born in the slave states). Similarly, $3x + y = 324$ (the total number of males born in the slave states), since it is assumed that males represented three out of every four runaways and that free men and women came to Canada West in more or less equal numbers. Solving for x and y allows us to determine the percentage of all blacks from the slave states who were fugitives.

27 If 80% of the fugitives were men, this figure drops to around 16%. The objection might be raised that perhaps the 744 who indicated their state of birth were not representative. But men made up a slightly lower proportion of those who registered 'United States' as their birthplace than of those who indicated a specific state (56% as compared to 58%), suggesting that the estimate of 20% fugitives is, if anything, marginally too high. It is worth noting that likely a small number of elderly blacks from the North had fled to Canada as slaves before emancipation was carried out in their individual states, and no doubt at least a few of the blacks from the West Indies were also fugitives.

28 In fact, the census does not specify family relationships. However, they can be inferred with what appears to be a reasonable degree of accuracy from the data recorded on individuals and households. For a discussion of the methodology involved, see Wayne, 'Blacks in the Canada West Census of 1861,' The schedules allow us to identify 2,851 children born in Canada living with both mother and father who were American and another 1,652 living with one parent from the United States. However, the need to use the person listed first in each household as the reference point for determining family relationships precludes the possibility of easily identifying sons and daughters of any individual who was not the household head – for example, a widow from Maryland who had moved with her children into the home of a married brother or sister.

29 Ripley et al., eds., *Black Abolitionist Papers: Volume II*, pp. 461–498; Drew, *A North-Side View of Slavery*; Howe, 'The Self-Freedmen of Canada West.'

30 Winks, *The Blacks in Canada*, pp. 156–162, 178–218; Pease and Pease, *Black Utopia*; Victor Ullman, *Look to the North Star: A Life of William King* (Boston: Beacon Press, 1969); Walton, 'Blacks in Buxton and Chatham'; Howard Law,

'"Self-Reliance is the True Road to Independence": Ideology and the Ex-Slaves in Buxton and Chatham,' *Ontario History*, vol. 77 (1985), pp. 107–121.

31 A county in Virginia was on average somewhat larger than a township, but considerably smaller than a county, in Canada West.

32 Winks, *The Blacks in Canada*, pp. 147, 156, 180, 205.

33 Ripley et al., eds., *Black Abolitionist Papers: Volume II*, p. 475.

34 Keep in mind, though, that approximately 40% of all blacks were native-born.

35 The census reported a total of 22,906 individuals born in 'Prussia, German States, and Holland.' *Census of the Canadas. 1860–1861. Personal Census. Vol. I*, pp. 78–79. This assumes that the data on birthplace in the published report are more reliable than the data on colour. Such an assumption is not necessarily invalid. Entries on colour were made in a separate column of the schedules with some but not all enumerators including totals at the bottom of the page. It seems that likely one of the reasons clerks understated the number of blacks in particular communities is that they made their tabulations on the basis of the listed totals. Where no total was listed, the clerk may have assumed no blacks had been found. The entries on birthplace, often varying from household to household and sometimes from person to person, allowed for no totals at the bottom of the page, and presumably clerks had no choice but to check individual entries in compiling the data.

36 George M. Fredrickson, *The Black Image in the White Mind: The Debate on Afro-American Character and Destiny, 1817–1914* (New York: Harper Torchbooks, 1971), pp. 58–96. David Roediger has recently made a compelling case for use of the term '*herrenvolk* republicanism' to describe the political ideology of American working men. See David R. Roediger, *The Wages of Whiteness: Race and the Making of the American Working Class* (London: Verso, 1991), pp. 59–60.

37 Quoted in James M. McPherson, *Ordeal by Fire: The Civil War and Reconstruction* (New York: Alfred A. Knopf, 1982), p. 100.

38 Needless to say, we know next to nothing about the relatively small number of blacks who came from outside North America.

39 James Oliver Horton writes in reference to the United States: 'Today almost all scholars accept the historical existence of a highly structured and dynamic community among antebellum free African Americans.' Horton, however, shares a mistaken impression with other scholars that, by the second quarter of the nineteenth century, blacks 'clustered in small urban communities in sizable cities.' Horton, *Free People of Color*, pp. 13, 2. As Kenneth Kusmer has observed, 'It is seldom realized that throughout most of the nineteenth century most blacks – like most whites – lived in rural areas or small towns.' Kenneth L. Kusmer, *A Ghetto Takes Shape: Black Cleveland, 1870–1930* (Urbana: University of Illinois Press, 1976), p. 24fn. The same was true of Canadian blacks. For a recent example of a Canadian study that makes community for-

mation central to its analysis, see Patricia J. Yee, 'Gender Ideology and Black Women as Community-Builders in Ontario, 1850–70,' *Canadian Historical Review*, vol. 75 (March 1994), pp. 53–73.

40 I have assumed that a husband and wife were married prior to their arrival in Canada if they were both recorded in the census as having American birthplaces and if their oldest child was also born in the United States. Of course, some of the married couples who came to Canada from the United States did not have children until after they settled in the province – some did not have children at all – while others had American-born children who were not living with them at the time of the enumeration. Hence, the figure 'almost one in five' is clearly understated, probably substantially so.

41 Charles J. Johnson, who settled in Toronto, was the son of a prominent free black tailor from Charleston who had owned six slaves. South Carolina's free black elite is discussed in Johnson and Roark, *Black Masters*. Correspondence involving the Johnson family can be found in Michael P. Johnson and James L. Roark, eds., *No Chariot Let Down: Charleston's Free People of Color on the Eve of the Civil War* (Chapel Hill: University of North Carolina Press, 1984). Patricia J. Yee has recently drawn attention to distinctions between the experiences of black men and women in 'Gender Ideology and Black Women.'

42 Ripley et al., eds., *Black Abolitionist Papers: Volume II*, p. 39.

43 Drew, *A North-Side View of Slavery*, p. 39.

'Self-Reliance Is the True Road to Independence': Ideology and the Ex-Slaves in Buxton and Chatham

HOWARD LAW

During the first half of the nineteenth century thousands of American black slaves stood poised on the brink of freedom. Black and white abolitionists alike pondered the difficult transition from slavery to a life of freedom. On the other hand ex-slaves often had their own notions of life without slavery. This paper explores the meeting of abolitionist ideals and ex-slave expectations that took place in Canada West during the

1840s and 1850s. In Chatham and the nearby village of Buxton, the struggle began for the ideological leadership of refugee blacks. In Buxton a white Presbyterian missionary philanthropist, the Reverend William King, directed an all-black community founded on his work ethic of independent and self-reliant homesteading. In Chatham an elite of black clergymen with an outlook similar to King's endeavoured to make the former slaves into the yeoman class that would be best suited to the homestead economy of the province. Both King and the black elite were determined that the refugees should leave their plantation work habits and social conduct behind them. King appears to have impressed his values upon the black villagers, but the black leaders of Chatham met with mixed success, their disappointments largely attributable to the demographic crisis created in the region by the post-1850 exodus of American blacks to Canada.

Escaping from northern racism[2] and southern slavery, American blacks journeyed northward throughout the early nineteenth century. The flow of northward emigration increased after 1850, when the American government enacted the Fugitive Slave Law, which provided for the strict re-enslavement of escaped slaves living in northern states. For that reason, runaway slaves were likely to flee all the way to the safety of Canada. In many places in Canada, like Chatham in the Thames River valley, frontier families were still subduing the wilderness, staking out their homestead farms, and planting their first crops. Consequently, agricultural opportunities were plenty. And in Canada, unlike the United States, there was no slavery and no discriminatory 'black code.' Legally, Canada was colour-blind.[3]

The blacks who arrived in this legally non-racist society were generally ex-slaves, along with a few free-born blacks.[4] They established themselves throughout Canada West, principally in the southwestern part of the province between Windsor and Toronto. By 1860 there were at least 11,223 blacks in Canada West.[5] In Chatham, always a major centre of black settlement, there were 200 blacks amid a town population in 1,100 as early as 1841. A decade later, the figures were 353 and 2,070 respectively.[6] In 1861, the black population numbered 1,259 out of 4,466, a jump from 17 per cent to 28 per cent of the town's population.[7] This was due to the increased flow of refugee slaves fleeing the Fugitive Slave Law of 1850. Meanwhile, in Buxton, a nearby agricultural village of blacks formed in 1849 by a white missionary, the Reverend William King, the population also grew. King reported forty-five families in 1851, totalling over two hundred persons. By September 1852 there were four hundred citizens of the community known variously by its legal name, the Elgin Association, and its Church-mission name, Buxton.[8]

The blacks of Buxton and Chatham had done well to settle in that particular district, for Chatham was an area of economic growth from 1840 to 1860. The town was perched at the headwaters of the Thames River, the commercial highway of the southwest. In 1854 the Great Western Railway was built through the region, bringing not only commercial growth but also many construction jobs for black men.[9] Generally, black employment was high.[10]

Like Chatham, Buxton was a prosperous home for blacks. It had been founded when the Reverend William King brought his fifteen Louisiana slaves to the area and manumitted and settled them on one thousand acres of uncleared land outside of Chatham. Beginning with this nucleus, King's model community grew. The new citizens planted a variety of crops while working in their sawmill and roofing and potash enterprises that they had built under King's direction.[11] The Buxton settlement was economically stable, and from 1853 to 1857 crop production rose 100 per cent with only a 50 per cent increase in population.[12] Even the economic depression of 1857 did not shake the foundations of Buxton's prosperity.[13]

If the Buxton and Chatham ex-slaves established themselves with considerable success during the 1840s and 1850s, how did neighbouring white settlers react to the sudden, and apparently permanent, influx of blacks? Perhaps because of the geographic proximity of town blacks and whites, and the relative isolation of Buxton blacks in their separate community, we should not be surprised to discover the race relations were strained in Chatham, but were smooth, after some initially rock patches, in Buxton.

As soon as blacks began arriving in Chatham in considerable numbers, the whites shut them out of the local public schools.[14] By 1840 a separate black school was erected.[15] In Buxton, King's endeavours to lay the foundations of his settlement were opposed vehemently by a prominent local racist, Edward Larwill, who mobilized over three hundred citizens to petition Governor General Elgin, the Legislative Assembly, and King's Presbyterian seniors in Toronto.[16] Citing threats to property values and the racial purity of whites, Larwill and his followers intimidated King during his visits to Chatham until it became clear that neither church nor state would prevent the birth of Buxton.[17]

After 1850, white hostility to Buxton appears to have died down: neither King nor later historians recorded any significant prejudice against this secluded all-black society.[18] But in Chatham, prejudice was rampant. Each decade from 1830 to 1860 saw at least one colonization scheme pop up in the Chatham community. These plans, which were never set in motion, recommended the emigration of local blacks to more 'suitable' surroundings in Trinidad, Jamaica, or Haiti. As J.K.A. Farrell has noted, they were sometimes formulated by blacks themselves, although the colonization idea was a manifestation as much of anti-black sentiment as of black frustration with white hostility.[19]

An Anglican missionary visiting Chatham in 1854 noted the continued racism:

Prejudice against the coloured people prevails here to a greater extent than I have anywhere else found. Some would even deny them the right of burial in the same graveyard with white men; and most owners of town lots would on no account let or sell a lot to a coloured man, but would dispose of it to a white man for half what such a one could offer. They are not, and would not on any account be admitted into the Public Schools.[20]

The last word on Chatham 'colour-phobia' was perhaps written by the black Reverend Henry Bibb, in April 1851, in his newspaper, *The Voice of the Fugitive*:

Colour-phobia is a contagious disease. It is more destructive to the mind than to the body. It goes hard with a person who is a little nervous. It makes them froth at the mouth as if the Bengal tiger were in them. Its symptoms are various. It makes them sing out 'darkey', 'darkey', 'nigger', 'nigger', 'long heel', 'long heel' ... It frightens them up from the dining table at Public Houses not because of a black man's cooking but because of his sitting down to eat ...

In Canada it gets hold of the very dregs of society. It makes them shudder at the idea of 'Negro Settlement'. 'They will ruin the country', etc. The objection brought up is that we shall have Negro lawyers, doctors, etc. It serves their imagination so much that they have become alarmed about amalgamation ... the white girls are all going to make choice of black men, and the white gents will be left without wives, and what then?[21]

In short, Chatham whites, generally speaking, were racists.

To sum up, we may compose a picture of Buxton and Chatham from 1840 to 1860. Buxton grew and prospered steadily throughout the 1850s and, once established, endured a minimum of white hostility. Chatham also grew rapidly, but its blacks suffered considerable prejudice at the

hands of their white neighbours. However, since black employment was
high in Chatham, these new Canadians had an incentive to stay there.

Why did the blacks remain in an area that, although admittedly prosperous, was often racist? I propose that these blacks, especially the
Chatham Afro-Americans, were driven by a desire to conform to certain
white standards of behaviour. In other words, deliberate and partial
acculturation was economically advantageous for the ex-slaves. White
philanthropists and black leaders of the time believed that the ex-slaves
had to adopt new attitudes towards work, theft, and drinking if they
were to adjust successfully to a life of freedom in Chatham and Buxton.
The Reverend William King and the black clergy clung to this belief
despite the fact that these new attitudes were to some extent alien to the
ex-slaves' plantation experiences.

William King's attitude was in many respects typical of the white abolitionists' approach to the blacks' transition from slavery to freedom. It
is important to underline the fundamentals of this thought. The cradle
of anti-slavery ideology was the transatlantic Quaker community. The
movement was particularly strong in England, where Quakers built the
network of anti-slavery news-sheets and meeting places from which
sprang the later evangelical brand of anti-slavery thought.[22] During the
late eighteenth century, the evangelicals were led by William Wilberforce and during the early nineteenth century by Thomas Fowell Buxton. This tradition of anti-slavery thought had no fundamental objection
to the exploitation of labour, as David Brion Davis points out, so long as
that labour was free and not enslaved. These thinkers believed that free
workers, including the English working class, were in dire need of discipline in their moral and working lives. Of course blacks were free of this
burden of the 'work ethic' while they were enslaved because they
'lacked responsibility for [their] own status.' But this exemption could
not be permitted to outlive slavery: 'Liberation from slavery did not
mean freedom to live as one chose, but rather freedom to become a
diligent, sober, and dependable worker who gratefully accepted his
position in society.'[23] In other words, the freed men and women were
expected to absorb the virtues of diligence, sobriety, regularity of work,
and deference to their employers.

Canadian adherents to this ideology were not difficult to find. One
was housed snugly in the Presbyterian Synod of Toronto: the Reverend
Michael Willis, Principal of Knox Presbyterian College in the early
1850s, became the first President of the Anti-Slavery Society of Canada,
established in February 1851.[24] The Synod appointed William King to

his first pastoral mission in St. Andrew's Church of Chatham in 1846.[25] Throughout the 1850s, King reported annually to the Synod on the progress of the Buxton mission.[26]

The Governor General, Lord Elgin, was also sympathetic to King's project. In 1849 he resisted all attempts by Chatham whites to block King's purchase of lands. He envisioned 'sober, industrious, and honest settlers [of the black race] always availing themselves of the best means of education.'[27] He was also engaged in a ferocious political battle with the local Tories, who were fighting his co-operation with the program of the Reform Party. It is interesting that Larwill, a vehement Tory, championed the Chathamites who wished to expel King's black followers. By supporting King, Elgin was able to spite a political enemy.

Another supporter of King and the settlement at Buxton was George Brown. As a prominent Reformer and zealous Presbyterian, Brown used his Toronto daily newspaper, *The Globe*, to defend King's policies in Chatham. He was also steeped in the anti-slavery tradition of transforming ex-slaves into fervent adherents to the work ethic of sobriety, discipline, godliness, and deference to their employers.[28]

King also spoke from this tradition of white philanthropy, which presented an ideological challenge to the ex-slaves in Buxton. Born in Ulster County, Ireland, in 1812, King was raised in a Presbyterian family and in a farming household.[29] In the 1830s he emigrated to America. Deciding to journey from his family's new home in Ohio to take up school teaching in the South, he refused to borrow $100 travelling money from his brother because he wished to be completely 'self-supporting.'[30] He became a school-teacher in Louisiana in 1835 and six years later married Mary Phares, the daughter of a nearby planter. Mary brought two female slaves to their new household, and because King had always been opposed to slavery while living in England and Ireland, this first contact with plantation slavery in Louisiana provoked much soul-searching. Years later, he wrote in his autobiography about his thoughts on slavery during his stay in Louisiana:

The evils of the system [of slavery] which were necessarily connected with it bore as heavily on the white families as on the black ... [T]he moral evils connected with it were such that it could not exist with Christianity. It would either destroy Christianity or Christianity would destroy it.[31]

Louisiana law, however, made voluntary manumission of slaves extremely difficult and, at any rate, the slaves belonged to King's wife.[32]

Instead of crusading against slavery, King concentrated on teaching and saving money to attend divinity school in Scotland. But the accumulation of slaves continued. Because his hired servants in his boarding school were undependable, in 1842 he purchased a twenty-year-old slave, Talbert, to supervise the staff. Later, he wrote that 'one could not get faithful and trustworthy servants unless you bought them.'[33] In 1843, in preparation for journeying alone to Edinburgh to attend divinity school, King bought five more slaves in order to establish Mary and their infant son on a farm. A year later, the estate of his deceased father-in-law rendered him six more slaves for a total of fourteen.[34]

In 1843 William King, the slave-holding abolitionist, left for Scotland. But before he could set sail, his wife and two children died suddenly. In the space of twenty-five months he had lost Mary, his children, and his father-in-law.[35] This personal tragedy helps to explain King's activities in Buxton, which he was often accused of running like his own plantation: a white paternal master, King, overseeing blacks.[36] It is possible that King was fulfilling the father-role he had lost and was trying to replace his family with the ex-slaves. There were writers in the anti-slavery pantheon like James Ramsay who suggested in 1784 that the positions of superiority and inferiority between master and slave were natural and appropriate: slavery was evil only because it lacked the slaves' liberty and consent to inferiority.[37] Treating a free man or woman as an inferior was not necessarily hypocritical in King's mind.

King's anti-slavery ideology was further developed during his stay in Scotland, where he witnessed the tumultous split of the Church of Scotland. In 1843 four hundred Presbyterian ministers and their congregations bolted the state-endowed Church because of excessive government interference in its affairs. By forsaking considerable economic assistance, the members of the new Presbyterian Free Church rid themselves of political dependence upon the government. King's years at the Edinburgh divinity school also gave him the opportunity to witness the appalling poverty of the local slums. He remarked upon the moral paralysis inflicted upon the poor by alcoholism and decided that only active moral philanthropy could cure it. He also participated in the neighbourhood mission schools, which required token tuition fees from their impoverished flock 'in order to cultivate a spirit of independence and self respect.'[38] Three of King's most basic values – sobriety, independence, and self-reliance – grew and matured during his years in Scotland.

Once King finished divinity school and was assigned to the Toronto Presbyterian Synod on his own request, he seized the opportunity to bring his slaves to a country where he could manumit them and prepare them for the difficult transition to a life of free labour. In 1846 he took up his job in Chatham, and by 1848 he was searching out suitable lands on which to settle his slaves and any other blacks who might be suited to his new community.

After purchasing the Elgin Association tract, King set down precise conditions for land tenure and home building and in this regard, he was dictatorial. There was no question as to who would sketch out the guidelines for the settlement. The lots were all the same size, and the houses were all the same distance from the road. Each homesteader bought his land at $2.50 an acre, which was cheap for that time in Canada West. The ex-slaves naturally paid for their land on credit, and they had ten years to repay King, who was the financial director of the Association. Individual homesteading was King's only plan.[39]

This individualism formed the cornerstone of King's moral philosophy. He often required letters of reference from blacks who applied for membership in the community so that their moral character was vouchsafed. His blueprint for a moral community of ex-slaves revealed two designs: that blacks be established as independent and self-reliant settlers and that recruits be found for missionary work to Africa, the womb of the slave trade.[40] Independence must have appeared to King as the most admirable moral framework for the freed men and women. Independence meant no charity, and it was the soliciting of charity that had soiled the reputations of earlier black communities in British North America.[41] King also believed that independence meant a break with paternalism. As David Davis explains above, to many heirs of the British anti-slavery tradition, black independence did not mean 'freedom to live as one chose, but rather to become ... diligent, sober, and dependable worker[s].' King, it should be noted, did not recognize the dependence of free black labourers on white employers. Yet he did favour diligence and sobriety, and his idea of independence entailed a break from any ex-slave expectations of material assistance from paternalist whites. Finally, independent, self-reliant land holding was part of the homesteading tradition of Canada West.

But economic self-reliance, King understood, could not be the only flux for the transition from slave to free life, from dependence to independence. Education was also imperative. The curriculum of King's school emphasized the rudiments of a classical and humanist education: Latin, languages, literature, mathematics, history, and Bible-reading (this was for boys; girls were given 'a common education' of reading and domestic sciences).[42] This was probably part of King's plan to educate black youngsters so that they might become candidates for the Presbyterian divinity school, Knox College of Toronto, and then voyage to Africa as missionaries. But for most blacks it meant the indispensable advantage of literacy, which, we might assume, was not only vital to Bible reading but was also an important step towards independence of mind and political acumen for the former slaves.

Independence for the ex-slaves, in King's estimation, meant economic self-reliance on a homestead, and literacy. His banner of independence never referred to the political, educational, and religious dependence of the blacks that was a consequence of his unquestioned leadership in the community. This created a curious philosophical mixture of paternalism and rugged individualism. King's career as a father figure – as a boarding-school teacher, slave owner, and community leader – was in direct contradiction to his encouragement of independence among the ex-slaves.

King appears to have enjoyed a dominant influence in Buxton. The booming productivity of the Buxton fields during the 1850s testifies to the success of his homesteading plan and its foundation of self-reliance. As for the ex-slaves' social conduct, it is still difficult to discover with any accuracy if the Buxton blacks crossed a moral threshold under King's tutelage. Certainly King had doubts about their moral fibre. When he informed his Louisiana slaves that they were about to journey with him to Canada and be manumitted, 'the good news seemed to have little effect upon them. They had come to consider that slavery was their natural condition. They did not know what freedom meant ... [T]hey thought that to be free was to be like their master, to go idle, and have a good time.'[43] King may have unintentionally exposed the nature of his own work habits in that passage, but more importantly he betrayed his fears that the freed slaves would be lazy. In a letter to Lord Elgin on August 29, 1848, he shuddered that young black children 'are growing up in ignorance and vice' and that the goal of the Buxton scheme was to 'meet their spiritual wants, and to improve their social and moral condition.'[44] King's Buxton schoolmaster, Alexander McLachlan, echoed this anxiety in April 1851 when, resigning his position (for personal reasons), he complained that Buxton blacks were 'just as deceitful and despretley wicked as [the] white man.' He did note, however, that 'the coloured man has a heart to feel that sin is a burden too heavy for him.'[45]

King's moral sketch of the slaves and McLachlan's codicil, however, were not necessarily accurate. Herbert Gutman has written of the successful efforts of slaves to preserve the integrity and unity of their families despite sales of individual family members and the daily humiliation of slavery.[46] Surely, this devotion to the family demonstrated some sort of moral courage and resilience, rather than degradation, among the slaves.

Secondly, African historians have commented upon the resurgence of religion, with a particularly moral tinge, among tribes that have faced the disruption of their socio-economic environments.[47] Perhaps the blacks who came to Buxton arrived with a determination to hold their families and their community together by observing strict rules concerning sobriety, theft, and hard work. Such values would have corresponded to King's notions of morality. In brief, it was quite possible that the Afro-Americans' moral state was not so debased as King might have suggested, nor so distant from the level to which he hoped to raise it.

At last even King was struck by the blacks' moral strength. In his autobiography he reported that in 1850 he had succeeded in persuading Buxtonites to refuse outside charity, as a threat to their self-reliance, and to boycott a local grocery store that sold liquor. It is unclear if King was so persuasive because many of the Buxton residents owed him money for their plots of land or because he and the blacks genuinely shared a moral consensus.[48] Whatever the case, it seems certain that King's ideology of independence, self-reliance, and sobriety succeeded not only because of his position of leadership but because of the ex-slave's natural inclination towards his philosophy. King's plan for the blacks' transition from slavery to freedom enjoyed considerable success in Buxton.

Little evidence of King's philanthropy could be found in white Chatham, where the whites were generally hostile and racist. How did Chatham blacks react to these white attitudes? How did they respond to an 'ideology' so different from the ideas that the Buxtonites encountered? As I suggested earlier, the combination of hostility with the economic incentives to settle in Canada produced among the black leaders an ardent desire to conform to white expectations. The spokespersons and leaders of the ex-slaves in Canada, the shepherds who hoped to lead the free men and women in a new land, were usually preachers or ministers of the church. Spiritual leaders always held a highly respected place in the slave quarters of the American South. As the standard-bearers of the slaves' central communal organization, slave preachers naturally found themselves in positions of leadership. As the heralds of the gospel to the slaves, the usually literate preachers offered their brethren a window to the outside world.[49] In Canada the foremost spokespersons of the black communities were Josiah Henson, Austin Steward, Samuel Ringgold Ward, and Henry Bibb. Steward, Ward, and Bibb were ministers; Henson was an illiterate preacher.

Before examining the ideologies of these men, however, it should be noted that black ministers usually held positions not only of social and political pre-eminence but also of economic privilege in their communities. They constituted a comfortable intellectual elite that did not necessarily share the same ideology or cultural outlook as their uneducated working parishioners. It was not surprising that these men were deeply concerned about the problem of 'uplifting' their ignorant brethren to a state in which they could live improved lives and, incidentally, conform better to white standards of behaviour.

These black leaders in Canada West hailed from a tradition of Afro-American leadership, a tradition with both a marked suspicion of white reformers and a moral commitment that spoke from the black experience. In *They Who Would Be Free*, Jane and William Pease make two points worth noting.[50] First, the idealism of black leaders differed from that of white radicals. While white American reformism of the antebellum period was often characterized by transcendentalism or utopian socialism, black leaders concentrated on moral reform, education, and especially temperance:

Thus [the blacks] espoused temperance not because alcoholism or drunkenness [was] a race preoccupation, but because abstinence so well represented the moral uplift and social control which lay at the heart of antebellum reform.

Secondly, these leaders insisted on 'hard work and plain living' as the key to racial improvement and white respect. This concept had a distinctively black dimension. As Martin Delany, a black author, wrote in 1852, blacks had to be industrious or they would always be dependent on whites. Clearly material independence from whites was of paramount importance to Afro-American leaders.[51]

Samuel Ward belonged to this tradition of black leadership. He was a well-travelled man, having toured the anti-slavery lecture circuit on both sides of the Atlantic. In Canada West he edited the black newspaper *Provincial Freeman*. He began publishing in the early 1850s in Windsor and by 1855 had moved the paper to Toronto and then to Chatham. The regular masthead inscription read in 1854, 'Devoted to

Anti-Slavery, Temperance, and General Literature.' A year later 'Emigration' was added.[52] In 1857 the masthead was completely revised to read 'Self-Reliance is the True Road to Independence.'[53]

The last phrase is reminiscent of William King's philosophy, and indeed, King was referred to in glowing terms by Ward's paper.[54] In his autobiography, Ward called King 'one of the most single-minded, straightforward, energetic, and philanthropic ... men I ever knew.'[55] King's ideas appear repeatedly in Ward's writings (or vice versa), evidence less of King's successful ideological hegemony over Ward than of a concert of interests.

Like King, Ward was concerned with temperance, the war against drunkenness, and he gave the issue as much space in the *Provincial Freeman* as the raging political debate over slavery in the United States. Ward believed that temperance was the key to the moral reform of the slaves.[56] He also believed that this 'new' black person needed a sound agricultural training so that he could live on an equal footing with his white neighbours. Upright and independent black yeomen were better suited to a world in which, lamented Ward, they endured the extreme prejudice of the 'native-born Canadians who [were] ignorant of genteel behaviour.'[57] In fact, the racism of Chatham whites, he concluded, was the worst in Canada West.[58] Perhaps he had met Edward Larwill.

Ward's emphasis on agricultural pursuits is significant. While he did not rule out professional or artisan careers for blacks, he feared the consequences of too many ex-slaves living in towns such as Chatham.[59] Unskilled urban dwellers, he warned, got only the worst jobs and therefore became dependent on whites. Thus independent agricultural careers were ideal. Here we can see a hint of a crucial concept articulated elsewhere by Martin Delany and locally by Austin Steward: economic independence not only meant moral improvement, as King stressed, but it also meant less dependence on racist whites.[60]

Both Josiah Henson and Henry Bibb, the editor of the *Voice of the Fugitive* newspaper, agreed with Ward on the importance of agriculture and independence. Bibb's journal advocated abolition, emigration of blacks to Canada, temperance, moral reform, and, he declared, 'the claims of agricultural pursuits among our people, as being the most certain road to independence and self-respect.'[61] His paper ran a regular column dedicated to agricultural education.[62]

Henson also firmly believed in the need to educate the ex-slaves in matters of husbandry. Black settlers were exploited by white landowners, said Henson. The landlords rented uncleared land to black tenants and then evicted them once the field had been cleared.[63] Moreover, Henson noted, blacks uneducated in the vicissitudes of the agricultural marketplace were victimized by the fluctuating prices.[64] Henson, like Ward, Bibb, and Steward, favoured educating the ex-slaves and settling them on independent plots of land.[65]

The theory was clear, but it was not easy to put into practice. While Buxton developed carefully under King's watchful eye during the early 1850s, Chatham was deluged, according to Bibb, by 'hundreds'[66] of fugitive slaves within a year of the passage of the United States Fugitive Slave Law. No longer were the economic incentives to conform to white expectations or the black ministers' ideal of yeoman bliss sufficient to cope with the reality of a demographic crisis. In town, Thomas Pinckney, a black preacher from South Carolina, observed that white prejudice against blacks rose as the district was flooded by a wave of refugees.[67] The new immigrants were probably poorer and less well-educated than the established Chatham blacks, and their poverty most likely fuelled white fears of a criminal black mob being released into their community.

If the influx of ex-slaves raised the temperature of race relations in Chatham, how did the black ideologues respond? How, they must have asked themselves, could blacks avoid white prejudice with such a handicap? The solution was to settle these immigrants on the land quickly. But these refugees, despite their extraordinary courage in journeying hundreds of miles to freedom, were almost certainly more accustomed to slave rhythms of work and dependence upon white masters than a rigorous life of individual cultivating that had been offered to them by established Canadian blacks.

The problem lay at the heart of the transition from slave to free labour. For men like King, Ward, Henson, or Bibb, this bridge from dependence and subordination in one's daily working life to independence and self-reliance was imperative.[68] Yet the slaves were used to the rhythm of the plantation. They toiled when ordered to; they worked in spurts of seasonal or weekly productivity, not in regular shifts; and they expected the master to care for them in youth, illness, and old age.[69] Furthermore, as Eugene Genovese comments, Afro-Americans differed from American whites in that they had no religious roots in the Protestant tradition that posed a 'stern doctrine of work as duty ... [W]orldly asceticism neither corresponded to the sensibilities shaped by the historic development from Africa to the New World nor could take root among a people who had no material stake in its flowering.'[70] In Canada, however, these ex-slaves were expected to become independent farmers, to work assiduously, and to expect no material relief from anyone.

That the ex-slaves could not make the instant jump from one world to another was made apparent by the fact that the leaders of the black community had to find ways to care for their less fortunate brothers and sisters. One controversial method was the solicitation of philanthropic charity. Henson favoured this method, but he was in a minority.[71] Bibb expressed the prevalent opinion of the black leaders when he raged against this 'begging' because of its deleterious moral consequences and the poor image of the blacks that it created in the eyes of the white community. Black craftsmen and artisans in Chatham, sensitive to white charges of indolence, were keenly opposed to begging on behalf of poorer blacks.[72]

A more popular solution to the problem of poverty was found in communal welfare. In January 1854, black women in Chatham formed the Victoria Reform Benevolent Association, with a private subscription list, to offer aid to sick or destitute women.[73] As well, both black men and women across the province established 'True Bands' to extend assistance to the ill and the poor. The Chatham chapter was explicitly opposed to begging outside the black community.[74] Another Benevolent Association was constituted by Bibb, Ward, and Henson, with the intention of settling fugitive slaves on twenty-five-acre farms.[75]

In addition to the poverty created by the post-1850 migration, black leaders were worried about the refugees' work habits. Bibb declared that he would 'discountenance idleness in coloured people, and especially ... induce every coloured man among us, who is not, to become a freeholder.'[76] Two comments by contemporary white observers suggest that Bibb had reason to demand that ex-slaves shed their plantation work habits. A white magistrate in Chatham remarked, 'Negroes are too lazy to work: but I must admit that they are industrious. They keep pottering about, and pick up a living somehow.'[77] An Anglican missionary wrote in 1854:

There are at least 2,000 [blacks] in the town and its vicinity and they are daily increasing, as Chatham may be called the great resting place of the fugitives after landing on the Canadian shore. They afterward make their way into the interior. Degradation, crime, idleness prevail among them here, to a greater extent that I have met with anywhere else. But it must not be forgotten that a large proportion of them just escaped from slavery, and for the first time in their lives they are able to call themselves free men.[78]

Apparently, many ex-slaves stuck to their cultural conceptions of earning a living when they arrived in Canada.

As well as the problems created by plantation work attitudes, Bibb worried about the danger of unacceptable social conduct that threatened the orderly establishment of Canadian blacks and their acceptance by local whites. Judging by the fierce opposition of Bibb and Ward to alcohol, it is possible that intemperance was a real social problem (although as the Peases observe above, the temperance crusade may have been a partly symbolic aspect of moral education). Furthermore, theft was indeed occurring. In the slave South it had been common for slaves to seize property belonging to the master. Among slaves, 'stealing' only applied to articles taken from one slave by another. The master, however, was fair game and stealing from him was known as 'taking.'[79]

It is unclear what kind of theft so alarmed the black leaders in the Chatham area. Bibb was undoubtedly troubled by black theft; whether or not he was an alarmist is uncertain. Bibb was rather an elitist among blacks and prone to condemning black mistakes.[80] Hoping to see pilfering ended, he announced his determination to fight theft in an issue of his *Voice of the Fugitive*. The same issue included a salutation to J.C. Brown, a prominent Chatham black, for turning burglars over to the law.[81] The records do not say from whom the black thieves stole. If it was from whites, it may be evidence of continued 'taking.' This would certainly have alarmed Bibb, who was dedicated to racial harmony and black conformity of Canada. Archival records reveal, however, that the threat of black crime did not in fact exist. Although unfortunately the minutes of the Western District Assizes do not note the colour of the defendants before the influx of fugitive slaves,[82] the register of the Chatham jail from April 1852 to March 1853 records the sex and colour of each prisoner. During that twelve-month period, eighty-one prisoners were incarcerated. Seventy-two of them were white; nine were black. In other words, in a city where the black population was rising steeply from 17 per cent of the total, blacks accounted for 12.5 per cent of reported crime.[83] If one assumes that black crime against whites would be religiously prosecuted (although theft among blacks may have been settled without recourse to the white man's law), then black crime was a less serious problem than white crime. This fact did not alter the sincerity of Bibb's fears of a degraded black slum class, but it does, in retrospect, increase our understanding of the black leadership's nearly paranoid concern that blacks conform to an overwhelmingly white environment.

In Buxton and Chatham the ideological leadership extended to the ex-slaves by the Reverend William King and the black clergy pointed down the same road: the road of self-reliance and independence. King was able to control the population and resources of Buxton, and, judging from Buxton's orderliness and prosperity during the 1850s, his leadership was successful. In Chatham, however, the post-1850 deluge of refugee blacks made it difficult for black leaders to gain acceptance for their ideas of proper work and social behaviour. To some extent the refugees were more accustomed to plantation life. They marched down a different road.

NOTES

This article is from *Ontario History* 77 (2) (1985). Reprinted with permission.

The author would like to acknowledge the helpful comments of Martin A. Klein and Michael Wayne of the University of Toronto, and Indhu Rajagopal of York University on earlier drafts of this paper.

1 Two excellent sources on the problem of transition are P.D. Curtin, *Two Jamaicas* (New York, 1955), for Jamaica, and Lawrence Powell, *New Masters* (New Haven, 1980), for the American South.
2 Leon Litwack, *North of Slavery* (Chicago, 1961), Chapter 4.
3 Ida Greaves, *National Problems of Canada: The Negro in Canada* (Montreal, 1930), pp. 29–34.
4 Jonathan Walton, 'Blacks in Buxton and Chatham, Ontario, 1830–1890' (Ph.D. diss., Princeton University, 1979), p. 27. See also Samuel R. Ward, *An Autobiography of a Fugitive Negro* (London, 1855), p. 154. Most Buxton and Chatham blacks, according to evidence collected by the journalist Benjamin Drew in *The Refugee* (New York, 1855), spent a period of transition in the free northern states.
5 Samuel G. Howe, *The Report of the Freedman's Commission* (Westport, 1866), p. 15.
6 *Census of the Canadas, 1851–2* (Quebec, 1853), vol. I, p. 50.
7 Walton, pp. 22, 61, 84.
8 Ibid., pp. 92–94.
9 Ibid., p. 67.
10 In 1851, 68 of 122 black adult males were employed in skilled or semi-skilled occupations: as tradesmen, craftsmen and their assistants, merchants, or clergymen. Forty-two of 122 were common labourers whose possible underemployment might have been alleviated by the introduction of the railways.

Two men were farmers, and only ten were listed in the census, as having no occupation; presumably they were unemployed. This constituted only an 8 per cent unemployment rate (a brief look at surrounding rural townships reveals that Chatham's black unemployment was in no way being exported outside the town limits). See Walton, p. 67 and *Census of Canada, 1851, Kent County,* Archives of Ontario, C11729. Note that adult men are defined as males aged seventeen to sixty-five. Women were rarely listed as holding any profession or employment.

11 William and Jane Pease, *Black Utopia* (Madison, Wisc., 1963), Chapter 5, and Walton, pp. 101–104.
12 Walton, p. 105.
13 Ibid.
14 Robin Winks, *The Blacks in Canada* (New Haven, 1971), p. 148. See also Fred Hamil, *The Valley of the Lower Thames* (Toronto, 1951), p. 118.
15 Walton, p. 24.
16 Ibid., p. 44.
17 Ibid., p. 46. See also Victor Ullman, *Look to the North Star* (Boston, 1969), p. 110. William and Mary Pease have also demonstrated that Larwill, despite his fanatical racism, had the support of large portions of Chatham's white population. See Pease, 'Opposition to the Founding of the Elgin Association,' *Canadian Historical Review* 37, no. 3, pp. 202–18.
18 It is interesting that King's school for blacks was of such high calibre as to attract neighbourhood whites who normally avoided sitting among blacks.
19 J.K.A. Farrell, 'Schemes for the Transporting of Refugee American Negroes from Upper Canada in the 1840s,' *Ontario History* 25, no. 1, pp. 246–49.
20 Quoted in J.K.A. Farrell, 'The History of the Negro Community in Chatham, Ontario' (Ph.D. diss., University of Ottawa, 1955), p. 167.
21 *The Voice of the Fugitive* (April 1, 1851), p. 1.
22 David B. Davis, *The Problem of Slavery in the Age of Revolution* (Ithaca, 1975), pp. 221–23.
23 Ibid. See also pp. 253, 350–58.
24 Farrell, *History of the Negro Community,* p. 92.
25 Ullman, p. 74.
26 Minutes of the Presbyterian Synod of Canada (Toronto, 1849–1860). Presbyterian Archives, Knox College, Toronto.
27 Ullman, p. 117.
28 Winks, pp. 253–54.
29 Ullman, p. 9.
30 William King, Autobiography (Public Archives of Canada, c. 1890), p. 21.
31 King, pp. 69–70.

32 Ullman, pp. 30–52.

33 King, p. 129.

34 Ullman, pp. 49–67. Before he set out for Canada with his slaves, he bought the infant of one of his female slaves. Ibid., p. 86.

35 Ullman, pp. 63, 74.

36 Winks, p. 218.

37 Davis, p. 378.

38 King, pp. 146–47, 163–64.

39 Ullman, p. 120.

40 The Presbyterian college offered a bachelor's degree in divinity and was skilled in the training of missionaries. King adopted Thomas Buxton's plan of combating slavery by striking at its heart, the slaving grounds of Africa. Buxton believed that a combination of agricultural education and Christianization of African tribes would kill the slave trade by weaning local headmen and rulers from the lucrative slave trade and encouraging them to raise cash crops. King planned in the late 1850s to send some of his students (enrolled in Knox by then) to Lagos (Minutes of the Presbyterian Synod (1857)), pp. 41–42.

41 A full explanation is in Pease, *Black Utopia*, Chapter 4.

42 Ullman, pp. 151–55.

43 King, p. 229.

44 William King to Lord Elgin, August 29, 1848, King Papers, Public Archives of Canada, MG 24 J14 C2223.

45 Alexander McLachlan to the Rev. Alexander Gale, April 4, 1851, King Papers.

46 See Herbert Gutman, *The Black Family in Slavery and Freedom* (New York, 1976).

47 See Georges Balandier, 'Messianism and Nationalism in Black Africa' in M.A. Klein and G.W. Johnson, eds., *Perspectives on the African Past* (Boston, 1972), p. 470. This point is also brought forward after discussions with Professor Martin A. Klein of the University of Toronto.

48 King, pp. 318–319.

49 Eugene Genovese, *Roll, Jordan, Roll* (New York, 1972), Book 2, Part 1.

50 Jane and William Pease, *They Who Would be Free* (New York, 1974).

51 Ibid., pp. 1–13, 97, 124–28, 130.

52 *Provincial Freeman*, March 24, 1854; October 4, 1855.

53 Ibid., February 14, 1857.

54 Ibid., April 15, 1854.

55 Ward, p. 212.

56 *Provincial Freeman*, March 24, 1854.

57 Ibid., October 2, 1855.

58 Ward, p. 201.
59 Ibid., p. 191.
60 Austin Steward, *22 Years a Slave: and 40 Years a Freeman* (Canadaigua, N.Y., 1869), p. 167.
61 *Voice of the Fugitive*, January 1, 1851.
62 Ibid., November 5, 1851.
63 Josiah Henson, *An Autobiography of Reverend Josiah Henson* (Don Mills, 1849, 1969), p. 89.
64 Ibid.
65 Henson had a slightly different view of the ex-slave's transition from slavery to freedom. He envisaged a more protracted period of change in which black communalism would play a large role.
66 *Voice of the Fugitive*, January 1, 1851. Winks (pp. 250–51) believes that the post-1850 blacks were *poorer* than their predecessors and very suspicious of whites.
67 Walton, p. 81.
68 Henson, p. 77.
69 See Genovese, Book 2, Part 2.
70 Ibid., p. 287.
71 Pease, *Black Utopia*, Chapter 4.
72 *Voice of the Fugitive* (April 23, 1851). For the similar response of the Amherstburg Baptist Association, see J.K. Lewis, *Religious Life of Fugitive Slaves* (New York, 1965), p. 80.
73 Walton, p. 69.
74 Ibid., p. 71.
75 Ibid.
76 *Voice of the Fugitive* (January 1, 1851).
77 Howe, p. 42.
78 Quoted in Farrell, p. 138.
79 See Genovese, Book 4.
80 Henry Bibb, 'Henry Bibb Tries "Conjuration"' in Willie Lee Rose, ed., *A Documentary History of Slavery in North America* (New York, 1976), p. 458.
81 *Voice of the Fugitive* (January 1, 1851).
82 *Minutes of the Western District Assizes*, Archives of Ontario, Toronto, MS 530, Reel 4.
83 *Register of Chatham Jail* (1852–1858), Archives of Ontario, Toronto.

Mary Ann Shadd and the Search for Equality

JASON H. SILVERMAN

Educator, orator, reformer, and the first black woman editor of a newspaper in North America, Mary Ann Shadd worked throughout her life for the social and political integration of blacks. She first sought to achieve integration in the northern United States, but when that goal was thwarted by white legal maneuvering, especially after passage of the Fugitive Slave Act in 1850, she decided that integration could better be achieved outside the United States. Thus, along with thousands of 'hunted blacks,' as W.E.B. Du Bois described them, Shadd moved to Canada in 1851. Unlike other emigrationists, though, she constantly held to an idea of integration with white society and white institutions as the only means by which blacks could achieve racial parity. Her uncompromising insistence on integration occasionally set her apart from other black leaders in both the United States and Canada, and because of this her leadership of the black community proved to be less effective, but more widely known, than it otherwise might have been.

Mary Ann Shadd was introduced to the black quest for civil equality by her father, Abraham D. Shadd. In 1819 Abraham Shadd inherited not only his father's occupation as shoemaker but part of an estate valued at $1,300. He successfully continued in the trade and subsequently acquired some property in Wilmington, Delaware. It was into this well-to-do free black family that Mary Ann was born, the eldest child, on October 9, 1823. Abraham Shadd had become an active abolitionist, at least by 1830, representing Delaware at the National Convention for the Improvement of Free People of Color in Philadelphia in 1830, 1831, and 1832. As president of that national convention in 1833, he condemned the American Colonization Society for its support of black expatriation to Liberia. He stressed instead the need for the Society to aid in educating blacks, for he believed that education, thrift, and hard work would enable blacks to achieve racial equality. Starting in the mid-1830s he also covertly opened his home to fugitive slaves going further north via the

Underground Railroad, believing that blacks must help themselves and each other if they were ever to achieve a better life.

Shadd had been forced to act on his self-help ideology seven years earlier, when he uprooted the family from Wilmington. In the 1820s Delaware had provided no educational opportunities for people of color. Consequently, the Shadds relocated in 1833 to West Chester, Pennsylvania, where they enrolled Mary Ann in Price's Boarding School, under the auspices of the Society of Friends. After six years of schooling, the sixteen-year-old Mary Ann demonstrated how profoundly she had been affected both by her denial of education in Delaware and by her father's attitude toward self-help when she returned to Wilmington to organize a school for black youth. For eleven years (1839–50) Mary Anne taught, first at the Wilmington school and subsequently at black schools in New York City and in West Chester and Norristown, Pennsylvania, everywhere echoing her father's views on black education, thrift, and hard work as the desirable means of achieving racial parity, and thus integration, in America.

Indicative of Mary Ann Shadd's views at this point in her career was a pamphlet on the elevation of her race that she published in 1849. *Hints to the Colored People of the North* pointed to the folly of black imitation of white conspicuous materialism and asserted that blacks would not profit or improve their condition by such a display of themselves. Following the legacy of her father's political activism, Mary Ann implored blacks to take the initiative in implementing antislavery reform without waiting for whites to provide their beneficence or support. By the age of twenty-six, then, Shadd had gained considerable recognition by articulating what would become her perennial themes: black independence and self-respect.

The situation for blacks in the United States significantly deteriorated by 1850, causing changes in black attitudes toward emigration. The passage of the Fugitive Slave Act, facilitating the return of runaway slaves to the South, suggested the precarious nature of black freedom in the North. Because of the increased risks, some black leaders, who until this point had largely eschewed emigration as a means to racial elevation, now became its vocal advocates. Lewis Woodson, a minister and teacher in Pittsburgh and a former slave, had written essays in the 1830s and 1840s calling for a national identity among blacks. He theorized that integration would not work in the United States and suggested as alternatives either the establishment of black communities, to be called Africanas, or emigration. These essays helped to promote the emigrationist movement of the 1850s, which was joined by Mary Ann Shadd and by such black illuminaries as Henry Bibb, Samuel Ringgold Ward, James T. Holly, Henry Highland Garnet, Alexander Crummell, and Martin R. Delany. With black leaders encouraging emigration and finding freedom in the northern United States increasingly fragile, thousands of blacks emigrated to Canada seeking freedom, security, and equality.

What American blacks found in Canada, however, differed considerably from what they had anticipated. Canadians undeniably gave refuge to thousands of fugitives, but they did not necessarily do so for philanthropic or humanitarian reasons. As the number of impoverished blacks entering Canada increased, so too did Negrophobia on the part of white Canadians. This sentiment manifested itself in educational, social, and religious discrimination that permeated all levels of black life. Although slavery had been abolished in Canada on January 1, 1834, blacks still were kept out of white schools, experienced great difficulty traveling on public transportation, lived in segregated areas of towns and cities, obtained few jobs, and participated in the political system infrequently at best. In the end, the ostensible Canadian Canaan at times strangely resembled the antebellum United States North.

Nevertheless, along with her brother Isaac, Mary Ann Shadd departed for Canada. Arriving in Toronto in the fall of 1851, she participated in a convention of distinguished black leaders gathered to discuss emigration, the repercussions of the Fugitive Slave Law, and the new environment in which American blacks now found themselves. Eminent emigrationists Martin Delany and Henry Bibb attended this convention, where Shadd quickly learned that she would have to defend her deeply held integrationist posture. While Delany and Bibb advocated emigration, they also buttressed Woodson's concept of a separatist black identity. Partially advanced by the belief that integration would fail no matter where it was attempted, black separatists contended that blacks should maintain their racial identity based on a common black experience, culture, and worldview. Both Bibb and Delany espoused this philosophy, with Delany becoming the most outspoken proponent of 'Africa for the Africans.' Shadd, however, maintained the principles that her father had taught her: that full black equality could ultimately be achieved only by integration with mainstream white society. As secretary of the convention, Shadd's perceptive account of the proceedings soon appeared in both American and Canadian newspapers, earning her the reputation of a knowledgeable black leader.

Over the issue of segregation in Canada, Shadd soon found herself embroiled in a bitter and persistent struggle with Henry Bibb. Born a slave in Kentucky in 1815, Bibb had seen his family sold one by one. He ultimately became such an incorrigible slave that he was sold to six different masters after attempting to escape the same number of times. In 1842 Bibb successfully escaped to Detroit, and eight years later, when Congress passed the Fugitive Slave Act, he joined many of his fellow fugitives in crossing the border into Canada. He and his wife, Mary, settled in Chatham, where they quickly assumed the leadership of the black community in Canada West. Besides establishing the bimonthly newspaper *Voice of the Fugitive*, the Bibbs founded a separate day school, participated in the building of a Methodist church, and assisted in the creation of educational, temperance, and antislavery societies as well as a society devoted to greeting and aiding newly arrived fugitive slaves. An influential and popular figure among Canadian blacks, Bibb would strongly support separate and segregated institutions.

Shadd's challenge to Bibb's leadership in Canada West arose immediately over the issue of integration. When the Toronto meeting adjourned, Shadd continued on to the town of Windsor, located at the opposite end of Lake Erie. She chose Windsor as the place to begin helping elevate the immigrants because it was one of the most destitute black communities in Canada West. Believing like her father that literacy constituted the first step on the road to self-sufficiency, Shadd at once created a private school for those denied an education by converting an old military barracks into a classroom. Opposition, however, came from within the black community itself when Shadd announced that her school would not segregate black children from white. Mary Bibb led the attack by suggesting that the black community petition for a separate public school instead of supporting an integrated private one. Popular black opinion ran in favor of Bibb's separatism rather than Shadd's integrationism, but to a great extent the question was moot as the existence of public schools for white children ensured that few would attend a private school for back fugitives. Indeed, though blacks were legally entitled to send their children to public schools, neither white Canadians nor black fugitives preferred that arrangement. Nevertheless, the principle of integrated schooling mattered much to Shadd. She felt that caste institutions would only exacerbate racial discrimination and distrust. She also observed that whites often abused the black alternative of building separate public schools for, in practice, whites ensured that blacks attended segregated schools only. In the face of opposition Shadd opened her theoretically integrated classroom and operated the night school for only eight weeks before it disbanded. The day school continued, however, but as more and more blacks disclaimed the idea of integration, choosing instead Bibb's vision of a self-contained and insulated existence, Shadd sadly observed, 'I stand alone in opposition to caste schools.'

Viewing all segregated institutions with nothing less than contempt, Shadd openly condemned those blacks who willingly subjected themselves to that kind of second-class citizenship. She believed that separate black schools, black utopian or vocational communities such as Elgin, Dawn, or Wilberforce, and the Refugee Home Society alienated whites even further both by their economic failure and by their perpetuation of old stereotypes that identified blacks as incapable of living a life of freedom. In frequent letters to newspapers in the United States, Shadd relentlessly criticized the organized and isolated black communal experiments in Canada for leading blacks to a life of segregation instead of encouraging them to integrate into mainstream Canadian society.

Yet writing letters provided, at best, only a fragmentary and incomplete refutation of the separatist philosophies of Henry Bibb and his followers. To express her views more fully, Shadd published, in the summer of 1852, a pamphlet entitled *A Plea for Emigration, or Notes of Canada West, in Its Moral, Social, and Political Aspect*. To encourage emigration to Canada, Shadd presented salient statistics and information about life north of the border. She revealed where land was available and its cost and explained the electoral process with great emphasis on the absence of discriminatory laws. Admonishing her black brethren in the United States, Shadd concluded that it would be naive for them to hope for a miraculous overthrow of slavery. On the contrary, she surmised, more ground had been lost to the slavocracy in the wake of the Fugitive Slave Act. She asserted that black spirit and pride would better be served by a decision to emigrate peacefully than by 'a miserable scampering from state to state, in a vain endeavor to gather the crumbs of freedom that a pro-slavery besom may sweep away at any moment.' By providing detailed information about Canada West, Shadd hoped to show that the province, as well as Mexico, the West Indies, and Vancouver Island, compared favorably to the situation facing blacks in the northern United States.

Shadd also attacked the growing separatist philosophy of blacks in Canada. In *Notes of Canada West* she prevailed upon blacks to emigrate to Canada in order to integrate with all free people under the protection of British law. Throughout the pamphlet Shadd's assimilationist philosophies abound. Recognizing the fundamental problem with separation from mainstream Canadian society, she maintained that exclusively black settlements would tend to identify blacks with 'degraded men of like color in the States.' That, in turn, would induce white Canadian estrangement, suspicion, and distrust of the fugitives. Lamenting that some blacks in Canada made a broad line of separation between themselves and the whites, Shadd castigated those separatists as perpetuating black prejudices against whites. She observed how black separatists construed and transformed even casual white remarks into Negrophobia, thereby influencing the recently arrived fugitives into believing that separatism would provide them with a better way of life. Moreover, Shadd feared that because of separatism blacks would seldom attend schools, and the result would be the ascendancy of whites over illiterate fugitives.

Despite the widespread circulation of *Notes of Canada West*, Shadd still functioned at a disadvantage when it came to disseminating her beliefs. With increased vehemence in the wake of the publication of Shadd's *Notes*, Henry Bibb attacked her assimilationist philosophies in his newspaper, *Voice of the Fugitive*. Able only to respond through letters, Shadd lamented the helplessness she felt in reaching her people. Still working full-time as a teacher, the thought of planning and establishing a newspaper of her own increasingly appealed to her. At that time just a few white women had entered the press world, and they, for the most part, submitted articles and letters in much the same fashion as Shadd. Pittsburgh native Jane Swisshelm changed that tradition, however, in 1848 when she founded and edited the antislavery newspaper *The Saturday Visitor*. Following Swisshelm's example, Shadd would soon cross both sex and color barriers to become the first black woman editor of a newspaper in North America.

Such a move did not come easily, however. Bibb's criticism of Shadd in the *Voice of the Fugitive* escalated. Indirectly attacking her for race betrayal, Bibb categorized anyone who shared 'the deluded sister['s]' integrationist beliefs as 'vile traitors who give "aid and comfort" to the enemies who attack us.' In the aftermath of this vituperation Shadd found it particularly difficult to marshal support for her undertaking. But by early 1853, with the timely help of Samuel Ringgold Ward, another prominent fugitive slave who had left the United States, and a committee of local luminaries, Shadd published the first edition of the *Provincial Freeman*.

Proclaimed editor of this bold venture, Ward actually lent only his name to the paper to generate interest and subscriptions. An excellent orator, the 'Black Daniel Webster' spent most of his time traveling extensively through Britain raising funds for various black causes. Although Shadd had taken no official title or position, she represented the driving force behind the new enterprise. She explained in the first issue the difficulties of Ward's titular editorship, noting that, because he was either traveling or residing elsewhere, he could not devote his attention to the paper. At no time, indeed, did Ward act as editor or invest his own money in the operation.

Staunchly assimilationist in tenor, the first issue of the *Provincial Freeman* appeared in March. Publication was then suspended for a year while Shadd traveled in the United States and Canada on a lecture tour to raise money for her fledgling endeavor. As a public speaker she blazed new paths. With the exception of Frances Ellen Watkins, very few other black women could, or did, take to the lecture circuit. Upon the completion of her tour, Shadd triumphantly returned to Canada as a foremost champion of black equality.

Now quite prominent in her own right, Shadd found sufficient support for the *Provincial Freeman* by early 1854 to resume publication. She chose Toronto as her new headquarters, most likely because of the large concentration of blacks there and the presence of several prosperous black businessmen who had expressed interest in her newspaper. In any event, in March 1854, with the motto, 'Self-Reliance Is the Fine Road to Independence,' the *Provincial Freeman* began appearing on a regular basis. Immediately directing her pen toward Bibb's separatism, Shadd stated uncategorically that the newspaper's raison d'être was to represent the intelligent choice of 'Colored Canadians' for integration. Perhaps, though, the fundamental difference between Bibb and Shadd was more subtly expressed by the very titles of their respective journals. On the one hand, the *Voice of the Fugitive* described blacks as actual fugitives and implied their temporary relocation in Canada. On the other hand, the *Provincial Freeman* obviously used Canada as the point of reference, imparting the feeling of a more permanent move. Toward this end, Shadd urged her fellow blacks to contribute their energy and industry 'to the weal of their adopted country.'

Bibb's death in the summer of 1854 deprived Shadd of her primary nemesis. By autumn, with Ward's name expunged from the masthead, Shadd directed the fortunes of the *Provincial Freeman* with her sister Amelia. Bereft of any benefits accruing from association with Ward's reputation, Mary Ann Shadd again began lecturing in Canada and the

United States to meet the newspaper's operational expenses. Returning to Toronto she unexpectedly met with public opposition to a newspaper run exclusively by women. Realizing that hers was the only black newspaper left in Canada, Shadd acquiesced and very reluctantly searched for a male editor to placate her opponents and prevent any disruption of her press. She settled on the Reverend William P. Newman, a rather innocuous individual, to act as nominal editor. Yet she sharply chastized her readership for their captiousness toward her as a woman editor. Cognizant of her own importance in breaking 'the Editorial ice,' she implored other black women to go into editing despite the obstacles.

The title of editor was all that Shadd surrendered. Her reputation as orator and equal rights champion firmly established, she journeyed to Philadelphia to attend the 1855 National Negro Convention, the first black woman to be admitted as a corresponding member to the colored convention movement. Her impressive address to that group moved Frederick Douglass to observe that she made 'one of the most convincing and telling speeches in favor of Canadian emigration I ever heard.' From Philadelphia, Shadd visited other areas of the United States generating interest in and subscriptions to the *Provincial Freeman*. When she again returned to Canada she moved the newspaper's offices to Chatham, a former Bibb stronghold, where a larger number of blacks had settled.

Shadd used her newspaper to comment on all aspects of black life in Canada, but she focused especially on problems of racial discrimination and segregation. Exposing discrimination wherever it occurred, Shadd publicized, much to the chagrin of many white Canadians, specific examples of their racist behavior. She described Wardsville, a town near London, Ontario, as a contemptible and disgraceful place because of the discrimination aimed at fugitives. As she did on numerous other occasions, Shadd warned blacks to avoid that area or experience 'lessons in colorphobia.'

So fervent an integrationist was Shadd that she had much difficulty comprehending why blacks should be subject to the peculiar detestation of white Canadians. In defense of her philosophy, she noted in an editorial the biblical precedent for leaving a land ruled by tyrants, comparing the black exodus from 'the hell of the continent' with the departure of the children of Jacob from Egypt. Her most telling analogy compared the Puritans as fugitives of Europe with blacks as fugitives from the United States. She observed that both kinds of emigrants were fugitives from oppression and contended that skin color alone differentiated the two. She then tried to proselytize both white Canadians and black fugitives to accept integrationism.

To implement her assimilationist policy, Shadd encouraged blacks to strive for financial independence in Canada. The *Provincial Freeman's* motto of self-reliance echoed her personal motto, as well as the lessons she had learned as a child about self-help. She wrote that the best way available to help the refugees was to employ such measures as would make them independent, self-sustaining laborers within the given social structure. Their success in this endeavor would thereby prove 'the fitness of the slaves for freedom ... and the perfect capability of the negro to live and to advance under the same government and upon terms of political and social equality with the anglo-saxon race or any other of the one great human family.' Success would also facilitate the abolitionist cause by serving as an example to American slaveholders. Black progress in Canada, according to Shadd, would be a triumphant refutation to racial prejudice everywhere.

While the *Provincial Freeman,* by its very publication, continued to provide some service to the fugitives, by 1856 it seemed that the venture would cease due to insolvency. Shadd worried about obtaining the 3,000 subscriptions necessary to maintain publishing. In the summer, a planned thirty-day hiatus to equip a new office evolved into a four-month disruption in publishing because of the shortage of funds. Of course, most black newspapers faced a similar situation at that time. As Shadd struggled to resume publishing operations, she noted that *Frederick Douglass' Paper* had been greatly reduced in size yet much improved in appearance. She applauded Douglass's changes as sensible and wrote to a friend that black newspapers must survive even if reduced to the size of one's hand.

Regular publication of the *Provincial Freeman* resumed in the fall of 1856, but with many of its subscribers in arrears the financial state of the journal again rapidly deteriorated. Shadd's husband of two years, Thomas F. Carey, a Toronto barber, began selling lamps to supplement the newspaper's income. A widespread depression during the late 1850s, however, hastened the paper's demise. Shadd managed to publish it sporadically until 1859, at which time the financial burden became too debilitating.

In the wake of the *Provincial Freeman's* demise, Shadd returned to full-time teaching at an American Missionary Association-supported school – an ironic twist of fate since Shadd had long been at odds with the A.M.A. With its money she had opened her first school in Windsor in

1851, but the A.M.A. withdrew its support in 1853, ostensibly because Shadd was not an Evangelical Christian. (Earlier a Roman Catholic, Shadd had joined the African Methodist Episcopal church but left it in Canada because of its segregated policies to become a Methodist.) The true reason the A.M.A. withdrew its support of her, Shadd believed, rested upon her sharp criticism of an association-affiliated project, the separatist Refugee Home Society, directed by her nemesis, Henry Bibb, and created to settle blacks on low-cost land in Canada. Shadd publicly accused all of the Society's agents of malfeasance, asserting that they cheated the fugitives by granting them five acres of land conditional upon the purchase of twenty more – clearly beyond the financial capacity of most blacks. She claimed the agents kept for administrative expenses between twenty and twenty-five percent of all funds solicited. By accepting the job at an A.M.A.-supported school, though, Shadd apparently went against her own idealistic rule of never allowing interest to become the master of principle.

No longer running her own enterprise freed Shadd to enter more actively into the abolitionist movement. With particular vigor she assailed those who sought to compromise in any way with slavery or who were prepared to allow blacks to accept temporary second-class citizenship. Singling out such abolitionists as Hiram Wilson, Josiah Henson, and the late Henry Bibb, Shadd opined in a letter to a friend that the antislavery cause consisted of too many 'pretended leaders.' Indeed, she predicted that all of their conventions and caucuses would be fruitless since they attended such meetings only for self-aggrandizement. As a Garrisonian, Shadd also had little use for John Scoble, secretary of the British and Foreign Anti-Slavery Society and manager of Dawn, a black community in Canada. Describing Scoble, Shadd wrote that his pomposity and petulance totally undermined his effectiveness. Nor did she have any kind words for the Canadian Anti-Slavery Society and its secretary, Thomas Henning. She recorded the hypocrisy of Canadian abolitionists and criticized 'this disgusting, repulsive surveillance, this despotic, dictatorial, snobbish air of superiority of white people over [black], by Canadian anti-slavery people.' Shadd repeatedly drew attention to those Canadians who verbally endorsed abolition but who never attended meetings, gave contributions, or assisted blacks in any tangible way. She thereby attempted to embarrass or harass them into changing their ways, but in that effort she succeeded only in proving her own self-righteousness. Her leadership at times seemed to consist only of carping criticism of those not meeting her expectations.

Shadd watched with great interest as the sectional crisis intensified in the United States. Her hope for the potential destruction of slavery by the impending conflict heightened upon John Brown's arrival in Chatham in the spring of 1858. Meeting with Brown, a group consisting of Shadd, her husband, her brother Isaac, and a friend, Osborne P. Anderson, became privy to the visionary's intended plans. So taken with Brown was Anderson that the young black joined him at Harpers Ferry and survived to record his memoirs in a volume entitled *Voice from Harper's Ferry*, edited and prepared for publication by Mary Ann Shadd. Shadd, who held Brown in highest regard, wrote the New York *Weekly Anglo-African* shortly after his death to eulogize the 'plucky' abolitionist.

Through the early years of the Civil War, Shadd continued to teach in an interracial school in Chatham, but she also wrote letters in support of abolitionism to many American newspapers. Not surprisingly, the activist grew tired of watching the American Civil War from a distance, and, anxious to assist in the Northern war effort, she accepted an invitation from Martin Delany, in late 1863, to serve as an enlistment recruiter. Without hesitation, Shadd returned to the United States to participate in the recruitment programs of several states, ultimately obtaining a commission as a U.S. recruitment officer from Indiana's governor, Oliver P. Morton. That she succeeded in this effort came as no surprise to her contemporaries. William Wells Brown wrote that she raised recruits with as much skill, tact, and order as any government recruiting officer and that her men were always considered among the best recruited.

Shadd agonized over whether to remain in the United States after Appomattox. Still hoping for an integrated Canadian Canaan, she had witnessed a steady exodus of blacks from Canada following the Emancipation Proclamation. With seemingly safe conditions in the United States, thousands of blacks, fatigued with broken promises and Canadian racism, returned to search for friends, relatives, and freedom. Shadd concluded that she could best serve her people by remaining in the United States to educate and help assimilate the millions of newly emancipated blacks. Toward this end, in 1869 she obtained an American teaching certificate and taught for a while in Detroit; shortly thereafter she relocated to Washington, D.C.

'The capital,' Shadd recorded, 'is the Mecca of the colored pilgrim.' Observing the numbers of recently freed blacks migrating to Washington, D.C., in pursuit of their fortunes, Shadd reflected that a great potential for racial equality now existed, if intelligence dictated action. And intelligence, to her, still meant racial uplift and advancement through education. This, of course, complemented her view that racial advancement should aim at and, in the end, produce acceptance and integration into the mainstream of American society. Toward this goal Shadd once again promulgated self-help in lectures to biracial audiences, for she felt that the greatest mistake blacks could commit would be to compromise themselves by relying on others' philanthropy. She had abandoned emigrationism but retained a belief that dependence on the benevolence of whites would emasculate the freedpeople and prevent them from integrating. In this she would recognize no middle ground.

The passage of the Thirteenth, Fourteenth, and Fifteenth amendments convinced Shadd that blacks would also have to be fully cognizant of the laws of the land were they ever to achieve equality in postbellum America. Hoping to serve as a role model, Shadd, at the age of forty-six, enrolled in the evening law school of the recently created Howard University – the first woman to do so. Intermittently she would study law, supporting herself by teaching, and would eventually receive her degree in 1883.

As she pursued her law degree, Shadd continued to write articles and letters to newspapers expressing her sociopolitical concerns. For example, she disparaged Reconstruction politics of both parties as tending to divide and exploit the black community. She noticed that white politicians, after adroitly pitting blacks against one another, complacently deprecated them for being so divided. Proposing a rather radical panacea given the times, Shadd encouraged blacks to unite in a boycott of discriminatory white businesses. They should demand that these prejudicial businesses allow black customers or else blacks would withdraw their patronage from all white businesses. The opinionated Shadd encouraged blacks to proclaim such a policy and then 'stick to it like grim death.'

Long recognized as a spokesperson for racial equality, Shadd increasingly turned her attention to gender equality. A fervent supporter of equal rights and equal opportunity for black women as well as men, she wrote often to Frederick Douglass's *New National Era*. In a series of articles in the spring of 1872, she chided black women for maintaining a frightened silence and by that silence condoning petty criminality and vagrancy in the black community. She noted that white women were gaining some power in the United States, and she implored black women likewise to speak out on social issues. One of a handful of black women leaders, Shadd felt that black women should establish a voice in those matters most directly affecting them.

Supporting rights for women, both black and white, Shadd actively participated in most women's rights conventions in and around Washington, D.C. Testifying before the House Judiciary Committee on behalf of women's suffrage, she praised the passage of the Fourteenth and Fifteenth amendments but declared that women all over the country still felt discriminated against by the retention of the word 'male' in the amendments. After all, she reasoned, millions of women shared with men the responsibilities of freedom. She encouraged legislators to expunge any sexist references from the amendments as expeditiously as possible and provide women with the franchise. Arguing that women were taxed and governed in other respects without consent, Shadd simply requested that the principles of the founding fathers be applied to women as well as to men.

On March 19, 1874, Shadd put her theories about equal rights into practice. Along with sixty-three other women in the District of Columbia, she attempted to register to vote in an approaching election. Anticipating the refusal, the women, both black and white alike, demanded that the clerks provide sworn, notarized affidavits stipulating they had been denied the right to vote. Armed with what any attorney would consider incriminating documents, Shadd penned a series of condemnatory exposes for the local press.

Recognized by Susan B. Anthony and Lucretia Mott as a valuable member of the movement, Shadd, upon invitation, addressed the National Woman's Suffrage Association convention in 1878. Caught up in the zeal to obtain the franchise for women, she temporarily forsook her long-held preference for integration in favor of what appeared to be separatism. Shortly after addressing the National Women's Suffrage Association, and with its support, Shadd founded the short-lived auxiliary organization called the Colored Women's Progressive Franchise Association. The fledgling organization attracted many to its first few meetings by advocating that black men and women in the District of Columbia create labor bureaus, cooperative stores, banking institutions, printing establishments, and lecture bureaus for their mutual benefit. The organization declared that while it would tolerate no gender discrimination, women would nevertheless have the controlling power since they had the most to gain. Shadd's organization received cautious coverage from Washington's black newspapers. The *People's Advocate*, for example, reported that Shadd had stated 'our leading men of color were always talking about providing for "our boys" but never a word did they say of "our girls."'

As activity in her organization waned, Shadd took to the lecture circuit to engender interest in and support for equal rights. Commenting on topics that ranged from race pride to the Republican party, from women's rights to the Ku Klux Klan, she addressed audiences both north and south of the Mason-Dixon Line. Until her seventieth year Shadd maintained an active schedule. Finally, enfeebled by rheumatism and cancer, she died in the summer of 1893. In the twilight of his own life, Frederick Douglass commented that Mary Ann Shadd proved the mental capacity and dignity intrinsic in black women. By her lifework he felt she had demonstrated 'the possibilities of her sex and class.' And indeed she had. Shadd surpassed her father's role in the abolitionist movement to become not only a prominent abolitionist but an emigrationist as well. Her lifelong goal was to see equality achieved for all black men and women. To achieve this she was ready at various times during her life to endorse emigration and even separate institutions. Throughout her career, though, she always retained her basic belief that through education, thrift, and hard work blacks could achieve integration. At times her personality made her a less effective leader, able to persuade or to cajole and not to convince. Nevertheless, Shadd spoke for all oppressed men and women by her actions. She aired her views as early as 1849, when she was only twenty-six. She emigrated, and then facilitated the way for others by authoring her *Notes of Canada West*. She became the first black woman editor of a newspaper, writing scathing editorials on those she thought had betrayed the fugitives. She actively participated in the women's suffrage movement, agitating alongside white women for something in which she believed. She lectured, published, and rarely compromised, and in so doing Mary Ann Shadd assuredly made her voice heard and her ideas known.

NOTE

This article is from *Black Leaders of the Nineteenth Century*, ed. Leon Litwack and August Meier. Urbana: University of Illinois Press 1988. Reprinted with permission.

TOPIC THREE
Settling the Canadian West: The 'Exotic' Continentals

When in 1904 Prime Minister Wilfrid Laurier said that the twentieth century would be Canada's century, he had good reasons for his optimism. Canada had weathered the harsh realities of world depression and begun to enjoy dramatic economic growth. International conditions favoured a sharp increase in the demand for Canadian exports, especially natural products like wheat, while encouraging the foreign investment needed for the development of newly discovered mineral resources. Domestic industries prospered, helped along by the protective tariff, the Canadian Pacific Railway, and a rapidly increasing population. In 1900, Canada's population stood at close to six million; by 1920, that number had nearly doubled.

Large-scale immigration explains some of this population growth. The early twentieth century brought mass immigration to Canada and contributed to the racial–ethnic diversification of Canadian society. Some 2.5 million newcomers had arrived by 1914: close to one million were from Britain, more than 750,000 were from the United States, and more than 500,000 were continental Europeans. Immigration to western Canada was a dynamic feature of this migration. Most immigrants who chose the 'last best west' were English-speaking, but large numbers of Germans, Scandinavians, and eastern Europeans also came. The latter included ethnic Ukrainians, Hungarians, Poles, and ethno-religious sects like the Doukhobors and Mennonites, from the Russian and Austro-Hungarian empires. Mostly midwestern farmers, the Americans included 'ethnic Americans,' or U.S.-born descendants of earlier European immigrants, including Scandinavians and Germans. Official restrictions on Asian admissions and the stalling tactics of immigrant agents determined to keep out African-American farmers kept these and other racial minorities to a minimum.

Immigration helped to make the prairies one of the most ethnically diverse and economically dynamic regions of the country. It had not always been so. From the time of Confederation, and even before, political leaders had considered the settlement of the prairie west with white, homesteading families a crucial prerequisite to the success of Canada as a white settler society. Such settlement, of course, meant the displacement of aboriginal peoples from these lands. Yet in the thirty years after Confederation, attempts to settle the prairies failed. Prospective immigrants from Europe preferred the American west. So did many Canadians, including farmers, who were attracted to the better climates, weather-resistant strains of wheat, and advanced farming techniques. Not only was the Canadian west not being filled with immigrants, the country actually faced a mass exodus of Canadian-born citizens.

The situation changed dramatically after 1896. Various global factors well beyond Canadian influences fuelled immigration to the Canadian west between the late 1890s and the First World War era (and later). These included the spreading industrial capitalism and persistent unfavourable land tenure systems pushing out Europe's rural artisans and peasants, the closing of the American frontier, and favourable world wheat prices. But Canadian authorities also tried to influence events, and successful experiments in dry farming techniques and aggressive recruitment of immigrants probably also played a role.

Federal politicians and bureaucrats actively encouraged immigration from the United States and abroad. Men like Clifford Sifton, minister of the interior in Laurier's first cabinet, used immigration policy to try to encourage and even influence the character of immigration. The official policy that was designed above all to encourage agricultural settlement, was highly selective, even discriminatory and racist. The ideal immigrant - usually depicted as belonging to a family unit of seasoned farmers – was one who not only fit into the government's economic designs, but also satisfied the prevailing assumption that Canada was a white nation, and should remain so. Hence the preference for Britons and white Americans. The 'exotic' continental Europeans were also accepted, particularly during Sifton's era, precisely because they fulfilled the declared need for experienced agricultural labour, even if as southern and eastern Europeans they were considered less 'desirable' than Britons or white Americans. Thus, ethnic tolerance went hand in hand with national self-interest, or the priorities of nation-building and economic development. At the same time, the growing 'foreign' face of the prairies engendered a racist backlash from both English- and French-speaking observers, who declared that Canada had taken in the refuse of Europe, and who issued dire predictions about the 'mongrelization' of the races.

But who precisely were these immigrant-settlers, and how did they face the risks and endure the hardships of pioneer life? Anne Woywitka's account of a Roumanian immigrant woman reminds us that the history of western settlement is also a history of ordinary people who demonstrated resilience and ingenuity in the struggle to survive pioneer life. In Woywitka's essay, women are at the centre of the immigration drama, a role traditionally reserved for men. How important was the family unit to prairie settlement? What were the particular skills and talents needed to survive pioneer life that women were able to provide? What sorts of survival strategies did settlers employ to 'make it' in the Canadian west?

By focusing on a numerically significant group, the Ukrainians, James Darlington's essay explores the complex dynamics by which families, extended kin, and co-villagers remade their lives on the marginal farmlands of the Canadian prairies. Moreover, he highlights the critical role that networks of information and support played in the migration and settlement process and the impact of the bloc settlement of Ukrainians on the physical and cultural landscape of the west. How immigrants found ways of transplanting and adapting (as well as discarding) familiar strategies, rituals, mores, and even artifacts to their new environment is a familiar theme in work on urban immigrants. Darlington has documented these themes for rural folk. His case study of Dauphin, Manitoba, describes the log-building and roof-thatching techniques and farming decisions of Ukrainian homesteaders, and charts the rise of self-help, commercial, and institutional structures that long characterized this tight-knit community.

Both Woywitka and Darlington alert us to critical issues for discussion, including the fact that homesteading, far from being an overnight enterprise, was a prolonged and labour-intensive process that demanded enormous commitment and work from all family members. Pioneer farming, furthermore, was often combined with some wage-earning. Why were men most likely to leave home to earn cash for their struggling farm families? Where did they find waged work? Students might also consider how the lives of homesteaders differed from those of the sojourners and urban dwellers described elsewhere in this book. How do descriptions of urban neighbourhoods and ethnic communities compare with Darlington's depiction of a Ukrainian-Canadian cultural landscape that took shape on a rural 'frontier'? Indeed, how does his training as a geographer distinguish his work from that of historians? As Darlington observes, bloc settlement was not exclusively a Ukrainian pattern, although in contrast to the government-organized settlements of Mennonites and other 'Continentals,' it was a voluntary process in which Old World farming practices and knowledge, individual choice and nostalgia for certain types of land, and ties of family and friendship infuenced patterns. How then, does he account for the eventual demise of the once successful settlement of Dauphin, Manitoba?

BIBLIOGRAPHY AND SUGGESTED READINGS

Avery, Donald H. *Reluctant Host: Canada's Response to Immigrant Workers, 1896–1994*. Toronto 1995.

Brown, R. Craig, and Ramsay Cook. *Canada, 1896–1921: A Nation Transformed*. Toronto 1974.

Burnet, Jean, and Howard Palmer. *'Coming Canadians': An Introduction to a History of Canada's People*. Toronto 1988.

Francis, Douglas, and Howard Palmer, eds. *The Prairie West: Historical Readings*. Edmonton 1985.

Friesen, Gerald. *The Canadian Prairies: A History*. Toronto 1984.

Iacovetta, Franca, Michael Quinlan, and Ian Radforth, 'Immigration and Labour: Australia and Canada Compared' *Labour/le Travail* 38 (Fall 1996).

Loewen, Royden. *Family, Church and Market: A Mennonite Community in the Old and New Worlds, 1850–1930*. Toronto 1993.

Luciuk, Lubomyr, and Stella Hryniuk, eds. *Canada's Ukrainians: Negotiating an Identity*. Toronto 1991.

Owram, Doug. *Promise of Eden: The Canadian Expansionist Movement and the Idea of the West*. Toronto 1980.

Palmer, Howard. *Patterns of Prejudice: A History of Nativism in Alberta*. Toronto 1982.

Palmer, Howard, and Tamara Palmer, eds. *Peoples of Alberta: Portraits of Cultural Diversity*. Saskatoon 1985.

Swyripa, Frances. *Wedded to the Cause: Ukrainian Women and Ethnic Identity, 1891–1991*. Toronto 1993.

Troper, Harold. *Only Farmers Need Apply*. Toronto 1972.

Woodcock, George, and Ivan Avakumovic. *The Doukhobours*. Toronto 1968.

A Roumanian Pioneer

ANNE B. WOYWITKA

Mrs. Veronia Kokotailo came with her parents to Canada in 1898 when she was four years old. Her father had decided to leave the village of Boian in Roumania because his native land could no longer offer sustenance to him and his growing family. He owned the house they lived in, plus a scrap of land no larger than a small city lot. Over the preceding generations, the original land holding had been divided and subdivided among members of his family so that there was hardly enough to grow a garden. How could he hope to raise a family on this meagre bit of land? Much less, how could he hope to give anything to his own children when they were ready to go on their own? For these reasons, he decided to emigrate to Canada. Four other families decided to join him, including his father-in-law with a wife by a second marriage.

The sale of his property in Boian brought him enough to pay their passage, but little was left over to re-establish them in the new land. They arrived in Canada in the summer of 1898 to settle in a district northeast of Willingdon which was to form the nucleus of the first Roumanian settlement in Alberta. Though they left behind them the poverty of the Old Country, they also left behind all things dear and familiar to them – their homes, relatives, and friends, church and their way of village life. In exchange, they hoped to establish a better life on the 160 acres of land the Canadian Government was giving away for $10 – never dreaming how hard the transition from 'rags to riches' would be, nor how long it would take to make a decent life for themselves.

They brought with them such tools as spade, shovel, axe, hammer, saw, scythe and sickle. One family brought a quern for grinding wheat into flour, another a spinning wheel and loom. They brought with them their bedding and personal effects. The little extra money they still had went for hiring teamsters and wagons to take them from Edmonton to the area they had chosen to settle. In truth, to them the place was a dot on the map which they chose because there were other settlements nearby – Willingdon, Shandro and Whitford. They planned to call the new settlement Boian, after their native village.

When their teamster dropped them off, they could see little else than a forest of poplar trees and a glimmer of sky above. So this was to be their home in Canada!

'Well,' said Veronia's father, 'at least we will never run short of wood here. There is more than enough for our buildings and even more for fuel and fences than we ever dreamt of in the Old Country!'

For economic reasons, they decided that for the first little while, it would be better for the two families to live together.

They immediately set to clearing a space in the woods for their primitive shelter which they called a 'burdey.' It was a dugout large enough to accommodate the family with a pole-roof like a tepee over it. The poles were covered with sedge and sod. The burdey afforded them shelter from wind and sun and even kept out most of the rains that fell frequently that summer.

The two men had no sooner completed the burdey and dug a well when they left the women and children in search of work. They had to earn a few dollars for winter food supplies.

As the women enlarged the clearing for a garden, the pile of logs grew. Then Veronia's mother saw the possibility of a log house. She resented living like an animal in a lair and had cried bitterly over it. She longed for the clean white-washed home she'd left behind. From then on she worked with the vision of a log house uppermost in her mind. Before the men returned in the fall, the house had been built.

Veronia recalls how hard her mother worked as she cut, limbed and sawed the logs into equal lengths. With the mother-in-law's help, they dragged the logs into place and set them upright into the soil, side by side, to make a wall. Her mother was young and her body was yet to be hardened by hard work. Before she was finished building the house, both her shoulders were a mass of raw bleeding flesh. But she refused to give up and in time all four walls were standing. The only thing that baffled her was the roof, for which she was forced to call for help from a neighbour.

She left a space for the door and arranged for a window on the south wall. In place of glass she used a linen pillow case. As a final touch to the house, she made a porch over the door. Its walls and roof were made by weaving willows over a frame. She then plastered everything, inside and out, using a mixture of clay and chopped sedge.

Later, when she discovered a deposit of white clay, she carted it home by hand and used it to smooth and brighten the dark walls. The dirt floor bothered her, but there was no way to improve on that other than to surface it with clay and tramp it down. She kept the loose dirt down by sprinkling it with water and sweeping it off with a broom made of birch switches.

Now there remained the problems of a door, a chimney and an oven. Again, the willow came in handy. For the door she made a cross frame over which she wove thick batts of sedge. She wove a willow frame for the chimney and plastered it thickly, inside and out. She made a clay bake-oven, the top of which served as a warm bed for the children on cold winter nights. She laid rocks for a cook stove but had to wait until she could get a galvanized iron sheet for the stove-top. Thus, without spending a penny and improvising as she went, Veronia's mother built them a home in which they lived for many years.

One day while the women worked and the children played nearby, a herd of wild range cattle wandered into the clearing. The children screamed in terror as they ran for their mother. Alarmed by the screams, the cows wheeled around to form a protective circle around the calves. This aroused the bulls so they roared and pawed the ground, throwing clouds of dust over their humped backs. Terrified at their first sight of wild cattle, the women grabbed the children and ran to the house, certain that their end had come. However, after a while, the animals wandered off and did not come back again.

That summer and fall they lived mostly off the woods and meadows around them, picking berries, mushrooms and edible roots. They had some flour and a bag of potatoes which they had used sparingly. Their supplies had to last indefinitely.

The men returned in the fall with enough money to replenish food supplies and to buy the barest necessities. Because it was necessary to live on one's homestead part of the year in order to 'prove' it, they built a shelter on the father-in-law's quarter and he moved into it with his wife. About this time, Veronia's mother gave birth to another child.

That fall and winter, Veronia's parents chopped down trees, enlarging the clearing around the house. Come spring they would hire someone to break it. They did not spare themselves as they worked. When the snows grew deep, they sawed stacks of firewood for fuel and trimmed trees for posts and fence rails. Young as she was, Veronia took care of the baby and her brother and kept the fire going.

Before the spring thaw came, the father went working again. The food supply was running short and they needed money to pay for the breaking and the seed. Soon after he was gone it became necessary to ration their food. When the last handful of flour had been used and the last potato had gone into the soup pot, death by starvation became a very

real possibility. The baby cried and the other children begged for something to eat. There was no one to whom the mother could turn for help,
knowing other settlers were all in the same predicament.

Without too much hope, she went into the woods looking for mushrooms, though it was still early in the season. However, she did find little yellow button-sized mushrooms growing. These she picked not
knowing whether they were edible or not. What difference if they died
of mushroom poisoning or by starvation? Beggars could not be choos-
ers. She added chopped green grass to the mushrooms in the pot and
boiled it. They ate that day and did not die. Then for two weeks without
a break, they ate the same unpalatable food. The mother cried each night
and prayed that they not wake when morning came. But every morning
they awoke, alive as ever and hungrier than the day before. The mother
would go into the woods again and hunt for more mushrooms and pick
more grass, and pray for the father to return.

At the end of the second week the father arrived home, carrying on
his back 50 pounds of flour and a pig's head. He had walked a hundred
miles over rough trails bringing food for his family. Later, the mother
earned her husband's displeasure when she cut off the ears from the
pig's head and gave them to her parents for a pot of soup.

They broke a plot of land that spring and planted it to potatoes, a bit
of garden, and the rest in wheat.

In the meantime, Veronia's mother and a neighbour woman, hearing
that a Mr. Johnson at Whitford had raised a log barn and was looking for
someone to plaster it, offered their services in hopes of earning a bit of
money. They walked twice a day to work through five miles of bush. It
was a back-breaking job and for lunch they were given raw carrots out
of the garden.

One evening on their way back home, they lost all sense of direction.
Wandering aimlessly, they began to despair of ever getting back home,
when they came upon a path with human excrement alongside it. They
fell on their knees thanking God for letting them know that there were
people around. They had been afraid they had wandered off into deep
wilderness and would never see home or people again. They finally
stumbled back to their homesteads late that night. Next morning they
took an axe with them and blazed their own trail. At the end of two weeks
of hard labour, they each received a pail of potatoes in lieu of payment.

Because her father was away from home so much of the time and her
mother worked outside the house, Veronia at the age of five had already
learned responsibility. She took care of the younger children and ran
errands for her mother.

In 1899, her mother harvested their first crop of wheat by sickle, tying it into sheaves and putting it in stooks to dry. The day she threshed, she took a panful of the precious grain, put it in a bag over Veronia's shoulder and sent her up the path to a neighbour's home where they had a quern. Veronia came back with the flour and by night-time they were eating buns and potato soup made from the produce of their own little bit of land.

It was a great day for rejoicing when Veronia's father bought a cow. Her grandfather had also bought one and when they purchased a plough, the two men teamed their animals. Now, not only did they have milk, but were able to break more land without hiring anybody.

The mother was heartbroken the day their cow died. They had come to depend on the milk, the bit of cream and cheese the cow had supplied them. It was hard to reconcile themselves to the loss. However, being a practical woman, she skinned the cow and tanned the hide. At least she had leather for making moccasins for her family.

Then, in time, her father bought another cow, and also an ox. This time he kept the cow for milking purposes only and used the ox for heavy work.

During those first years they were always only a step away from hunger and starvation. Mostly, they lived off the land. Meat was almost an unknown commodity. Though wild game was plentiful, her people were not hunters. Without a gun, they had no way to get the ducks and upland game-birds to their table.

One day when Veronia was on an errand to a neighbour's home, she sniffed the heavenly aroma of meat cooking on the stove. As she waited hopefully to be invited to eat, her attention was drawn by a cat yowling at the door.

The old woman turned to the door.

'Oh, there's my Machko back home. Be a good girl and let him in. He's been out all morning,' she said to Veronia.

Veronia opened the door and drew back with a gasp. She had never seen such a large cat before. He was twice the size of an average tom. His face and ears were nicked with battle scars, the end of his tail bitten off. On the doorstep lay a fat prairie chicken he had brought home. Padding softly into the house, he went straight to his mistress, rubbing himself affectionately against her legs and purring like a distant thunderstorm.

While the woman bent over to fondle the cat, speaking endearingly and praising him, the wheels in Veronia's head began to turn madly. She did not think the woman had seen the prairie chicken. Though she had never stolen anything before, hunger did not leave her much choice. Through the half-open door she could see the dead bird. It lay there, tempting her with visions of broth and succulent meat. Maybe if she snatched it and ran ...? Surely the woman could not miss something she had not seen? Besides, Veronia told herself convincingly, there was meat bubbling in her pot already. She did not know what it was to be hungry.

Putting her thoughts in action, the little girl slid out of the door, grabbed the prairie chicken under her arm and ran. But she had not gone far before she heard the woman shouting:

'What are you doing? Where are you going with that chicken? It's mine. Wait till I tell your mother what you did. Just wait.'

Caught in the act red-handed, Veronia dropped the bird and dived into a tall growth of green, too scared to look where she landed. Immediately, she felt the sharp sting of nettle on her legs and arms, but mostly on her bare buttocks. She scrambled out of the nettles even faster and ran home crying, shedding tears of shame and humiliation combined with a painful itch of nettle stings. She shrivelled inside when she thought of her mother's wrath. Now even hunger seemed preferable.

The neighbour came to their door later in the day carrying the plucked bird in her hand. The little girl looked for a place to hide but saw none. Hanging her head in shame and resignation, she waited for the sky to fall on her. But as it turned out, the neighbour had a heart after all. While Veronia watched fearfully, the woman handed the bird to her mother.

'Perhaps you would like to make some soup. My cat is a hunter and brings me more than I can use.'

No word or mention of what had really happened.

Veronia's mother seized the old woman's hand and kissed it. Her eyes were bright with unshed tears. 'God will repay you for this! My husband is not home and my children are hungry. Thank you! Thank you so much!'

The neighbour nodded sadly. 'Forgive me! But like the saying goes, the well fed do not know the hungry.'

The lean years continued. What little income rolled in from the father's work was ploughed back into the homestead. The clearing in the woods grew ever larger. The family increased and so did the mother's responsibilities. Soon Veronia was to shoulder much of the work her mother had done before. She helped clear land, picked roots, and learned to work with the machinery her father had acquired. They grew a large garden and laid in a store of potatoes, dried peas, beans and broadbeans. They krauted cabbage, picked saskatoons and dried them for the winter. The whole family contributed to the welfare of the home for there was no room for a drone in their midst.

As more settlers came in, they brought with them various things like an oil press, mortar, and a grist mill. Her mother availed herself of their use, making oil from poppy seed, sunflower seeds and mostly from the oil rich seed of the cannabis, all of which she grew in her garden. She used the oil in all her baking and her cooking. She used the mortar to take the coarse hulls off the barley, wheat and millet and used the hulled grains to cook as cereal or as filling for cabbage rolls. They caught fish in the river using box-traps. These fish they pickled for later use or salted and dried them for winter eating. They picked mushrooms and dried them.

From the cannabis or hemp plant, they processed a coarse fibre which they wove into horse blankets. From these same fibres, they made strong rope. The mother made her own soap using waste fat and lye made from ashes. She scrubbed clothes on a wooden scrub board. She sewed and mended, first by candlelight, later by the light of a kerosene lamp.

In times of sickness, Veronia's mother reverted to the use of herbs and roots to make her own medicinal teas and salves. As a carryover from the Old Country she, like the rest of the settlers, believed in the power of witchcraft and the 'evil eye.' Usually in every district of Central European settlers, there was an old woman versed in the art of 'pouring wax' or 'throwing coals,' which was supposed to be able to relieve many aches and pains as well as take away illnesses of an emotional nature. These may have been primitive practices but the power of believing in them was strong and seemed to help in many instances.

By 1910 Veronia's father had horses for working on the land, a breaker for turning the sod, a plough, a disc, drill, harrows and a binder for harvesting.

The Boian Marea school was opened in 1909, and though fifteen-year-old Veronia wanted to go, her father felt that she was too old for that. Besides, he needed her help on the homestead. Three of the oldest children missed school because they were needed at home. The father felt that though he was illiterate, he had done well. Why waste time on school when there was still more land to be cleared, more work to be done? Perhaps that was why, when Veronia married and had children of her own, she made certain that no sacrifice on her part was too great in order to give them the education she had missed.

Veronia grew into a hard-working, spirited girl who enjoyed life in spite of the hardships. In her own words, she was as 'black as a crow,' wind-burned and suntanned by her life outdoors. At sixteen, she did not know how to boil a pot of potatoes when she fell in love with the man she was later to marry. In order to impress him, she was determined to have a new blouse to wear for the Easter celebrations in church. She wheedled some linen from her mother and took it to her godmother's to embroider and sew into a blouse.

Because Easter holidays came late that year, people were already working on their land. It was Saturday, the day before Easter. Veronia's father had gone to the blacksmith's in Willingdon and left her harrowing the field in preparation for seeding. It seemed an opportune time to go and pick up the blouse. She tied all the horses but one to a fence, gave them hay and rode that one bareback to her godmother's. But she was not back soon enough, for her father had returned.

Upon inquiring of her mother, he discovered she had gone to her godmother's on the horse. He shook with anger. Instead of stopping to feed the horse and letting it rest, she had further played him out. He was waiting for her when she got back.

'Where have you been?' he shouted at her.

There was no way out but to tell the truth. 'I had to get my blouse!'

'Your blouse! Do you realize the horse will be too tired to work this afternoon?'

'But I had to get it! What am I to wear to church tomorrow? A quilt on my back?'

That did it! Not only had she misused the horse but she had dared to talk back. That day she received a beating she was to remember for the rest of her life.

A few months later when the young man decided to ask for her hand, he sent a 'starosta' (matchmaker) to her father's home. It was her mother who tried to talk her out of it for several reasons. But Veronia stuck by her decision and made a good marriage of it that lasted for more than half a century. She and Thomas Kokotailo were married in 1913. Her father made her a wedding, inviting all their neighbours, and as was the custom among her people, they presented the newlyweds with 25 hens, 20 bags of grain, including wheat, oats and barley, three ducks and two geese. Her father gave her a cow and calf, her mother pillows and a featherbed. They moved into a small house on their homestead at Eagle Tail Hill and Veronia began to learn to keep house.

She worked along with her husband as she had with her father. The grain presented to them on their wedding day yielded well on the new land and that fall they bought a new binder. Never having worked with a binder before, Tom found he did not know how to put the binder-canvas on. When Veronia tried to show him how it was done, it became a battle of the sexes.

'You must think I'm stupid,' said young Tom. 'What do you know about it? You're only a woman!'

While he struggled and sweated with the canvases, Veronia watched impatiently but dared not say anything. It was a dry harvest day and a shame to have it wasted but her husband refused to let her show him how it was done. In the end he succeeded, proving once and for all his male superiority!

Their life on the homestead was full of hardships. They cleared land, bought machinery and raised a large family. Veronia still had to do all the things her mother had done before her. She grew a large garden, took care of the house and babies, hulled grains for cereals, baked bread, made her own oil and learned to cut corners like all pioneer women. Her work began at daybreak and ended late at night. She scrubbed clothes by hand. She sewed and mended by night.

Few women had any money to call their own, not because their husbands were tightwads but because the land came first. If the land was to ever support them, then it must, first and foremost, be developed. This took money.

The farm woman's financial emancipation came with the arrival of the country peddler with his democrat loaded with empty crates and cases. He bought eggs and old hens and, for the first time, a bit of money found its way into Veronia's pockets. It was never frittered away and it helped to bring back her self-respect. With it she bought embroidery thread and poured out her re-awakening love of color and beauty into embroidered aprons and pillow cases. With a few cents worth of crepe paper, she made dozens of roses and decked her drab walls with the flowers. For the first time in a couple of decades, she was able to buy a few extras for herself and her children without being beholden to her husband.

It took a lot of work and money to raise her eight children. At one time, Veronia had all eight going to school. Many a time, she wracked her brains to figure out what to give them for their lunches. She baked twenty loaves of bread or more at a time. Sometimes there was nothing but a sprinkling of sugar to go with the bread, and a bottle of cold tea.

'Mrs. Kokotailo,' an elderly woman teacher who used to come to her house said, 'how do you manage? How do you manage?'

When George, the oldest son, started university, Mrs. Kokotailo spent most of her nights lavishly embroidering shirts with cross-stitch work for which she had ready buyers. It took a month and more to embroider one, and the $25 it brought helped her son through a few weeks. Altogether she made 35 shirts. When George was finished, he helped the younger brothers to get their education. Today, George is a research scientist in New Jersey. Three other boys finished university and are scattered throughout Canada. The rest received a high school education.

The early settlers survived and made good because of the industry and character of their women. The men would have never lived through the rigours of those frontier days without their support. They were the ones who bore the brunt of work and worry. The man worked hard, but his woman worked even harder.

NOTE

This article is from *Alberta Historical Review* 21 (4) (1973). Reprinted with permission.

The Ukrainian Impress on the Canadian West

JAMES W. DARLINGTON

A journey through the western interior of Canada, in the zone where the grasslands mix with the aspen-poplar forest, reveals extensive districts that stand out as one of the most distinct ethnic landscapes to be found anywhere in Canada and indeed in all of North America. They are the areas settled by Ukrainian immigrants and their descendants who began arriving in western Canada one hundred years ago. To uninitiated travellers, the onion-domed churches with their detached bell towers provide perhaps the strongest clue that they have entered a different ethnic environment. Closer inspection reveals additional features found predominantly, if not exclusively, in the Ukrainian districts. The more prominent elements include clusters of whitewashed crosses that mark the numerous graveyards, a preponderance of log buildings of various kinds, the frequent occurrence of houses and other structures painted pale blue and light green both on the farms and in the small communities, and a disproportionately high number of crossroad hamlets containing a church, a general store, a community hall, and a house or two. These and other features that set the areas of Ukrainian settlement apart from the surrounding districts have not gone unreported in both the popular and the academic press.[1]

As distinctive as the present-day Ukrainian-Canadian settlement landscape is, there is ample evidence that it was even more distinct in times past. 'When less than five miles of our journey [from Lamont] was covered,' wrote a visitor to the Edna-Star district of Alberta in 1911, 'we entered a district as typically Russian [sic] as though we dropped into Russia [sic] itself. Here and there beside the winding trail loomed up groups of buildings, low browed, and heavily thatched. These always faced south. The houses were all of rough logs, rough hewed and chinked with a mortar made of clay and straw. Some were plastered on the exterior, and almost all of them had been lime-washed to a dazzling whiteness.'[2] Although this description is of a rural area in Alberta, it could just as easily apply to contemporary Ukrainian districts in Manitoba or Saskatchewan.

But the visual presence of Ukrainian immigrants and their descendants in western Canada extends beyond the individual cultural elements in the landscape. For example, one of the most impressive aspects of the Ukrainian landscape is its geographic extent. With few exceptions, Ukrainian immigrants settled among their countrymen in what came to be extensive, nearly homogeneous, and often densely inhabited tracts. The Ukrainians were not the only ethnic group to settle in this manner. Throughout North America, immigrants and other long-distance migrants commonly settled among people of similar background, so much that such behaviour was more conspicuous by its absence than by its presence. In western Canada, the Mennonites and Icelanders were two of the groups that established large, ethnically exclusive settlements.[3] But the federal government facilitated the establishment of bloc settlements by both these groups by setting aside sizeable reserves for their exclusive use.[4] In contrast, the Ukrainians received no such government assistance. The development of their settlements was essentially voluntary, the result of a combination of related concerns.

The economics of survival was one of these. With few exceptions the Ukrainian immigrants arrived in Canada with limited financial resources and were not able to purchase improved farmland in previously settled areas of the prairies.[5] They had little choice but to seek out free homesteads, the bulk of which were located at or near the settlement frontier.[6] But rather than consider unclaimed sections of prime wheat-growing land in the extensive grasslands of the southern prairies, most new arrivals, to the consternation of immigration agents, turned instead to the wooded, moderately to extremely poor lands within the parkland.[7] The decision to settle on such marginal land, which other settlers had rejected or bypassed, led to economic disaster, but at the time it made eminent sense to a financially destitute people.

The parkland belt, where the vast majority of Ukrainians settled, held a number of advantages in the form of raw materials that the open prairies could not supply in equal abundance. Among these items were timber for building, fuel, and fencing, marsh grass for roofing, water for stock, and wild game and fish to supplement a limited diet.[8] All of these were put to immediate use by the Ukrainian immigrants, who were well acquainted with log-building and roof-thatching techniques.[9] Further, the parkland provided an opportunity to earn much-needed cash from seasonal work in nearby lumber camps or from the sale of cordwood or seneca root cut or dug on the homestead.[10]

Like other immigrants, the Ukrainians arrived with preconceived ideas as to what constituted valuable and productive land. Coming as they did from a part of Europe where woodland was the prized possession of the upper class, it is not surprising that these people of peasant stock would be attracted to treed land. And if they perceived the lack of trees on the prairie as a sign of infertility, then certainly they were not alone. Many farmers from the forested eastern half of the continent or from northwest Europe came to the same conclusion, only to change their minds later.[11] Their logic was as consistent as it was straightforward: 'bareness equals barrenness equals infertility equals uselessness for agriculture.'[12] Even if the Ukrainian immigrants did perceive the true potential of the grasslands and bush, the logic of their choice of the woodland remains unchanged when one takes into account their limited knowledge of commercial agriculture as practised in North America at the time. Peasant farms in Western Ukraine were marginal at best. The average farm in Galicia had less than twelve acres (five hectares) and still less in Bukovyna.[13] So, even if the wooded land did hold less agricultural promise than the prairie land, surely all but the meanest 160 acres of Canadian woodland could be made to outproduce the average farm in Western Ukraine. From this perspective it is small wonder that many Ukrainian settlers during the early period tried to subdivide their allotments.[14] Further, since few of the immigrants had experience with commercial agriculture, it is unlikely that they foresaw the economic consequences of their locational decision.

For some, nostalgia played a role in the selection of land. John Lehr cites a group of Hutsuls, or Carpathian highlanders, who chose to homestead in the wooded country near Hafford, Saskatchewan, because it reminded them of their homeland.[15] Another group of Ukrainian highlanders who came from three neighbouring villages in the Galician district of Kolomyia selected land south of Dauphin, Manitoba, and several townships removed from the principal area of Ukrainian settlement for the same reason. In the words of one member of the group, 'We chose to settle in the part of the district because the mountains, woods, streams, and meadows very much resembled our native Carpathian scenery.'[16] In the second instance, the land chosen was part of the Riding Mountain Timber Reserve and therefore not open to homesteading, a fact the settlers were soon made aware of. But they nonetheless persisted and after six years of debate with the government managed to gain title to their farms.[17] The point suggests the strength of the settlers' emotional attachment to the land.

New immigrants were guided by more than their own instincts and perceptions in their efforts to select land. In 1895, Dr Osyp Oleskiv, professor of agriculture at Lviv, Galicia, visited the Canadian prairies in order to identify areas suitable for Ukrainian settlement. Impressed with what he had seen, Oleskiv returned to Lviv, where he immediately published a pamphlet entitled *O emigratsii* (On emigration) in which he offered encouragement and advice to prospective emigrants. The publication quickly achieved wide circulation among the Ukrainian rural population in the Austrian provinces of Galicia and Bukovyna. In this and subsequent publications, Oleskiv, cognizant of the emigrants' limited financial resources and the advantages of woodland, advised them to select land in the parkland as opposed to the open prairie.[18] Oleskiv also served as an unofficial emigration officer for many groups of Ukrainians bound for western Canada and in that capacity at times urged emigrants to select homesteads in specific locales.[19]

Once the vanguard of Ukrainian settlers became established in an area, an additional set of factors entered into the decision making of subsequent immigrants. With rare exception, later arrivals tried their utmost to settle among family or friends or, if this was not possible, among people from the same district or province of Western Ukraine.[20] In many instances the desire to locate near friends or relatives overrode any concern about the quality of the land with the result that large tracts of marginal land were occupied.[21] From an economic perspective this pattern of behaviour was disastrous. Not only was this the case on the poorer lands where entry into commercial agriculture was seriously delayed, but the resultant high density also restricted expansion into areas of better land. On the other hand, the fact that the Ukrainians did settle close to family and friends meant that strong social ties existed within the new communities from the very beginning. Ironically, the marginal conditions the settlers faced only served to strengthen those ties and to enhance social support structures, which in turn made it more difficult for these people to leave the area and thus alleviate the situation.[22]

The combination of a marginal agricultural base that hindered economic success and an exceptionally strong social structure that encouraged the population to look inward was a major cause of a third characteristic of the Ukrainian-Canadian landscape, its persistence over time. Whereas other cultural groups accepted the Anglo 'norm,' the Ukrainians resisted it. And whereas the reasons for this resistance are numerous and include forces internal and external to the Ukrainian culture itself, from the perspective of landscape the result is a series of regions within the parklands of the Canadian prairies that remain today decidedly different from the surrounding countryside.

As the citations referred to above indicate, many aspects of the Ukrainian-Canadian cultural landscape have been examined individually or in combination. Yet there have been few attempts to consider these various elements as they have persisted or evolved over the years within a single bloc settlement. The remainder of this paper will examine the development of the cultural landscape created by Ukrainian settlers and their descendants in the area north of Dauphin, Manitoba.

The Initial Wave of Settlers

In the late summer and early fall of 1896, eight Ukrainian families from the Austrian province of Galicia stepped off the train in Dauphin. They came on Oleskiv's advice to file homestead claims in the area. Following the lead of one of the first arrivals, Basil Ksionzik, all eight families filed a homestead claim in the western half of Township 26, Range 20 W, approximately a dozen miles northwest of Dauphin village (fig. 1).[23] The quarter-sections, clustered along the Drifting River, were, aside from some small scattered areas of marsh, mostly covered with stands of

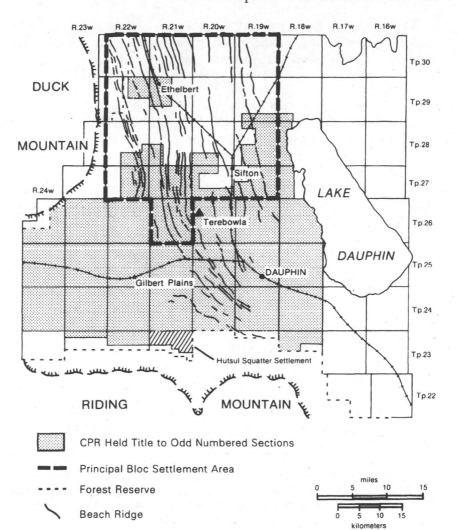

CPR Held Title to Odd Numbered Sections

Principal Bloc Settlement Area

Forest Reserve

Beach Ridge

FIGURE 1 Ukrainian bloc settlement, Dauphin region

good-sized poplar and willow. Although a few patches of trees had been killed by fire several years earlier, the supply and quality of the timber was adequate for use as logs in house and barn construction. In addition, the quarter-sections were all close to a cart-track that led back to Dauphin.[24]

Shortly after their arrival, the settlers began calling the rural neighbourhood Terebowla, after the district of Galicia from which Ksionzik and several of the others had come. Over the course of the winter several more Ukrainian families arrived, and by the early spring of 1897 the settlement had grown to fifteen families. Father Nestor Dmytriw, a touring priest who visited the growing community that April, reported that seventy-eight Ukrainian immigrants were living there.[25] This modest group of Ukrainian settlers grew rapidly in the months and years that followed. Between 30 April and 22 May of that year, for example, three steamships carrying over a hundred Ukrainian families bound for the Dauphin region docked in eastern Canada.[26] By the end of the summer, more settlers had arrived, and the government was prompted to order the construction of an immigration shed at Dauphin. The stream of Ukrainian migrants into the region continued unabated during the next several years, and in 1901 J.O. Smith, the commissioner for immigration in Winnipeg, estimated the Ukrainian population in the greater Dauphin district to be 5,500 and growing.[27]

The vast majority of these immigrants filed for quarter-sections north or west of the original settlement at Terebowla. And, although Ukrainian settlement eventually extended from the shores of Dauphin Lake on the east to the lower elevations of the Duck Mountain escarpment in the west and to the end of the arable land in the north, settlement activity concentrated in townships 26, 27, 28, and 29 and ranges 19, 20, 21, and 22 W. The land immediately to the south of this bloc was of better quality, but much of it was already in the hands of English and Scottish homesteaders who had moved into the area several years before the first group of Eastern Europeans arrived.

Physical Setting

The country the Ukrainians chose to occupy in the Dauphin region is similar in many ways to that found in the other areas of extensive Ukrainian settlement. The eastern two-thirds or more of the Dauphin bloc settlement are flat and low-lying and as a consequence poorly drained. A major contributing factor to the poor drainage is an extensive series of gravel ridges that cut across the area in a northwest-southeast trending fashion. Composed primarily of sand and gravel, the ridges are remnant beach lines of glacial Lake Agassiz. Within the area where they exist, these modest ridges provide the only recognizable relief aside from some localized downcutting of the streams that flow east across the area. In contrast, the western third of the area is gently to moderately rolling country that stands roughly two hundred feet higher in elevation than the area to the east and is as a result better drained (fig. 1).

At the time of initial occupancy the better-drained portions of the entire area of Ukrainian settlement were largely covered by stands of poplar and willow intermixed with occasional bluffs of spruce. Sizeable patches within these areas were reported by government surveyors in the years immediately before settlement as having been recently burnt over, and other areas that had presumably burnt some years earlier were, at the time of survey, covered with bush. The wettest areas were covered with marsh grass and occasional stands of tamarack and black spruce.

From an agricultural standpoint, the quality of the land within the bloc settlement varies considerably. The soils that offer the greatest potential in the district are confined almost exclusively to a strip four to eight miles wide on the broad shoulder of elevated ground that extends along the base of the Duck Mountain escarpment. And, while many of the soil associations within this portion of the bloc settlement are classed as being of high or good productivity, a notable proportion of these soils is also stony. East and west of this band of better agricultural land, indeed throughout the rest of the bloc settlement, the soil is of moderate quality or worse. Today extensive areas are deemed suitable only for hay production or grazing.[28]

Land Selection

Its limited agricultural potential notwithstanding, much of the land within the bloc settlement was ultimately homesteaded. A section-by-section examination of the land taken by Ukrainians reveals that ultimately only the very worst land failed to attract settlers. There is nothing to suggest that this behaviour was the result of indifference. New immigrants did not take the first piece of land available for settlement. Indeed, some spent a considerable amount of time checking conditions before selecting a quarter-section. Jacob Maksymetz, for instance, arrived in the region in late April 1898 and checked possible homestead sites for over a month before filing a claim in early June.[29] New arrivals sometimes traversed considerable amounts of territory looking for the right combination of environmental factors before deciding where to locate. For example, Dmytro Romanchych was a member of a party of Hutsuls who set off on foot from Dauphin in search of land the day after their arrival in the spring of 1897. Spades and axes in hand, they headed cross-country in a northwesterly direction, stopping occasionally to dig a pit so as to check the quality of the soil. Proceeding in this fashion, they reached the vicinity of the present-day village of Ethelbert on the second day. Not satisfied with what they had seen, most of the group decided to turn back south and investigate the higher ground nearer the base of the Duck Mountain escarpment. Several members of the group found homestead sites to their liking near the hamlet of Venlaw, but most continued on and eventually selected land much further to the south in Township 23, Range 20, along the north slope of Riding Mountain. For these individuals the exploratory trek took the better part of a week and covered at the very minimum 70 miles (112 kilometres) and in all likelihood much more.[30]

The actions taken by this group of highlanders to settle together also illustrate the importance of social ties in the selection of land. The mutual support members of this party of Ukrainian settlers must have felt for one another undoubtedly influenced their decision to settle away from the principal bloc settlement and to risk the possible consequences of squatting. This desire to settle among relatives, friends, or, at the very minimum, persons from the same district or region was also repeatedly demonstrated within the main settlement bloc. Besides the initial group of settlers from Terebowla, immigrants from other Galician districts including Borshchiv, Sokal, and Husiatyn showed the same tendency.[31] Kinship ties were understandably stronger than community ties in most cases, and in numerous cases throughout the Dauphin bloc settlement relatives settled near or even next to one another. One example that stands out in this regard is the Negrych family. In 1897 six members of the family settled on quarter-sections located on three contiguous sections of Township 27, Range 22. Four family members filed homestead claims in section 14 alone.[32] As part of the initial wave of settlers in the area, the Negryches were in a reasonably good position to fulfil the twin desires of reasonable quality land and proximity to other family members. Later arrivals had fewer options. More often than not one or the other concern could be met but not both.[33]

External forces, primarily government regulation, played a critical role in determining the pattern of settlement. The federal government placed definite restrictions on where these people could settle. With rare exception new arrivals were not in a position to buy land. This left them with the options of filing a homestead claim or squatting. At the time of initial occupancy lands of a typical township were designated as follows: even-numbered sections, with two exceptions, were designated by the government as homestead land; odd-numbered sections, with two exceptions, were reserved for selection as railway grants; the Hudson Bay Company held title to section 8 and all but the northeast corner of section 26, which was available for homesteading; and sections 11 and 29 were reserved as school lands. Thus, sixteen and a quarter of the thirty-six sections contained in a standard township were set aside for homesteading and therefore available for a ten-dollar registration fee. The rest of the lands in a township were either held in reserve or available for purchase. These conditions resulted in a checkerboard pattern of settlement with alternate sections of land standing vacant until such time when additional lands were made available for homesteading or the settlers had established themselves well enough to purchase more land. The year-by-year sequence of land alienation in two adjoining townships in the western portion of the Dauphin bloc settlement illustrates this process (fig. 2).[34] All of the appropriate railway lands were held in reserve until 1903, when, by order of the Privy Council, the Canadian Pacific Railway relinquished its claim to all sections except those in the southeast corner.[35] Between settlement in 1897 and 1903 eighty-five quarter-sections were occupied, all but two of them homestead land. In the seven years that followed, the trend continued. An additional forty-two quarter sections were occupied; four were purchased, the rest homesteaded.

Clearly the locational decisions made by the Ukrainian immigrants were based on a number of factors. Some had to do with the physical or social environment; others were imposed by governmental and other agencies. Although the multi-dimensional concerns and restraints were no doubt present throughout the period of initial land alienation, it should be pointed out that the examples cited all occurred during the first wave of settlement in the region.

Creating a Farm

Having selected a quarter-section of land, the immigrant family faced an immediate need for shelter. Normally a lean-to of sorts was erected to

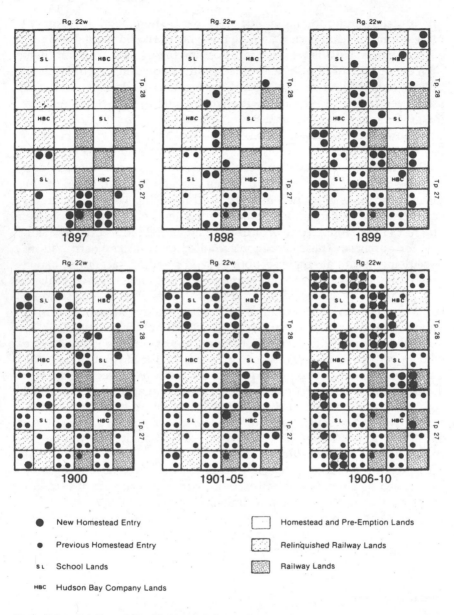

FIGURE 2 Land disposition, Mink Creek–Venlaw area, 1897–1910.

serve that purpose for a few weeks until a more substantial structure could be built. Most often this second shelter was a simple sod-roofed dug-out modelled after the *staia*, a type of hut used by Hutsul shepherds in the Carpathians. Crude and cramped as this structure was, it provided many a newly arrived family with modest protection from the elements through the first Canadian winter or until such time when a more substantive home could be built.[36]

Within a year or two, a modest log house reminiscent of those found in the builder's home region was built near the *staia*. A large majority of these were of horizontal log construction with saddle or dovetail corner notching. Occasionally, when the quality of timber necessitated, frame and fill, or Red River Frame, was used instead. Vertical log construction or *poteaux-en terre*, a building technique used by Ukrainian settlers elsewhere in the province, appears to have been rarely used in the Dauphin district.[37] Once the walls were in place, the building was covered with a thatched roof made from marsh grass gathered from nearby sloughs.[38] The walls were covered, inside and out, with a plaster made of mud mixed with straw or dung. In turn, the plaster was covered with a coat of lime-wash, which Galicians often tinted by adding laundry bluing. The dirt floor was also coated with a layer of mud and animal urine, which made it hard and easy to keep clean. With rare exceptions, the resultant one-storey, rectangular house was oriented with its roofline running east-west and the single entryway and most of the windows located on the southern exposure. Inside, the house was commonly divided into two or sometimes three rooms. These were known as the *velyka khata*, or 'big room,' the *mala khata*, or 'little room,' and the *seeny*, or entry hallway.[39] The *mala khata* contained a massive earthen stove, or *peech*, used for both cooking and heating. Besides serving as kitchen, the *mala khata* was also both common meeting room and children's bedroom. The *velyka khata* traditionally occupied the eastern half of the house and served as the parents' bedroom, but was otherwise reserved for use on special occasions. The east wall of this room was normally decorated with icons, family photographs, and religious calendars.

On many farms, these initial log houses were replaced later by larger and more carefully constructed log structures. These second-generation houses were more apt to be made of hewn timber held in place with wooden pegs and dovetail corner notching. The first of these second-generation dwellings were otherwise very similar to the old. But as the economic situation improved the Ukrainian settlers began to introduce different materials: sawn lumber was used for doors, window frames, and plank floors; wood shingles replaced thatch; a cast-iron stove replaced the *peech*; and brick replaced wattle chimneys. Despite the changes, these second-generation farmhouses remained very much a reflection of Ukrainian culture. In room arrangement, general orientation, and wall treatment the houses remained as before. Upon completion of the new farmhouse, the old one was invariably relegated to use as a summer-kitchen, storage shed, or animal shelter.

Before a second-generation log house could be contemplated many other tasks had to be carried out. Land had to be cleared and broken; crops had to be planted and harvested; barns and other outbuildings had to be raised; a well needed to be dug; and fences had to be erected. Homestead inspection reports and other scattered evidence make it possible to discern the rate at which individual farms took form. In June 1898, one year after the group of Ukrainian highlanders squatted on the timber reserve lands south of Dauphin, a survey was made of their progress. Of the twenty-three families that had settled in the area the previous June, all had built a house; seventeen had erected a stable; the same number had dug a well. Each family was reported to be cultivating between one and six acres, the average being slightly less than three.[40] In the spring of 1901 a number of these families petitioned the government in an attempt to gain legal title to the land. In that document the petitioners described the status of each farm. In nine cases the descriptions can be traced back to the previous list, and comparisons can be made. During the two and a half years the average number of acres broken rose from approximately 2.7 to 7.6. The number of outbuildings on the nine farms increased from seven to twenty-four, the number of cattle from fifteen to fifty.[41] Progress was clearly being made.

The rate at which land was cleared increased once the essential structures were in place and more time and effort could be devoted to clearing operations. This pattern is demonstrated by three of the original families that homesteaded in the Terebowla area in 1896. According to the colonization report of 1899, these three families had, in addition to erecting several essential buildings, cleared or ploughed eight, five, and one acre on their farms.[42] Three years later, in 1902, a similar report identified these same families as having respectively 32, 32, and 18 acres under cultivation. By that date, the first two families had also seen fit to purchase an additional 160 acres of land, thus doubling the size of their farms.[43] These two families were not the only ones to experience enough prosperity to invest in more land. A more extensive record exists for Jacob Maksymetz, who filed a homestead claim on a quarter-section

(SW 34-27-22) in the Venlaw region in June 1898. Five years later, a growing family, a modest amount of financial success, and some keen foresight prompted him to purchase an adjoining quarter-section (NW 27-27-22) from the CPR. The family continued to prosper, and in 1918, encouraged by high commodity prices brought on by the First World War, purchased two quarter-section farms from neighbours (SW 4-28-22 and SE 4-28-22).Two years later two more farms came under family control, one of 60 acres (SW 27-27-22) and another of 160 (NE 28-27-22). In 1921 the family purchased yet another quarter-section (SW 26-27-22), thereby bringing its total holdings to 1,020 acres.[44] The Maksymetz family was not the only one to buy land with the profits made during the war years. The combination of hard-won financial success and population pressure led a number of Ukrainian families to purchase Anglo farms located on the better lands along the southern margin of the Ukrainian settlement tract.[45] The post-war recession cut this venture short for some, but most who made the move managed to survive and ultimately gained from their decision.[46] Others responded differently to the heightened population pressure. Rather than seek to expand their acreage, they subdivided their quarter-section homesteads in an effort to accommodate more families. This latter practice appears to have been most common on the worst lands, where only subsistence agriculture was possible.[47]

Under both scenarios, however, the amount of cleared land rose and with it farm production. As crop acreage expanded and livestock multiplied, the need for ancillary farm buildings increased accordingly. By 1910, for example, the Wasyl Negrych farmstead, settled in 1897, contained nine buildings: a substantial, three-room house, two barns, two granaries, a chicken coop, a hog shed, a summer-kitchen, and a storage shed.[48] The progress made by the Ukrainian settlers in the area and their imprint on the farm landscape was noticed by a Manitoba school inspector who wrote in 1900, 'I drive from Ethelbert across to Sifton, through the heart of Galician settlements. I was impressed with [the] prosperous appearance of most of the farms. The country is flat and uninviting – once the ridge upon which Ethelbert is situated is left – but in spite of the apparently unfertile nature of the soil, the little homesteads are surrounded by patches of wheat, rye and hemp and invariably a good vegetable garden. Most of the houses are small but with their thatched roofs and heavy overhanging eaves, on plastered walls, they are quite picturesque. I saw some quite large houses too.'[49]

Although farmsteads were springing up everywhere, not all the

Ukrainian settlers met with success. Among 425 known homestead claims filed by Ukrainian settlers in the Dauphin region between 1896 and 1899, 350, or approximately 82 per cent, were granted patent.[50] Of those individuals or families who failed to receive patent, some purchased land elsewhere in the region. A few, it seems, filed a second homestead claim in the area. Others left the area.[51]

Creating the Sacred Landscape

The landscape beyond the homestead was also being transformed during this period, as various social groups established facilities to meet community needs and service centres containing a variety of commercial enterprises appeared in response to actual and projected opportunities. Of all the social institutions, none was more important than the church. The prominent role religion played in the lives of Ukrainians before and after immigration to Canada is well documented.[52] Churches invariably appeared within a few years of settlement,[53] and the first Ukrainian parish in the bloc settlement north of Dauphin was established at Sifton in 1900.[54] The following year St Michael's Ukrainian Catholic Church was erected seven miles west and two miles north of the present village of Sifton. Although very modest in size, the structure was centrally located within the Ukrainian district. More churches appeared throughout the region during the following decade. The dates of construction of many of them have been lost, but a least five were built before 1910. In the years that followed the residents of the area organized more congregations, and by 1940 at least thirty-four Ukrainian churches existed in the area (fig. 3). The structures themselves exhibit various levels of architectural sophistication and design, cultural transfer, and monetary expenditure.[55]

Distributed throughout the bloc settlement, standing in rural isolation and small urban centre alike, these houses of worship with their distinct onion-shaped domes offer tangible evidence of the importance of religion in the lives of the Ukrainian immigrants and their descendants. Their number, however, reflects more than unbending religious faith, and is certainly greater than population size or poor travel conditions would warrant. The Ukrainians who settled in the Dauphin district mostly came from Galicia and were, with few exceptions, members of the Uniate, or Ukrainian Catholic, faith.[56] The majority of the churches built in the area give credence to that fact, but the significant number of Orthodox churches suggests that the religious homogeneity that charac-

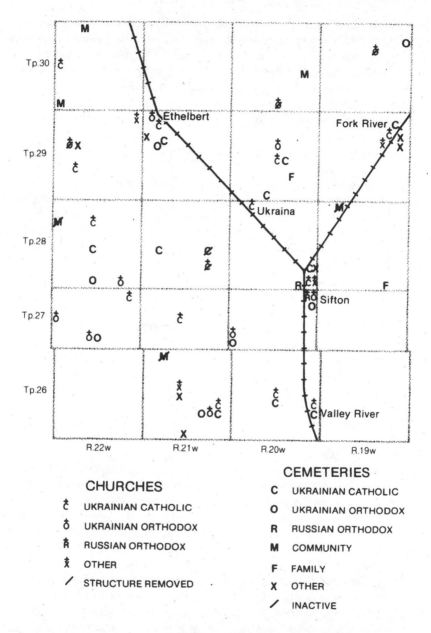

FIGURE 3 Religious landscape: churches and cemeteries.

terized Galician society did not survive the journey to Canada intact. Indeed, the Ukrainian community was buffeted by religious turmoil during the first several decades of settlement. The history of the various religious denominations that attracted a following among the Ukrainian settlers during the early years is long and complex and goes well beyond the scope of this paper. Suffice it to say that the early settlers were thwarted, largely through no fault of their own, in their efforts to attract Ukrainian Catholic clergy. Out of frustration, and at times despair, many Ukrainian settlers in the Dauphin region, as elsewhere on the Canadian prairies, turned to other religious groups. The Roman Catholic church, the Russian Orthodox church, and the Independent Greek church were all involved in this competition for souls. In the case of the Independent Greek church, an organization founded in Winnipeg in 1905 with the surreptitious moral and financial support of the Presbyterian church, the intent went beyond religious conversion to include deliberate efforts to acculturate or 'Canadianize' the Ukrainian population.[57] All of these religious denominations established congregations and erected churches in the area around Sifton during this early period of settlement.

By the outbreak of the First World War the Independent Greek church was defunct, the Russian Orthodox church was in rapid decline, and some Ukrainian Catholics increasingly disapproved of the Roman Catholic church's powerful influence on Ukrainian Catholic affairs. This dissatisfaction among a sizeable segment of the Ukrainian population led to the formation of the Ukrainian Greek Orthodox Church of Canada in 1918. Across the prairies as a whole, the new church drew most of its adherents from the Bukovynian settlers, who were, by tradition, followers of the Orthodox faith. In the Dauphin district, however, most members came from the dissolved Independent and Russian churches or were dissatisfied members of Ukrainian Catholic congregations. In regard to the latter, a number of congregations split in dispute over church ritual and calendar.[58] In several instances these schisms resulted in the construction of a new church building, at times within sight of the old. Indeed, in the case of the congregation north of Ashville, the second church was built immediately across the road from the first. Ironically, the large number of churches in the Dauphin bloc settlement was a manifestation not only of profound religious feeling but also of a social fabric that had been deeply torn. A legacy of bad feeling remains to this day.

Cemeteries constitute another major element of the religious landscape of a region. As on most frontiers, the earliest burials in the Dauphin district took place near the family farmstead. But within a few years of settlement, as the community developed, a farmer would donate a portion of his land for use as a community cemetery. Both Catholic and Orthodox church law requires that a burial site be consecrated by a priest before a member of the faith can be interred there. As a consequence, many of the cemeteries in the area became tied to a specific church congregation. Where this is the case, the church and graveyard are frequently situated adjacent to or within a short distance of each other. Most often than not the cemetery was in existence some time before the church was built. Thus the site of the cemetery influenced the location of the church.[59]

The most conspicuous display of the religious character of Ukrainian cemeteries is not their association with specific churches, but with the symbolism displayed on the individual grave markers. The cross stands out in this regard. Regardless of their religious background, Ukrainian settlers brought with them the long-standing tradition of denoting graves with free-standing crosses that were of Eastern, Latin, or, in a few cases, Greek form.[60] The earliest of these were made of wood, but the impermanence of that material soon led to the use of wrought iron and cast cement. By the 1920s a modest number of carved stone monuments had begun to appear. A large majority of these monuments maintained the same free-standing or at least partially free-standing cross form. In a few cases, however, the stone or cast-cement monument was in the shape of an obelisk or block, and the cross was displayed in bas-relief rather than in silhouette. These adjustments in grave monument material and style reflect more than changing tastes among the Ukrainian settlers. The material from which the monument is made mirrors the economic well-being of the family of the interred, and the basic change in design indicates an acceptance of Anglo grave monument design and thus a desire to acculturate.[61]

Creating the Social Landscape

Within a few years of settlement secular features that reflected the growing social cohesion in the region began to appear in the public landscape. Some of the resulting facilities were more distinctly Ukrainian that others, but all fulfilled critical social needs. The most obvious of these were schools. Shortly after their arrival in the area, the Ukrainian settlers began agitating the provincial government for educational facilities. Unfortunately for the Ukrainian districts in the province, a lack of local funding and a shortage of qualified instructors who could speak Ukrainian slowed the government's response.[62] Aware of the situation, the Presbyterian Home Missionary Society financed the construction and staffing of the first school in the district. Located at Terebowla, the one-room school opened around 1900. By 1903 the Presbyterians had opened additional schools at Sifton and Ethelbert.[63] Before the end of the decade, publicly funded schools were also operating across the region, and more were being added annually. By the early 1920s at least twenty-eight primary, principally one-room, schools were serving the Ukrainian area (fig. 4). The school buildings looked the same as school buildings found elsewhere in the province and thus were not culturally distinct. But in some instances they were given Ukrainian names, such as 'Bohdan,' 'Halicz,' 'Kulish,' 'Zelena,' and 'Zoria,' which came to identify rural neighbourhoods and which remain in use today long after the schools have closed and in some cases have disappeared from the landscape.[64]

The Prosvita, or community hall, was another important element that first appeared in the public landscape during these early years. With the establishment of a *chytalnia*, or reading hall, at Sifton in 1903, Ukrainian settlers throughout the area began to organize enlightenment or reading societies. Modelled after the self-help associations established in Ukraine in 1868, these societies had the purpose of cultivating education and cultural identity. In 1905 a reading hall was established at Venlaw. The following year two more were organized in the district, and in the year after that another two. By 1910 there were at least nine cultural societies with their respective community halls scattered across the area, and more would be built in the years to come (fig. 4).[65] Throughout the early years and into mid-century these community halls and the reading clubs, drama societies, and other organizations affiliated with them helped maintain Ukrainian culture and encouraged public interchange of ideas.

Creating the Commercial Landscape

Commercial enterprise followed close on the heels of settlement in the Dauphin region as it did in the other Ukrainian settlements on the prairies. In 1897 a railway line was built through the eastern portion of what was to become the Ukrainian bloc settlement, extending north from Dauphin to Winnipegosis. The stations along it became the site of almost instant commercial development. In the same year the railroad

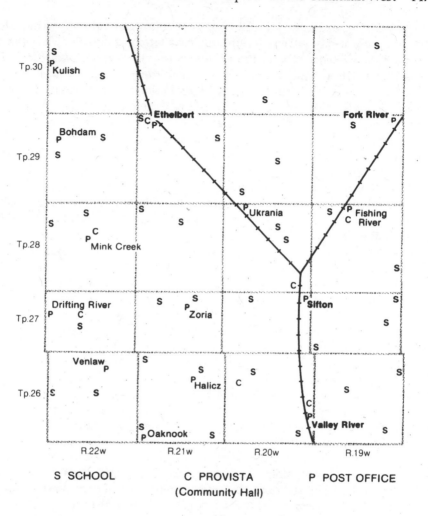

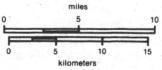

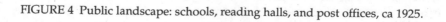

S SCHOOL   C PROVISTA   P POST OFFICE
                      (Community Hall)

FIGURE 4 Public landscape: schools, reading halls, and post offices, ca 1925.

was built, for example, John Kennedy opened a general store at the site of the present-day village of Sifton. A year later the village of Ethelbert came into existence when a branch line was extended northwest from a point near Sifton. The other train stations in the area also attracted commercial activity. Valley River, Fork River, Dnieper (later Fishing River), and Ukraina all owed their location, if not their very existence, to the railroad. Besides a store or two, each of these places soon had a post office and, with the exception of Ukraina, eventually one or more grain elevators. Dnieper and Ukraina stand out in another way. Modest though they were, they constitute the largest centres in the region with names that reflect the Ukrainian presence in the area.

Not all of the region's commercial activity took place along the railroad. Soon after settlement, enterprising farmers began to open small general stores. Basil Ksionzik, for example, is reported to have been operating a store (which was probably nothing more than a room in his house) in the Terebowla neighbourhood in 1899, just three years after his arrival.[66] Unfortunately, few details are available concerning the number or location of the other stores that operated in the Dauphin region. But what occurred in the Ukrainian bloc settlement of east-central Alberta suggests that Ksionzik's store was not the only one established during this pioneer period. More came into existence in the 1910s, after some of the more entrepreneurial settlers had managed to accumulate a bit of savings.[67]

Like the store and the railroad station, the post office marked a community's social and commercial links with the larger world. Postal services within the Ukrainian tract north of Dauphin expanded in a fashion parallel to that of country stores. Sifton received mail service in 1898, and by 1905 all of the railroad communities aside from Ukraina had a post office, as did the rural community of Venlaw in the southwest corner of the bloc. In response to a growing population and increased demand, six more post offices were opened between 1911 and 1915, all in the western or central portions of the district (fig. 4). The similarity in the pattern of post offices and stores was in at least some instances more than just coincidence. A store proprietor often doubled as the postmaster, thereby assuring the store customer traffic. In the early years, the sites of the central place functions not anchored to a train stop tended to shift from time to time. Some began as part of a private farmhouse. Later it became common for the country store and the post office to be located at a crossroads, frequently in conjunction with some other central place function such as a church, school, or community hall. The result was a hamlet containing three to six establishments that constituted a tangible manifestation of Ukrainian community life. In Ukraine community life centred around the *selo*, or village, where farmers lived and churches and various services were located. In Canada the township and range survey system and the federal government's refusal to suspend the section of the Homestead Act that stated that each homesteader must reside on his or her homestead hampered the immigrants' attempts to re-create their traditional settlement pattern. Rather than acquiesce entirely to the situation, the settlers located rural central place functions at the corners of four adjoining survey sections, thereby achieving the maximum amount of clustering possible given the circumstances. Sometimes a less compact settlement form evolved. In either case, however, the result was a hamlet that served as the focus for both social and economic activities in the neighbourhood.

A more detailed picture of the economic growth of the bloc settlement during the first few critical decades can be gained by examining the commercial expansion of the village of Sifton. At the turn of the century, the community consisted of a train station, a general store, and a post office. By 1902 a second general store had been added along with a farm implement dealership and a livery stable. A grain elevator was built in 1905, and the next year the village could boast of its own newspaper, the *Sifton Gazette*. As the name of the paper implies, the early residents and businessmen of the budding community were Anglo. One of the first exceptions to this trend was the Ruthenian Trading Company (Ruska Torhovelna Spilka), which opened for business shortly after the turn of the century.[68] In 1919, according to a fire underwriters' map, Sifton had a population of approximately 250 persons and contained two flour mills, two grain elevators, two lumberyards, a Bank of Commerce, numerous stores, a Presbyterian mission hospital, several schools, and at least three churches – a Ukrainian Catholic, a Ukrainian Orthodox, and a Presbyterian (later United) mission church. The last served mostly the merchants and businessmen of the community.[69] By this time more of the businesses were in the hands of Ukrainians, who now constituted a majority of Sifton's population.

By 1920 the Ukrainian settlers' imprint on the cultural landscape in the Dauphin bloc settlement was at or near its greatest extent. Land alienation had for all intents and purposes ceased. The population in the original area of Ukrainian settlement had reached its peak of 7,587 persons, a 128 per cent increase over the figure for 1901.[70] Clearly the pioneer stage had passed, and the social and economic infrastructures of the district were in place. On the farms, second-generation log houses had been erected and the farmsteads expanded to include sizeable clusters of special use buildings. Substantial acreages of land stood clear of trees and bush, and much of that acreage was under crop. The majority of the region's churches, schools, and community halls were in place, as were most of the economic institutions.

The Inter-war Years and Later

The 1920s and 1930s were a period of gradual economic and social adjustment for the Ukrainians in the bloc settlement north of Dauphin. The population declined slightly from its high of 1921, but overall remained stable. This was also a time of transition within the local economy. The production capabilities of individual farms continued to increase during the 1920s as more of the previously alienated land was cleared and planted. The First World War had provided many of the area's farmers with the opportunity to enter into the agricultural market economy for the first time. Having enjoyed the high commodity prices of those years, many Ukrainian farmers invested in new equipment in an effort to improve their efficiency. The more venturesome expanded operations by purchasing additional land from their Ukrainian neighbours or from Anglos residing on better land directly to the south of the bloc settlement. Some farmers found themselves overextended when the post-war recession struck and as a result suffered a setback, but most managed to weather the economic downturn and were in a more advantageous position when the commodity markets improved a few years later.

By the late 1920s and early 1930s evidence of this shift away from a self-sufficient farm economy and towards a market-oriented one could be seen in the landscape. Besides investing in more modern farm equipment, many farmers took the opportunity to make improvements to their homes. Thatch roofs were replaced by shingle roofs of lower pitch. Additions of various sorts were built on existing houses using milled lumber rather than logs. Existing log structures were sheathed in wood siding. In some instances entirely new houses were erected using milled lumber. These new buildings often deviated in other ways besides building materials from the traditional Ukrainian houses built a generation earlier. Sometimes the house form or room arrangement was modified, and even when the basic form was maintained, traditional features like large overhanging eaves were no longer incorporated in the design since the building's wooden siding did not need to be protected from rain the way mud-plastered walls did.[71] Builders became less concerned with orienting the front of the house to the south and more with orienting it to the road. The outbuildings constructed at this time were also frequently built with milled lumber. New barns sported gambrel roofs that allowed farmers to store feed hay in the loft rather than under a hay barrick or out in the open.[72] This innocuous change in a barn's roofline was clear evidence of a desire to make the farm operation more efficient and cost-effective.

Not everyone was in a position to benefit from the upscale farm prices of the war years. This was most decidedly the case for the farmers who occupied the more marginal lands. For them full integration into the market economy remained more a hope than a reality. For many in this position, off-farm employment remained an important, if not essential, activity. Not surprisingly, it was most frequently these marginal farm operations that were the first to be sold or abandoned.

This was also a time of technological transition. The radio and the telephone helped to break down the barriers of physical and social isolation and expedited the process of acculturation. But it was the internal combustion engine that had the greatest impact on the region, just as it did throughout North America. The internal combustion engine did two things for the farmer: it put him on a tractor that allowed him to farm more efficiently with fewer hands, and it put him behind the wheel of an automobile that allowed him and his family to travel greater distances for everyday goods and services. The impact of this technology was not felt overnight, of course, but by 1940 a third of the post offices in the bloc settlement had been closed, no doubt in part because of improved travel conditions.

The high farm commodity prices during the Second World War brought greater prosperity for those living in the Dauphin bloc settlement. Even the most marginal farmland in the region could be used to turn a profit. Outstanding debts could be retired, and by the war's end some farmers had accumulated enough savings to make major investments in their farms or to move their farming operations elsewhere. The war-time economy and the limited supply of labour meant that those without savings could leave the region feeling confident they would find employment. By the end of the Second World War the Dauphin region had been drawn into the national economy, and the people of Ukrainian heritage in the settlement were in a position to become fully integrated into Canadian life.[73]

The Dauphin Bloc Settlement Today

Today the Ukrainian settlement north of Dauphin is far different from what it was nearly a hundred years ago, when the first Ukrainian immigrant stepped off the train in that town, or even at mid-century. The population has declined precipitously in recent years; many of the local residents, especially the younger ones, have left for better opportunities elsewhere. Depopulation is writ large on the land in the form of vacant and abandoned houses and farm buildings. Agriculture remains the mainstay of the economy, but aside from some of the better land in the southern and particularly southwestern portion of the original settlement district, farming has shifted almost entirely away from grain farming to livestock raising – principally cattle. Average farm size has increased, but the Manitoba government has bought extensive areas of what were once private farms for use as community pasture. The more prosperous farms can be identified by modern houses, many of which were built in the 1960s or 1970s, when the farming economy was particularly strong. Once again the former farmhouse was recycled, so that it is now possible to see three generations of farmhouse on at least a few of the farmsteads.

Most of the churches stand vacant, some in a very sad state of repair. Several have been completely removed from the scene. The Ukrainian Catholic churches at Sifton and Mink Creek are the only ones in the entire area that remain active, and then only on a biweekly and monthly basis. Anyone who wishes to hear mass more frequently must travel to Dauphin or Winnipegosis. The rural schools have long been abandoned, and two years ago the elementary school at Sifton was closed. Now all the children in the region are bussed outside the original bloc settlement to Dauphin, Gilbert Plains, or Winnipegosis. The community halls are all boarded up, and the rural post offices have closed. The country stores at Mink Creek and Venlaw remain open, but only on an irregular basis since the owners of both have essentially retired. A drive down the main street of the once bustling town of Sifton reveals more of the same. Of the dozen or so commercial and public buildings, only the post office, the credit union, and Kennedy's general store remain open. The last also serves as the local gas station. The only other commercial functions that continue to operate are a grain elevator and a lunch counter that doubles as a beer parlor. All the other commercial buildings and some of the houses stand derelict. The population, now about two hundred, is a third of what it was as its peak in the late 1940s. Most of the residents who are not retired commute to Dauphin to work. In the face of all of this decline the community has experienced a small amount of new construction. A twelve-unit retirement home has gone up in the past few years, as have half a dozen new houses in a small housing tract recently laid out on the edge of town.

Most of the cemeteries in the region remain active, and it is here that the most complete picture of the area's social transition during the past forty years can be seen. A survey of the grave markers reveals a number of important changes that extend well beyond the graveyard. The typical grave marker erected in the mid-1940s was made of cement in the shape of a cross inscribed in the Cyrillic alphabet. Today stone, most notably granite, has all but completely replaced cement, a clear sign of improved economic conditions. The style of the monument has also shifted from a free-standing cross to a block essentially identical in size and shape to those found in Anglo cemeteries. Simultaneously, the crosses have diminished greatly in size and are now shown in bas-relief on the face of the monument. All of this points to a decline in the importance of religion within Ukrainian society. Perhaps the most telling transition has been the dramatic drop in the use of the Ukrainian language. In the mid-1940s well over 80 per cent of the monuments were inscribed in Ukrainian. That figure remained over 50 per cent until the 1960s, but by the mid-1970s, Ukrainian had all but disappeared. The acculturation process was, for all intents and purposes, complete.

Conclusion

The creation and evolution of the cultural landscape in the Ukrainian bloc settlement north of Dauphin, Manitoba, like cultural landscapes everywhere, has been a long and involved process. The incidents and decisions that transformed this region from an unsettled wilderness to an entrenched ethnic community to a relic agricultural district are, of course, unique, but the general pattern by which the landscape of the Dauphin bloc settlement evolved is not unlike that of many of the other tracts of marginal land settled by Ukrainian immigrants at the end of the nineteenth century.

Considered from hindsight, the Ukrainian settlers' occupation of the treed lands of the parkland proved to be mixed blessing. Given their financial constraints, environmental perceptions, and economic expectations, the decision to occupy less than ideal – but nonetheless arable – farmland seems to have been a prudent one for the first wave of

Ukrainian pioneers. For those who came later, the decision to settle on what was at times clearly sub-marginal land in order to be close to relatives and acquaintances turned out to be extremely shortsighted in most instances.[74]

Regardless of where they settled, powerful forces of acculturation confronted Ukrainians upon their arrival in western Canada. The disruptive effects of migration and exposure to a dominant culture that spoke a different language, practised a different religion, and functioned under different social, economic, and political systems induced the settlers to modify and ultimately abandon many of their traditional practices and cultural traits. Many of these practices were not given up easily. At times acculturation was simply imposed, as in the basic settlement system, which disallowed the creation of traditional farm villages. The overall lack of economic landscape features that are distinctly Ukrainian within the region lends support to the contention that acculturation was most rapid in those aspects of life that were most closely linked to commercial activity. Buffered though they were by an environment that allowed them to remain partly self-sufficient, when it came to making a living the Ukrainian settlers had little choice but to adapt as quickly as possible to the Canadian system.[75] They were better able to retain their identity in those aspects of culture that were further removed from the marketplace. In the public landscape this was evident in the establishment of community halls, which served a social function within the community, and even more pronounced in the construction of churches, which functioned as symbols of ethnic as well as religious identity. An analogous situation developed around the ethnic landscape features erected on the basis of personal or familial decisions. The design and construction of the first- and second-generation Ukrainian farmhouse are the most obvious statement of ethnic identity of this sort. Grave markers comprise a second set of features that display personal attitudes as they relate to social and economic as well as religious matters.

Research on immigrant communities elsewhere in North America suggests that several factors slowed the rate of loss of cultural traits. One was the physical size of the ethnic community: the larger an ethnic community's territorial base the greater its ability to resist assimilation.[76] A second factor was the isolation imposed by the cultural distinctiveness of the ethnic group. A third was a strong sense of cohesiveness among the minority group in regard to common community or family background. Finally, strong ties between the immigrant church and the community encouraged the retention of some cultural traits.[77] All these factors certainly came into play among the Ukrainians who settled in the Dauphin district. Indeed, the factors reinforced one another, thereby increasing the immigrants' will to resist acculturation. Add to these the settlement district's limited potential for commercial agriculture, which not only restricted external economic influences but also helped bind the Ukrainian community together in the face of economic adversity, and it is small wonder that the Ukrainian cultural landscape remains to this day as extensive and conspicuous as it is.

This landscape remains visible to all who wish to see. Most of the old farmhouses are gone, many bulldozed to make room for other things, but a scattering of second-generation houses can still be found, along with some log outbuildings. A larger proportion of the public structures has survived. The situation is much the same in Ukrainian bloc settlements elsewhere. There have been modest efforts to preserve old Ukrainian buildings in the Dauphin area by moving them to a common site in an effort to create a 'theme' park.[78] Unfortunately, although a few buildings are preserved by such efforts, the geographical setting within which the collected buildings are displayed is totally artificial, a gross distortion of the actual settlement environment as it existed. Instead of moving a few select buildings to a designated site, the buildings, along with their associated artifacts, need to be preserved *in situ*, thereby capturing a far more comprehensive and authentic perspective not just of the buildings but of the cultural landscape as well. Historic landscapes can be protected only by creating rural preservation districts. None at present exist in Canada, but heritage conservation districts are in place in the United States and Europe.[79] There is no reason why such an arrangement could not be used to preserve representative cultural landscapes in one or more of the Ukrainian blocs of western Canada. The fact that this type of preservation effort need not require immense amounts of government funds adds a further incentive. However, a critical time is rapidly approaching in regard to the Ukrainian ethnic landscapes of the region. Unless something is initiated within the next few years, much of what is worth preserving will be lost, and the whole of Canada will be the poorer for it.

NOTES

This article is from *Canada's Ukrainians: Negotiating an Identity*, ed. Lubomyr Luciuk and Stella Hryniuk. Toronto: University of Toronto Press, 1991. Reprinted with permission.

1 By far the most prolific writer on the various aspects of the Ukrainian-Canadian landscape is John C. Lehr. See, for example, 'Ukrainian Houses in Alberta,' *Alberta Historical Review* 21 (1973), 9–15; 'Ukrainian Vernacular Architecture,' *Canadian Collector* 11 (1976), 66–70; 'The Log Buildings of Ukrainian Settlers in Western Canada,' *Prairie Forum* 5 (1980): 183–96; 'Colour Preferences and Building Decoration among Ukrainians in Western Canada,' *Prairie Forum* 6 (1981): 203–6; 'The Landscape of Ukrainian Settlement in the Canadian West,' *Great Plains Quarterly* 2 (1982): 94–105; 'The Ukrainian Sacred Landscape: A Metaphor of Survival and Acculturation,' *Material Culture Bulletin* 29 (1989): 3–11; and 'Preservation of the Ethnic Landscape in Western Canada,' *Prairie Forum* 15 (1990): 263–76. Others have also reported on the Ukrainian presence in the prairie provinces: Cathy Chorniawy, *Commerce in the Country* (Edmonton: Historic Sites Service, Alberta Culture and Multiculturalism, 1989); James W. Darlington, 'The Evolving Ukrainian-Canadian Landscape: A Driving Tour of the Dauphin Block Settlement Region of Manitoba,' *Proceedings of the Prairie Division of the Canadian Association of Geographers 1990* (forthcoming); Lubomyr Y. Luciuk and Bohdan S. Kordan, *Creating a Landscape: A Geography of Ukrainians in Canada* (Toronto: University of Toronto Press, 1989); Edward M. Ledohowski, *Ukrainian Farmsteads in Manitoba: A Preliminary Investigation* (Winnipeg: Manitoba Culture, Heritage and Recreation, Historic Resources Branch, 1987); and Basil Rotoff et al., *Monuments to Faith: Ukrainian Churches in Manitoba* (Winnipeg: University of Manitoba Press, 1990).
2 Miriam Elston, 'The Russian in Our Midst' (journal and date unknown), as cited in John C. Lehr, 'Changing Ukrainian House Styles,' *Alberta History* 23 (1975): 26-7.
3 C.A. Dawson, *Group Settlement: Ethnic Communities in Western Canada* (Toronto: Macmillan, 1936).
4 Hansgeorg Schlichtmann, 'Ethnic Themes in Geographical Research in Western Canada,' *Canadian Ethnic Studies* 9 (1977): 10-14; Dawson, *Group Settlement.*
5 According to one survey, 50 per cent of the Ukrainians arrived in western Canada penniless, and another 42 per cent had less than five hundred dollars. See J.S. Woodsworth, 'Ukrainian Rural Communities,' Report of Investigation by Bureau of Social Research, Governments of Manitoba, Saskatchewan, and Alberta (Winnipeg, 1917), 73–94. One copy of the report is at the National Archives of Canada, Ottawa (hereafter cited as NAC).
6 Lehr, 'The Landscape of Ukrainian Settlement,' 94.
7 See, for example, the correspondence between William F. McCreary of the Immigration Office in Winnipeg and James A. Smart, Ottawa, 14 May 1897,

RG 76, vol. 144, file 34214, pt. 1, NAC; and the telegram from C.W. Speers, Saskatoon, 19 May 1898, ibid.

8 John C. Lehr, 'The Government and the Immigrant: Perspectives on Ukrainian Block Settlement in the Canadian West,' Canadian Ethnic Studies 9 (1977): 42–52.

9 Roman Fodchuk, 'Building the Little House on the Prairies: Ukrainian Technology, Canadian Resources,' Material History Bulletin 29 (1989): 89–97.

10 The prospect of seasonal employment in the lumber camps located in the Riding Mountain Timber Reserve was one of the reasons for the establishment of the Shoal Lake–Strathclair bloc settlement south of what is now Riding Mountain National Park. C.W. Speers, Winnipeg, to Frank Pedley, Ottawa, 10 June 1899, RG 76, vol. 144, file 34214, pt. 3 (83911), NAC. For non-agricultural sources of income see John C. Lehr, '"The Peculiar People": Ukrainian Settlement of Marginal Lands in Southeastern Manitoba,' in David C. Jones and Ian MacPherson, eds., Building beyond the Farmstead (Calgary: University of Calgary Press, 1985), 34.

11 See, for example, James M. Richtik, 'The Agricultural Frontier in Manitoba: Changing Perceptions of the Resource Value of Prairie and Woodland,' Upper Midwest History 3 (1983): 55–61.

12 J. Wreford Watson, 'The Role of Illusion in North American Geography: A Note on the Geography of North American Settlement,' Canadian Geographer 13 (1969): 16.

13 For figures on Galician farm acreage see Emily Greene Balch, 'Slav Emigration at Its Source,' Charities and the Commons, 16 (May 1906): 179; for Bukovynian farm size see A.M. Shlepakov, Ukrainska trudova emihratsiia v SShA i Kanadi: Kinets XIX–pochatok XX st. (Kiev: Akademiia nauk Ukrainskoi RSR, 1960), 23.

14 See, for example, N. Wagenhoffer, 'Some Socio-economic Dynamics in Southeastern Manitoba with Particular Reference to the Farming Communities within the Local Government Districts of Stuartburn and Piney' (MA thesis, University of Manitoba, 1972), 55; and Kaye, Early Ukrainian Settlements, 139.

15 John C. Lehr, 'The Rural Settlement Behaviour of Ukrainian Pioneers in Western Canada, 1891–1914,' in B.M. Barr, ed., Western Canadian Research in Geography: The Lethbridge Papers, BC Geographical Series, No. 21, Occasional Papers in Geography (Vancouver: Tantalus Research, 1975), 59.

16 Kaye, Early Ukrainian Settlements, 203.

17 Ibid., 201–3.

18 Iosyf Oleskiv, O emigratsii (Lviv: Obshchestvo Mykhaila Kachkovskoho, 1895), 39.

19 For one such example see Kaye, Early Ukrainian Settlements, 179.

20 John C. Lehr, 'Kinship and Society in the Ukrainian Pioneer Settlement of the Canadian West,' *Canadian Geographer* 29 (1985), 207–19; see also Luciuk and Kordan, *Creating a Landscape*, map 4, 'District, village, and kinship ties in Manitoba, 1901.'

21 Lehr, 'Kinship and Society,' 216–17.

22 For an analogous situation in coal-mining communities see Ben Marsh, 'Continuity and Decline in the Anthracite Towns of Pennsylvania,' *Annals of the Association of American Geographers* 77 (1987), 337–52.

23 Kaye, *Early Ukrainian Settlements*, 184–8.

24 Department of the Interior, 'Plan of Township 26 Range 20 West of First Meridian,' Department of the Interior, Topographic Surveys Branch, 1891, NAC.

25 Kaye, *Early Ukrainian Settlements*, 185–6.

26 The three ships were the SS *Scotia*, docked in Halifax 30 April 1897 with thirty-five single men or families bound for Dauphin, the SS *Arcadia*, docked in Quebec City 2 May 1897 with thirty-five single men or families bound for Dauphin, and the SS *Prussia*, docked in Halifax 22 May 1897 with fifty-nine single men or families bound for Dauphin. Vladimir J. Kaye, *Dictionary of Ukrainian Canadian Biography: Pioneer Settlers of Manitoba 1891–1900* (Toronto: Ukrainian Canadian Research Foundation, 1975), 2–118.

27 J. Obed Smith, Commissioner of Immigration, Winnipeg, to the Secretary, Department of the Interior, Ottawa, 1 February 1901, Reports on Immigration Operations, NAC.

28 W.A. Ehrlich et al., *Report of Reconnaissance Soil Survey of Grandview Map Sheet Area*, Soils Report No. 9, Manitoba Soil Survey, 1959.

29 *The Maksymetz Family Reunion* (Np: Privately printed, 1982), 12.

30 Dmytro Romanchych, 'Ukrainski kolonii v okruzi Dauphin, Manitoba,' in Semen Kovbel, comp., and Dmytro Doroshenko, ed., *Propamiatna knyha Ukrainskoho narodnoho domu u Vynypegu* (Winnipeg: Ukrainskyi narodnyi dim, 1949), 514–16; and Kaye, *Early Ukrainian Settlements*, 203.

31 Luciuk and Kordan, *Creating a Landscape*, map 4, 'District, village, and kinship ties in Manitoba, 1901.'

32 Michael Ewanchuk, *Pioneer Settlers: Ukrainians in the Dauphin Area, 1896–1926* (Winnipeg: Privately printed, 1988), 28.

33 Lehr, 'Kinship and Society,' 214.

34 Township 28, Range 20 W, is a standard township containing thirty-six sections; Township 27, Range 20 W, is a modified township of only twenty-four sections. Both were surveyed according to the Third Dominion Land Survey system. See John L. Tyman, *By Section, Township and Range: Studies in Prairie Settlement* (Brandon: Assiniboine Historical Society, 1972), 12.

35 Ibid., 160–1.
36 Ledohowski, *Ukrainian Farmsteads in Manitoba*, 9. Kaye, *Early Ukrainian Settlements*, 139, provides a description of the construction of a dug-out in the Stuartburn region of Manitoba. See also Andriy Nahachewsky, *Ukrainian Dug-out Dwellings in East Central Alberta* (Edmonton: Historic Sites Service, Alberta Culture and Multiculturalism, 1985).
37 Ibid., 186.
38 Fodchuk, 'Building the Little House on the Prairies,' 93.
39 *Khata* refers both to a house and to the rooms within it. Thus *velyka khata* can be translated as 'big house' or 'big room,' and *mala khata* as 'little house' or 'little room.'
40 Thomas Young, Forest Ranger, Dauphin, to E.F. Stephenson, Winnipeg, 18 June 1898, Immigration, Dominion Lands Branch, file 480870, NAC, as quoted in Kaye, *Early Ukrainian Settlements*, 206–8.
41 Thirteen petitioners from Township 23, Range 20 W, to Thomas Young, Homestead Inspector, Dauphin, Man., 10 March 1901, Immigration, Dominion Lands Branch, file 621566, NAC, as quoted in Kaye, *Early Ukrainian Settlements*, 216–17.
42 C.W. Speers, General Colonization Agent, Portage la Prairie, to Frank Pedley, Superintendent of Immigration, Ottawa, 27 March 1899, Reports on Immigration Operations, file 78733, NAC, as quoted in Kaye, *Early Ukrainian Settlements*, 187–8.
43 9 April 1902, Reports on Immigration Operations, file 198189, NAC, as quoted in Kaye, *Early Ukrainian Settlements*, 188.
44 *Maksymetz Family Reunion*, 12–14.
45 See *Cummins Rural Directory: Manitoba: 1923*.
46 Michael H. Marunchak, *The Ukrainian Canadians: A History* (Winnipeg: Ukrainian Free Academy of Sciences, 1970), 352.
47 Charles H. Young, *The Ukrainian Canadians* (Toronto: Thomas Nelson, 1931), 97.
48 Personal communication with Stephen Negrych, son of the original owner, September 1990.
49 Report of the Department of Education of Manitoba for 1900, 31–2, Provincial Archives of Manitoba, Winnipeg.
50 The figures were compiled from Kaye, *Dictionary of Ukrainian Canadian Biography*.
51 Ibid.
52 The important role that the Greek Catholic church played in the Ukrainian community is discussed in John-Paul Himka, 'The Greek Catholic Church and Nation-Building in Galicia, 1772-1918,' *Harvard Ukrainian Studies* 8

(December 1984): 426–52; and Paul Yuzyk, 'Religious Life,' in Manoly R. Lupul, ed., *A Heritage in Transition: Essays in the History of Ukrainians in Canada* (Toronto: McClelland and Stewart, 1982), 143–72. The church was important in the life of other immigrant groups as well. See, for example, Robert C. Ostergren, 'The Immigrant Church as a Symbol of Community and Place in the Upper Midwest,' *Great Plains Quarterly* 1 (1981): 225–38.

53 Lehr, 'Landscape of Ukrainian Settlement,' 99.

54 Marunchak, *The Ukrainian Canadians*, 103.

55 The numbers and dates are provided by *Ukrainian Churches of Manitoba: A Building Inventory* (Winnipeg: Manitoba Culture, Heritage and Recreation, Historic Resources Branch, 1987). See also Basil Rotoff et al., *Monuments to Faith*.

56 Of the 451 families that settled in the Dauphin region and are listed in Kaye, *Dictionary of Ukrainian Canadian Biography*, only two gave Bukovyna as their home province; the rest named Galicia.

57 Yuzyk, 'Religious Life,' 147–52; and Orest T. Martynowych, '"Canadianizing the Foreigner": Presbyterian Missionaries and Ukrainian Immigrants,' in Jaroslav Rozumnyj, ed., *New Soil – Old Roots: The Ukrainian Experience in Canada* (Winnipeg: Ukrainian Academy of Arts and Sciences in Canada, 1983), 33–57.

58 Yuzyk, 'Religious Life,' 155–6.

59 Field-work by the author.

60 Bohdan Medwidsky, 'Ukrainian Grave Markers in East-Central Alberta,' *Material History Bulletin* 29 (1989), 72–5. See also A.M. Kostecki, 'Crosses of East Slavic Christianity among Ukrainians in Western Canada,' *Material History Bulletin* 29 (1989): 55–8.

61 Luciuk and Kordan, *Creating a Landscape*, map 16, 'The Religious Landscape in Manitoba.'

62 Paul Yuzyk, *The Ukrainians in Manitoba: A Social History* (Toronto: University of Toronto Press, 1953), 144–5.

63 Frances Swyripa, 'The Ukrainians and Private Education,' in Lupul, *A Heritage in Transition*, 245.

64 Marunchak, *The Ukrainian Canadian*, 120–1.

65 Ibid., 166–7; and Luciuk and Kordan, *Creating a Landscape*, map 17, 'Prosvitas.'

66 C.W. Speers to Frank Pedley, 27 March 1899, Reports of Immigration Operations, file 78733, NAC, as quoted in Kaye, *Early Ukrainian Settlements*, 187.

67 Orest T. Martynowych, *The Ukrainian Bloc Settlement in East Central Alberta 1890–1930: A History* (Edmonton: Historic Sites Service, Alberta Culture and Multiculturalism, 1985), 225.

68 Marunchak, *The Ukrainian Canadians*, 236.

69 The Western Canada Fire Underwriters' Association, 'Fire Insurance Plan for Sifton, Man.' (Winnipeg, 1919).

70 Dominion Bureau of Statistics, *Census of Manitoba, 1936: Population and Agriculture* (Ottawa, 1938).

71 Lehr, 'Changing Ukrainian House Styles,' 28; and Ledohowski, 'Ukrainian Farmsteads in Manitoba,' 19.

72 Ledohowski, 'Ukrainian Farmsteads in Manitoba,' 20.

73 William J. Carlyle, 'The Relationship between Settlement and the Physical Environment in Part of the West Lake Area of Manitoba from 1878 to 1963' (MA thesis, University of Manitoba, 1965), 172, has identified the mid-1940s as the end of the economic transition period for the Ukrainian settlement immediately to the east of Riding Mountain.

74 Lehr, 'Kinship and Society,' 217.

75 In this respect the Ukrainian settlers behaved like most other immigrants in North America. See Robert C. Ostergren, 'A Community Transplanted: The Formative Experience of a Swedish Immigrant Community in the Upper Middle West,' *Journal of Historical Geography* 5 (1979): 208.

76 D. Aidan McQuillan, 'Territory and Ethnic Identity: Some New Measures of an Old Theme in the Cultural Geography of the United States,' in James R. Gibson, ed., *European Settlement and Development in North America: Essays on Geographical Change in Honour and Memory of Andrew Hill Clark* (Toronto: University of Toronto Press, 1978), 136–69.

77 John G. Rice, 'The Role of Culture and Community of Frontier Prairie Farming,' *Journal of Historical Geography* 3 (1977): 155–75; and Ostergren, 'A Community Transplanted,' 189–212.

78 Two such arrangements exist in the Dauphin area. The more ambitious project is located south of Dauphin at Selo Ukraina, the site of the Canadian National Ukrainian Festival. The second site involves several buildings that have been incorporated into a roadside picnic area at Terembowla. The same approach to preservation has also been followed in Alberta at the Shandro Historical Living Village and Pioneer Museum at Willingdon and the Ukrainian Cultural Heritage Village at Elk Island.

79 Lehr, 'Preservation of the Ethnic Landscape,' discusses this idea more thoroughly.

TOPIC FOUR
'Women's Work': Paid Labour, Community-Building, and Protest

In her autobiography, *The Stream Runs Fast*, Nellie McClung recounts an incident told to her by the friend of her domestic servant, Anna. Anna's friend Mary, a live-in domestic servant from Europe, was one day informed by her employer that she was not to use the family bathtub, but could take her bath at the YWCA. Mary was amenable to the idea, but worried that to bathe daily at the YWCA, located a mile away, would take up too much time from work. Her mistress's response was to tell Mary that 'One bath a week is plenty for you, and you can take it on your day out.' Mary replied curtly: 'No bath, no work.' In the end, Mary got her way. McClung ends the story with Mary singing happily away, in the family tub.[1]

Although McClung could hardly have known it, Mary's story reflects the different approaches of scholars who have studied immigrant domestics. On the one hand, the attempt by her 'mistress' to control where and when Mary could bathe fits neatly the framework of many scholars who have documented and emphasized the exploitative features of domestic work. The lack of freedom, the isolation and loneliness, and the low status accorded domestic service by society at large have long combined to keep many Canadian women away from the occupation and to make it a female 'job ghetto' for immigrants. Mary's defiant refusal to submit to her mistress's order, on the other hand, appeals to historians who, like Varpu Lindström, highlight the resourcefulness, agency, and even defiance of immigrant women as they negotiated the demands and constraints of domestic work.

Immigrant maids have been the subject of much scholarly attention. How could they not be? Since the nineteenth century numerous streams of female domestics have entered Canada. Between Confederation and the onset of the Great Depression, more than 250,000 women immigrated to Canada with the stated intention of working as a domestic servant. Thousands more entered the country under other pretenses, either alone or with their families, but many of them eventually found work in the homes of others. Most were young, single women – in many instances, teenagers. And their services were in high demand. So great was the demand for female domestics in the late nineteenth and early twentieth centuries, and so severe the shortage, that newspaper reports of the day regularly spoke of 'the servant girl problem.' No wonder, then, that federal and provincial governments actively recruited young women, mostly from Britain and Europe, to work in the homes of upper- and middle-class Canadians. Such recruits were among the few groups of unaccompanied female immigrants to be so courted. Indeed, between 1870 and 1930, domestic servants were considered 'preferred' immigrants, along with farm families and single male farm labourers.

Lindström suggests the ways in which one group of immigrant domestics, the Finns, found ways of adapting to and challenging their exploitative conditions. Adaptation, she suggests, came through a positive self-image and pride in their hard work, their diligence, and the clean homes they kept. For a good many Finnish women, moreover, socialist politics held out the hope of improved working conditions. Their racial status as 'white ethnics' is also a factor worth considering, especially when we contrast the experiences of white British and European domestics reruited in the years before the Second World War to those women of colour from the West Indies and other so-called non-white sources. While the former gained entry as landed immigrants, the latter were (and still are) recruited as temporary guest workers who face serious barriers to gaining permanent settlement in Canada.[2]

Considerably less scholarly attention has been paid to immigrant women as community-builders and to their lives beyond home and workplace. Paula Draper and Janice Karlinsky focus on charity and political work within the ethnic community – in this case, Canada's Jewish community. They break new ground by putting women at the centre of their work to demonstrate how, for an entire generation of middle-class Jewish women, charity and community work became 'a way of life,' an extension of the domestic duties traditionally associated with women within the patriarchal social order of Judaism. Moreover, whereas immigration historians have tended to portray ethnic communities as relatively insular, cohesive, and internally unified, Draper and Karlinsky highlight the gender, class, and ideological conflict that divided Canadian Jewry despite the common experience of anti-Semitism. When, for example, Jewish women's involvement in philanthropy failed to supplant the male dominance of benevolent and communal associations, some Jewish women created their own gender-exclusive organizations devoted to religious instruction, charity activities, and child-care.

The essays offer us two case studies of immigrant women's work roles and suggest that we expand our conventional notions of what constitutes 'women's work.' How might we use these essays as a basis for discussing more generally the varied experiences of immigrant women and the characteristics of their family, work, community, and political lives? To what extent were the politics of the Finnish and Jewish women depicted in these essays shaped by their position as women, wives, and mothers? How did relations with male kin and male colleagues and comrades affect women's public and private lives?

NOTES

1 Nellie L. McClung, *The Stream Runs Fast: My Own Story* (Toronto 1945) 259
2 On post-1945 domestics, see, for example, Agnes Calliste and Makeda Silvera, below, and the introduction to topic 8.

BIBLIOGRAPHY AND SUGGESTED READINGS

Barber, Marilyn. *Immigrant Domestic Servants in Canada* (Ottawa 1991)
– 'The Servant Problem in Manitoba': Help for Farm Homes: The Campaign to End Housework Drudgery in Rural Saskatchewan in the 1920s.' *Scientia canadensis* 9:1 (June 1985).
– 'Below Stairs: The Domestic Servant.' *Material History Bulletin* 19 (Spring 1984).
Burnet, Jean, ed. *Looking in My Sister's Eyes: An Exploration in Woman's History.* Toronto 1986.
Calliste, Agnes. 'Canada's Immigration Policy and Domestics from the Caribbean: The Second Domestic Scheme.' In Jessie Vorst, ed., *Class, Race and Gender in Canada*. Toronto 1985.
Harney, Robert F., ed. *Gathering Place: Peoples and Neighbourhoods in Toronto, 1834–1943*. Toronto 1989.
Lacelle, Claudette. *Urban Domestic Servants in 19th Century Canada*. Ottawa 1987.

Lindström, Varpu. *Defiant Sisters: A Social History of Finnish Immigrant Women in Canada*. Toronto 1992.

Loewen, Royden. *Family, Church, and Market: A Mennonite Community in the Old and New Worlds, 1850–1930*. Toronto 1993.

Luciuk, Lubomyr, and Stella Hryniuk, eds. *Canada's Ukrainians: Negotiating an Identity*, Toronto 1991.

Ramirez, Bruno. *Les Premiers Italiens de Montréal*. Montreal 1984.

Silvera, Makeda. *Silenced*. Toronto 1988.

Speisman, Steven. *The Jews of Toronto*. Toronto 1979.

Tulchinsky, Gerald. *Taking Root: The Origins of the Canadian Jewish Community*. Toronto 1992.

Zucchi, John. *Italians in Toronto: The Development of a National Identity*. Montreal 1988.

'I Won't Be a Slave!': Finnish Domestics in Canada, 1911–1930

VARPU LINDSTRÖM

It is with deep sorrow and longing that I inform you of the death of my beloved daughter Siiri Mary who became the victim of a terrible death in her place of employment in Nanaimo, B.C. on the first of May at 04:00 in the morning. As she was lighting the fire in the kitchen stove with kerosene it exploded and the fire ignited her clothes and she burnt so badly that on the fifth of May she died in the Nanaimo hospital at 11:30 in the evening. She was born on January 1, 1906 and died on May 5, 1922 at the age of 16 years 4 months and 4 days. Father remembers you with bitter sadness and longing.[1]

This touching funeral notice reveals some of the dark realities about domestic service in Canada. Why was the sixteen-year-old girl having to start her work day at 4:00 A.M.? What knowledge did she have of kerosene? And what protection in case of an accident? Who could she turn to for advice, or what avenues for complaint did she have? While the domestic servant looked after all the members and guests of the household, who looked after her? These questions were hotly debated in the various organizations established for Finnish maids in North America. Despite the many negative aspects of domestic work, it was the most common occupation for Finnish immigrant women.

The domestics themselves are quick to point out the many positive features about their life as a *haussi-meiti* (housemaid). From the discussions emerge important differences in the society's view of domestic service as a low-status occupation and the maid's own view of her work. This article will probe into both the positive and negative aspects of life as a domestic, taking the examination beyond the work place and into the community. In the process the study will discuss the organizations and communication networks which were established to assist the Finnish domestic servants.

Supply and Demand

The University of Toronto probe into the conditions of female labour in Ontario in 1889 noted that the demand for domestic servants exceeded the supply and that it was necessary to import domestic servants from the British Isles.[2] Barber's thorough examination of the recruitment and settlement of the British domestic servants as the most welcome women shows to what great extent the government and employers would go to recruit domestics.[3] Young girls, often orphans from England, were brought to Canada through various benevolent agencies and ended up as domestic servants.[4] Still, as poignantly illustrated by Makeda Silvera's book, *Silenced*, the chronic shortage of domestic servants has continued until the present day.[5] There have, of course, been periodic fluctuations in the demand, and some communities felt the shortage of domestic workers more severely than others, but generally the supply of maids did not meet the demand.

After the turn of the century, Finnish domestics were enticed to come to Canada. The federal government bent immigration regulations for women who promised to work as domestic servants.[6] In fact, it was the only category, in addition to farm worker, in which a single woman from Finland during the twenties was allowed to enter the country.[7] Like the British, they too were welcome. The following riddle in a Finnish paper illustrates the point:

I am not beautiful,
Yet, I am the most wanted woman.
I am not rich,

Yet I am worth my weight in gold.
I might be dull, stupid,
Dirty and mean,
Yet, all the doors are open for me.
I am a welcome guest
All of the elite compete for me.
I am a maid.[8]

Finnish women entered the industry during its 'transitional period,' when the proportional importance of domestic service as a major occupation for women was declining. In 1921 domestics represented only 18 per cent of all employed women in Canada. New opportunities were enticing Canadian women away from domestic service and the resulting gap was partially filled by newly arrived immigrants.[9] The largest proportion of foreign domestic workers still came from the British Isles – 75 per cent before World War One and 60 per cent during the 1920s.[10] Among the other ethnic groups, the Scandinavians and Finns showed an exceptionally high propensity for domestic work. While the British women, who were able to speak English, also had other opportunities for employment, the Finnish women were almost exclusively concentrated in the service industry. In Finnish jargon 'going to work in America' became synonymous with 'going to be a domestic in America.'[11] During the twenties, the Finnish domestic servants made up 7–8 per cent of all female immigrants classified as 'female domestics.' In the fiscal year ending March 31, 1929, for example, 1,288 Finnish women arrived in Canada under this category out of a total of 1,618 adult female immigrants from Finland.[12] This does not necessarily mean that all women actually settled into their declared occupations in Canada. In fact, the Finnish Immigrant Home Records indicate that there was considerable diversity of skills among these 'excellent domestic servants.' Letters of recommendation from Finland often included revealing additions such as 'she is also an experienced seamstress,' or 'this woman is a skilful masseuse.'[13] The domestic service category was simply the most convenient for immigration purposes.

Nevertheless, the vast majority of working women in Finnish communities were maids. Calculations based on the two largest urban centres indicate that of all the Finnish immigrant women employed outside the home during the twenties at least 66 per cent were maids in Toronto and Montreal.[14] Except for a handful of women who worked in restaurants, 'all Finnish women in Winnipeg were maids.'[15] This single, overpowering concentration of Finnish women in domestic work had a great impact on the community which had to adapt to the life patterns of the maids. Just as mining, lumbering and construction work coloured the life of Finnish men, influenced their economic status, settlement location and political thinking, domestic work shaped the world-views of the Finnish women.

The nature of domestic service was also changing from the predominance of live-in maids around the turn of the century to 'day workers' by the depression. For example, the percentage of laundresses in the service occupations doubled between 1901–11.[16] It was becoming increasingly difficult to find women willing to live in and, consequently, more of this work was left to the newly arrived immigrants – the greenhorns – whose occupational choices were limited. The Finnish women knew upon arrival that there would be no problem in finding a job. 'I could have worked thirty hours a day, eight days a week,' commented one tired woman;[17] and a man shamefully recollected:

There was no work for me, nothing, but my wife was always able to get work as a live-in cook. What to do? I had to take women's work. Oh, I didn't like it. I was to look after the liquor, but in the morning I had to do some dusting too. I hated women's work and the pay was not good either, but we had a place to live and food to eat. As soon as I could get man's work, I left.[18]

The consequent role reversal, which heightened during periods of economic slow-down, was a bitter pill for many men to swallow. 'My mother worked,' remembered a dynamic leader of the Finnish community, 'she could always find work in the houses, and my father stayed home with the children.' Then she laughed, 'He never liked it, but he did a good job!'[19] By 1928 when the Great Depression had hit the lumbering industry – one of the biggest employers of Finnish men – the frustrated 'house-husband' syndrome spread beyond the urban centres. Letters to Finland explained how 'women are the only ones who find work and men stay home to look after the children.'[20] Women gained in status as 'they were the only ones with money to spend.'[21] Even during the depression in 1937 when all doors to immigration were shut, the government launched a special scheme to bring in 'Scandinavian and Finnish Domestics.' Most of the women who came under this plan were Finnish and in their late twenties and early thirties.[22]

Thus, the Finnish women who came to Canada from 1900–30 when the supply of domestics was dwindling and the demand for live-in maids still strong were in good economic position. They came mainly as single, mature women who were used to hard work, and many had been domestics prior to emigrating. This combination, the availability of work and the ability to do it, was the main reason why Finnish women, both in the United States and Canada, were found in such large numbers in domestic service. In addition, there were other positive features about domestic work which attracted the newcomers.

The Bright Side of Domestic Work

The most pressing concerns of newly arrived immigrants included where to live and where to work. As a live-in maid both worries were taken care of at once. While the Finnish men spent much of their first years in Canada in rooming-houses or bunk-houses, or roaming around in search of work, the live-in maids at least had a solid roof over their heads. Their homes might only be damp cellar quarters, or, more commonly, cold upstairs rooms, but they could also be sunny rooms in luxurious mansions, with beautiful gardens and comfortable feather beds. Lice-covered blankets, hair frozen to the bunk-house wall, or the unpalatable smell of dozens of sweaty socks were not part of the maid's experience. Instead, the domestics usually lived in middle- and upper-class homes in safe and relatively clean neighbourhoods. No time was spent looking for housing and no initial investment needed to buy furniture or basic kitchen utensils.

The maid's limited free time was carefully monitored by the employers. 'The family' was sure to report any unexpected absences or late arrivals of the maids. In case of serious trouble or illness at least someone would notice and beware. The stories of unidentified Finnish men found dead by railroad tracks, lost in the bush, or dying alone from an illness did not have their female counterparts. Someone, whether from reasons of moral concern or meanness, was keeping tabs on the maid's whereabouts and routines. For many younger women, the employers became the surrogate family, disciplining and restricting their social activities. This, of course, was a double-edged sword. One summer evening when a Finnish maid in Toronto failed to come home from the local dance at the agreed-upon time of eleven, the employers swiftly called the police. In her case the alarm was too late as her beaten-up body was found on the outskirts of Toronto in 1916, but her friend was saved from a similar fate.[23] While appreciating any genuine concern, many women resented the strict scheduling of their free time. A Port Arthur maid remembers her first evening off in 1910:

I have been rebellious ever since I was a child. On my only evening off, I was supposed to be back at 10:00 P.M. Well, I went to the hall to see a play and to dance afterwards and didn't get back until one in the morning. I found the door bolted down from inside and my blood rushed to my head. They treated me just as if I was a small child incapable of looking after my own affairs. I banged on that door so hard that they finally opened it, and I shouted in my broken English: 'I not dog! I Sanni! I sleep inside!'[24]

In addition to a safe 'home' the domestics received regular meals. Many farm girls who were used to hearty dinners, however, complained of the small portions served. They had to sneak extra food from the kitchen. Others went to a local Finnish restaurant on their afternoon off 'and stuffed themselves with pancakes' so that for at least a day they would not go hungry.[25] One woman noted an ideological difference about eating and explained in a letter to her mother: 'Canadians don't give enough food to anybody. They are afraid that if you eat too much you get sick and the Finns are afraid that if you don't eat enough you get sick.'[26] Others complained of the miserly manner in which the mistress checked all food supplies. In one millionaire's home in Montreal, the maids were not allowed to have cream in their coffee. 'When the lady asked for the hundredth time if there was cream in the coffee,' explained one frustrated maid, 'my friend took the entire cream pitcher and threw it against the wall.' With a thoughtful sigh she added, 'We Finns, you know, we have such temper – that *sisu* – has caused many a maid to lose her job.'[27] On the other hand, many women were fed good balanced diets, were introduced to white bread, various vegetables and fruits unknown in their own country. Not only did they receive regular meals, they learned to 'eat the Canadian way.'

Living with a Canadian family they also learned to speak some English, usually enough to manage in the kitchen. Jokingly they described their language as *kitsi-Engelska*. Many were taught by their employers who found communication through a dictionary too cumbersome, others took language classes provided by the Finnish community during the 'maid's day.' The maids themselves realized the importance of learning the language:

... I am so thankful that right away I was placed in a job where there are only

English-speaking people so that I just have to learn when I don't even hear anything else and here that is the main thing to learn to speak English first even
when looking for work they don't ask if you know how to work but if you know
the language of the country ...[28]

Along with language skills, the maids were also given an immersion
course on Canadian home appliances, customs and behaviour. On-the-
job training included the introduction to vacuum cleaners, washing
machines and the operation of gas oven. The maids attentively observed
the 'ladies' and were soon acquiring new role models. In amazement
Finnish men complained of the profusion of make-up used by the maids
who had started to *playata laidia* (play the lady).[29] Women's clothing
reflected the new image – hats, gloves and silk stockings being among
the first items of purchase. Having obtained these symbols of Canadianization, the maids rushed to the photography studios and sent home
pictures of themselves lounging on two-seater velvet sofas, sniffing at a
rose and revealing strategically placed silk-stockinged legs. Other pictures showed women with huge hats, the likes of which could only be
worn by the nobility or the minister's wife in Finland.[30] We can imagine
what effect these photographs had on the relatives back home, or on the
girlfriends still wearing tight scarves and wool stockings. Only one
month in Canada, and the photographs showed a total transformation
of a poor country woman into a sophisticated 'lady' sipping tea from a
silver pot, some needlepoint resting on her knee.

The reality, of course, was much different from the illusion created by
the props in the photographers' studios. Undeniably, there were many
advantages to being a live-in maid – an instant 'home,' on-the-job training and immersion in the country's language and customs. On the other
hand, there were also serious complaints.

The Proud Maid

A recent study of domestic service in Canada blames the long working
hours, hard work, lack of privacy and low status of domestic work for
the unpopularity of the job.[31] The Finnish immigrant women certainly
agreed with many of these complaints, but because of their cultural
background, their position in the community and their special immigrant conditions, their view of domestic work was somewhat different.

Historians have suggested that for the young Irish girls in Boston domestic work actually represented upward mobility, since they had been unable to obtain any kind of work in Ireland. A study of Swedes in Chicago indicated that domestic work was reputable and accepted as the norm for the first-generation Swedish women who were almost exclusively working as maids.[32] This trend is evident among the Finnish domestics in Canada. When the community was so overwhelmingly composed of domestic servants, comparisons with other occupations became irrelevant. Instead the domestics created their own internal hierarchy. Their status came from a job well done and they took pride in their honesty, initiative and ability to work hard 'to do what previously had taken two women.'[33] Together they worked to create a sound collective image and to improve their working opportunities. Any deviance from this norm, any Finnish woman perceived as 'lazy' or dishonest, was severely chastised in the Finnish-Canadian press for ruining the reputation of Finns as 'most desirable and highly paid domestic servants.'[34]

On an individual level, pride in their work – in their profession – is reflected in the comments of the domestics interviewed for this project. 'My floors were the cleanest on the street,' or 'my laundry was out the earliest every morning' are typical of the self-congratulatory mood. Comparisons with other women were used to illustrate these points:

Nobody had scrubbed that dirt off, did they look at me when I took off my only pair of shoes, got on my knees and scrubbed that muck till you could have eaten from the floor. Women weren't supposed to show their naked ankles, but heck, I wasn't about to ruin my shoes. Another Finlander, they thought![35]

They worked hard to gain the trust of their employers, and then they boasted, 'If I said the sky was green, then the sky was green.'[36] Finnish women often showed a strange mixture of an inferiority and a superiority complex. While they might have respected the position of the 'Missis,' they often felt great disdain for 'her inability to do anything right.' Helmi, who worked for a wealthy family in Sault Ste. Marie during the early twenties, is a prime example of the confidence and control that shines through from many of the stories told by domestics:

When that Mrs. noticed that I could take care of all the cleaning, all the dishes and all the cooking, in fact, I ran the entire household, she became so lazy that she started to demand her breakfast in bed. Healthy woman! Just lying there and

I had to carry the food to the bed. Oh boy, that hurt the Finlander's *sisu* that a woman makes herself so shamefully helpless. What to do, what to come up with, when there was no point to *kikkia* [kick back]. So I started making the most delicious old-country pancakes, plenty of them and thick, and I added lots of butter and whipped cream. Every morning I carried to the Mrs. a huge plateful, and the Mrs. ate until she was as round as my pancakes. The Mr. ordered her to go on a diet, and Helmi no longer had to take breakfast to bed![37]

When Nellie McClung chose to make a Finnish domestic the heroine of her novel *Painted Fires*, she agreed with the image that Finnish domestics had of themselves. Having had a Finnish maid, she was surprisingly familiar with their manners, pride, temper and customs. The Finns, on the other hand, greeted the book with exalted praise as it showed the Finnish maids 'exactly as we like to think we are.'[38] The novel was promptly translated into Finnish and sold thousands of copies. The heroine, whose name was also Helmi, was honest to a fault, loyal, extremely clean and hard working. She was also strong, stubborn and defiant. For example, in one scene Helmi slams the dishtray on the head of another domestic who had not pre-rinsed the greasy plates. In the ensuing chaos the employer asks, 'Isn't that kind of behaviour so typical of the Finns, Maggie? They are clean, swift, but so hot-headed.'[39]

McClung's stereotype of a spirited Finnish domestic finds many counterparts in the literary tradition of Finland and of Finns in North America. Because of the Finnish women's love of theatre, of acting and performing, they were often in the position to choose and even write plays for the stage. Invariably the maid was portrayed as 'intelligent and honest,' constantly involved in her self-improvement while the masters were corrupt, lazy and often stupid. In the Finnish-Canadian socialist literature, the class struggle is depicted through scenes of superior servants suffering under less capable masters. The beloved poems of Aku Päiviö, the best known Finnish-Canadian socialist writer, reinforced the superiority of the victim. One woman confided: 'Every time I read the poem "Woman's Day," I just cried. It was so true that I could feel it in my bones. The book, you know, was censored by the government, so I removed a tile from the kitchen floor and hid it. When I was in the kitchen by myself, early in the morning, I would read the poem over and over again. It was my private source of strength.'[40]

Another woman, Sanni, describes the Finnish domestics by taking examples from the writings of Minna Canth and Juhani Tervapää. The latter's play *Juurakon Hulda* (Hulda from the Stump District) gave Sanni her inspiration and role model. Hulda was a poor farm girl who took employment as a domestic servant, but through hard work and persistent studying in the middle of the night, she eventually outshone her employers in wit, intelligence and honesty.[41] 'You might be a servant,' said Sanni,'but it doesn't mean you are dumb':

When you can read, a whole new world opens up for you. It doesn't matter where you live, how far from civilization, or in what poverty. Once I got started, I read everything I could get my hands on ... Finnish women are like that Juurakon Hulda, they come from such poor circumstances with nothing in their name, but through hard work and self-education they try to get ahead, find dignity, learn to see beyond their own neighbourhood.[42]

Of course, not all Finnish domestics fit this collective image. Many a woman quietly cried herself to sleep, 'too tired to get a handkerchief.'[43] The image, however, did create a role model of a domestic that Finnish women ought to emulate, and if they reached this goal, if they convinced their friends and the community that they had earned the respect of their employers, they also gained the support and respect of the community. A maid who was not afraid to take the household reins into her hands had high status in her community. Many bizarre stories emerge when women explain that really they were the ones in control in such families as the Molsons, Otises and Masseys. Perhaps the most outrageous comes from a woman who served the widow of a Governor General in Quebec. She discovered that her living quarters on the first floor of the house were infested with rats. Having spent the entire night catching them, she laid the seven fat specimens on the breakfast table.[44]

Within the social hierarchy of the domestics, those who specialized and worked for the 'millionaires' had the highest status within the community. The salaries reflected the experience and the nature of the work, ranging from $15 a month before the First World War and during the twenties to as high as $50 a month. The cooks were at the top of the hierarchy and so too were nursemaids and companions. Chamber-maids, kitchen helpers and 'generals' followed in that order.[45] For women with a Finnish cultural background, domestic service was not necessarily a 'low status occupation.' Furthermore, the maid's own view of her work and the community's response to it might indeed see it as reputable, well paid and even independent work.

'When You Are a Domestic You Are Nothing but a Slave'

While the generally perceived low status of domestic work was not a serious deterrent to the Finnish immigrant women, the demand for submis-
siveness was almost impossible for Finns to meet. The most serious and
persistent complaints came from those domestics who bemoaned their
lack of privacy, their loss of individuality, their sense of being totally controlled by a strange family. Domestics who stayed with the same family
for a long period of time lost their chance to have a family of their own.
Children and husbands were seldom tolerated by the employers. Those
lucky couples who were able to hire themselves out as butler-maid teams
were rare exceptions.[46] Not many husbands were satisfied to have a part-
time wife who was available only every other Sunday and one afternoon
a week, although such 'hidden' marriages did exist. More often, the maid
became an extension of somebody else's family and an integral part of the
daily routines, but not necessarily any part of the emotional life. As years
went by and the maid aged, the chance of ever having a family of her own
became an impossible dream. The exceptionally high age of the women
giving birth in Montreal to illegitimate children – 37.6 in 1936–39 – suggests that some women made a deliberate decision to have a child of their
own while it was still physically possible.[47]

   A Finnish pastor of the Montreal congregation during the late seventies regretted the fate of some of his parishioners, most of whom were
women who had worked as live-in domestics in Montreal during the
twenties and thirties, and now were totally alone.[48] The families did not
provide pensions, nor take much interest in the whereabouts of a retired
maid. To make matters worse, the maid had no family, no home, no life
of her own. 'All my life, I just worked and worked, I seldom went anywhere or met anybody,'remembers one resident of a Vancouver old-age
home, 'and now I know nobody, I am just wondering why God keeps
me alive?'[49] The tremendous personal sacrifices demanded from a reliable domestic, the willingness to become a shadow, a quiet figure in the
corner tending to the household tasks, was described by one maid as
'equal to being buried alive.'[50]

   This sad fate fell on some Finnish domestics, but many others vigorously fought against it. The free time, the precious Wednesday or Thursday afternoon off, when the maid was allowed to exercise her own will,
to be a decision-making person and to meet people of her choice, was
carefully planned in advance. Here the Finnish community was of special help and support.

Community Support

The Finnish communities quickly adjusted to the maid's unusual time schedules in order to have some social activity. Finnish organizations, which until the thirties were largely socialist locals of the Finnish Organization of Canada (FOC), scheduled their social occasions, gymnastics practices, theatre rehearsals and dances during the 'maids day.' The halls kept their doors open so that the maids could relax after their weekly pilgrimage to Eaton's. They could go and have coffee, meet each other, discuss the work situation, find out about new job opportunities and for a few brief hours escape from their employers. The FOC locals were not the only groups vying for the maid's attention. Finnish congregations, especially in Toronto and Montreal, also catered to them, scheduling their services for Wednesday and Sunday evenings and providing social coffees and reading-rooms for the maids.

When the Finnish consul of Canada, Akseli Rauanheimo, tried to convince Canadian industries, railroads and government to contribute to the building of a Finnish immigrant home in Montreal, one of his chief concerns was the welfare of the maids. 'Many of them have nothing to do in their afternoons off except sit alone on park benches.' The home was not only to be used for entertainment, it could also function as a refuge for those women who were mistreated by their employers and who had no other 'home' to go to then.[51] Similarly, such temporary shelters for maids in other major communities were usually provided by those women who ran the maids' employment services.[52] Thus, the Finnish domestics could have a sense of belonging to a community, they could share their work experiences with other domestics, and they knew that if their conditions became intolerable other options were open – they could quit and leave and know that they didn't have to spend the night on the street.

This added to the bargaining power of the Finnish domestics who knew that their services were in demand and who had the means to contact new employers. Most Finnish maids did take advantage of their ability 'to slam the door so that the chandeliers were shaking,' or alternately to 'sneak out of the backdoor so that nobody would notice.' During their first year as domestics in Canada, the women changed jobs frequently. For example, the Finnish immigrant home in Montreal accommodated women who were changing their jobs for the sixth time within a year.[53] Similarly the biographies and interviews concur that at first women took almost any work and then shopped around until a suitable family came along.

The Finnish employment agencies were the key to the domestic's flexibility. They were quick to advise the women not to accept intolerable working conditions. Many enterprising women kept rooms for just such a purpose, and there is every indication that they kept close watch on the 'greenhorns' who were most vulnerable to exploitation. Still, even with a helpful Finnish woman, the hiring was a harrowing experience. Elli remembered it vividly:

The first lady who came picked me up because I was obviously the cheapest and strongest one, she wanted a greenhorn who would work like a dog ... I cried and washed her floors and I was always hungry, but I stayed there for four months until I went back to Mrs. Engman ... She got me a new job right away, but this time I quit after one crazy day, sneaked out secretly ... In my third place I stayed for seven and a half months and was able to demand $35.00 a month, but I quit that place too ... because I had to be home at eleven o'clock and it broke my heart to leave the dances during the intermission and see my good-looking boyfriend stay behind.[54]

As the maids gained confidence in their ability to work, they became more defiant in the work place and often refused to be treated like slaves. Hilja explained:

In one place where I worked the lady started to shout at me because I hadn't got up early enough to do the washing at 6:00 A.M. I told her that nobody shouts at me and I quit. I decided to take that day off and went to stay at Ilomaki's [home for the maids], but as soon as I got there the phone rang for me. It was the employment office calling, they figured that I quit because my lady had called for a new maid. They phoned me to let me know that a new job was already waiting for me. Next day I was working again.[55]

In addition to the private agencies which received payment for every maid they placed, the Finnish Immigrant Home and many churches arranged for employment for the maids. The system was the same kind of 'cattle auction.' Ida remembers that 'the women just stood in a line and the ladies came to pick which one they wanted.'[56] While most Finnish-Canadian sources claim that the Finnish maids were sought-after workers, there were also examples to the contrary: 'There were places that would take only Finns, but there were also places that wouldn't take a Finn for any money. Once I was told bluntly that "We won't hire Finns, because they are all red and stubborn."'[57]
One woman remembers being told to quit singing the 'International'

while washing the kitchen floor. 'I'll sing what I want,' she replied and with that lost her job.[58] Nellie McClung also referred to the reputation of Finnish maids as socialists and trouble-makers.[59] But on the whole the employers were not interested in the private lives of their maids, not to speak of their political opinions, as long as the floors were scrubbed, the laundry washed and the family fed. Edna Ferber vividly describes the family's ignorance of the maid's private world in her short story of a Finnish maid in the United States.[60]

The Class-Conscious Maid

To some Finnish domestics, the availability of work and the supportive networks within the community were not enough. Instead they sought a more elusive goal – a strong collective spirit.

Class consciousness, unlike such characteristics as temper or shyness, is acquired through experience, cultivated by self-study and cemented by daily injustices. Finland was swept by a socialist fervour during the first two decades of the nineteenth century and the question of maids was hotly debated in both the legislature and media. Special homes for maids were established where women could acquire domestic skills. A newspaper, *Palvelijatar* (Maid), discussed at length 'maids rights' and suggested protective measures. The paper's editor, Miina Sillanpää, a Social Democratic member of Parliament since 1907, raised the grievances in the Finnish legislature.[61] Thus it is highly possible that many maids who arrived in North America had already learnt to accept the socialist world-view in Finland.

Because domestic service was the major occupation for Finnish women, it received much attention from the Finnish socialists in North America. The socialist leaders were worried that the live-in domestics would adopt the 'capitalist outlook of their employers when they are clearly an indistinguishable part of the working class.'[62] They were baffled as to how to organize the domestics who were serving thousands of different 'bosses' all over Canada. In the end, the main impetus was placed on raising the individual consciousness, making each maid fight for her own rights within her particular place of employment, while the community would provide her with the best possible support: knowledge, training, cooperative housing and minimum guide-lines for wages and working hours. Unsuccessful efforts at unionizing the maids were also made in major working areas.

The key to bringing the maids into the socialist fold was to give them hope of improved working conditions by frankly discussing the problems and solutions throughout the Finnish North American press. In this the socialist women's newspaper, *Toveritar*, which had over 3,000 subscribers in Canada in 1929, played a vital role.[63] In a special issue for the maids, on May 9, 1916, the editor Selma Jokela-McClone, analysed the situation:

1 While the factory worker is seldom in direct contact with her employer, the maid has personally to face her boss on a daily basis and negotiate her undefined work.
2 A maid is a highly skilled worker, yet she has no possibility to learn her trade before she starts working.
3 Maids do not necessarily work for the big capitalists, many serve the middle class and even the more prosperous working class, which can confuse the issue of class struggle.

To deal with these problems Jokela-McClone suggested that:

1 Because the maid meets her employer as a human being she must have the self-confidence and the sense of self-worth to demand decent human treatment.
2 Maids must become professionals by improving their skills to the utmost of their ability. The key to successful bargaining is the ability to perform well.
3 They must organize maids' clubs, cooperative homes, employment exchanges and raise the class-consciousness of the maids before they can put forth strong demands.[64]

These guide-lines were adopted by Finnish socialist women's groups in Canada, but not without a debate. Many questioned 'the need for special skills,' or the argument that a maid was a professional, or a highly trained worker. There were those who saw the maid as an 'appendix to the parasite class' and not a trustworthy member of the working class. Maids themselves asked what good would training centres or clubs do when the maids didn't have the free time to attend them. Despite the scepticism, attempts were made to implement the plan.[65]

In New York and San Francisco well-organized and highly effective maids' cooperative homes were established. These were seen as a model for other communities to emulate. In Canada the cooperative maids' home movement among the Finns had sporadic support at best. The need for such homes in Canada was partially met by private establishments which provided temporary housing when necessary. The employment exchange for Finnish maids was also in the hands of Finnish women who were generally trusted and reliable, unlike the situation in Manhattan, for example, where several large American agencies 'competed for Finnish maids.'[66] Besides, in 1916, both the United States and Canada were experiencing shortages of domestic servants, 'giving the maids great opportunities to be selective.' In 1922 an article in *Vapaus* concluded that obtaining work was the least of the maids' problems, but rather the inhumanly long working days.[67]

By the mid-1920s, when socialist activity among the Finns had taken a more radical turn toward communism, the question of maids' unions and organizations rose again. This time, the response was at least lukewarm. The first Palvelijatar Yhdistys (Maids' Organization) was founded in Toronto on December 6, 1925.[68] Prior to this the Finnish Organization of Canada's Toronto local had given their Don Hall free of charge for the maids to use on their afternoons off. In 1926 the organization placed a permanent advertisement in the *Telegram* and set up a job exchange at the hall. Later the advertisement was only placed in the paper if someone was in need of work. At times the organization had over twenty paying members and then it seemed to 'go to sleep.' The last time it was 'woken up' was on January 6, 1929, under the name of 'Finnish Domestic Club.'[69] A year earlier the Chinese community of Toronto had established a union of domestic workers at 87 Elizabeth Street complete with an employment exchange. Among the Finns a cooperative home for the maids was discussed, but it never materialized.

In 1927 Vancouver women also decided to establish a cooperative home and employment exchange for the maids. They set up a fund for this purpose, but by the end of 1928 gave up the idea. Instead, they decided to investigate the possibility of joining the existing Domestic Servant's Union, mainly made up of Chinese domestics. Nothing came of this joint venture.[70]

The largest Finnish maids' organizations was established in Montreal, where the need for protection was the greatest since the city was the immediate recipient of all the newly arrived maids coming off the transatlantic steamers. Here a cooperative home was not only discussed but also established in 1930, only to be dissolved within two years by the depression. This home and job exchange was in competition with the Finnish Immigrant Home established by the Consul of Finland and the Seamen's Mission in 1927. From the beginning the housing co-op had over thirty members.[71] In 1928 an article in *Vapaus* pointed out that the city had about 500 Finnish women of whom less than 2 per cent were housewives; the rest were all working as maids or in the service industries. A newly arrived maid might only receive a wage of $20 a month, and the only weapon used by Finnish women to improve their working conditions was to change jobs constantly in search of a better employer.[72] The maids' organization was founded in September 1928 and was quite active. The success of actually getting a cooperative home off the ground was not unbiased because: 'so many of the women who joined up were former members of the workers' organizations and unions in Finland and thus, right from the beginning were able to have experienced, capable women to carry on the cause.'[73]

Similar maids' groups were established in Sudbury in 1928, in Sault Ste. Marie in 1929 and more sporadically in Port Arthur and Timmins during 1928–30. Common to all these maids' organizations was the desire to achieve minimum wage levels. The women in Sault Ste. Marie all swore that they would not 'scab' for lower wages.[74] In Sudbury the maids were keen to establish insurance schemes for the sick and unemployed.[75] In all locations great emphasis was placed on self-education, not in domestic skills, but in class-consciousness and in understanding the role of women in a communist society.

In total, a rough estimate would suggest that about 200 Finnish domestics belonged to the organizations designed for the specific purpose of promoting maids' interests. The small numbers suggest that domestic servants did not have the time or will to give their only afternoon off for meetings, especially since other Finnish women's groups could carry on the task. In northern Ontario the Timmins domestics suggested total integration of women's organizations instead of splintering women into small interest groups.[76] Finnish men 'did not take the organizations seriously,' and the groups were not strong enough to have any concrete impact on wages. 'Despite this,' concludes a published assessment of the maids' organizations, 'they had great impact in making the maids realize that they too were part of the working class and most welcome in socialist circles.'[77]

No matter how good the family you work in, when you are a maid, you are nothing but a slave. I won't be a slave![78]

Domestic service, the greatest employer of Finnish women, clearly had many problems such as long hours, hard work and lack of privacy. Still, it continued to attract Finnish women, at least initially, because of the perceived advantages of room and board and learning the language and customs of the employers. It was also work that Finnish women were able and accustomed to doing, and the pay was sufficient to meet their immediate demands. Women could see considerable upward mobility within the hierarchy of domestic service and could conceivably double their wages within a year. The stigma of low-status work was not very relevant in the Finnish community where most women were, or had been domestics. Furthermore, the number of Finnish maids in the urban centres was great enough to force the community to set up their activities around the maids' schedules, thus lessening the pain of isolation.

While the Finnish communities could claim that many of their maids were class-conscious workers, they did not succeed in establishing long-term unions or cooperative homes. Still, by collectively keeping up their good image, Finnish domestics were some of the highest paid in the country. The more informal arrangements of maids' meeting-rooms, employment exchanges and private 'homes' increased the flexibility of the Finnish domestics and gave them greater bargaining power with the employers. Yet domestic service demanded great personal sacrifices which most women were unwilling to make. As soon as other opportunities presented themselves, Finnish maids left their live-in situations and tried to find more independent work.

NOTES

This article is from *Looking into My Sister's Eyes: An Exploration in Women's History*, ed. Jean Burnet. Toronto: Multicultural History Society of Ontario, 1986. Reprinted with permission.

1 *Vapaus*, 30 May 1922, signed by Adolf Leaf.
2 Ramsay Cook and Wendy Mitchinson (eds.), *The Proper Sphere: Women's Place in Canadian Society* (Toronto, 1976), pp. 172–74.
3 Marilyn J. Barber, 'Below Stairs: The Domestic Servant,' *Material History Bulletin*, No. 19 (Ottawa, 1984); Marilyn Barber, 'The Women Ontario Welcomed: Immigrant Domestics for Ontario Homes, 1870–1930,' *Ontario History*, vol. LXXII, no. 3 (September 1980).
4 Joy Parr, *Labouring Children* (London, 1980); Kenneth Bagnell, *Little Immigrants* (Toronto, 1980); Gail H. Corbett, *Barnado Children in Canada* (Woodview, Ont., 1981).
5 Makeda Silvera, *Silenced* (Toronto, 1983).
6 Ibid., pp. 11–40; Genevieve Leslie, 'Domestic Service in Canada, 1880–1920,' in Janice Acton, Penny Goldsmith and Bonnie Shepard, eds., *Women at Work* (Canadian Women's Educational Press, 1974), pp. 71–125; in 1985 live-in domestic servants are allowed to enter Canada without immigrant status as temporary foreign workers.

184   Varpu Lindström

7 'Emigration from Finland 1893–1944,' New Canadian Immigration Regulations concerning emigration from Scandinavia and Finland, RG 76 vol. 651 C 4682, Public Archives of Canada.
8 *Toveritar* 10 Feb. 1925, poem by Arvo Lindewall.
9 Leslie, 'Domestic Service in Canada,' Table A, p. 72.
10 Barber, 'Below Stairs,' p. 38.
11 The term in Finnish is *piikomaan Amerikkaan*.
12 Dominion of Canada, Report of the Department of Immigration and Colonization for the Fiscal Year ended March 31, 1929.
13 'Finnish Immigrant Home Records,' MG 28 V 128 Vol. 1 File 1.
14 For Montreal figures see Varpu Lindström-Best, 'Finnish Immigrants and the Depression: A Case Study of Montreal,' Ph.D. II paper (York University, 1981) and for information on Toronto see her 'Tailor-Maid: the Finnish Immigrant Community of Toronto before the First World War,' in Robert F. Harney, ed., *Gathering Place: Peoples and Neighbourhoods of Toronto, 1834–1945* (MHSO, 1985).
15 Interviews with Martta Norlen and Mary Syrjälä, Winnipeg, 1983.
16 Census of Canada, 1911, Volume VI, Table I, 'Occupations of the people compared for all of Canada.'
17 Interview with Tyyne Pihlajamäki, Timmins, 1982.
18 Interview with Rolph Koskinen, Parry Sound, 1983.
19 Interview with Helen Tarvainen, Toronto, 1978; see also Joan Sangster, 'Finnish Women in Ontario, 1890–1930,' *Polyphony,* vol. 3, no. 2 (Fall 1981).
20 American Letter Collection, LOIM:IV Letter from Aino Kuparinen, a maid who came to Toronto in 1924.
21 Interview with Lahja Söderberg, Vancouver, 1983.
22 'Scandinavian and Finnish Domestics,' RG 76 Vol. 436 File 654504.
23 Interview with Martta Kujanpää, Toronto, 1978.
24 Interview with Sanni Salmijärvi, Thunder Bay, 1984.
25 Interview with Martta Norlen, Winnipeg, 1983.
26 American Letter Collection, EURA:XXVI Letter from Aino Norkooli, who immigrated to Fort William, Ontario in 1923.
27 Taped recording of Ida Toivonen's reminiscences in Thunder Bay, 1983 and her handwritten notes, both in the author's possession.
28 American Letter Collection, KAR:CXXVI, letter from Sylvia Hakola in Schreiber, Ontario dated 06.09.1926.
29 Carl Ross, 'Finnish American Women in Transition, 1910–1920,' in Michael G. Karni, ed., *Finnish Diaspora II: United States* (MHSO, 1981).
30 For example, see Varpu Lindstöm-Best and Charles M. Sutyla, *Terveisiä Ruusatädiltä: Kanadan suomalaisten ensimmäinen sukupolvi* (Helsinki, 1984), especially the chapter on 'Valokuvaajalla' (At the Photographers), pp. 143–56.

31 Leslie, 'Domestic Work in Canada,' p. 85; *Toveritar*, 20 June 1916, an article explaining why women do not like to be domestic servants.
32 Ulf Beijbom, *Swedes in Chicago*, Studia Historica Upsaliensia XXXVIII, especially pp. 197–98.
33 'Consulate of Finland Correspondence,' MG8 G62 Vol.2, File 59.
34 Interview with Hilja Sihvola, Parry Sound, 1983.
35 Ida Toivonen Recordings, Thunder Bay, 1983.
36 Interview with Lahja Söderberg, Vancouver, 1983.
37 Interview with Helmi Vanhatalo, Sault Ste. Marie, 1981.
38 Nellie L. McClung, *Painted Fires*, was translated into Finnish by Väinö Nyman, *Suomalaistyttö Amerikassa* (Helsinki, 1926).
39 Copies of related correspondence courtesy of J. Donald Wilson.
40 Aku Päiviö poem 'Naisten Päivä.'
41 Juhani Tervapää, (Hella Wuolajoki) *Juurakon Hulda* (Helsinki, 1937).
42 Interview with Sanni Salmijärvi, Thunder Bay, 1984.
43 Interview with Saimi Ranta, Niagara Falls, 1974.
44 Ida Toivonen Recordings, Thunder Bay, 1983.
45 Interview with Rolf Koskinen, Parry Sound, 1983.
46 Butler-maid, cook-chauffeur, etc., combinations were especially popular during the depression when men could not obtain any other kind of work.
47 'St. Michael's Finnish Ev. Lutheran Church,' Province of Quebec Registration of a Live Birth, MG 8 G62 Vol. 7, files 23–25.
48 Discussion with Rev. Markku Suokonautio, Montreal, 1979.
49 Interview with Impi Lehto, Toronto, 1974.
50 Interview with Marrta Huhtala, Waubamik, Ontario, 1983.
51 'Consulate of Finland Correspondence,' MG8 G62 Vol. 2, File 59.
52 In Toronto alone, there were at least twelve women who took in maids and found them jobs on a more or less permanent basis.
53 Immigrant Home Registers for Women list a total of 3,044 women between 1927 and 1931, MG 28 V128 Vol. 6 Files 1–3.
54 Interview with Elli Mäki, Parry Sound, 1984.
55 Interview with Hilja Sihvola, Parry Sound, 1983.
56 Ida Toivonen Recordings.
57 Ibid.
58 Interview with Sanni Salmijärvi, Thunder Bay, 1984.
59 McClung, *Painted Fires*; the heroine is often confused in the novel with a socialist Finnish woman who has the same last name but a reputation as a trouble-maker.
60 Edna Ferber, *Every Other Thursday*, a short story about the life of a Finnish Domestic in New York City.

61 Oma Mäkikossa, *Yhteiskunnalle omistettu elämä: Miina Sillanpään elämän ja työn vaiheita* (Helsinki, 1947).
62 *Toveritar*, 18 Jan. 1916.
63 *Toveritar*, 9 May 1916; see also Varpu Lindström-Best and Allen Seager, '*Toveritar* and the Finnish Canadian Women's Movement 1900–1930,' a paper presented in Frankfurt, West Germany, February 12–15, 1985.
64 *Toveritar*, 9 May 1916.
65 *Toveritar*, 6 June 1916.
66 Ross, 'Finnish American Women,' pp. 239–55.
67 *Vapaus* article, 'Nais palvelijain asema Kanadassa' (The position of female domestics in Canada) was also printed in *Toveritar*, 30 May 1922.
68 *Vapaus*, 6 Dec. 1925.
69 *Vapaus*; 18 Jan. 1926; 26 Jan. 1926; 28 Dec. 1926; 18 Jan. 1927; 29 Jan. 1929.
70 *Vapaus*, 19 June 1926; 07 June 1927; 05 June 1928; 12 Feb. 1929; the organization stopped earlier on Dec. 1928.
71 'Finnish Organization of Canada Correspondence with Montreal,' MG V46 Vol. 11 File 7.
72 *Vapaus*, 15 Aug. 1928.
73 *Vapaus*, 24 Sept. 1928.
74 *Vapaus*, 01 Oct. 1929.
75 *Vapaus*, 29 Jan. 1929.
76 *Vapaus*, 18 Mar. 1930.
77 *Vapaus*, 20 Dec. 1929.
78 Interview with Sanni Salmijärvi, Thunder Bay, 1984.

Abraham's Daughters: Women, Charity, and Power in the Canadian Jewish Community

PAULA J. DRAPER AND JANICE B. KARLINSKY

For I have singled [Abraham] out, that he may instruct his children and his posterity to keep the way of the Lord by doing what is just and right.

(Gen. 18:19)

However important the role of women and their associations has been in Jewish life, being female has translated into powerlessness in the political structure. Jewish women – energetic, skilled and committed as many have been and continue to be – operated on the periphery of the community. Without women, synagogues, schools, hospitals, homes for the aged, fund-raising organizations and representative federations would have been hard pressed to function effectively. Through fund-raising, women provide the bulk of the finances that enable the community to undertake social welfare programs. Yet within these community associations women have generally been barred from the decision-making process.[1]

While an examination of the status of women in Judaism is outside the confines of this study,[2] the relationship between religion and the position of Jewish women within their community structure should be recognized. Traditionally the role played by Jewish women has not differed significantly from the general role of women in Western society. Domesticity controlled women, kept them subservient and restricted their opportunities. Exclusion from education solidified their secondary status. Yet within the European Jewish family structure, women were the undisputed rulers of the household. Although their absence from synagogue-centred ritual activity and their secondary legal status kept them outside the sphere of real power in the community, many Jewish women were the economic as well as spiritual mainstays of their families. Women were delegated responsibility for the moral development of their children and often their economic support while their spouses withdrew to study and pray. But the weight given to the cultural significance of the role of women in the family was deceptive. Religious celebrations were presided over by fathers; male children studied long hours under exclusively male tutelage. The Jewish woman in eastern and central Europe often worked outside the home, her materialistic role always being secondary to but supportive of the male pursuit of spirituality.

In a world which excluded Jews from property ownership, participation in certain trades, political activity and even citizenship, the sphere of Jewish women was necessarily limited. Only with the emancipation of Jews in the eighteenth and nineteenth centuries did Jewish women in western Europe taste liberation. Daughters of the well-to-do benefited from a combination of the Enlightenment and traditional Jewish values which prized education.[3] Indeed Jewish women often surpassed their Gentile sisters in a society which valued intellectual astuteness as a social grace. Many Jewish women quickly overtook their husbands in the race for acculturation, which often led to the conclusion that only conversion to Christianity would enable them to obtain complete acceptance. For however well-educated and freed from household duties upper-class Jews became, strong social and religious barriers remained.

Meanwhile, the growth of the Reform movement in Germany freed Jewish women from many traditional religious restraints. The movement's ideology opposed many of the barriers which limited female participation in religious ceremonies, and efforts to eliminate them began to be implemented.[4] Yet political power in the community eluded women. They were still regarded as enablers who worked for the benefit of husbands and sons; their role remained family centred. Satisfying their own personal psychological need was regarded as selfish, often by men and women alike. It was with this modernized yet still ethnocentric baggage that the first permanent Jewish women settlers arrived in Canada.

As an identifiable ethnic group, Jewish immigrants had a head start in the formation of self-perpetuating community institutions. Unlike most other ethnic groups, they were coming from countries wherein they had always experienced minority status. They arrived with a pre-established minority mentality and frameworks for cultural and religious institutions. The British and German Jews who came to Canadian cities like Toronto in the nineteenth century found a New World in which conversion was not the only means to integration.[5]

Mostly middle class themselves, Jewish women adopted the new perception of religion as a feminine field. Absorbing male-imposed stereotypes, women accepted the notion that their nurturing qualities made them uniquely qualified to relieve suffering. Jewish women had a new vocation, a logical extension of their family role – charity. One of the cardinal precepts of Judaism, the concept of *tzedekah*, or charity, obliged every Jew to give to the less fortunate. Indeed the Hebrew translates as either 'righteousness' or 'justice,' and it has been central to Jewish life from biblical times. Social assistance was institutionalized in European Jewish communities through charity boxes, soup kitchens, the giving of clothing and burial societies. Boxes were circulated in homes, in the synagogue, in the cemetery – wherever Jews assembled. Taxes for relief of the poor were often levied on communities in order to care for orphans, the sick, handicapped and aged, to school the poor and provide low-interest or interest-free loans. This central theme of Jewish life, previously dominated by men, now tied Jewish women into the widening female sphere. The relative wealth and high degree of acculturation of Jews from western Europe allowed for rapid adjustment to New-World feminine ambitions, just as it reinforced their fear of any threat to their integration into Canadian life.

Women of the Jewish establishment were fuelled by a desire to Canadianize the new immigrants from eastern Europe. Yet they failed in their attempts to make these new Canadian Jews over in their own image. Indeed, by 1920 the character of Canadian Jewry had been completely transformed. Anti-Semitism intensified and the position of Jews in Canada suffered irreparable damage. Jews strove to succeed in Canada but found with each advance that growing anti-Semitic sentiment curtailed their prospects and hindered their assimilation.

The community turned inward, and women became essential participants in blossoming communal organizations. Jewish women enthusiastically took over the philanthropic demands of Jewish life. They created Ladies Hebrew Benevolent Societies. Charity as an extension of home duties became a way of life for a whole generation. But since the devotion of Jewish women to social welfare work could not overcome the traditional male dominance of benevolent and communal associations, they soon moved to create their own. In so doing, the militant social reformers of the turn of the century became 'professional volunteers.'

The unique nature of each major women's organization resulted from its ability to fulfill the particular social needs, language, religious and political orientation of its members. The first such Canadian women's organization, the Nation Council of Jewish Women (NCJW), was formed in 1897 in Toronto, just four years after its establishment in the United States.[6] At the American organizing conference, the religious justification for this new sphere of women's work was clarified. 'All Israel suffers in the degradation of its poor,' stated an organizer. 'Woman is the Messiah come to deliver them from their second bondage of ignorance and misery. She is the educator, the reformer, and the reward of her labor will be the evolution of a nobler race of worthy citizens and respected members of society.'

The National Council of Jewish Women was devoted to religious philanthropic and educational activities considered to be female pursuits. NCJW volunteers served the larger community through the provision of schooling, scholarships, orphanages, recreation and summer camps for children and working girls, childrens' libraries, scientific research and clubs for the aged. During the Second World War services were provided for both Jewish and non-Jewish servicemen, mobile blood donor clinics were established, and bundles sent to Britain. Postwar activities saw this volunteer sector extend its programs from social welfare and immigrant and refugee absorption to contemporary Jewish affairs, social legislation and even international affairs. Throughout its history, however, the NCJW has remained an association of women, not particularly feminist-oriented, with as its basis the principle of charity as women's work.

For first-generation western European Jewish immigrant women, social reform was a revolutionary and fulfilling role. For their daughters in the 1920s – the professional volunteers – self-esteem and a sense of career were equally rewarding. But the 1930s saw a narrowing of their activities as paid professionals, most of them male, took over the social action aspects of their work and left them with the grass-roots tasks of organizing and fund-raising. Middle-class Jewish women, who neither needed nor sought employment, discovered themselves relegated to organizations which began to operate as female social clubs. Postwar options with the Jewish communal structure were increasingly limited, while higher education for women and the decline of anti-Semitism opened new doors in secular Canadian society.

While Jewish immigrants from western Europe and their daughters followed a pattern of community work best exemplified by the activities of the National Council of Jewish Women, their eastern European sisters organized their own groups. Indeed the creation of social service work as a field for women resulted from an urgent societal need.

The Toronto chapter of the Zionist Hadassah organization was established in 1917 by women who had settled in Canada in the 1880s and 1890s. These women and their daughters had risen into the ranks of the middle class yet saw themselves as worlds apart from the acculturated, North-American educated and leisured National Council women. Hadassah was founded by the daughter of a Baltimore rabbi, Henrietta Szold. After visiting Palestine in 1909 she became a determined advocate of the provision of modern health care for the peoples of Palestine. Her intelligence and indomitable spirit inspired thousands of Jewish women to focus on the concerns of building a Jewish state as an outlet for their talents. Within the Zionist Movement, however, the women of Hadassah were often referred to as 'diaper Zionists.' They had to struggle to maintain a separate voice, a voice which they expressed through control and allocation of the funds they raised.

While the NCJW concentrated its work for the benefit of Canadian Jewry, Hadassah focused on the creation of a Jewish homeland in Palestine. Hadassah had no particular ideological bent; its concerns were directed at the provision of social services, particularly health care, to Jews in the Holy Land. Hadassah's stated principle was that: 'Women understand the art of healing, and nation building is only an abstraction.'[7] Motivated solely by benevolence, Hadassah members gave no formal recognition to the important political and social role of Jewish women in the rebuilding of the Jewish homeland.

This was not the case for a third segment of Canadian Jewish women. Immigrant working-class women – Yiddish-speaking, politicized and religiously unaffiliated – joined the Pioneer Women's Organization (PWO),[8] a left-wing Zionist group affiliated with the Labour Zionist (Poale Zion) movement.[9] These women came from backgrounds that rendered them socially and philosophically unsuited for membership in organizations composed of the wives of their husbands' bosses. In eastern Europe their mothers laboured with their fathers in small family businesses. Modern liberal thought spurred many youths to trade traditional Judaism for equally fervent beliefs in socialism and political Zionism. They turned their backs on Judaism but not on Jewishness. Many secular Jews observed Jewish holidays and kept kosher as a means of maintaining their commitment to Jewish culture and peoplehood. Education acted as a catalyst. One Pioneer Woman explained: 'Books lit my mind on fire. Herzl and Marx made me think about my life and the life of the Jews. They made me so mad that we had waited so long and suffered so much. I got many ideas and became free of religion.'[10]

Many future Pioneer Women were involved with formal Zionist and socialist organizations in Europe. Socialism showed them the dignity of labour; Zionism pointed to labour as the means for cultural, social and economic redemption of the Jews as a nation. They became infused with new expectations of participating in the task of nation-building. They carried these expectations to Canada.

Arrival in Canada often meant the end of formal schooling for immigrant women. Many worked in factories or cared for their children, finding little time and energy to attend English classes. Yiddish remained their primary language and for this reason many shied away from joining English-speaking groups, like Hadassah. Likewise, they would not consider joining secular organizations for they maintained strong ties to Jewish culture if not religious observance. Canadian experience, especially with trade unionism, further distanced these women from pre-existing Jewish organizations. So they joined the Labour Zionist Movement, which had been formed in 1904. This male-dominated orga-

nization raised money for Palestine, supported the activities of organized labour in Toronto and sponsored social and educational activities
for its membership. By 1925 women in the movement had become dis-
illusioned by their exclusion from its political process. Encouraged by
the success of other women's organizations, the women created the
Pioneer Women's Organization (PWO). Its purpose was to educate children in the Labour Zionist tradition and promote women's participation
in building the Jewish state. The PWO became the most ideologically
based Jewish women's organization in North America. Its founding
members felt part of an historic event in women's history. This feeling is
reflected in the preamble to its constitution:

The Jewish woman who occupies so distinguished a place in the life of our people has a great mission to fulfill in this period of our national rebirth and the
reconstruction of Palestine ... as part of the Jewish people, which suffers most,
she has the high duty to place herself in the front ranks of a great movement for
the rehabilitation of our national, cultural and political life.[11]

The formation of the PWO was in direct response to the exclusion of
women from power in the Labour Zionist Movement rather than the
urge to fulfill a feminine role. 'We felt like second-class citizens,' one
member recalled.[12] 'Major decisions were made by men, women weren't
consulted ... They didn't think women capable of making political decisions.'[13] Once the split was effected, however, Pioneer Women pursued
a truly feminist goal: becoming the first Jewish women's group, outside
Palestine,[14] to focus on the role of women. Funds raised by the PWO
were to go to help women and children in Palestine and to raise the cultural level of women in Canada so they could make more valuable contributions to Jewish life. Through the PWO, women would finally have
the opportunity to enter the front ranks of the Zionist movement. For
the next twenty-five years, the PWO grew in membership, including
English-speaking second-generation women, and it played a vital part
in the creation of the Jewish state.

Two generations of women joined the PWO in Toronto. The initial
members were inspired by the early women's movement and political
enfranchisement. They were also searching for personal fulfillment.
'Homemaking is very important and dignified work,' wrote an early
American member, 'but homemaking alone for these women who had a
revolutionary background with its keen interest in humanity, that was
not enough for them ... In our organization, these women found their

place and an opportunity for self-expression.'[15] The women who joined the PWO in its formative years wanted both to benefit others and derive recognition from the community. The PWO offered them a role which neither synagogues, male-dominated organizations, the NCJW, nor Hadassah could. One women explained that: 'I once attended a Hadassah meeting. But, coming here, being a greenie, I felt out of place. Hadassah didn't suit me socially. Maybe they were too big for me, I mean rich.'[16] In the PWO Yiddish language and cultural values were shared, and meetings were held in evenings or on weekends, so working women and those with small children could attend.[17]

The Second World War and the virtual end to eastern European immigration to Canada limited traditional sources of PWO membership just as the needs to raise funds for Jews in Palestine intensified. The organization looked to their daughters. Most of these women had participated in youth groups run by the Poale Zion and were familiar with the ideology and organizational life of Labour Zionism. They became a new and dynamic element in the PWO, for they had lived with the ideology since birth.

In 1939 a new chapter was formed comprising fourteen women who had grown up together within the Labour Zionist Movement. Most had married men from the same backgrounds. 'Everything we did revolved around the Labour Zionist movement,' explained one early member. 'We were so tightly knit that if we came to a dance with someone who was not in the movement, we were boycotted by the other Young Poale Zion members ... We used to tell each other who to date.'[18] The movement shaped their politics as well. 'We were very idealistic, and very dedicated to the Labour Zionist principles.'[19] These principles also shaped their view of secular Jewish life. 'We never felt the need to join synagogues or temples. Belonging to the movement gave us our fulfillment.'[20] In short, they joined the Pioneer Women because to do otherwise would have been an unnatural break with family and friends. Membership allowed them to continue their way of life, to work as a team and perhaps an extended family – with their parents, husbands and friends – for Labour Zionism and its ideals. It represented the vehicle through which they could become formally involved in a social and political group that represented their interest in the public sphere.

By the late 1940s the PWO had once again reached a plateau in its growth. Fortunately, its desire to attract still more members coincided with an increased interest on the part of Jewish women in joining Zionist organizations in light of the formation of the State of Israel. Although new members were often the same age as existing members, one women explained: 'I never had anything to do with Labour Zionism till I joined the PWO. I never knew anything like that existed.'[21] Some of the new members had been in Hadassah in other cities; some were from orthodox religious families, and others were the daughters of Jews from England who had little or no Yiddish cultural background. They were all there because they wanted to work for Israel. 'After the Holocaust, how could we not work for Israel? Working for Israel became very important.'[22] Yet these women were not Labour Zionists. Their social activities took place outside the Labour Zionist milieu. They were affiliated with synagogues and did not socialize with other PWO members outside of meetings. One old-timer complained that 'after they joined, it just wasn't the same; I think everybody felt that.'[23]

The Holocaust and the creation of Israel caused a major shift in ideology and attitude for all North American Jewry. Old-World ties were destroyed and a new identity, focused on political nationhood, began to take shape. For those women not willing to re-establish themselves in Israel, Zionist organizations offered an avenue for expression of new concerns. Few new members carried on a family tradition of Zionist or political activity. The PWO offered a chance for socializing with friends while fulfilling the traditional charitable function, nothing more. Despite the fact that the cohesion of the PWO suffered, the new members were vital to the organization. Without them, it could not have raised as much money for Israel.

What the PWO did not lose sight of were its feminist goals. From its inception, it laid emphasis on the need to increase women's political and social awareness in Palestine and North America. Articles it published, such as 'The Progress of Working Women in the Depression,' 'International Women's Movement' and the 'Housewife and the Histadruth,' were intended to generate women's interest in 'raising the economic, social and cultural level of Jewish women.'[24] Although the Pioneer Women in Toronto did not consciously design their program with these goals in mind (this was the rhetoric of the leaders, not the rank and file), the women understood, as one member protested, that 'men didn't know everything and shouldn't do everything in Palestine.'[25] They understood that women had an important part to play in the building of the Jewish state and that the PWO was working to equip women to do their share, whether in North America or in Palestine.

Through its practical program, the PWO encouraged women to think about things beyond their homes and families. While many members 'were not consciously thinking about raising the level of women,'[26] they believed that they succeeded in doing so. One women explained: 'The PWO succeeded in raising the Jewish women up a little more. When you're a Pioneer Woman, and you go and think about your people, that makes you more than just a plain woman that sits at home.'[27] The Toronto Pioneer Women also participated in the annual celebration of International Women's Day. While they did not take seriously the requests by national leaders to 'identify with the women's movement throughout the world,'[28] they did feel a strong bond with women in Palestine. One member vividly recalled, 'Years ago we didn't talk so much about women's rights and equality. At that time we had one aim – to help build Israel and help the women there to live and work.'[29]

One activity managed to bridge the gap between ideology and practical programing – fund-raising. Money collected would shape the experience of women in Palestine and assist in national self-realization. The first generation of Pioneer Women took their financial responsibility to Palestine very seriously and raised money in every way they could. In the beginning, no matter what the weather was like, they canvassed door to door to collect coins to fill their assigned quotas. Although the average contribution was fifty cents, they persisted year after year and sometimes they were especially fortunate. As one woman recalled: 'We went to one man; he asked us if we had a cheque book. I said we have receipts for 25¢, 50¢ and $1.00. He said I need a cheque, so my partner ran to get him one. The man donated thirty dollars! We nearly went crazy. We started to dance in the streets.'[30]

The Pioneer Women were aggressive fund-raisers. One woman had a particularly effective scheme: 'I used to go to one chicken dealer and show him the receipt from the other. He'd have to match the donation to save his face.'[31] Sometimes the women's enthusiasm got them into awkward situations:

I once went collecting with a friend. One woman I went to, she knew I had bad feet and it was hard for me to climb the stairs to her place. Well, I got there and she said 'I'm not giving you any money.' So my friend gave her hell and she called the police. Later the PWO told us we shouldn't insult people.[32]

Working class and often poor themselves, Pioneer Women actually displayed great compassion and understanding while canvassing:

Once I went collecting and the woman at the home was old and sick. I said to her, we're out for house collection for women and children in Palestine. She gave me two pennies. My heart was aching. She was so poor, I thought to give her money instead, but I didn't want to hurt her feelings.[33]

Other schemes included selling light bulbs and oranges and donating a day's wages or selling baked goods.

Fund-raising was also done collectively. The PWO's largest undertaking was its annual bazaar, preparations for which were elaborate and time consuming. They baked hundreds of pieces of gefilte fish and other delicacies for the food stand and collected saleable goods from generous businessmen. One bazaar was barely over before preparations began for the next. Other annual projects included teas, Hannukah parties and Passover celebrations. Women would prepare food and plays to entertain their guests who in turn were expected to make donations. When representatives of the Moetzet Hapoalot (a Palestinian women's organization) came to Toronto, the PWO charged admission to their lectures. In 1929 the most famous member of Moetzet Hapoalot, Golda Meir, brought in six hundred dollars for the Toronto branch.[34]

The PWO gave its members many things in return for their devotion, including confidence in group dynamics. Besides fund-raising techniques, women learned organizational skills. One member recalled how 'women came in raw, took positions and learned how to be organizers.' Commenting on the members' increasing ease as public speakers, she further explained that 'I learned how to get up at a meeting and talk.'[35] The PWO also gave its members 'something to believe in, something to live for'[36] outside of their families and homes. Involvement in the organization gave them purpose and meaning. In return they received recognition from the community and praise from their families. 'My children are so proud,' said one member, 'that I don't sit around and play cards all day.'[37] Through meetings and special programs many women, denied secular education in their youth, were now able to learn. The educational activities of the PWO made information from the English-language newspapers accessible to women who could not read English, kept women informed about important issues and expanded women's knowledge of Palestine and the world. Women who were recent immigrants relied heavily on the PWO to satisfy their thirst for knowledge:

The greenies needed the PWO very much. Speakers, seminars was their way to understand what was going on. They couldn't read a newspaper and they didn't go much to the movies and things like that. They couldn't afford it. There wasn't much things for them to do except for the Pioneer Women.[38]

At local and national conventions women heard a variety of prominent speakers and exchanged ideas with women from across North America. Conventions also prepared women for leadership roles through exposure to organizational structure and procedure.

For first- and second-generation immigrant members in particular, the PWO was a formative and progressive experience. 'To me,' explained one women, 'the Pioneer Women's Organization was very important. I lived out my life there, socially and politically. All my activities were there. I knew no other life.'[39] Yet changes in membership, the PWO's consistent relegation to a female and, therefore, secondary role in the Zionist movement in Canada and the new political reality which followed the creation of the Jewish state moved the organization away from its roots and gradually destroyed its appeal.

Ironically, the establishment of Israel brought a crisis of ideology which has never been overcome. Some Pioneer Women did take up the challenge and emigrate. This was, of course, the logical conclusion to a program which focused on supporting women in state-building by establishing day-care facilities and training women for agriculture and industry. The ideals which differentiated Pioneer Women from other voluntary associations, however, were disappearing. Israel replaced the Yiddish secular culture (which was destroyed by the Holocaust) as a source of Jewish identification. Zionism, originally a political and nationalist ideology for creating a state, became a philosophy for support, largely financial, of Israel. The PWO no longer enjoyed a monopoly on Zionist passion. Meanwhile the membership had slowly moved into the middle class, and they had lost interest in the problems of working women. Its feminist dimension was quickly dissipating. Concerns shifted to children, their welfare and education in Israel. Yet the most devastating shift in ideology was the loss of socialist commitment. Although their pro-labour sympathies were unaltered, Pioneer Women were often no longer working and their children were becoming professionals. The creation of a Jewish state in which Labour Zionist principles played a major role, the increasing preponderance of Jews in the middle class and the increase in government sanctioned welfare legislation and unionism dissipated socialist fervour. With the winding down of the socialist component, the transformation of Zionism into a synonym for Jewishness and the devaluation of its feminist dimension, the PWO was in danger of losing its identity and its appeal.

The PWO was truly pioneer. It was the first Zionist women's group to separate from a male-dominated organization. It actively supported political causes long before other Jewish womens' groups did. Rather than depending on the established Jewish community or the NCJW, the PWO taught immigrant women that they had organizational skills and talents, encouraged a distinctly feminist outlook and fostered public speaking and political awareness among them.

Today the PWO appears to be an association which has lost its ideology and, therefore, its prestige. It has become a social club, a female ghetto whose previous functions have been taken over by the Jewish state. Yet its problems seem to be tied to the basic issue of women's powerlessness in the Jewish community.

Women took over the voluntary aspects of Jewish life and made significant contributions to its qualities, yet they were taken for granted. Women, and therefore volunteerism, have not been held in high esteem. Women have remained subservient in every sphere of Jewish life while providing the enthusiasm and funding to maintain its structural base. Meanwhile presidents of women's associations run multi-million dollar budgets and organize huge networks of regional groups.[40] Yet they are seldom given access to the ladder leading to communal decision-making. Historically, that power has been kept in the hands of perhaps 16–20 men in large urban centres – successful and wealthy businessmen and professionals in their sixties and seventies.[41] With only a few exceptions, the Jewish establishment in cities like Toronto has always been completely male. Likewise, in community organizations composed of men and women, virtually all important decision-making positions are monopolized by wealthy men.[42]

In 1975 – the UN International Women's Year – a female member of the National Executive of the Canadian Jewish Congress (CJC) noted that only sixteen of the 116 members of Canadian Jewry's governing body were women and that that imbalance was perpetuated nationwide at every level of the community. She advised that immediate steps be taken to rectify this injustice.[43]

In 1983 at the Congress Plenary Session, a women's workshop was forced on the organizers and, despite omission from the program, on the last day of the Plenary, 300 people packed the room to listen to speakers attack discrimination against women by the Jewish religious and political establishment. A survey vividly demonstrated under-representation in positions of power by women in both the volunteer and paid sec-tors.[44] On May 5, 1985 a women's workshop, 'Involving Women in the Political Process,' was presented at the Canadian Jewish Congress's Ontario regional conference. Women were urged to utilize their experience as organizers to achieve positions of power. The obstacles to overcome – to remove wealth as a prerequisite for power and to convince men to step aside – were no small tasks.

Jewish women, their perceptions altered by the feminist movement and increasingly professional, no longer see voluntary work in feminine ghettos as viable expressions of their Jewish commitment. If Canadian Jewry is to survive, the community must redefine the role of women. Neither can their traditional roles be minimized or overlooked.[45] As a former president of the Toronto chapter of the NCJW wrote in her book *Three Cheers of Volunteers*:

Women are responsible for a great wave of compassionate action. The weak, the fallen, the aged, the young, the sick, and the lonely are all benefiting from the deeds of women. Without women, much that is planned would never be realized, and much that is dreamed would never come into being.[46]

NOTES

This article is from *Looking into My Sister's Eyes: An Exploration in Women's History*, ed. Jean Burnet. Toronto: Multicultural History Society of Ontario, 1986. Reprinted with permission.

1 For an examination of the role of Jewish women in the United States see June Sochen, 'Some Observations on the Role of American Jewish Women as Communal Volunteers,' in *American Jewish History* 70; no. 1 (September 1980), pp. 23–34.
2 For recent evaluations of the role of women in Judaism see: Charlotte Baum, Paula Hyman, and Sonya Michel, *The Jewish Woman in America* (New York: Plume Books, 1977); Susannah Heschel, ed., *On Being A Jewish Feminist* (New York: Schocken Books, 1983); Elizabeth Koltun, ed., *The Jewish Woman. New Perspectives* (New York: Schocken Books, 1976) and Sally Priesand, *Judaism and the New Woman* (New York: Behrman House, 1975).
3 For in-depth studies of the effects of emancipation and the Enlightenment on European Jewry see Jacob Katz, *Out of the Ghetto* (Cambridge: Harvard University Press, 1973) and Michael Meyer, *The Origins of the Modern Jew* (Detroit: Wayne State University Press, 1967).
4 For the effects of the Reform movement on Jewish women see Ellen Uman-

sky, 'Women in Judaism: From the Reform Movement to Contemporary Jewish Religious Feminism' in Rosemary Ruether, and Eleanor McLaughlin, eds., *Women of Spirit. Female Leadership in the Jewish and Christian Traditions* (New York: Simon and Shuster, 1979).

5 Early Jewish life in Toronto is examined in Stephen A. Speisman, *The Jews of Toronto* (Toronto: McClelland and Stewart, 1979).

6 See Ethel Vineburg, *The History of the National Council of Jewish Women* (Montreal: National Council of Jewish Women, 1967).

7 Hadassah Organization of Canada, *Hadassah Jubilee Book* (Canada: 1927), p. 131.

8 This examination of the Pioneer Women's Organization is based on Janice B. Karlinsky, 'The Pioneer Women's Organization: A Case Study of Jewish Women in Toronto' (M.A. thesis, University of Toronto, 1979).

9 By the end of World War One many different brands of political Zionism had evolved. Labour Zionists (also known as the Poale Zion or Socialist-Zionists) shared the conviction that Jewish national redemption could not be separated from the movements aiming at the liberation of oppressed classes in all nations. They adapted Marxist determination to the General Zionist slogan: 'If you will it, it is no dream' by explaining the establishment of a Jewish state as the inevitable result of the Jewish proletariat's search for a base from which to conduct the class struggle. The new Jewish state would give rise to a cooperative socialist society built by Jewish labour.

10 Karlinsky, 'The Pioneer Women's Organization,' p. 19.

11 *Pioneer Woman* (New York), March 1927.

12 Karlinsky, 'The Pioneer Women's Organization,' p. 49.

13 Women in the Poale Zion in the United States faced the same problem: 'We were ... active *chaveras* [members], but as usual, it was our male comrades who did all the planning ... We merely helped.' Recollections of a founding member in *Pioneer Woman* (New York), October 1945.

14 The Moetzet Hapoalot was the women's branch of the Histadrut in Palestine, also a Labour Zionist group. This became the PWO's sister organization and funds raised in North America supported their projects.

15 *Pioneer Woman* (New York), November 1945.

16 Karlinsky, 'The Pioneer Women's Organization,' p. 104.

17 The daytime scheduling of events and meetings by Jewish women's organizations has once again become a significant factor, causing membership to remain dominated by middle-aged, leisured women as increasing numbers of young women remain in the work-force after marriage and children.

18 Karlinsky, 'The Pioneer Women's Organization,' p. 119.

19 Ibid.

20 Ibid.
21 Ibid., p. 124.
22 Ibid., p. 125.
23 Ibid., p. 127.
24 *Pioneer Woman* (New York), February 1934, December 1935, December 1936, March 1927.
25 Karlinsky, 'The Pioneer Women's Organization,' p. 111.
26 Ibid., p. 112.
27 Ibid.
28 Ibid.
29 Ibid.
30 Ibid., p. 113.
31 Ibid.
32 Ibid.
33 Ibid., p. 114.
34 Ibid., p. 115.
35 Ibid.
36 Ibid.
37 Ibid., p. 116.
38 Ibid., p. 117.
39 Ibid., p. 118.
40 See Sochen, 'Some Observations on the Role of American Jewish Women.'
41 See Waller, 'Power in the Jewish Community.'
42 For a discussion of the situation of Jewish women in a North American perspective see Amy Stone, 'The Jewish Establishment is not an Equal Opportunity Employer,' in *Lilith* 1, no. 4 (Fall/Winter 1977–78).
43 Dorothy Reitman, 'What are the Roles CJC Women are Playing?' in *Congress Bulletin*, September 1975.
44 Telephone conversation with Judy Feld Carr, 25 April 1985; *Canadian Jewish News*, 5 May 1983, p. 5.
45 For further discussion of the historical background of Canadian Jewish women see Paula J. Draper, 'The Role of Canadian Jewish Women in Historical Perspective,' in E. Lipsitz, ed., *Canadian Jewish Women of Today. Who's Who of Canadian Jewish Women, 1983* (Toronto: J.E.S.L. Educational Products, 1983), pp. 3–10.
46 Ruth Hartman Frankel, *Three Cheers for Volunteers* (Toronto: Clarke and Irwin, 1965), p. 15.

TOPIC FIVE
Men without Women: 'Bachelor' Workers and Gendered Identities

Throughout the early twentieth century, Canada's official immigration policy remained agriculturalist in orientation. Yet these years also witnessed the arrival of thousands of immigrants from Europe and Asia who did not settle on the land. Alongside the flow of agriculturalists who entered Canada before 1930 were two parallel streams of immigrants whose labour was also much in demand: female domestic servants and industrial male workers. This section considers the latter group, namely, the non-British foreign-born men who filled the ranks of Canada's industrial proletariat during the late nineteenth and early twentieth centuries.

The significant presence of Chinese and central and southern European workers in such large-scale enterprises as railway, mining, and logging reflected the influence of employers and investors in Canada's resource and transportation industries, who were keen to recruit large pools of low-skilled, seasonal, and comparatively cheap labour. By the early 1900s tens of thousands of men were involved in completing two new transcontinental railroads, building numerous colonization roads into remote but mineral-rich regions, and double-tracking the main line of the Canadian Pacific Railway. The racial–ethnic diversity of the labour force, where Canadian, British, and non-British workers toiled in the same workplaces, was a distinguishing feature of these workplaces. Slavic and Italian workers could be found in the coal mines of western Canada; Finns, Poles, Ukrainians, and Italians diversified the workgangs of northern Ontario's lumber, gold-mining, and railway camps; and Chinese labourers gave the British Columbia railway navvy a distinctly Asian face. By 1911 close to 60 per cent of mine workers in Canada were immigrants; in the Rocky Mountain coal-mining regions of

British Columbia and Alberta, their proportion reached 88 per cent. These worksites were also distinguished by highly exploitative class relations, risky and dangerous jobs, and low and insecure wages. Immigrant workers also confronted middlemen (both immigrant and Canadian) who extracted money for various services rendered. Far from being merely passive pawns of industrial capitalism, however, the immigrant recruits had their own reasons for enduring such harsh conditions. They also sought to protect their manly pride or create 'bachelor' communities amid a usually hostile environment.

As the readings demonstrate, despite their diverse origins, continental European and Asian immigrant industrial workers in Canada shared many similar experiences. Whether fathers or sons of families left behind, these men were largely low-skilled rural villagers with little formal education, and they were expected to tolerate low wages and poor working and living conditions in Canada's industrial hinterlands. These men often lived and worked in largely gender-exclusive surroundings, physically and emotionally separated from women. 'Men without women' is how Robert Harney describes the Italian male sojourners who came to Canada before the Second World War. These men migrated abroad temporarily in order to earn wages to augment dwindling farm family incomes, and they intended to return home once their objectives were met. However, in the case of the Chinese men whom Anthony Chan studies, the condition of gender exclusivity was imposed upon them. Severe anti-Chinese sentiment and, later, government-introduced head taxes on Chinese admissions meant that many Chinese labourers were unwilling or unable to bring their family members to Canada. Married men with wives and children back home were thus formed de facto 'bachelor' immigrant workers in Canada. Nancy Forestell shows how prevailing assumptions about proper gender roles, as reflected in government legislation that prohibited female employment in the mines, ensured the male exclusivity of mining work in the Porcupine district of northern Ontario. In this way the town of Timmins was born a 'bachelors' town,' virtually by government decree.

If the readings share the theme 'men without women,' they also share the theme 'men not alone.' Living in overcrowded bunkies or boarding-houses, these labourers forged what Forestell calls a 'homosocial working class culture.' Beyond the workplace, their lives revolved around such same-gender activities as gambling, sports, and drinking. (Some men also engaged in same-sex practices.) Though frequently illegal, these various activities could offer necessary relief and help to nurture a male culture. However, as Harney observes, the absence of women and children in the workcamps, the brutal conditions of the work world (where both filth and filthy language could prevail), and the easy accessibility of diversions (such as drink and prostitutes) that quickly drained away a man's wages and destroyed his family's dreams also constantly threatened to transform the migrant into a 'brute' and a failure. By the same token, though, as the essays by Chan and Forestell suggest, even when lone men acted as model migrants, contemporary racist and anti-immigrant stereotypes of foreign men could unfairly lead outsiders to dismiss all-male immigrant communities as threatening and degrading places.

The essays combine a discussion of the recruitment of immigrant workers and their experiences. What factors best explain the heavy reliance of Canadian industrialists on 'foreign' labour? Why did the Canadian government permit the admission of immigrants into Canada who did not fit the ideal portrait of the rural homesteader? How have the various authors calculated the physical, emotional, and psychological effects of the remote and almost exclusively same-sex environment on the men under study? What was the nature of the limited male–female contact that did take place in and around the work camps? What can we say about the women left behind in the towns and villages of Europe and Asia? Did those women continue to influence the male sojourner abroad? Finally, how did the racial–ethnic diversity of these male work worlds affect labour solidarity and working-class culture in these locales?

BIBLIOGRAPHY AND SUGGESTED READINGS

Avery, Donald. *'Dangerous Foreigners': European Immigrant Workers and Labour Radicalism in Canada, 1896–1932*. Toronto 1979.
– *Reluctant Host: Canada's Response to Immigrant Workers, 1896–1994*. Toronto 1995.
Bradwin, Edmund. *The Bunkhouse Man: A Study of Work and Pay in the Camps of Canada, 1903–1914*. Toronto 1972.
Chan, Anthony. *Gold Mountain: The Chinese in the New World*. Vancouver 1983.
Dubinsky, Karen. *Improper Advances: Rape and Heterosexual Conflict in Ontario, 1880–1929*. Chicago 1993.
Harney, Robert F. 'Boarding and Belonging: Thoughts on Sojourner Institutions,' *Urban History Review* 2 (1978): 8–37.

- 'Montreal's King of Italian Labour: A Case Study of Padronism,' *Labour/Le Travail* 4 (1979): 57–84.
Li, Peter. *The Chinese in Canada*. Toronto 1988.
Morton, James. *In the Sea of Sterile Mountains: The Chinese in British Columbia*. Vancouver 1974.
Radforth, Ian. *Bushworkers and Bosses: Logging in Northern Ontario 1900–1980*. Toronto 1985.
Roy, Patricia. *A White Man's Province: British Columbia Politicians and Chinese and Japanese Immigrants, 1858–1914*. Vancouver 1989.
Zaslow, Morris. *The Opening of the Canadian North, 1870–1914*. Toronto 1971.

Men without Women: Italian Migrants in Canada, 1885–1930

ROBERT F. HARNEY

In July of 1908, the lead article of the *Rivista di Emigrazione* described emigration as the 'greatest social phenomenon of our epoch whether one is speaking of the demographic impact on the country, its economy, its moral condition, levels of criminality, state of public health, in fact, of any aspect of the people's life.'[1] Since that time, both in countries of emigration and in immigrant-receiving countries, historians have created a rich literature about migration's demographic and economic impact. From Robert Foerster's *Italian Emigration of Our Times* (1919) to recent studies of remittances and *ritornati*, we have been shown the way in which emigration affected class structure in the Italian South.[2] Much less has been said of emigration's impact on the people's morale.

The reasons for this silence are numerous. Having seen the damage wrought first by racists and restrictionists, and then by a few insensitive social scientists, the historian is disinclined to emphasize the disruptive and pathological aspects of migrating. It is far safer to describe migration as simply the first step in the journey to assimilation or as an orderly advance by means of which families and villages adjust traditions in order to maintain their commonweal.[3] However, not since the turn-of-the-century debate on emigration in Italy which generated writings like those of Fortunato, Nitti, Pasquale Villari, Adolfo Rossi, Amy Bernardy, and Leonello De Nobili has the Italian migrant himself been at the centre of study.[4]

In the *inchieste*, polemics, and studies concerning these writers, the abnormality of leaving one's home place and the caprice of the world economy which moved men about was demonstrated. Such writers understood that the social history of the European agrotown or village was one with that of the history and vicissitudes of the migrants in North America. Somewhere that integrity of view has been lost. Preoccupied with issues of assimilation, the North American historian has worked within a framework which limited debate to questions of uprootedness and persistence of ethnicity. The sojourner's physical commitment to the place from whence he came needs to be considered.

This essay concentrates on the Italian emigrant as a man of his family and of his *paese* (agrotown or village). It suggests that his intentions when he began his sojourn in North America defined whether or not the length of his stay caused extraordinary stress on him and also on those he had left behind. For, just as the hometown remained at the centre of his concern, so the migrant retained his place in the social organization of the village or in the inheritance structure and plans for the family. The debate over the role of nuclear and extended families in South Italian life is tedious, but all would agree that family members were expected to suppress their indivualism and to work for what Constance Cronin had labelled a synthetic person, the family.[5] Such a view of the family is not, of course, uniquely Italian. The family as a functioning economic until occurs in most rural and pre-industrial settings. Boguslav Galeski puts the point most simply: 'For the rural family is a collective producer, sometimes also a collective entrepreneur and common owner of a small plot.'[6]

The decision to migrate, then, was not usually made by the individual, particularly not if he was a young man: 'The actual decision itself is thrashed out in the nuclear family.'[7] (The corollary would be that the decision to end a sojourn abroad will also not be the result of individual decision). In fact, the migrant, like the cash remittances and the *ritornati*, was a constantly accounted-for unit of the family and town which he left behind.[8]

The mayor of a small town in Basilicata informed a parliamentary committee in 1907 that 'the population [of his town] was 2400 souls of whom about 600 were in America.' At first glance that is an extraordinary view to take of the fact that one quarter of the population, and probably at least half of the productive men and boys, were residing in foreign lands.[9] But the mayor did not see those men as future Canadians, Americans, or Argentinians. They remained in his mind the husbands, sons, fiancés, and fathers of the women in his town. In this essay, we try to share the mayor's perspective. The role of the migrants as cheap foreign labour and potential Canadian or American citizens has been studied; their role as wage earners and sources of 'cash money' for the Italian South is receiving more attention now. Here we look at the impact of emigration on family life, on morals, health, and the state of mind of the migrant and his people.

Italian critics of emigration felt that it engendered that most pompous and portentous of Italian crimes, *'delitti contro il buon costume e l'ordine delle famiglie.'*[10] Perhaps if we look more closely at the personal and family issues raised by migration, we can see what truth lay in that charge. The so-called 'target migrant' – the man who goes abroad or to the city in search of cash money for a specific family objective – expects certain things of his sojourn away from the village and plans to be away for a certain amount of time. In turn, his family and dependents expect certain things of him and have at least a rough estimate, based on local folk wisdom, of how long it should take him to achieve these objectives.[11] Obviously, a sojourn which goes beyond the customary time causes anxiety for all involved. The daughter awaiting a dowry, the empty conjugal bed, the aging parent, or just a Mediterranean spring missed – all put pressure upon the migrant. In this essay we will be dealing with migrants betrayed, thwarted in their schedule by the Canadian economy, by dishonest men, and by harsh winters. The betrayal turned seasonal migration into long-term sojourning and turned momentary success in achieving the financial goal of migration into new depths of indebtedness. Unexpectedly long separation brought disruption and perhaps some of the social pathology which the critics of emigration feared.

How long could commitment to family obligations survive the great distance and increasing time that lay between the sojourner and his origins? One Lithuanian who came as a migrant to Canada in the 1920s told me that when he returned to Vilnius after fifty years in Canada, he went immediately to his sister in order to apologize for failing to send her dowry money to her a half-century earlier.[12] Did young migrants from Calabria have a less filial or familial sense of duty than that?

A tradition of happy endings has grown up to obscure the disruption and pain caused by long sojourning abroad. The *ritornato*, the rich *cafone*, the *Americano* with the diamond stickpin who returns to buy the land that he once sharecropped and to marry the girl of his dreams or take up with the wife whom he has not seen for many years – both the latter as virginal as when he left for America – is migration study's version of the Western melodrama.[13] In the same genre, of course, are the happy vineyard owners who send to Italy for brides who have been fluttering expectantly for many years: 'In his absence, members of the extended family or clan will provide protection and supervision for his immediate family. He can return at any time, assured of a physical home, a social niche and at least some income.'[14] How does that sanguine view of the modern migrant correspond to De Nobili's survey of Calabria in 1907? 'Adulteries, infanticides, and vendettas are the order of the day – manifestations of that abnormal social state brought on by emigration and the consequent disequilibrium of the sexes.' One critic clearly understood the difference between inheriting the earth and losing one's soul: 'The country is covered with houses, the houses of the new landowners, but from their houses and those of the former owners is banished an ancient heritage and an ancient nobility – the moral integrity of the *focolaio*.'[15] The same cash money which confused and brought mobility to the social and cadastral structure also deeply affected family structure.[16] However, the physical absence of the migrant himself, especially if it was unexpectedly prolonged, ravaged any dream of a well-ordered future for South Italian families. It changed the distribution of inheritances, the meaning of marriage alliances, and the feelings of people toward one another.

Canada had a higher percentage of 'target migrants' in its Italian immigration after 1900 than the United States did. There were sound economic reasons for that, but there was also terribly fraudulent advertising of work and exploitation of migrants, so Canada also had a very high percentage of seasonal and 'target migrants' trapped into longer sojourns. The gap between the intention of the sojourner and his fate seems particularly great when one looks back at Canada in the 1900s. In that sense, it becomes an especially fruitful setting for the study of the impact of long-term sojourning.

One reason that Canada had more migrants and fewer immigrants than the United States was that neither the Dominion nor the Italian government encouraged settlers from Italy. The Italian Commissariat of Emigration issued several *bollettini* on conditions in Canada which pointed out that the country was not suitable for colonizing except by wealthy peasants. In 1901, the Italian consul in Montreal went so far as to fault 'the lightheartedness with which the Canadian government seeks to people the desert plain of the Dominion.' He concluded that Canada was no place for 'experiments with our peasantry.'[17] Nor did Sifton, the Dominion's powerful Minister of the Interior, view Italians as useful immigrants.[18] So the climate of opinion was as frigid as the climate itself. Nonetheless, a well organized system of seasonal migration to Canada developed at the beginning of the century.[19] Before World War I, thousands of Italian labourers, particularly from Calabria, the Abruzzi, Basilicata, and Friuli were induced to migrate to Canada. There is little doubt that most of those who came through the network fit the definition of 'target migrants.' They came intending brief sojourns, usually hoping for a summer's work in the railway, timbering, and mining camps of the Canadian North.[20]

False newspaper reports were printed in Montreal and distributed throughout Calabria. Workers were led out of Italy overland through Chiasso and Switzerland and then on to the Channel ports and England where they made the crossing on Cunard, CP, and Beaver Lines ships. They were escorted by a variety of sinister labour and travel agents, and so they reached Canada much in the manner of migrants travelling with a foreman to seasonal work on the European continent. Solimbergo, the Italian consul in Montreal, 'found out that of all Italian emigrants who were already in Canada not one thought it of any use to become a colonial ... the emigrants are going to Canada in order to find work.'[21] At first the seasonal work offered by the great Canadian labour-intensive employers such as the railroad, mining, and lumber companies served the interests of the target migrants well.[22] Struggle for control of the labour pool, though, led to dislocation in the system. Every year a certain number of seasonal migrants became a winter residue in the country. In some years, for example, 1901 and 1904, simply too many migrants were brought over.

Men who had come for single 'campaigns' found that crooked bankers, foremen, boardinghouse keepers, and late thaws made it impossible to hold to their family and community schedule for migration.[23] The same commerce of migration which made the system efficient and drew the target migrants, also led to cutthroat competition between *padroni* and dishonest labour bureaux. That in turn led to imbalances in the labour supply and lost time for the migrants. In 1901, a correspondent for the *Corriere della Sera* accompanied a group – 'almost entirely young men, representing the best portion of our country population of the South.' He soon learned how the system could fail the target migrant and his family plans. His group was met in Montreal, where they had been promised work, by agents of the Donnor Emigration Company, which had sponsored their crossing. The migrants were told that they could only have work in British Columbia. Most had no idea where that was. 'Those who refused the terms were abandoned. Those that remain here,' he went on, 'seek to house themselves as best they can. Many found their way into different houses, and when it came to paying were driven into the streets as they had no money, their belongings having previously been retained.'[24]

Canadian immigration statistics are virtually useless for the study of return flows to Italy, so it is difficult to estimate the number of migrants caught in the country each year as winter approached.[25] If a man did not get home at season's end, it was quite likely that he would not do so for another year, and perhaps many more. The boardinghouses were run by *padroni*, the camp commissaries were exorbitant and dishonest, and there was little or no work for foreigners in the winter except city snow removal. Some were lucky and found factory work or steady work in street railway construction; many others never escaped the seasonal cycle of work and consequently found their sojourn becoming a form of exile.[26]

It is a truism of migration studies that people who reared themselves as sojourners, regardless of how long they dwell in a host country, continue to think of the problems and needs of their home town as paramount.[27] Translated into national assimilation measurements, the same idea is expressed in Eisenstadt's statement that 'the analysis of the immigrant's motive for migration and his consequent "image" of the new country is not of historical interest alone, but is also of crucial importance for understanding his initial attitudes and behaviour in his new setting.'[28] If it is true that the sojourner was preoccupied with what he had left behind, then we should study him not just as an urban problem or a potentially assimilable immigrant, but also in his own existential frame of reference. Italian migrants were, first and foremost, men away from loved ones and familiar places. They were men entrusted with responsibilities who sensed the proximity of failure, usually failure to bring family levels of existence into harmony with rising expectations. They were men with the increase and natural suspicion that things would not be, indeed could not possibly be, as they should be when and if they managed to get back home.[29] The abnormality of their own existence had to have, they thought, its mirror image in the *paese*.

This essay speculates on the impact of separation and uncertainty on the sojourner. It does not matter whether each migrant eventually became a rich and respected *ritornato* with many children and a Fascist party card, or sent for a wife and became part of the Italian-Canadian bourgeoisie. Any seasonal or 'target migrant' who did not return after the first season slipped into an abnormal existence; so did the people left behind.

One reason historians have shied away from studying the turn of the century in terms of migration disruption is distrust of the sources. We do not have much chance to employ the survey and interviewing techniques used by the anthropologists and sociologists who study contemporary migration.[30] Only bits of oral history material survive, along with risky inferences from migration statistics, to suggest the migrant's real frame of mind. What we are left with is the very suspect literature of those opposed to emigration in Italy and of the missionaries, social workers, and restrictionists in North America. Obviously, with such sources it is too easy to paint a picture of emigration and the migrant's life as pathological. What follows is not a vindication of such literature, but the modest suggestion that it makes sense to think of the man separated from his people as being in an abnormal situation and to use the questions raised by the anti-immigrant literature to propose avenues of research.

We know the economic consequence of the migrant's commitment to his hometown – that willingness to be crowded in cheap boarding-houses, to depend on *padroni*, to show little interest in the host country, and to risk no 'cash money' on North American situations. Now we must look at the migrant's frame of mind itself. Let us begin with his hometown world which concerns him so much. His failure to return after a season's work may have been eased by remittances (although more often than not, it was lack of funds which made him stay in Canada). Then, too, there are things money can't buy. If he was a young man, the girl of his choice may not have waited. If he was a father and a husband, he worried about the virtue of his womenfolk.

Anti-emigration literature concentrated on the impact of sojourning on sexual morality. As migration increased, there apparently was an increase in cuckolding and bastardy in the Italian countryside, as there was of prostitution in the cities.[31] Giuseppe Scalidi, writing about Calabria in 1905, claimed an absolute correlation between emigration rates and the increase of *'delitti contro il buon costume e l'ordine delle famiglie.'* Another moral opponent of emigration put it more bluntly: 'It is a sad fact but one well known to everyone who knows the regions of heavy migration that the wives and fiancées of the "Americani" take the place of prostitutes.' In fact, in a grand analogy to the *commercio di carne umana* which exploited the menfolk, the author goes on to describe such women as ignorant, inexperienced, and improverished, who sadly *'si gettano nel grande mercato della carne femminile.'*[32]

What is one to make of such evidence? Obviously such writers believed that emigration caused massive social disruption. Their writing also reflected an old Mediterranean assumption that healthy people left alone copulate, and that women particularly are helpless in the face of temptation. 'Modesty is not natural in women but imposed on them (Il pudore è atteggiamento più coattivo che spontaneo della donna). The emigration of men, fathers, brothers, husbands, lovers, eliminates the coercion and lets natural and unbridled instincts emerge.'[33] The author's view of women and their instincts was primitive, but one can wonder whether it was more so than that of the young, under-educated, rural men and jealous husbands who were the migrants themselves. Moreover, one can also assume that, among men thrown together in work gangs, camps, and boardinghouses, such a view of women became accentuated. The coarse jokes, thwarted young appetites, the dreams of women left behind and inaccessible women seen in the host country, the banter about *cornuti*, the fragmentary news from home, all colluded to paint a picture of the hometown which would increase the migrant's tension.[34] The reality of the impact of migration on the countryside hardly mattered as much as the imaginations of those abroad in causing tension and misunderstanding.

It is unlikely that simply the absence of men would destroy the inbred, umbertine, and Catholic values of most peasant women. Moreover, few towns or families were so completely decimated by migration that some older guardian of the family's good name was not about to cluck over impropriety:

Even the logistics are impossible. Overpopulation is not conducive to trysts. When husband and wife share their room, often their bed, with their children, and grandmother sleeps just the other side of the partition, it is hard to have a private fight, let alone arrange a secret meeting. On the few occasions when the street is empty there is always an old woman peering through the cracks in her 'dutch' door. Empty fields do not exist ... Where becomes almost unsolvable.[35]

So the possibilities of family disintegration, cuckolding, and dishonour haunted men whose sojourn grew uncontrollably and the phantom that lived with them was, at least in part, created by fear and guilt about how well they were fulfilling family obligations.

Of course, not all the migrants had the same social and familial stress upon them. Many young men had only limited responsibility and had in some sense been ejected from the family inheritance structure with a cash settlement which paid their fare in the New World. (If, however, they were beyond puberty, they might already have had the pressure from a potential bride and the need to meet the property conditions of forming a new nuclear family.) Nonetheless, some young men clearly fit Osborne's category of 'escaping' rural migrants,[36] and many married men had become such multiple migrants that they managed to return once a year, beget children, settle family affairs, and thus mitigate the burden of uncertainty that came with long-term sojourning.[37]

All sojourners were under some pressure and the Commissariat of Emigration doctors saw that as a cause of insanity in *ritornati*:

Il disagio economico, l'ansia della ricerca del meglio, la preoccupazione dell'ignoto, associati allo strapazzo fisico alle privazioni alle fatiche e disagi de ogni sorta e in fine assai de frequente alle delusioni piu amare, sono il doloroso fardello che di solito accompagna l'emigrante nella sua odissea.[38]

There is no need for us to believe that large numbers of men buckled completely under such pressure in order to make the case for the abnormal life style of migrants.[39] One index of the charges which came with leaving the village was the degree to which one could conceive of and practice marital infidelity or be promiscuous.

The Italian critics of emigration, just like racist restrictionists in North America, saw the male sojourner as a dangerous and amoral beast preying upon North American women. The fear and jealousy of the sexual prowess of strangers along with an almost colour racism against Italian bachelors makes it impossible to study this aspect of the migrant's life through the layers of prejudice in North American sources. For example, Toronto's local muckracking newspaper, *Jack Canuck*, carried lurid accounts of Italian labourers having carnal knowledge of young girls and infecting them.[40]

Years ago, Robert Forester remarked that 'plenty of testimony exists to show that loose living on the part of male Italians abroad is common. Our witnesses, who are generally also critics, affirm that there is often a ready frequenting of prostitutes, a class of persons all but absent from the Italian countryside and village.'[41] Perhaps the Italian literature deserves more attention since it has no racist edge. The critics of emigration, as umbertine Italian gentlemen, held the rather simple physical and ecological view of sex which we spoke of when dealing with the family without its menfolk. Illicit sex would take place if physical and social barriers were not erected against it. To the critics, the migrants abroad were men with the barriers removed. They would be unfaithful to wives and fiancées. They would spend in bordellos money earned for a sister's dowry or saved for a few *tomoli* of land. So,

... freed from sexual control ... which long habit and religious anathema hurled against the flesh by the clergy enforced, that the physical exhaustion of their bodies, the jealousy of the wives, and the ferocious surveillance of the gossipy village also enforced ...

they would run amok, especially when they encountered the flirtatious American women and the free atmosphere of cities. Perhaps with an insight only possible for a conservative, the same critics remarked that this phenomenon which happened to migrants in North America was an exact analogy to the decline of respect for property.[42] The corollary was that America's negative moral and physical impact on Italy could be shown by detailing the rising incidence of madness, alcoholism, syphilis, and tuberculosis in areas of heaviest emigration.[43]

No doubt travelling only with other males produced an earthy camaraderie typical of a peasant work force. Whatever the culture or education of the sojourners, life in isolated work camps brutalized them in the truest sense of the word. Men became *bestie* (brutish) under the impact of conditions, and work camp life in Canada was usually worse than in the United States.[44]

The decline into brutishness which took place was not one into unbridled sexuality. The workers were too isolated, tired, frugal, and the host society too prejudiced against them for moral decline to take that form. Rather, the failure came in terms of personal dignity, outward appearance, language, and manner. The process enabled North American racists to remark that such conditions could only be imposed on victims who were 'the sons of backward civilization and know not what twentieth-century living is.'[45]

Interviews with men who were young migrants in those isolated camps refer over and over to becoming *bestie*, to feeling inadequate and inferior not just to the Anglo-Celtic Canadians but to city folk generally.

Men came to feel like the *forese*, 'the man who lives *fuori*,' those too poor and brutish to live in a nucleated agrotown, the unclean, impoverished shepherds and others who held their head downcast when they entered town, 'and in the face of *stranieri*, nearly always more educated and civil than they, felt themselves humiliated by their ignorance, as men and as Italians.'[46]

They were men who had not eaten anything but stew on mouldy bread and sardines for months on end, and had only eaten in the company of other men. They were men who were 'deprived of the refining influences of women and the soothing touch of childhood.' And their decline was not just in concern for their physical appearance:

Camp life is an unnatural life, and in it the coarse, vulgar elements of human nature come to the surface; the indecent story, the vulgar joke and the immoral picture are introduced and passed around. If intoxicants are within reach, the men will drink and gamble.[47]

The quote may have the speech rhythm of a born-again preacher or Salvation Army sergeant, but there is no reason to doubt its essential truth.

In general, the brutalization of foreign migrant workers was worst in the most isolated settings. Even in those settings, though, controls existed to keep them from the immorality and sexuality which the critics in Italy assumed. First of all, the very system which drew 'target migrants' to Canada kept them in groups based upon their *paese*. Employment of sub-bosses, foremen, and *agenti* from each *paese* was the way in which the large-scale *padroni* in Montreal and Toronto used *campanilismo* to advantage.[48]

This meant that often the eyes of the village followed the migrant into the remotest setting. If a man became a drunkard, consorted with the rare prostitutes to be found in the North, dabbed in perversion, or just seemed to go a little crazy, word might get back to the family and town. (It would be interesting to be able to show that those who were not 'target migrants' but 'rural escape migrants' or immigrants fell away from scrutiny first.) As the modern students of rural-urban migration put it, 'rural norms and customs are most likely to be obtained precisely among those who plan to return home in the foreseeable future.'[49] The other powerful force which kept most of the 'sins against chastity' of the migrants at the level of fantasy was the deep prejudice toward them among their hosts. Literature about 'dirty foreign navvies' abounds and would seem to imply that the migrants were unlikely to find female

companionship among the natives easily or without a price.[50] A quotation about those who left the labour camps for the city has more bravado
than historical detail:

However, Toronto had little appeal for the young, rugged, Italian labourers
without families. There were no enjoyments, no drinks during the week, and
few girls. Montreal had all that. It was the centre of attraction for Italians who
came from the west. Instead of facing a dull winter in Toronto they pushed on to
the gay port city.[51]

The story was much more one of demeaning assaults on manhood by
the natives and the constant fear of getting into trouble for offending
Anglo-Saxon custom. This plus lack of confidence and langauge difficulties impelled the migrant toward the lowest classes of female companionship or left him at the level of vain flirtation and coarse inference:

Down below there was more noise than it is possible to describe. Everyone was
busy preparing his bed or sleeping. Five or six were running and throwing potatoes at each other. Two German girls sleeping in the same compartment were
obliged to leave shortly after owing to the stupid remarks by two Calabresi who
were in the vicinity.[52]

'Stupid remarks' – the innocence of it rings true – from the first rejection
of attention on the boat to the veteran *ritornato* who 'came back to marry
– no women in America, *ostia* – las'time I wer six year in America, work
in backwood, for two year never see a woman.'[53] The abnormality of life
for the migrants came not from promiscuity but from total physical and
cultural frustration. The same was probably true for the vast majority of
women left behind in the *paese*. Perhaps the substitutions were just as
debilitating for the family structure. Commissionaires in most camps
sold alcohol. The U.S. Industrial Commission of 1901 claimed that
unemployed Italians spent 'almost all the idle time ... in the saloons and
in other resorts of their countrymen,' a strange new image for an abste-
mious wine-drinking people and one, as we have seen, that the critics of
emigration in Italy had been quick to notice.[54]

In the long run, the same combination of external and internalized
social coercion which guarded the *villagio pettegolo*, 'the gossipy village,'
existed in the migrant camps. The backbiting *paisano* or solicitous relative, the hostile women of the host society, combined with levels of filial
piety, parental duty, and morality in the migrant to serve as a brake on

his decline into brutishness. He might drink more, he might find a prostitute, he certainly became coarser and more vulgar than he had been when he left Italy, but he probably had not broken faith with the commitments which had sent him forth. He still worked to send money home for specific purposes; he still intended to marry someone from his *paese* (most often someone whom he or his family had chosen before he left), or to return to his wife.

Each migrant seems to have measured time differently according either to his nature, or to the original purpose of his sojourn, and to the situation in his town or origin. To the extent, though, that migration was a form of suspended animation, the sojourn had no time dimension. If a young man were a bachelor, he was held between youth and manhood in regard to marriage, inheritance, and indeed to carrying weight with family and *paesani*. Oral history interviews with immigrants from half-a-dozen countries show that what Arensberg said of the Irish countrymen held true in most rural communities. 'The "boy" reaches adult status when he marries and inherits the farm. The family and the land are both involved in the crucial reorganization.'[55] Young men who had married but had no children before they migrated were often just like bachelors. Their counsel was worth little, and until they had saved money to start a household, would not increase in value. Their absence was a temporary solution to problems of space and fecundity even if the larger problem of owning arable land could only be solved by a long and successful sojourn. Fathers of families worried more; they had more that could go awry or dishonour them at home. For all these men seasonal migration, repeated trips across the oceans, and even accepting immigration were options; the degree to which they entertained each option was entangled with their fortunes in America and the nature of news from home. Out of that cluster of concern emerged the real measurement of each man's sojourn time.[56]

If a man escaped the confined world of labour camps in summer and large *padrone*-owned boardinghouses[57] in winter and still had not found means to return to Italy or continued to have a 'target' need for cash, he might begin to look for a change to become *bordante*[58] in one of the larger cities with a family from his *paese*. This meant that some of his job transience had declined and usually coincided with the transition to city street work or factory work.[59] The value of the system to husband and wife was obvious. It provided sheltered work at home which enabled her to continue her economic role in the family. The increase in the atmosphere of *civile e gentile* for the migrant *bordante* was also obvious, but what did the system of *convivenza* mean for the moral life of the migrant and for the maintainance of his commitments to his village of origin?

In the first place, if each good-sized Little Italy was a combination of many little *paese*, the little *paese* broke down further into houses where families took in *paesani* and relatives. Historians have long known this, but have not thought about these homes as outriders of the goals and mores of the *paese*. It is through the households and neighbourhoods that 'the high proportion of temporary migrants ... often associated with large numbers of apparently "broken" or "incomplete" families and of people living with friends and relatives rather than their nuclear family'[60] began the process of reasserting the social controls of the village and some of the original goals of migration. The Italian Mission (Methodist) in Toronto, 1908, complained that 'there are so many home-less men in this community it makes it necessary for every woman to accommodate as many boarders as she can crowd into her house.'[61]

Moving from camps and working-class hotels to live with families did not just reflect the emergence of job opportunities in the city. The price of home-cooked food and family chatter, clean clothes and a safe mailing address was that migrants themselves had to clean up, to overcome cafonism, and to make conversation without constant vulgarity. In the city, living with families or visiting families from the *paese* on Sundays marked either the settling-in for a long sojourn or the beginnings of thinking about true immigration. Married men had been unable to envisage their womenfolk living near most non-urban Canadian work sites.[62] Becoming *bordante* also meant that the decline into brutishness and the constant but idle chatter about sex ended. The family with whom one boarded, particularly *la padrona*, might know the boarder's family as well as his commitments at home and his dreams. Often the lady of the house had her own dream of playing matchmaker. If the *bordante* was not betrothed or married, there was invariably a niece of the household who could be sent for as a bride. In such simple human terms the needs of the old country family and of the *paese* itself were served. No one who boarded with a landlady from his own village had much chance of being either promiscuous or exogamous.

Often the lady of the house was as young as the youngest boarders, but if they were *paesani*, they most likely addressed her as *zia* (auntie). Respect, recognition of her connection with the Old World family structure, and a guarantee of propriety were all in the use of the word auntie.[63]

Probably that proximity to the occasion of sin which so exercized the critics of emigration came into play occasionally between *la padrona* and the *bordante*, although in the home as in the village and camp, the problem of *where* remained complex. The chance arrival of husbands, children, neighbours, other boarders, visiting city nurses, water meter readers, settlement house workers, and Methodist missionaries could make a farce of the most passionate scenario. The central actors themselves also made passionate scenarios unlikely. Whether from morality and familial honour or a good sense of status and self-preservation, trysts were not likely. Amy Bernardy, one of the most insightful of Italian travellers, in her address to the first Congress of Overseas Italians at the Campidoglio, claimed that she could not speak in a language fit for a congress about the fruits of the *promiscua servitù* which the system of *convivenza* imposed on Italian women in North America,[64] but that was merely rhetoric.

Short of a survey or a statistical analysis, we may never know how effective the safeguards against the 'near occasion of sin' were. Certainly good order in a home with boarders had something to do with the immediacy of kinship and hometown ties between the boarder and the family. The word *paesano* is quite misleading in this context, since being Calabrese together hardly constituted a strict relationship with social safeguards built in. On the other hand, being from Cosenza and related by marriage obviously imposed reciprocal obligations.

There obviously were cases of hanky-panky, but how many? A social worker at Central Neighbourhood House in Toronto reported that 'a child came with a story of immoral relations between mother and one of the boarders. Case investigated – Reported to Juvenile Court.' Of fourteen other Italian social cases that day, all others refer to problems of health or rents; of four Anglo-Canadian cases, one was a fourteen-year-old 'living an immoral life' and a second was a husband's desertion.[65] It is difficult to draw conclusions about the effect of an abnormal and transient lifestyle on Italian peasants from such material. Certainly there are no suggestions of even the practical promiscuity of the *zadruga* system among South Slavs, and certainly none of the sly humour which exists in the Hungarian–American concept of the 'star boarder' could have developed among Italians if it is true that the first purpose of accepting boarders was to find women work where there was no threat to chastity.

At any rate, the social and moral structures of the *villagio pettegolo* which had been weakened but never vanished in the all-male work camps recovered in the city's Little Italy. The Rev. Taglialatela, Methodist colporteur to the Italians of Toronto, saw social abnormality in transience itself: 'They are not under the eyes of their friends and relatives and do not feel obliged to look better and act well.' He, of course, thought that they had improved with time in the city; perhaps the sense of the *paese* and its controls simply reasserted itself through family and campanilist density.[66]

Vecoli's 'Contadini in Chicago,' a decade ago, noted the crucial place of the family in Little Italies: 'If the South Italian retained a sense of belongingness with his fellow townsmen the family continued to be the focus of most intense loyalties.'[67] The point, I think, could be pushed further. Just as the village or agrotown was a collectivity of families, so potentially were the *colonie* of the *paese* in North America. A migrant or sojourner was at all times within the system whether as a potential *ritornato* or as a colonist of the new *piccolo paese*. He was also at all times a member of a family, nuclear and extended. In fact, families – new ones, old ones, broken ones, potential ones in the form of young sojourners, girls awaiting dowries, husbands, fiancées, sons with insufficient inherited land, fathers toiling abroad so that family status kept pace with fecundity – were the impelling cause of migration.

Remittances made one economic world of the village and the many faraway lands where there were migrants sojourning. In the same way, families and neighbours in the New World reimposed the social coercion, jealousies, and affectionate familiarity of the *paese*:

Most of the Cinisari in the 69th St. group intend to return to Sicily. The town of Cinisi is forever in their minds: 'I wonder if I can get back in time for the next crop? ... I hope I can get back in time for the festa ...' They receive mail keeping them informed as to the most minute details and about all gossip that goes on in Cinisi; in addition, they keep their hometown informed as to what is going on here. They write home of people here who have transgressed home custom: 'So and so had married an American girl. The American girls are libertines. The boy is very disobedient.' He has married a stranger ... that is, an Italian of another town. In this way they blacken a man's name in Cinisi so that a bad reputation awaits him on his return.[68]

We have long known about this pattern of contact between a specific *paese* and a specific part of some American city. The instances of it are very numerous.[69] Such networks of communication and transit existed between most towns of emigration and their *colonie*, but perhaps we have spent too much time looking at the remittances or prepaid tickets which were the chief items transmitted through the communication system. 'Cash money' was rarely the end purpose of 'target migration.' Settlement of family or land questions almost always was. The abnormality of the migrant condition came, as we have seen, not from decline into boorishness or unbridled sexuality, but from the suspended animation in matters of marriage, sex, and inheritance which came with separation. The logical end of sojourning was either creation of a new nuclear family or reconstitution and completion of one. This could come about by 'going home,' sending for a wife or bethrothed, or marrying endogamously in the new land.[70] Whatever the solution, the real messages carried along the communications network were the details of family life:

In the old country there is no such thing as a person not married; every men he is born when he is little, he grow up he marry, then a little while and he die. I never hear of no person not marry in old country.[71]

Different cultures obviously have different tolerance levels about bachelorhood and different proper ages for marriage. It is difficult to say how much the tradition of migration affected such cultural predispositions. Certainly inheritance systems affected the age of marriage more. The ethnic groups who provided the shock troops for turn-of-the-century industrialization – Italians, Hungarians, Greeks, South Slavs, Poles, Lithuanians, Finns, and Chinese – all had tremendous imbalances of male over female in the sex ratio of their migration statistics. And the boardinghouse stereotypes of rowdiness, insobriety, ignorance of English, and transience persist to one degree or another about all these groups, but perhaps less so about the Italians than the others.

While most Italian communities in North America have a few old unmarried 'uncles' and *cafoni* who are the fossils of that earlier abnormal life style, Italian culture has not been tolerant of bachelorhood.[72] Then too, despite the difficulty of U.S. and Canadian quotas and of Facism, the *paese* to *piccolo paese* communications network which carried gossip, matchmaking, and prepaid tickets was fully interrupted only briefly during World War II. Unmarried sojourners alone or in groups were always whittled away by that family and village desire to make the future by creating new nuclear families.

If immigration was a matter of intention and attitude rather than duration of sojourn, one is tempted to suggest that true immigration did not really commence until the questions of marriage and inheritance

were settled. A migrant's search was ended when he had fulfilled his
target, but his target was almost always to live a normal life, i.e., married life, among his own kind, somewhere in the psychical world of his
paesani where he could make a living.

The ideas in this essay owe more to ethnologists and students of
developing nations than to historians. This is fitting, because the study
of sojourners should be centred on the people themselves. Moreover,
their commitment to the *paese* may come as close as one can to 'ethnicity'
defining daily existence. Sex ratios in migration and other statistical
tools provide a rough correlation to migrant intentions, but folk truth,
acquired from the 'memory culture' of the former migrants themselves,
is a more useful guide to the sojourner's frame of mind.[73]

The real history of the sojourners and of Canadian Little Italies will
only be within our reach when all the possible archival and statistical
sources are used along with the 'memory culture.' Church records, minutes of *mutuo soccorso* and other benevolent societies, stub books of payment, receipts and remittances from immigrant banks, and the sparse
records of *paese* clubs are the internal ethnic sources we need to use.
Photographs and city directory analysis also help to show the place of
the migrants and *bordanti* in the birth of a *paese*'s colony.[74]

Much of this essay should be read as a plea and perhaps an agenda for
further study – study of the villages and towns of emigration and study
of the migrant's mind set as a key to his North American experience.
Until studies of such topics as changes in marriage and betrothal patterns, cuckolding, alcoholism, mental problems among *ritornati*, endog-
amy rates among sojourners, and a myriad of attitudinal and cultural
subjects are done, plausible constructs such as this essay provide our
glimpse of the men who entered Canada in the 1900s.

We have at least been freed from seeing every man in North America
as somewhere on a scale of assimilation. The work was begun by those
who realized that the migrant was not 'uprooted' and those who,
through 'return flow' rates and study of remittances, saw the economic
consequence of families and towns reaching out across the ocean for
survival or improvement. What we must do now is study more closely
the preoccupation with family and status which was the motive behind
world-wide search for 'cash money.' If we do so, I am sure that we will
discover new and useful perspectives about emigration, about ethnic
persistence and identity, as well as about the pace of assimilation. Historians, like the migrants, may take courage from some verses of a poet
from my *paese*, Robert Frost, who writes in *Wilful Homing*:

Since he means to come to a
door he will come to a door
Although so compromised of aim and rate
He may fumble wide of the knob a
    yard or more,
And to those concerned he may seem
    a little late.

NOTES

This article is from *The Italian Immigrant Woman in North America*, ed. Betty Boyd Caroli, Robert F. Harney, and Lydio F. Tomasi. Toronto: Multicultural History Society of Ontario, 1978. Reprinted with permission.

1 Leonello De Nobili, 'L'Emigrazione in Calabria. Effetti dell'emigrazione in generale,' *Revista di Emigrazione* 1:5 (July, 1908).
2 R. Foerster, *Italian Emigration of Our Time* (Harvard, 1918). See F. Cerase, *L'Emigrazione di Ritorno* (Rome, 1971); Betty Boyd Caroli, *Italian Repatriation for the U.S., 1900–1941* (New York, 1973); T. Saloutos, *They Remember America* (Berkeley, 1956).
3 O. Handlin, *The Uprooted* (New York, 1951), and John Baxevanis, *Economy and Population Movements in the Peloponnesus of Greece* (Athens, 1971).
4 See, for example, F.S. Nitti, *Scritti sulla questione meridionale* (Bari, 1959); Amy Bernardy, *Italia randagia attraverso gli Stati Uniti* (Torino, 1913); G. Fortunato, *Il Mezzogiorno e lo stato italiano, Discorsi politici, 1880–1910* (Bari, 1911); A. Rossi, 'Vantaggi e danni dell'emig. nel mezzogiorno d'Italia. Note de un viaggio fatto in Basilicata e in Calabria del R. Commissario dell'emigrazione,' *Bollettino dell'Emigrazione* Anno 1908 No. 13; D. Taruffi, L. De Nobili, and C. Lori, *La questone agraria e l'emigrazione in Calabria* (1907).
5 C. Cronin, *The Sting of Change: Sicilians in Sicily and Austria* (Chicago, 1970), pp. 85–89. C. Ware, *Greenwich Village, 1920–1930*, p. 197: 'A child would be expected to sacrifice his own ambition and advancement to the interest of the family group.' Pitkin shows the obverse of this: the parents' duty to *sistemare* their children's lot. See D. Pitkin, 'Marital Property Considerations Among Peasants: An Italian Example,' *Anthropological Quarterly* 33:1 (Jan., 1960): 37.

    An earlier view of emigration as disruptive to the family is in N. Douglas's *Old Calabria* (New York, 1928), p. 63: 'What is shattering family life is the speculative spirit born of emigration. A continual coming and going: two

thirds of the adolescent and adult male population are at this moment in
Argentina and the U.S.'

6 B. Galeski, 'Social Organization and Rural Social Change,' *Peasants and Peasant Societies*, ed. T. Shanin (London, 1971), p. 120.

7 C. Cronin, *The Sting of Change*, pp. 58–59; Baxenavis, *Economy and Population Movements*. See especially Chapter IV, 'The Decision to Migrate.'

8 This, of course, can be seen from the perspective of the 'stem family' or from the person's own sense of family responsibility as a 'target migrant.' The clearest discussion of migrant intentions that I have found is in Joan M. Nelson's *Temporary versus Permanent Cityward Migration: Causes and Consequences* (Migration and Development Study Group, MIT, 1976).

9 The response of the mayor of Albano di Lucania to commissioners is in A. Rossi's *Vantaggi e danni dell'emigrazione*, p. 1550.

10 Dr. Angelo Alberti, 'La psicologia dell'emigrati,' *Rivista di Emigrazione* 1:9 (Nov., 1908), or Dr. Antonio D'Ormea, 'Per la profilessi psichica dei nostri emigrati,' *Revista di Emigrazione* 11:2 (Feb., 1909).

11 See testimony about timing and length of sojourn throughout. A. Rossi's *Vantaggi e danni dell'emigrazione*. An anthropological study of a Lebanese village shows that there was both a real and ideal pattern of migration deviation and income. See L. Sweet, 'The Women of Ain ad Dayr,' *Anthropological Quarterly* Vol. 140: 171.

12 Taped interview with Mr. Jones Yla, former Lithuanian-Canadian newspaper editor (Multicultural History Society of Ontario collection, 1976).

13 Typical would be the idyll in G. Fortunato's *Il Mezzogiorno* 11:502: 'But the peasant, oh the peasants pick up the zappa and the vanga willingly again, happy enough to be free from the usurious slavery of rents, of being able to acquire for himself and for his a bit of his own and a piece of land.'

14 J. Nelson, *Temporary versus Permanent Cityward Migration*, p. 37.

15 De Nobili, 'L'Emigrazione in Calabria,' p. 7, and A. Milani, 'L'Emigrazione e una partita del suo bilancio morale passivo,' *Rivista di Emigrazione* 1:7 (Sept., 1908): 17.

16 Again the contemporary Lebanese case study echoes the many cases recorded by Nitti, Fortunato, De Nobili, etc., in the 1900s: 'Then some families have land but not labour, some have sheep and goats but no land, some have both, and many receive money from overseas which aids the exchange of food and work necessities among all.' Sweet, 'Women of Ain ad Dayr,' p. 173.

17 Some of the more damning *bollettini* about Canada were D. Viola's 'Le condizioni degli opera: italiani nel distretto minerario di Cobalt nella provincia di Ontario,' Anno 1910 no. 13; E. Rossi's 'Delle condizioni del Canada rispetto all'immigrazione italiana,' Anno 1903 no. 4; B. Attolico's 'L'agricoltura

e l'emmigrazione nel Canada,' Anno 1912 no. 5. There were also complaints in the Italian parliament in 1901 which led to the *Corriere della Sera*'s investigative reporter accompanying immigrants.

18 See D. Avery, 'Canada's Immigration Policy and the Foreign Navvy, 1874–1914,' *The Canadian Historical Association, Historical Papers* (1972), pp. 135–156.

19 The best account of this 'commerce of migration' through Chiasso to Canada is in B. Brandenberg's *Imported Americans* (New York, 1903). His is the only account of the notorious E. Ludwig who operated on the Swiss-Italian border as a labour agent for a number of Canadian companies.

20 The testimony of many labourers before the Royal Commission of 1904 confirms their transience and 'target' intention. See *Royal Commission appointed to inquire into the Immigration of Italian Labourers to Montreal and the Alleged Fraudulent Practices of Employment Agencies* (Ottawa, 1905).

21 *Corriere della Sera*'s report, 'Emigration of Italian Peasants to Canada' (March 18, 1901), includes *Solimbergo's Report*, Public Archives of Canada, Immigration Branch, RG 76, Vol. 128, File 28885:1.

22 See *Royal Commission* (1904) for details.

23 See reports to the *Corriere della Sera* through 1901. Some 'target migrants' apparently even found themselves recruited to fight for Great Britain in the Boer War.

24 *Corriere della Sera*, 'In Canada the Landing of the Emigrants New Delusion,' Quebec May 3rd and the despatch of May 5th in PAC, Immigration Branch, RG 76, Vol. 129, File 28885:1.

25 See W.D. Scott, 'Immigration and Population,' in *Canada and Its Provinces*, ed. A. Shortt and A. Doughty, VII: 561 (Toronto, 1914) for the system of counting immigrants. Since so many Italian migrants to Canada came and went through U.S. ports, the figures are particularly unreliable. The sex ratio in Italian migration to Canada in the 1900s overpoweringly suggests seasonal and target migration. In 1906–1970, 5,114 Italians arrived in Canadian ports in steerage, 17 in other classes; 4,430 were men and 384 were women. Some reconstruction of such arrivals can be made from the annual immigration reports in Parliamentary sessional papers, but they cannot answer questions about Italian migration between U.S. Little Italies and Canada. Even in Toronto, where there should have been more balance between the sexes, there were three times as many Italian men as women according to the Census of 1911.

26 The 'memory culture' describes many South and East European bachelor migrants being caught in a cycle of inadequate summer work, winter indebtedness, and thus, no opportunity to end the sojourn. For some, the turn-of-the-century 'reconnoitring of North America elided with the Depression

years.' The impact of harsh winters on the seasonal migrant continued a traditional problem of Canadian social history. See Judy Fingard, 'The Winter's Tale: Contours of Pre-Industrial Poverty in British America, 1815–1860,' *The Canadian Historical Association Historical Papers* (1974), especially p. 67.

27 See R. Berrier and T. Wolf, *Internal Migration*, a selected bibliography (Migration and Development Study Group, MIT, 1975).
28 S. Eisenstadt, *The Absorption of Immigrants* (London, 1954), p. 4.
29 The concern could range from the health of a parent to that of a fig tree, but it tended to involve jealousy about property and female virtue. Foerster, in *The Italian Emigration*, quotes Coletti as claiming that in 'some parts of South Italy men who marry just before emigrating sometimes, by way of precaution, leave the wives immaculate,' p. 441.
30 For examples of a literature which put the migrant himself at the centre of study, see J. Berger and J. Mohr, *A Seventh Man* (London, 1975); Jane Kramer 'Invandrare,' *New Yorker Magazine* (22 March 1976). Ann Cornelisen's *Women of the Shadows* (Boston, 1976) provides a good picture of those left behind.
31 T. Cyriax, *Among Italian Peasants* (Glasgow, 1919), pp. 216–217.
32 A. Milone, 'L'emigrazione e una partita,' p. 7.
33 Ibid., p. 10.
34 A brilliant, if a bit cruel, analysis of the relationship between South Italian male sexual fantasizing and banter on the one hand, and their feelings of poverty and powerlessness on the other can be found in A. Cornelisen, *Women of the Shadows*.
35 Ibid., p. 35.
36 Ann Osborn, 'Migration from the Countryside in the Absence of Consent: Escape as an Alternative,' in *The Political Economy of Urban Development in Latin America*, ed. W. Cornelius and F. Trueblood (Sage Publications no. 5, Los Angeles, 1975).
37 See the pattern described by V. Nee and his wife in San Francisco's Chinatown where men actually did go home only to beget sons or to bring them to America when they reached puberty: *Longtime Californ. A Documentary Study of an American Chinatown* (Boston, 1973), pp. 60–124.
38 A. D'Ormea, 'La Pazzia negli emigranti rimpatriate,' *Rivista di Emigrazione* 17 (Sept., 1907). One doctor noted that not just emigration but the emigration of parents 'passa gia costituire essa medesime un carrattere degenerativa.'
   Translation of quote in text: 'The economic discomfort or poverty, the worry of seeking a better life, the preoccupation with the unknown, together with physical exhaustion from privation, fatigue, and discomforts of every kind, and finally, the frequent, bitter disappointments make up the burden which usually accompanies the immigrant in his odyssey.'

39 It is almost impossible to confirm this from remittances which tend to decline with length of sojourn anyway. See Valeriote Store stub books and receipts (Multicultural History Society of Ontario collection).
40 See S. LaGumina, *Wop: A Documentary History of Anti-Italian Discrimination in the United States* (San Francisco, 1973). See *Jack Canuck* 1:12 (25 Nov. 1911), City Archives of Toronto.
41 Foerster, *The Italian Emigration*, p. 441.
42 A. Milone, 'L'emigrazione e una partita,' pp. 15–16.
43 E. Duse, 'Pellagra, alcoolismo ed emigrazione nella Provincia de Belluno,' *Rivista pellagrologica italiana* (1909). See D'Ormea, 'La Pazzia negli emigranti,' p. 99. Supporters of emigration tended to see such vices as older than emigration. See P. Villari, *Seritti sulla emigrazione e sopra alti argomenti vari* (Bologna, 1909).
44 See P. Roberts, *The New Immigration* (New York, 1914), for U.S. work camps; E. Bradwin, *The Bunkhouse Man* (New York, 1928), for Canadians. Neither account details the degradation as well as the Italian *bollettini* and some of the oral 'memory cultures' do. See note 17.
45 Roberts, *The New Immigration*, p. 112.
46 Notiziario in *Rivista di Emigrazione* 1:3 (May, 1908). See John Davis, 'Town and Country,' *Anthropological Quarterly* 42:3 (July, 1969). This view was confirmed very forcefully by all the former migrants interviewed. Davis' local study is based on Pisticci which happened to be the hometown of many Italians who came to Toronto.
47 Roberts, *The New Immigration*, p. 115.
48 See *Royal Commission* (1904), and R.F. Harney, 'The Padrone and the Immigrant,' *Canadian Review of American Studies* V:2 (Fall, 1974).
49 Nelson, *Temporary versus Permanent Cityward Migration*, p. 63.
50 The limits of the 'memory culture' and of oral history sources generally are discovered when one asks about sex habits among the migrants. Even the oldest survivors will talk about the heterosexual prowess of their youth, but little else.
51 A.V. Spada, *The Italians in Canada* (Ottawa, 1969), p. 265.
52 Report to *Corriere della Sera*, 'On board the "Lake Megantic"' (24 April 1901), PAC, Immigration Branch, RG 76, Vol. 129, File 28885:1.
53 T. Cyriax, *Among Italian Peasants*, p. 90.
54 U.S. Congress, *Reports of the Industrial Commission* (Washington, 1901), XV:498.
55 C. Arensberg, *The Irish Countryman, An Anthropological Study* (New York, 1968), p. 77. Interviews with Poles, Macedonians, Ukrainians, Italians, Lithuanians, and Croats confirm this view.
56 J. Baxevanis, in *Economy and Population Movements*, writes that 'Emigration is

the historical solution to land fragmentation,' p. 67. The point is true but not subtle enough for the Italian situation. For some, 'target migration,' for others, seasonal migration, and for others, longtime sojourning were the alternatives, not simply emigrating. The Italian folk song, 'Quando Saro in America,' shows how complicated the matter was. See T. Cyriax, *Among Italian Peasants*, p. 196–197.

57 On the complicated question of whether the *padrone*, steamship agent, and boardinghouse keeper were one and the same, see testimony before *Royal Commission* (1904), p. 167. A comparative study of the role of women in Slavic, Hungarian, and Italian boardinghouses would be very useful.

58 In North America, the usual usage was *bordante* or *bordisti* although variations of the Italian *covivenze* were used as well.

59 J. MacDonald and L. MacDonald, 'Chain Migration, Ethnic Neighbourhood Formation and Social Networks,' in *An Urban World*, ed. C. Tilly (Boston, 1974), p. 230. The MacDonalds view the *bordanti* more as the product of serial migration than as migrants from the camps coming to the city.

60 Nelson, *Temporary versus Permanent Cityward Migration*, p. 62.

61 *Missionary Outlook* (June, 1908), XXVLLL:6: 141. 'As these are not employed all the time in winter, but spend the idle hours around the house, it gives the housekeeper much extra work and makes it hard to leave and attend meetings.'

62 John Davis, 'Town and Country,' p. 174: 'and the very strong associations of women with town make it difficult for men to accept that the women should work in the country.'

63 The use of terms of respect or affection for *la padrona* came out in many interviews. One of the most detailed accounts was that of Mrs. M. Caruso about her grandmother (taped interview, 7 Dec. 1976, MHSO collection). Mrs. Gina Petroff remembers that as a young wife, she always referred to her older boarders as uncle (taped interview, 27 Oct. 1976, MHSO collection).

64 'The congestion of Italian American households is more dangerous to women and children than the factory or the street ... cases of incest are more frequent than one could believe – boarders are in truth an economic resource but are also the principle cause of congestion, filth, degeneration of domestic life of the immigrant family.' Bernardy goes on to blame the spread of syphilis on boarders. 'Da un relazione di Amy Bernardy su l'emigrazione delle donne e fanciulli italiane nella Stati Uniti,' *Bollettino del'Emigrazione* (1909). Contrast her view with that of the MacDonalds that the system of *bordanti* became popular because women could work at home and avoid the 'threat to their chastity' that outside work, especially as domestics, posed. MacDonald and MacDonald, 'Chain Migration,' p. 231.

65 *Report of My Day* by Headworker (Sept. 23, 1918), Archives of Central

Neighbourhood House, Toronto. A. Vazsony's 'The Star Boarder. Traces of Cicisbeism in an Immigrant Community,' in *Tractata Altaica* (Weisbaden, 1976), is a wonderful ethnological foray into the morals of Hungarian boardinghouses.

66 A Taglialatela, 'Our Italian Citizens,' *Missionary Outlook* (April 10), XXX:4.

67 R. Vecoli, 'Contadini in Chicago,' in *Journal of American History* LI:3 (Dec., 1964): 409.

68 Cusumano account of Cinisi colony in New York. R. Park and Miller, *Old World Traits Transplanted* (New York, 1921), pp. 150–151.

69 See C. Bianco, *The Two Rosetos* (Indiana, 1974); L.W. Moss and S.C. Cappannari, 'Patterns of Kinship Comparaggio and Community in a South Italian Village,' *Anthropological Quarterly* 33:1 (Jan., 1960), and the bibliographical references in MacDonald and MacDonald, 'Chain Migration.'

70 Endogamous marriage, to have real meaning for this essay, would have to be between people from the hometown or surrounding villages. Marriage between people from the same province is really out-marriage in *paese* terms. Unfortunately, priests in North America, to avoid the difficulties of following canon law – the prescription that records be sent of the marriage to the parishes where a couple were baptized – usually simply wrote 'Italy' into parish registers.

71 Quoted in 'Women and Settlement Work,' in *St. Hilda's Chronicle* (Michaelmas, 1915), University of Toronto Archives, p. 7.

72 John Kosa's *Land of Choice* (Toronto, 1957), p. 28, describes the place of the bachelor among Hungarian immigrants. The bachelor is accepted. He may be irresponsible, gamble, drink, and play by different rules, but that is because he remains 'a boy' no matter what his age.

73 In fact, we in Canada have already neglected oral sources too long and much of what one can gather about the sojourner frame of mind has to come from survivors of the 1920s migration, not the true 'target migrant' of the turn-of-the-century.

74 The Multicultural History Society of Ontario has found many sources to be richer than assumed and others to be disappointing. As we noted earlier, parish records fail to give the hometown or parish of baptism of most of the Italians who married in Toronto. (Russian and Macedonian Orthodox Churches, however, kept very exact records of town or village of origin.) *Paese* club records were apt to be destroyed when the secretary-treasurer's pants were washed and he had forgotten to clean his pockets. On the other hand, *banchisti*, stores, and steamship agencies kept, for obvious reasons, thorough accounts of debts, remittances, and prepaid tickets.

Bachelor Workers

ANTHONY B. CHAN

The trip from Hong Kong to Victoria took about 35 days under normal weather conditions. Depending on the quality of the ship and its crew, a one-way ticket cost between 15 and 20 Hong Kong dollars. A diet of rice, dried fish and preserved cabbage and other provisions added another 45 to 50 dollars. These expenses were paid by the labor contractors to the immigration brokers and shipping companies before the laborer left Hong Kong. Once the laborer began collecting a wage, a small portion, usually 2.5 per cent, would go to the contractor to repay the cost of his own passage.[1] Often, gold seekers travelled under the same arrangements as contracted laborers; those who were lucky were able to repay their fare with their first strike. Merchants emigrating to Gold Mountain sailed with their families in comparative luxury and at their own expense; often they would have had a hand in the labor contracting trade.

Port of Entry

The first view many immigrants had of their new homeland was Victoria's harbor. Before the arrival of the gold seekers, Victoria, lorded over by Vancouver Island's governor, James Douglas, was a quiet hamlet of 300 white inhabitants. It was a place marked by Sunday picnics, intimate garden parties and theatrical dabblings - attempts to recreate an English atmosphere.[2] On Sunday, April 25, 1858, Victoria's somnolence was shattered by the arrival of the *Commodore*, a wooden side-wheeler steamer, carrying 500 men from San Francisco.[3] Overnight, a tent village sprang up in Victoria.[4]

Douglas was not perturbed by the influx of fortune seekers; he saw them as a boon to the local economy and a source of revenue for his fledgling administration. By designating Victoria as the sole port of entry to British Columbia for gold seekers, Douglas forced all miners to detour through Victoria en route to Fort Langley, the major link to the gold fields. Without awaiting British approval, Douglas levied a 10 per cent duty on every import destined for the mainland, while products destined for Vancouver Island remained tax exempt. Further, merchants buying or selling goods in the Fraser Valley had to pay $7.50 a month for a trading license. Despite these levies, a substantial profit could be made selling provisions to the growing number of miners on the Fraser River: a barrel of flour would command $25 at Fort Langley, $36 further up the river at Hope, and $100 at the gold fields near Spuzzum. Prospectors also had to pay $5 dollars a year for their license and $1 a pound for beans, sugar, salt and rice.[5] These high prices, entrance fees, customs duties and steep commercial taxes were the official welcome awaiting Canada's* first immigrants from China.

By the summer of 1858 Victoria was a cluster of tents, strung out in uneven rows, housing 6,000 immigrants. This tent town had little sanitation, no law enforcement to speak of, and severe food and housing shortages. By the end of that year, Chinese immigrants formed their own small community amidst this tent town, whose population had levelled off to about 3,000. The press welcomed the new citizens. The *British Colonist*, founded on December 11, 1858, by Amor de Cosmos, the future British Columbia premier who quickly worked up a hatred for Asians, began referring to the Chinese community as 'Little Canton.'[6]

The Chinese in Victoria banded together for protection as a result of the mistrust, suspicion and race hatred that had been their experience in California. Chinatown quickly expanded around Johnson Street, where Jewish merchants, auctioneers and tailors had earlier set up shop. Chinatown's first laundry opened for business in July, 1858. Later that year the Kwong Lee Company – Importers and Dealers in all kinds of Chinese Goods, Rice, Sugar, Tea, Provisions, Etc., Etc. – was established by a San Francisco merchant, Chong Lee, who later expanded his business to Vancouver. In the spring of 1860 the steamer *Pacific* brought Lee's wife and children from China.[7] Mrs. Lee was the first Chinese woman in Victoria, and her arrival marked the beginning of the Chinese family in Canada. The frontier Chinese family blended Confucian values with Christian teachings; these families were to provide stability and continuity in a Chinese community that was overwhelmingly made up of bachelor workers.

By the end of 1860 Victoria's Chinatown was augmented by laborers and prospectors who had arrived from Hong Kong in 1859, and immigrants who continued to stream into the city from San Francisco.[8]

---

*Although Canada did not come into being until 1867, reference to British North America as Canada before 1867 is used for the sake of continuity.

Men without Women

By January, 1860, 1,195 Chinese gold hunters on their way to the Fraser River had passed through Victoria.[9] An individual like Chang Tsoo, the gold prospector, could stop off at Chong Lee's trading post and stock up on rice, tea, tobacco, silk goods, matting, clothes, shoes, opium and joss paper and sticks. For entertainment, he could head down to Fantan Alley and Theatre Lane, two side streets linking Fisgard and Cameron Streets at the centre of Chinatown. Too much entertainment could be a problem, but with the arrival in June, 1859, of Ay Kay, the first Chinese doctor on Canadian soil, remedies were available for physical ailments ranging from headaches caused by intoxicants to serious medical problems. From his office on Johnson Street, Ay Kay dispensed his knowledge of traditional Chinese medicine to all comers.[10]

By the spring of 1860 the Chinese population on Vancouver Island was 1,577. The rise in population would spark anti-Chinese sentiments among the 2,884 whites, whose numerical domination was dwindling. Women formed less than 1 per cent of the Chinese population. Even in 1902, when the Chinese population in Victoria was 3,283, the number of women did not exceed 96; 61 were married to merchants while 28 were wives of laborers, 2 had interpreters for husbands and 1 was a minister's wife. The remaining 4 had no occupation and were accused by the white population of being prostitutes.[11]

The low ratio of women to men was seen by anti-Chinese agitators as an indication that few Chinese immigrants intended to settle in Canada. If they did, they argued, their wives and children would have left China for Canada long ago and Chinese families would be the norm in Chinatown. But as Sing Cheung Yung, a Nanaimo market gardener, explained: 'I have been here twelve years. My wife and two children are in China. They are eleven and nine years old. I would like to bring my wife and children here.'[12] These sentiments were echoed by Won Alexander Cumyow, who in 1861 became the first Chinese born in Canada.[13] A native of Port Arthur, British Columbia, he told the Royal Commission on Chinese and Japanese immigration that 'the Chinese have a very high regard for the marriage relationship. They usually marry at from sixteen to twenty years of age. Many of those who are here are married and have wives and children in China. A large portion of them would bring their families here, were it not for the unfriendly reception they got here during recent years which creates an unsettled feeling.'

Alexander Winchester, a Presbyterian clergyman, reported that many Chinese saw Canada as their home. He told the Royal Commission, 'I have met Chinese who had expressed a desire to become citizens, but claim they could not do so and maintain their self-respect. In explanation they said they could not bring themselves to belong to a nation that treated another nation so unfairly, instancing the unwarrantable attacks made upon Chinese in the press. Some Chinese who had become naturalized, hoping to bring relief from this treatment, had been disappointed.'

Winchester, who at the time of his appearance before the Royal Commission was pastor of Knox Presbyterian Church in Toronto, also said that 'there is hope of Chinese becoming permanent settlers if treated the same as other nationalities. At present Chinese allege that they are afraid to bring their wives and children to this country.'[14]

Rather than expose their wives and children to the anti-Chinese hatred, many Chinese immigrants opted to remain bachelors in Canada for the rest of their lives. None wanted a life away from their families. But the profusion of racist agitators – like John Robson, editor of the New Westminster *British Columbian*, Amor de Cosmos, who became British Columbia's second premier in 1872, Victoria city councillor Noah Shakespeare, and F.L. Tuckfield of the Knights of Labour – all calling for more taxes, fewer jobs or straightforward exclusion based on fear of Chinese competition prevented the development of a social climate suitable for settling peacefully and raising a family.

Racism at the top emboldened those who preferred less genteel outlets for their hostility. A market gardener on his way to work could expect to be met with a volley of stones or name calling from young toughs and local neighborhood Johnny Canucks. Queue pulling, and taunts of 'chinky, chinky, Chinaman,' were almost daily events. No Chinese, then or now, has been immune from such street racism.

Products of a Civil War

British Columbia, with its anti-Chinese feelings, was inhospitable, but to many, China in the 1870s offered little hope of even a subsistence livelihood. South China was going through a period of reconstruction following the Taiping Rebellion. More than 20 million people died during that war, which had lasted from 1850 to 1865; many more had been left homeless. In 1873 (the year the first anti-Chinese society was established in Victoria), South China was on the brink of ruin. For the poor Chinese worker or peasant, the choice was between leaving China or staying behind and perishing in the agony of poverty.

Southeast Asia, close by and less alien, seemed the most promising and congenial locale in which to build a new life. But an emigrant's destination was determined by district and clan ties. If you grew up in Fujian province, you were likely to emigrate to Southeast Asia.[15] North America was your likely new home if you were from Guangdong counties like Taishan, Zhongshan, Xinhui, Shunde, Haoshan or Nanhai. The racial hostility and economic uncertainty of Gold Mountain was usually preferable to the fate awaiting in South China.

Labor and Wages

In contrast to the decades following the Taiping Rebellion, a laborer could still find work during the Taiping rebels' march northward to Nanjing in the 1850s. By going from one village to the next during harvest time, he could earn between two and a half and five cents a day. Those who were hired on permanently received three meals a day consisting of rice, pork fat, cabbage and rice wine. At the end of the year they would receive ten 'stone,' or about 2,000 pounds, of grain, worth about twenty silver dollars.[16] But by 1865 the fertile Yangtze River valley was 'strewn with human skeletons, [its] rivers polluted with floating carcasses, no hands were left to till the soil.' Another witness reported that many 'have been driven to cannibalism to satisfy the craving of hunger.'[17] For the many Chinese struggling against starvation, the call for men to build railways in North America was difficult to resist, and those who were still able signed on for the transpacific voyage. From 1876 to 1880, 3,326 immigrants arrived in Victoria; in 1885, six ships from Hong Kong brought 1,739 passengers. Not all of these laborers were able to start work immediately; about 10 per cent had developed scurvy, caused by poor food and lack of ventilation on board ship. Because of the raging seas and stormy weather, the Chinese were kept below deck with the hatches bolted.

The workers who arrived in British Columbia from the United States by land were in much better health because they were not subjected to a transpacific voyage. Adding to the Hong Kong total were 387 from the Puget Sound area and another 387 from San Francisco. During the entire five-year construction period, about 15,000 rail hands were hired by Andrew Onderdonk to build the tracks linking British Columbia with the rest of Canada.[18]

Unlike the independent gold hunters of 1858, the Chinese laborers from the United States were under contract Chinese compradores in San Francisco. The compradores originated in China's treaty ports after the Opium War in 1842, when they had been hired by foreign trading houses in China to deal with the Chinese side of their business. Usually bilingual, they acted as intermediaries between the foreign merchant and the huge Chinese domestic market. In the Americas, the compradores still functioned as go-betweens, but they were often independent of any foreign control.

The most active compradore firms in securing railway workers were the companies of Lian Chang, Tai Chong and Lee Chuck. Their Victoria offices became the final stop-off point for all of the workers contracted out of San Francisco and Hong Kong.

Immigration brokerage, however, was in white hands. In June, 1881, most of the 6,676 laborers arriving from Hong Kong were consigned to non-Chinese immigration brokers – 5,297 to the firm of Stahlschmidt & Ward, and 450 to Welch & Rithet.[19] The only Chinese company able to compete with the white brokers was Lian Chang, through its contracts with Onderdonk for 2,000 workers in 1881. Much of the profit from the trade in Chinese muscle during this time did not go into the coffers of the compradores.

Because labor brokers' profits depended on workers arriving in Canada in good health, the ships carrying Chinese workers upgraded their food and living conditions after 1882. The *Colonist* reported that on November 15, 1881, the *Volmer* arrived in Victoria with '224 Chinese who had been aboard for 50 days. They lived on a pound and a half of rice, a half pound of meat, and a half pound of vegetables per man per day, with an allowance of fruit or lime juice.'[20] Because their strong backs were needed to fulfil John A. Macdonald's pledge to unite Canada by rail, Chinese laborers were temporarily indulged.

Boss Onderdonk

This Chinese role in the construction of the Canadian Pacific Railway began at eleven in the morning on May 14, 1880, with the firing of a blasting cap near Yale, British Columbia. Central to the working lives of all the Chinese employed on the rail line was Andrew Onderdonk, whose imposing presence dominated the British Columbia chapter of the CPR story. A civil engineer by trade, his towering figure commanded such respect among even the white laborers that they would tip their caps when he passed by on the railroad.

A reserved and detached figure who was always impeccably dressed in the latest Wall Street fashions, Onderdonk was the ideal contractor for the CPR's stretch run to the Pacific. His experience in the United States – by age 37 he had already organized the construction of San Francisco's seawall and ferry boats – revealed him as an efficient, no-nonsense achiever whose only interest besides the task at hand was profits.[21] Like many other employers, Onderdonk imported Chinese muscle because he believed 'that 99 per cent of the Chinese here are industrious and steady' and that the 'development of the country would be retarded and many industries abandoned' if Chinese laborers were not allowed to work in North America.[22] Onderdonk eagerly sought compradores who could ferret Chinese workers out of the decaying corners of the streets of Hong Kong and the market gardens and laundries of San Francisco.

Their reputation as the best labor money could buy started with the building of the Central Pacific Railway in the United States. Gathered together by Charles Crocker, the Central Pacific's labor contractor, the Chinese were hired to supplement the Irish-American rail hands. It started as an experiment involving 50 unemployed miners, laundry workers, market gardeners, domestic servants and laborers. After seeing the cleanliness of the Chinese camp, their ability to adapt to the thin air of the Sierras, and their toughness in handling a pick and shovel, Crocker hired 6,000 more by 1866 at $35 a month (board and lodging were not supplied; white workers received board and lodging in addition to their pay of about a dollar a day). During its most hectic period of construction, between 1866 to 1869, the Central Pacific obtained about 90 per cent of its 10,000 rail hands from the Chinese labor market, thereby saving itself $5.5 million.[23]

By the time Onderdonk began laying tracks for the Northern Pacific in Oregon in 1880 and the Southern Pacific in California in 1881, the Chinese rail hand had earned a reputation as the most able and least expensive worker available. Sir Mathew Begbie, the British Columbia chief justice, declared that the four personal qualities of the Chinese were 'industry, economy, sobriety, and law-abidingness.'[24] And J.A Chapleau, a cabinet minister of the Conservative Canadian government who along with J.J.C. Abbott and Joseph Tasse had incorporated the 88-mile Montreal and Western Railway and later sold it to the CPR, wrote in 1885 that the Chinese worker had 'no superior as a railway navvy.' He also noted that the money saved by paying the Chinese lower wages than whites found its way into the profit ledger of railway companies.[25] Perhaps the most famous endorsation of the Chinese laborer was made by Prime

Minister John A. MacDonald, who in 1882 told parliament that although the Chinese were 'alien' and would never assimilate into the 'Aryan' way of life, stressed that 'it is simply a question of alternatives: either you must have this labor or you can't have the railway.'[26]

Politicians and railway investors grudgingly admitted that the Chinese worker was valuable and even necessary, a conclusion based almost entirely on dollars and cents. When profits and savings on wages motivate the builders of the country, they tend to become color-blind.

Virulent attacks on the Chinese worker came from the Knights of Labour, an early organization of skilled workers, which attacked the Chinese 'as a low, degraded and servile type, the inevitable result of whose employment in competition with free white labor is to lower and degrade the latter without any appreciable elevation of the former.' Competition, however, was not the main objection. Rather, the Chinese were 'the willing tools whereby grasping and tyrannical employers grind down all labor to the lowest living point.'[27]

If there was any degradation in the value of white workers because of the hiring of the Chinese, it did not show up in their pay envelope or accommodations. In April, 1880, Onderdonk assured the Anti-Chinese Society that white workers would always be given preference in hiring; once this labor pool was exhausted, he would turn to French Canadians and finally he would 'with reluctance, engage Indians and Chinese.' Consequently, according to Onderdonk's engineer Henry Cambie, unemployed clerks, 'broken-down bar-keepers or one of that class' as well as 'rough necks' and 'sand-lot hoodlums' from San Francisco were given higher wages and better camps than Chinese.[28] Onderdonk paid his white laborers $1.50 to $1.75 a day, and a skilled worker got between $2 and $2.50 per day. He also provided cooks, cooks' helpers and other amenities to accommodate the taste of his white employees.

In contrast, Chinese workers all received the same wage – $1 per day, regardless of the work they performed. For provisions, they were given a choice between inflated prices at the company stores and competitive prices at local trading houses, if there were any nearby. They had to buy their own provisions, bringing their daily wage down to 80 cents. There were other expenses too. The Chinese laborer, unlike his white counterpart, had to dig into his own pocket for camping equipment and cooking items. Chinese rail hands would travel light, carrying all of their needs on their backs. They could quickly break camp, trek as far as 25 miles and set up a new camp within 24 hours. According to Michael Haney, Onderdonk's general manager, 2,000 Chinese laborers could be moved such a distance within a complete day. The same number of white laborers needed about a week to move camp. The advantages of Chinese mobility did not escape Onderdonk's attention.[29]

It was not the Chinese who were responsible for the white workers' low standards of living; it was Onderdonk, and bosses like him, who decided the pay structure and living arrangements for both white and non-white workers. Compared to the Chinese, white laborers were pampered, getting better wages and housing. But the white rail hand in British Columbia was getting 25 cents less per day than his American counterpart, and skilled white laborers for American railways received $1 a day more than did Canadian skilled workers. Beside the discrepancy in wages, Onderdonk's workers had to lay tracks on difficult terrain, in mountainous areas and alongside fast-rising rivers, in areas where the population was sparse and unsettled.[30]

Onderdonk's section of the CPR was bankrolled by American tycoons, mostly bankers. They included Darius O. Mills, H.B. Laidlaw, Levi P. Morton and S.G. Reed of the Oregon Railway and Navigation Company. Because of Onderdonk's family connections he was privy to the board rooms of the eastern establishment in the United States. Since the prime objective of this banker's syndicate was maximum profit, Onderdonk had to secure majority interest in, or complete control of, the British Columbia rail route. Fortunately for him and his bankers, the Canadian government had a policy of encouraging private construction in certain areas of the country. Land grants and a large sum of cash subsidies sweetened the taste for railway construction west of Winnipeg.[31]

Onderdonk had to eliminate equally avaricious rivals to win the contracts for the British Columbian section of the CPR. In his tenders for the four contracts involved, well-placed friends and allies in Ottawa saw to it that even the lowest bidders had little chance of success. Among Onderdonk's Ottawa friends was Charles Tupper, who as Canada's minister of railways had to cope with the failures of badly financed railway contractors. Recognizing the financial power of Onderdonk's American connection, Tupper supported his bid for the four British Columbia contracts.

Beyond patronage, a successful bid depended on an impressive track record, experience in labor relations and the ability to balance the books. In all these aspects, Onderdonk's company was the best of the competition. More importantly for Onderdonk, Tupper was inclined to award the four contracts to one firm, thus sparing Ottawa from dealings with more than one company. Onderdonk's monopoly on railway construction gave him *carte blanche* in the buying of labor and materials, a powerful bargaining position with British Columbia politicians and anti-Chinese racists. The bureaucratic efficiency that went with needing only one paymaster and merchant, one time table and work schedule, and one arbiter and boss, added to Onderdonk's power.

His 1880 contract covered the lower Fraser and main Thompson rivers, east and west of Lytton. It included the entire 127 miles from Emory's Bar at the mouth of the Fraser Canyon to Savona's ferry near Kamloops. In 1882, the government also awarded Onderdonk the Emory's Bar-Port Moody extension.[32]

The 'Chinese Pacific' Railway

The 15,000 Chinese laborers who worked for Onderdonk between May 14, 1880, and completion of the railway on July 29, 1885, saved his company $3–5 million.[33] At first, they were organized into mobile gangs of 30 workers, lorded over by a white overseer, or herder. Later, when they settled into camps, a cook, a cook's helper and a bookman were assigned to each gang. The bookman was responsible for collecting the wages from the company and paying them to the workers, and representing his gang to the employer. His most immediate contact with the railway company was the herder, Onderdonk's representative at the grass roots level. Another task of the bookman was to buy provisions for the workers at the lowest possible price.

Because of the salary differences, the Chinese laborers usually lived on a monotonous diet of rice and stale ground salmon while his white counterpart ate fresh meat and vegetables. The result was a growing list of scurvy victims, unable to receive medical help in the camps. No doctors or medicine were available for the workers; compradore firms knew that such services cost money and would do nothing to enhance their profits. As long as unemployment in China was severe, human muscle was readily available.

The construction company, too, was indifferent to the workers' health needs; Onderdonk benevolently refused to interfere in Chinese affairs. The sick, injured or dying lived either in the same bunkhouses in the permanent Chinese camps or in segregated tents along the construction line. Entertainment was limited to fantan and other gambling activities. A total of 15,000 Chinese worked on Onderdonk's railway but only 7,000 were on his payroll at any one time, so turnover among the rail hands was high, and news of China and Chinese communities in Canada circulated freely and rapidly.

Some Chinese laborers supplemented their income by selling to the white workers a potent homebrew know as 'Chinese gin.'[34] But generally Chinese contact with whites and native Indians was minimal; each new crew lived and worked by an unwritten rule of segregation. Most Chinese workers communicated with whites only through their bookman, if at all. Knowledge of the English language was not a necessity and there was little incentive to learn it. Even if a Chinese did want to learn the language, English teachers were hard to find at a railway construction site. There was the bookman, but he had no interest in teaching other Chinese English; his knowledge of English gave him access to the white world, and, as the major intermediary between the white and the Chinese worlds, a position of power in the latter. A white rail hand, because of his antipathy towards his Chinese colleague, was as likely to teach a Chinese English as he was himself inclined to learn Chinese.

Divide and Rule

The tense, suspicious relations between the races prevented understanding and respect between Chinese and white workers. Company bosses never spoke of using these racial differences as an instrument of control, but racial animosity did prevent Chinese and whites from joining together into an effective union that could demand fair wages, better housing and job safety. In the absence of such a union, Onderdonk and his syndicate profited from the racial differences. They kept Chinese wages low, but not so low that they did not infuriate white workers. Vital to Onderdonk's policy of divide and rule was the constant flow of anti-Chinese propaganda thrown at the white laborer by journalists like John Robinson, politicians like Amor de Cosmos and Noah Shakespeare, and labor leaders like F.L. Tuckfield. Focusing on the Chinese as a foreign threat to the 'free' white labor market helped to deflect grievances white workers might have against their bosses. The propagandists, whose interest was supposedly in the betterment of white labor, emphasized that each successful Chinese meant the failure of one white worker. But Onderdonk was not beloved by them either, even though he did benefit from their invectives; they opposed the hiring of Chinese rail hands.

For some like Noah Shakespeare, involvement in racist organizations like the Anti-Chinese Society was a tool for their own political advancement. Shakespeare's election pledge to rid Canada of the Chinese menace brought him the mayoralty of Victoria and a seat in parliament in

Ottawa. Because the political flavor of the times was so anti-Asian, no politician with ambitions could risk dissociating himself from racist views. Like the white workers, politicians attacked everything Chinese – dress, speech, customs, pay, packages, etc. They preyed on the insecurities of the white laborer, harping on the 'strangeness' of the Chinese. They pointed to his cotton shoes, his Chinese-style worker's jacket with cloth buttons, and his loose cotton trousers. But they failed to point to his meagre wages, which prevented a Chinese rail hand from buying expensive Western apparel, should he wish to do so.

A 'Chinaman's Chance'

The work assigned to Chinese laborers was the most backbreaking and dangerous on the railway. Initially, the Chinese were assigned to the task of grading – cutting out hills to fill ravines and gullies. Later, the more dangerous jobs of tunneling and the handling of explosives were given to the Chinese. It was they who opened the frontier for the white rail hands who were responsible for the lumber work, for the construction of bridges and tunnels and the laying of track.

Conflicts between Chinese and white workers were not infrequent. In August, 1880, a dynamite explosion near Yale killed or maimed nine Chinese laborers standing on a rock directly below the charge. No warning had been given by the white herder, who claimed the Chinese had misunderstood his orders. An angry, pick-wielding group of Chinese rail hands forced the terrified herder to scramble to safety up the side of a hill. No inquiry was convened to investigate this incident. From this and similar events, the Chinese came to realize that the concepts of justice and fair play, so praised by the English, did not apply to them.

In another incident, several Chinese asked the overseer for permission to light a fire to boil water for tea along the line. His refusal so angered them that the entire gang threw down their picks and shovels and left for Yale.

Sometimes clashes between Chinese and whites resulted in bloodshed. Once, a herder tried to fire two Chinese without consulting their bookman. This disagreement exploded into an attack by the Chinese work gang on the foreman, bridge superintendent, time keeper and teamster; a retaliatory night raid by white workers left the Chinese bunkhouses burnt to the ground and several Chinese beaten. One died the next day.

The bookman who led his workers' protests against any pay deductions was a powerful individual. Once, in the early days of construction at Yale, the Chinese found that their pay packages were a penny an hour short. After a long and heated discussion in the company's stores, the 'mistake' was admitted and the money was paid.

However, the bookman was not always on the workers' side. At times he was the object of the enmity of his workers, as when they suspected that he had pocketed part of their wages. In one occurrence, a bookman was attacked for cheating his workers during the building of the Grand Trunk Railway to Hope in 1874.

Chinese laborers would also take on Chinese companies if they thought they had been cheated. One time, the trading company belonging to Lee Chuck had agreed to supply rice for the workers outside Yale. On the day of delivery, the workers discovered that the agreed-upon price had been raised to include a 2 per cent deduction from their salaries. The unauthorized increase, as well as a deficiency in the quality and weight of the cargo, drove 200 laborers to storm and destroy Lee Chuck's warehouse in Yale.[35]

Many Chinese deaths resulted either from premeditated negligence or simple incompetence on the part of the herders, other white laborers or the company itself. Failure to warn Chinese rail hands of imminent explosions, inadequate protection from falling boulders and rock slides, and the lack of safety precautions against cave-ins gave rise to the saying in Canada's Chinatowns that 'for every foot of railroad through the Fraser Canyon, a Chinese worker died.' At least 600 laborers gave up their lives so that John A. Macdonald's dream of a Canada united from coast to coast could be realized.[36] Even in death, the Chinese could be worth money; an Irish entrepreneur named Big Mouth Kelly was able to secure a monopoly on burying the Chinese dead.[37]

Labor Used, Labor Discarded

Completion of the CPR forced thousands of Chinese to migrate across Canada in search of work. The trek eastward was caused in part by Andrew Onderdonk's refusal to honor his pledge to provide railhands with a one-way ticket back to China.[38] Many laborers were left destitute and stranded in a foreign land.

The art of saving their meagre wages taxed the mental agility of even the most frugal, especially when the typical salary of a Chinese worker was $25 a month. Because typically there was no work for three months each winter, his annual income would be $225. From this had to be deducted $130 for provisions and clothing, $24 for room rent, $10 for tools and transportation, $5 for revenue and road taxes, $5 for religious fees, $3 for doctors and medicine (if they were available), and $5 for oil, light and tobacco. That left a grand total of $43 for everything else.[39] A worker toiling for five years on the Onderdonk section could have saved $215; food and passage back to China cost $70. But those who were able to save even that were few; most ended up, as the *Island Sentinal* reported, 'in the buildings along Douglas Street [Yale's Chinatown], some of them in very poor communities.'[40] There was also a story about desperate workers scrambling for frozen potatoes thrown out on Yale's Front Street.[41]

By the time Donald A. Smith, a major CPR stockholder and director whose influence had proven so crucial, drove the railroad's final spike at Craigellachie, B.C., on November 7, 1885, most of the 2,900 Chinese had already drifted out of the construction camps toward the west coast, the United States, or eastward toward the Maritimes in search of work. There were also doctors, barbers, vegetable sellers, butchers, wood cutters and cafe owners who had provided services to the railway workers and who had to move now that the construction sites were dismantled. Some of these immigrants settled in the small towns along the rail line instead of heading for the west coast or out of B.C. Doctors set up practices in places like Soda Dog Creek, the Lillooet district and Yale. Merchants established themselves in every village and town along the line, and miners found work in Hope, Cassiar, Lytton, Lillooet, Dog Creek and as far north as the Cariboo and Quesnel Forks.[42]

Most of the Chinese who moved west eventually reached Victoria, still the best source of work because it possessed the oldest and most firmly-established Chinatown in Canada. As well, Victoria remained the most important seaport linking China and Canada. While Vancouver would eventually outstrip it in population and influence during the 1930s, Victoria was still the clearing point for all Chinese travellers leaving or returning to Canada, Seattle or Portland.

Those rail hands who headed east passed through the Rockies to Lethbridge and on to Calgary, Edmonton, Medicine Hat or Saskatchewan. Some in Alberta found work as miners, but most took up the only jobs left to them: in laundries and cafes. A few became grocers, bunkhouse cooks, market gardeners and servants to the white elite.

In self-defence, the Chinese in Alberta, as in other provinces, congregated in Chinatowns. By the turn of the century, Calgary had Alberta's largest Chinatown. Because of urban expansion and the inability of the Chinese to buy any land outright, Calgary's Chinatown was forced to move twice between 1900 and 1910. By 1911, its population leveled off at 1,700.[43]

If the racism of white Albertans, or simple bad luck, persuaded Chinese immigrants to move on to Swift Current, Saskatchewan, along the rail line, they would find a tiny speck of a community which by January, 1923, had a total of 23 bachelors operating laundries and restaurants, one woman who was a maid to the only Chinese merchant in town, and two teenage boys. One of them, Deep Quong, was among the last Chinese immigrants to arrive in Canada before the exclusion act of 1923. The son of a Chinese official in the Qing government who moved to Toronto after World War II, he probably also caught a glimpse of Moose Jaw on his way to Swift Current. By 1911 a growing Chinese community of 160 people and 20 businesses made Moose Jaw the largest Chinese community in Saskatchewan; Regina, Saskatoon and Battleford also had Chinatowns of their own.[44]

Leaving Saskatchewan, a traveller passed through Brandon, with its small Chinese community, to Winnipeg, where old-timers would tell of their city's first Chinese, who arrived in the late 1850s. (The Winnipeg *Free Press*, however, reported that on November 18, 1877, four workers who came to Manitoba by stagecoach from the United States were that city's first Chinese.) By the time of the exclusion act, Winnipeg's Chinese population consisted of more than 790 bachelors and 22 women. The surnames of Lee, Wong and Mah dominated; there were only four families in the entire city. Many came from the Guangdong provincial districts of Haoshan, Taishan, Nanhai, Panyu and Shunde.[45]

Leaving Manitoba for Toronto, Chinese itinerants passed through small patches of Chinese communities in Kenora, Port Arthur (now Thunder Bay), Sudbury and finally into Toronto, the capital city of Ontario. In contrast to Victoria's close community of 3,280 in 1884, a traveller found Toronto's population of 100 Chinese laborers and merchants scattered throughout the city. Some immigrants were said to have arrived as early as 1877 or 1878; in 1881, 10 Chinese settled in Toronto, and were soon followed by about 90 more after work on the CPR ended.

By 1900, a Chinatown was forming between Parliament and Yonge along Queen Street. Since it was located close to the business heart of the city, Toronto developed in and around Chinatown. In 1911, 228 businesses, mostly laundries, employed many of the 1,031 Chinese settlers in a Toronto which now had a population of 130,000. Four years later, Chinatown expanded westward toward Bay Street and the old city hall, where a large market community was located. Cafe owners, launderers, grocers, barbers and market gardeners were able to stabilize their businesses in this area, which formed the hub of the Chinese community until 1936, when Chinatown moved again. By the late 1920s, Chinatown was a community of a little over 2,000 people, working, raising families, exercising in athletic associations, acting in dramatic societies and betting in the merchant-run gambling halls.[46]

Southwest of Toronto, Chinese communities sprang up in Hamilton, London and Windsor. Of the three, Hamilton was the most important because of its proximity to Toronto. The first immigrant reached the city, probably from Toronto, in 1880 or 1881. By 1901, an energetic community was developing in the city centre, near city hall, the market area, the train station and the main highway heading toward Toronto. Despite the economic depression then affecting Hamilton, the Chinese community was able to develop a firm and stable base. The community's leadership was assumed by merchants such as Fong Young, who at 26 moved from Ottawa and established Hamilton's first Chinese-owned restaurant, and John G. Lee, a laundry owner who was the president of a marriage bureau for bachelors called the Chinese Women's Organization. The marriage bureau was especially important for the growth of Chinatown because its main objective was to establish settled families in Hamilton, thus helping to eliminate the myth of the transient associated with the bachelor life.

Hamilton's Chinatown grew steadily until 1910, the year the city's alderman passed two by-laws aimed at preventing its further growth. By-law 73 prohibited the setting up of laundries in areas where such businesses already existed. This prevented the establishment of new laundries in Chinatown, where the laundries' clientele lived, and where it was least expensive to set up a business. Operating costs in other neighbourhoods were prohibitively higher, and businesses would be slower. The effect of by-law 73 was to halt the growth of business in Chinatown.

The other anti-Chinese regulation, by law 74, prohibited a laundry from using its premises for lodging or gambling. Travellers and newly-arrived Chinatown residents were frequently put up in laundries for short periods of time; additionally, it was well known to Hamilton's police that laundries also served as leisure time recreation areas for the community's bachelor workers. This second by-law thus attempted to control the activities of the Chinese, and together with the first, destroyed Chinatown as a compact community. A traveller arriving in Hamilton in 1920 would find a declining Chinese community scattered throughout the city.[47]

Continuing eastward, the next large Chinatown would be found in Montreal. On the way, a traveller could stop off at small Chinese settlements in Kingston and Ottawa, whose Chinese population in 1902 was 100. In 1880, the Montreal *Star* reported that the city's Chinese community was 30 residents, working in laundries and other businesses. By 1921, there were about 600 businesses and 1,603 Chinese settlers in Montreal.

In Quebec City could be found another small Chinese community of 60 bachelor workers living around Cote d'Abraham in 1910 and later on east St. Vallier. In 1911, the community absorbed 50 Chinese newcomers. By 1940, the Chinese population reached 230, with 50 working in laundries and the rest in restaurants. But Quebec City's Chinese community grew slowly because, like Edmonton and Saskatoon, it did not lie along the CPR's route.[48]

Those who ventured east past Montreal found only sparse Chinese settlements in the Atlantic provinces. By the 1930s, only about 300 Chinese made their homes in New Brunswick, with the majority living in Fredericton.[49] In Nova Scotia and Newfoundland, the Chinese settlements revolved around the family of entrepreneur Fong Choy. Leaving his village in the Enping district of Guangdong province, Fong set out for England in the 1880s. From Europe, he managed the Atlantic crossing and settled in Montreal, the port of entry on the east coast. Later he moved to Halifax, where he and a relative opened a laundry in 1895. In time, immigrants with surnames other than Fong began arriving in Halifax by way of Victoria, Toronto and Montreal. By 1916, about 100 bachelors lived in Halifax, most running laundries and restaurants. Three years later, the wife of a laundry owner named Lee joined her husband and son, Chuck, and the Lees became the first Chinese family in Nova Scotia's capital.[50]

Fong Choy also had a hand in building the Chinese community in Newfoundland. In the same year that he opened a laundry in Halifax (which he later sold), Fong set up a laundry with a partner named Wang Chang in St. John's. They announced that 'Sing Lee & Co. Chinese laundries will be ready to receive work on Monday at their laundry, 37 New Gower Street, corner Holdsworth Street.' The notice, printed in local newspapers, was dated August 24, 1895.

By 1904, the Lee Wah Laundry at 239 New Gower Street and the Kam Lung Laundry at 11 Cochrane Street began to rival Sing Lee & Co. for business. But work was still plentiful until 1906, the year the Newfoundland house of assembly created a head tax of $300 for all new Chinese settlers. At this time, the population of the Chinese community stabilized between 120 and 130.[51]

Some of the more fortunate ex-rail hands moved to Victoria in search of work and human company. Once there they headed straight for Chinatown, which took in four blocks around Fisgard Street. By 1884, they would have found other Chinese workers in many occupations. While Victoria alone had 130 Chinese bootmakers, the most common jobs were in the laundries, restaurants and domestic service. But in British Columbia as a whole, the Chinese found work in many other areas. In 1884, 7,200 of the entire Chinese adult male population of 9,870 was employed on the railways and farms and in mining, mills and canning. The other 2,670 were working as cooks, domestics, merchants, store employees and in laundries. In addition, there were the self-employed who provided services in Chinatown as barbers, doctors, butchers and other occupations.[52]

In 1902, Victoria's Chinatown was still located within the city limits. Its population had levelled off at 3,280 (less during the canning season). It was able to serve all the common laborer's needs.

NOTES

This article is a chapter from *Gold Mountain: The Chinese in the New World*, by Tony Chan. Vancouver: New Star Books, 1983. Reprinted with permission.

1 *Royal Commission, 1885*, pp. xxviii, lxxvi, 46, 161.
2 Harry Gregson, *A History of Victoria, 1842–1970* (Vancouver: J.J. Douglas, 1977), p. 12.
3 Li, *Jianada*, p. 59; Chen Tien-fan, *Oriental Immigration in Canada* (Shanghai: Commercial Press, 1931), p. 33; James Morton, *In The Sea of Sterile Mountains: The Chinese in British Columbia* (Vancouver: J.J. Douglas, 1974), pp. 5–7; G.P.V. Akrigg and Helen Akrigg, *British Columbia Chronicle, 1847–1871* (Vancouver: Discovery Press, 1977), p. 108.
4 Margaret A. Ormsby, *British Columbia: A History* (Toronto: Macmillan, 1971), p. 130.
5 Akrigg, *British Columbia Chronicle*, pp. 119, 115, 165, 247.
6 Gregson, *Victoria*, p. 12; Akrigg, *British Columbia Chronicle*, p. 105.
7 Li, *Jianada*, p. 81; Morton, *Sterile Mountains*, pp. 7–8.
8 Gregson, *Victoria*, p. 21.
9 Victoria, *British Colonist*, January 26, 1860.

10 Li, *Jianada*, p. 92.
11 *Report of the Royal Commission on Chinese and Japanese Immigration, Session 1902* (Ottawa: S.E. Dawson, 1902), pp. 12–13, 22.
12 Ibid., p. 65.
13 Robert Edward Wynne, 'Reaction to the Chinese in the Pacific Northwest and British Columbia, 1850–1911,' (PhD dissertation, University of Washington, Seattle, 1964), p. 145.
14 *Royal Commission, 1902*, pp. 236, 36.
15 Edgar Wickberg, *The Chinese in Philippine Life, 1850–1898* (New Haven: Yale University, 1965); Yen Ching-hwang, *The Overseas Chinese and the 1911 Revolution* (London: Oxford University, 1976).
16 Wakeman, *Strangers at the Gate*, p. 110n.
17 *Journal of the North China Branch of the Royal Asiatic Society* (1865), 2, p. 143; *North China Herald*, April 30, 1864.
18 Ormsby, *British Columbia*, p. 281; Morton, *Sterile Mountains*, pp. 55, 106.
19 Morton, *Sterile Mountains*, p. 94; Li, *Jianada*, p. 127.
20 Victoria *Colonist*, November 15, 1882.
21 Pierre Berton, *The Last Spike* (Toronto: McClelland & Stewart, 1971), pp. 182–185.
22 *Royal Commission, 1885*, pp. 84–85, 149; Gustavus Myers, *A History of Canadian Wealth* (Toronto: James Lewis & Samuel, 1972), p. 270.
23 *Royal Commission, 1885*, pp. 313–314; Ronald T. Takaki, *Iron Cages: Race and Culture in Nineteenth Century America* (New York: Alfred A. Knopf, 1979), pp. 229–230.
24 *Royal Commission, 1885*, p. 71.
25 Cited in Berton, *The Last Spike*, p. 198.
26 Canada, *House of Commons Debates*, 1882, p. 1476.
27 *Royal Commission, 1885*, p. 156.
28 Morton, *Sterile Mountains*, p. 77; Berton, *The Last Spike*, p. 196.
29 Berton, *The Last Spike*, p. 196.
30 Ibid., pp. 196–197.
31 Myers, *Canadian Wealth*, pp. 245–246.
32 Norman Thompson and J.H. Edgar, *Canadian Railway Development: From the Earliest Times* (Toronto: Macmillan, 1933), pp. 138–139; Berton, *The Last Spike*, pp. 196–197.
33 Berton, *The Last Spike*, p. 206.
34 Ibid., p. 213.
35 Morton, *Sterile Mountains*, p. 84; Berton, *The Last Spike*, pp. 200–201.
36 Li, *Jianada*, p. 131.
37 Berton, *The Last Spike*, p. 212.

38 Joseph Krauter and Morris Davis, *Minority Canadians: Ethnic Canadians* (Toronto: Methuen, 1978), p. 61.

39 *Royal Commission, 1885*, p. 366.

40 Berton, *The Last Spike*, p. 204.

41 Ibid.

42 *Royal Commission, 1885*, pp. 363–365.

43 Paul Voisey, 'The Chinese Community in Alberta: An Historical Perspective,' *Canadian Ethnic Studies*, II (1970), p. 18; Ban Seng Hoe, *Structural Changes of Two Chinese Communities in Alberta, Canada*, National Museum of Man, Mercury Studies, Paper 19 (Ottawa: Canadian Centre for Folk Cultural Studies); Howard Palmer, 'Anti-Oriental Sentiment in Alberta, 1880, 1920,' *Canadian Ethnic Studies*, II (December, 1970), pp. 31–57; J. Brian Dawson, 'The Chinese Experience in Frontier Calgary, 1885–1910,' pp. 124–140 in Anthony W. Rasporich and Henry C. Klassan, eds., *Frontier, Calgary: Town, City, and Region, 1875–1940* (Calgary: McClelland & Stewart West, 1975).

44 Interview with Deep Quong, Toronto, Ontario, April 13, 1981; *Project Integrate, An Ethnic Study of the Chinese Community of Moose Jaw*, Report of a Summer O.F.Y. Project. 1973, p. 9. (mimeographed).

45 Julia Kwong, 'Transformation of An Ethnic Community: From National to a Cultural Community,' in K. Victor Ujimoto and Gordon Hirabayashi, eds., *Asian Canadians and Multiculturalism: Proceedings, Asian Canadian Symposium IV of the Canadian Asian Studies Association*, Université de Montréal, Montréal, Quebec, May 25 to 28, 1980, pp. 87–88.

46 Lau Bo, 'Hostages in Canada: Toronto's Chinese (1880–1847),' *The Asianadian*, I (Summer, 1978), pp. 11–12; Paul S. Levine, 'Historical Documentation Pertaining to Overseas Chinese Organizations' (MA thesis, University of Toronto, Toronto, 1975) pp. 78–83; *Royal Commission, 1902*, p. 37.

47 Gao, 'Hamilton: The Chinatown that Died,' pp. 15–17.

48 Ban Seng Hoe, 'The Assimilation of the Sino Quebecois,' *Chinatown News*, XXVI (August 3, 1979), pp. 5, 25.

49 Lawrence N. Shyu, *The Chinese in New Brunswick*, p. 4. (mimeographed).

50 Interview with Chuck Lee, *Minority Perspective*, Channel 10, Dartmouth, Nova Scotia.

51 Margaret Chang, 'Chinese Come to Newfoundland,' *St. John's Evening Telegram*, February 11, 1978, p. 17.

52 *Royal Commission, 1885*, p. viii.

Bachelors, Boarding-Houses, and Blind Pigs: Gender Construction in a Multi-Ethnic Mining Camp, 1909–1920

NANCY M. FORESTELL

Mining communities scattered across the North American industrial frontier in the latter part of the nineteenth century acquired a reputation for violence and lawlessness. Drunken brawls between men were supposedly everyday occurrences, while gambling and prostitution were 'wide open.' Social and political commentators, journalists, and even novelists of that era constructed a portrait of the mining camp as a place of social disorder.[1] The mining towns that sprang up in northern Ontario during the early twentieth century shared a similar image. Despite the best efforts of northern Ontario businessmen and provincial government bureaucrats to provide an alternative picture of northern resource communities as peaceful and law-abiding, they continued to be viewed, particularly by those living in the southern half of the province, as centres of vice and corruption.[2] The fact that many of the region's inhabitants were male, working-class, and immigrant, with a tendency towards political radicalism, directly contributed to its perception as a dangerous and chaotic place.[3]

The communities situated within the Porcupine goldmining district did not escape this negative assessment. During the early years of the mining camp, the Porcupine quickly became known not only for its great potential as a gold producer, but also for the easy availability within its jurisdiction of liquor, gambling, and prostitutes. Describing the missionary efforts by the Presbyterian Church in the Porcupine district in 1911, Reverend J. Byrnes[4] noted that 'the forces of evil with a hundred agencies are organized to defeat the purposes of the Church, and we realize something of the difficulties which the missionary must face.'[5] Journalists from Toronto, Montreal, and New York who descended on the 'New Eldorado'[6] in its initial years claimed that violence and lawlessness were not as pervasive as in mining communities in the west. Nonetheless, they still wrote stories about white slavers and professional gamblers invading the district and about the 'uncivilized' and primitive living conditions in the region.[7] One Montreal newspaper article went so far as to print an unsubstantiated story of cannibalism in the Porcupine camp.[8]

An in-depth examination of social relations in the Porcupine camp's most populous settlement, Timmins, reveals a more nuanced picture. Economic and social conditions that existed in Timmins during its initial years resulted in the formation of a community whose inhabitants were primarily lone working-class men, a significant proportion of whom were recent European immigrants. With no resident families and living in the cramped quarters of boarding-houses or drafty shacks, the male working-class population in this town created a life for themselves outside of work which revolved around same-gender communal activities. Extending out from the masculine environment of the mine, a homosocial working-class culture was formed that involved a range of male-centred pursuits such as drinking, gambling, sports, and associational life.[9] While a number of these actitivities were illegal and occasionally ended in violence, they offered sociability and companionship to a transient male population of immigrants and Canadian migrants. At the same time, though, these pursuits upheld a public culture based on self-indulgence and male privilege. Moreover, they reinforced a male gender identity that placed a greater emphasis on 'rough' expressions of masculinity, and less on 'respectable' elements such as breadwinning.[10] In the context of a frontier mining town such as Timmins, what could be viewed from one perspective as disorder can be seen from another as a reordering of gender relations within a multi-ethnic and almost exclusively male working class.

Previous Canadian historical work has largely overlooked the significance and interconnectedness of gender, class, and race/ethnicity as a means of better understanding social relations within mining communities. One of the first and most influential pieces on the settlement of the mining frontier argued that the physical qualities of the mineral being extracted largely determined development in a region.[11] Subsequent works have tended to focus on the question whether a unique society was created in the hinterland or whether economic and cultural institutions were transplanted there from metropolitan centres.[12] Although valuable, much of this literature lacks any detailed analysis of the internal dynamics of frontier settlements.

The works of labour and working-class historians have greatly contributed to our knowledge of the class-based struggles of Canadian miners in the workplace and in the community; unfortunately, this literature reveals little about the domestic and social lives of miners.[13] The experiences of lone male sojourners have been the subject of considerable attention by immigration historians. Yet what many of these scholars have tended to characterize as immigrant behaviour, as behaviour of 'men without women' who became coarse and vulgar, should be depicted more broadly in certain contexts as male migrant behaviour.[14] Without negating cultural distinctions or the impact of the immigration process, this article will explore the significance of similarities as well as differences among men in this community.

A number of recent studies have demonstrated the importance of an approach that simultaneously considers gender and class in the lives of working-class men and women.[15] These studies emphasize that men as well as women make the history of gender relations, and that masculinity as well as femininity is constructed 'in particular social and temporal settings,' not only in the workplace, but also in the home and in the community. Recognizing the additional significance of race and ethnicity, I will illustrate that such relations could be shaped, and assume specific meanings, in the boarding-house and the blind pig, in the relative absence of women, and in a northern frontier environment.

Gold Rush on the Resource Frontier

In the spring of 1909 several prospecting parties uncovered gold veins in the vicinity of Porcupine Lake, touching off Ontario's first and largest 'gold rush.'[16] Within months, thousands of men and a small number of women journeyed to this isolated region of northern Ontario (some 230 kilometres north of the silver-mining town of Cobalt, and 70 kilometres west of the Temiskaming and Northern Railroad) to prospect or to labour for others working on mining claims. Unlike the mining of silver in Cobalt, which had required relatively little investment, equipment, or labour for sizeable profits to be made, the low-grade ore bodies being uncovered in this gold-mining district meant that large-scale capital investment and a significant labour supply were necessary.[17] Only in fictional accounts of the Porcupine gold rush would the figure of the impoverished prospector who struck it rich appear.[18] Three mining companies with substantial capital resources quickly assumed dominant positions in the camp: Dome, Hollinger, and McIntyre.[19]

During the very early stages of mining development the gold camp managed to attract the necessary skilled and unskilled labour from a variety of sources. With production in the silver mines of Cobalt noticeably on the decline by 1910, experienced miners left for the Porcupine in significant numbers. Although some of these men were immigrants from continental Europe, including Finns who had earlier migrated from mining communities in the United States and Ukrainians who had previously worked in Sudbury, most of the experienced miners were English Canadians originally from Nova Scotia, or British immigrants.[20] Other important sources of labour for the new mining camp proved to be French Canadians from rural areas of Quebec and eastern Ontario, as well as English Canadians from small towns and rural areas of southern Ontario. Large numbers of Finns, Poles, Ukrainians, and Italians also arrived from the small lumber and railway camps scattered across northern Ontario, drawn by the promise of higher wages in mining as well as better working and living conditions.[21] As social investigator Edmund Bradwin observed, new mining centres such as the Porcupine, 'pulsing with the hopes of new-found gains,' lured many immigrant workers from the isolated work camps.[22] While the Porcupine did not draw the same numbers of immigrants as did the Alberta coalfields, approximately half of the men working in the gold mines during this time were born outside Canada, most of them in continental Europe.[23] A pattern of hiring was established early on whereby non-British immigrants constituted the largest proportion of unskilled labourers as seasonal surface workers and underground as muckers, trammers, or machine-helpers, while Canadians (both English and French) and British immigrants regularly filled the more skilled positions of machine-runners, shaftmen, timbermen, mechanics, carpenters, and millmen.[24]

From the outset, moreover, regulations stipulated in the Mining Act of Ontario ensured not only the male exclusivity of mining work in the Porcupine, but, just as important, that much of the labour (both skilled and unskilled) would be performed by adult men. The prohibition of women's employment, which had been specified in general terms decades earlier, was further clarified in an amendment to the act passed in 1912:

Except as a stenographer, book-keeper or in some similar capacity, no girl or woman shall be employed at mining work or allowed to be for the purpose of employment at mining work, in or about any mine.[25]

Although the hiring of adolescent boys remained commonplace in coalfields throughout Canada (at least prior to the strict enforcement of child labour and compulsory schooling legislation in the 1920s), they were rarely employed in the hard-rock mining camps of northern Ontario.[26] At the time of the Porcupine gold rush, existing provisions in the Mining Act restricted underground labour to males seventeen years and over. In 1919 the legal age limit was raised to eighteen years. Although government regulations allowed companies to hire younger teenagers for surface work, these positions were most often filled at local gold mines by men who were too old or incapacitated to withstand the physical demands of underground work.[27]

With the financial backing of a group of men who had already grown rich from the Cobalt silver rush, and with a plentiful supply of labour, the Hollinger Consolidated Mining Company became the camp's biggest gold producer. The company experienced an initial setback when a series of fires swept through the Porcupine area in the spring and summer of 1911. The fire of 11 July was especially devastating, as it killed over seventy people and destroyed most of the townsites and mine buildings in the district.[28] In the process of rebuilding its camp, Hollinger management decided that a town site named after the company's president and co-founder, Noah Timmins, would be erected nearby.[29]

Bachelors' Town

Like many other towns situated along the northern Ontario resource frontier during the early twentieth century, Timmins was the creation of a single private corporation.[30] Without any direct government assistance or interference (provincial or municipal), Hollinger management set the parameters for the early stages of the community's development by establishing a clear separation between the mine site and the community as well as commissioning a rudimentary town plan.[31] The company did not seek to retain monopoly control, however, over property within the town's limits; instead, through a Hollinger subsidiary, the Timmins Townsite Company, lots were auctioned off beginning in the fall of 1911 in an area designated the 'Hollinger Home' district.[32] Although the prices for residential lots here were not exorbitant, from $5 to $10, few mine workers actually bid on them, given the much larger amount needed to build an adequate house on the site. Some men pooled their financial resources and purchased a single lot with the collective intension of residing together, but they were few in number. Those miners who actually bought properties often could only afford to erect small, crudely built structures.

While Hollinger built well-constructed single-family dwellings for its office and supervisory staff in an elevated area of the community known as 'the Hill,' the company did not assume any major responsibilities or expenses for housing its blue-collar employees. Initially, it financed the construction of several boarding-houses, but subsequently contracted out the operation of these buildings.[33] Even then, the company never intended that its boarding-houses would provide sufficient accommodation for all the men working at the mine, but reasoned – correctly, as it turned out – that local businesswomen and men would take the risk of building additional boarding-houses to meet the increasing demand for accommodation in town. Despite repeated announcements over the next ten years that Hollinger would soon initiate a large-scale construction project of single-family dwellings for its wage-earning employees, such a scheme did not materialize until the 1920s.[34]

The population of Timmins expanded rapidly during the first decade of the town's existence, reaching 3,843 by 1921.[35] Much of this increase can be attributed to the expanding labour force employed at Hollinger. By 1914 an average of 546 men worked at the mine, and by 1916 their number had risen to 1,056.[36] While the First World War seriously disrupted the supply of labour to the entire Porcupine mining camp, Hollinger managed to maintain a force of just over a thousand men for the duration of the conflict.[37] The transformation of Timmins into the major 'payroll town' for the Porcupine camp also spurred growth. Retail stores opened and services were offered that catered to the needs and desires not only of Hollinger employees, but also of mine workers from all over the mining district. On paydays men could spend a portion of their wages on consumer items, on a haircut and shave, or perhaps on the wide array of available leisure pursuits.

The predominance of working-class bachelors (primarily single men, but also married men without resident families) continued to be a key feature of the population in Timmins throughout this period. The community's middle class, which was composed of mine management and technical staff, retail store owners, and professionals, remained only a small proportion of the town's inhabitants.[38] The near absence of a female population during the community's earliest years would only begin to alter noticeably by the end of the 1910s. Population figures from the 1911 census, which are only available for the Porcupine district, reveal there were 1023 males for every 100 females. Yet a decade later a significant gender disparity continued. In the town of Timmins this imbalance had been reduced substantially, but there were still 163 males for every 100 females.[39]

Ongoing economic and social conditions, precipitated in large part by mining-company policy, offered very few inducements for single working-class women or for wives and children of miners to relocate permanently in the community. In a resource-based, single-industry town such as Timmins, job opportunities for working-class women were quite limited. Prohibited by law as well as local custom from working at Hollinger, or at any other mine in the Porcupine camp, women were confined to a small range of service, clerical, and retail jobs. Language qualifications for certain jobs could narrow employment opportunities even further. Many retail stores, for example, required their sales clerks to speak both in English and in French so that they could better serve English- and French-speaking residents in the community.[40] European immigrant women unable to speak either language fluently found themselves confined to positions in businesses that catered to their particular ethnic group.[41] Other ways of earning an income, such as prostitution and/or bootlegging, were potentially quite lucrative with such a predominantly male population; but these were risky ventures, given that women could be arrested for such activities.[42]

Miners who wanted to bring wives and children to Timmins were confronted with almost insurmountable difficulties during the initial years of the mining camp. The most serious obstacle to relocating families continued to be a lack of housing. Although cheap boarding-house rooms were plentiful, single-family dwellings were constantly in short supply.[43] The local board of trade acknowledged that this situation was a serious problem, but offered no solutions. At a meeting in November 1915 one board member observed, 'There are scores of married men in Timmins living in indifferent lodgings who would bring their wives and children here if housing accommodation could be secured. This certainly is not as it should be.'[44] Members of the local mining union consistently drew attention to the necessity for more housing in Timmins during and after the First World War, but the situation was not alleviated. There were rarely houses for sale, or even for rent, and when they did become available they were expensive. One four-room house lacking running water and electricity advertised for $25 a month in March 1916; that sum would have represented approximately one-third of an unskilled worker's earnings. Not only was owning or renting a house costly, but Timmins' remoteness from any major metropolitan centre meant that the prices of most consumer items were exorbitant. An October 1916 report in the local newspaper indicated that the cost of living in Timmins was at that point 27 per cent higher than in Toronto.[45] Mine workers rightly complained that they simply could not afford to bring their families to town, given the rate of wages and the cost of living.[46] At a hearing of the Royal Commission on Industrial Relations in 1919, an executive member of the Porcupine Miners' Union testified that, at the current scale of wages being paid in the district, men could not possibly maintain a family.[47] Since job opportunities for women were so scarce in Timmins, there was little likelihood that wives could supplement the wages of their husbands by securing paid work.

Inadequate health care proved to be another serious drawback for relocating wives and children. While Hollinger provided medical and hospital treatment for its employees at a cost to them of ninety cents per month, the company did not extend coverage to workers' families. Moreover, the only hospital in the community, which had been financed and built by Hollinger, was reserved for the exclusive use of mine workers. Any family member of a Hollinger employee or any other resident of Timmins needing hospital care had to travel to Haileybury (220 kilometres away) or, in some instances, as far south as Toronto.[48] Despite repeated pleas by town officials and the mining union,[49] Hollinger would not agree to make hospital facilities open to the public until 1925.[50] Just as important, the community lacked the provision of necessary educational institutions for miners' children. A Catholic primary school served as the sole educational institution in town until a public school was constructed in 1920; the first high school was opened in 1924.[51] Hollinger management spoke on occasion about wanting a more stable workforce of married men with families in the community, but they did very little to accomplish this goal until the early 1920s.

While some men did manage to find a house and scrape enough savings together to send for their families from as close as southern Ontario or as far away as Europe, they were relatively few in number. Some were immigrant sojourners who never intended to settle permanently in the community; but for many others, the obstacles were insurmountable. The relative absence of resident families for both single and married men directly contributed to the transient nature of the working-class community in Timmins. This population was continually being reconstituted as new men arrived in town while others left on an almost daily basis. Like the coalfields of Alberta, the Porcupine gold camp in general and Timmins in particular served as only a temporary stopping-place for migrants and immigrants in search of work.[52] Hollinger established a 'loyal service' bonus in September 1913 as a means of reducing at least some of the labour turnover at the mine. Under the provisions of this plan, mine workers received 15 cents extra per day after working one year for Hollinger, an additional 30 cents the second year, and 45 cents after three years.[53] This financial incentive, however, did not significantly reduce the exodus of workers. As one local businessman observed, 'There is an underlying feeling of restlessness at all times among the men here to be on the move. They come into the camp to work for a few months and as they have no social ties the novelty wears off and having seen all there is to see their "feet get itchy" and they seek new fields.[54] According to the municipal assessment roll for 1915, close to 80 per cent of the mine workers in town neither owned nor rented property in Timmins; they were designated non-householders. Five years later the same situation persisted.[55] Not bound by the constraints of having family members living in the community or the responsibilities of owning or renting property, men moved on to new jobs and relocated in other towns.

The formation and perpetuation of this bachelors' town was not an inevitable consequence of mining development on the industrial frontier. In conjunction with government regulations, Hollinger not only created an exclusively male workplace, but also played a key role in shaping a community of lone, working-class men. With its most immediate priority being intense mine development, and with the long-term prospects of the Porcupine camp still uncertain, this goldmining company was uninterested at this point in creating a more permanent workforce or a more settled community.

All Men Together: Group Living Arrangements

In the absence of resident families, the peripatetic working-class bachelors who inhabited this community during its early years congregated primarily in boarding-houses and collective households.[56] Boarding-houses served the accommodation needs of transient workers, male immigrants, and Canadians alike. Such places provided working-class men with a bed in a shared room at little expense. One of the more noticeable differences between and among such lodging places derived from the ethnic composition of the clientele, which was usually, although not exclusively, determined by the ethnicity of the owner. For example, the boarding-house run by Sasha Sannovitch and her husband Dan attracted Russian men, while French Canadians stayed at the one operated by Marie Dubois. Some form of exclusionary process may have occurred whereby immigrant men, especially those from eastern and southern Europe, were 'unwelcome' at some boarding-houses. This was certainly the case during and immediately after the First World War, when 'enemy aliens' in the community were looked upon with considerable suspicion. Still, the practice of specific boarding-houses accommodating particular ethnic groups was potentially beneficial for the men, as it offered them the opportunity to live and socialize with others who spoke the same language and shared the same cultural values. In certain instances they also shared a similar political orientation. As Robert Harney has observed, lodging places for immigrant sojourners 'served as the focus of "fellow feeling," of gossip and news.'[57]

Further variation existed between lodging places in terms of the services offered by boarding-house keepers, most of whom were women, and the domestic labour their male clientele were willing or able to perform.[58] Annie Buzowski provided her Ukrainian immigrant boarders with a full range of meals, including the lunches they took to work, and regularly did their laundry.[59] Fernanda Spadafore cleaned the rooms and washed the clothes of her *bordanti*, but the men bought and prepared their own food.[60] At another boarding-house occupied by Italian immigrants in Moneta, the Italian section of town, an informant recollected cooking and cleaning 'for all of them.'[61] During this era there were also a number of cooperatively run Finnish boarding-houses. Under this type of arrangement a group of men would buy shares in a house, which entitled each of them to a bed and meals for a small weekly charge. These cooperatives usually hired Finnish immigrant women to do much of the required domestic work.[62] Still other *poika talot* (boarding-houses) were privately operated by Finnish women such as Helmi Laakso, who 'did everything' for her male lodgers.[63] This type of diversity would appear to be attributable less to possible cultural differences and more to the adaptability and mutability of group household domestic arrangements, characteristic of the town generally in its early decades.

From the glimpses available of daily life inside the boarding-houses, a picture emerges of men talking, arguing, and sometimes fighting among themselves,[64] of men constantly leaving for or returning from one of the three shifts at Hollinger, of men lacking privacy in often overcrowded quarters, and of the incessant labour of female boarding-house operators. Living conditions in these boarding-houses were initially not much better than those encountered in the bunk-houses of isolated lumber and mining camps of that era. Provincial health officials complained constantly that boarding-houses in town were overcrowded, improperly ventilated, and quite dirty.[65] 'Foreign' boarding-houses were targeted as the worst offenders, though one official also admitted they offered the cheapest accommodation. Yet, ironically, some of these same establishments were supposedly serving so much food to lodgers during the First World War that their owners were accused of contravening federal food board regulations as well as winning 'trade away from law-abiding restaurants and hotels.'[66] Moreover, poor living conditions existed throughout the working-class district of Timmins; houses often were without running water or adequate provisions for sewage disposal, and mud was continually tracked inside from unpaved streets. With the exception of Finnish boarding-houses, which often had saunas, many lacked bathing facilities. As a public health nurse declared in a letter to her superiors after searching in vain for temporary lodgings in Timmins and encountering none that she could live in, 'this is a place for miners.'[67]

While boarding-houses accommodated a large proportion of the male working-class population in Timmins, another form of group household was popularly adopted whereby approximately three to six men would collectively pool their resources and rent or buy a house together.[68] Such households were common enough in the community that locals termed them 'bachelor families.'[69] These men usually knew one another prior to their arrival in Timmins, having come from the same village in Nova Scotia, for example, or having travelled together from the same region of Italy. Some bachelor households were composed entirely of men related to one another. As an article in the community newspaper made clear, these were not 'normal family households.'[70] Not only was the gender composition in these residences atypical, but many of the 'reproductive' functions of the 'normal' nuclear family had been removed. Without female kin present, bachelor families tended to assume some of the responsibilities of domestic work themselves,[71] but in many instances the more important and labour-intensive tasks were performed outside the household. In particular, many working-class men sent their clothes to the laundry and ate at least some of their meals in restaurants. Interestingly enough, both of these local businesses were owned and operated primarily by Chinese male immigrants.[72] Local laundries appealed directly to bachelors with advertisements such as the following: 'Most all the boys are having their sweaters washed by the Sanitary Steam Laundry because they don't run the colors.'[73] The prevalence of eating in restaurants can be inferred from a lengthy article by the editor of the *Porcupine Advance* criticizing the poor quality of food in local restaurants. He argued that this problem was particularly serious because so many men in the community were 'forced by necessity to patronize the restaurants and to trust the proprietor to supply them with wholesome food.' The editor went on to explain that such necessity arose because these men lacked the privileges of a 'home situation.'[74]

The physical environment of many of these bachelor households certainly would have conjured up few images of a 'home.' Their residences were often little more than poorly constructed shacks, lacking even a rudimentary separation between sleeping and eating spaces. Donat Bastien occupied a one-room house with several other men in which a small cook stove offered the sole source of heat.[75]

In the specific context of this newly formed mining community, the boundaries between public and private were blurred and the traditional gendered division of domestic labour was – temporarily, at least – redrawn. Lacking the unwaged labour of female family members, numerous working-class men did some necessary domestic work themselves. Not unlike the female millworkers of Paris, Ontario whom Joy Parr has so deftly analyzed, however, miners here turned frequently 'to the market,' where an expanding commercial sector offered lodging, food, and clean laundry on a cash basis.[76] The gendered contours of this particular community meant that reliance on commercial services was actually far greater here, evidence of working-class men's willingness to avoid the more onerous and time-consuming aspects of domestic labour.

Adding another dimension to the local situation, this paid domestic labour was partially carried out by women, but also notably by Chinese male immigrants who worked in the restaurants and laundries.[77] Their gender and race had contradictory implications for this group of men. On the one hand, as a small racial minority in the community who routinely and exclusively performed 'women's work,' they were not perceived as being masculine.[78] Yet, on the other hand, these Chinese male immigrants were definitely viewed as men in terms of the supposed sexual danger they posed to women in town. Community leaders queried at various points the propriety and the legality of Chinese men employing 'white' waitresses at restaurants in town because of the implied sexual threat these men posed to the women.[79] At a July 1915 meeting of the Timmins Board of Trade concerns were raised about the possibility of 'white girls' being 'corrupted' by Chinese men while working in these establishments. According to the published report of this meeting, board members discussed whether any legal provisions could be applied to restrict Chinese immigrant men from hiring women. Apparently none existed.[80] A decade later the municipal council would threaten to pass a by-law prohibiting the employment of non-Chinese women in all local restaurants 'unless [the owners] arranged to have the girls leave before the late hours than have hitherto been arranged.' Although no such by-law was ever drafted, the chief of police was subsequently directed by the council to enforce an 11 o'clock 'curfew.'[81]

In addition to domestic labour, sexual relations were also largely a matter of monetary exchange in the public realm between male working-class residents and female prostitutes in the early years of Timmins. As historians of sexuality such as John D'Emilio and Estelle Freedman have argued, wherever single men have congregated in large numbers they have often generated a significant demand for sexual commerce. Scholars of American frontier mining towns have fully documented the sizeable local markets for heterosexual services which were created in these centres.[82] The scope of prostitution in this community is difficult to gauge. Much of the documentary evidence offers only fragmentary clues to the scale of sexual commerce, or, just as important, to the interactions between male customers and the women themselves. The sources do suggest that prostitution was neither well organized nor contained within a discrete geographical area or 'red light' district. Instead, women were dispersed in several of the hotels in the central business area, and more commonly in shacks along the Mattagami River beyond the town boundaries.[83] Yet the informal tolerance of prostitution by the local police and the community at large, discussed in detail below, points to the widespread tacit acceptance, if not the existence, of heterosexual commerce.

It would be oversimplifying the situation, though, to present relations with female prostitutes as the only form of sexual expression available to, and pursued by, men in this community. As a number of recent historical studies have made clear, same-sex relationships between men have existed alongside, but have often been obscured by, the more dominant and culturally accepted practice of heterosexuality.[84] Some miners in this community certainly engaged in sexual relationships with other men, yet the paucity of available evidence makes it impossible to gauge the extent or significance of such practices.[85] Further research and additional sources will be necessary to determine exactly how permeable sexual boundaries might have been in this type of context.

Rough Stuff: A Homosocial Bachelor Culture

During this time period the physical and ideological importance of the private sphere as represented by a home and family was greatly diminished in the daily lives of most mine workers residing in Timmins.[86] While few married men shirked their financial obligations to families living elsewhere, most were not bound by the day-to-day responsibilities of being breadwinners or by the necessity of spending time with wives and children. In addition, with single working-class women in such short supply, single men had few opportunities for mixed-gender socializing. In other communities marital status had important social implications. As Joy Parr has shown in the case of men in the furniture-making town of Hanover, for example, 'fine distinctions' were made between those who were 'family men and males who were not.'[87] In Timmins, however, such distinctions were not yet made. In addition, while long-standing patterns of male exclusive leisure pursuits were giving way elsewhere to more mixed gender socializing, there was neither much opportunity nor much inclination for such activities in this mining town.[88] Consequently, a bachelor culture was constructed which included both single and married working-class men. This public culture expanded out from the male work environment and lodgings, and involved homosocial leisure pursuits.[89] The sites of these activities varied among different ethnic groups, but the rhythms of daily life in the community for most working-class men were remarkably similar. Still, these divisions reflected the beginnings of different ethnic subcultures, and also allowed for the simultaneous expression of gender, class, and ethnic identities among immigrants and Canadians alike.

This bachelor culture was shaped as much by those who did not participate in it as by those who did. For the Chinese male immigrants who worked in the laundries and restaurants of Timmins, both race and gender elements combined to bar them from being included in the predominant masculine culture. Compounding ongoing and pronounced racial discrimination against them, these men were not engaged in what could be considered masculine work – the common claim for much of the rest of male population. The small Chinese community instead constructed its own separate and racially distinct 'bachelor society' by spending time outside of work engaged in such homosocial activities as opium-smoking, gambling, and a mutual aid association.[90]

In the 'manly' context of this mining town, moreover, the small number of working-class women who resided in Timmins appeared largely on the margins of community life. Unlike the situation in southern Ontario industrial centres, where a generation of young working-class women entering the labour force in ever greater numbers were fundamentally altering the urban cultural landscape, women in this northern town lacked both the numerical strength and the economic influence to shape the social contours of Timmins more favourably.[91] Certainly there were few 'respectable' social spaces where women could congregate among themselves or socialize with husbands or boyfriends.[92] There were dances, picnics on public holidays, and the occasional house-party, but such events were sporadic.[93] And, with the exception of those women who were prostitutes and bootleggers, few participated in any of the 'rough' amusements.[94] Yet even prostitutes, who assumed a visible and public presence in other frontier mining towns, made only brief appearances in this overwhelmingly masculine environment.

In keeping with the proclivities of working-class men elsewhere, drinking played a central role in the social activities of mine workers in Timmins.[95] Local circumstances, however, made this pastime less respectable as it simultaneously made it more important.[96] During the period under examination, the sale and consumption of liquor was prohibited by one means or another throughout the entire Porcupine camp. A brief explanation of this situation is necessary, since it had a major influence on the location, legality, and apparent morality of consuming liquor. Under an amendment of the Ontario Mining Act passed in 1906, liquor licences could not be issued for any tavern or shop within six miles of a mine or mining camp.[97] Whereas miners in Cobalt could travel a short distance outside their mine limit to licensed hotels in Haileybury or New Liskeard, no such option existed for men in the Porcupine.[98] Saloons in South Porcupine and Timmins were permitted to sell only temperance beers, appropriately named 'soft' drinks, which consisted of 2 per cent alcohol. The importation of liquor to the district for personal use was also forbidden. The passage of the Ontario Temperance Act in 1916 superseded the provisions of the Mining Act by extending prohibition throughout the province. While the OTA closed all drinking establishments and banned the sale of liquor, a loophole in the legislation allowed individuals, who managed by whatever means to purchase alcohol, to keep it legally in private households.[99] Since all boarding-houses and single-family dwellings with more than three lodgers were specifically excluded from the definition of 'private' in this legislation, it meant that most working-class men in Timmins who wished to continue drinking alcohol would have to do it illegally.[100]

Rather than inhibiting the consumption of alcohol, however, the terms of prohibition stimulated a flourishing trade in illicit liquor which revolved around so-called blind pigs.[101] At these unlawful establishments alcohol could be obtained from a bootlegger for an inflated price.[102] These locales provided an accessible supply of liquor, and, initially, one of the few places in the community where working-class men could congregate. Most operated in private residences, but, ironically, they offered much needed 'public' places for men to gather and socialize. Writing to the *Cobalt Nugget* in April 1912, one Timmins resident pointed out that 'The blind pigs are the sole source of recreation for the men working in the mines.'[103] The same year an editorial in the newspaper suggested that as many as ninety of them were located within the Porcupine mining district.[104]

Yet even when other places of leisure became available, the appeal of these establishments remained. Like the boarding-houses, individual blind pigs in this community tended to lure male customers from one particular ethnic group. They provided space for men from similar ethnic backgrounds who spoke the same language to meet, to exchange gossip, and to drink. In the case of Italian men, for example, these bars represented the continuation of a tradition of visiting with *paesani* in one's free time.[105] Blind pigs were also enticing because they accommodated the work schedules of miners by staying open for extended hours and on Sundays. Miners finishing an afternoon shift at Hollinger around 11 P.M. and wanting some place to relax could easily find a bootlegger open for business long after other legitimate establishments were forced to close. When the town police raided a blind pig one Monday night in August 1918, the scene they encountered was described as follows: '[The owner] and some friends were sitting in a friendly way around a table on which was a whisky jug and some glasses.'[106] The report also mentioned that the men were playing poker.

The attraction of card games proved to be still another reason drawing working-class men to blind pigs. When and where drinking occurred, gambling also seems to have been prevalent. Accusations surfaced occasionally that professional gamblers were fleecing miners 'of their hard earned money,' but most of the gambling in these establishments took place between peers for small stakes.[107] While drinking liquor was illegal all of the time, gambling was against the law only part of the time. The federal Lord's Day Act prohibited gambling of any form on Sundays but on no other days of the week.[108] Thus a friendly game of poker that began on Saturday night became an illegal act when prolonged into the early hours of Sunday morning.

Far from undermining this homosocial culture based on drinking and gambling, the advent of commercial business ventures in Timmins focusing on entertainment and recreation only served to reinforce it. Businesses opened in Timmins that catered to the predominantly male working-class population. The proliferation of poolrooms was particularly noticeable. By way of comparison with other northern Ontario communities, one local resident suggested somewhat sarcastically that 'in poolrooms this town has Sudbury or any other place beat seven ways.'[109] They became yet another place in town where men could congregate, obtain liquor, and place a bet, only in this instance on a game of pool. Several theatres opened and brought vaudeville acts to town, and regularly sponsored boxing and wrestling matches. The sporting events consistently drew large crowds by setting a local 'favourite son' against a known outsider. The spectators at these events were primarily working-class men, as revealed by the manager of the Empire Theatre when he postponed one match from a Tuesday to a Saturday night. He explained that the latter night was more convenient, since 'the men do not have to get up for work at the mine the next day.'[110] Beyond their immediate appeal as 'clever exhibitions in the manly art,' boxing and wrestling offered an additional outlet for gambling. One wrestling match at the Timmins Coliseum in September 1915 was expected 'to carry a side bet of one hundred dollars.'[111]

Of course, prostitution represented another notable commercial venture that catered to a large population of bachelors. As noted earlier, sexual relations (along with domestic labour) were relegated primarily to the public realm during the town's first decade as a matter of monetary exchange. Prostitutes were dispersed throughout the community and, in some instances, were also part of the operation of blind pigs. The presence of prostitutes afforded men the opportunity to engage in heterosexual relations, albeit infrequently. Given the expense of a single sexual encounter, which reportedly could cost anywhere from $2 to $4, or more than a day's pay at the higher end of the scale, most mine workers could afford sexual relations only sporadically.[112] Many working-class men typically visited a prostitute after receiving their biweekly wage packet. One informant recalled the common sight on paydays of men congregating in the hallway of a local hotel waiting for 'their turn.'[113]   These activities served to uphold – at least the public appearance of – a prominent component of this male homosocial culture: heterosexual masculinity.[114]

During this initial stage of the community's development the local authorities made notable distinctions in terms of how they attempted to regulate these male-centred 'vices.' The police went to considerable lengths when it came to enforcing legal provisions restricting drinking and the prohibition of gambling on Sundays.[115] Indeed, they repeatedly tried to 'clean up' these pursuits by arresting both operators and customers.[116] None the less, they were completely unsuccessful in eradicating these activities. In part, this failure can be attributed to the relatively small size of the local and provincial police forces who were responsible for enforcing the law.[117] Just as important, the male working-class population openly obstructed the police in their attempts to eliminate them. In fact, special agents, or 'spotters,' were brought into the community to infiltrate illegally run drinking establishments because residents so often tipped off operators when the police were sighted nearby.[118] Inhabitants also proved quite reluctant to provide evidence in court. Police officials and local community boosters on occasion tried to allege that 'foreigners' were the main culprits, but police court reports demonstrate that Canadian and immigrant men from all ethnic groups were well represented among those who were actually arrested.[119]

The police took a quite different approach with regard to prostitution in Timmins. Although prostitution was not legalized or even formally condoned here, as was the case in some frontier mining towns in the Canadian and American west, the evidence suggests that it was informally tolerated.[120] A careful reading of published court reports fails to reveal any organized raids of houses of 'ill fame' conducted by the police. Arrests were made on occasion, although never of male customers, usually as a result of local citizen complaints. Newspaper reports indicate that neighbours usually lodged complaints because of noisy disturbances at these residences rather than out of any sense of moral outrage.[121] In some instances the women were not even arrested in such circumstances, but simply asked to leave town:

Three women of an undesirable type who have been living in a house on Station street have recently been annoying the good people of the neighbourhood by the noise and rowdyism created at unearthly hours of the late night and morning. Several complaints have been made to the police, the latter gave the undesirables a few hours to leave town, and consequently the neighbourhood has been freed from the nuisance.[122]

As further evidence of the toleration of prostitution, one informant recalled the weekly visits of medical doctors to several of the hotels to ensure that the women were free of venereal diseases.[123]

Yet why were some of these illicit activities tolerated while others were not? It would appear that local authorities attempted to clean up drinking and gambling because they wanted to inhibit working-class men from engaging in certain 'bad habits.' There was no such concern about regulating the activities of the women involved in prostitution. Indeed, it is possible to argue that these prostitutes provided an essential service in a community of bachelors.

While there is no indication that Hollinger necessarily approved of any the illicit social activities, the company did not actively engage in any efforts to restrict them.[124] With ongoing problems of high labour turnover during the first decade, the corporation seems to have adopted the position that as long its economic interests were not threatened it would not directly intercede to limit such activities. Hollinger did attempt, however, to offer a more 'healthy and wholesome'[125] outlet for its employees during their non-working hours through the construction of several recreational facilities and the encouragement of various team sports.[126] The company built an arena as well as an athletic field, and sponsored both a hockey and a baseball team. Without question these sports proved to be a popular pastime for working-class men in this community. While not all them participated in hockey or baseball, many watched and cheered for their local teams. During the long northern Ontario winter, men in Timmins played hockey on nearby lakes and, by 1914, in the local arena. By that time a district league had been organized for the entire Porcupine camp which included teams from a number of the larger mines, one of them being Hollinger.[127] A measure of the popularity of these league games can be found in the sports pages of the local newspaper. Reports mentioned consistently that attendance at district hockey games reached between four and five hundred spectators. As these reports also remarked on occasion that fights broke out between men rooting for rival teams, clearly the intensity of the competition on the ice sometimes spilled over into the stands.[128] In the summer months attention shifted to baseball. A district league was also established for this sport, with many of the same mining companies fielding a baseball team. Swarms of blackflies periodically marred the enjoyment of baseball games for participants and spectators, but both groups were willing to withstand some discomfort in exchange for the opportunity to play or see their team play.[129] Gambling again proved to be one of the appeals of attending such events, as many wagered on games.[130] In all likelihood Hollinger additionally intended for team sports to instil greater loyalty and discipline within its workforce; while they may have had some success in achieving the first goal, it would appear that the second as yet remained beyond reach.[131]

Although these particular team sports attracted working-class men from all ethnic backgrounds as spectators, it is worth noting that the players were almost exclusively anglophone and francophone Canadians. The children of European immigrants in this community would later grow up playing hockey and baseball, but the sojourners of this era chose to participate in traditional sports of their country of origin. Finnish residents, for example, skied downhill and cross country during the winter, and in the summer they competed with one another in a range of track and field events.[132] Italian men groomed several vacant lots in Moneta where they played *bocci*.[133] And even British immigrants, who so often were found in the company of English Canadians, played soccer against one another.[134] Rather than representing a discrete alternative to other male-centred recreational pursuits, sports signified just one of a range of activities in which men could experience pleasure and express competitiveness and a particular form of tough 'masculinity.'[135]

Another component of this homosocial culture involved associational life. During this first decade working-class men initiated a process of forming gender-exclusive groups that offered both mutual aid and sociability.[136] Confronted by a dangerous work environment and lacking the financial and physical support of resident family members, bachelors derived much-needed benefits from these organizations in the form of a small income for temporary illnesses and burial costs in more unfortunate circumstances. Transiency militated against large or sustained memberships at this time, but various societies were organized, primarily along ethnic and religious lines. European immigrant men created self-described mutual aid associations,[137] while English Canadian and British Protestants established a number of fraternal orders.[138] Since Catholic clergy frowned upon fraternal orders because of their secret rituals and, at times, their anti-Catholicism, men of this religion instituted their own organization, the Knights of Columbus, which was loosely affiliated with the Catholic Church.[139]

Saturday night marked the end of a long work week for most miners and the beginning of an extended period of leisure. For some men, Sunday represented a day of rest and spiritual obligation; but for many others it provided them the opportunity to engage in a lengthy card game or visit with friends at one of the local bootleggers. For several years after Timmins' inception, Protestant and Catholic church services were irregular, as they depended upon the presence of missionaries serving settlements scattered across wide expanses of northern Ontario.[140] In a letter that appeared in the *Christian Guardian*, a Methodist missionary described his attempts at holding a service in a local boarding-house in the spring of 1912:

When I went in I found a number of men gathered around the old table, watching four others playing a game of cards known as 'poker.' I went over and watched them play for awhile, then I asked them to come and have some singing when they were through with their game; some of them laughed; some of them cursed but I took no notice.[141]

Regular services began with the arrival of permanent clergy and the construction of church buildings, but these developments still did not guarantee strict Sunday observance. While the religious needs of English Protestants as well as French and English Catholics were addressed, immigrant Finns, Russians, Ukrainians, and Italians lacked resident clergy.[142] The Finnish and Ukrainian radicals, who constituted most of the socialists in the community, refused contact with any church.[143] Clergymen in the community observed, however, that infrequent church attendance was characteristic not only of immigrant residents, but of the male population as a whole. Young working-class men, as a recent study by Lynne Marks has illustrated, have historically been the least likely to attend church.[145]

In the decades that followed, the Sabbath would become a 'family day' for the wage-earning men of Timmins; but for now it signified the continuation of activities engaged in on Saturday nights, outbursts of drunken revelry being especially prevalent. With some humour, the local newspaper included such reports as the following: 'It was a fine day on Sunday but it got noisy as the hours wore along until around midnight there was considerable din and clamour, strong words, and stronger breaths in the main part of town.'[146] Under the Lord's Day Act poolrooms and theatres were forced to close, leaving the blind pigs one of the few places of recreation on the Sabbath. Acknowledging that 'amusements were scarce,' one town official nevertheless urged men to 'take a true vacation on Sunday and get into the open, breathe the good air, instead of sitting around in a stuffy back room swigging down a few drinks.'[147] Yet organized sporting events also contravened the federal legislation on Sunday observance. In a number of instances when baseball and hockey games were held on the Sabbath,[148] this information was somehow brought to the attention of members of the Lord's Day Alliance in Toronto, who subsequently complained to provincial police.[149] Legal prosecution never resulted, but local police officers were directed to prevent further such sporting events from taking place. Informal matches may have continued, but these measures successfully inhibited organized games on Sundays.

Local male businessmen and clergy tried at various times to organize a social club which would provide an alternative to the specific temptations of the blind pigs and generally improve moral standards.[150] Their efforts were primarily directed at the male working-class population, as middle-class men already had access to private tennis, golf, and social clubs in the community. At a meeting of the local Board of Trade in September 1916, one retail merchant emphasized the need 'to establish a permanent club with attractions for young men to spend their evenings sociably.'[151] While other board members concurred, nothing came of the suggestion. Subsequent proposals during the war also proved futile, but with the substantial influx of men into Timmins after the Armistice, civic leaders were encouraged to try again. Separate meetings were initially held at the Catholic and Presbyterian churches to consider the formation of a club that would provide 'wholesome and elevating recreations and environments for the men here in increasing numbers.' The organizers envisioned a 'home centre' that would entice men 'whose spare moments very often consist of poker playing and the consumption of bootleg whisky' by including a billiard room, bowling alley, refreshment parlour, and library in their plans. Further discussions took place between and among town officials, clergy, and businessmen about raising money for a club building, but no concrete strategy materialized.[152] Less than a year later concerned citizens again called a meeting 'for those who see or feel the need for wholesome places in the Camp for men, and especially for those whose homes are not here.'[153] The only outcome of this appeal was the formation of a small group that held infrequent 'literary and social evenings' in the basement of the Presbyterian church. Individuals also made repeated appeals to the Young Men's Christian Association to establish a branch in Timmins, but as the secretary of the National Council pointed out in responding to one of these requests, without sufficient local interest and financial resources nothing could be done.[154] Hollinger had been approached about donating funds for a YMCA centre in Timmins, but the company had declined. Perhaps not surprisingly, a corporation whose president and major stockholder was Catholic would be unwilling to support a Protestant organization such as the YMCA. The company also showed no interest in stepping into the breach to finance any other project. In the absence of financial and moral support from Hollinger, no large-scale project materialized.

By the mid-1920s the composition of the working class in Timmins began to alter noticeably. Ever great numbers of married miners were settling permanently in the community with their wives and children. Lone men would continue to account for a significant proportion of the working class, but they would no longer constitute the majority. These changes did not affect in any way the male exclusivity of mining work, but it did influence the location, remuneration, and gender of domestic labour. Reproductive labour largely reverted to the home, where unpaid housewives did the necessary work. At the same time, the bachelor culture was gradually dismantled as married men spent a portion of their leisure time involved in family-centred recreational activities and single men had greater opportunities to socialize with single women. As part of an ongoing process of social and economic transformation in this community, gender identities and gender relations within the working class were reconstituted and reordered.

NOTES

1 For a discussion of contemporary views of frontier mining towns in the United States, see Duane Smith, *Rocky Mountain Mining Camps: The Urban Frontier* (Bloomington: Indiana University Press, 1979), 78–98; see also Ralph Mann, *After the Gold Rush: Society in Grass Valley and Nevada City, California, 1849–1870* (Stanford: Stanford University Press, 1982).

2 Karen Dubinsky, *Improper Advances: Rape and Heterosexual Conflict in Ontario, 1880–1929* (Chicago: University of Chicago, 1993), 152.

3 *Ibid.*, 156; see also Karen Dubinsky and Franca Iacovetta, 'Murder, Womanly Virtue, and Motherhood: The Case of Angelina Napolitano, 1911–1922,' *Canadian Historical Review* 72:4 (December 1991), 505–31.

4 In order to ensure the privacy of residents who agreed to oral interviews and those referred to in other documentary sources, pseudonyms have been devised. In the case of well-known public figures who were involved in business, political, or religious activities, actual surnames have been retained.

5 Rev. J. Byrnes, *Greater or Northern Ontario*, Women's Home Missionary Society of the Presbyterian Church in Canada, 1911.

6 Investors in the mining camp created this term to denote its great potential as a gold producer.

7 See, for example, *Cobalt Nugget*, 19 February 1910; 20 July 1910; 4 March
   1911; 21 April 1911; 1 September 1911. *Porcupine Advance*, 9 August 1912.
8 *Cobalt Nugget*, 19 February 1910.
9 On other aspects of miners' lives outside the workplace, see Nancy
   Forestell, 'All That Glitters Is Not Gold: The Gendered Dimensions of Work,
   Family and Community Life in the Northern Ontario Goldmining Town of
   Timmins, 1909–1950' (PhD thesis, University of Toronto, 1993).
10 The meaning and importance of respectability for working-class men varied
   somewhat among different ethnic groups, occupations, regions, and even
   countries. Nevertheless, during the early twentieth century some shared
   principles were recognized. By this time respectability was less dependent
   on skill definition than it had been in the nineteenth century, and more
   dependent on the ability of individual workers to provide for their families
   as breadwinners. For a discussion of the rough and respectable in the nineteenth century, see Peter DeLottinville, 'Joe Beef of Montreal: Working-Class
   Culture and the Tavern, 1869–1889,' *Labour/Le Travailleur* 8–9 (Autumn/
   Spring 1981–2), 9–40; and Bryan Palmer, *Working-Class Experience: The Rise
   and Reconstitution of Canadian Labour, 1800–1980* (Toronto: Butterworths,
   1983), 29–39; Lynne Marks, *Revivals and Roller Rinks: Religion, Leisure, and
   Identity in Late Nineteenth-Century Small Town Ontario* (Toronto: University
   of Toronto Press, 1996), 81–90. For a discussion of working-class male
   respectability in the twentieth century, see Suzanne Morton, *Ideal Surroundings: Domestic Life in a Working-Class Suburb in the 1920s* (Toronto: University
   of Toronto Press, 1995), 108–30.
11 Harold Innis, 'Settlement and the Mining Frontier,' in A.R.M. Lower and
   H.A. Innis, *Settlement of the Forest and Mining Frontier* (Toronto: Macmillan,
   1936).
12 See J.M.S. Careless, 'Frontierism, Metropolitanism and Canadian History,'
   Canadian Historical Review 35:1 (March 1954), 1–25; S.D. Clark, 'Mining
   Society in British Columbia and the Yukon,' in *British Columbia: Historical
   Readings*, ed. by Peter Ward and Robert McDonald (Vancouver: Douglas
   and McIntyre, 1983), 215–30; and Morris Zaslow, *The Opening of the Canadian
   North, 1870–1914* (Toronto: McClelland and Stewart, 1971). For a more
   recent piece within this debate, see Doug Baldwin, 'Imitation vs Innovation:
   Cobalt as an Urban Frontier Town,' *Laurentian University Review* 11:2
   (February 1979), 23–43. See Jeremy Mouat, *Roaring Days: Rossland's Mines
   and the History of British Columbia* (Vancouver: University of British Columbia Press, 1995).
13 Allen Seager, 'A Proletariat in Wild Rose Country: The Alberta Miners,
   1915–1945' (PhD thesis, York University, 1982); Allen Seager, 'Class

Ethnicity and Politics in the Alberta Coalfields, 1905–1945,' in *'Struggle a Hard Battle': Essays on Working-Class Immigrants*, ed. Dirk Hoerder (De Kalb: Northern Illinois University Press, 1986), 304–25; David Frank, 'The Cape Breton Coal Miners, 1917–1926' (PhD thesis, Dalhousie University, 1979); David Frank, 'Company Town/Labour Town: Local Government in the Cape Breton Coal Towns, 1917–1926,' *Histoire sociale/Social History* 27 (May 1981), 77–96; Ian McKay, 'Industry, Work and Community in the Cumberland Coalfields, 1848–1927' (PhD thesis, Dalhousie University, 1983). Steven Penfold's discussion of the Cape Breton coal strikes in the 1920s represents an important departure: see 'Have You No Manhood in You? Gender and Class in the Cape Breton Coal Towns, 1920–1926,' *Acadiensis* 23:2 (Spring 1994), 21–44.

14 See especially Robert Harney, 'Men Without Women: Italian Migrants in Canada, 1885–1930,' in *The Italian Immigrant Women in North America*, ed. Betty Caroli et al. (Toronto: Multicultural History Society of Ontario, 1978), 79–101. For an excellent overview and analysis of Canadian immigration history, see Franca Iacovetta, 'Manly Militants, Cohesive Communities and Defiant Domestics: Writing about Immigrants in Canadian Historical Scholarship,' *Labour/Le Travail* 36 (Fall 1995), 217–52.

15 Joy Parr, *The Gender of Breadwinners: Women, Men and Change in Two Industrial Towns, 1880–1950* (Toronto: University of Toronto Press, 1990), 9. Historical studies of working-class masculinity are rapidly expanding. See, for example, Mark Rosenfeld, '"She Was Hard Life": Work, Family Politics and Ideology in the Railway Ward of a Central Ontario Town, 1900–1960' (PhD thesis, York University, 1990); Marks, *Revivals and Roller Rinks*; Morton, *Ideal Surroundings*; Chris Burr, '"That Coming Curse – The Incompetent Compositres": Class and Gender Relations in the Toronto Typographical Union during the Nineteenth Century,' *Canadian Historical Review* 74:3 (September 1993), 233–66; Cecilia Danysk, '"A Bachelor's Paradise": Homesteaders, Hired Hands, and the Construction of Masculinity, 1909–1925,' in *Making Western Canada: Essays on European Colonization and Settlement*, ed. Catherine Cavanaugh and Jeremy Mouat (Toronto: Garamond, 1996), 154–85; Ava Baron, 'An "Other" Side of Gender Antagonization at Work: Men, Boys and Remasculinization of Printers' Work, 1830–1920,' in *Work Engendered: Toward a New History of American Labour* (New York: Cornell University Press, 1991), 47–69; Paul Willis, 'Shop-Floor Culture, Masculinity and the Wage Form' in *Working-Class Culture: Studies in History and Theory* (New York: St Martin's Press, 1979), 185–200. For a historiographical discussion, see Steven Maynard, 'Rough Work and Rugged Men: the Social Construction of Masculinity in Working-Class History,' *Labour/Le Travail* 23 (Spring

1989), 159–70; Ava Baron, 'On Looking At Men: Masculinity and the Making of a Gendered Working-Class History,' in *Feminists Revision History*, edited by Anne-Louise Shapiro (New Brunswick: Rutgers, 1994), 146–71; Michael Roper and John Tosh, 'Introduction: Historians and the Politics of Masculinity,' in *Manful Assertions: Masculinities in Britain Since 1800*, ed. Michael Roper and John Tosh (London: Routledge, 1991), 1–24; John Tosh, 'What Should Historians Do with Masculinity? Reflections on Nineteenth-Century Britain,' *History Workshop Journal* 38 (Autumn 1994), 179–202; Joy Parr, 'Gender History and Historical Practice,' in *Gender and History in Canada*, ed. Joy Parr and Mark Rosenfeld (Toronto: Copp Clark, 1996), 8–28. For a theoretical discussion of masculinity see Lynne Segal, *Changing Masculinities, Changing Men* (New Brunswick, NJ: Rutgers, 1990); R.W. Connell, *Masculinities* (Berkeley: University of California Press, 1995); Rowena Chapman and Jonathan Rutherford, *Male Order: Unwrapping Masculinity* (London: Lawrence and Wishart, 1988); Andrea Cornall and Nancy Lindisfarne, 'Dislocating Masculinity: Gender, Power and Anthropology,' in *Dislocating Masculinity: Comparative Ethnographies*, ed. Andrea Cornwall and Nancy Lindisfarne (London: Routledge, 1994), 11–47.

16 Ontario, *Annual Report of the Bureau of Mines, 1909*, 120. Romanticized accounts include D.M. Bourdais, *Metals and Mines: The Story of Canadian Mining* (Toronto: McClelland and Stewart, 1957), and A. Pain, *The Way North: Men, Mines and Miners* (Toronto: Ryerson, 1964).

17 Innis, 'Settlement and the Mining Frontier,' 349.

18 Phil Moore, *Slag and Gold: A Tale of the Porcupine Trail* (Toronto: Macmillan, 1924).

19 Innis, 'Settlement of the Mining Frontier,' 350.

20 Ibid., 326.

21 Peter Vasiliadis, *Dangerous Truth: Interethnic Competition in a Northeastern Ontario Goldmining Center* (New York: AMS Press, 1989), 64; James Di Giacomo, 'The Italians of Timmins: Micro and Macro Ethnicity in a Northern Resource Community' (MA thesis, York University, 1982), 45; Allen Seager, 'Finnish Canadians and the Ontario Miners' Movement, *Polyphony* 3:2 (Fall 1981), 35–45.

22 Edmund W. Bradwin, *The Bunkhouse Man: A Study of Work and Pay in the Camps of Canada, 1903–1914* (Toronto: University of Toronto Press, 1972). Originally published 1928.

23 According to census data for 1911, 47.1 per cent of the operatives in Ontario gold-mining that year were born outside of Canada, while in 1921 immigrants accounted for 53.4 per cent of the workforce. Since most gold production in the province took place in the Porcupine before, during, and

after the First World War, one can surmise that these percentages accurately represent the workforce over this period. See Canada, *Fifth Census of Canada, 1911*, vol. 6, table 5; and Canada, *Sixth Census of Canada, 1921*, vol. 4, table 6.

While native men were employed as casual labour in resource-industry jobs elsewhere in northern Ontario, none of the documentary or oral sources reveal their presence in the Porcupine. This situation can be attributed, at least in part, to the sparse Cree population, indigenous to this area of the North, in the district surrounding the Porcupine goldfields. On the employment of native men in mining and lumbering, not only in British Columbia, but also in Ontario, see Rolf Knight, *Indians at Work: An Informal History of Native Indian Labour in British Columbia, 1838–1930* (Vancouver: Star Books, 1978), 144–65. A detailed history of the social and economic impact of the advancing resource industry frontier on native peoples in northern Ontario has yet to be written.

24 Ontario, *Annual Report of the Bureau of Mines, 1911*, 14; S. Price, 'Limitations of the Hours of Labor of Underground Workmen in the Mines of Ontario,' *Sessional Papers, 1913*, vol. 13, no. 82, 10.

25 Ontario, An Act to Amend the Mining Act of Ontario, 1912 (1912) 8 Edw. VII, c. 21. In various localities in Britain during the nineteenth century, women were hired to work both below and above ground in coal-mining. Legislative restrictions were placed on their employment by the British Parliament from the 1880s onwards. As far as can be determined, women were never employed in any mining operations in Canada. On British women in coal-mining, see Angela John, *By the Sweat of Their Brow: Women Workers in Victorian Coal Mines* (London: Routledge and Kegan Paul, 1984).

26 On child labour in Canadian coal mines, see Ian McKay, 'The Realm of Uncertainty: The Experience of Work in the Cumberland Coal Mines, 1873–1927,' *Acadiensis* 16:2 (Autumn 1986), 3–57; Lynne Bowen, *Boss Whistle: The Coal Miners of Vancouver Remember* (Latzville, BC: Oolichan Books, 1982), 43–7; and Robert McIntosh, 'The Boys in the Nova Scotian Coal Mines: 1873–1928,' *Acadiensis* 16:3 (Spring 1987), 35–50. For a gendered analysis of the transformation of an occupation into adult men's work, see Baron, 'An "Other" Side of Gender Antagonism at Work,' 47–69.

27 Prior to 1919, boys fourteen years of age and over were allowed to work on the surface. After an amendment was passed in that year, the age limit rose to sixteen years. An Act to Amend the Mining Act of Ontario, 1919 (1919) 2 Geo. V, c. 8. As tangible evidence for the absence of adolescent boys, published census data from 1921 on the provincial gold-mining industry broken down by age groups tabulated only 2 out of 1,533 operatives under sixteen

years of age. Even in the sixteen-to-seventeen age group there were just 16. Canada, *Sixth Census of Canada, 1921*, vol. 4, table 4.

28 Ontario, *Annual Report of the Bureau of Mines, 1911*, 62.

29 For a history of Hollinger Consolidated Gold Mines Limited and its president, Noah Timmins, see N.A. Timmins, 'A Reminiscent History,' *Canadian Mining Journal* 56 (September 1935), 353–62. See also Bourdais, *Metals and Men*, 158–60.

30 Gilbert Stelter and Alan Artibise, 'Canadian Resource Towns in Historical Perspective,' *Plan Canada* 18 (1978), 11.

31 The provincial government, however, played an active role in encouraging the development of the gold-mining industry through a variety of incentives that economically benefited mining companies. For a detailed discussion on this topic, see H.V. Nelles, *The Politics of Development: Forests, Mines and Hydro-Electric Power in Ontario, 1849–1941* (Toronto: Macmillan, 1974), 110–32.

32 Timmins Lions Club, *The Book of Timmins and the Porcupine: Official Publication of the Celebration of Timmins' Silver Jubilee, 1937* (Timmins, Ont.: Lions Club, 1937), 40.

33 *Annual Report of Hollinger Gold Mines Limited, 1911*, 14.

34 On the paternalistic policies of Hollinger in the operation of Timmins as a company town in the 1910s and 1920s, see Forestell, 'All That Glitters Is Not Gold,' chapter 2.

35 *Cobalt Nugget*, 2 January 1912; Canada, *Sixth Census of Canada, 1921*, vol. 1, table 8.

36 *Annual Report of Hollinger Gold Mines Limited, 1914*, 5, and 1916, 18.

37 Ibid., 1917, 16, and 1918, 11.

38 Derived from Timmins Municipal Archives (TMA), Municipal Assessment Roll, 1915; Municipal Assessment Roll, 1915; Municipal Assessment Roll, 1920.

39 Canada, *Fifth Census of Canada, 1911*, vol. 6, table 2; Canada, *Sixth Census of Canada, 1921*, vol. 1, table 8.

40 Advertisements such as the following appeared regularly: 'Wanted for store work. Must speak English and French.' *Porcupine Advance*, 15 November 1915.

41 See interviews with Edna Anduchuk, born 1910, and Peggy Boychuck, born 1913. Aili Schneider, who was employed for a time in her father's bakery, noted in her published autobiography that it took her a long time to learn English because 'We had very few customers who did not speak English.' See Aili Gronlund Schneider, *The Finnish Baker's Daughter* (Toronto: MHSO, 1986), 28. Domestic service was one notable exception to this pattern. Since

domestic work did not entail 'serving the public,' immigrant women could get by with only limited second-language abilities. Finnish women in particular pursued domestic service work. Advertisements placed by Finnish women seeking work as domestics appeared continually in the local newspaper. See *Porcupine Advance*, 13 August 1915; 4 June 1916; and 22 January 1919. For a discussion of the general trend of Finnish immigrant women as domestics, see Varpu Lindström-Best, *Defiant Sisters: A Social History of Finnish Immigrant Women in Canada* (Toronto: Multicultural History Society of Ontario, 1988), 84–114.

42 For examples of court cases involving women found guilty of prostitution or bootlegging, see *Cobalt Nugget*, 2 November 1912; and *Porcupine Advance*, 15 September 1915; 6 April 1916; 1 July 1916; 23 March 1917.

43 *Porcupine Advance*, 18 September 1914. An article in this issue suggested that 'never has there been a time when there were nearly enough houses to meet the demand.'

44 Ibid., 12 November 1915.

45 Ibid., 11 October 1916.

46 *Miners' Magazine* (Butte, Montana), June 1917. Cole Harris describes a similar situation in Slocan, BC. See Cole Harris, 'Industry and the Good Life Around Idaho Peak,' *Canadian Historical Review* 66:3 (1985), 315–43.

47 Canada, Royal Commission on Industrial Relations, 1919, Minutes of Evidence, 3, 1787.

48 Ibid., vol. 3, 1843.

49 The Porcupine Miners' Union complained to the Ontario Board of Health about this situation as early as June 1914. See Ontario, *Annual Report of the Provincial Board of Health, 1914*, 59. For subsequent discussions by the miners' union and the town council on this matter, see *Porcupine Advance*, 10 January 1917 and 1 May 1918.

50 *Porcupine Advance*, 12 September 1921.

51 Ibid., 31 June 1918; 17 May 1920; 5 February 1924.

52 Seager, 'A Proletariate in Wild Rose Country,' 81.

53 Innis, 'Settlement and the Mining Frontier,' 360.

54 *Porcupine Advance*, 30 August 1916.

55 Derived from TMA, Municipal Assessment Roll, 1915; Municipal Assessment Roll, 1920.

56 According to the assessment rolls, there were 19 boarding-houses in Timmins in 1915 and 25 in 1920. These figures do not include more informal arrangements where families had one or two boarders. See TMA, Timmins Municipal Assessment Rolls, 1915 and 1920.

57 In a pioneering piece on this subject, Robert Harney has argued persua-

sively that boarding-houses constituted an important ethnic institution for all sojourners. See Robert Harney, 'Boarding and Belonging,' *Urban History Review* 2 (1978), 29. The secondary literature on this crucial aspect of migrant life is quite sparse and has tended to focus on specific immigrant ethnic groups. See Lillian Petroff, 'Sojourner and Settler: the Macedonian Presence in the City, 1903–1940,' in *Gathering Place: People and Neighbourhoods in Toronto, 1934–1945* (Toronto: Multicultural History Society of Ontario, 1985), 177–203; Isabel Kaprielian, 'Women and Work: The Case of Finnish Domestics and Armenian Boarding-house Operators,' *Resources for Feminist Research* 12:4 (1983), 51–4.

58 From the point of view of the operators, boarding was a 'form of entrepreneurship' for some 'settlers,' as Robert Harney has argued: 'Boarding and Belonging,' 11. The Timmins assessment rolls for 1915 and 1920 reveal that among the boarding-houses that could be identified some were owned by working-class couples. The husband was usually listed as being employed at the mine, thus indicating that his wife was principally responsible for the operation of the boarding-house. See TMA, Timmins Municipal Assessment Rolls, 1915 and 1920.

59 This establishment first opened in 1918. The household had eight to ten men living on the premises at any one time, while several dozen other men just had their meals there. See interview with her daughter Molly Buzowski.

60 Interview with her daughter Theresa Del Guidice.

61 As cited in Di Giacomo, 'The Italians of Timmins,' 44.

62 For a further discussion of these boarding-houses, see Vasiliadis, 'Dangerous Truth,' 86–7; and Lindström-Best, *Defiant Sisters*, 87–8.

63 TIM, Porcupine Historical Society (PHS), interview with her daughter Martta Laaksa Johnson.

64 The local newspaper reported instances of fights breaking out between boarders. See *Porcupine Advance*, 26 April 1916, 30 April 1919, and 3 November 1920.

65 Ontario, *Annual Report of the Provincial Board of Health, 1913*, 297; Ontario, *Annual Report of the Provincial Board of Health, 1914*, 42; PAO, RG 62, Ontario Provincial Board of Health, Series 1-B-D, Box 446, File Health District 6, Memo from Dr W. George, 3 August 1914; memo from Dr W. George, 1 May 1917.

66 *Porcupine Advance*, 7 August 1918. Three boarding-house keepers ended up being fined $100 each for serving too much meat.

67 PAO, RG 62, Series F-1–6, Box 477, File Public Health Nurse Reports, District 6, Letter from A.L., 30 December 1920.

68 The assessment rolls proved to be unhelpful in quantifying these house-

holds, since they could only be identified when men bought and registered the property together.

69 *Porcupine Advance*, 25 July 1917.
70 Ibid.
71 The ethnic literature has provided numerous examples of immigrant men fending for themselves in other contexts. Among Macedonian immigrant men in Toronto, Lillian Petroff has discovered a rather elaborate code of conduct ordering domestic work. In a number of households she has studied a distinguishable hierarchy existed whereby younger men did the chores. See Petroff, 'Sojourners and Settlers,' 184–5; see also Iacovetta, *Such Hardworking People*, 55–7.
72 For a brief history of the Chinese in Timmins, see Lawrence Lam, *'The Whites Accept Us Chinese Now': The Changing Dynamics of Being Chinese in Timmins* (Toronto: Institute for Behavioural Research, 1983), York Timmins Project Working Paper no. 4.
73 *Porcupine Advance*, 27 August 1915.
74 Ibid., 9 August 1916. A newspaper report in December 1925 recalling Christmas celebrations a decade earlier mentioned that 'many a man yearning for home' had to be satisfied with a meal in a local restaurant. See ibid., 24 December 1925.
75 TIM, PHS, interview with Donat Bastien. See also PHS interview with Matti Laitinen.
76 Parr, *The Gender of Breadwinners*, 94.
77 The gender composition of the Chinese immigrant community in Timmins as of 1921 was fifty men and no women. Government immigration restrictions, including an ever-increasing 'head tax,' discouraged the immigration of Chinese families to Canada during the late nineteenth century and early twentieth century. Much of the discussion on immigration policy and racism has focused largely on the western Canadian provinces. See Peter Ward, *White Canada Forever; Popular Attitudes and Public Policy Toward Orientals in British Columbia*, 2d ed. (Montreal: McGill-Queen's University Press, 1990); Howard Palmer, *Patterns of Prejudice: A History of Nativism in Alberta* (Toronto: McClelland and Stewart, 1982); and Patricia Roy, *A White Man's Province: British Columbian Politicians and Chinese and Japanese Immigrants, 1858–1914* (Vancouver: University of British Columbia Press, 1989). For one of the few works on Chinese immigrant women see Dora Nipp, '"But Women Did Come": Working Chinese Women in the Interwar Years,' in *Looking into My Sister's Eyes: An Exploration in Women's History*, ed. Jean Brunet (Toronto: Multicultural Historical Society of Ontario, 1986), 179–94.

78 Lam, 'The Whites Accept Us Now,' 14. In other locations Chinese immigrant
   men were hired as mine-workers. Lynne Bowen has documented that
   Chinese men were employed in coal mines on Vancouver Island from the
   1870s onward. During the early decades of the twentieth century, however,
   they were barred from one mine after another. See Bowen, Boss Whistle, 68–
   78. While Chinese men were never formally excluded from employment in
   the Porcupine gold mines, the documentary sources reveal the presence of
   only a handful. See PAO, F 1350, Box 14, File Wage Scales, Memo re Personnel of Men Employed at the Mines of the Porcupine Camp, 1940. That year
   there were only three Chinese men in a mining labour force of over eight
   thousand.
79 See Porcupine Advance, 2 July 1914. On the construction of Chinese immigrant men as dangerous sexual offenders and the 'yellow peril' narrative,
   see Mariana Valverde, The Age of Light, Soap and Water (Toronto: McClelland
   and Stewart, 1991); Carolyn Strange, Toronto's Girl Problem: The Perils and
   Pleasures of the City, 1880–1930 (Toronto: University of Toronto Press, 1995);
   and Madge.Pon, 'Like a Chinese Puzzle: The Construction of Chinese Masculinity in Jack Canuck,' in Joy Parr and Mark Rosenfeld, eds, Gender and History in Canada (Toronto: Copp Clark 1996).
80 Porcupine Advance, 2 July 1915.
81 Ibid., 24 September 1925 and 12 November 1925. Other municipalities did
   implement municipal by-laws prohibiting the employment of 'white' waitresses in Chinese restaurants. Sudbury, for example, passed this provision
   in 1926: as cited in Dubinsky, Improper Advances, 189.
82 John D'Emilio and Estelle Freedman, Intimate Matters: A History of Sexuality
   in America (New York: Harper and Row, 1988), 136. On prostitution in western American mining towns, see Mary Murphy, 'The Private Lives of Public
   Women: Prostitution in Butte, Montana 1878–1917,' Frontiers 7:3 (1984), 31–
   5; Paula Petrik, No Step Backward: Women and Family on the Rocky Mountain
   Mining Frontier, Helena, Montana, 1865–1900 (Helena: Montana Historical
   Society Press, 1987) 25–58; Marion S. Goldman, Gold Diggers and Silver Miners: Prostitution and Social Life on the Comstock Lode (Ann Arbor: University of
   Michigan Press, 1981); Anne M. Butler, Daughters of Joy, Sisters of Misery:
   Prostitutes in the American West, 1865–1890 (Urbana: University of Illinois
   Press, 1985). In Canada, see Bay Ryley, 'Gold-Digers of the Klondike: Prostitution in Dawson City, Yukon, 1898–1908' (MA thesis, Queen's University,
   1995). For a popular but sometimes offensive historical study of prostitution
   in western Canada, see James Gray, Red Lights on the Prairies (Toronto: Macmillan, 1971).
83 Beyond their names, available documents offer few clues as to the ethnic or

racial background of prostitutes in this community. Sylvia Van Kirk has discovered that at the time of the Cariboo gold rush native women were prominent among the area's prostitutes. While it is entirely possible that some
native women may have been prostitutes in Timmins, given the large native
population in the Ontario northeast, the sources are entirely silent on this
issue. See Sylvia Van Kirk, 'A Vital Presence: Women in the Cariboo Gold
Rush, 1862–1875,' in *British Columbia Reconsidered: Essays on Women*, ed. Gil-
lian Creese and Veronica Strong-Boag (Vancouver: Press Gang Publishers,
1992), 21–37.

84 See, for example, George Chauncey Jr, *Gay New York: Gender, Urban Culture
and the Makings of the Gay Male World, 1890–1940* (New York: Basic, 1994);
George Chauncey Jr, 'Christian Brotherhood or Sexual Perversion? Homo-
sexual Identities and the Construction of Sexual Boundaries in the World
War I Era,' in *Hidden from History: Reclaiming the Gay and Lesbian Past*, ed.
Martin Duberman, Martha Vicinus, and George Chauncey Jr (New York:
Meridian, 1989), 294–317; Thomas W. Laquer, 'Sexual Desire and the Market
Economy during the Industrial Revolution,' in *Discourses of Sexuality: From
Aristotle to Aids*, ed. Domna Stanton (Ann Arbor: University of Michigan
Press, 1992), 185–215; see also Maynard, 'Rough Work and Rugged Men,'
159–70.

85 Susan Lee Johnson has noted the difficulty of locating 'unambigious'
sources on this topic. See Susan Lee Johnson, 'Bulls, Bears, and Dancing-
boys,' 25–6; see also Margaret Creighton, 'Davy Jones' Locker Room: Gender and the American Whalemen, 1830–1870,' in *Iron Men, Wooden Women:
Gender and Seafaring in the Atlantic World, 1700–1920*, ed. Margaret Creighton
and Lisa Norling (Baltimore: Johns Hopkins University Press, 1996), 128–30.
With regard to sources for these studies, two well-publicized cases of two
miners charged with sodomy provide the only concrete evidence of same-
sex male relations. See *Porcupine Advance*, 19 November 1917; 5 January
1919.

A number of South African historians have documented the practice of
'mine marriages,' which existed in the completely enclosed compounds
adjacent to gold mines in that country, whereby men would form emotional
and sexual bonds with one another. See T. Dunbar Moodie (with Vivienne
Ndatshe and British Sibuyi), 'Migrancy and Male Sexuality on the South
African Gold Mines,' *Journal of Southern African Studies* 14:2 (January 1988),
228–56; Patrick Harries, 'Symbols and Sexuality: Culture and Identity on the
Early Witwarersand Gold Mines,' *Gender and History* 2:3 (Autumn 1990),
318–36.

86 For working-class men in other communities, the importance of the private

sphere was increasing. See Rosenfeld, '"She Was a Hard Life,"' 97–147; and Parr, *The Gender of Breadwinners*, 187–205.

87 Parr, *The Gender of Breadwinners*, 205.

88 See Kathy Peiss, *Cheap Amusements: Working Women and Leisure in Turn-of-the-Century New York* (Philadelphia: Temple University Press, 1986).

89 Robert Harney has suggested in the case of Italian immigrant sojourners that these 'men without women' were not men with all moral barriers removed. Without female family members around they did, however, become coarser and more vulgar. See Robert Harney, 'Men Without Women: Italian Migrants in Canada, 1885–1930,' in *The Italian Immigrant Women in North America*, ed. Betty Caroli et al. (Toronto: Multicultural History Society of Ontario, 1978), 79–101.

90 See Lam, '*The Whites Accept Us Now*,' 15–19. For a general description of a 'bachelor society' among the Chinese in Canada, see Anthony Chan, *Gold Mountain: The Chinese in the New World* (Vancouver: New Star, 1983), 74–85.

91 See Strange, *Toronto's Girl Problem*. For similar analyses in American cities, see Kathy Peiss, *Cheap Amusements: Working Women and Leisure in Turn-of-the Century New York* (Philadelphia: Temple University Press, 1986), and Joanne Meyerowitz, *Women Adrift: Independent Wage Earners in Chicago, 1880–1930* (Chicago: University of Chicago Press, 1988).

92 Public spaces for middle-class women were also lacking, but as reports of social events in the local newspaper revealed, they had spacious homes wherein they could entertain other women and couples. See, for example, *Porcupine Advance*, 5 September 1915, 23 April 1916, and 29 December 1916.

93 See, for example, ibid., 5 April 1912; 28 June 1912; 9 July 1915 and 21 August 1918; and 21 January 1920.

94 Respectability for working-class women was defined quite differently from that of working-class men. As Elizabeth Roberts has observed, female respectability during the early twentieth century was defined by an adherence to cleanliness of the body (sexual morality), clothing, and language, as well as of the home. See Elizabeth Roberts, *A Woman's Place: An Oral History of Working-Class Women, 1890–1940* (London: Basil Blackwell, 1984), 14–17. See Ellen Ross, 'Not the Sort That Would Sit on the Doorstep: Respectability in Pre World War I London Neighbourhoods,' *International Labor and Working Class History*, 27 (Spring 1985), 39–59. The location and frequency of drinking, whether in public or in private, also became an issue in defining respectability.

95 For an example in the Canadian context, see Rosenfeld, '"She Was a Hard Life,"' 75–82; For an example in the American context, see Roy Rosenzweig, *Eight Hours for What We Will: Workers and Leisure in an Industrial City, 1870–*

1920 (Cambridge: Cambridge University Press, 1983), 181–9. A useful overview of the international historical literature on drinking is provided by Cheryl Krasnick Warsh, '"John Barleycorn Must Die": An Introduction to the Social History of Alcohol,' in *Drink in Canada: Historical Essays*, ed. Cheryl Krasnick Warsh (Montreal: McGill-Queen's University Press, 1993), 3–26.

96 The male-centred activity of drinking in neighbourhood saloons was being replaced in Canadian and American urban centres at this time by leisure pursuits that involved both men and women. For a detailed analysis of this process, see Peiss, *Cheap Amusements*. In many North American mining communities this transition occurred somewhat later. See Mary Murphy, 'Surviving Butte: Leisure and Community in a Western Mining City, 1917–1941' (PhD thesis, University of North Carolina, 1990), 1–50. A recent contemporary sociological study of the northern Ontario city of Thunder Bay has demontrated that public drinking remains an important element of male working-class culture. See Thomas Dunk, *It's a Working Man's Town: Male Working-Class Culture in Northwestern Ontario* (Montreal: McGill-Queen's University Press, 1991), 68–70.

97 Mining Act of Ontario (1908), 8 Edw. VII, c. 21.

98 Haileybury and New Liskeard were far enough away from Cobalt to fall outside the six-mile limit. See Baldwin, 'A Study in Social Control,' 101.

99 The provincial government also significantly undermined the impact of prohibition by permitting breweries and distilleries to continue production. For a more detailed discussion of the Ontario Temperance Act, see Graham Decarie, 'The Prohibition Movement in Ontario, 1894–1916' (PhD thesis, Queen's University, 1982).

100 Ontario Temperance Act (1916) 6 Geo. V, c. 50.

101 During this period provincial police officers in northern Ontario seem to have spent most of their time trying to uncover the almost infinite number of methods employed to conceal liquor being transported to large mining centres such as Cobalt and the Porcupine. See PAO, RG 23, Series B-12, File 1.1, Annual Report, 1911; Annual Report, 1912, Annual Report, 1913–14; Annual Report, 1918–19.

102 Ibid., Annual Report, 1912.

103 *Cobalt Nugget*, 12 February 1912.

104 Ibid.

105 Di Giacomo, 'The Italians of Timmins,' 60.

106 *Porcupine Advance*, 21 August 1918.

107 PAO, RG 23, Series E-46, File 1.2, Letter 4 October 1912, From C.B. Dale to

Supt. Rogers, OPP. In this letter Dale complained that professional gamblers were inducing 'working miners to come into the games.'

108 The Lord's Day Act, which was passed by the federal parliament in March 1907, attempted to restrict Sunday trade, labour, and recreation.

109 *Porcupine Advance*, 24 November 1920.

110 Ibid., 3 September 1915.

111 Ibid.

112 These prices were referred to in police court reports involving women arrested for prostitution: *Porcupine Advance*, 27 September 1916 and 20 October 1920. See also Lindström-Best, *Defiant Sisters*, 112.

113 TIM, PHS, interview with Walter Mattinen, born 1895.

114 Steven Maynard, among others, has argued that heterosexuality is an important component of a particular form of masculinity and masculine cultures. See Maynard, 'Rough Work and Rugged Men,' 166.

115 In a 1950s study of placer gold-mining communities in British Columbia and the Yukon during the nineteenth and early twentieth centuries, the sociologist C.D. Clark has concurred with these views. See Clark, 'Mining Society in British Columbia and the Yukon,' 215–30. William Morrison, however, has recently argued that while certain aspects of the gold rush mythology have an element of truth – 'the painted ladies, the gold dust, the hard drinking' – the Yukon was quite unlike the American frontier in that it was 'remarkably free of violent crime, mostly due to the authoritarian presence of the police.' See William Morrison, 'Policing the Boom Town: The Mounted Police as a Social Force in the Klondike,' *The Northern Review* 6 (Winter 1990), 85.

116 For reports of large-scale raids of blind pigs by police, see *Porcupine Advance*, 22 January 1912, 27 July 1914, 10 June 1917, and 26 May 1920. Some raids were scheduled on Sundays so the police could arrest men for both activities. See, for example, ibid., 29 May 1918.

117 Several provincial police constables were initially the sole law enforcement authorities in the area. It should be pointed out, however, that the provincial government was willing to send several dozen constables into the district on occasion, as it did during a district-wide mining strike in the winter of 1912–13. In 1915, the Timmins municipal council created a local police force with a chief and three constables. Local and provincial police authorities often cooperated with one another in conducting raids.

118 Newspaper reports also mentioned that the spotters from various ethnic backgrounds were hired for this type of work. *Porcupine Advance*, 20 August 1915; 20 September 1916; 10 April 1918; 14 February 1917.

119 See, for example, ibid., 11 June 1915, 10 January 1917; 15 August 1917;
     30 January 1918. Not surprisingly, criticisms of the supposed criminality
     and immorality of European immigrant men increased in frequency during
     the First World War and even for several years afterward. In the local case,
     at least, the 'enemy alien' and the 'foreigner' were conflated in the minds of
     some middle-class residents. As one local newspaper editorial in January
     1918 noted: 'There are enough and too many aliens in this country already.
     Too many of them cut no other figure in a public way than in public court
     cases. For example, in Porcupine today the vast majority of those securing a
     livelihood from gambling, blindpigging and other forms of graft are of alien
     nationalities and many of them even of enemy origin.' See *Porcupine
     Advance*, 23 January 1918. In Sudbury, European immigrant men were also
     singled out as both the producers and consumers of vice. None the less,
     they were not over-represented for criminal offences in the Sudbury police
     court records. See Peter Kratz, 'The Sudbury Area to the Great Depression:
     Regional Development on the Northern Resource Frontier' (PhD thesis,
     University of Western Ontario, 1988), 224–6. Politics also played a role in
     such concerns, as evidenced by other reports which emphasized the need to
     get rid of 'Bolsheviks' in town. For a fuller discussion of the intersection of
     ethnocentrism and politics, see Donald Avery, *"Dangerous Foreigners": Euro-
     pean Immigrant Workers and Labour Radicalism in Canada, 1896–1932* (Toronto:
     McClelland and Stewart, 1979), 65–89; for an early and important work on
     this issue in the American literature, see John Highham, *Strangers in the
     Land: Patters of Nativism, 1860–1925* (New York: Atheneum, 1985; reprint of
     original, 1973).

120 See, for example, *Cobalt Nugget*, 7 September 1911; and *Porcupine Advance*,
     19 January 1912; 27 September 1916; 1 August 1917, 5 September 1917;
     20 October 1920. Lynne Bowen has documented that in the coal-mining
     town of Nanaimo, BC, the local municipal government formally tolerated
     prostitution until the Second World War. See Bowen, *Boss Whistle*, 218–19. In
     the United States, see Mary Murphy, 'The Private Lives of Public Women:
     Prostitution in Butte, Montana 1878–1917,' *Frontiers* 7:3 (1984), 31–5; Petrik,
     No Step Backward, 25–58; and Goldman, *Gold Diggers and Silver Miners*,
     62–75.

121 See, for example, *Porcupine Advance*, 27 September 1916; 5 September 1917;
     20 October 1920.

122 Ibid., 1 August 1917.

123 TIM, PHS, interview with Eva Desanti, born 1894.

124 Although mining company owners in other national contexts actively

encouraged drinking and gambling as a means of subduing and impover-
ishing their labour force, Hollinger does not appear to have been operating
under such an agenda. See Charles van Onselen, *Chibaro: African Mine
Labour in Southern Rhodesia, 1900–1933* (London: Pluto Press, 1976).

125 One newspaper report used this phrase as the aim of Hollinger in reference
to the 'keen' interest the mine manager had been taking in sports. See *Porcupine Advance*, 16 July 1916.

126 Later in the century mining companies assumed much greater financial
responsibilities in providing recreational facilities for their employees. See
Thompson, *New Industrial Towns*, 86.

127 *Cobalt Nugget*, 16 February 1914.

128 *Porcupine Advance*, 13 February 1912; 12 January 1916; 3 December 1920.

129 See, for example, ibid., 7 July 1920.

130 See, for example, ibid., 14 February 1916 and 7 July 1917. Alan Metcalf has
argued that gambling was central in all working-class sports. See Alan
Metcalf, 'Leisure, Sport and Working Class Culture,' in *Leisure and Working-
Class Cultures*, ed. Hart Cantelon and Robert Hollands (Toronto: Garamond,
1988), 68. See also Ross McKibbin, *The Ideologies of Class: Social Relations in
Britain, 1880–1950* (Oxford: Clarendon Press, 1990), 101–38.

131 Joan Sangster has recently argued that the 'actual meaning sports had for
players might differ from the intentions of team promoters.' See her, '"The
Softball Solution": Female Workers, Male Managers and the Operation of
Paternalism at Westclox, 1923–60,' *Labour/Le Travail* (Fall 1993) 167–99.

132 Finns actually formed their own athletic club, the Comets, in 1917: *Porcupine
Advance*, 20 June 1917.

133 Di Giacomo, 'The Italians of Timmins,' 48. This sport resembled a form of
bowling.

134 *Porcupine Advance*, 15 July 1917; 22 August 1918.

135 For an excellent discussion of the historical importance of sports in shaping
male gender identities, see Colin Howell, *Northern Sandlots: A Social History
of Maritime Baseball* (Toronto: University of Toronto Press, 1995).

136 Unfortunately, few sources exist which offer details of the membership or
operation of any of these organizations. The records of such groups do not
appear to have survived, or at least have not made their way into any archival repository. The foreign-language press might have provided additional
information but, lacking translators, these sources remain inaccessible. I
have therefore had to rely largely upon local newspaper reports.

137 Italians, Ukrainians, and Finns each had their own mutual benefit society. In
the latter two instances membership in these groups overlapped with membership in Ukrainian and Finnish socialist political groups. *Porcupine*

Advance, 3 March 1917; 22 May 1918; 17 November 1918. See also Vasiliadis, *Dangerous Truth*, 112–20. For a discussion of the importance of the mutual aid association as an aspect of different ethnic immigrant cultures, see the entire issue of *Polyphony* 4:1 (Spring/Summer 1982); and Lizabeth Cohen, *Making A New Deal: Industrial Workers in Chicago, 1919–1939* (Cambridge: Cambridge University Press, 1990), 64–75.

138 With regard to fraternal orders, locals of the Masons and the Odd Fellows were instituted. *Porcupine Advance*, 7 January 1916; 15 March 1916.

139 Although anglophone and francophone Catholic men would later separate into different groups when an English Catholic parish was formed in the 1920s, for the time being both linguistic groups were members of this organization. *Porcupine Advance*, 14 November 1917.

140 For an account of missionary activities in northern Ontario by the Presbyterian church, see Byrnes, *Greater or Northern Ontario*, 4–9; for accounts of missionary activities by the Methodist church, see United Church Archives (UCA), Records of the Home Department of the Methodist Church, Missionary Society, Box 2, File 3, Letter 10 August 1911, from E.J. Adams to Rev. C. Manning; Box 2, File 4, Letter 13 September 1911, from E.J. Adams to Rev. C. Manning.

141 *Christian Guardian*, 17 April 1912.

142 Vasiliadis, *Dangerous Truth*, 70; Di Giacomo, 'The Italians of Timmins,' 47.

143 Lindström-Best, *Defiant Sisters*, 72.

144 *Cobalt Nugget*, 24 April 1914.

145 Marks, *Revivals and Roller Rinks*, 27–30.

146 *Porcupine Advance*, 19 May 1920.

147 Ibid., 2 August 1912.

148 Since a small admission was charged at all such events, this made it a commercial sporting event and thus contrary to the provision of the Lord's Day Act.

149 See, for example, PAO, RG 23, Series E-18, File 1.21, Letter 10 July 1914, from Rev. R.M. Rochester, Lord's Day Alliance, to J.E. Rogers, Superintendent, OPP. Rochester complained that baseball had been played between teams from Timmins and South Porcupine (another small town in the Porcupine gold district) 'for some four or five Sundays past.'

150 Although on a modest scale, these moral reform efforts indicate that masculine dominance of community life may have carried over into the middle class, as evidenced by the complete absence of women. Mariana Valverde has observed that in large urban centres during this period middle-class women were an integral aspect of moral reform. See Valverde, *Age of Light, Soap and Water*, 44–76.

While local chapters of the Women's Christian Temperance Union were organized in Cobalt and Cochrane in 1918, this temperance organization was never established in Timmins. An examination of WCTU records and publications reveal that the organization's 'missionary' for New Ontario visited the Porcupine on a number of occasions during the 1910s, but her main focus remained on lumber and railway camps. In a state of decline, the provincial union no longer employed a missionary for this type of work in northern Ontario after 1920. See *White Tidings* (Toronto), 1 November 1913; also PAO, F 1202, Women's Christian Temperance Union, 8408.11, *Report of the Thirty-Fifth Convention of the Ontario Women's Christian Temperance Union, 1912,* 119; MU 8409.1, *Report of the Thirty-Seventh Annual Meeting of the Ontario Women's Christian Temperance Union, 1918,* 121.

151 *Porcupine Advance,* 20 September 1916.
152 Ibid., 19 February 1919.
153 Ibid., 3 December 1919.
154 PAO, F 1814, National Council of the Young Men's Christian Association in Canada, Series A, Box 35, File Timmins. Letter 24 March 1919, S. Brent, Sec. YMCA, to Dr D.L. Honey, Timmins. A YMCA was not established in Timmins until 1946, but this file is filled with requests by town residents appealing for a branch of the YMCA and subsequent responses from the organization.

TOPIC SIX
Demanding Rights, Organizing for Change: Militants and Radicals

In the late 1970s, the U.S. radical historian Gabriel Kolko issued his now classic lament regarding the weakness of the American working class.[1] For Kolko, and for an entire generation of North American scholars, ethnic and racial differences among workers, as well as successive waves of immigrants and temporary migrants (or sojourners), proved the Achilles heel of American labour, dividing workers and hindering collective protest. Similar arguments have been made for Canada, and not without reason. From the start, the Canadian working class was ethnically diverse. This heterogeneity was perpetuated, as in the United States, by successive waves of migrants, many of them sojourners with no intention of settling here and thus reluctant to join Canadian workers in campaigns to protest working conditions or to unionize. Also, ethnic differences and the temporary nature of the North American work experience of many migrants did at times impede working-class protest and stifle potential radicalism. At the turn of the century, for example, employers regularly imported foreign-born workers to act as strikebreakers. Some groups of migrant workers, such as the Italians and the Chinese, actually earned a reputation early in this century as willing strikebreakers and unwilling unionists. (In earlier decades, bitter regional and religious antagonisms had hampered class solidarities among groups like the Irish.)

But there is more to the story. As the readings demonstrate, a new generation of immigration and labour historians has shown how Kolko's arguments went too far in one direction, ignoring the ways in which transplanted Old World communal traditions and resistance strategies could both help preserve ethnic identity and promote class solidarity among immigrants in North America. It is worth stressing that immigrants, both British and non-British, have in their varied ways contributed greatly to the history of union-building and labour protest in Canada.

Ruth Frager's account of the strike of Jewish garment workers at Eaton's in 1912 highlights a rare instance of male solidarity with female workers, the product of coinciding interests of class and ethnicity among Toronto's East European Jewish immigrants. Ian Radforth takes us into the woods of northern Ontario to show how pre-migration traditions of labour militancy and radicalism encouraged and sustained the Finnish immigrant radicals, mainly men, who led the class struggle against employers in the first half of the twentieth century. Both Frager and Radforth focus on a single group of immigrant workers. Carmela Patrias's account of a Depression-era strike by immigrant workers employed on relief projects in the southern Ontario town of Crowland broaches the neglected theme of inter-ethnic relations. In the 1930s, Crowland was a multi-ethnic blue collar town, and the 1935 strike reflected – indeed, was the product of – the inter-ethnic collaboration that had obtained in the area since early in the twentieth century. What were the bases of inter-ethnic harmony in Crowland? In what ways was the relief strike of 1935 similar to other instances of inter-ethnic collaboration on the picket line? How was it different? To what extent is the history of the Finnish and East European Jewish radicals representative of the working-class immigrant experience in Canada? Do you think the Canadian labour movement has been seriously handicapped by ethnic diversity? Or has diversity been its greatest strength?

NOTE

1 Gabriel Kolko, *Main Currents in American History* (New York 1976).

BIBLIOGRAPHY AND SUGGESTED READINGS

Avakumovic, Ivan. *The Communist Party in Canada*. Toronto 1975.
Avery, Donald. *'Dangerous Foreigners': European Immigration, Workers, and Labour Radicalism in Canada*. Toronto 1979.
Frager, Ruth A. *Sweatshop Strife: Class, Ethnicity, and Gender in the Jewish Labour Movement of Toronto, 1900–1939*. Toronto 1992.
Seager, Allen. 'Class, Ethnicity and Politics in the Alberta Coal Fields,' in Dirk Hoerder, ed., *'Struggle a Hard Battle': Essays on Working Class Immigrants*. De Kalb, Ill. 1986.

Kealey, Linda, and Joan Sangster, eds. *Beyond the Vote: Canadian Women and Politics*. Toronto 1989.

Lindström, Varpu. *Defiant Sisters: A Social History of Finnish Immigrant Women in Canada*. Toronto, 1992.

Patrias, Carmela. *Patriots and Proletarians: The Politicization of Hungarian Immigrants in Canada*. Kingston and Montreal 1994.

Radforth, Ian. *Bushworkers and Bosses: Logging in Northern Ontario, 1900–1980*. Toronto, 1987.

Finnish Radicalism and Labour Activism in the Northern Ontario Woods

IAN RADFORTH

During the first half of the twentieth century a large proportion of activists in Canada's labour movement and left-wing parties were immigrants, many of them 'foreigners' from continental Europe. Jewish, Ukrainian, and Finnish immigrant groups provided leaders and the vast majority of recruits for the Communist Party of Canada (CPC) in the interwar period. New immigrants frequently became labour militants, striking to defend their group interests on the job. In strikes, recent arrivals from diverse European backgrounds sometimes acted in solidarity with one another and with Anglo-Celtic and French-Canadian workers. In certain locales and industries, however, a particular ethnic group dominated labour unionism and strike activity. Such was the case in the northern Ontario logging industry.[1]

From the First World War until the early 1950s, Finnish immigrant men spearheaded the class struggle that radicals waged against employers in northern Ontario's logging industry. As we shall see, traditions of labour militancy and radicalism originating in Finland thrived amid a vibrant, radical, immigrant culture in northern Ontario. Male woods-workers immersed in, and sustained by, this ethnic radicalism built unions and fought bitter strikes that made Finns notorious among employers, as well as among some woods-workers of different backgrounds and outlook. Nevertheless, the Finns' commitment to worker solidarity laid the foundations for an enduring union presence in Ontario's logging industry. Their conflicts and achievements warrant study and explanation. Furthermore, Finnish radicals in northern Ontario provide a vivid illustration of some of the broader patterns of immigrant radicalism in Canada during the first half of the twentieth century.

Finnish immigrants began settling in northern Ontario at the turn of the twentieth century, a time when there was a large exodus from Finland and work opportunities were expanding on the emerging industrial frontier of northern Ontario. Population pressures and a changing rural economy pushed people from their homes in Finland. Many came to North America seeking paid work or the chance to homestead. A majority of Finnish emigrants left with the hope of coming back to Finland better off, but only about 20 per cent ever returned. Whatever their intentions, then, Finns overwhelmingly became settlers in North America rather than sojourners. Some Finns came to the new world as families, but a large proportion were young single men and single women. While single women sought jobs principally as domestics in large Canadian cities such as Montreal, Toronto, and Vancouver, single men gravitated to so-called unskilled labouring jobs down the hard-rock mines or in the lumber woods of northern Ontario and northwestern Quebec. The pace of immigration from Finland to Canada quickened in the 1920s, when U.S. quotas diverted migrants to Canada, and then it fell off sharply during the Depression and the Second World War. By 1931 the Census of Canada showed 43,885 Finns living in Canada, about three-fifths of them in Ontario.[2]

Most Finnish woodsmen in northern Ontario combined seasonal waged employment in logging with periods of work on their own bush farms. Finnish immigrants found it particularly appealing to homestead in northern Ontario, where the forested districts looked like home, where immigrants could settle together and form their own ethnic communities, and where the men could earn wages by logging during farming's off-season.[3]

The Finns came to specialize in pulp cutting – felling spruce and other conifers and making them into four- or eight-foot logs destined for the province's pulp and paper mills. Most of the work took place in fall and winter, when there was little other employment and, in winter at least, farm duties were few. The tools, which were provided by the bushworkers themselves, were simple and inexpensive: an axe and a bucksaw – a type of handsaw with a narrow blade set in a wooden (later a steel) frame. In this industry neither a formal education nor facility in English were required; physical strength and stamina were the crucial assets. While the work could be learned on the job, many Finnish men already had excellent woods skills upon arrival in the logging industry. Finns showed a preference for cutting pulpwood rather than sawlogs (destined for lumber mills) because of the opportunity for higher incomes. The pulp and paper companies (or their subcontractors) paid a few dollars a cord for logs cut and piled in contrast to lumber companies, which paid wages based on time – so much per month. With their well-honed skills and experience at pacing themselves for heavy labouring tasks, the Finns could expect to make more money from piece-rates than from monthly wages.[4]

Finns made up only a minority of northern Ontario's logging labour force, but they dominated woods employment in particular places, including areas west of Sudbury, near Cochrane, north of Sault Ste-Marie, and in the vicinity of Thunder Bay. In these places there were numerous all-Finnish camps, many of them under the authority of a Finnish foreman or logging subcontractor who showed an ethnic preference when hiring. The Finns, like virtually all men in the Ontario logging industry, lived in camps housing fifty to one hundred men and located within walking distance of work sites in the forests. The shanties were crudely built of logs and designed to last perhaps a couple of seasons until the surrounding timber had been harvested. Primitive living conditions prevailed because employers saw little point in providing comforts or luxuries when there were plenty of men eager for work and willing to settle for simple facilities. Most camps were made up entirely of men who for a season at least were living apart from their families. Daily they risked exceptionally dangerous work routines, and they endured tough living conditions – such as the early morning experience of waking up with hair frozen to the log walls of the shanty. The hazards and hardships, and the all-male experience, contributed to the loggers' reputation for rugged manliness.

Finnish logging camps in northern Ontario had certain distinctive features that set them apart from camps manned by others. When Finns went to a camp, the first thing they did was build a sauna bath so they could be clean and enjoy a familiar pastime. It was easy enough to construct a sauna because logs could be readily made and a simple shack erected. For heat, a wood-stove was made from a tin barrel. Every other night, and certainly on Saturday evenings, the fire would be lit and the men would gather to have their baths. The Finns' cleanliness contrasted sharply with many old-stock Canadians, whose custom it was to abstain from taking a bath of any kind during their sojourns in the camps. The unusual presence of laundresses in the Finnish contractor camps also made for superior hygiene among Finnish pulp-cutters, and vermin such as lice and bedbugs were not nearly so prevalent as elsewhere. Similarly, Finnish women cooks and 'cookees' – assistants who peeled potatoes, served meals, and washed the dishes – took pride in maintaining a spotless cookery. 'Not a man could stand half up to the Finnish women,' recalls an Anglo-Celtic former bush-worker. 'God, they even used to scrub the benches the guys sat on.' Finnish bush-workers loved the familiar, old-country dishes that the Finnish women prepared. Finnish camps also differed from the rest because of the way some men spent their evenings in the bunkhouse. 'At the camp our entertainment was to argue over politics,' recalls Toivo Tienhaara. 'If there were Finns, there were Reds and Whites. I was a White. Even though I was indisputably in the minority, I always spoke my mind. Sometimes there were men all around my bunk trying to convert me.' What were the sources of that political consciousness?[5]

A substantial minority of the Finns who settled in northern Ontario during the period 1900–1930 had already been radicalized in the old country. They began to leave Finland for northern Ontario early in the twentieth century, at the very moment when radicalism was rapidly spreading in Finland. The country was gripped by problems arising from industrialization and from a program of Russification imposed by the czar who ruled Finland with no respect for the national culture. Many of those men and women who eventually came to Canada were first forced from their farms by population pressures and the commercialization of agriculture. They sought relief from hardship by turning to wage labour in Finland's growing industrial centres. There they found erratic employment, overcrowded housing, and poor wages and working conditions. The burgeoning Social Democratic Party, which sought redress of these problems, recruited enormous numbers of such people. Effective marshalling of anti-Russian sentiments also helped the party to expand. But when relief did not come quickly, thousands of the new socialists emigrated, many of them to northern Ontario.[6]

Like immigrants of every background, the Finns sought familiar company and surroundings. They settled near one another and established cultural institutions. For the radical Finnish immigrants that meant building socialist halls for mutual help, recreation, education, and political action. Leadership generally came from highly motivated Finnish leftists, some of them well-educated intellectuals and all of them seasoned labour activists. Such leadership was greatly strengthened in the early 1920s by the arrival in the north of numerous Red emigrés. In December 1917, with the czar recently toppled from power, Finland declared its independence, and the Social Democrats, who predominated in Parliament, formed a government. The ensuing civil war brought much bloodshed and saw the Whites triumph over the Reds. Many Red activists were driven into exile, some to Canada. Even Oskari Tokoi, the prime minister of Finland's short-lived socialist government, and some members of his cabinet found temporary refuge in a logging camp near New Liskeard in northeastern Ontario.[7]

Yet it is likely that a majority of the Finns who came to Ontario during the first three decades of this century were upon arrival either untouched by radicalism or active anti-socialists. Most settlers came from rural areas remote from the Social Democratic Party's strongholds in and around Helsinki. The more politically active from these rural areas were apt to have backed the Whites or served in the White Guard. In North America many of them continued to hate the Reds, shun the socialist halls, and play an active part in church activities or in anti-Communist organizations such as the Loyal Finns of Canada. More surprisingly, a significant proportion of the apolitical immigrants were radicalized in the northern Ontario communities where their social life was dominated by highly motivated leftists.[8]

Two cultural developments enabled leftists to recruit substantial numbers of Finns who had not been radicalized at home. First, the church that Finnish immigrants had known, the Lutheran Church, was weak in northern Ontario, and few newcomers were brought under its conservative influence. Because the powerful state Lutheran Church in Finland condemned emigration, it gave little support to struggling congregations in Canada. The few Finnish-speaking pastors who ministered in Ontario preached an otherworldly theology and a strict moral code that had little appeal for many young people who had been bold enough to venture to Canada. When freed from the restraints and disciplines of their homes in the old country, the habit of church attendance could be easily thrown off.[9] Second, and by contrast, the socialist halls dotting the north served as lively centres of activity and drew many to their doors.

Finnish radicals in northern Ontario shrewdly recognized that in order to build a strong socialist movement that could challenge capitalism they would need to enlist the active support of large numbers of working-class people who might otherwise remain apathetic. Socialist halls in local immigrant communities could serve the vital function of drawing people together. Immigrants living in a strange land and in isolated frontier communities hungered for social activities and familiar cultural experiences. Once brought together at a Finnish community hall, men, women, and children would be educated by leftist leaders and develop a sense of solidarity. Organizations based at the hall might then mobilize working people to take action in the class struggle. Activists believed that the bosses could be challenged, the powerful influence of capitalists on mainstream political parties exposed, and one day a socialist system introduced that would bring fundamental social equality and production for use instead of profit.[10]

Every socialist hall had an amateur theatre group that attracted many participants and spectators. The groups performed popular classics, as well as plays written by talented Finnish radicals living in Canada. One such playwright was Alf Hautamäki, a left-wing activist who skilfully portrayed events of local interest while providing painless lessons in socialist principles and practices. In his musical, *Erämaiden Orjat*, or *Slaves of the Wilderness*, he combined a call for worker solidarity with dramatic material about logging-camp life, strikes, a theft, love affairs, alcoholism, and a lost husband.[11]

'Hall socialism,' as it came to be called, also attracted adherents through sports clubs and other such activities. Gymnastics and cross-country skiing had been popular in the old country, and they proved no less so in northern Ontario. Here, too, athletes and spectators at meets came together for enjoyment, but left activists encouraged them to think about such matters as team spirit and solidarity or sports as an outlet for competitive urges that capitalism encouraged in a ruthless marketplace. Popular sporting events, like the theatricals, were opportunities to raise funds for political activities and for strike support. Similarly, popular weekly dances at the hall provided chances for building a sense of community or comradeship and raising money for socialist causes.[12]

Closely linked to the halls were Finnish cooperative restaurants and stores. In communities where services were generally inadequate, these co-ops were highly welcome. For single men living in town when bush jobs were unavailable, the restaurants became daily haunts. Co-ops also provided a concrete example of alternatives to capitalist enterprise. Moreover, their profits could be directed towards political projects and their services used to relieve hungry strikers – the infantry in the class war.[13]

Newspapers and magazines produced by Finnish radicals reported regularly on hall events, and as essential socialist educational tools they were worthy of funds raised through hall activities. The Finnish-Canadian left read several newspapers, each one associated with a left organization. Finns in Port Arthur published *Työkansa* ('Working People') from 1907 to 1915. For several years it was the organ of the Finns who belonged to the Social Democratic Party of Canada, a national party that, during the first two decades of the twentieth century, brought together socialists and social democrats from a variety of ethnic backgrounds. One of the longest running newspapers was *Vapaus* ('Freedom' or 'Liberty'), which began publication in 1917 in Sudbury by the Finnish Socialist Organization of Canada, soon renamed the Finnish Organization of Canada. During the 1920s *Vapaus* expressed the viewpoint of the large number of Finnish radicals who belonged to the Communist Party of Canada. *Industrialisti* was published in Duluth, Minnesota, by a rival left organization close to the Industrial Workers of the World (IWW) – a radical industrial union that sought to destroy capitalism through workplace militancy and general strikes. That there were competing organizations among the Finns and newspapers expressing different positions on the left was typical of the left more generally in Canada and elsewhere.[14]

Hall socialism and the many left organizations supported by the Finns served as a springboard for launching union drives in industries such as logging, where the Finns' presence was strong. Central to the ethnic identity of the Red Finns was a political commitment to building a powerful mass movement of all workers. In the Ontario logging industry, doing so meant rallying immigrants of diverse backgrounds, as well as French- and English-speaking Canadians from rural areas where leftist traditions were unknown. To organize loggers who were neither compatriots nor political allies would prove a formidable task for the Finnish Reds, and not just because of the fierce opposition of employers and the state. A cultural gap yawned between the radical Finns and other northern woods-workers. Language played a part; few first-generation Finnish Canadians had facility in English or French. Moreover, the Finns' preference for clustering in all-Finnish logging camps reduced further the opportunities for contacting and inspiring other workers. Even the very vitality of hall socialism, ironically, could make launching successful union drives more difficult. Involvement with like-minded members of one's ethnic group at hall events was simply more appealing than spending time persuading sceptical workers of the advantages of unionism or the correct Marxist analysis. Loggers of other backgrounds at times would follow the lead of militant Finns, but at other times they would find the Finns' proud leftism unfamiliar and uninspiring, if not downright weird and off-putting.

At the turn of the twentieth century, Ontario's bush-workers lacked a tradition of collective action. On occasion lumberjacks had come together to fight for scarce jobs, resist a wage cut, or protest bad camp food, but such actions had always been spontaneous and had never given rise to organization. In the forest industry, only employees in saw-mills and pulp and paper mills had formed unions. They had been able to do so because steady work and valued skills gave them bargaining power. By contrast, the sheer abundance of workers with woods skills and the seasonality of logging meant that bush-workers had no such advantages. Draughty bunk-houses, bedbugs, pay cuts, dangerous work, unfair foremen – bush-workers had had plenty to complain about in Ontario's woodlands. As individuals they had frequently protested by 'jumping' from one bush camp to another or by going on a binge in town. Yet the unionization of the province's woods-workers came about slowly, after many years of apparent inactivity followed by two decades of persistent struggle spearheaded by Finnish radicals.[15]

During the second decade of the twentieth century, Finns in northern Ontario made sporadic efforts to organize bush-workers. In 1911 at Port Arthur (now part of Thunder Bay), there was organized the Ontario Lumber and Railroad Workers Ring, or *Ontarion Metsä-ja Rautatiety-öläisten Rengas*. From its name it is apparent that the Finns hoped to organize into one unit workers in two seasonal industries – logging and railway construction – where seasonal labour demands dovetailed and where many immigrants found jobs. Little came of the union. Serious progress in the unionization of bush-workers began when several camps at the Lakehead were organized during the First World War. Finns like A.T. (Tom) Hill, at that time a recent immigrant and itinerant worker, had come into contact with the IWW when working seasonally in the United States. In 1915, while working on the wheat harvest in the American midwest, Hill learned that the IWW had a branch, known as the Lumber Workers Industrial Union no. 120, that organized bush-workers. It was under the auspices of this union that Ontario woods-workers were first organized.[16]

The IWW had an obvious appeal for Ontario's Finnish bush-workers. Since its founding at Chicago in 1905, its greatest strength had been in the West among migrant so-called unskilled workers, many of them recent immigrants of diverse backgrounds. Though many of its members were also socialists, as an organization the IWW shunned political action, stressing instead direct action at the workplace. Like the syndicalists of Europe, the Wobblies, as they were called, combined a commitment of achieving immediate improvements in wages and working conditions with a long-range goal of overthrowing capitalism. Equally opposed to business and the state, they hoped that by joining together in a fiercely democratic 'one big union' and fighting for better wages and conditions, a solidarity would develop that would one day prove powerful enough to emancipate capitalism's 'wage slaves.' Finns working in the mines, lumber camps, and harvest gangs of the American midwest had come into contact with the IWW, and they brought the idea with them into Canada. Moreover, Finns living in northern Ontario read about the Wobblies in the U.S.-based Finnish-language newspapers that circulated widely in the province.[17]

The activities of the IWW were scrutinized closely by officials in Canada and the United States because both governments hoped to repress what they perceived as a dangerous, anarchistic movement. The Bolshevik Revolution in Russia in 1917 intensified the concerns of state officials here, and the fact that Canada was at war gave the state additional authority to repress so-called threats to internal security and the war effort. The IWW, the Finnish Socialist Organization of Canada, and the Finnish-language press were all outlawed in 1918. Authorities tried to cut off Canada's supply of radical pamphlets published in the United States. At one point, an Ontario Provincial Police (OPP) constable at Port Arthur wrote with exasperation to his superior: 'Now the Finns are the worst foreigners we will have to deal with regarding this bolsheviki plague. They are very cunning and hard to catch.' The constable had recently discovered that local Finnish Wobblies had received through the mail banned literature disguised in Chinese wrapping-paper and with Chinese writing on it![18]

Police had spies at meetings of bush-workers who were organizing a union at camps along the Algoma Central Railway, north of Sault Ste-Marie. A police translation of union minutes taken in Finnish and dated 25 March 1918 shows that organizers were attempting to coordinate the tactics of river-drivers who were planning to demand improved wages and conditions. The meeting had decided that 'the fight' would be carried out simply in the name of 'the working class.' Perhaps this was an attempt to avoid public association with the IWW and the consequent police repression. The commissioner of the OPP, nevertheless, believed that this development was 'part and parcel of the I.W.W. business.'[19]

Once the war was over, union organizing in the Ontario bush took off, as it did in so many other industries at the time. In 1919 workers throughout Canada were eager to see incomes catch up with the spiralling cost of living, they were fired by wartime rhetoric about 'a world fit for heroes,' and they had been released from wartime restraints. In the same restless summer as Winnipeg's giant general strike was fought, there emerged a Canadian-based industrial union, the One Big Union (OBU). Its key leaders were socialists, and its membership was made up largely of former locals of conservative U.S.-based unions. These locals had joined the OBU in the hope that it could build a more effective industrial union movement in Canada. In British Columbia that year a new, independent union of loggers and sawmill workers had been formed and had spread 'like a forest fire.' That organization soon affiliated with the OBU, becoming the Lumber and Camp Workers Industrial Union of the OBU. From the west organizers arrived in northern Ontario to unionize bush-workers. Walter Cowan, a British-born socialist from Vancouver, worked closely with Finnish socialists in the north, and *Vapaus* gave much news coverage and support to the union drive among woods-workers. Most of the Finnish camp organizations of the IWW soon joined the new union as going concerns, although a few resisted amalgamation.[20]

During the logging season of 1919–20, the union movement in the Ontario bush grew well beyond its Finnish base. Developments can be followed in the Lumber and Camp Workers' newspaper, *Le Travailleur / The Worker*. From the paper's title and the occasional article in French, it is evident that organizers hoped to reach French- and English-speaking bush-workers – the great majority of woodsmen across the province. To some extent they succeeded. There are many reports of camp committees that sought recognition from camp foremen, the (shorter) eight-hour day at higher wages, and better camp conditions. The union also led a campaign to pressure the Ontario government, a generally sympathetic Farmer-Labour government formed in 1919, to enact and enforce tougher regulations regarding sanitation and medical care in logging camps. Quite a number of the camp reports in *The Worker* are translations from Finnish, and it is evident that some of the most active camp committees were Finnish ones.

Almost as quickly as it began, the union surge in the Ontario bush came to a temporary halt. As in so many other industries in 1920 and

1921, unemployment levels rose and employers succeeded in forcing wage cuts. Support for unions declined, and as one observer of Ontario lumber camps said in December 1920, it was 'the foreman's day.' Bush-workers had grown 'subdued, work well, and know too well that a complaint means discharge, and discharge no job, and very little prospect of another.' Amid these discouraging conditions, union activists squabbled and accomplished little.[21]

The task of rebuilding the labour movement in the Ontario bush was taken up during the 1920s by Finns who formed two rival unions that competed for support. One of the unions evolved along syndicalist lines, maintaining ties at one time or another with the OBU and the IWW. The other was closely associated with the emerging Communist movement in Canada. The dichotomy reflected a sharp division within the Finnish-Canadian left of the 1920s.

The syndicalist union among Ontario bush-workers was supported by one group of Finnish leftist halls. At the beginning of the decade, when the OBU nationwide had vitality, these halls, located at northern Ontario centres such as Port Arthur, Nipigon, the Sault, Timmins, and Sudbury, called themselves *OBU:n Kannatusrengas*, or OBU Support Circles. As the OBU withered during the mid-1920s, the Wobblies gained control of these left halls and the bush-workers' union locals. This is remarkable, given the successful repression and the collapse of the IWW virtually everywhere else in North America. *Industrialisti*, the newspaper of Finnish-American Wobblies, helped maintain an IWW presence in the north, where it was read by many. Finnish-speaking Wobbly activists fleeing state authorities in the United States also kept the organization alive in northern Ontario. In 1925 several halls joined to form a new organization known as the CTKL, or *Canadan Teollisuusunianistien Kannatusliitto* (Support League of Canadian Industrial Unionists), which soon expanded to include twenty-three halls in Ontario. It remained close to the IWW and in the logging industry played a crucial role building locals of the Lumber Workers Industrial Union no. 120. In the mid-1920s it had a membership of approximately 1,500 woods-workers, most of them Finns who had been active for a time in the OBU.[22]

The other bush-workers' union formed in Ontario during the 1920s was built by Finnish leftists who had been inspired by the Russian Revolution and the world Communist movement formed in its wake. Some activists like A.T. Hill, who had once supported the IWW, now opposed that organization, as well as the OBU. Instead, they had become active supporters of the Communist Party of Canada (CPC), which was founded in 1921 and known as the Workers Party of Canada from 1922 to 1924. Hill, in fact, was present at the party's founding and headed the Finnish group, later the Finnish Section, within the CPC. The Finnish Organization of Canada had joined the Workers Party as an organization, its members automatically becoming members of the new party. Thus, the many FOC halls in northern Ontario became centres of Communist activity. They lent support to a new industrial union that Hill and other activists such as Kalle Salo and Alf Hautamaki began to build among bush-workers. In early 1924 they launched organizational drives for what became, in 1925, the Lumber Workers Industrial Union of Canada (LWIUC), a Canadian union that remained closely tied to the Communist Party. Thanks largely to the strength of the FOC halls, a few thousand members were soon recruited to the LWIUC. December 1925 saw the appearance of *Metsätyöläinen* ('The Forest Worker'), the organization's Finnish-language monthly magazine which was creatively edited by Hautamaki.[23]

Metsatyolainen announced the LWIUC's strategy for organizing, and it attempted to rally workers to the cause. The plan was to begin the unionization drive in Ontario's pulpwood logging sector, where sympathetic Finns were most numerous, and then move to the province's sawlog camps, and finally to use the base in Ontario to launch a campaign in neighbouring Quebec. *Metsatyolainen* articulated the complaints of many bush-workers and sought to make them conscious of their exploitation. The paper stressed that camp bosses bullied workers, treating them like 'feudal slaves.' Bosses cheated woodsmen by breaking oral agreements on wages, deducting extra, fictitious expenses from their pay, and failing to provide promised medical services. It maintained that the status of lumberjacks had been declining: 'Now even the lowliest female dishwasher won't speak to lumberjacks, and so they must go to the saloons and brothels for amusement.'[24]

Monthly issues of *Metsatyolainen* included entertaining and inspirational stories and poems as well. One short story recounted how an irresponsible, drunken lumberjack who had been injured went to a hospital where he began reading left-wing literature. Eventually he became a fine unionist. Poems by Aku Päiviö, renowned in the radical Finnish-Canadian community, powerfully expressed the union's central message:

Rise you sinuous men against those who would steal your strength!
Rise by the thousands, like the forest itself!
That will be your only salvation.[25]

The organizing tactics of the LWIUC resembled those of the IWW. Union delegates or organizers took jobs in the logging camps, where they were supposed to avoid harassment from the boss by 'work[ing] in secret, pretending to be ordinary workers.' Edwin Suksi recalled his days as an organizer for the LWIUC in the Thunder Bay district in 1926 and 1927. 'It was tough. There's not much friendliness. You have to walk from the railroad 28 to 30 miles in through the bush, and when you get there you get a very cold reception from the camp foreman ... One time, I walked into the camp at one o'clock and had to leave by evening.' Like nearly all the union delegates, who were men under thirty 'in the best of manhood,' Suksi learned the art of organizing as he went along. He soon discovered that 'in the camps when organizing, mainly you talked bread-and-butter issues, not politics.' The men were interested in pay first and camp conditions second. With the exception of recalcitrant White Finns, Suksi found his countrymen the easiest to organize because they 'were radical immigrants; they got solid unity.' Once workers signed union cards and paid their small initiation fee and monthly dues, they elected a camp committee. It would negotiate for immediate improvements with the camp boss and maintain contacts with the union as a whole in preparation for district-wide bargaining, as well as strikes to enforce the demands.[26]

The northern Ontario logging industry was the site of several big strikes from 1926 to 1929, a time when workers elsewhere in Ontario were scarcely striking at all. The first large strike began in late September 1926 as some 700 pulp-cutters, many but not all of them Finns, walked off their jobs in the Thunder Bay district. Preparations had begun in the summer, when Wobbly and LWIUC camp delegates met jointly to set wage demands. Employers rejected the demand to raise monthly wages on average from about $40 to $60. A test of strength ensued. For a few weeks the employers refused to negotiate. Meantime, the inexperienced strikers and the union did remarkably well at cutting off the supply of strikebreakers and providing food and accommodation for all needy strikers. Finns, Slavs, French Canadians, and others enjoyed the aid of the left-wing Finnish community as both CTKL and FOC halls rallied to the cause. By the end of October some of the employers had agreed to the demands, while others insisted on a compromise and paid fifty dollars per month. Even this amounted to a significant advance which leftists hailed as the start of 'a new chapter in the history of our movement here in Canada.'[27]

In the years immediately following the 1926 breakthrough, no other strike involved as many workers or brought the union such favourable results. Strikes fizzled in the Cochrane area in 1927 and near Kapuskasing the following year. LWIUC activists blamed these defeats on their failure to take account of the lack of commitment among the predominantly non-Finnish bush-workers of these areas. They also pointed to 'the deceit' of unionists from the IWW. Inter-union rivalries were intense.[28]

The unions and their camp committees had their quickest victories and their most thoroughgoing defeats when confronting employers who were Finnish subcontractors, or 'jobbers.' Certain of the jobbers were neither materially far removed from the bush-workers nor culturally at odds with the socialist perspective. Such contractors could be comparatively easily persuaded to negotiate with camp committees and provide inexpensive improvements in living conditions. However, the narrow profit margins allowed for in the jobbers' contracts with the big pulp and paper companies gave the subcontractors little or no latitude in wage bargaining. If some contractors were reasonably cordial with the unionists, other Finnish jobbers – particularly those who had been Whites in Finland – resisted the unions with every imaginable tactic.

The most dramatic and tragic incident involving woods unionists and Whites grew out of a failed strike in the Thunder Bay district during the fall of 1929. Two Finnish-Canadian organizers from the LWIUC were at the centre of the drama: Viljo Rosvall and John Voutilainen, an experienced trapper and woodsman. In an attempt to extend the stalled strike to additional camps, the two men, perhaps unrealistically, agreed to try to organize about one hundred men at the Onion Lake camps of Pigeon Timber Company contractor Leonard Maki, or *Pappi* (Reverend) Mäki, as the one-time lay preacher was known. Rosvall and Voutilainen knew it was a dangerous mission, for the vehemently anti-union Mäki employed mostly White Finns like himself. On 18 November they set out for the Onion Lake camps, but the union never heard from them again. Mäki admitted to having talked to the two men on their first day out, but union-organized search parties in the woods could find no trace of them. Eventually, in mid-April 1930, a search party found the organizers' bodies in a creek flowing out of Onion Lake. At coroners' inquests in which confusing testimony was heard, jurors quickly returned verdicts of accidental drowning. But LWIUC leaders, and the Finnish-Canadian left in general, rejected this finding. It was impossible for them to believe that two experienced woodsmen, one of them very familiar with the area, could have drowned in shallow water. Also not accounted for was a blow Rosvall had received to his skull. The Finnish unionists were convinced that a gang of Whites from Mäki's camp had murdered the organizers.[29]

On 28 April 1930, the day of Rosvall and Voutilainen's funeral, a giant procession of several thousand people followed the pallbearers through the streets of Port Arthur. In the front of the procession, union delegates carried a red ribbon with the union cards of the two organizers pinned to it, followed by the FOC brass band playing Chopin's *Funeral March*. The event was further dramatized by an eclipse of the sun, which even the atheist radicals found eerie. Thereafter, the Finnish-Canadian left and the woods-workers' union hailed Rosvall and Voutilainen as martyrs of the bush-workers' organizing struggles and as heroic victims of the class war.

About the time of the failed strike at Thunder Bay in 1929, the Great Depression set in and union organizing ground to a halt. Union drives were ineffective at least for a few seasons during the worst years of the Depression, when unemployment levels soared and logging operations were drastically reduced. No one could have succeeded at building a union under such circumstances. Nevertheless, prospects for unionization were made even worse by two developments on the left.

Finnish-Canadian radicalism, and the LWIUC in particular, were seriously weakened by the emigration in the early 1930s of more than two thousand Finnish Canadians to Soviet Karelia. These people were inspired to assist the Soviet authorities in developing the forest industry of Karelia. Many of the most experienced bush-workers, and the most radical, went. In April 1932 the Timmins district LWIUC representatives reported that the local leadership of the union had had to be replaced three times because of departures for Karelia, and membership had 'fallen significantly; the work of the locals ha[d] just about ceased.'[30]

Second, there were disruptions on the Communist left that had implications for the LWIUC. The Communist International – that is, the international Communist movement based in Moscow – and the central leadership of the Communist Party of Canada had in the late 1920s adopted a policy they called Bolshevization. Beginning in 1929 a concerted effort was made to eliminate the power of the ethnic blocs (of Ukrainians, Finns, and Jews) within the party. Members were now to be Communists first, rather than to think and act as cultural separatists. The new policy did not go down well with many Finns, and a few of their leaders became deeply disenchanted when the central party leadership attacked them.

Meantime, the party had revised its union organizing strategy. In

1930, following directives from the Communist International, a new central organization of unions was formed in Canada, the Workers Unity League (WUL), with which the LWIUC affiliated. The union now came under the authority of central CPC leaders, such as Tom Ewen, a Scot who was not afraid to criticize the Finnish leadership of the LWIUC. At the 1931 convention of the Workers Unity League, Ewen lashed out at Hautamaki's 'pessimism and defeatism,' and insisted, following the main policy of the WUL, that strikes should be called. The central purpose of the WUL unions was to agitate among workers and the unemployed, encouraging them to harass employers and governments. In this way, the stability of capitalism would be upset and capitalist countries would be distracted from any interest they might have in declaring war on the Soviet Union, the home of communism.[31]

In northern Ontario, however, effective strikes were impossible until the industry began to recover somewhat in mid-1933. At that point the LWIUC began a concerted campaign of agitation, and efforts were made to unionize all bush-workers, reaching beyond the Finnish base. The LWIUC produced a new English-language newspaper, The Lumber Worker, and J. Gillbanks, an English-speaking Communist Party member from the Lakehead, was elected to assist the Finnish leaders. Beginning in the summer of 1933 and for the following two years, the LWIUC played a key role in a series of large, militant strikes in which Finnish activists rallied substantial numbers of French and English Canadians, Swedes, Slavs, and others – men who worked in every logging district of the north.

The strikes of the mid-1930s held to a common pattern. Camp committees and union delegates prepared a list of demands, which were presented to employers along with a threat to strike if the demands were not met almost immediately. Employers, acting together, refused to meet or otherwise recognize unionists and made no concessions in response to demands. A strike then ensued. Despite the urging of provincial and federal government officials, employers would continue to refuse to deal with the unionists, branding them as Reds and outside agitators who were fomenting trouble in an otherwise peaceful setting. Picketing strikers frequently scuffled with police as the pickets tried to block strikebreakers from reaching the camps. After a few weeks, employers would concede on some of the demands, but refuse to sign a contract with the union. Labour activists would then claim a victory, even though it was partial.

The Finnish role in the strikes of the mid-1930s was crucial. Finnish radicals manned the camp committees, coordinated pre-strike planning, acted as leaders during the strikes, and provided the lion's share of strike support, as well as many of the most militant pickets. The Finnish halls served as meeting places for strike committees, workshops for preparing propaganda, and bases for flying squads of pickets. Employers saw the Finn halls as the nerve-centres of agitation, the heart of enemy territory. When strike committees were at their most provocative, they would insist that employers come to negotiate at the Finn hall rather than some public building or other neutral ground. As a point of honour, employers always refused to meet at the Finn hall.[32]

The halls also served as centres for strike support. Countless strikers, who of course had left their seasonal homes in the camps, found free shelter at the theatres, which now served as dormitories. These same large rooms were used for dances held to raise strike support funds and to maintain morale and for bazaars that women's groups hosted to make money to contribute to the strike fund. At the cooperative restaurants, women volunteers served pickets cheap or free food, much of it donated by local Finnish farmers. Gertie Grönroos recalled: 'If the farmers hadn't supported those strikers heaven knows what would have happened ... Money was hard to come by, but they did have food.'[33]

The strikes of the mid-1930s were notoriously combative events, and the violence associated with picketing drew the attention of daily newspapers in the north and elsewhere. Bloody confrontations sometimes occurred deep in the bush, as strikers tried to extend the strike to additional camps where woodsmen were continuing to work. During the first big strike of 1933, for instance, newspapers reported that radicals were preventing workers from going to their jobs, that militants had threatened to burn down the camps of holdouts, and that 'one camp was seized by strikers who only were ejected when provincial police were called in.' During a later dispute, it was reported that 250 striking employees of the J.A. Mathieu Lumber Company had boarded a train in Fort Frances carrying some fifty strikebreakers and coach windows were smashed, two policemen were injured, and Mathieu himself received three broken ribs. Nevertheless, the strikers gained sympathy and support from some members of the public. In the Mathieu strike, the Winnipeg *Tribune* held that the strikers of northern Ontario had '100 per cent public sympathy and support on their side,' because employers had taken advantage 'of the state of the labor market to an almost criminal degree.' The town of Chapleau had maintained strikers on local public relief, so great was the town's sympathy.[34]

Just as controversial as the violence was the strikers' so-called foreign-ness. Employers sought to discredit the strikers in the eyes of the public by portraying the militants as foreigners come to disrupt peace-loving Canadians. For instance, during a dispute in the Cochrane area in 1934, A.E. Wicks, an owner of a large logging concern, publicly charged that 150 strikers, all of them 'foreigners armed with spiked clubs, a rifle and several revolvers, swooped down on [a] pulp-cutting camp.' They ordered the forty Canadian workers 'to march 22 miles to Cochrane on five minutes notice.' Government investigators reported confidentially to Queen's Park authorities that the real instigator in the dispute was Wicks, who had assumed from the start 'a pugnacious attitude towards the strikers,' and who was 'endeavouring to make a racial issue of the matter.' In March 1934 George Nicholson, the member of Parliament for East Algoma and a prominent Conservative and lumber company owner, thundered in the House of Commons about Moscow-financed Communist agitators who had caused a strike in his riding. In reply, a spokesman for the strikers felt compelled to insist on both his legitimacy as a striker and as a Canadian. Ellard Connolly declared that the bush-workers 'here want only a living wage and civilized living conditions,' and he made it known he was 'a Canadian citizen of British pioneer stock, born, reared, and schooled in Bromely Township, Renfrew County.' The debate on the foreignness and Soviet connections of strik-ers also took on a partisan edge. Opposition Liberals at Queen's Park and Ottawa criticized Conservative governments both for the heavy-handed use of police and for their willingness to resort to nativism and virulent anti-Communism in an attempt to discredit legitimate protest.[35]

Nativist and anti-Red Finn sentiments were forcefully expressed by a propagandist par excellence who tried to forge a new union in the Ontario bush, one that would offer an alternative to the radical unions. In 1933 and 1934 George Salverson, a former Port Arthur alderman and member of a conservative railwaymen's union, launched the Canadian Bushmen's Union. He maintained that Canadian workers had decided that 'these Bolsheviki side shows shall cease.' His organization, it was reported widely, had been organized by 'Canadian-minded workers of several nationalities.' He tried to rally White ('Canadian-minded') Finns and 'Anglo Saxons' in a blatantly nativist and anti-Red movement. It appears likely that he had financial and other support from some employers. The LWIUC took the threat seriously, but in the end the Canadian Bushmen's Union never got off the ground.[36]

1935 proved to be a turning-point in the history of Finnish radicalism in the northern Ontario woods. The period of intense labour agitation drew to a close. This was partly a result of policy changes initiated by the Communist International and the CPC. It was decided that everywhere the Communists would abandon their vigorously militant, sectarian unions – like those of the Workers Unity League – and instead Communists would work from within mainstream trade unions. In 1935 the LWIUC was thus disbanded, and Communists succeeded in developing locals of the Lumber and Sawmill Workers Union, a branch of the Indianapolis-based craft union, the United Brotherhood of Carpenters and Joiners.

Finnish bush-workers still provided most of the membership for the new union locals in the north, as well as many of the leaders, including men such as A.T. Hill and Harry Raketti. Yet at this juncture a new leader came to the fore, Bruce Magnuson, who was a Communist, but Swedish rather than Finnish and with a stronger command of English than his predecessors. Even improved facility in English did not eliminate the cultural gap between the activists and many ordinary bush-workers: the gap was not just ethnic but political. A Toronto-born man who began logging in the north in 1937 recalled much later: 'Those first union organizers in the bush must have been brainwashed somewhere. They were new birds to us, a strange species. We'd listen to them and most of what they said didn't make sense – that Marxist philosophy they spouted. "Solidarity forever" and all that crap!'[37]

In the late 1930s the Lumber and Saw, as the new union was known locally in the north, sought to establish a collective bargaining relationship with employers. For the unionists, strikes and agitation became less a goal in themselves, and more a tactic of last resort in order to win union recognition and a collective agreement from employers. This strategy was assisted by state initiatives of the day. In 1935 the provincial Liberal government introduced the Industrial Standards Act, which brought employers and union representatives together at the bargaining table and helped to established certain minimum wage levels, as well as work and camp standards. The process continued during the Second World War, when the federal government became paramount in the field of labour relations as part of the national war effort. For the war's duration, the federal Regional War Labour Board for Ontario brought woods employers and union representatives together to negotiate wages and conditions.[38]

Full-blown collective bargaining came to the Ontario bush in 1946. That fall the Lumber and Saw took advantage of an acute shortage of woods-workers, which was related to the war's end, and it won the biggest strike in the industry. In step with developments in many industries at the time, the major corporations in the provincial pulp and paper industry signed formal collective agreements with the union. A pattern of collective bargaining was set that would last for four decades.

Finnish activists played an important role in the developments from 1935 to 1946 that brought collective bargaining to the bush. Finns served on the executives of union locals throughout the period, and in the important strikes of the late 1930s and 1946 they were once again conspicuous for their militancy. These strikes were much less Finnish-dominated than earlier ones, however, and from the 1950s the Finns were increasingly on the periphery of union matters.

There were a few reasons for the Finns' waning influence in the Ontario woods after 1950. The most active among the Finns, those still serving on the executives of locals in the immediate postwar years, were driven from office, along with non-Finnish radicals such as Magnuson, by the anti-Communist hysteria of the Cold War. Meantime, the base for radicalism was eroding. The generation of bush-workers that had been so active on the left was growing old, and the old-timers were retiring from their strenuous bush jobs. Their places in the camps were taken by new immigrants from diverse backgrounds and with varying political commitments. Few among them were Finnish. The children of the immigrant Finns were equipped to take jobs that were less physically onerous and hazardous than those in logging, and their interest in radical politics was in any case much less marked than their parents'. After all, the second generation had grown up in Canada, and their lives were shaped in fundamentally different ways. Furthermore, during the Cold War links to radicalism became embarrassing, even dangerous.

For a generation, however, the radical Finns in northern Ontario had developed a vibrant culture, one that made the province's logging industry the site of some of the most militant and sustained labour unrest in the country. Their radicalism had kept them apart from their Finnish compatriots who had supported the Whites in the old country, and it had differentiated them from most of the other woods-workers who came from other backgrounds. The Finnish radicals were not always able to overcome their own ethnic separateness or successfully mobilize the majority of bush-workers, but nevertheless they played the key role in the labour unrest in the Ontario woods during the interwar years. Their part was crucial, too, in the 1946 breakthrough that brought true collective bargaining to the pulpwood industry. As a result, thousands of workers during the following four decades had a voice at the workplace, enjoyed the protection of a union and collective agreements, and won significant improvements in wages and employment conditions. Radical leaders had perceptively met the cultural needs of immigrants on the frontier and moulded the immigrant workers into a formidable force for labour activism. On their part, the newcomers had gained a sense of belonging in a new place, a measure of dignity on the job, and pride through their struggle for a better deal and for social change.

NOTES

1 Donald Avery, 'Dangerous Foreigners': European Immigration, Workers, and Labour Radicalism in Canada, 1896–1932 (Toronto 1979); Ivan Avakumovic, The Communist Party in Canada: A History (Toronto 1975); for examples of multiethnic militancy, see Allen Seager, 'Class, Ethnicity, and Politics in the Alberta Coalfields, 1905–1945,' in Dirk Hoerder, 'Struggle a Hard Battle': Essays on Working Class Immigrants (Dekalb, Ill. 1986), and Carmela Patrias, Relief Strike: Immigrant Workers and the Great Depression in Crowland, Ontario, 1930–1935 (Toronto 1990); on single group militancy, see Ruth A. Frager, Sweatshop Strife: Class, Ethnicity, and Gender in the Jewish Labour Movement of Toronto, 1900–1939 (Toronto 1992).
2 Reino Kero, Migration from Finland to North America (Turku 1974); Keijo Virtanen, Settlement or Return? Finnish Emigrants (1860–1920) (Helsinki 1979); Varpu Lindström, The Finns in Canada (Ottawa 1985); Varpu Lindström, Defiant Sisters: A Social History of Finnish Immigrant Women in Canada (Toronto 1992), chapter 1.
3 Bay Street Project no. 2, A Chronicle of Finnish Settlements in Rural Thunder Bay (Thunder Bay 1976); M. Rasmussen, 'The Geographic Impact of Finnish Settlement on the Thunder Bay Area of Northern Ontario,' MA thesis (University of Alberta 1978).
4 On logging methods and labour in northern Ontario, see Ian Radforth, Bushworkers and Bosses: Logging in Northern Ontario, 1900–1980 (Toronto 1987), and his 'The Shantymen' in Paul Craven, ed., Labouring Lives (Toronto 1995).
5 Confederation College Archives, Thunder Bay Labour History Project, Buzz Lein, taped interview by Jean Morrison, 1974; Multicultural History Society of Ontario [MHSO], Oral History Collection [OHC], Toivo Tienhara, interviewed by Lennard Sillanpaa, 1977 (translation by Varpu Lindström).
6 D.G. Kirby, Finland in the Twentieth Century (London 1979).
7 Anthony F. Upton, The Finnish Revolution, 1917–18 (Minneapolis 1981);

Oskari Tokoi, *Sisu 'Even Through a Stone Wall': The Autobiography of Oskari Tokoi* (New York 1957).

8 Mauri Amiko Jalava, '"Radicalism or a 'New Deal'?": The Unfolding World View of Finnish Immigrants in Sudbury, 1883–1932,' MA thesis (Laurentian University 1983); Varpu Lindström-Best, 'Central Organization of the Loyal Finns in Canada,' *Polyphony* 3:2 (Fall 1981), 81–90.

9 A. William Hoglund, 'Breaking Religious Tradition: Finnish Immigrant Workers and the Church, 1890–1915,' in *For the Common Good* (Superior, Wisc. 1977), 23–64; Markku Suokonautio, 'Reorganization of the Finnish Lutherans in Canada,' *Polyphony* 3:2 (Fall 1981), 91–6.

10 Hall socialism is discussed in Lindström, *Defiant Domestics*; Jalava, '"Radicalism or a 'New Deal'?"; Peter V. Kratz, '"Sudburyn Suomalaiset": Finnish Immigrant Activities in the Sudbury Area, 1882–1939,' MA thesis (University of Western Ontario 1980); William Eklund, *Builders of Canada: History of the Finnish Organization of Canada, 1911–1971* (Toronto 1987).

11 Taru Sundsten, 'The Theatre of the Finnish-Canadian Labour Movement and Its Dramatic Literature, 1900–1939,' in Michael G. Karni, *Finnish Diaspora*, vol. I (Toronto 1981), 77–92; Arja Pilli, *The Finnish-Language Press in Canada, 1901–1939* (Turku 1982), 67–9.

12 Bruce Kidd, 'The Workers' Sports Movement in Canada, 1924–40: The Radical Immigrants' Alternative,' *Polyphony* 7:1 (1985) 80–8; Jim Tester, ed., *Sports Pioneers: A History of the Finnish-Canadian Amateur Sports Federation, 1906–1986* (Sudbury 1986).

13 Mauri A. Jalava, 'The Finnish-Canadian Cooperative Movement in Ontario,' in Karni, *Finnish Diaspora*, vol. I, 93–100.

14 Pilli, *Finnish-Language Press*.

15 A fuller discussion of the history of unionism in the Ontario logging industry may be found in Radforth, *Bushworkers and Bosses*, chapters 6 and 7.

16 Public Archives of Canada [PAC], Finnish Organization of Canada Collection [FOCC], MG 28 V46 vol. 143:1; Pilli, *Finnish-Language Press* 67; Thunder Bay Historical Museum and Archives, A.T. Hill papers, A.T. Hill, 'Historical Basis and Development of the Lumber Workers' Organization and Struggle in Ontario' (typescript 1952) and his 'Autobiography' (typescript n.d.).

17 A.R. McCormack, 'The Industrial Workers of the World in Western Canada, 1905–1914,' Canadian Historical Association, *Historical Papers* 1975, 167–90; Mark Leier, *Where the Fraser River Flows: The Industrial Workers of the World in British Columbia* (Vancouver 1990); Melvyn Dubofsky, *We Shall Be All: A History of the Industrial Workers of the World* (New York 1969); Douglas Ollila, 'From Socialism to Industrial Unionism (IWW): Social Factors in the Emergence of Left-Labor Radicalism among Finnish Workers of the Mesabi, 1911–

1919,' in Michael G. Karni et al., eds, *Finnish Experience in the Western Great Lakes Region* (Turku 1975); John Wiita, 'A Finnish-American in Canada, 1918–23,' in J. Donald Wilson, 'The Canadian Sojourn of a Finnish American Radical,' *Canadian Ethnic Studies* 16:2 (1984) .

18 Ontario Archives [OA], Ontario Provincial Police Records, RG 23 E-30 1.6, Constable A.W. Symons to Supt James E. Rogers, 5 April 1919; Arja Pilli, 'Finnish Canadian Radicalism and the Government of Canada from the First World War to the Depression,' in Karni, *Finnish Diaspora*, vol. I, 19–32; Gregory S. Kealey, 'State Repression of Labour and the Left in Canada, 1914–20: The Impact of the First World War,' *Canadian Historical Review* 7:3 (Sept. 1993), 281–314.

19 AO, OPPR, RG 23 E-30 1.6, transl. of minutes of meeting, enclosed in James E. Rogers to A.W. Caldron, 23 April 1918.

20 David J. Bercuson, *Fools and Wise Men: The Rise and Fall of the One Big Union* (Toronto 1978), 57–108; Dorothy Steeves, *The Compassionate Rebel: Ernest Winch and the Growth of Socialism in Western Canada* (Vancouver 1977) 46; Radforth, *Bushworkers and Bosses*, 114–15; Gordon Hak, 'British Columbia Loggers and the Lumber Workers Industrial Union, 1919–1922,' *Labour / Le Travail* 23 (Spring 1989), 67–80.

21 University of Toronto Archives, Faculty of Forestry Collection, Logging Report no. 28 by J.A. Brodie and F.T. Jenkins..

22 Radforth, *Bushworkers and Bosses*, 119–20.

23 Ibid., 120–1; Edward W. Laine, 'The Finnish Organization of Canada, 1923–40, and the Development of a Finnish-Canadian Culture,' *Polyphony* 3:2 (Fall 1981), 81–90.

24 *Metsätyöläinen* 1926, no. 2, no. 3, no. 5 (translated by Varpu Lindström).

25 Ibid., 1926, no. 2 and 1929, no. 1 (translated by Varpu Lindström).

26 Ibid., 1926, no. 3; MHSO, OHC, Edwin Suksi, interviewed by Lennard Sillanpää, 1977, and Suksi interviewed by Ian Radforth and Varpu Lindström-Best, Sudbury 1980.

27 *The Worker* (Toronto), 13 November 1926; PAC, Strikes and Lockouts Files, RG 27 vol. 337 76; PAC, FOCC 143:3, Financial Report, 1 April 1926–20 February 1927.

28 *The Worker*, 11 January 1930; PAC, Strikes and Lockout Files, RG 27 334 98.

29 Satu Repo, 'Rosvall and Voutilainen: Two Union Men Who Never Died,' *Labour / Le Travailleur* 8 / 9 (1981–2), 179–202; Radforth, *Bushworkers and Bosses*, 124–5.

30 PAC, FOCC, 143:6, Minutes of the Timmins District Meeting, L&AWIUC, 10 April 1932; Jalava, 'Radicalism,' 231–53; Reno Kero, "The Canadian Finns in Soviet Karelia,' in Karni, *Finnish Diaspora*, vol. I, 203–14.

31 On Bolshevization, see Jalava, 'Radicalism,' 194–208; Ian Angus, *Canadian Bolsheviks: The Early Years of the Communist Party of Canada* (Montreal 1981), 273–88. On the Workers Unity League, see John Manley, 'Communism and the Canadian Working Class during the Great Depression,' PhD thesis (Dalhousie University 1984). The criticism of Hautamaki is from PAC, FOCC, 143:16, minutes of the L&AWIUC convention 2–5 May 1931 (transl. by Varpu Lindström).

32 Radforth, *Bushworkers and Bosses*, 125–32; Livo Ducin (pseud.), 'Unrest in the Algoma Lumbercamps; the Bushworkers' Strikes of 1933–34,' in *50 Years of Labor in Algoma* (Sault Ste-Marie 1978).

33 MHSO, OHC, Gertie Grönroos, interviewed by Helena Doherty, 1979.

34 Fort William *Times-Journal*, 8 June 1933; Port Arthur *News Chronicle*, 1 December 1933; Winnipeg *Tribune*, undated clipping in PAC, Strikes and Lockouts Files, RG 27 353 166; Canada, House of Commons, *Debates*, 12 March 1934, 1415–17.

35 Toronto *Daily Star*, 28 September 1934; AO, Department of Labour Records, RG 7 II-1 vol. 12, L.A. Dent to J. Marsh, 25 September 1934; L.A. Dent, 'Report of Conditions in the Woods,' and 'Final Report,' 23 October 1934; Canada, House of Commons, *Debates*, 26 March 1934, 1883–5, and Connolly read into *Debates*, 26 March 1934, 1916–20.

36 AO, Department of Labour, RG 7 II-1, vol. 10, clippings, and E. Hutchison to J. Marsh, 26 September 1934; *Metsätyöläinen* 1934, no. 1.

37 Confederation College Archives, Thunder Bay Labour History Interview Project, Buzz Lein, interviewed by Jean Morrison, 1972.

38 For these and subsequent developments, see Radforth, *Bushworkers and Bosses*, chapter 7.

Sewing Solidarity: The Eaton's Strike of 1912

RUTH A. FRAGER

'Mr. John C. Eaton, "King of Canada" as he is generally called, is being taught the A.B.C.'s of Industrial Democracy by the striking Cloak Makers of Toronto,' proclaimed the International Ladies' Garment Workers' Union (ILGWU).[1] It was 1912, and the Jewish workers who laboured in the Toronto garment factory of the T. Eaton Company were locked in combat with one of the most powerful employers in the country. The ILGWU charged that:

... in this very Kingdom of the Eaton Company, frail children of fourteen years, in busy seasons, work from 8 a.m. to 9 p.m. ... in slack season, skilled working women, connected with the firm for six, eight or more years, can earn only Five, Four or even less Dollars per week ... girls are forced at times to take 'homework' to do at night, after the long day in the factory; ... foremen and forewomen have power to discriminate most flagrantly in favor of their friends, or vice versa, and may cut wages, ruinously, by intention, or from careless distribution of piece work; and this is not the half of the story of wrongs.[2]

'Insults to Girls' (i.e. sexual harassment) and 'Graft for Foremen' were other complaints against Eaton's.[3]

Eaton's was no worse than many other employers in this period. Nevertheless, this strike is outstanding because it provides a rare example of male solidarity in support of women workers. The strike began in one department of the firm's clothing factory when sixty-five male sewing machine operators refused to follow new orders to sew in the linings of women's coats on their machines. Although the large Eaton's garment factory was not a union shop, all of these men were members of the ILGWU. They had been making 65¢ per garment without sewing in the linings, and they were now being asked to do the extra work without any increase in pay. Previously, the linings had been sewn in by hand by female workers who were known as finishers. So the new order from management amounted to more than a pay cut for the men – it meant women were going to lose their jobs. Male self-interest and female self-interest now coincided, and the strike became an expression of male solidarity with women workers.[4]

This solidarity was emphasized by the Toronto District Labour Council when it passed a resolution objecting to Eaton's locking out workers for refusing 'in the interest of their sister workers,' to do work which did not belong to them.[5] Indeed, this solidarity between men and women became the main theme of the strike. 'Remember,' stated Joe Salsberg, a Jewish immigrant who became a left-wing labour activist, 'the Jewish tailors in Toronto went on their first big strike in defense of *undzere shvester* – our sisters.'[6] Salsberg explained that:

The reasoning of the men who worked at Eaton's was a simple one: that these [women workers] will lose their jobs, and [...] maybe they felt they didn't want to do these jobs that the women are now doing, maybe their wages will come down [if the men were to sew in the linings by machine] because the rates fixed for those operations were always traditionally lower because women did [those operations] ... I never rule out the element of selfishness and self-interest – which is also human.

But [one of the strike slogans] became the folksy expression of simple, honest working men ... in Yiddish particularly: 'Mir vellen nisht aroycenemen dem bissle fun broyt fun di mayler fun undzere shvester.' [In English:] 'We will not take the morsel of bread from the mouths of our sisters.'[7]

The solidarity displayed by the men was not a simple matter of self-interest. According to the ILGWU's newspaper, union officials believed that 'management would have increased the price of operating [on] the garment, but the operators, with admirable solidarity, insist that the finishers shall not be deprived of their share of the work.'[8]

When the sixty-five male operators refused to sew in the linings, Eaton's management fired them and physically threw them out onto the street. Almost immediately, over one thousand of their fellow workers from Eaton's factory went on strike to support them. About a third of these strikers were women, and the ILGWU's head office sent two women organizers to Toronto in order to help lead the women strikers. The sympathy strike spread beyond the ILGWU to include members of the United Garment Workers who worked in the men's clothing departments of the Eaton's factory. And it spread beyond Toronto: workers at the Eaton's clothing factory in Montreal also struck in sympathy with the Toronto workers, and Hamilton's garment workers threatened to join the strike if any of Hamilton's clothing firms attempted to do any work for the T. Eaton Company.[9]

The attack on 'Fort Eaton' was reinforced by the call for a nation-wide boycott of the company's goods. The labour press warned its readers not to 'go after cheap Eaton bargains' because 'bargains at the expense of manhood, womanhood and childhood are expensive in the extreme.'[10] The boycott was particularly effective within Toronto's immigrant Jewish community. This was due largely to the support of Jewish women, for they were the ones who were primarily responsible for the family shopping. Here, women's role as consumer was used strategically to support the struggles of male and female producers. In addition, Eaton's mail order business suffered as customers from across the country mailed back their Eaton's catalogues in protest.[11]

Further appeals for support were made to women's groups outside of the Jewish community. The Toronto District Labour Council asked 'Women's Clubs [and] Suffrage Associations ... to defend the rights of the [Eaton's] workers.'[12] The ILGWU's newspaper optimistically reported that 'Women's Lodges and Women's Auxiliaries of men's trade unions, and associations of leisure class women' promised to support the strike.[13]

Meaningful solidarity between women appears to have stopped at the class border, however. Alice Chown, a women's rights activist, described the considerable difficulty she had when she tried to persuade non-working-class women's groups to support the Eaton's strikers:

I tried to interest the various women's clubs, but I was amazed because they had no sympathy with the strikers, unless I had some tale of hardship to tell. The common, everyday longings for better conditions, for a life that would provide more than food, clothes and shelter, were not recognized as justifying a strike. I had to tell over and over the old, old story of the bosses who favored the girls whom they could take out evenings, girls who had to sell themselves as well as their labor to get sufficient work to earn a living.[14]

Chown also indicated that many women suffragists were unwilling to support women strikers fearing that strike support work would tarnish the appeal of their main cause:

During the [Eaton's] strike I had to preside at a meeting of the Women's Political League. I asked [the women], who had been sent from New York to conduct the strike, to speak to our association. She made a very wise and illuminating speech. I did not expect an audience who had never considered that justice to working people was a higher virtue than charity, to respond any more cordially then it did. As soon as the discussion started I closed the suffrage meeting, and asked all who were willing to try to awaken interest in the strike to remain. I though I made it quite clear that with the adjournment of the suffrage meeting a new meeting came into existence, but I aroused a great deal of hard feeling amongst the zealous suffragists, who were afraid that their pet cause would be hurt through being linked with an unpopular one.[15]

The unpopularity of the strikers' cause in Chown's circles was also because the vast majority of the Eaton's strikers were East European Jewish immigrants – and English Canadians were often intensely ethno-centric and suspicious of foreigners.[16]

The Jewish nature of the strike was a central issue. The ILGWU's newspaper was to the point:

Those affected [by the dispute at Eaton's] are almost entirely Jewish: and the chief slogan by which it was hoped to cut off public sympathy was the report ... that this is 'only a strike of Jews.' The appeal to race and creed prejudice has succeeded, too, in so far as it has prevented the Gentile Cloak Makers from joining in the sympathetic strike.[17]

The failure of Eaton's non-Jewish workers to join the strike was part of a wider pattern of tension between Jews and non-Jews in Toronto's garment industry. Considerable ethnic tension also existed within the labour movement more generally. Garment manufacturers attempted to capitalize on these divisions, by trying to pit non-Jewish workers against Jewish workers, particularly in strike situations. In the Eaton's strike, the non-Jewish strike-breakers protected 'Mr. Humpty Dumpty Eaton' from his downfall.[18]

Despite the formidable solidarity between male and female workers and despite the vigorous support of the working-class Jewish community, the 'King of Canada' prevailed. After four months, the workers were forced to admit defeat. The effect on Jewish workers was devastating. The ILGWU was seriously weakened, and 'for a long time [after this strike],' a union official recalled, 'the T. Eaton Company would not hire any Jews.'[19]

Workers' defeats were not uncommon in this period. What is outstanding here is the potential for working-class power that this strike illuminates. Without the unusual solidarity between men and women and without the mobilization of consumers to boycott Eaton's, the strike would never have developed the powerful momentum it did. If the solidarity between the sexes and the solidarity between producers and consumers had been supported by greater solidarity between Jewish and non-Jewish workers, the 'King of Canada' would indeed have gotten 'the surprise of his life.'[20]

This strike provides a glimmer of what might have been the basis of a much more powerful labour movement. It highlights the critical need to overcome the deep divisions within the working class.

NOTES

This updated article is from *Canadian Woman Studies/Les cahiers de la femme* 7 (3) (1986). Reprinted with permission.

1 ILGWU, *The Ladies' Garment Worker* (New York), April 1912, p. 1. For a more

detailed analysis of this strike, see Ruth A. Frager, 'Class, Ethnicity, and Gender in the Eaton Strikes of 1912 and 1934,' in Franca Iacovetta and Mariana Valverde, eds., *Gender Conflicts: New Essays in Women's History* (Toronto, 1992).

2 Ibid., pp. 1–2.

3 United Garment Workers, *The Weekly Bulletin of the Clothing Trades* (New York), 29 March 1912, p. 3.

4 Canada, Department of Labour, *Labour Gazette*, March 1912, pp. 856 & 897–901; *Toronto Daily News*, 15 Feb. 1912, p. 13; *Toronto Star*, 15 Feb. 1912, p. 5 & 16 Feb. 1912, p. 2; *Industrial Banner* (London, Ontario), March 1912, p. 1; Toronto ILGWU's Cloakmakers' Union, *Souvenir Journal, 1911–1936*, A. Kirzner's speech (in Yiddish) and Charles Shatz's speech (in Yiddish); & Toronto ILGWU's Cloakmakers' Union, *Souvenir Journal, 1911–1961*, S. Kraisman's address & Max Siegerman's address.

5 Toronto District Labour Council Minutes, 15 Feb. 1912, Labour Council of Metropolitan Toronto Collection, vol. 3, Public Archives of Canada, Ottawa. See also, 7 March 1912.

6 Interview with Joe Salsberg, Toronto, 1984.

7 Ibid.

8 *The Ladies's Garment Worker*, March 1912, p. 14.

9 Toronto District Labour Council Minutes, 7 March 1912; *The Weekly Bulletin of the Clothing Trades*, 22 March 1912, p. 3. 29 March 1912, p. 1. & 12 April 1912, p. 1; *Industrial Banner*, March 1912, p. 1; *Labour Gazette*, March 1912, pp. 856 & 897–901; *Souvenir Journal, 1911–1936*, A. Kirzner's speech (in Yiddish); *The Ladies' Garment Worker*, March 1912, p. 14 & April 1912, pp. 2 & 18; & *Toronto Daily News*, 15 Feb. 1912, p. 13.

10 *Hamilton Labour News*, cited in *The Weekly Bulletin of the Clothing Trades*, 3 May 1912, p. 2 & *The Ladies' Garment Worker*, June 1912, p. 25.

11 *Souvenir Journal, 1911–1936*, A. Kirzner's speech (in Yiddish) & *Industrial Banner*, April 1912, p. 4. On the ways in which immigrant Jewish women frequently made strategic use of their power as consumers, See Ruth A. Frager, *Sweatshop Strife: Class, Ethnicity, and Gender in the Jewish Labour Movement of Toronto, 1900–1939* (Toronto, 1992), pp. 36–7.

12 *The Ladies' Garment Worker*, April 1912, pp. 2–3.

13 Ibid., p. 3.

14 Alice A. Chown, *The Stairway* (Boston, 1921), pp. 151–152.

15 Ibid., p. 153.

16 On the prevalence of anti-Semitism in Toronto in this period, see *Sweatshop Strife*, pp. 12–14.

17 *The Ladies' Garment Worker*, April 1912, p. 2.

18 The reference to 'Mr. Humpty Dumpty Eaton' is from *The Ladies' Garment Worker*, April 1912, p. 4. On the tension between Jews and non-Jews in Toronto's garment industry, see *Sweatshop Strife*, pp. 77–97.
19 *Souvenir Journal, 1911–1936*, A. Kirzner's speech (in Yiddish). (The translation from the Yiddish is my own.)
20 The quotation is from *The Ladies's Garment Worker*, April 1912, p. 2.

Relief Strike: Immigrant Workers and the Great Depression in Crowland, Ontario, 1930–1935

CARMELA PATRIAS

On 2 April 1935, relief recipients from over a dozen ethnic groups employed on public works projects in Crowland, Ontario, laid down their tools in an effort to obtain 'fair' compensation from their labour. Over the next month their strike became the source of consternation far beyond the boundaries of the small southern Ontario township. It was the subject of front-page stories in newspapers across Ontario, and it occasioned three visits from Premier Mitchell Hepburn, in the company of such key cabinet members as David Croll, minister of labour and welfare, and Attorney General Arthur Roebuck. The premier, who less than two years earlier had denounced the decision of his predecessor, George Henry, to use the militia against strikers in Stratford, now sent Ontario provincial policemen to Crowland. Admitting that 'serious developments' could ensue from the arrival of OPP reinforcements in the township, Hepburn stated emphatically that unless strikers returned to work, it was 'battle to the bitter end.'[1]

A visit to Queen's Park by Crowland officials who declared themselves unable to deal with the strike was the immediate reason for Hepburn's actions.[2] Amidst the mounting discontent and unrest among the unemployed throughout Ontario and Canada, however, Hepburn had clearly chosen to make an example of the Crowland strike, to turn it, in the words of the St Catharines' *Standard*, into a 'test strike between the unemployed and provincial authorities.'[3] Although the press spoke of 'mobs,' 'rioting,' and 'considerable violence' in Crowland, and although Hepburn accused the strikers of 'terrorization' and of 'breaking heads and damaging property,' the relief strike was largely peaceful. What appeared so dangerous to Hepburn and to local officials was rather that the Crowland strikers took a firm stand on wages for relief work, and that they managed to hold out for weeks, despite the fact that municipal authorities withheld relief allotments on which they and their families depended for survival. Officials also worried about the prominence of Communists among the strike's leaders.

That some one hundred unemployed workers challenged local and provincial authorities is itself noteworthy. The Crowland relief strike was but one particularly dramatic example of the sense of basic rights and dignity among unemployed Canadian workers that fuelled their agitation for useful work for wages even during the depth of the Great Depression. What makes the strike truly remarkable, however, is that it required collaboration among immigrant workers from a wide variety of European backgrounds. Interwar Crowland was one of the most ethnically heterogeneous communities in southern Ontario. In 1931, more than two-thirds of the township's five thousand inhabitants were continental Europeans.[4] The decisive force behind the strike was the recognition by immigrant workers that they shared grievances and goals that transcended ethnic boundaries. An analysis of the strike thus tells us not only about the struggle of Canadian workers against unemployment during the Depression, but also about the relationship between ethnicity and class in this struggle.

The nature of this relationship, which is of crucial importance for understanding the history of Canada's multi-ethnic population, has rarely been studied. Most studies in the field focus on individual immigrant or ethnic groups. Although such studies are important, the single-group focus is potentially distortive. With the exception of certain rural group settlements, no group of continental European immigrants in Canada lived or worked in isolation. In large cities and in small towns, they settled in ethnically heterogeneous neighbourhoods. Most of Canada's immigrants during the late nineteenth and twentieth centuries, moreover, were peasants and workers. They worked in mines, railroad gangs, construction gangs, and factories alongside men and women of diverse ethnic backgrounds. Those studies that do consider immigrant sojourners help to explain why so little attention has been paid to instances of interethnic collaboration in Canada.[5] Migrant workers who planned to return to their homelands with savings had little incentive or opportunity to make common cause with fellow workers of any nationality. Such efforts made more sense after immigrants settled down in Canada and their primary attachment shifted from the Old World to the New.

Studies of immigrant labour in the United States[6] suggest that despite linguistic and other cultural differences, immigrant workers were capable of taking collective action on the basis of shared class interests.[7] Allan Seager's work on polyglot mining communities in Alberta suggests that shared class interests could override ethnic divisions in Canada as well, at least in towns dependent on extractive industries, where exploitation was particularly visible, and where immigrants formed a large proportion of the workforce. In these communities immigrant workers united before the Second World War in support of radical unions, and they repeatedly voted for socialist and Communist candidates.[8] The 1935 Crowland relief strike shows that immigrant workers in urban–industrial centres in Canada could also overcome ethnic differences to take collective action on their own behalf.

Urban Crowland

Crowland Township surrounds the town of Welland in the Niagara peninsula. Until the first decade of the twentieth century, Crowland was a rural community of Loyalist, Pennsylvania Dutch, and British immigrant stock, who did not find the land particularly fertile.[9] The township became a polyglot industrial centre as a by-product of the relatively late and rapid industrialization of Welland. Despite its access to five different railway lines and the Welland canal, large industries employing hundreds of workers arrived only after cheap hydroelectric power became available from DeCew Falls and Niagara Falls in the town in the early 1900s. The Plymouth Cordage Company, Page Hersey Iron Tube and Lead, Ontario Iron and Steel,[10] the Electrometallurgical Company, Union Carbide, and the Empire Cotton Mills were the largest among them. As land within Welland was limited and expensive, some plants were built just outside the town's boundaries, in Crowland township.[11]

The need for unskilled labourers and machine-tenders in these new mass-production plants was met by the agriculturalists who were arriving by the thousands at the same time from southern and eastern Europe. They also supplied unskilled labour for the erection of workers' housing, for road and railroad building, and for the construction of the fourth Welland canal between 1913 and 1932. Some of these immigrants were brought to the area by contractors and employment agents; others were recruited by the new industrial concerns from other parts of Canada and from the United States, while still others came on their own, drawn by rumours of job opportunities.[12] Many of those who came to the area before and after the First World War stayed. Although no building-boom resembling that of the 1905–13 period would occur again in Welland-Crowland, and factory jobs fluctuated considerably, employment opportunities for unskilled workers were more plentiful than in most other parts of Canada. Until the coming of the 1930s depression, workers were not idle for long. They found seasonal employment in agriculture, canning, and construction to tide them over until they were rehired by the local plants. Niagara's comparatively moderate climate also made this region appealing.

Many of these workers settled in Crowland Township because lots and houses were cheaper than in most Welland neighbourhoods and located next to the factories that employed them. 'There was nothing but fields,' commented a Polish woman who came to Crowland in 1909. 'Houses were few to be seen ... The fields reminded me of my home in Poland.'[13] Few immigrants, however, became farmers; by and large, farming in Crowland remained in the hands of the descendants of British and Pennsylvania Dutch settlers.

Gradually, a new working-class neighbourhood emerged in the shadow of the factories, which I shall call 'urban Crowland' to distinguish it from the rural portion of the township. On several occasions during the 1920s, the separation of urban and rural Crowland was discussed, but no agreement could be reached on the boundaries of the new communities. By the 1930s the two distinct communities were still uncomfortably united under Crowland Council, which was comprised of a reeve, a deputy reeve, and three councillors.[14] The rural representatives tended to dominate, by allying themselves with the urban office-holders who were the descendants of old Crowland families.

By 1935, 87 per cent of the inhabitants of urban Crowland were blue collar workers, 11 per cent skilled workers of various kinds, and 76 per cent labourers. The remaining 13 per cent of the population was composed primarily of small businessmen: grocers, barbers, poolroom owners, and others who catered to the needs of the community but were not much better off economically than their working-class customers. Significant differences none the less existed between Anglo-Celtic and 'ethnic' residents. In 1935, when 83 per cent of the residents of European background were unskilled labourers, only 49 per cent of their Anglo-Celtic counterparts fell into this category. Moreover, almost all the skilled jobs in construction and industry – jobs that offered greater security and better wages – were held by Anglo-Canadians or British immigrants.

Owing to hasty, careless development, urban Crowland was not the most salutary of neighbourhoods. Smoke from the factories polluted air and coated workers' homes with soot. Many workers' homes remained unconnected to water and sewage lines until well into the 1930s, and the absence of proper sanitary facilities created serious health problems in urban Crowland.[16] A number of subdivisions lacked adequate fire protection. Township schools, moreover, were not large enough to accommodate the children of new arrivals, many of whom, even in the 1920s, were forced to attend classes in ethnic halls and in private buildings.[17]

The residents of urban Crowland, whatever their ethnic background, were united in seeking fire protection, sidewalks, sewers, and an independent waterworks system for their community.[18] Their demands brought to the surface the conflict of interests between urban and rural Crowland. Although the farmers of Crowland Township welcomed, even solicited, the arrival of industry,[19] they were unprepared to pay for the consequences of industrial growth – streets, sanitation, water supply, health services, education, and police and fire protection.

Suspicion, fear, and prejudice accentuated the division between urban and rural. Although both Anglo-Celtic and immigrant workers settled in urban Crowland, the more established residents associated urban growth and its attendant problems with immigrants. The local press and officials dubbed urban Crowland the 'foreign section' or 'foreign quarter.' They condemned the overcrowding and unsanitary conditions of ethnic boarding-houses[21] and the unruliness of immigrants, who were frequently arraigned for fighting, drunkenness, and Sabbath-breaking.[22]

Because of their better economic status, Anglo-Celtic workers were better able than 'ethnic' workers to escape the problems of urban Crowland by moving where the air and services were better. By 1935, 79 per cent of urban Crowland residents were continental European immigrants and their children; all but one of the small businesses were owned or operated by immigrants.[23] Prejudice made a move away from urban Crowland unappealing for immigrants. Indeed, during the early stages of Crowland's development, local land promoters hoped to exclude 'foreigners' from the new subdivisions.[24] But newcomers also generally preferred to settle next to those who spoke their language and shared their traditions. Ethnic clustering permitted the establishment of social and cultural networks that facilitated adjustment to the New World.

The largest ethnic groups developed formal associations to serve their varied needs. As early as 1917, the local Polish community established the Society of St Stanislaus Kostka to serve the sick and poor, and to cover funeral costs of deceased members. In 1927 mutual aid within this community was taken over by the Canadian-Polish Society. In a hall constructed by the society's members, Polish language classes for children were held and plays mounted. Frequently held dances and dinners were not simply recreational but served to unite the ethnic group.[25] The Croatian Sons Association fulfilled a similar role for Croatian immigrants.[26] Even the tiny Jewish community had its own synagogue, and the Hebrew Culture Club brought together the politically divided group with remarkably rich educational and cultural programs.[27]

Not all ethnic groups were united around a single association. The organizational structure of the Ukrainian community, for instance, reflected political and religious fragmentation within it. During the 1930s, two leftist groups, the Ukrainian Labour and Farmer Temple Association and the Ukrainian Workers' Mutual Benefit Association, were active in the community.[28] Church-going Ukrainians attended the Ukrainian Greek Orthodox Church, the Ukrainian Greek Catholic Society, or St Peter and Paul Roman Catholic Church. Crowland's Hungarians were divided among Roman Catholics, Presbyterians, Baptists, and United Church members. Three secular associations were also active within the community: The Welland-Hungarian Self Culture Society, the Hungarian Workers' Club, and the Independent Mutual Benefit Federation. Of these groups, only the Hungarian Presbyterian Church was located in Crowland. The rest were in Welland.

Despite this ethnic diversity and the existence of intragroup tensions, a common identity emerged among Crowland's foreign-born inhabitants and their children, based on shared experiences and lifestyles and reinforced by daily contacts in the neighbourhood and workplace. Perhaps the strongest integrative force among them was the discrimination they all faced from the host society. As Helen Gerencser recalls, 'They couldn't tell you apart if you weren't English.'[29] Others remember being called a variety of derogatory names, such as 'dagos,' 'polacks,' or 'hunkies.' The immigrants and their children recall as well that the best jobs in the local plants were held by the 'English' or 'Scotch.'[30]

Although the local establishment became somewhat more respectful by the late 1920s, job discrimination continued. Adam Ferioli, for example, the Canadian-born son of Italian immigrants, was denied permission to transfer from the job of craneman in the hot, unpleasant furnace-room at the Electrometallurgical plant to the position of derrick-driver in the yard, where the air was better. His foreman claimed that people in the yard would not work with him 'on account of [his] nationality.'[31] Until the Second World War, the children of immigrants who sought white-collar jobs outside industry encountered similar obstacles. For example, Wanda Lusina, who was born and educated in Crowland, was refused a teaching job in a school in urban Crowland because of her Polish background. Members of the school board claimed that she had an accent and therefore was unsuited to a career in teaching.[32]

Crowland's immigrants also shared a tolerance for behaviour that offended the sensibilities of the more established residents of Welland-Crowland. Sabbath observance, for example, did not form part of the cultural background of southern and eastern Europeans. They were thus understandably confused and angry when they were taken to court for playing ball on Sunday,[33] or for continuing on Sunday a wedding celebration begun on Saturday evening.[34] Confectioners, restaurants, and pool halls opened on Sundays because that was when workers had free time to enjoy ice-cream, visit a restaurant with the family, or play pool.[35]

Most immigrants found teetotalism just as unfamiliar as Sabbatarianism. Even Protestant immigrants, such as Hungarian Presbyterians, viewed the consumption of alcohol as an essential part of merrymaking, and they got into trouble with church authorities for selling such beverages during fund-raising events for their hall on the Lord's Day. Some ethnic restaurateurs, poolroom owners, and boarding-house keepers supplemented their earnings by bootlegging.[36] Indeed, small bootlegging establishments, or 'social clubs,' as they were called, constituted important social institutions in urban Crowland. Their hours were more flexible than those of local hotels, and they provided immigrant workers with a friendlier environment.

The immigrants also maintained some of their agricultural practices in urban Crowland. Most of their houses were surrounded by vegetable gardens, and most families kept livestock. Almost everyone had hens and pigs. In the tradition of European villages, many families also had cows and employed a cowherd to take them to graze in the neighbouring bush. Every spring a meeting would be called to determine the cowherd's wages. In a manner reminiscent of eastern European villages, pedlars, many of them Jewish, would visit urban Crowland and offer their wares from house to house. Every spring a Jewish butcher would come to slaughter cattle.[37]

Urban Crowland was actually too small to permit the emergence of enclosed cultural islands. No matter how strong their sense of group loyalty, people came into daily contact with those of other ethnic groups. While the boarders in the Santone household, for instance, all came from an Italian town in Campobasso province, their neighbours included Rumanians, Yugoslavs, Jews, Poles, Hungarians, Ukrainians, and even Scots, and the Santones maintained friendly relations with them all. Men from various ethnic groups met in neighbourhood pool halls and barber shops,[38] while immigrant women of different backgrounds encountered each other at local grocery stores. They did not necessarily patronize grocers from their homelands. Crowland's immigrants also met at work. While a few immigrant 'straw bosses' in the plants preferred to hire their own countrymen exclusively, few departments that employed foreign-born workers were composed of a single ethnic group.

Even stronger integrative forces were at work among the immigrants' children. They attended ethnically mixed public schools – now recalled fondly as 'a regular United Nations.'[39] While many of them attended language classes at ethnic halls every other day after school, they also played with children of other ethnic backgrounds on the street. Adolescent gangs were based on neighbourhood rather than ethnic ties. Teenagers of all ethnic backgrounds attended the dances held at various clubs. Some of them dated and even married across ethnic lines.[40] By the late 1920s the children of immigrants employed in the local plants were even more likely to form workplace friendships across ethnic lines and to join multi-ethnic athletic leagues and 'social clubs.'

The shared experiences and lifestyles of all immigrants combined with linguistic or religious affinity to permit a special kind of rapport between certain ethnic groups. Serbians and Croatians overcame Old World national antagonism, and lived in apparent harmony in the same Crowland boarding-houses.[41] Amicable relations also prevailed among Ukrainians and Poles from Galicia.[42] Slavic and Lithuanian immigrants founded the Polish, Slovakian, Russian-Lithuanian Society of Fraternal Brothers (Towardzystwo BratniejPomocy Polsko-Slowacko Rusko-Litewskie) in 1912, at the initiative of Polish immigrants, to provide sickness and death benefits and to organize a Roman Catholic parish in Crowland.

Even institutions of the host society contributed to the development of a distinct, shared identity among Crowland's immigrants. For example, the Roman Catholic parish of St Peter and Paul brought together Slavic Roman Catholic immigrants. The United Church's Maple Leaf

Mission, led by Harvey Forster and Fern Sayles, played an important unifying role. Given the emphasis placed by scholars on the role of Protestant churches in promoting Anglo-conformity in Canada, it is worth noting that Forster and Sayles were not proselytizers. Their mission offered invaluable services to immigrants without demanding religious conformity in return. The athletic Sayles built a gymnasium with the help of community members and encouraged children of all nationalities and religions to join teams that met there. He also showed movies at comparatively cheap rates.[44] As oral testimonies reveal, the mission attracted immigrants, even ones who were not religious, because its ministers combined community work with an unswerving support for labour.[45] Sayles' open support for left-wing politics undoubtedly contributed to the legitimacy of the left in Crowland.

During the interwar years, the Communist Party's mass organizations in Welland and Crowland, the Ukrainian Labour and Farmer Temple Association (ULFTA), the Hungarian Workers' Club and the Independent Mutual Benefit Federation, and the Yugoslav Workers' Club also contributed to the emergence of an identity that transcended ethnic boundaries among Crowland's immigrant workers. Although each of these organizations sought to preserve certain aspects of the distinct ethnic culture of its members, they all encouraged cooperation among immigrant workers in accordance with the precept of proletarian internationalism. Some members of these radical organizations espoused proletarian internationalism before the establishment of the Communist Party of Canada (CPC), possibly even before they immigrated to Canada. The members of the Welland branch of the Ukrainian Social Democratic Federation, for example, who established the ULFTA in Crowland, provided an organizational base for Crowland workers as early as 1920. In June 1920, striking workers at Page Hersey held their meetings at the Ukrainian Labour Temple.[46] The majority of immigrant workers, however, became politicized only after they joined these radical organizations, and their attitudes were shaped by CPC policies. The party systematically employed cultural and mutual aid organizations to transmit its ideology to immigrant workers,[47] and the promotion of inter-ethnic collaboration formed an important part of the party's program throughout Canada. In Crowland the party's internationalist orientation was particularly influential. As the 1935 relief strike reveals, the members of Communist-led ethnic organizations provided disciplined, energetic leadership during periods of unrest and protest in Crowland. The particular ethnic mix of the township's population helped them in this task. Ukrainians, Hungarians, Serbians, and Croatians – precisely those groups with whom they communicated most easily – formed more than a third of Crowland's population, and a considerably higher proportion of residents of urban Crowland.

Unemployment and Relief

During the 1930s both tensions and solidarities among ethnic groups were accentuated in Crowland. The hardships brought by the depression intensified the conflict between rural and urban Crowland. Yet they also strengthened the sense of shared grievances and objectives among the immigrants who now composed the majority of urban dwellers, and even brought some of Crowland's Anglo-Celtic workers together with these immigrant workers.

While no factories in Welland-Crowland failed as a result of the depression, all of them – save for Atlas Steel – cut back production.[48] In 1930 the Empire Cotton Mill first employed all workers only two days a week, and later laid off half of them. By the mid-1930s its fate improved, and it was the only plant to hire significant numbers of workers during the depression. In 1932 Page Hersey was operating at half its normal capacity; in 1934 its seamless department was shut down indefinitely.[49]

All Crowland workers suffered as a result of these cutbacks. The more fortunate among them worked for fewer hours; the less fortunate were laid off. Unemployed factory workers were unlikely to find jobs elsewhere, since by 1930 construction on the fourth Welland Canal was coming to an end, and there was a general slowdown in the construction industry.[50]

Local employers exploited the desperation of working-class families, and their behaviour no doubt sharpened workers' consciousness of the injustices inherent in industrial relations in Welland-Crowland. The Empire Cotton Mill, notorious for underpaying workers of all ages, preferred to employ children between the ages of fourteen and sixteen because they could be paid less than adults.[51] Adult textile-workers also felt compelled to accept up to a 25 per cent cut in wages.[52] Although the company complained of poor business throughout the depression, it insisted that its employees continue to work fifty-five hours a week, arguing that it would lose its competitive edge if shorter hours prevailed. Workers who voiced dissatisfaction with these policies were fired, declared to have 'violent Russian red sympathies,' and were then easily replaced.[53] At the Electrometallurgical plant four six-hour shifts were replaced by three of eight hours, but the wages were not increased accordingly. Because of extreme heat and noxious fumes in some departments, the longer shifts were almost unbearable for the workers, but widespread joblessness enabled the company to disregard their complaints.[54] At the Page Hersey plant, where foremen were rewarded for maintaining production with a minimal crew, employees faced speed-ups. The plant's unskilled workers did not know from one day to the next whether they had work. They appeared at the plant gates at seven o'clock every morning, but only a small number, selected at the whim of the foreman, got work. Men who bribed foremen with money or whisky, who dug their garden or helped them make wine, stood a better chance than those who kept their distance. Such practices predated the depression, but economic hardship during the 1930s lessened the possibility of resistance and increased the workers' sense of helpless rage.[55]

The income of women and children from berry-picking, corn-husking, and other seasonal agricultural jobs, which had constituted an important addition to the family economy before the depression, became even more critical after 1930, as did the gardens and livestock kept by most Crowland families. Some women earned a little extra cash by selling milk locally.[56] Despite such resourcefulness, the poverty of some families was so great that they stole coal from railroad cars in order to keep warm.[57]

Our only accurate figures on relief recipients suggest that Crowland was not as badly off as many other southern Ontario communities. While 52.6 per cent of the population of East Windsor, 26.3 per cent of the population of Kingston, and 21.2 per cent of the population of Niagara Falls depended on relief at the beginning of 1932, at the end of that year, when unemployment was much higher, only 14 per cent of Crowland residents did so.[58] What these figures do not reveal, however, is that Crowland's relief recipients were almost all from the urban section. Although Crowland's farmers – most of whom owned small farms of two hundred acres or less – found it difficult to pay local taxes, they apparently did not qualify for relief. Thus the Great Depression accentuated the cleavage between urban and rural Crowland. Some urban residents continued to pay municipal taxes and thus to contribute towards relief, but local farmers were aware only of the large number of relief recipients in urban Crowland. Despite the fact that Crowland remained solvent during the depression, thanks largely to the assessments paid by industrial plants, farmers argued that the township was mostly rural and that they were carrying its burden of taxation. While critical of the provincial and federal governments for not assuming full responsibility for relief, most of their resentment was focused on relief recipients. Some farmers, probably unaware of the desperate plight of many relief recipients, believed that families on relief managed to live as well as those of many local farmers. They believed that able-bodied men forced to rely on relief were somehow responsible for their own predicament.[59]

These attitudes played a crucial role in shaping Crowland's relief program. The provision of relief fell within the jurisdiction of municipal governments, and between 1930 and 1933 Crowland Council was dominated by representatives from the rural section. Provincial and federal funds covered two-thirds of Crowland's relief costs. As in other municipalities, however, the eligibility for and the amount of relief was determined locally. Since Crowland Council's major concern was to spare its supporters, the farmers, by avoiding an increase in taxes, it instituted the most economical program possible, to the detriment of the unemployed.[60] The inexperience of local officials in administering relief and the slowness of the two higher levels of government in elaborating and funding their share of relief programs also contributed to the difficulties faced by relief recipients.

Crowland Council's initial reaction to the great increase in the numbers of residents requiring aid was piecemeal and lacked any awareness of the magnitude of the problems that it and every other local government in the country would have to face for some years. In January 1930 council put indigents to work shovelling snow for 25 cents an hour.[61] During the fall of 1930, Crowland Council received only $5,000 of the $42,000 it had applied for from a new provincial fund to build sewers.[62] These funds were quickly spent. By June 1931 a committee of concerned citizens and local officials sought work for the unemployed with the Welland Rural Hydro commission, but it employed an extremely narrow definition of eligibility. Thus, when two hundred unemployed workers applied for relief work, the committee declared only thirty of them to be 'in circumstances of actual want.' These relief workers got cash for their work. However, in some cases, 'where the breadwinner has demonstrated his inability to spend his earnings in the interests of his family,' the committee made the worker sign over his wages to them to 'see that the money is spent to the best possible advantage.'[63] Earnings from relief work were supplemented by direct relief, in the form of groceries and fuel. A few single unemployed travelled to northern Ontario to take advantage of the work projects established by the provincial government there.[64]

In the same year, the township established a special committee to administer the allocation of relief and to raise the local share of relief costs through voluntary donations. The Reverend Fern Sayles of the United Church was put in charge of the committee. Significantly,, much of the money raised by the committee during 1931 came from employed workers in Welland and Crowland plants. The handful of Crowland's white-collar workers – teachers, Ontario Hydro employees, and bank clerks – also contributed generously to the fund. The contribution of local industries was rather meagre by comparison.[65] Most of this money was used to obtain groceries, clothes, fuel, and other necessities, which were then distributed from a relief depot to families only. Crowland Council agreed to help relief recipients with their rent payments only after it received assurances of aid from the provincial government.[66] In exchange for the relief they received, male household heads were expected to work approximately two days a week.[67]

The depot arrangement meant that goods could be purchased cheaply in bulk. However, this new relief system threatened to ruin local merchants, who had extended credit to many of their unemployed customers. Grocers, bakers, and butchers depended on those customers who were now receiving aid from the township. With the opening of the depot this business was lost to them.

The program was just as unsatisfactory from the perspective of the beneficiaries. In the interest of economy the food and coal purchased for the relief depot were of very poor quality. The clothing did not fit, and people had to wait unduly long for it. Food allowances, though calculated by family size, were so parsimonious that they did not meet the needs of larger families.[68] Many recipients did not receive the amount of food that the schedules called for. Nor were relief allocations adequate to pay for the labour performed by recipients, supposedly at an hourly rate of 30 cents. A recipient calculated that while the relief for an eight-hour day should have amounted to necessities valued at $2.40, they received on average 70 cents a day.[69]

To qualify for this meagre aid the unemployed had to submit to humiliating treatment by relief officials. The Reverend Mr Sayles, who was kindly disposed towards the unemployed, did not have enough time to administer the relief program efficiently. Much to the misfortune of recipients, that job was actually carried out by relief investigator Edward Semley and several youths employed at the relief depot.[70] Semley and the depot workers were arbitrary, disrespectful, and impatient in their dealings with the men and women who turned to them for aid.

When a woman asked Semley if she could get fuel to keep her family warm, he told her that she did not need it because the sun was shining.[71] Semley found another applicant ineligible when he discovered that the man had three suits. He told the unemployed man that he would be able to provide for his family if he sold his suits.[72] A woman who came to the depot to get underwear was publicly humiliated: a pair of women's bloomers was held up to her in front of a crowd of men and she was asked, 'There, how will these fit?'[73] Many others were simply turned away with the explanation that nothing suitable was available for them.[74]

The single unemployed, whose number was expected to reach three hundred by the winter of 1932, did not qualify for the type of aid offered to men with families. The township council opened a soup kitchen and expected them to work for the food they received.[75] Local authorities throughout Canada were reluctant to offer relief to the single unemployed because they feared that generous relief would attract additional members to this relatively mobile group. In Crowland the rationale for this position was that single men could always find farm work in exchange for room and board.

If non-naturalized immigrants, married or single, lost their jobs, they fared even worse than the single unemployed. When relief workers received cash wages, preference was given to British subjects.[76] Moreover, in November 1931 Crowland Council passed a motion instructing the township clerk to 'report all persons who become a public charge to the immigration authorities and recommend them for deportation provided they are not citizens and have been in the country not over five years.'[77] In neighbouring Welland, several Anglo-Celtic aldermen decried the injustice of such deportations.[78] It is impossible to say exactly how this ruling effected Crowland's immigrants.[79] In the face of chronic unemployment, some immigrants actually welcomed deportation. Rather than living off their hard-earned savings, they declared themselves destitute and relied on the Canadian government and on steamship companies to transport them home free of charge. Others, who intended to stay on, were warned by the Welfare Board that they faced deportation if their names appeared on the relief rolls.[80] By 1935 no immigrant who had resided in Canada less than five years received relief in Crowland. Fear of deportation may explain why immigrants were underrepresented among relief recipients. While more than two-thirds of Crowland's inhabitants were of European background, relief rolls show that only 59 per cent of relief recipients were immigrants from continental

Europe. Of the remaining recipients 13 per cent were born in Great Britain, 2 per cent in the United States and 26 per cent in Canada.[81] According to the local Hungarian Presbyterian minister, even immigrants who had been eligible for relief 'would sooner starve than ask for charity.'[82]

Unemployed Organizing

All of Crowland's unemployed, regardless of ethnic background, were highly dissatisfied with the design and implementation of their council's program. During the fall of 1932 they began to discuss their grievances at well-attended meetings in various ethnic halls and in the basement of a local school.[83] The make-up of the committees of unemployed elected to speak on their behalf to Crowland Council suggests that those who flocked to these meetings represented a cross-section of urban Crowland.

The Communist Party of Canada attempted to unite Canada's unemployed in the National Unemployed Association. This initiative contributed to the organization of the unemployed in Welland and Crowland. From 1931 on, party speakers and organizers travelled there to gain the support of local workers for the party's programs. Their ability to influence Crowland's workers was largely due to the community networks of support provided by the party's local ethnic organizations. Until 1934, John Strush coordinated efforts to organize the unemployed in Crowland and Welland with the plans of the Workers' Unity League. Strush, a Ukrainian-born member of the ULFTA, had been sent to Crowland early in 1930 to direct cultural and educational programs at the Labour Temple.[84] He received help in distributing leaflets and organizing meetings from members of the ULFTA and the Hungarian Workers' Club.[85] In 1934 Frank Haslam went to Crowland to recruit more Anglo-Celtic members and inherited these support networks. With the help of Ukrainian and Hungarian organizations and the local branch of the Communist-led Canadian Labour Defense League, the two organizers attracted from two hundred to five hundred workers to meetings and demonstrations organized to protest against unemployment and deportations.[86]

John Kowal's election to various committees of Crowland's Unemployed Association during 1932 and 1933 suggests that Crowland's unemployed appreciated the Communists' efforts on their behalf. A thirty-seven-year-old labourer who had immigrated to Canada from Poland in 1910 and had settled in Crowland in 1930, Kowal openly promoted affiliation with the Communist Party, claiming that 'the Communists were the only body who stood up for the workers.'[87] This appreciation would grow during the months that led up to the strike. By 1934 the Crowland Unemployed Association was formally affiliated with the National Unemployed Council.[88]

Since local and provincial authorities tried to discredit the legitimate demands of the unemployed by blaming unrest in Crowland on outside agitators, it is worth noting that CPC workers Strush and Haslam had much in common with Crowland's unemployed. Like many of the Ukrainian immigrants, John Strush had received only three years of schooling before leaving his native Galicia in 1912 at age eleven. He and his family initially settled on a homestead in northern Manitoba, where they tried unsuccessfully to eke out a living from infertile soil. Strush later joined the ranks of thousands of immigrant navvies employed by the CPR, and worked as a miner. Frank Haslam, who came to Canada from England in 1914, also had little formal education. He started to work at the cement plant in Port Colborne at age fourteen. Before being sent to Crowland by the CPC, Haslam travelled far and wide in search of work like many other Canadian workers. He worked at Union Carbide in Crowland in 1917–18, returned to the Port Colborne cement plant from 1919–23, moved to Detroit to work in a Ford plant, travelled to the Canadian prairies for the harvest season, and found various jobs around the Niagara peninsula during the late 1920s and early 1930s.[89]

While these Communist organizers enjoyed considerable support in urban Crowland, they were not alone responsible for organizing the unemployed. Two leaders of the relief recipients, John Dennis, president of the Crowland Unemployed Association between 1932 and 1934, and Thomas Martin, perhaps the most prominent spokesman for the unemployed, belonged to the Welland CCF club.[90] Moreover, the Unemployed Association had the backing of the Ukrainian Workers' Educational Society, an outspoken critic of the Communist Party during the 1930s. The Canadian-Polish Society, which had close ties with the Roman Catholic Church in Crowland, also lent its support to the association. Thus, the ideological leanings of the association's members were as diverse as their ethnic backgrounds.[91] Indeed, collaboration between the Communists and these other groups occurred in Crowland even while some party organizers still pursued the pre-Popular Front sectarian line that had characterized their party's policies through the 1920s and early 1930s.[92]

The diverse members of the Crowland Unemployed Association were united by more than a desire for increased relief benefits. Unemployed 'through no fault of their own,' they insisted on retaining their full rights as citizens of Crowland and on being accorded respect.[93] They believed that their representatives should have a say in deciding who was eligible for relief and how relief should be allocated. As workers, they had the right to perform work that was useful to the community for a fair cash wage. Because such work would permit them 'to retain their proper independence,' they could not be viewed as public charges.[94]

To lend strength to their demands and show support for their spokesmen, the unemployed packed council meetings, which were held at the police station, whenever the question of relief was discussed. When Crowland Council failed to respond to their complaints, the Unemployed Association entered local politics. The Crowland Ratepayers' and Tenants' Association had been established in 1928; by 1932 it had 374 members from various ethnic backgrounds. Merchants and the unemployed formed special committees within it.[95] The association's members were keenly aware of the differences between urban and rural Crowland, and sought to alter the composition of the council so that the interests of urban Crowland would be served. A more equitable treatment of the unemployed was paramount among these interests. The association's efforts to gain control of Crowland Council constituted the first instances of self-assertion by the working-class community.

Although the candidates supported by the Ratepayers' and Tenants' Association were not successful during the 1932 elections, the association's campaign did bring about the complete reorganization of Crowland's relief program. In March 1933 the independent Welfare Board was discontinued.[96] Its role was assumed by the township council, which, at least in principle, was more accountable to the community, and hence to the unemployed. At first the newly elected council seemed responsive to complaints from urban Crowland. Recognizing the plight of Crowland merchants, it closed the relief depot and issued vouchers that could be exchanged for groceries at any local store. A delegation of local officials and the unemployed went to the Ontario Hydro-Electric Commission in Toronto to request lower hydro rates for the unemployed.[97] One of the newly elected councillors from rural Crowland, Louis Whitaker, even declared that he would sooner pay higher taxes than see the children of the unemployed go hungry.[98]

However, the majority of the council supported Reeve Frederick J. Schneider in his efforts to keep taxes down. The salaries of township officials and teachers were reduced.[99] Those most affected by the cost-cutting, however, were the unemployed. Food rations, fuel, clothing, and allocations for light and shelter were still insufficient to meet their needs. Disregarding the dietary habits of recipients, officials still specified what foods they should obtain.[100] In the summer of 1933, grocery vouchers were cut in half so as to force recipients to seek seasonal work 'outside the township's jurisdiction.'[101] The single unemployed remained ineligible for relief through most of 1933. To add insult to injury, council retained the unpopular investigator E.F. Semley.

The unemployed continued to hold regular meetings and to protest against the relief program. The township council seemed increasingly disturbed by the militancy of the unemployed. For the first time it blamed outside agitators for local unrest. Two resolutions intended to stop organized protest by Crowland residents were passed. The first instructed the township solicitor to draw up a by-law prohibiting parades and the distribution of handbills and the posting of signs on or along the highway of Crowland unless sanctioned by the police. The second proclaimed that any member of any family receiving aid, 'who in the opinion of the Welfare Board takes part in any agitation in respect to relief will be refused further consideration and all relief will be refused the entire family, until such time as agitation ceases.' The first by-law was blocked by the township solicitor, who explained that council had no authority to prohibit parades. However, another by-law to license halls and public places 'with a view to prohibiting treasonable language or any plot or plan against the public health, safety, morality or welfare' passed.[102]

The local police chief attempted to obstruct the activities of the Unemployed Association by attending its meetings in an apparent effort to intimidate members. On occasion the association was denied the right to meet in the basement of a local school – the only public meeting place open to it. At least on some occasions, persons suspected of radicalism were denied relief.[103]

By 1934, the council also began its efforts to break the ranks of the unemployed. Reeve Frederick Kilgour ascribed all unrest in the township to outside agitators and declared that council members 'were prepared to co-operate with the unemployed at all times, but they would pay no attention to demands and agitation by outsiders.' By year's end this policy struck a responsive chord among a minority of the unemployed. The poverty of Crowland's relief recipients was reaching alarming proportions. Not only did they continue to find their food and clothing allowances inadequate, but many of them were in desperate

need of such household necessities as blankets, mattresses, cooking
utensils, and stovepipes, for which no allowance was made by council.[104] Facing this situation, some relief recipients chose the moderate
route and adopted Crowland Council's position that 'outside agitators'
were responsible for the growing tensions. The moderates seceded from
the Unemployed Association to form the Indigent Committee. All the
members of this committee were Anglo-Celtic. Although they did not
make anti-Communist pronouncements, they limited participation in
their meetings 'to unemployed residents of Crowland,' thereby effectively excluding the Communist organizers Frank Haslam and William
Douglas. The Indigent Committee also abandoned the struggle to obtain
relief for the single unemployed. However diluted the demands of this
group may have been, they were not strictly economic. They sought not
only a 25 per cent increase of relief vouchers, but also the participation
of the representatives of the unemployed in determining eligibility for
relief. As a gesture of confidence in the willingness of Crowland Council
to reform its relief program, the committee endorsed council members
who sought reelection during the winter of 1934–5.[105]

The majority of the unemployed and a substantial proportion of the
population of urban Crowland reacted quite differently to the council's
politics. Following the secession of the 'moderate' minority, the remaining members of the Unemployed Association elected eight representatives to a radical committee, which included the Communist organizer
Haslam. Six of the committee's eight members were men with Slavic
names. Crowland's unemployed immigrants and even some Anglo-
Celtic relief recipients had come to believe that no local politician had
their interests at heart. The members of the Ratepayers' and Tenants'
Association had reached the same conclusion. Together, the two associations put forward a 'United Front' slate in the township elections of
1934–5.

Judging from the horrified response of the local press and local officials, the United Front slate was more radical than any slate of candidates previously put forward in a Crowland election. It included Nick
Zenchuk, a baker and prominent ULFTA member who spoke explicitly
about class struggle during his campaign. 'Today's society,' he stated, 'is
divided into two classes, the workers and exploiters, whose interests
clash. All those present belonged to the former.' William Kupnitzki, a
local grocer also known as Bill Cooper, pledged to work in the interests
of 'workers and poor peasants.' Significantly, while Zenchuk and Kupnitzki spoke in the name of workers, both were shopkeepers. The slate

also included Robert Gatfield, an electrician running for reeve; Mike Tabacki, a barber and one of the trustees of the Ukrainian Labour Educational Association, who sought the post of assistant reeve; and Frank Soos, a Hungarian labourer. While the election of this slate would have meant the transfer of political control from rural Crowland to the working-class urban community, the contention of the United Front's rivals that its members sought to bring 'Communist theories into municipal affairs' was an exaggeration.[106]

United Front candidates enjoyed broad support among Crowland's immigrants and their children for reasons that were explained by Reverend Fern Sayles in a letter to the *Welland Tribune* just prior to the election.[107] The letter was a response to the *Tribune's* condemnation of the United Front for its allegedly Communistic orientation: 'The issue really is – shall life or property come first? Since all that the poor have left is life the radical is their champion, while the economically secure "with a stake in the community," and likewise from self-interest are the loyal defenders of property, at whatever cost to life.' Although the United Front candidates were not elected, they carried the two polling subdivisions where foreign-born residents dominated.

By March 1935 even the moderate members of the Indigent Committee had cause to regret their secession from the Unemployed Association. Despite their electoral support for the candidates now in office, the moderates were permitted neither to take part in the administration of relief nor to act as intermediaries between the unemployed and the township council. Indeed, despite meetings and parades organized by the unemployed to protest against the relief system,[108] the new council refused to increase allotments on the grounds that 'recipients were satisfied with the relief they were obtaining.'[109] Faced with this attitude, the Indigent Committee disbanded and its members now advocated collaboration with the radicals. They had come to believe that local officials would be willing to make concessions to the unemployed 'only as long as the Unemployed Association showed signs of strength.'[110]

Relief Strike 1935

At this point, Crowland Council instituted a new relief program. As of 1 April 1935, relief recipients would have to work more for the same amount of relief. Until then all heads of families on relief, regardless of family size, worked approximately two six-hour days for the relief they received. Under the new system the amount of work to be done would be calculated according to the value of relief – food, clothing, shelter, medical aid – that their families received the previous month. Since the value of food given to a family of five – the average size of Crowland families on relief – alone amounted to five dollars weekly, the new program, which set hourly rates for relief work at thirty-five cents, actually meant an increased workload for most relief recipients.[111]

The council's actions infuriated the unemployed. They insisted that a 25 per cent increase in relief was essential to meet minimum nutritional requirements and that relief should be extended to the single unemployed. Since Crowland Council paid only for part of this relief, they argued, it could require the unemployed to work only for the share of relief it directly provided. Its insistence that they work for 100 per cent of the benefits constituted an attempt to exploit men on relief. When the council refused to hear these complaints on the grounds that there were outside agitators among them, relief recipients decided to strike.[112] On 2 April 1935, thirty-nine of the forty-seven men who worked on the Beatrice sewer, about one-fifth of all relief recipients in Crowland, laid down their tools. The former moderate leader of the unemployed, Tom Martin, claimed: 'The Welfare Board is responsible for this fight, not the unemployed.'[113] Soon their example was followed by virtually all relief recipients. The Unemployed Committee claimed to represent 98 per cent of Crowland unemployed.[114]

The outbreak of the strike strengthened the township council's resolve to divide the ranks of the unemployed and to force them into submission. After a single meeting with the strikers' representatives, at which local officials reiterated their accusations against 'outside agitators,' council decided to cut off relief to the strikers and their families. On 8 April, Crowland's unemployed, many of whom had received their last vouchers on 4 April, found the doors of the relief office closed. The next day the strikers, their families, and their supporters surrounded the relief office in an attempt to force Crowland Council to meet with the strikers' delegates. Despite the anger over the council's move, the demonstrators were initially orderly. When a woman demonstrator accosted relief inspector Semley as he was approaching the relief office, Frank Haslam and others quickly prevailed upon her to let him go. Only when it became clear that the council did not intend to meet the demonstrators did some of the strikers attempt to force their way into the relief office, arguing that as a public building it could not legally be closed to them. The local police responded by hitting those closest to the door – among them a ten-year-old child – with clubs and by throwing tear gas among those who surrounded the building. The demonstrators dispersed quickly. Some of them had vented their frustration by breaking four windows in the building.

That night the police arrested Frank Haslam, William Douglas, Adolph Gagan, and Robert Lougheed, the strike's supposed leaders. They were charged with being members of an unlawful assembly and with creating a riot. Bail was posted by a number of foreign-born Crowland residents, and the four were released the next day.[115]

Over the next weeks, local officials tried to divide the ranks of the strikers much as they had tried to weaken unemployed organizing before the strike. They branded strike leaders 'outside agitators' and blamed their 'pernicious communist doctrines' for the strike. The strikers, however, were unswayed. They repeatedly demonstrated their support for the accused, two of whom, Haslam and Douglas, were Communists. When the four men appeared in court (only to be remanded for another two weeks), the strikers and their supporters paraded two miles from Crowland to the Welland police court, filling the courtroom to capacity. The Unemployed Association explained that Haslam and Douglas were 'as thousands of other young men in Canada, unemployed,' and that they had earned the support of Crowland's unemployed because 'through their actions' they had 'proven' to be 'honest and sincere.' It also effectively identified these attacks as tactics designed to undermine the legitimacy of their organization and their demands.[116]

The council's red-baiting proved ineffective because the influence of popular local Communists increased as a result of their conduct during the strike. Whether or not they were unemployed, the members of the ULFTA and the Hungarians Workers' Club adopted the Communist Party's popular front policy and gave their full support to the strikers, whatever their religion or political orientation.[117] Indeed, the Ukrainian Labour Temple served as the strike's headquarters, and, after the strikers were cut off relief, a soup kitchen was opened there to feed them.[118] As experienced organizers with connections outside Crowland, Frank Haslam and William Douglas played a key role in shaping the strikers' tactics and strategies. Far from inciting violence, Haslam was a moderating influence throughout the strike, repeatedly impressing upon the strikers the importance of non-violent, orderly protest. When it became clear that the strikers could make no headway with the council as long as Haslam and Douglas were among their representatives, the two agreed to step down.

To get community support, strikers went from house to house in Welland and Crowland to collect food and used clothing. 'It wasn't simply a question of food,' Haslam explained fifty-two years later, 'but it was something to get publicity.'[119] Contrary to insinuations in the press that the strikers used the threat of violence to force local grocers to provide food after the township council withheld relief vouchers, the grocers repeatedly demonstrated their commitment to the strikers' cause. They promised to support the strikers 'to the limit of their resources,' and contributed money to the Unemployed Association for the publication of leaflets appealing for the support of local taxpayers.[120] Food for the strikers was also donated to the ULFTA by dairies, bakeries, and private individuals.[121] The Crowland Ratepayers' and Tenants' Association, which represented urban Crowland, was unequivocally behind the strikers. The association approved the strikers' demands, gave financial support to publicize their cause, decried the use of tear gas against them, and demanded that the 'frame-up' charges against Douglas, Haslam, Lougheed, and Gagan be dropped.[122]

The solidarity of the strikers is particularly impressive in light of their great ethnic heterogeneity. In fact, the strike provided the occasion for the first public expression of the solidarity that had developed in urban Crowland. Responding to accusations directed against it by local councillors, the Crowland Unemployed Association stated: 'The solidarity of the unemployed in this strike, irrespective of their different nationalities, religions, political viewpoints, completely discredits statements that the strike is caused by a few agitators ... Men, women, and children do not parade the streets every day because they like it. Nor do they face tear gas, clubs and midnight arrests merely to cause trouble.'[123]

The strikers' supporters included even residents whose politics were normally conservative. Louis Lusina was a Polish grocer who had been active in the Conservative party. Now he sided with the unemployed, no matter how radical their leadership. As a grocer he knew that the foodstuffs allowed on the relief vouchers were not what immigrants ate. His store was opposite the relief office where the strikers and their supporters assembled daily. Lusina permitted them to use the washrooms behind his store and used his truck to obtain food for them. When provincial police attempted to disperse the demonstrators by barricading the entrance to these washrooms, he was infuriated. Ignoring accusations that he was a Communist, he took down the barricades and successfully stood up for the strikers at a hearing that followed, claiming that the police had no right to barricade his property.[124]

The community-based nature of this strike was also indicated by the active involvement of women and children. They were in the forefront of daily parades designed to bolster strikers' morale. Following a clash with police at the relief office, the strikers resumed picketing the Beatrice Street sewer. Women and children lined both sides of the sewer daily, determined to prevent any efforts to break the strike. Their presence undoubtedly contributed to the failure of efforts by Crowland Council to lure unemployed workers back to work. Two weeks after the strikers had been cut off relief, Reeve Kilgour promised that any striker who showed 'a willingness to work' would be given a relief voucher. Seventeen policemen were posted daily by the sewer that was being picketed to guarantee protection to anyone who wished to go to work. Women and children responded by booing and deriding the police and sometimes even pelting them with dirt. Women climbed to the top of a tool-box by the sewer to address the crowds that gathered there daily.[125] 'I had a glass of water for breakfast,' said one woman in response to the foreman's call that strikers return to work. 'What did you have – nice bread and butter?' 'How can we work,' said another. 'We got no shoes or stockings or food.' Acknowledging that they were all hungry, they still insisted that there were no scabs among them.[126]

Communist-devised tactics, such as school boycotts, contributed to community participation in the strike.[127] On the day that the Crowland relief office was closed, many children stayed away from school to picket and demonstrate alongside their parents. At Matthews School in immigrant-dominated Industrial Park, 30 to 40 per cent of the pupils were absent.[128] On 24 April, forty-one children aged eight to fourteen were sent to Toronto at the urging of Toronto organizers of the National Unemployed Council and billeted with working-class families. The National Unemployed Council also organized a children's demonstration in Queen's Park, where Minister of Labour David Croll refused to see 'these lilliputian Lenins.'[129] Such public displays of solidarity, which had precedents in the European labour movement, proved effective in attracting attention to the plight of Crowland unemployed. All major Ontario newspapers carried stories, frequently with illustrations, about the Crowland children who travelled to Toronto in an open truck carrying a banner that read 'Hungry Crowland to be fed by Toronto Workers.' The generosity of Toronto workers boosted the morale of Crowland strikers.[130] Had the children been permitted to stay in Toronto more than three days, it would also have alleviated the strikers' economic difficulties. Premier Hepburn, however, forced the children's return to Crowland and threatened to charge the parents with infractions of the Truancy Act.[131]

Communist connections brought more help. The Workers' International Relief Association sent two truckloads of provisions to the Crowland Ukrainian Labour Temple, while unemployed workers from the Niagara region organized a 'solidarity' concert there.[132]

Even after they were denied relief, the strikers and their sympathizers were remarkably disciplined. The most violent action at the Beatrice Street sewer was actually carried out by the police. When strikers refused to allow the project's foreman to open the tool-box that was located on site, police fired gas among them. More than three weeks into the strike, striker Adam Wakuniuk broke ranks and returned to work. Although clearly disappointed with Wakuniuk's actions, Robert Lougheed, president of the Unemployed Association, nevertheless offered his personal guarantee that nobody would molest the worker, his family, or home.[133]

A torchlight parade held on the night of 24 April most clearly illustrates the widespread community support for the strike and the workers' capacity for disciplined protest. Shortly after midnight a crowd of three hundred strikers, family members, and sympathetic workers gathered. They filed past the houses of the township officials and the sole strikebreaker, booing, hooting, thumping old tubs and pans and pelting some houses with dirt. This dramatic protest was not shaped by CPC tactics. The ethnic heterogeneity of the strikers makes it impossible to discover its exact pedigree, but the nocturnal setting and the 'rough music' through which the marchers censured local officials places the parade in the tradition of the charivari, a form of popular protest employed since the late middle ages in Europe to assert community norms and values.[134] But even this charivari-like parade was rather restrained.

It was the strength and determination of the strikers and their supporters, not their violence, which local officials found so menacing. The strikers' ability to hold out despite the council's hard policy threatened to undermine the hegemony of Anglo-Celtic rural Crowland for the first time in the township's history. Three weeks into the strike Crowland officials declared the strike out of control; they travelled to Toronto to seek Premier Mitchell Hepburn's intervention.

The fears of local officials were echoed outside Crowland. Despite the strikers' disciplined behaviour, major Canadian newspapers reported 'rioting mobs' in Crowland, lawlessness, and threats to constitutional authority.[135] The city of Welland made available its police force, and Welland Council appropriated five hundred dollars for the maintenance of law and order in the township.[136] Premier Hepburn made three visits to the township along with key cabinet members between 17 April and 10 May 1935. His decision to send OPP reinforcements to Crowland suggests that he too considered the situation in Crowland grave.

These fears were generated in part by conditions outside Crowland – namely, the growing unrest among the unemployed throughout Canada. In April 1935 the most significant strike by Canadian relief workers occurred when hundreds of workers from the relief camps of British Columbia descended on Vancouver to protest against wages and conditions in these 'slave camps.'[137] This was a prelude to the 'On-to-Ottawa' trek. Still, circumstances peculiar to Crowland – above all, urban Crowland's ethnic composition – were even more important in making this a 'test strike between the unemployed and provincial authorities.'[138] By the time of Premier Hepburn's intervention, the Crowland strike was one of the longest relief strikes in Ontario and had developed into a grim standoff between unemployed workers and municipal officials. The decision of Crowland Council to retaliate against the strikers by withholding relief from them for the duration of the strike was unparalleled in its harshness anywhere in the province.[139] It can be explained by the gulf that separated rural from urban Crowland. Even those officials who lived in urban Crowland had adopted the perspectives of the township's Anglo-Celtic farmers. That the strikers could hold out for weeks despite these harsh measures also distinguished this relief strike and frightened its opponents.

Crowland farmers were evidently genuinely afraid of the strikers' radicalism, and it confirmed their views about the indolence of the urban unemployed. They seemed to believe that socialism or communism provided a rationale for this indolence. Louis Whitaker, the farmer who had showed some sympathy for the unemployed while he served on Crowland Council, said that Communist agitators told the unemployed: 'It's all yours, demand that it be given to you.'[140] Farmers feared the strength of the strikers. On 9 April, when violence erupted between police and strikers, local farmers organized to lend a hand to police.[141] A few days later they sent a delegation to Toronto to inform the Ontario government that the strikers threatened constitutional authority in Crowland and to call for intervention from provincial authorities.[142]

Premier Hepburn gave expression to what was implicit in the standoff between rural and urban Crowland when he accused the strikers of having been tricked by 'professional agitators' who hoped 'for the day when Canada will be a Communistic state with themselves as autocratic rulers.' 'That day,' Hepburn predicted confidently, 'will never come in this or any other Anglo-Saxon country with the majority of people rural dwellers.'[143] Hepburn was determined to prove to the strikers and the province as a whole that radicalism and militancy had no place in Canadian society. Not only did he attempt to discredit the strike's radical leaders, he also explored the possibility of having them deported.[144]

Ultimately, concerted action by local and provincial authorities succeeded in breaking the strikers' resolve. On 29 April, when Hepburn offered to consider their demands if they returned to work, the strikers agreed to a kind of armistice, but retained their fighting stance. They would return to work for one week, but would resume the strike if council did not meet their demands for food vouchers 25 per cent above those recommended by the Campbell report. They also insisted that task work beyond the value of food vouchers be ended and demanded open clothing vouchers, food and rent vouchers for the single unemployed, the liquidation of debts to merchants, and the dropping of charges against the arrested strike leaders.[145] Hepburn responded that he would not comply with any ultimatum.[146] The Crowland unemployed committee then withdrew its demands and the strikers' unanimity began to crumble. A week later, their resolve stiffened briefly when Hepburn rejected most of their demands. Two hundred strikers and sympathizers voted unanimously to resume the strike. The next day, however, the strike was over. About thirty men returned to work, led by former moderate Tom Martin.

Several factors combined to undermine support for the militant position. First, just when the strikers were debating Premier Hepburn's offer, the main leaders, Haslam and Douglas, were detained in jail for several days. Welland County's Crown attorney had advised that they be refused bail to keep them from 'further upsetting the men's passions.'[147] By his own admission, Tom Martin used that time to convince some of the strikers to return to work. Second, Tom Martin himself, who on 30 April 1935 still supported a militant stance, suddenly got a job.[148] Overnight he became the principal advocate of returning to work. The timing of his unexpected good fortune and a letter overflowing with gratitude from Martin to Hepburn suggest that the premier was instrumental in producing Martin's change of heart.[149] Finally, the township council announced that it was willing to make concessions to those strikers who agreed to return to work. Food vouchers would be increased by 10 per cent and would be broken into one-dollar units that could be used in different stores. The task of supplying women and children with clothing would be taken over by Josephine di Martile, the daughter of Italian immigrants, and steps would be taken to improve the service. When strikers weighed these promises against threats by local officials and Hepburn that no concessions would be made if the strike was resumed, some of them clearly decided that it would be better to accept partial fulfilment of their demands than to risk losing all by resuming the strike.[150]

Indeed, in the immediate aftermath of the strike, the militant stand adopted by Crowland's immigrant workers appeared discredited. The strike's radical leaders paid a heavy price for the modest gains made. The Ukrainian Labour Temple, the strikers' headquarters, burned to the ground on 5 May 1935. Although ULFTA members rebuilt it that fall, Crowland Council refused to renew their licence.[151] When the Temple's manager, Nick Zenchuk, defiantly opened the new building, he was arrested.[152] On 13 June 1935 the strike's leaders were tried for rioting and participating in an unlawful assembly. The two Communists among them, Haslam and Douglas, were found guilty and sentenced to the Ontario Reformatory for one year definite and three months indefinite. Robert Lougheed and Adolph Gagan received suspended sentences on the grounds that they were misled and had not intended to break the law.[153]

These developments led some of Crowland's immigrants publicly to dissociate themselves from the radicalism adopted during the strike. At the trial of the strike leaders, for example, Mike Blazetich, a Polish-American and Crowland's superintendant of waterworks, denounced the activities of the 'red' strikers as un-Canadian.[154] Apparently fearful of being found guilty by association, leaders of Crowland's Ukrainian Greek Catholic Society protested the rebuilding of the Ukrainian Labour Temple.[155]

The subsequent history of the township suggests, however, that Crowland's immigrant workers continued to believe in collective struggle as a way of gaining fairness and equality. In September 1935, striking employees at Page Hersey supplemented their demand for higher wages and union recognition by insisting on the eligibility of all workers 'irrespective of their trade, nationality, race, creed or political opinions in his native language.'[156] Despite widespread unemployment, the company recognized the union, but only to smash it six months later by firing its organizers and establishing a company union.[157] Still, company opposition merely delayed the unionization of Crowland's plants.

Workers at Union Carbide and Page Hersey Tubes responded with enthusiasm to the invitation of the radical ULFTA and Hungarian Workers' Club to join the Communist-led United Electrical, Radio and Machine Workers (UE) in 1942–3.[158] Even those with little sympathy for communism supported the UE, and their support was not based on economic ends alone. According to Mary Karas, the union provided job security by curbing the power of the foreman over workers.[159] Stephen Bornemissza, a long-time employee of Page Hersey, emphasized that the union gave workers a voice so that they 'could speak up when they didn't like something' without fear of being fired.[160] Mike Bosnich, UE business agent for many years, best explains why rank-and-file workers supported his Communist-led union. Once a committed CPC member himself, Bosnich admits that in the late 1940s few Crowland workers were members. They supported the union not for its specific ideological bent, but because it 'overrode nationalities,' enabling immigrant workers 'to have a say in their wages, working conditions, and to have some modicum of control over their futures.' That the union gave them 'the chance for self-respect and ... decency,' Bosnich believes, 'was more important to them than even the money or the seniority.'[161]

Crowland's immigrant workers also elected men from their own ranks to the township council and the school board until well into the 1940s.[162] Even those foreign-born residents and their children who were not otherwise sympathetic to the Communist Party voted for candidates who were active in local Communist organizations, such as John Petrochenko, Nicholas Zenchuk, Joe Husar, and Mike Bosnich. Such voters believed that these radical candidates would best serve the interests of 'ethnics' and of 'working class people.'[163]

Conclusion

The Crowland relief strike was the first instance of collective action by Crowland's immigrant workers to change their working and living environment. This solidarity had developed gradually during the first decades of the twentieth century as the community of urban Crowland matured. Despite their ethnic diversity, similarities existed in the backgrounds of peasant immigrants from southern and eastern Europe, and in their lifestyles once they settled in Crowland. The township's small size, the high proportion of immigrants among its inhabitants, and their concentration in large plants ensured daily contact across ethnic lines, thus contributing to an awareness of common grievances and goals among Crowland's residents of continental European background. The strongest integrative force among them, however, was the discrimination they faced. It was not surprising that the first expression of solidarity by Crowland's immigrants occurred during the Great Depression, when in addition to suffering from unemployment or underemployment, 'foreign' workers were subjected to special indignities. The particular ethnic mix of Crowland's participation contributed to the militancy of the immigrants' protest. Radical Ukrainians, Hungarians, and Serbians – the members of three ethnic groups with strong Communist-led factions in Canada – frequently played key roles in strikes, unionizing efforts, and local politics. Immigrant workers, including many non-Communists, accepted their leadership because local Communists seemed to be the most committed and capable advocates of their cause.

While firm conclusions about the national relevance of this case study must await further studies of inter-ethnic collaboration in other Canadian locales, the election of 'ethnic' Communist politicians such as William Kolysnik and Jacob Penner in Winnipeg and J.B. Salsberg in Toronto suggests that working-class immigrants in these cities developed a sense of shared identity similar to that of Crowland's 'foreign' residents. The behaviour of Crowland's immigrant working class brings into question the widely used model that locates immigrant adaptation on a continuum somewhere between complete adoption of the ways of the host society and defensive reliance on social networks and behaviour patterns imported from the Old World. Without denying their unique ethnic traditions, Crowland's immigrants developed a new sense of identity based on their shared condition as workers and newcomers in Canada. It was uniquely Canadian, and it had a distinct class component.

NOTES·

This abbreviated article is from *Relief Strike: Immigrant Workers and the Great Depression in Crowland, Ontario, 1930–35*, by Carmela Patrias. Toronto: New Hogtown Press, 1990. Reprinted with permission.

Acknowledgments are due to the men and women who permitted me to interview them, especially Flavio Botari, Mike Bosnich, and Nick Petrochenko; the Social Sciences and Humanities Research Council and Multiculturalism Directorate of Secretary of State for generous financial assistance; the staff of the Welland Public Library and the Welland Museum, and John Burtniak of Brock

University Library; the Labour Studies Research Group of Toronto, especially Craig Heron; the editorial board of New Hogtown Press; and Wayne Thorpe. I also acknowledge Franca Iacovetta's efforts in abbreviating the original essay for inclusion in this reader.

1 *Toronto Globe*, 30 April 1935.
2 *Toronto Daily Star*, 25 April 1935; *St Catharines Standard*, 25 April 1935.
3 *St Catharines Standard*, 25 April 1935.
4 Brock University, Special Collections (henceforth BU, SC], Crowland Relief Rolls, 1934–6.
5 For example, Donald Avery, *'Dangerous Foreigners'* (Toronto 1979); Jean Morrison, 'Ethnicity and Class Consciousness: British, Finnish and South European Workers at the Canadian Lakehead Before World War I,' *Lakehead University Review* 9 (Spring 1976); Craig Heron, *Working in Steel* (Toronto 1988).
6 Victor Greene, *The Slavic Community on Strike: Immigrant Labor in Pennsylvania Anthracite* (Toronto 1988).
7 James R. Barrett, 'Unity and Fragmentation: Class, Race and Ethnicity on Chicago's South Side, 1900–1922,' in D. Hoerder, ed., *'Struggle a Hard Battle'* (De Kalb. 1986); William Kornblum, *Blue Collar Community* (Chicago 1974).
8 Allan Seager, 'Class, Ethnicity, and Politics in the Alberta Coalfields, 1905–1945,' in *'Struggle a Hard Battle.'*
9 James Gordon Nelson, 'Crowland Township, a Study in Land Utilization,' MA thesis (McMaster University, 1985).
10 In 1911 Ontario Iron and Steel merged with Montreal Car and Foundry and was renamed Canada Steel Foundries. *Peoples Press* and *Welland Telegraph*, 17 January 1911.
11 Norman Richard Young, 'The Economic and Social Development of Welland, 1905–1939,' MA thesis (University of Guelph, 1976).
12 *Tribune*, 7 April 1910, 8 December 1911, 11 January 1912; Paula Esposito, 'The Italian Community in Welland; an Oral Sources Study,' unpublished paper, Geography, McMaster University, n.d., 4–6, 12.
13 Natalie Wieczorek, 'The Polish Community of Welland, 1900–1939,' MA thesis (OISE, 1978), 82.
14 *Tribune*, 22 September 1910; *People's Press*, 14 December 1909; *Tribune*, 14, 19, 28 January 1928; 2, 25 February 1928; 13, 27 March 1928, 3 January 1929.
15 BU, SC, Assessment rolls, Crowland Township, 1935.
16 Interviews with Ann Hunka, Welland Heritage Council and Multicultural Centre Collections (WHCMC); W.K., 4 December 1986, Welland; Peter Santone and sisters, October 1985, Welland; *People's Press* 19 August 1913.

17 Fiftieth anniversary publication, Matthews Public School, 1929–79; *People's Press*, 17 November 1914.

18 *Tribune*, 21 December 1942, 2 August 1928, 28 September 1929.

19 *People's Press*, 14 December 1909; *Tribune*, 22 September 1910.

20 For example, *People's Press*, 14 December 1909; *Tribune*, 22 September 1922.

21 For example, *People's Press*, 25 October 1910, 24 March 1908.

22 Interview with Peter Santone, October 1985, Welland.

23 Based on Assessment Rolls, Crowland Township, 1935.

24 See, for example, *Tribune*, 28 March 1912.

25 Wieczoreck, 114, 119. William Makowski, *History and Integration of the Poles in Canada* (Niagara: Canadian Polish Congress 1967), 75; Minute Books of Welland-Canadian Polish Society, 1927–49; interview with Mrs Gibbons, 7 March 1986, Welland; Maria Karas, 26 November 1986, Welland; Hedwig Fitkowski, 3 December 1986, Welland; V.S., 3 December 1986, Welland.

26 WHCMC, *The Croatians of Welland* (Welland 1979), 29.

27 Interview with Dr J. Ennis, Toronto; *Tribune*, 22 May 1930, 15 August 1930.

28 RCMP informants in 1920 described the Ukrainian Workers' Mutual Benefit Association as anarchist. National Archives (NA), MG27 II D 19, Arthur Lewis Sifton papers, vol. 9, Notes of C.I.B. Division for week of 4 November 1920, 18. (I am indebted to Jim Naylor for this reference.) In 1934 the association hosted an anti-Stalinist speaker with Trotskyist sympathies. *Tribune*, 2 May 1934. For information on the origins of the association, I thank Philip Crouch, QC, Welland, the son of a founding member.

29 Interview with Stephen Bornemissza and Helen Gerencser, 25 November 1986, Welland.

30 Unfortunately, no company records are available to confirm this.

31 Interview with Adam Ferioli, 10 October 1985, Welland. See also interviews with John Durley, 2 December 1986, Welland, and Mike Bosnich, 11 October 1985.

32 Interviews with Mrs G. Gibbons and Helen Gerencser.

33 *People's Press*, 24 March 1908.

34 Ibid., 25 October 1910.

35 Ibid., 30 June 1914.

36 *Tribune*, 18 September 1913; *Tribune*, 13 July 1931, 6 March 1935.

37 Interview with Nick Petrochenko, 10 December 1986, Welland.

38 Interviews with John Durley and Peter Santone.

39 For example, interview with Pearl Kalynuk, 20 February 1986.

40 Unfortunately, no precise records are available to indicate the extent of exogamy in Crowland.

41 Interview with Mike Bosnich, Welland, 20 September 1987.

42 Interview with John Durley and Mr and Mrs W.K. Most Poles and Ukrainians in Crowland came from Galicia.
43 Wieczorek, 110.
44 Interviews with Mike Bosnich, Pearl Kalynuk, W.K., 4 December 1986, John Kozlowski, 8 December 1986, Ann Hunka, 21 February 1986, Chester Malaguti, 3 October 1985, Pina Riddel (née Orsini), 30 January 1986.
45 Interview with Pearl Kalnuk, 20 February 1986, Welland.
46 Fern Sayles, *Welland Workers Make History* (published privately 1963) 123.
47 On this theme see Carmela Patrias, *Patriots and Proletarians: The Politicization of Hungarian Immigrants in Canada, 1923–1939* (Montreal: McGill-Queen's University Press, 1995).
48 As Crowland was too small to attract the attention of investigators, we must rely on scattered announcements in the local press to gauge the extent and duration of these cutbacks. On Atlas, see *Tribune*, 5 June 1934.
49 *Tribune*, 30 August 1930, 12 November 1930, 15 April 1932, 1 August 1934.
50 Ibid., 20 May 1930.
51 Interviews with Mrs Ferioli, 10 October 1985, Elsie Malaguti, 3 October 1985, M.B., 24 November 1986, Welland.
52 Company practices came to light during a bitter strike in the winter of 1936–37. For example, see *Tribune*, 22 December 1936.
53 Ibid., 27 October 1933.
54 See the letter from a Hungarian employee in the *Kanadai Magyar Munkas*, 2 April 1935.
55 Interview with Mike Bosnich, Welland, 11 October 1985; *Tribune*, 15 April 1932.
56 Interview with Mr and Mrs W.K., 4 December 1986, Welland.
57 See, for example, *Tribune*, 28 March 1933.
58 Cassidy, 45–6; *Tribune*, 16 December 1932.
59 Interview with Frank Haslam and Nick Petrochenko, Port Colborne, 10 December 1986.
60 Sayles, 125.
61 Minutes, Crowland Township Council (henceforth CTC), 13 January 1930.
62 *Tribune*, 14 November 1930.
63 Ibid., 18 June 1931.
64 Minutes, CTC, 28 November 1930; *Tribune*, 23 November 1931.
65 *Tribune*, 18, 21, and 25 November 1931; 7 December 1931.
66 Ibid., 17 August 1932.
67 Minutes, CTC, 29 April 1932.
68 Judging from the 1934–6 relief records, the average family size of relief recipients in Crowland was larger than in other Ontario communities.

69 *Tribune*, 13 December 1932.

70 Ibid., 19 February 1925.

71 Ibid., 28 March 1933.

72 Interview with Maria Karas, 2 December 1986.

73 *Toronto Worker*, 2 May 1935.

74 *Tribune*, 26 November 1932, 28 March 1933; Sayles, 126–7.

75 Minutes, CTC 30 October 1931; *Tribune*, 29 October 1932.

76 *Tribune*, 1 August 1931.

77 Minutes, CTC, 17 November 1931.

78 *Tribune*, 5 August 1931.

79 The only surviving record suggest that in early 1933 the names of twelve companies were submitted to the Department of Immigration by Crowland Council. It is not clear if the Department deported those named. See Minutes, CTC, 20 February 1933.

80 *Tribune*, 30 November 1932.

81 Figures based on BU, SC, Crowland Relief Rolls, 1934–6.

82 *Tribune*, 3 June 1931.

83 *Welland Tribune*, 14 December 1932.

84 Archives of Ontario (AO), Communist Party records, CP 2A 1210, National Executive Secretary, WUL, to John Strush, 15 June 1931; ibid., CP 2A 1296, Strush to A. Horvat, 20 July 1931.

85 Ibid., CP 2A 1279, D. Kozlowsky, Chairman, Workers Unemployed Organization, Welland, to Workers Unity League, 15 July 1931.

86 See, for example, *Tribune*, 17, 20 June 1931, 29 December 1931, 15 April 1933, 2 May 1934, 20 August 1934, 11 February 1935.

87 *Tribune*, 3 February 1933. For biographical information, see Crowland Relief Rolls.

88 *Tribune*, 15 March 1934, 20 December 1934. By 1932 the National Unemployed Council replaced the National Unemployed Workers Association.

89 Interviews with John Strush and Frank Haslam.

90 *Tribune*, 25 September 1933, 2 February 1934.

91 For example, *Tribune*, 1 October 1934.

92 For example, the *Tribune* of 2 May 1934 describes the condemnation of the CCF by Niagara regional organizer James Bryson.

93 *Tribune*, 13 April 1935.

94 Ibid., 26 November 1932; 14, 17 December 1932; 2 February 1934; 16 March 1934; 15 January 1935; 13, 22 April 1935; Minutes, CTC, 27 March 1933; *Toronto Daily Star*, 30 April 1935.

95 *Tribune*, 17 December 1932.

96 Ostensibly for lack of funds. Minutes, CTC, 1 March 1933.

97 *Tribune*, 25 February 1933, 25 March 1933.

98 Ibid., 28 March 1935.

99 Ibid., 10 and 18 January 1933.

100 Ibid., 28 March 1933; 8 April 1933.

101 Sayles and Forster claimed that these cutbacks could not be justified, for work in the area was far from plentiful. Minutes, CTC, 7 and 23 June 1933; *Tribune*, 30 June 1993

102 Minutes, CTC, 22 April 1933; *Tribune*, 29 April 1933.

103 Minutes, CTC, 22 April 1933; *Tribune* 29 April 1933; Sayles, 126.

104 *Tribune*, 21 December 1934.

105. Minutes, CTC, 29 November 1934; *Tribune*, 18 and 29 December 1934; 12 and 15; January 1935.

106 *Tribune*, 3 December 1935; 2 and 5 January 1935.

107 Ibid., 5 January 1935.

108 Ibid., 10 January 1935; 13 and 20 February 1935; 5 March 1935.

109 Ibid., 15 March 1935.

110 Ibid., 5 and 15 March 1935.

111 Ibid., 1 April 1935; for food allotments, Minutes, CTC 7 March 1935. The average size of families on relief was calculated on the basis of the Crowland relief rolls.

112 *Tribune*, 1 April 1935; AO, Attorney General Records, RG 4, Series 4–32, File no. 1771, 1935, *Rex v. Haslam et al.*, evidence taken at trial, Welland, 13 June 1935, page 153; *Tribune*, 13.

113 *Worker*, 6 April 1935.

114 *Tribune*, 13 April 1935.

115 Ibid., 11 April 1935.

116 Ibid., 22 April 1935.

117 *Ukrainski Robitnichi Visty*, 17 April 1935.

118 *Toronto Daily Star*, 26 April 1935; *Ukrainski Robitnichi Visty*, 15 April 1935.

119 Interview with Frank Haslam, Port Colborne, 10 December 1986; interview with Ann Hunka, Welland, 21 February 1986.

120 *Tribune*, 11 April 1935.

121 Ibid., 13 April 1935.

122 Ibid., 12 and 20 April 1935.

123 Ibid., 13 April 1935.

124 Interview with Mrs G. Gibbons, Welland, 7 March 1986.

125 *Toronto Daily Star*, 17 April 1935.

126 Ibid., 26 April 1935.

127 For example, *Toronto Worker*, 22 April 1933; 16 and 18 November 1933.

128 *Tribune*, 9 April 1935.

129 *Toronto Daily Star*, 27 April 1935.
130 *Kanadai Magyar Munkas*, 8 May 1935.
131 *Toronto Daily Star*, 27 April 1935.
132 *Tribune*, 29 April 1935.
133 *Toronto Daily Star*, 27 April 1935.
134 Natalie Z. Davis, 'The Reasons of Misrule,' in *Society and Culture in Early Modern France* (Stanford 1975) 97–123; E.P. Thompson, '"Rough Music": le charivari anglais,' *Annales: economies, societes, civilisations* 27 (March–April 1972); Bryan Palmer, 'Discordant Music: Charivaris and White-Capping in Nineteenth-Century North America,' *Labour/le travail* 3 (1978), 5–62.
135 *Globe*, 10 and 26 April 1935; *Toronto Telegram*, 18 and 28 April 1935.
136 Young, 111.
137 See Ronald Liversedge in Victor Hoar, ed., *Recollections of the On to Ottawa Trek* (Toronto 1973).
138 *St Catharines Standard*, 25 April 1935.
139 NA, RG 27, Department of Labour, Strikes and Lockouts files, files on unemployment relief strikes; *Tribune*, 13 April 1935.
140 *Tribune*, 11 April 1935.
141 Ibid., 9 April 1935.
142 *Ibid.*, 11 April 1935.
143 Ibid., 10 May 1935; Neil McKenty, *Mitch Hepburn* (Toronto 1967) 103.
144 AO, Hepburn papers, RG 3, General Correspondence, Box 192, L.B. Spencer, Raymond, Spencer and Law, Welland, to Hepburn, 30 April 1935; Hepburn to W.A. Gordon, minister of immigration and colonization, 'Crowland Jobless,' 30 April 1935.
145 Ibid., Oliver Edwards, secretary, Unemployed Association, Crowland, to Hepburn, 'Crowland Jobless,' 27 April 1935.
146 *Toronto Globe*, 30 April 1935.
147 AO, Attorney General records, RG 4, Series 4–32, Criminal and Civil Files, 1935, 1222, T.D. Cowper, county crown attorney, Welland, to I.A. Humphries, Department of Attorney General, 7 May 1935.
148 *Toronto Daily Star*, 30 April 1935.
149 AO, Hepburn papers, RG 3, General Correspondence, Box 192, 1935, Thomas Martin to Hepburn, 19 May 1935.
150 *Tribune*, 11 May 1935.
151 Minutes, CTC, 29 May 1935.
152 *Narodova Gazeta*, 14 Marchch 1938.
153 *Rex v. Haslam et al.*, supra note 112, 220.
154 *Rex v. Haslam et al.*, ibid., 111f.
155 Minutes, CTC, 29 May 1935.

156 Sayles, 136.
157 Ibid.
158 Interviews with Lawrence Kovacs, Welland, 6 March 1986; Nic Dziobak and
    Ann Hunka, Welland, 21 February 1986.
159 Interview with Maria Karas, Welland, 26 November 1986.
160 Interview with Stephen Bornemissza, Welland, 25 November 1986.
161 Interview with Mike Bosnich, Welland, 11 November 1985.
162 Interview with Santone family, Welland, October 1985.
163 Interviews with John Kozlowski, 9 December 1986; Santone family, Mr and
    Mrs W.K., 4 December 1986; Mrs G. Gibbons, 7 March 1986, Welland.

TOPIC SEVEN
Encountering the 'Other':
Society and State Responses,
1900s–1930s

On the eve of the First World War, the project of constructing a nation-state in the northern half of North America was on track. Between 1900 and 1914, Canada's population had increased by about 40 per cent, its gross national product and wheat production had more than doubled, and vast tracts of territory had been settled into homesteads. Canadians were also well on their way to becoming a predominantly urban population. By 1921 more Canadians lived in cities than in rural areas. Urban growth was due in part to immigrants who increasingly congregated in the city, despite official attempts to confine them on farms or isolated work camps. Newcomers continued to enter Canada in ever larger numbers as the century progressed. Between 1900 and 1930, close to five million immigrants arrived in Canada. It would take the Great Depression of the 1930s to reduce the flood of newcomers to a trickle.

How to make a 'nation' in a state that was home to so many nationalities, with their seemingly peculiar or even threatening religious, social, and political customs, traditions, and institutions? This was a question that in the decades before the Second World War both English and French Canadians asked aloud. As the readings suggest, no matter how important they were economically and politically to the process of nation-building, newcomers encountered suspicion, fear, hostility, discrimination, exclusion, and sometimes even violence at the hands of mainstream Canadians. Making matters worse for newcomers during these years was the fact that foreign-born workers seemed to dominate the ranks of militant labour organizations and radical political organizations such as the Communist Party of Canada. This presence gave the heightened militancy of the Canadian labour movement during the era of the First World War a distinctly 'foreign' flavour. The First World War provided the pretext for the Canadian state to deal with foreign-born labour radicals through disenfranchisement and deportation of even naturalized Canadian citizens. Gregory Kealey's article suggests, however, that the 'mechanisms of repression' employed by the state against foreign radicals after 1917, including the infamous War Measures Act, were more a response to class conflict and the fear of socialism than an expression of ethnic chauvinism.

Before, during, and after the First World War, the drive to assimilate newcomers and their Canadian-born children was pursued with dogged determination. Important in this campaign from the perspective of the host society were teachers, clergymen, and social workers, as well as the Protestant missionaries whose activities among South Asian immigrants to Canada are examined by Ruth Compton Brouwer. Of course, Protestant missionaries were but one group among the hundreds that carried the banner of 'Anglo conformity' into immigrant neighbourhoods and homes during this period; but, according to Brouwer, their (limited) sensitivity to the immigrants they served made them an anomaly in the increasingly xenophobic atmosphere of the late 1920s and 1930s. Perhaps no group suffered more from this xenophobia than Jews. In fact, so pervasive was anti-Semitism in Canada during the 1930s that when Nazi Germany began to rid itself of its Jews, Canadians – including ordinary citizens, immigration bureaucrats, and politicians – showed little desire to make their country a safe haven for European Jewry. Consequently, as Irving Abella and Harold Troper document, Canada agreed to accept only a paltry number of Jewish refugees. Many of the Jewish women, men, and children who were refused entry into Canada ended up on trains headed for Auschwitz and other Nazi death camps.

The readings reveal a host society that was ambivalent at times to newcomers, allowing for varying degrees of sensitivity and hostility. The essays also reveal the Canadian state employing its monopoly of force and its control over citizenship to deal summarily with those deemed 'subversive' and thus dangerous to the state and its capitalist underpinnings. Was the state justified in deporting foreign-born radicals and in suppressing foreign-language publications that spread a socialist message during the First World War and in the interwar era? Was it class conflict or ethnic chauvinism that motivated the state to take these actions? How do we explain Canada's decision to accept so few Jewish refugees when other countries took tens of thousands more? Finally, what about the subjects themselves, be they foreign radicals, South

Asian immigrants, or Jewish refugees? How did they respond to the pressures and challenges they faced?

BIBLIOGRAPHY AND SUGGESTED READINGS

Abella, Irving, and Harold Troper. *None Is Too Many: Canada and the Jews of Europe, 1933–48*. Toronto 1982.
Avery, Donald. *'Dangerous Foreigners': European Immigrant Workers and Labour Radicalism in Canada, 1896–1932*. Toronto 1979.
Bercuson, David. *Confrontation at Winnipeg: Labour Industrial Relations and the General Strike*. Montreal, 1974.
Granatstein, Jack, et al., *Nation: Canada since Confederation*. 3d ed. Toronto 1990.
Israel, Milton, ed. *The South Asian Diaspora in Canada: Six Essays*. Toronto 1987.
Palmer, Howard. *Patterns of Prejudice: A History of Nativism in Alberta*. Toronto 1982.
McCormack, A.R. *Reformers, Rebels and Revolutionaries: The Western Canadian Radical Movement, 1899–1919*. Toronto 1977.
Roberts, Barbara. *When They Came: Deportation from Canada, 1900–1935*. Ottawa 1988.
Valverde, Mariana. *The Age of Light, Soap and Water: Moral Reform in English Canada, 1880s–1920s*. Toronto 1990.

A Disgrace to 'Christian Canada': Protestant Foreign Missionary Concerns about the Treatment of South Asians in Canada, 1907–1940

RUTH COMPTON BROUWER

'Seriously, how is it that these flabby philanthropists, these goody-good sloppy sentimentalists invariably champion the cause of foreigners against their own people and kin, as in this case?' The author of this question was a 1912 letter-writer to *Saturday Night* magazine who identified himself (?) only as 'Far West.' The 'foreigners' in this instance were immigrants from India. Unless they were stopped, 'Far West' warned, they would continue to flee their own overcrowded homeland for British Columbia. There, given their willingness to accept low wages and live cheaply 'in dens not fit for a swine,' they would soon flood the labour market and drive out white workers. The 'flabby philanthropists' were Canadian Protestant missionaries, who had offended the letter-writer with their claims to expertise on the immigrants, as well as their sympathy for them.[1]

Historians of Asian immigration have made Canadian students familiar with such negative stereotypes of 'Orientals' as the one reported above. With the exception of Peter Ward, however, they have not argued that missionaries, as a group, were notably more sensitive than other Canadians to the rights and needs of Asian immigrants.[2] This paper takes up Ward's theme, concentrating on the missionary response to immigrants from South Asia. It deals particularly with the activities of missionaries and missionary bureaucrats in the Presbyterian Church and, after 1925, the United Church of Canada.

Immigration to Canada from China and Japan during the early twentieth century far exceeded that from South Asia. In British Columbia, the province with by far the largest Asian population, residents of Chinese origin comprised 5 per cent of the population in 1911, those of Japanese origin 2.2 per cent, and those of 'East Indian' origin only 0.58 per cent.[3] Presbyterian and United Church outreach to the latter group was correspondingly small in scale. It found practical expression in small missions to South Asian communities in Vancouver and Victoria and in a variety of efforts to make Canadian public opinion and federal and British Columbia government policies more favourably disposed towards them. The decision to reach out to the South Asian immigrants was prompted by several motives: a concern to protect the churches' missionary enterprise in India (and to a lesser extent the Raj itself) from the anti-missionary and nationalist backlash created by the immigrants' harsh treatment in Canada; a desire to convert the immigrants to Christianity and an Anglo-Protestant way of life; and, more immediately, a desire to demonstrate the social meaning of the Christian faith by offering a variety of forms of practical assistance. The present study concentrates on the initial period of missionary outreach to the immigrants and on the years of the First World War, when the backlash created by the *Komagata Maru* affair and the escalation in Indian nationalism gave the missionaries' work particular urgency. It deals more briefly with the decline of the work in the postwar years and with its abandonment as an organized church endeavour in 1940. The study supports Ward's thesis that Protes-

tant missionaries to Canada's Asian immigrants held more positive attitudes towards them than did other Protestant leaders or Canadian
society at large. It provides new insights, however, by focusing specifically on South Asian immigrants, the group least studied by Ward. In
doing so, it demonstrates that Presbyterian–United Church interest in the
immigrants was related not only to humanitarianism and the churches'
concerns for Canada's future but also to their overseas missionary commitments and their support for the imperial cause.

The first South Asian immigrants began arriving in Canada in 1903.
They were chiefly men of the Sikh faith. Their homeland was the Punjab
region of India, but they had been working for years in Hong Kong or
one of the other British colonial possessions in the Far East. By 1908,
more than five thousand South Asians had come to Canada, settling
almost exclusively in British Columbia. Male Sikhs were still in the vast
majority, but after 1905 they came directly from the Punjab, where a
decline in the size of family landholdings and, frequently, a period of
travel and service in the British Indian army had made increasing numbers of young Sikhs receptive to the idea of emigrating.[4] The sudden
surge in numbers arising from this new pattern gave rise to concerted
opposition to the immigrants and led in 1908 to a federal order in council implementing the infamous 'continuous journey' regulation. The regulation, which was directed against Japanese workers who had been
making the trip to Canada from Hawaii, as well as against South Asians,
required a continuous journey to Canada from the immigrants' country
of birth. Though it sounded less offensive than the head tax on Chinese
immigrants, such a requirement was, in practice, even more restrictive
than the head tax.

Opposition to South Asian immigration reached a dramatic climax in
1914. In May of that year Gurdit Singh, a Sikh activist and businessman,
chartered a Japanese freighter, the *Komagata Maru*, and brought 376 South
Asians to Vancouver from ports of embarkation in the Far East in defiance
of the ban on such immigration. After two months of tense confrontations
between immigration officials and spokesmen for the South Asians, the
would-be immigrants were forced to return to Hong Kong and ultimately
to India. With the exception of 22 returnees, none of the *Komagata Maru*'s
passengers had been allowed even to disembark despite illnesses and a
shortage of food and water on board the aging vessel.[5]

Two Canadian Protestant churches – the Presbyterian and the Baptist
– had conducted foreign missionary work in India from the 1870s and

thus had a particularly strong reason for taking an interest in immigrants from that country. The Presbyterian Church, the larger of the two denominations, demonstrated an early concern for the immigrants. More accurately, a few retired and furlough missionaries from the church's large mission field in Central India and from its mission to indentured East Indian labourers in Trinidad directly expressed their own concern and sought to interest their fellow Presbyterians in the South Asians' well-being in Canada.

The first systematic effort to make contact with the immigrants came in 1907 when the medical missionary Alexander Nugent, home on furlough from Central India, took up residence in Vancouver and began visitation work among them. In letters to his church's Foreign Missions Committee, Dr Nugent spoke of the desirability of establishing a permanent mission among the East Indians, especially given their increasing numbers. Nugent also challenged negative stereotypes of the immigrants that were already becoming common currency. Dismissing complaints that they were rowdy, he argued that in fact no body of labouring men could compare to them for being law-abiding and sober. (He did favour a ban on the sale of alcohol to the immigrants, as to Canadian Indians, in order to nip in the bud the risk of their becoming dependent on the solace of liquor.) Despite all that was being written about 'Hindoo paupers,' there was, Nugent maintained, no likelihood of Canadians having to support the immigrants, since the majority had obtained jobs the day after their arrival.[6] Nugent regretted very much the discriminatory attitude of 'select whites,' an attitude that had prompted his landlord to forbid him from receiving any South Asian visitors in the quarters he was renting. Overall, Nugent's letters revealed a genuine concern for the immigrants' spiritual and temporal welfare. Like other missionaries who wrote about them, he depicted the Sikhs as a particularly worthy and hardworking community of Indians, and implied that they were more at risk from than a threat to the larger Canadian society.[7]

In a formal report on Indian immigrants in the Vancouver area, prepared for the Presbyterian Church in 1907, Nugent provided information on the immigrants' background and goals and described the opposition they were encountering. He singled out the local press and the mayor's office and especially labour representatives as significant sources of hostility to the immigrants, but went on to suggest that many citizens were sympathetic to their plight and many employers eager to hire them. Indeed, some employers were prepared to pay them the same wages as white workers if only organized labour did not prevent their doing so. Speaking of his own involvement with the immigrants, Nugent reported that they had received his overtures gladly, as those of a friend whom they had met unexpectedly in a foreign land. Finally, in what was to be a frequently repeated theme in India missionaries' correspondence, he spoke of the likely harmful effect on missionary work in India and on Britain's political control in that country if work of the immigrants' harsh treatment in Canada got back to their homeland. Canada was also making the imperial task harder, he warned, by asking the British government to prevent Indian immigrants from seeking entry to Canada.[8]

Back in India in 1908, Nugent continued to be interested in the immigrants. He was critical of information on South Asian immigration patterns provided to the federal government by Deputy Minister of Labour William Lyon Mackenzie King. King's contention that the number of immigrants was declining, and that many of those who had come to Canada were returning home, was wrong, he asserted. Indeed, some two hundred South Asians had landed at Vancouver from Hong Kong on the very day in 1907 when King had assured the federal government that their interest in Canada was declining. King's figures and predictions, he implied, reflected wishful thinking rather than reality. Like King, many local clergy were woefully ignorant of the real numbers and circumstances of the immigrants, he wrote. Finally, Nugent pointed out that what he had anticipated with regard to reaction in India to the immigrants' harsh treatment in Canada had in fact come to pass. '[T]he native press,' he wrote, 'is full of the immigration question.'[9]

Nugent's India colleague W.A. Wilson was also on furlough in Canada in 1907. He too spent time with the immigrants, though he did not work among them in as regular a way. Like Nugent, Wilson wrote to foreign missions officials about the desirability of setting up full-time mission work, both for the immigrants' 'individual good' and also '[to] help our work in India when they return to their own land.' (In contrast to Nugent, he believed that the majority were only sojourners in Canada.) Wilson spoke favourably about the immigrants' character and industry, as Nugent had done. En route back to Canada by way of China, he had travelled aboard the *Tartar* with a large contingent of new arrivals, and in Vancouver had accepted an invitation to attend the establishment of a place of worship and give an address. Nugent had already 'done a good deal' in getting jobs for the immigrants and in providing other forms of practical assistance, Wilson reported, and in so doing had gained their

confidence, so that the time truly was opportune for establishing permanent missionary work among them.[10]

The Reverend J. Knox Wright, a former Trinidad missionary, was also
much concerned about the plight of the South Asians, despite the fact
that he had a full-time ministry with a Vancouver-area congregation.
Wright echoed the two India missionaries' favourable assessment of the
South Asian immigrants and urged the importance of full-time work
among them. Like Nugent, he believed that Mackenzie King's predictions of only temporary stays by the immigrants, and of declining numbers of new arrivals, were based on inadequate information and wishful
thinking. Many of 'the better class' would remain, he insisted, citing as
evidence the fact that they had already built a temple costing about six
thousand dollars.[11]

At the time that Nugent, Wilson, and Wright were calling for the
opening of permanent missionary work among the immigrants, the
specific Presbyterian Church body to which they were looking was
the Toronto-based Foreign Missions Committee. Until 1912, when it was
reconstituted as the Board of Foreign Missions (BFM), the Foreign Missions Committee (FMC) was responsible for mission work among Asian
and Jewish communities within Canada as well as for overseas missions.[12] In May 1908, FMC officials received a petition from the Synod of
British Columbia formally recommending the appointment of a missionary to labour among the South Asians.[13] Later, they also received
direct and indirect communications from educated representatives of
the South Asian community and from some concerned Methodist clergymen in British Columbia on the subject of the need for better treatment for the community.[14] Given these expressions of interest, it seems
appropriate to ask why no permanent mission work was started among
the immigrants until 1913 and why the FMC was reluctant to initiate or
support strong calls for changes in laws and practices injurious to their
welfare.

The FMC's initial response to Asian immigration generally, and to
South Asian immigration in particular, came, most typically, from the
Committee's veteran full-time secretary, R.P. MacKay, or from his associate, A.E. Armstrong. Both men, but especially MacKay, showed a tendency to be inconsistent in their thinking and writing on the subject.
MacKay veered between sympathy for the plight of Asian immigrants in
Canada and apprehension lest the country be 'orientalized' by their
admission in unchecked numbers. In their sympathetic mode, the two
secretaries were consistent in their desire to show preference for the

'better class' of Asian immigrants, and for those meriting special consideration on compassionate grounds. Thus, in 1909 MacKay wrote to Mackenzie King to express the FMC's satisfaction that the government was planning to exempt Chinese students from the head tax on other Chinese immigrants.[15] And in 1911 the committee evidently joined other Canadian mission boards in asking the minister of the interior to respond favourably to a petition from Dr Sundar Singh, an educated Sikh activist, seeking changes in the legislation that was preventing the wives and children of immigrants from joining them in Canada. The same letter suggested that Sikhs deserved especially favourable consideration as immigrants, given their fine record of military service to the British Empire.[16]

At the same time, there were countervailing tendencies that militated against early and sympathetic action on the part of FMC officials. The fact that there were conflicting reports from clergy and missionaries in British Columbia about the size and long-term stability of the South Asian communities there led the Toronto-based officials to hesitate about establishing a permanent mission among them. In early 1912 there were further concerns when Principal John MacKay of the Presbyterian Church's Westminster College in Vancouver declared that Dr Sundar Singh, far from being a legitimate spokesman for the Sikhs, was a fraud (though the fact that John MacKay was a well-known opponent of Asian immigration may initially have made his testimony about Dr Singh somewhat questionable in the eyes of FMC officials).[17]

Most significant, perhaps, in explaining the FMC's hesitation was R.P. MacKay's acknowledgment in 1912 that, like 'Canadians generally,' he himself was changing his attitude and 'rather falling in with the exclusive sentiments of British Columbia' on the matter of Asian immigration. In a letter to the India missionary A.G. McPhedran he stated that while he sympathized with the needs and ambitions of the would-be immigrants, he thought that Canada had the potential, given its resources, to become 'the greatest country in the world,' if only it continued to develop along Anglo-Saxon lines.[18] MacKay would continue to be torn between two conflicting responses to Asian immigration. As secretary of his church's Foreign Missions Committee, he was drawn to a Protestant mission-building vision that emphasized the desirability of assisting Asian immigrants within Canada if missions in their homelands were to prosper. But as an ordinary Canadian citizen, he was also drawn to a much more widely held nation-building vision, one whose narrow purview could not accommodate substantial numbers of non-Anglo-Saxon immigrants.[19]

As strong as his commitment to Anglo-Saxon nation-building was at this time, R.P. MacKay was not prepared to associate himself with Principal John MacKay's calls for the future exclusion of all Asian immigrants, and in March 1913 he wrote to the Toronto *Daily Star* to make that point clear when the newspaper mistakenly attributed Principal MacKay's views to him.[20] But neither was he willing to support pleas for better treatment for South Asian immigrants if those pleas came from individuals or groups about whose character or motives he was at all uneasy. Thus, neither he nor A.E. Armstrong endorsed a pamphlet entitled *An Appeal for Fair Play for the Sikhs in Canada,* written in 1913 by one of their church's retired India missionaries, Isabella Ross Broad. In the pamphlet Broad argued strongly for the rights of the Sikhs, as British subjects, to equitable treatment in Canada, and warned that the persecution to which they were being subjected would create a backlash against missionary work in India. The latter argument was, as noted, one that carried considerable weight with the two FMC officials. But Broad's approach to mission politics made them uncomfortable. She was, MacKay observed, 'a good deal of the new woman type.' Moreover, it appeared that the money she had channelled into the pamphlet and into other literature in support of the Sikh immigrants' cause had come from funds which she had obtained from the Women's Missionary Society on grounds of personal need.[21] Her association with Dr Sundar Singh further undermined her credibility.

It was within this broad context – furlough and retired missionaries agitating for better treatment for the immigrants and for a permanent mission to them; foreign missions officials vacillating in their attitudes between sympathy for and fears about the immigrants; and some prominent Presbyterian churchmen joining the chorus of Canadians calling for a total ban on all Asian immigration – that small-scale but permanent mission work was opened among South Asians in Vancouver in 1913 under the administrative umbrella of the church's Board of Home Missions (BHM). The man appointed to the Vancouver work was Kenneth Grant, an elderly, retired Trinidad missionary. A year later another former Trinidad missionary, W.L. Macrae, would begin similar work in Victoria.[22]

Foreign missions officials did not lose interest in the South Asian immigrants when responsibility for work among them passed to the BHM. The *Komagata Maru* affair in early 1914 and the outbreak of the First World War some months later ensured that. As a result of these events, their India missionaries became increasingly concerned about the hostile treatment being meted out to South Asian immigrants in Canada and the potentially negative effects of that treatment on missionary work and British rule in India.[23] In their initial response to the *Komagata Maru* affair, the two BFM secretaries argued that the Canadian government had a right and a duty to enforce the country's immigration laws and that it should not be pressured into admitting unlimited numbers of immigrants. But they regretted the fact that the immigrants had been detained aboard ship in the harbour at Vancouver and ultimately turned away. 'The Komagata Maru incident,' A.E. Armstrong wrote, 'makes all true Canadians feel humiliated.'[24] While this scarcely constituted an outpouring of compassion, it reflected a more humane response than that shown in an editorial on the subject in the May 1914 issue of *The Presbyterian Record*, the church's official paper. Rather than allow immigrants from Asia to come in and drag Canadians down to their level, the editor declared, it would be 'best for Canada, best for India and China, best for the world that the Western gate should not be opened ... In the meantime let there be earnest effort to send these people that Truth which alone can enable them to [use] their new found liberty to the best advantage in fitting them to take their places among the nations.'[25] Its hypocrisy apart, this editorial was substantially in line with popular and journalistic attitudes expressed in the secular press. In the more moderate tone of their comments, then, and in favouring a 'gentlemen's agreement' with India on the number of immigrants to be sent to Canada annually, rather than a policy of total future exclusion, both foreign secretaries seemed to be at least a step beyond their church's official paper – and popular opinion – in terms of their response to the *Komagata Maru* crisis.[26]

As the war continued, the impact within India of Canada's inhospitable treatment of immigrants from that country became clearer to the two foreign missions secretaries. Not only their own missionaries but those from other denominations and other countries worried about the future effects of Canada's harsh immigration policy on mission work in the subcontinent.[27] At the level of imperial politics, it became evident just how important Canadian racism was to furthering the cause of a small group of radical Indian nationalists who were seeking by violent means to overthrow British rule in India. Indeed, some of those same nationalists had been sojourners and activists in North America and had been detained and arrested on their return to India.[28] It behooved foreign missions officials, then, to increase their support for more generous treatment of South Asian immigrants, not only to protect the Protestant churches' missionary efforts in their homeland but also as a means of preventing the erosion of British control in wartime India.

It would be misleading to suggest that strategic considerations alone prompted the two BFM secretaries to express a greater degree of concern about the immigrants' plight during the war years. The sympathetic attitude of their missionaries and numerous reports of the Indian Army's outstanding contribution to the war effort seem to have increased their ability to think of the immigrants in fraternal terms rather than simply as dangerous foreigners or potential converts. Nevertheless, it does appear that it was the pragmatic and public relations elements that were uppermost in their minds as, during the course of the war, they became somewhat more active in trying to effect alterations in public opinion and government policies with regard to the immigrants. Nothing perhaps demonstrated that pragmatism as clearly as A.E. Armstrong's 1916 proposal to University of Toronto President Robert Falconer that the Nobel-Prize-winning Indian writer, Rabindrinath Tagore, who was then travelling in the United States, be invited across the border and awarded an honorary degree by the university as a way of offsetting the damage done to Canada's reputation in India by the *Komagata Maru* affair.[29]

Despite their increased concern about the difficulties faced by South Asian immigrants in Canada, MacKay and Armstrong were not willing to participate in any significant cooperative strategies with educated spokesmen from within the immigrant community. Indeed, in 1915 they distanced themselves from Dr Sundar Singh and from some Canadian men and women who had associated with him in a renewed effort to secure the entry into Canada of immigrants' wives and children.[30] Like Principal John MacKay several years earlier, and many others subsequently, R.P. MacKay and Armstrong had become convinced that Singh was a self-serving agitator who had exploited members of his own immigrant community as well as sympathetic Canadians.[31] Nevertheless, the cause of reuniting immigrants with their families was one that continued to commend itself to foreign missions officials. In 1916 the Presbyterian General Assembly forwarded a memorial on the subject to the federal government. Prompting had come from the General Assembly of the Presbyterian Church in India through the medium of the BFM,[32] as well as from missionaries on the ground in British Columbia. The latter spoke of moral problems and intense personal suffering among the immigrants as inevitable results of their being deprived of the opportunity for normal family life. Kenneth Grant, for instance, reported that three Vancouver men had recently been charged with committing acts of sodomy, one of them while in a state of complete intoxication. In an interesting reversal of the common view that Asian male immigrants constituted a moral threat to white women, the Reverend J.S. Henderson maintained that of eight South Asian men who had recently married white women, it was 'in every instance to their hurt, industrially, socially and morally.'[33]

The BFM's most positive intervention in the life of the South Asian community came in 1915 when it agreed to assist the BHM in financing missionary work in Victoria by the Reverend Alexander P. Ledingham, who was home on extended health leave from Central India. Between 1916, when he began systematic work in Victoria, and late 1918, when he returned to India, Ledingham proved to be a compassionate advocate and friend of the South Asians. In a letter to R.P. MacKay written in July 1916, he made two general points about the community, the first calculated to inspire hope, the second a warning that the church should have limited expectations. The immigrants, he wrote, appreciated the Presbyterian Church's outreach to them, and it *was* helping to heal the wounds created by the opposition they had encountered. But at the same time, that opposition had created much more of a sense of religious and national community among them than would otherwise have been the case. It had effectively solidified them into a cohesive group, determined to maintain their religious and national identity.[34]

Ledingham adopted various strategies for assisting the immigrants. '[I]t seemed that our only thing to do was to lay ourselves as fully as possible at the disposal of these men in any way in which they might think we could help them,' he wrote in February 1917. 'We encouraged them to come to classes and taught English writing & arithmetic or the vernacular and read in the Bible with any who would read with us. Our classroom was used in the afternoon and evening.' Ledingham also visited the men in their dwellings and invited them to his home, 'day or evening and specially Sabbath afternoon.' He opened a 'kind of club or Rest Room' in Victoria for them as a drop-in centre, since they were barred from most hotels.[35] In company with his colleague W.L. Macrae and nine other members of a deputation, he called on the premier of British Columbia in an effort to persuade the province to press the federal government to let the immigrants' families join them. Describing the latter effort shortly after it had taken place, he told R.P. MacKay, 'I am hopeful that not only the smaller question of the families, but that the whole question of Indian Immigration may be taken up.'[36] Subsequently, he learned that British Columbia's political leaders were not prepared to present any such case to the federal government, and that federal politicians in any event were in no mood to consider such a proposal.[37] He attempted to publicize the General Assembly's memorial urging the reunion of immigrants and their families, both as a strategy for bringing more Christians on side for that cause and as a way of convincing the immigrants themselves of the existence of at least *some* concerned Christians. In order to challenge the hypocrisy of the situation whereby Indian immigrants were described as British subjects and yet denied all citizenship rights, he accompanied an educated Indian who met the usual requirements for naturalization to the registrar's office and asked first about getting him naturalized and then about his right to vote.[38]

As a devoted family man himself, Ledingham agonized over the dilemma of immigrants deprived for years on end of the comforts of family life. In a letter to R.P. MacKay he graphically described the plight of one such man:

One day shortly after my coming I said to one man whose hair was an iron gray well – are you living fairly comfortably in our land? He hesitated but finally said well Sahib with no wife to cook my food and keep my house tidy and no children to make merry it is not much comfort a man can have without these. On further talk it turned out that his son was that very day being married in India and the father was not there to oversee the festivities and hospitalities of such an occasion. There is not a heathen civilization on the face of the earth so far as I know that makes a law that comes in and separates the father and husband from the children & wife. That is reserved for Christian Canada. The family relationships of the whole round earth cries [sic] out against this kind of stupidity and inhumanity – and we are slowly it may be but none the less surely blackening our national name and our Christian name in the great land of India.[39]

In what appears to have been his last letter to R.P. MacKay on the subject of the immigrants before his return to India, Ledingham made two final points, one reflecting the insight of a sensitive Christian missionary, the other a political judgement. In attempting to Christianize the East Indian immigrants instead of the Canadian population, he wrote, the church had been adopting the wrong approach:

I have been compelled to see more and more that we have been putting our main strength on the wrong end of the work. We have been working chiefly among the

Hindus [Indian immigrants] themselves. I have felt right along that our first work is among and with ourselves. It is we who are wrong in our attitude to the East Indians. We need as a whole to understand this and take the means to get right and show the East Indians that we are working in this direction.

It was, he continued, 'useless' to preach the gospel to men under the existing conditions. 'They say first show us the spirit of the gospel then preach the gospel. I simply acknowledge our wrong – and I say Our Christian people send me here to acknowledge this wrong. We are moving as we can to mend matters. But their hope has been sorely tried and Hope deffered [sic] maketh the heart sick.'

Turning briefly to the political impact of Canada's immigration policy, Ledingham stressed that better treatment of South Asians in Canada would result in peaceful rather than acrimonious relations with the independent India of the future. 'If Canada could now be just and generous, world-wide not provincial,' he wrote, 'what a different position she would be in with India when she gets the controlling power in her own hands.'[40]

The compassion and indignation that were evident in Ledingham's letters about the immigrants seem to have left R.P. MacKay largely unmoved. Indeed, by the spring of 1918 MacKay appeared to have retreated to the cautious position of the immediate pre-war years in terms of his attitude towards more liberal immigration laws and improved treatment for the South Asians. He was reluctant to see significant pressure put on the federal government to alter its immigration regulations regarding South Asians before the end of the war. Even on the matter of admitting wives, he had become convinced that the government's plan to consider applications strictly on an individual basis was the only feasible one, since only in that way could government officials prevent the admittance of 'other women ... who are not bona fide wives.'[41]

With Ledingham's return to India in 1918, much of the heart went out of the Presbyterian Church's work among the South Asian immigrants. Ledingham's recently retired India colleague, W.A. Wilson, was posted to Vancouver to replace Kenneth Grant, who had returned to his native Nova Scotia in 1917. Wilson's main interest, however, was still in the kind of intellectual and theological work he had done as head of the Central India mission's seminary in Indore. He was not temperamentally equipped to give the Vancouver work the kind of personal and practical day-to-day commitment that its effective prosecution required.[42] When Wilson withdrew from the work in 1922, the BHM provided no one to take his place. W.L. Macrae was left to carry on alone in both Victoria and Vancouver, holding services in the two cities on alternate Sundays, attracting an average attendance of about thirteen in the former city and very little better in the latter.[43] For its part, the BFM by now had so little commitment to the work that when the outstanding Indian Christian leader Yohan Masih was visiting Canada in 1923 under BFM sponsorship, R.P. MacKay was unprepared to promise Macrae that he could spare Masih for even a brief visit to his missions among the immigrants.[44] Nor, apparently, did either home or foreign missions officials join in criticism of Mackenzie King when in 1923, as prime minister, he declined to commit himself to the enfranchisement of South Asian immigrants when that subject was raised in Parliament and at the Imperial Conference.[45]

From a purely pragmatic point of view, the waning of the Presbyterian Church's commitment to the South Asian community in British Columbia made sense. By 1924 the community had reportedly dwindled to somewhere around eight hundred or nine hundred people, and the expectation was that it would continue to decline.[46] It had yielded virtually no returns in the form of Christian converts, and because it was almost entirely a womanless and childless community, it offered few possibilities for the future. The absence of women and children, in turn, had meant that there had been no formal involvement by the church's women's missionary societies, unquestionably the most important collective force for the stimulation of missionary zeal within Canadian Presbyterianism.[47] With a temporary lull in nationalist activity in India, there perhaps seemed less reason than during the war and immediate postwar years to be concerned that a neglect of the immigrants' interest would have negative consequences for the church's work there.[48] Finally, in a period of declining financial support for missionary work,[49] the South Asian immigrant community had become, quite simply, a poor investment.

When the United Church came into existence in 1925[50] it took over most of the Presbyterian Church's extensive missionary enterprise, including its Central India mission and its work among the South Asians in British Columbia. No additional personnel were provided for the British Columbia work. The United Church era began, however, with hopeful signs of a new spirit of tolerance of the immigrants' way of life as well as an ongoing willingness to provide them with some practical assistance. Commenting on a multicultural Vancouver church service held several months after church union, a reporter for *The United Church Record* noted that Sikhs, Chinese, and Japanese had been in attendance. Though people seemed unable to mix racially, he observed, they could come together in the search for the Kingdom of God: 'All roads that lead to God are good. And as the years go on, those roads seem to be drawing closer together.'[51] In *Orientals in Canada*, published by the United Church Board of Home Missions in 1929, S.S. Osterhout, the church's Vancouver-based Superintendent of Oriental Missions for western Canada, advocated a public education policy that would introduce 'the ancient literature and language of the Orient' into the schools of western Canada. Osterhout was openly critical of the federal government's immigration legislation, especially that affecting immigrants from China and India. '[I]t should not be impossible,' he wrote, 'to evolve laws more in keeping with the high ideals and traditions of the British Empire and the Dominion of Canada, laws free both from the suggestion of subterfuge and the element of unfairness.'[52]

Yet *Orientals in Canada* also reflected some of the same unease about Asian immigration evident in the larger Canadian society. The need for special restrictions on Asian immigrants was taken for granted, as was the undesirability of racial intermarriage among Asians and English-Canadians as a way of achieving cultural cohesion. As for Osterhout's advocacy of Oriental languages and literature in the public schools, it was evidently a kind of pre-emptive strategy, designed (like federal multiculturalism in the 1970s) to forestall more vigorous cultural assertions – in this case, schools established by the Asian communities themselves where religious and cultural ideas antithetical to Canada's Anglo-Saxon Christian values might be introduced.[53]

The section of Osterhout's book dealing specifically with the United Church's missionary work among South Asians was written by W.L. Macrae. Macrae's account made it evident that his practical and undeniably helpful work (translating, writing passport applications, etc.) was accompanied by a condescending attitude towards the Sikhs' religious beliefs. At a time when the more sensitive of the church's foreign missionaries were abandoning terms like 'paganism' and 'heathen darkness' in speaking of non-Christian cultures, Macrae continued to employ such language in reference to the Sikh community. And he stoutly defended his Indian associate, Kanshi Ram, formerly a high-caste Brahmin, when the latter, with all the zeal of a recent convert, deeply offended the South Asian community with his vigorous denunciations of India's 'heathen' religions.[54]

When the Reverend C.F. Andrews came to Canada in 1929, Macrae opposed the proposal that he should visit Vancouver despite the fact that South Asians there were eager to invite him. Andrews, an Englishman and Anglican missionary, was the best-known western exponent of the national and spiritual views of Mohandas K. Gandhi, India's revered pacifist advocate of independence from Britain. A.E. Armstrong, who had become head of the United Church's Board of Foreign Missions and who was much more in touch than Macrae with the new, conciliatory approach to nationalist movements and non-Christian religions in international missionary activity, had commended Andrews' visit to the elderly missionary. He also urged him to welcome Rabindrinath Tagore, who, like Andrews, was travelling in Canada, and in so doing 'to delight the hearts of the Indians in British Columbia.'[55] Macrae did not indicate in subsequent correspondence whether he had met Tagore, but following Andrews' visit he complained that the Englishman had befriended the very men who had led the harassment of Kanshi Ram.[56]

Foreign missions bureaucrats like Armstrong were prepared to make diplomatic gestures towards the South Asian immigrant community as appropriate opportunities arose, particularly with an eye to the impact of such gesture in India. But neither they nor home missions officials were prepared to invest scarce resources in that small community, especially in the face of so many more pressing demands. South Asian mission work in the 1930s, therefore, was characterized by a series of expedients designed to keep the mission alive at minimum cost.

In 1934, with financing cobbled together from several sources, the recently retired India missionaries James S. MacKay and Jean Sinclair MacKay became involved in the work. Mrs MacKay, it was thought, would be able to interest the United Church Woman's Missionary Society in the work. And now that the community contained a few more women – an estimated seventy-five to eighty in 1929 as a result of the admission of some immigrants' wives during the 1920s – there appeared to be an opportunity for new forms of outreach. But neither the MacKays' own ministry nor their proposal to bring a converted Sikh from India to work among the South Asians found favour with Macrae, who was fiercely loyal to Kanshi Ram despite his generally acknowledged ineffectiveness. At the beginning of 1937, therefore, the MacKays opted to withdraw from the work.[57] Meanwhile, in 1933, the Reverend Simon Fraser, like Macrae an elderly veteran of missionary service in Trinidad, had begun working among South Asians in Victoria. But in 1937 both he and Macrae died.[58]

The death of Macrae was a particularly severe blow to the work. However out of fashion and unrealistic his evangelistic zeal had become, his devotion to the immigrants and their practical needs had been unquestionable. He had travelled for years throughout British Columbia to visit small groups of South Asians and by his very presence had kept open lines of communication between the United Church and the South Asian community.[59]

Despite these setbacks, and despite the fact that he was also responsible for the United Church's work with the much larger Chinese and Japanese communities in British Columbia, S.S. Osterhout was not yet ready to give up on the South Asian community. He appealed to national church headquarters to find another India missionary and/or a college-educated Indian to work among them. Even more audaciously, he asked for funds for a chapel, a missionary's residence, and a kindergarten building. The WMS, he reported, had offered to supply at least a part-time kindergarten teacher to work among the young children who were starting to become a noticeable element within the community.[60]

But not only were church officials in Toronto unwilling to invest further resources in the South Asian work, they were prepared to abandon it. Guided by the (mistaken) assumption that the mission opened by Canadian Anglicans in the Punjab in 1912 involved work among the Sikhs, George Dorey, the United Church's associate home missions secretary, suggested to Osterhout that local Anglican officials be approached about taking over the mission. Nothing came of that suggestion or of a subsequent one, originating with the Victoria Presbytery, ·that an effort be made to have Canadian Baptists take responsibility for the British Columbia work. The Vancouver Presbytery issued one last call for a retired India missionary to take up the work. Then it too gave up. In April 1940 BHM officials accepted its recommendation that work among the South Asians be discontinued 'as a national mission' and left to local volunteer effort.[61]

The thirty-three years of Presbyterian and United Church involvement with the South Asian immigrant community in British Columbia constitute a small and somewhat inglorious chapter in Canadian Protestantism's history of missionary activism. A few concerned missionaries, of whom A.P. Ledingham was the most outstanding, had been moved by humanitarianism as well as evangelistic and strategic considerations to work on behalf of the immigrants. But the interventions of foreign missions officials appear to have been inspired chiefly by pragmatism;

hence their sporadic quality. For their part, home missions leaders had seldom developed much enthusiasm for work among the South Asians. Admittedly, both sets of officials had faced the problem of trying to cope with increased responsibilities in an era of scarce resources. Still, as one educated spokesman for the South Asians had shrewdly observed in April 1914 in asking the Presbyterian Church to provide his community with a missionary, there was something deeply ironic in the fact that the church could find the resources to send many missionaries to Indians in India but almost nothing for work among those who had come to live within Canada.[62] Moreover, once one moved beyond the small circle of missionaries and missions bureaucrats, there were prominent and respected clergy (during the Presbyterian era, at least) whose preferred strategy for dealing with would-be immigrants from India was simply to exclude them from Canada's shores.

Nevertheless, during a period when much of the rest of 'Christian Canada' had reacted to the newcomers with hostility or indifference, the two churches, through their missionary representatives, had provided at least some sort of testament to a socially relevant Christianity. Prompted by a desire to protect their overseas missionary enterprise and the interests of the Raj as well as by a concern to Christianize and Canadianize 'the foreigner,' they had reached out to a group of men who, despite their nominal status as British subjects, had arguably been subjected to greater humiliation and deprivation than any other immigrant group.

In the face of the hostility they encountered in Canada, the South Asians did not adopt the role of 'passive Orientals.' Nor did they abandon their religious and national identity. Instead, they closed ranks and they learned to do what many another missionized group inside and outside Canada had long since learned to do: gain strength from the services and friendships provided by Christian missionaries without necessarily yielding to their ultimate religious and cultural goals. By the time the United Church ran out of workers – and zeal – to assist them at the end of the 1930s, the South Asians had been in Canada for more than a generation. During that interval they had developed the leadership and resources to meet their own social service needs.[63]

NOTES

This is a slightly amended version of a paper presented to the Canadian Historical Association's annual meeting held in Victoria in 1990. Financial assistance in the preparation of that paper was provided by a Social Sciences and Humanities Research Council of Canada Postdoctoral Fellowship. Katherine Ridout commented helpfully on an early draft of the paper.

1 'Far West' [author], 'A B.C. View of the Sikh,' *Saturday Night*, 9 March 1912, 2.
2 W. Peter Ward, 'The Oriental Immigrant and Canada's Protestant Clergy, 1858–1925,' *BC Studies*, 22 (Summer 1974), 40–55.
3 W. Peter Ward, *White Canada Forever: Popular Attitudes and Public Policy towards Oriental in British Columbia* (Montreal: McGill-Queen's University Press 1978), 171. 'East Indian' was the most commonly used designation for immigrants from South Asia.
4 Norman Buchignani and Doreen M. Indra with Ram Srivastiva, *Continuous Journey: A Social History of South Asians in Canada* (Toronto: McClelland and Stewart 1985), chapter 1. See also Hira Singh, 'The Political Economy of Immigrant Farm Labour: A Study of East Indian Farm Workers in British Columbia,' in Milton Israel, ed., *The South Asian Diaspora in Canada: Six Essays* (Toronto: Multicultural History Society of Ontario 1987), 94, 97–9.
5 Buchignani and Indra, *Journey*, 8, 18, 23–4, 53–8. For a book-length account of the *Komagata Maru* affair, see Hugh Johnston, *The Voyage of the Komagata Maru: The Sikh Challenge to Canada's Colour Bar*, 2d ed. (Vancouver: University of British Columbia Press 1989).
6 During the early twentieth century the terms 'Hindoo' and 'Hindu' were frequently used to refer to any immigrant from India, though, as indicated, few South Asians who were Hindu by religious and cultural identity came to Canada in this period. Many immigrants had been finding jobs in sawmills, railway construction, and land clearance; see Buchignani and Indra, *Journey*, chapter 2, and note 7 below.
7 United Church / Victoria University Archives, Toronto (hereinafter UCA), Presbyterian Church in Canada, Foreign Missions Committee, Western Section, Central India Mission, General Correspondence (hereafter India Correspondence), box 7, file 95, Nugent to A.E. Armstrong, 19 and 20 June 1907.
8 UCA, Presbyterian Church in Canada, Board of Foreign Missions, Mission to East Indians in British Columbia (hereinafter Mission to East Indians), 'Report Re Hindoos at Vancouver,' 1907. In 1907, Britain's rule in India, its proudest colonial possession, was still largely undisturbed by the popular nationalist challenges that would develop in the wake of the First World War and the return from South Africa of Mohandas K. Gandhi. But the Indian National Congress was already pointing to the restrictions on Indian workers in South Africa, which Gandhi was effectively publicizing, as an instance

of Britain's failure to protect expatriate Indians in its white-run dominions. A
ban on Indian immigration to Canada would therefore add fuel to Congress
grievances.

9 India Correspondence, box 7, file 97, Nugent to Armstrong, 25 March 1908.
The report by King to which Nugent referred was evidently an informal prelude to King's two official reports to the federal government in 1908 on the
subject of Asian immigration.
10 Mission to East Indians, file 1, W.A. Wilson to Armstrong, 11 May 1907.
11 Ibid., Wright to Armstrong, 13 November 1907; and file 2, Wright to Armstrong, 12 February 1908.
12 'The Church's Budget,' *The Presbyterian Record*, 39 (January 1914), 19. The
practice of assigning responsibility for mission work among non-European
immigrants and native peoples to foreign missions officials also prevailed for
many years within the Methodist Church. Even after 1912, the BFM retained
responsibility for work among the Chinese in Canada.
13 Mission to East Indians, file 2, extract from record of seventeenth synod of
British Columbia.
14 Ibid., file 3, draft letter to the Hon. R. Rogers, minister of the interior,
23 December 1911, from Prof. Taja Singh, L.W. Hall, et al.; and letter to
R.P. MacKay from Egerton Shore, 23 December 1911, endorsing the letter to
Rogers.
15 UCA, Presbyterian Church in Canada, Foreign Mission Board, General
Correspondence (hereinafter General Correspondence), box 3, file 50, 27 May
1909, MacKay to King.
16 Ibid., box 4, file 60, Canadian Mission Boards to Rogers, 26 December 1911.
Regarding Sikhs in British military service, see Buchignani and Indra,
Journey, 7, 11.
17 General Correspondence, box 4, file 60, A.E. Armstrong to Rob Monro,
27 February 1912.
18 India Correspondence, box 10, file 113, MacKay to McPhedran, 1 April 1912.
19 The increasing pessimism expressed by MacKay and other Canadians about
the potential of Indians to become good citizens of Canada was probably
reinforced by negative assessments of their capacity for full citizenship in
their own country. See, for instance, Canada Club of Vancouver, *Addresses*,
for several speeches on this topic between 1908 and 1913.
20 General Correspondence, box 5, file 71, R.P. MacKay to *Daily Star*, 19 March
1913.
21 Isabella Ross Broad, *An Appeal for Fair Play for the Sikhs in Canada* (Victoria:
Victoria Society of Friends of the Hindu 1913); India Correspondence, box 12,
file 143, MacKay to W. Leslie Clay, 4 October 1915.

22 *The Acts and Proceedings of the Forty-First General Assembly of the Presbyterian Church in Canada* (hereafter *Acts*, with year of assembly), 1915, appendix, 52; Mission to East Indians, file 7, K.J. Grant, 'Hindus in Canada,' 15 August 1917. Macrae's involvement with South Asian immigrants went back to 1906, when, as a minister in Golden, British Columbia, he had begun doing volunteer work among some 150 sawmill workers; see S.S. Osterhout, *Orientals in Canada: The Story of the Work of the United Church of Canada with Asiatics in Canada* (Toronto: United Church of Canada 1929), 195.

23 For example, India Correspondence, box 11, file 131, J. Fraser Campbell to R.P. MacKay, 23 October 1914.

24 Ibid., file 130, Armstrong to F.J. Anderson, 28 September 1914; also R.P. MacKay to J. Fraser Campbell, 12 September 1914.

25 'Oriental Immigration,' *Presbyterian Record* 39 (May 1914), 193.

26 India Correspondence, box 11, file 130, R.P. MacKay to J. Fraser Campbell, 12 September 1914. The kind of 'gentlemen's agreement' the BFM secretaries had in mind was one similar to the arrangement made with Japan in 1908. By the terms of that agreement Japan had agreed voluntarily to restrict the number of Japanese emigrating to Canada annually in order to maintain access to Canadian markets; see Patricia Roy et al., *Mutual Hostages: Canadians and Japanese during the Second World War* (Toronto: University of Toronto Press 1990), 11.

27 Mission to East Indians, R.P. MacKay to J.F. Steele, 9 March 1914; see also E. Stanley Jones, *The Christ of the Indian Road* (Toronto: McClelland and Stewart 1926), 125.

28 Buchignani and Indra, *Journey*, 59–61; India Correspondence, box 12, file 137, W.A. Wilson to R.P. MacKay, 29 April 1915, and file 139, F.J. Anderson to MacKay, 11 June 1915.

29 India Correspondence, box 13, file 154, Armstrong to Falconer, 28 September 1916. As the son of a former Trinidad missionary and an Empire enthusiast himself, Falconer may well have shared Armstrong's concern, but since Tagore at the time was unwilling to visit Canada the suggestion bore no fruit.

30 Mission to East Indians, file 5, R.P. MacKay to Arthur Hawkes, 23 April 1915; see also file 4, Armstrong to S. Singh, 22 January 1914. The Canadians associated with Sundar Singh included a group of Toronto Quakers and members of an organization called the 'Canadian Hindu Imperial Committee.'

31 Ibid., file 5, Armstrong to Principal MacKay, 16 April 1915, and R.P. MacKay to W.L. Macrae, 4 May 1915. See Johnston, *Komagata Maru*, 13, for a reference to suspicions about Sundar Singh's motives even within the immigrant community.

32 *Acts,* 1917, Minutes, 57, 95; Mission to East Indians, R.P. MacKay to A.P. Ledingham, 10 August 1916.
33 Mission to East Indians, file 6, K.J. Grant to R.P. MacKay, 1 June 1916, and A.P. Ledingham to Armstrong, 7 March 1916; J.S. Henderson, 'Orientals in B.C.,' *Presbyterian Record,* 41 (June 1916), 247.
34 India Correspondence, box 13, file 152, Ledingham to MacKay, 28 July 1916.
35 Ibid., box 14, file 159, Ledingham to MacKay, 3 February 1917.
36 Ibid., 2 February 1917.
37 Ibid., 3 February 1917; box 14, file 166, Armstrong to A.P. Ledingham, 7 September 1917.
38 Ibid., file 159, Ledingham to R.P. MacKay, 3 February 1917, and file 171, Ledingham to Armstrong, undated.
39 Ibid., file 159, Ledingham to MacKay, 3 February 1917.
40 Ibid., file 173, Ledingham to MacKay, 9 April 1918. For a variant on Ledingham's view that priority in missionary work should probably be given to teaching Canadians the true spirit of the Christian gospel rather than trying to convert East Indians, see Kenneth James Grant, *My Missionary Memories* (Halifax: Imperial Publishing 1923), 189.
41 India Correspondence, box 14, file 173, MacKay to A.P. Ledingham, 9 May 1918.
42 See, for example, box 15, file 190, W.A. Wilson to R.P. MacKay, 19 September 1919. Wilson had retired from his work in India only because of his wife's ill health.
43 *Presbyterian Witness,* 1 March 1923, 8.
44 Mission to East Indians, file 8, MacKay to Macrae, 17 December 1923.
45 Buchignani and Indra, *Journey,* 80–1; *Canadian Annual Review,* 1923, 46–7, 136; 'The Imperial Conference,' *Queen's Quarterly* 31 (November 1923), 215. Because South Asians in British Columbia were kept off the provincial voting list, they were also unable to vote federally. V.S. Srinivasta Sastri, a moderate Indian nationalist who visited Canada in 1922, had urged King to enfranchise Canada's South Asian residents, reminding him that they were fellow subjects of the British Empire. But both in his letter of response to Sastri and at the Imperial Conference in 1923 King attempted to downplay the problem, declaring that in eight of the nine Canadian provinces South Asians did have the federal franchise. Commenting on this characteristically evasive tactic, the author of the *Queen's Quarterly* report observed, 'Every person sufficiently interested to realize the existence of a problem knows that conditions in the ninth province are alone of practical concern.'
46 'Church Life and Work,' *Presbyterian Witness,* 11 September 1924.
47 Regarding these societies, see Ruth Compton Brouwer, *New Women for God:*

Canadian Presbyterian Women and India Missions, 1876–1914 (Toronto: University of Toronto Press 1990), chapter 2.

48 Judith M. Brown, *Modern India: The Origins of an Asian Democracy* (Delhi: Oxford University Press 1985), 223–6; Ruth Compton Brouwer, 'Canada, India and the Missionary Link: Canadian Presbyterian Missionary Responses to the Growth of Indian Nationalism,' paper presented to a symposium on 'The Presbyterian contribution to Canadian life and culture,' part 2, held at Toronto on 17 May 1989, 20–1.

49 Many Presbyterians who opposed their denomination's participation in church union discussions withheld donations to missions at this period: John S. Moir, *Enduring Witness: A History of the Presbyterian Church in Canada*, new ed. (n.p. 1987), 229.

50 The United Church of Canada resulted from a union of Methodists, Congregationalists, and Presbyterians. It became the largest Protestant denomination in the country despite the fact that approximately one-third of Presbyterians declined to become a part of it; N. Keith Clifford, *The Resistance to Church Union in Canada* (Vancouver: University of British Columbia Press 1985).

51 *United Church Record* 1 (January 1926), 21.

52 Osterhout, *Orientals in Canada*, 9, 4.

53 Ibid.

54 Ibid., 193, 200; UCA, United Church of Canada (UCC), BFM, Central India Correspondence, box 2, file 62, copy of article by Kanshi Ram, accompanying Macrae's 'Report of East Indian Work for 1928.'

55 Ibid., Macrae to Armstrong, 26 February 1929; Armstrong to Macrae, 5 March 1929.

56 Ibid., Macrae to Armstrong, 26 June 1929.

57 Osterhout, *Orientals in Canada*, 192; UCA, UCC, BFM, General Correspondence, box 8, file 159, S.A. Fraser to Osterhout, 20 March 1930, and J.S. MacKay to Dr Arnup, 4 August 1934; box 10, file 198, J.S. MacKay to Armstrong, 18 January 1937.

58 UCA, UCC, BHM, General Files, series II, section I (hereinafter General Files), box 12, file 304, Osterhout to George Dorey, 31 August 1937.

59 Osterhout, *Orientals in Canada*, 196; UCA biographical file for Macrae. An obituary in the *New Outlook* (24 December 1937) noted that the eighty-three-year-old Macrae had been visiting the home of East Indians in New Westminster on the day of his death.

60 General Files, box 12, file 304, Osterhout to George Dorey, 31 August, 1937.

61 Ibid., Osterhout to Dorey, 11 December 1937; UCC, BHM, Minutes, Series I, 29 and 31 March 1939, 3–5 April 1940, 966, 997, 1109, 1136.

62 Mission to East Indians, K.S. Akali to 'Dear Sir,' 1 April 1914.
63 Buchignani and Indra, *Journey*, chapters 5 and 6. ·

State Repression of Labour and the Left in Canada, 1914–1920: The Impact of the First World War

GREGORY S. KEALEY

For the Canadian working class, as for workers the world over, the experience of the First World War proved momentous. Not surprisingly, the Canadian bourgeoisie also learned important lessons from the process of organizing for war, not least of which was the potential power of the state apparatus to respond to serious threats from within as well as from without its borders. The Canadian labour revolt of 1917–20, which joined the international proletarian upsurge of those years, represented the first significant nationwide working-class challenge to bourgeois rule.[1] It met with a stern response, which established the parameters for state repression in the interwar years and set the pattern as well for the return to war in 1939. The Canadian state found itself unprepared initially to deal with labour radicalism in the late years of the First World War, but the solutions it devised, building on the mechanisms of repression developed for other purposes early in the war and on the similar experience of other Allied countries, proved successful and durable. When similar crises arose later during the Great Depression and the Second World War, the state would turn again to measures initiated in the years 1914–20 and to the institutions, such as the Royal Canadian Mounted Police, founded in the aftermath of the war.

The Canadian state faced twin crises in those years. First came the obvious necessity of orchestrating the grim organization of the nation for war. Far less appreciated was the second challenge of these years: the defence of the country's capitalist system against the connected threats of labour militancy and socialism.[2] This conception of twin crises explains the actions of the Borden government in these years far better than the more conventional historical accounts, which have focused

TABLE 1 Strike Activity in Canada, 1912–21

Year	Number of Strikes	Number of Strikes with Complete Data	Number of Workers Involved (000s)	Days Lost (000s)
1912	242	190	43	1,136
1913	234	164	41	1,037
1914	99	67	10	491
1915	86	69	11	95
1916	166	131	27	241
1917	218	163	50	1,124
1918	305	239	83	657
1919	427	350	149	3,402
1920	457	335	77	814
1921	208	172	28	1,050

Source: All strike data in this paper are drawn from recalculations of the general Canadian statistical series in Donald Kerr and Deryck W. Holdsworth, eds., *Historical Atlas of Canada*, vol. 3 (Toronto 1990). These recalculations are based on the addition of Maritime provinces' material compiled by Ian McKay of Queen's University and on the careful re-examination of all the 'incomplete' files available in the NA, Department of Labour, Strikes and Lockouts files. This work, commenced by Peter DeLottinville, was completed by Douglas Cruikshank. For the new national strike series see G.S. Kealey and Douglas Cruikshank, 'Strikes in Canada, 1891–1950,' *Labour/Le Travail* 20 (1987): 85–145, and *Historical Atlas*, vol. 3, plate 39.

largely on the exigencies of winning the war and have emphasized the national tensions between Quebec and English Canada over the prosecution of the war. In the process, class tensions have been largely ignored.[3] This paper will emphasize that class conflict, rather than the national question or ethnic tensions, fuelled the Borden government's major wartime policies. The largely immigrant composition of the Canadian working class allowed some government actions to be justified in terms of ethnic chauvinism, but the state's willingness to move against Canadian-born and British immigrant workers with equal vigour suggests that class, not ethnicity, motivated its actions.[4]

This paper will not document in any detail the contours of the labour revolt that have been well described elsewhere. Table 1, however, illustrates its magnitude and emphasizes the decline of prewar labour militancy during the economic downturn that continued through 1915. A return to job actions came in 1916 and increased rapidly thereafter, peaking in 1919 with the Amherst, Toronto, and Winnipeg general strikes and the national wave of sympathy strikes that followed the arrest of the Winnipeg leaders.[5]

For organizational purposes, these years can be divided into three distinct stages – 1914 to 1917, 1917 to mid 1919, and mid 1919 to 1920. Organizing for war characterized the first period; fighting on two fronts – domestic and overseas – the second; and pacification, the third. By tracing five overlapping issues through these three periods, we shall see how closely intertwined were the two crises facing the Borden government. 'Enemy aliens,' censorship, national security, labour policy, and recruitment for the armed forces represented significant problems from the war's outset and constituted the terrain on which this two-front war was fought.

The exigencies of fighting the First World War, especially given its unexpected duration, necessitated a mobilization by the state that was unprecedented in Canadian history. Once conventional political differences had been set aside with the emergence of the Union government in 1917, which effectively marginalized Quebec liberals and labour, the hawks of the Borden government began to listen more carefully to their war-time bureaucrats such as Joseph Flavelle, E.J. Chambers, C.F. Hamilton, and, even for a short period, C.H. Cahan. While this paper cannot deal at any length with the role of such outsiders in Ottawa, they did bring into the burgeoning bureaucracy a set of business and media linkages previously missing. In the process they pioneered a number of repressive innovations, which either remained in place thereafter, such as the Royal Canadian Mounted Police and its security and intelligence apparatus, or remained as ideas to be drawn on again in later emergencies such as internment, censorship, and conscription.[6]

Organizing for War

In May 1914, with war clouds on the horizon, the Borden government gave an early indication of its future directions. Its British Nationality, Naturalization, and Aliens Act radically changed Canadian naturalization practice. Until the passage of this act a sworn affidavit testifying to three years' residence in Canada had sufficed to gain immigrants their naturalization. After its passage, immigrants were required to prove both five years' residence and an adequate knowledge of English or French to a superior court judge. In addition, the secretary of state received absolute discretionary power to deny naturalization to any individual deemed a threat to the 'public good.'[7] In light of what was to come, this act was but a mild initiative.

Among the first actions of the Borden government after the declaration of war, the War Measures Act gave the executive almost unlimited powers: 'The Governor in Council shall have power to do and authorize such acts and things, and to make from time to time such orders and regulations, as he may by reason of the existence of real or apprehended war, invasion or insurrection deem necessary for the security, defence, peace, order, and welfare of Canada.' Unprecedented in the annals of parliamentary government, the act went even further and specified, inter alia: 'a) censorship and the control and suppression of publications, writings, maps, plans, photographs, communications and means of communication, b) arrest, detention, exclusion, and deportation.' Thus, the Borden government assured itself the maximum power possible to pursue the course of the war. Significantly, the legislation also possessed neither time limit nor independent mechanism for termination. While technically to apply only during war, invasion, or insurrection (real or apprehended), the executive's prerogative to end the act itself gave it a truly extraordinary mandate.[8] Thus, as Arthur Lower argued in *Colony to Nation*, Canada replaced parliamentary government during the First World War with order-in-council government.[9]

The government wasted little time in exercising this remarkable power. Even before the War Measures Act's passage through parliament, it had issued an order in council to regulate the flow of 'enemy aliens' (its phrase for citizens of enemy countries resident in Canada during the war) out of the country. It simultaneously assured these 'foreign aliens' that their property and businesses were indeed safe, and then the very next day by order in council demanded that they surrender all fire arms and explosives.[10]

In late October the government took a far more dramatic step, demanding that all 'enemy aliens' appear for registration and examination. Special registrars were appointed in major centres, while elsewhere police authorities were empowered; all this came under the mandate of Sir Percy Sherwood, the chief commissioner of the Dominion Police. On registration and examination, 'foreign aliens' regarded as nonthreatening were either allowed to leave Canada or to remain free under condition that they report monthly to the registrar; those considered dangerous were interned as prisoners of war. Their compatriots who either failed to register or who refused the examination soon joined them.[11] To supervise the anticipated flood of internees, the government appointed retired Canadian general Sir William Otter as director of internment operations. In an initial wave of enthusiasm, some 6000 aliens found themselves interned, most of whom were Ukrainians, not

Germans. The fact that most Canadian Ukrainians passionately hated the Austro-Hungarian Empire made no difference. While most of these internees were released in 1916 when the Canadian economy recovered and a general labour shortage developed, the entire experience understandably embittered Canadian Ukrainians.[12]

Most mainstream Canadian historical writing about the First World War internment has diverged dramatically from the discussion of the similar Japanese experience in the Second World War, which has been almost universally deplored. In the case of the Ukrainians, historians' conventional wisdom has argued that the massive initial internment of late 1914 and 1915 represented charity to indigent, unemployed foreigners.[13] Indeed, Brown and Cook argue in *A Nation Transformed* that the Borden government actually aimed 'to safeguard the rights of aliens' against nativist hostility. In a final rationalization, they conclude 'that the government's actions held in check the unrestrained enthusiasm of native Canadians to persecute their fellow citizens.'[14] Internment seems a peculiar method of protection. Not surprisingly, younger Ukrainian-Canadian historians have not shared this sympathetic view of the Borden government.[15] Furthermore, as we shall see, the internment process had explicit political uses that had little to do with the First World War or nativism.

The second major problem facing the Canadian government at war involved censorship. Initially censorship was divided between the military, with responsibility for cables, and the press and the post office, with authority over the mails. Canada's deputy chief censor, Lieutenant-Colonel C.F. Hamilton, handled both cables and the press until June 1915, when the government created the office of chief press censor to which it appointed Major Ernest J. Chambers in July.[16] Since Chambers's office reported to the secretary of state, it created a confusing departmental censorship triumvirate.

Press censorship, while handled by Hamilton, remained ineffectual. The appointment of Chambers, however, changed that. In his first years of operation Chambers depended largely on personal contact to establish his authority and to exercise as much influence as possible on foreign-language editors, to whom he devoted most of his attention. His lack of power to order a paper's closure largely dictated this style of operation. Only his minister, the secretary of state, possessed the power of closure and, much to Chambers's chagrin, the minister was reluctant to use this power. On frequent occasions, Chambers expressed dissatisfaction with the cabinet's caution and indicated clearly that, if allowed, he would have shut down the entire foreign-language press. In the one area where the censor's hands were not tied, bans were invoked vigorously and, by 17 August 1918, some 184 non-Canadian, almost all American, publications had been proscribed. The list included sixty-five books or pamphlets and 119 serials. Of the serials, forty-nine were in the English language, while seventy were not. Only three Canadian publications had met the censor's veto – an obscure book published in Toronto, *The Parasite*; and English-language paper, *The Week*, from Victoria, BC; and Toronto's *Zemla i Wola*, a Ukrainian paper edited by Ivan Stefanitsky.[17] The ever-increasing pace of Chambers's censorship can also be traced. In 1914 only two items were banned. This increased in 1915 to sixteen, but then leaped ahead under Chambers to fifty-two in 1916, fifty-eight in 1917, and fifty-nine in the first eight months of 1918.[18] This increase, however, derived as much from changing definitions of objectionable matter as from Chambers's growing zeal. The original orders in council of 1914 primarily restricted materials directly harmful to the war effort. The Consolidated Orders Respecting Censorship of 1917 both specified examples of materials harmful to the war effort and extended the ban to include hostility to conscription. Finally, in May 1918 the rules were yet again extended to cover the government's conduct of the war and, more pointedly, to include anything that might spread discontent or weaken the people's unanimity behind the war effort.[19] As we shall see later, even this Draconian measure proved inadequate for the government's purpose.

Translation represented a major, albeit often amusing, difficulty that the chief press censor encountered in his zealous pursuit of the foreign-language press. While the historian of the Finnish press assumes that this problem was unique to his community's newspapers, the difficulty actually cropped up frequently. For example, Frederick Livesay, the press censor for Western Canada, resorted to using Pavlo Krat as his Ukrainian translator while Krat not only belonged to the Ukrainian Social Democratic party but also still edited *Robotchyi Narod*.[20]

In the related field of national security almost as much confusion prevailed. While the Dominion Police had traditionally held responsibility in this area, their efforts had been amateurish and extremely limited at best. In effect, they lacked adequate resources and personnel to fulfill their mandate, especially as their duties multiplied in wartime conditions. The Dominion Police had traditionally functioned through cooperation with the existing municipal and provincial police forces and, when necessary, by hiring private detectives from standard United

States agencies such as Pinkerton and Thiel. This latter method proved blatantly inappropriate under war conditions, although that did not prevent its continued use. The Royal North-West Mounted Police received their initial security work in 1914 simply as the provincial police force of Alberta and Saskatchewan, working under Dominion Police supervision. In addition to the Dominion Police under the minister of justice, the minister of militia and defence had a military intelligence apparatus, which grew rapidly during the war, and the Immigration Department had developed a security operation, especially in British Columbia. Meanwhile, information from British and empire intelligence agencies was supplied through the offices of the governor general. Thus, Canadian security depended on extremely decentralized operations that were collectively held responsible for the gathering of domestic intelligence through the early years of the war.[21]

The government basically had no general labour policy in the early years of the war. Owing to the deep depression Canada had entered in 1913, the economy remained stalled for 1914 and much of 1915. Rampant unemployment both helped military enlistment and, as we have seen, provided a rationale for extensive internment. With economic recovery, however, new problems quickly manifested themselves. Built initially on the munitions industry, the boom started in central Canada but soon spread to the whole country. The flooded labour markets of 1914 suddenly dried up and the country faced a significant shortage of workers. In this new context, 'foreign aliens' found themselves freed from internment.[22] More important in the long run than the labour shortage, however, the Borden government failed in two significant areas to supervise the war economy. Its sole focus on financing and supplying the war effort let to run-away inflation, which it did almost nothing to check.[23] In addition, it refused to bring munitions production under its own fair-wages policy.[24] The combination of rampant inflation, ineffectual and apparently insincere labour policy, and the growing perception of massive corruption and war profiteering would all return to haunt the government in the war's next phase.

As table 1 demonstrates, labour remained relatively passive in the early years of the war. With the economic upturn of 1916, this quiescence began to change dramatically and to challenge seriously the Borden government's inactivity in the realm of labour policy.

In the early months of the war recruitment for the armed forces posed few problems. With the economy in a serious recession and with extremely high unemployment rates, many workers, especially British immigrants, joined the army in an initial wave of war enthusiasm.[25] Nevertheless, as early as the summer of 1915, even before the economy had fully recovered, recruiters began to complain bitterly of difficulties in attracting adequate numbers of soldiers. By 1916, as the war wore on relentlessly and the horrible costs of trench warfare became ever more apparent, the government faced mounting difficulties in attempting to meet its manpower commitments to the British imperial forces. Under heavy pressure from various bourgeois patriotic groups, the Borden government in August 1916 passed an order in council creating a National Service Board (NSB) and appointing a director-general of National Service. In October the new NSB announced its intention to take a national inventory of manpower, which it initially proposed as a compulsory registration program. The Borden government, sensitive to working-class opposition in this realm, instead mandated a voluntary scheme, to be carried out by means of a postal survey. In the face of considerable labour criticism of even this voluntary scheme, Borden issued assurances that the national service schemes 'are not connected with Conscription. Rather the idea was to make an appeal for voluntary National Service which would render unnecessary any resort to compulsion.'[26] The Trades and Labour Council (TLC) leadership accepted these vague assurances and recommended compliance to their members. This apparent surrender of the labour movement's purely voluntarist stance led to renewed opposition to the TLC leaders, especially in Quebec and the west, but also in Ontario. The leaders' abandonment of their renewed anti-conscription mandate, which they had sought and received in August 1916, brought to the fore the deepening split in the labour movement about the progress of the war.[27]

A War on Two Fronts

In the years 1917 to 1919, the war came home with a vengeance. War at home certainly did not await the return of the Canadian troops after the November 1918 armistice.[28] Indeed, their return simply added waves to an already turbulent sea of unrest that swept across the country in the wake of the Bolshevik Revolution and the fall 1917 election of a new Union government, which united proconscription Liberals with the Tories in a prowar coalition government. Without doubt the Bolshevik Revolution and the subsequent tide of revolts across Europe stimulated Canadian socialists. Equally it aroused the fears of the Canadian government and set off a Canadian Red Scare of significant proportions.[29]

Internment, which had been used less and less in 1915 and 1916, made an instant recovery. Now the 'enemy' was not only German but also Bolshevik. Although there had been some harassment of socialist and pacifist opponents of the war in its early years, these efforts grew massively in 1918. 'Foreign aliens' charged with anything related to radical politics – possession of prohibited literature, attendance at illegal meetings, membership in an illegal group – found themselves whisked away to internment camps.[30] Indeed, in February 1919, months after the war's end, the government had extended the camps' potential considerably by allowing any county or district court judge on summary complaint from a municipal authority or any reasonable citizen to intern on grounds no greater than 'a feeling of public apprehension entertained by the community.'[31] The 'foreign alien' need not be present at the hearing and was explicitly denied the right to legal counsel. This proved quite convenient in dealing with radicals. Some thirty-three 'aliens,' for example, were interned at Kapuskasing in the aftermath of the Winnipeg General Strike.[32] Any expectation that the Armistice would bring a quick end to the camps proved sadly mistaken. The camps remained open until February 1920, fifteen months after the armistice, and the Internment Operations Office formally closed only in June 1920.[33]

When finally closed, the camps had imprisoned 8579 men, 81 women, and 156 children. The men included 2009 Germans, 5954 'Austrians' (Ukrainians), 205 Turks, 99 Bulgarians, and 312 'miscellaneous.' Of these, by Otter's own estimate, no more than 3179 could be considered even remotely as conventional prisoners of war. Some 80,000 other foreign-born Canadians had passed through the registration and examination procedures without being interned. Robert Coats's 1919 apologia for the operation as 'conceived throughout in the broad spirit ... of looking forward to the day when the people under restraint shall resume the purpose for which they came in the peaceful upbuilding of the country' provides a sad comment on contemporary Canadian sentiments.[34]

As dramatic as internment, however, was the drastic extension of censorship. We have already noted the growing mandate of the chief press censor, but in September 1918 his earlier wishes finally came true. PC 2381 of 25 September 1918 'respecting enemy publications' quite simply banned all 'publications' in an 'enemy language.' Notable here was the inclusion of Finnish and Russian on the 'enemy' list.[35] Contravention of this order ('prints, publishes, delivers, receives, or has in his possession') brought a fine of up to $5000 or imprisonment of up to five years, or both. Thus, at one fell swoop, Chambers's job became much simpler. In the spirit of the times he too became quite active and in the latter half of 1918 and 1919 explicitly moved against a number of Canadian publications not necessarily covered by the above, including *Canadian Forward* (Toronto, Social Democratic party,) *Western Clarion* (Vancouver, Socialist Party of Canada), the *Marxian Socialist* (Toronto, Socialist Party of North America), and *Die Volkstimme* (Winnipeg, Yiddish).[36] While these papers maintained the honour of a specific ban, all publications of the organizations banned under PC 2384 were also prohibited.

The debate that followed PC 2381 and its subsequent amendments made painfully clear that the intended target was socialism and had little to do with the war. While a case could perhaps be made for the inclusion of Russia and Ukraine given the intervention of Canadian troops in the Civil War in the Soviet Union on the side of the whites, this position was never even argued. Indeed, Canadian embarrassment about military involvement in the Soviet Union mounted quickly.[37] The Canadian intervention in Siberia met with considerable opposition from Canadian workers.[38]

Thus in a series of amendments, which commenced even before the Armistice, the 'enemy' language press was permitted to publish under strict guidelines. Initially this involved the parallel publication of an English translation of all stories for specific papers licensed by the chief press censor to reappear. In April 1919 restrictions were lifted against all but German, Turkish, Bulgarian, and Hungarian papers and, finally, in December 1919, they too became legal.[39]

All Finnish and Ukrainian papers, radical or not, were banned by PC 2381. For the Yiddish press there was no uniform ban, but Winnipeg's *Volkstimme* came under specific ban on 5 July 1919, in the aftermath of the Winnipeg General Strike.[40] Needless to say, the paper had enthusiastically supported the strikers. Its editor, Moses Almazov, belonged to the Social Democratic party and wrote regularly for New York's *Jewish Daily Forward* as its western Canadian correspondent. Charged with other strike leaders on 21 June 1919, he faced deportation hearings but was eventually freed.[41]

The Finnish experience involved the suppression not only of the socialist *Vapaus* but also of the right-wing paper *Canadan Uutiset*. In the latter prohibition there was considerable poetic justice, since its editor, J.A. Mustonen, had played a major part in promoting the banning of *Vapaus*.[42] Mustonen had a cozy relationship with chief press censor Chambers and, from his paper's inception he had issued reassurances that it would publish 'in a thorough Canadian spirit.'[43] So helpful was

Mustonen that he supplied Chambers with one of his Finnish translators, Herman W. Niinimäki, as well as providing evidence in support of
the suppression of the radical Finnish-American press.[44] Mustonen's
activities proved doubly ironic because not only was his paper banned
in October 1918, but also his earlier actions in eliminating the Finnish-
American socialist papers had led the Finnish Socialist Organization of
Canada (FSOC) to perceive far more urgently the need to replace *Työkansa*, the socialist paper that had failed in the summer of 1915, with a
new Canadian socialist paper.

Canadan Uutiset, however, successfully played on its loyal image to
become one of the first 'enemy-language' papers to reappear under the
modified orders in council. This involved gaining the special permission
of the censor and publishing all articles in parallel translation. *Canadan
Uutiset* reappeared in December 1918 and published in bilingual format
until the ban was lifted in April 1919. In a self-congratulatory note on
the reappearance of the paper, the editors noted that 'we fought like des-
peradoes for our rights, and in the end of two months untiring struggle
we won'; further, this victory represented 'a public admittance on the
part of the Government of Canada that *Canadan Uutiset* is indispensable
educational material for Finns in Canada.'[45] This exaggerated claim can
be questioned given that permission to publish by special licence of the
censor was granted to some twenty other papers. The condition, in addition to the required English translation, was a basic demonstration of
right-wing politics in line with the Borden government's world view.

Vapaus, the paper of the FSOC, enjoyed no such privilege. Following
the banning of the Finnish-American papers in 1917, the FSOC decided
to publish a new paper. Considerable difficulty ensued, however, owing
to its inability to find a printer willing to produce the paper. When none
could be found in Port Arthur, the FSOC tried Sudbury, only to experience the same problem. Only after some months' negotiations, including
sending a delegation to Ottawa to meet Chambers, was it able to gain
his assent and a guarantee that the printer would not be liable.[46] With
that agreement in place, the paper finally appeared on 6 November
1917.[47]

For the following year the paper attempted to stay clear of the censor,
perceiving that being shut down would be no great achievement.
Despite translator Niinimäki's best efforts, Chambers initially found little to object to, especially since his terms in late 1917 still involved only
the war effort narrowly conceived. This attitude changed, however, in
May 1918 with the extension of censorship to cover spreading internal

unrest in Canada. Nevertheless, *Vapaus* kept publishing until all 'enemy-language' papers fell under the censor's ban.[48] Unlike *Canadan Uutiset*, however, *Vapaus* did not receive a permit to publish before the lifting of the ban in April 1919. This refusal came despite the FSOC's efforts both to legitimate its organization, which had been banned by PC 2384, and to get permission to publish. Negotiations with C.H. Cahan, Borden's director of the Public Safety Branch of the Department of Justice, succeeded in gaining recognition of a new Finnish Organization of Canada (FOC), supposedly nonpolitical.[49] Their attempts, however, to convince Chambers to allow the FOC to publish a bilingual version of *Vapaus* failed totally.[50] After negotiations with the government failed, the FOC organized a national campaign appealing to labour throughout the country to come to its support. In this national appeal, J.W. Ahlqvist, FOC secretary, noted the partisan political nature of the ban:

Amendments made to the Orders-in-Council made it permissible, under certain restrictions, to issue newspapers in a foreign language. The conservative element among the Finns, as well as among some other nationalities, promptly received a permit to issue publications according to the new regulations. The Finnish organizations of labouring people, however – in spite of their efforts to obtain a similar permit ... have so far been denied a similar right.[51]

No doubt *Canadan Uutiset*'s continuous attacks on the Finnish socialists had hurt the quest for a permit, especially, for example, their critique of the new FOC as nothing but the old socialist society under a new name.[52]

The debates within the Ukrainian community took on additional complexity after the Russian Revolution. The clear left-right split, of course, intensified, and the events of the October Revolution and its aftermath increasingly led to the emergence of a left-wing nationalist position that favoured the Ukrainian Central Rada and opposed the Bolsheviks. Again the ideological niceties of such debate mattered little to the Canadian authorities, and all Ukrainian papers were prohibited under PC 2381. This ban shut down both the Ukrainian Social Democratic party's (USDP) *Robotchyi Narod*, which had become increasingly pro-Bolshevik, and *Robitnyche Slovo*, the Toronto paper of Ivan Stefanitsky and latterly of Pavlo Krat. While numerous right-wing Ukrainian papers received permission to publish under censor's permit, the left papers did not. Instead, a series of attempts in Toronto to issue successors to *Robitnyche Slovo* fell under the censor's ban.

In the aftermath of the government prohibitions, the USDP enjoyed a stroke of good fortune. Since it already possessed a cultural organization, the Ukrainian Labor Temple Association, it could easily switch its organizational efforts there and thus avoid the need to create a new organization and to debate its merits with the Ottawa authorities. Just before the ban on publication ceased in April 1919, the ULTA commenced a new paper, *Ukrainski Robitnychi Visti (Ukrainian Labor News)*. Interestingly, this paper received the endorsement of the Winnipeg Trades and Labor Council, suggesting the emerging ties between the left-wing immigrant socialists and the mainstream labour movement. *Ukrainski Robitnychi Visti*, under an editorial triumvirate of Matthew Popovich, Danylo Lobay, and Ivan Navizivsky (John Navis), took a strong pro-Bolshevik line.[53]

By mid 1919, then, the Canadian state had effectively suppressed the entire Canadian foreign-language radical press. Owing to a combination of mounting protest, the six-month hiatus after the Armistice, and some slight civil libertarian sentiment from Liberal elements of the Union Government, especially Newton Rowell and Thomas Crerar, it slowly started to re-emerge. It still existed at the whim of the censor, and he issued warnings to *Vapaus*, for example, on numerous occasions throughout 1919.[54]

More striking than even PC 2381 and its suppression of freedom of the press was the simultaneous PC 2384, which effectively banned freedom of association, assembly, and speech for a select group of Canadians, most of whom were foreign immigrants.[55] The confusing list of named societies and parties, replete with errors, soon had to be amended to add the FSOC and the Socialist Party of North America (SPNA), while deleting the Social Democratic party (SDP).[56] Notable in its absence from either the original or the amended list is the Socialist Party of Canada (SPC), whose leadership would play crucial roles in the labour revolt of 1919. Edward Laine's conclusion that the SDP and the SPC escaped persecution because of their English-Canadian character is one possible explanation, although that characterization applied equally to large elements of the IWW and the Socialist Labour party (SLP) and most certainly to the SPNA, which was largely an organization of British immigrants, and they did not escape the ban. It might equally be argued that a familiarity with the actual ideological line of both the SPC and the SDP might have justified their exclusion. Bolshevism would prove to have limited appeal to a considerable component of the SPC membership and to almost the entire non-European immigrant elements of the

SDP. Yet it must be noted that such fine ideological distinctions were not common among Canadian government officials. Moreover, such niceties ceased to matter in the aftermath of the Winnipeg General Strike when SPC members gained most of the state's repressive attention.

PC 2384, of course, did not simply ban these organizations. It also made it illegal to 'sell, speak, write, or publish anything,' 'to become or continue to be a member,' 'or wear, carry or cause to be displayed ... any badge, insignia, emblem, banner, motto, pennant, card, or any device whatsoever' indicating membership. Illegality, in effect, became retroactive, and in any prosecution 'it shall be presumed in the absence of proof to the contrary' that the defendant was a member if, since the outbreak of the war, the person had 'repeatedly' attended meetings, spoken publicly, or distributed literature. Further clauses outlawed possession of any prohibited literature or attendance at illegal meetings, which initially included any meeting except religious services held 'at which the proceedings or any part thereof are conducted in the language of any country with which Canada is at war or ... the languages of Russia, Ukraine, or Finland.' All such offences were punishable by fines up to $5000 and prison sentences of up to five years.[57]

No systematic study of the resultant repression exists. In the literature there are numerous individual examples of the extraordinary wave of arrests, prosecutions, convictions, and internments that followed.[58] Strikingly at variance with the western radicalism thesis propounded in much of the older Canadian labour history, which located the west as the unique nexus of militancy, most of this repression took place in central Canada under the auspices of the Dominion Police.[59]

While vague in detail, it is clear that these efforts were orchestrated nationally. Ontario Provincial Police superintendent Joseph Rogers, for example, complained in February 1919 that federal efforts commencing in the fall of 1918 had not gone far enough. He wrote: 'The Police of Canada are pretty familiar with the whole situation but it seems impossible to impress the authorities at Ottawa with the seriousness of the situation. The police brought great pressure to bear on the Government at Ottawa and I was one of three representatives who waited on the Minister of Justice last summer [1918], when we told them in no uncertain terms what was coming.'[60] Claiming personal credit, he noted that PC 2381 and 2384 'practically gave us proper law to operate with.' In their aftermath, he described a 6 October 1918 conference held in Dominion Police chief commissioner Percy Sherwood's Ottawa office intended 'to formulate a general line of action.' 'At this meeting, it was decided that a

TABLE 2 Sentences for 'Bolshevik Propaganda' or
Membership in Prohibited Organization

Fines	144
under $10	20
$11–50	29
$51–100	29
$101–500	56
over $500	10
Jail	35
Interned	15
under 1 year	8
1–2 years	10
3–5 years	2
Jail and fine	10
$500 + 1 month	1
$500 + 6 months	2
$500 + 2 years	2
$500 + 3 years	1
$1000 + 3 months	1
$1000 + 3 years	2
$4000 + 5 years	1
Suspended sentence	20
Dismissed	5
Total	214

Source: NA, RG 18, vol. 2380

systematic raid should be made by the police from the Atlantic to the Pacific.' While he approved of the ensuing execution of this plan, he complained bitterly that it had not been carried further for 'the spirit of Bolshevism is strong among the aliens in this country and the Russians and the Finns are the class that requires the most attention.'[61] Such police policy led to numerous arrests. A preliminary analysis of one major list entitled 'Bolshevik Propaganda' includes 214 cases involving 199 men and six women between the fall of 1918 and June 1919.[62] The charges, primarily for possession of prohibited literature, also included eighteen for attending illegal meetings, thirty-one for membership in a prohibited group, four for general breach of orders in council, and one for creating discontent. The sentencing pattern is summarized in table 2, which shows a wide range but demonstrates that many defendants received severe treatment.

The geography of charges is displayed in table 3, which graphically

TABLE 3 Geographic Distribution of Violations of War Orders in Council

	By Province	
	Number	Per Cent
Quebec	3	1.0
Ontario	154	73.0
Manitoba	1	0.5
Saskatchewan	23	11.0
Alberta	13	6.0
British Columbia	15	7.0
Unknown	1	0.5
Total	210*	99

	By City (5 or more only)			
	Number			Number
Toronto, Ont.	27		Cobalt, Ont.	8
Windsor, Ont.	21		Kamsack, Sask.	7
Timmins, Ont.	20		Medicine Hat, Alta.	7
Vancouver, BC	15		Regina, Sask.	7
Sudbury, Ont.	15		Tisdale, Sask.	6
London, Ont.	13		Brantford, Ont.	5
Sault Ste Marie, Ont.	11		Copper Cliff, Ont.	5
Hamilton, Ont.	11			

Source: NA, RG 18, vol. 2380
* Varies from table 2 owing to multiple convictions versus some individuals.

suggests that not all worrisome radicalism stemmed from west of Lake Superior. Indeed, what the geographic distribution suggests is that the Dominion Police with security responsibilities in eastern Canada resorted to these prosecutions with far more enthusiasm than did the Royal North-West Mounted Police operating in the west. For the moment this contrast remains unexplained, although a few months later RNWMP commissioner A.B. Perry made it clear that he preferred implantation to prosecution. One obvious characteristic of this list is its high immigrant composition. Any attempt to attribute nationality based on the police-rendering of Slavic and other unfamiliar European surnames seems pointless, but a list of ten picked at random should demonstrate the obvious: Mike Bokla (Timmins, 23 October 1918); Pantely Ealarvegn (Ford City, nd); Tom Hobin (Sault Ste Marie, 30 October 1918); Mike Kustryn (Timmins, 5 September 1918); Ernest Lindberg

(Vancouver, 11 December 1918); Sofia Maitelinen (Cobalt, 18 December 1918); Ernest Rossiter (Stratford, 19 December 1918); John Stepanitsky (Toronto, 20 November 1918); Fred Trechuba (London, 29 October 1918); and John Sabo (Hamilton, 27 March 1919).[63] A perusal of the entire list makes quite clear the high proportion of Finnish men and women who were prosecuted under these orders in council, as well as the Slavs who figure prominently in this sample.

The origins of PC 2381 and PC 2384 deserve our attention because they originated to some degree out of the Borden government's confusion as unrest increased throughout in the country. The complete variance in reports received from the Dominion Police and from Military Intelligence in early 1918 had led to the commissioning of Montreal lawyer C.H. Cahan to draw up a report on left-wing activities in Canada.[64] Cahan reported to the minister of justice in September confirming the government's worst fears about foreign agitators and Bolshevik agents. As a result, the government moved quickly and passed PC 2381 and 2384. There had been mounting veterans' pressure for foreign-language press censorship even before his report, but nativism was not the major cause here.[65] In addition, Cahan himself accepted a new position as director of the Public Safety Branch of the Department of Justice, with an ambiguous mandate to advise the government on security matters. He held this position only until January 1919 when he resigned, later complaining to Borden at the height of the Winnipeg crisis: 'I tried in vain, after your departure [for the Paris Peace talks], to obtain a hearing from your colleagues; but they restated my representations with such contemptuous indifference, that there was for me no alternative but to retire quietly and await events.'[66]

Cahan's career, no matter how brief, demonstrated the high profile that some government figures now gave to security and intelligence. The Winnipeg General Strike and the wave of sympathy strikes it inspired fully confirmed this position.[67] Moreover, while Cahan may not have been satisfied with the cabinet's response to his efforts, certainly the new security forces were hard at work in the early months of 1919. The Dominion Police's high-profile arrests were accompanied by extensive secret service work with the placing of agents in Sault Ste Marie, Toronto, Windsor, Montreal, Welland, and Hamilton. One Toronto agent was 'in good with the foreign element – he is able to speak several of the foreign languages and only a few days ago was requested to make a speech in the Russian language at one of the meetings.'[68] There was complete cooperation between company spies hired through American detective agencies, especially Thiels, and the various levels of police. In Hamilton, for example, a Thiel detective employed by Stelco provided reports that were passed on from the steel company to Hamilton local police, to Superintendent Joseph Rogers of the Ontario Provincial Police in Toronto, and selectively by him to the acting Dominion Police commissioner, A.J. Cawdron, in Ottawa. In one case, for example, a report by the Thiel detective warning against the pending release from internment of one Kowalashen led to a series of letters from Hamilton to Toronto, and from there to Ottawa, culminating in Cawdron's assurance that he had passed the concerns on to his director of internment, General Otter.[69] The full extent of such corporate spying and of its relationship to 'legitimate' police activities remains an open question. Equally striking was a series of reports on the Montreal police attack on a Social Democratic party meeting on 1 June 1919 and the subsequent harassment of 'enemy aliens' that followed.[70] To some degree at least the overemphasis on the west in the Canadian literature on radicalism has stemmed from recourse to the more readily available Royal North-West Mounted Police files at the National Archives of Canada and the failure to see the total security picture that went far beyond the Mounties' responsibilities in the west.[71]

A complete overview of the total Canadian internal security operation remains an important historical task. From the available RNWMP materials, however, one can construct clearly the birth of the modern Canadian security apparatus in 1919, which would be turned solely over to the Mounted Police under a new act of November 1919. This act gave the force complete jurisdiction in the area of federal law enforcement and national security, and explicitly banned trade-union rights to members of the force. The older Dominion Police force was quietly merged into the larger body.[72] The new Royal Canadian Mounted Police began its national role in February 1920.

Pacification

In the aftermath of the Winnipeg General Strike, there was much talk of the carrots as well as the far more evident sticks of state repression. Most of the conciliatory talk stemmed from the Royal Commission on Industrial Relations that had had the dubious task of holding hearings across Canada during the worst 'industrial relations' crisis in the country's history. The final report, with its enthusiastic endorsement of Whitley Council schemes, was carried forth by Borden's minister of labour, Senator Gideon Robertson, with an initial display of support. These schemes, however, ran into a frigid response from most elements of Canadian capital at the September 1919 National Industrial Conference, which had been intended as 'a domestic peace conference.' For all intents and purposes, significant state participation in such promotion then came to an end. In effect the slow-to-develop state wartime economic role, with its limited concession to the TLC, was being dismantled in general, and the massive victory of Canadian capital in 1919 speeded the process along.[73] After Winnipeg and in the subsequent economic downturn capital would make no concessions and would instead try to retake ground lost in 1917–1919.

Foreign immigrants of a radical leaning would need to live carefully for the next sixteen years because, under the spring 1919 pressures, the government had introduced significant amendments to the Immigration Act that allowed for the automatic deportation of anarchists and any other advocates of revolution. Further, under the direct pressure of the Winnipeg General Strike, the government had further amended the Naturalization Act to allow the revoking of the naturalization of anyone, even of British lineage, who fomented revolution. Amendments to the Criminal Code also made prosecution possible for anyone deemed to be promoting change outside of peaceful, parliamentary channels.[74]

In addition, the conviction and jailing of the Winnipeg strike leaders under basically trumped-up charges made only too clear the state's power. While such charges would not be used again so broadly until the prosecution of the Communist party leadership in 1931, the potential for such legal action remained. Moreover, the state's domestic intelligence ability grew far more sophisticated with the development of the RCMP security service.[75] For example, when the chief press censor's office was shut down, a summary of its activity was passed on to the RCMP with a clear indication of which papers the censor felt should be watched. This list included the *BC Federationist* ('incite[d] the public to violence and revolt against constituted authority'), *Calgary Searchlight* ('needs watching'), *Camp Workers* ('extremely revolutionary in tone'), *Labor* ('of a revolutionary socialist character'), *New Democracy* ('radical socialist'), *One Big Union Bulletin* ('revolutionary and opposed to constituted authority'), *Ukrainian Labor News* ('objectionable Bolshevist publication ... worth watching closely'), *Vapaus* ('socialistic'), and *Western Labor News* ('created feeling of unrest and discontent').[76] In general, as Chambers's comments to the RCMP make clear, he continued to favour some form of censorship. Needless to say, the RCMP would continue the surveillance part of this work.[77]

The RCMP cut its teeth in 1919 and established a clear trajectory in security and intelligence work, but so did the revolutionary movement. For the Finns and Ukrainians the way forward remained quite clear, and the FOC and the Ukrainian Labour-Farmer Temple Association (ULFTA) moved directly into the emerging Communist Party of Canada. This direction proved most appealing for most left-wing Jews as well, although there was a significant residual social democratic grouping in that community. The radical press of the three communities became dominantly communist in the 1920s. In the aftermath of 1919 the SDP disappeared as its immigrant members moved into the CPC, while some of its British and native Canadian elements moved into labourism.[78] The SPC eventually split on the issue of joining the Third International, with a majority becoming members of the CPC and the others maintaining the SPC.[79]

This article has covered much ground in an attempt to review the interaction of the Canadian working class and the state in the fiery crucible of the First World War. The Canadian state initiated a whole new set of repressive measures and agencies during this war and in its immediate aftermath in response to the significant challenge mounted by Canadian workers. The state's position on the battlefield of class war, which had remained hidden to large segments of Canadian labour before 1914, now stood exposed. The economic climate of the 1920s, however, was to prove unpropitious for further labour gains. The state's new repressive apparatus, operating out of the Departments of Immigration and Justice and through Military Intelligence and the Royal Canadian Mounted Police, remained alert. These practices, initiated in the First World War and its aftermath and continued during the 1920s, would again come to the fore during the Great Depression, the next period of nationwide worker militancy.

NOTES

This abridged article is from *Canadian Historical Review* 77 (3) (1992). Reprinted with permission of University of Toronto Press Incorporated.

I would like to acknowledge the helpful comments of Bryan Palmer, Linda Kealey, and participants in the Memorial University Graduate History Seminar, and the financial support of the Social Sciences and Humanities Research Council of Canada.

1 On the labour revolt see G.S. Kealey, '1919: The Canadian Labour Revolt,' *Labour/Le Travail* 13 (1984): 11–44, and Allen Seager, 'Nineteen Nineteen: Year of Revolt,' *Journal of the West* 23, 4 (1984): 40–7.

2 The US experience has received far more attention owing, perhaps, to academic concern about McCarthyism and later about FBI excesses during the late 1960s. See F.C. Luebke, *Bonds of Loyalty: German Americans and World War I* (DeKalb, Ill. 1974); Robert K. Murray, *Red Scare: A Study in National Hysteria* (New York 1964); and William Preston, Jr, *Aliens and Dissenters: Federal Suppression of Radicals, 1903–1933* (Cambridge, Mass. 1963).

3 For standard accounts see Robert Craig Brown, *Robert Laird Borden, A Biography,* vol. 2 (Toronto 1980), 162–7; Robert Craig Brown and Ramsay Cook, *Canada, 1896–1921: A Nation Transformed* (Toronto 1974), 212–27, 239–43, 309–14; Roger Graham, *Arthur Meighen*, vol. 1 (Toronto 1960), 229–44; and Margaret Prang, *N.W. Rowell: Ontario Nationalist* (Toronto 1975), 266–9, 298–303. Brown's most apologetic effort by far, however, is his '"Whither are we being shoved?" Political Leadership in Canada during World War I,' in J.L. Granatstein and R.D. Cuff, eds., *War and Society in North America* (Toronto 1971), 104–19.

4 In making this bald argument I am not dismissing ethnic chauvinism as an important ingredient in the war and postwar repression. It clearly played a significant role. I am, however, trying to emphasize that the same policy direction would have been pursued even if there had been no immigrant workers to blame.

5 David Jay Bercuson, *Confrontation at Winnipeg: Labour, Industrial Relations and the General Strike*, rev. ed. (Montreal 1990), offers a new preface xi–xii, and a new, entertaining conclusion, 196–205, which basically argue that his book as written almost twenty years before stands in need of no modification. His major complaint, other than an unapologetic dismissal of Marxist historical writing, is that many strikes do not equal a revolt. This is not the place to debate the significance of 1919, but it seems clear that the Canadian bourgeoisie and its state did not share Bercuson's perspective. For them, the organization of such groups as mass-production workers, the public service, and the police, international events, and the growth of labour and socialist politics at home all combined to create tangible fear.

6 While I do not want to bore readers with a theoretical digression on the state, I would identify my perspective as roughly coincident with that of Leo Panitch in his article in *The Canadian State* (Toronto 1977). I would add, however, that his renewed emphasis there on coercion seems to demand renewed empirical demonstration. This article and the larger work from which it is derived is intended to pursue this question. For other works that

have influenced my view of the state see Ralph Miliband, *The State in Capitalist Society* (London 1973), and his *Marxism and Politics* (Oxford 1977), and Peter B. Evans et al., eds., *Bringing the State Back In* (Cambridge 1985).

7 For a discussion of this act see Orest Martynowych, 'The Ukrainian Socialist Movement in Canada, 1900–1918,' *Journal of Ukrainian Graduate Studies* 1 (1976): 27–44, and 2 (1977): 22–31, and Peter Melnycky, 'The Internment of Ukrainians in Canada,' in Frances Swyripa and John Herd Thompson, eds., *Loyalties in Conflict: Ukrainians in Canada during the Great War* (Edmonton 1985), 1–24.

8 David Edward Smith, 'Emergency Government in Canada,' *Canadian Historical Review* 50 (1969): 429–48; Brown, 'Whither are we being shoved?' 104–19.

9 Arthur Lower, *Colony to Nation* (Toronto 1969), 473. For an excellent discussion of the implications of this act see F. Murray Greenwood, 'The Drafting and Passage of the War Measures Act in 1914 and 1927: Object Lessons in the Need for Vigilance' (unpublished paper, University of British Columbia 1987).

10 Inter alia, see PC 2086, 7 Aug. 1914; PC 2128, 13 Aug. 1914; PC 2150, 15 Aug. 1914; and PC 2283, 3 Sept. 1914. A number of these and later provisions are conveniently collected in Swyripa and Thompson, eds., *Loyalties in Conflict*, 171–81.

11 For details see Robert H. Coats, 'The Alien Enemy in Canada: Internment Operations,' in *Canada and the Great World War* (Toronto 1919), II, 144–61; Desmond Morton, 'Sir William Otter and Internment Operations in Canada during the First World War,' *Canadian Historical Review* 55 (1974): 32–58; Morton, *The Canadian General: Sir William Otter* (Toronto 1974), 315–68; Jean Laflamme, *Les Camps de Detention au Québec* (Montreal 1973); Melnycky, 'Internment of Ukrainians,' 2–3; Joseph A. Boudreau, 'Western Canada's Enemy Aliens in World War I,' *Alberta History* 12, 1 (1964): 1–9, and 'The Enemy Alien Problem in Canada' (PhD dissertation, University of California at Los Angeles 1965).

12 For first-hand experiences see Helen Potrobenko, *No Streets of Gold: A Social History of the Ukrainians in Alberta* (Vancouver 1977), 131–6. For a useful, albeit uncritical, eyewitness account see Watson Kirkconnell, 'Kapuskasing – An Historical Sketch,' *Queen's Quarterly* 28 (1921): 264–78.

13 While certainly true of Coats, 'The Alien Enemy,' this argument is also echoed in Morton, 'Sir William Otter,' and Boudreau, 'The Enemy Alien.'

14 Cook and Brown, *Canada*, 224–7, quotations at 226

15 Potrobenko, *No Streets of Gold*, 103–30; Myrna Kostash, *All of Baba's Children* (Edmonton 1977), 45–55; Melnycky, 'Internment of Ukrainians,' 1–24

16 On censorship see Allan L. Steinhart, *Civil Censorship in Canada during World*

406   Gregory S. Kealey

War I (Toronto, 1986); Charles Hanburry-Williams, 'The Censorship,' in *Canada and the Great World War*, 238–41; Herbert Karl Kalbfleisch, *The History of the Pioneer German Language Press of Ontario, 1835–1918* (Toronto 1968), 105–6; Werner A. Bausenhart, 'The Ontario German Language Press and Its Suppression by Order-in-Council in 1918,' *Canadian Ethnic Studies* 4, 1–2 (1972): 35–48; W. Entz, 'The Suppression of the German Language Press in September 1918,' *Canadian Ethnic Studies* 8, 2 (1976): 56–70; and Arja Pilli, *The Finnish-Language Press in Canada, 1901–1939* (Turku 1982), 85–95. The key early order was PC 1330 (10 June 1915). The general discussion in John Herd Thompson, *The Harvests of War: The Prairie West, 1914–1918* (Toronto, 1978), 33–5, fails to take this issue seriously enough.

17 On these two papers see Peter Weinrich, *Social Protest from the Left in Canada, 1870–1970* (Toronto 1982), no. 5150 and no. 5218. *The Week's* strong pacifist and anti-conscription position as well as its general muckraking, pro-labour stance appalled the censor. When it began to republish on May Day 1920, its editor, W.E. Pierce, recalled the ban of two years before and his three-month jail sentence and $1000 fine. *Week*, 29 June 1918, 1 May 1920.

18 Ernest J. Chambers, *Revised List of Publications the Possession of Which in Canada Is Prohibited* (Ottawa, 19 Aug. 1918). National Archives of Canada (NA), RCMP Records, RG 18, vol. 2380. For an accessible but unaccountably incomplete list see Weinrich, *Social Protest*, 471–4.

19 See PC 2070 (6 Aug. 1914); PC 2821 (6 Nov. 1914); Consolidated Orders Respecting Censorship, 17 Jan. 1917; and PC 1241 (22 May 1918).

20 Pilli, *Finnish-Language Press in Canada*, 88; Nadia Kazymyra, 'The Defiant Pavlo Krat and the Early Socialist Movement in Canada,' *Canadian Ethnic Studies* 10, 2 (1978): 47

21 S.W. Horrall, 'The Royal North-West Mounted Police and Labour Unrest in Western Canada, 1919,' *Canadian Historical Review* 61 (1980): 169–90, provides useful background. A popular version is John Sawatsky, *Men in the Shadows: The RCMP Security Service* (Toronto 1980), esp. chap. 5. See also Carl Betke and S.W. Horrall, *Canada's Security Service: An Historical Outline* (Ottawa 1978), acquired through an access request to CSIS in 1991. On British Columbia see Hugh Johnston, 'The Surveillance of Indian Nationalists in North America, 1908–1918,' *BC Studies* 78 (1988): 3–27.

22 Kirkconnell, 'Kapuskasing,' 269

23 R.T. Naylor, 'The Canadian State, the Accumulation of Capital, and the Great War,' *Revue d'études canadiennes* 16, 3 and 4 (1981): 26–55; Terry Copp, *The Anatomy of Poverty* (Toronto 1974); Michael J. Piva, *The Condition of the Working-Class in Toronto* (Toronto 1979); Gordon Bertram and Michael Percy, 'Real Wage Trends in Canada, 1900–1926,' *Canadian Journal of Economics* 12

(1979): 299–3212, and Eleanor Bartlett, 'Real Wages and the Standard of Living in Vancouver, 1901–1929,' BC Studies 51 (1981): 3–62

24 D.J. Bercuson, 'Organized Labour and the Imperial Munitions Board,' Relations Industrielles 28 (1974): 602–16; Peter Rider, 'The Imperial Relations Board and Its Relationship to Government, Business, and Labour, 1914–1920' (PhD dissertation, University of Toronto 1974), esp. chap. 9; Michael Bliss, A Canadian Millionaire: The Life and Business Times of Sir Joseph Flavelle, Bart., 1858–1939 (Toronto 1978), esp. 270–2, 280–4, 320–5, 378–81; and Myer Siemiatycki, 'Munitions and Labour Militancy: The 1916 Hamilton Machinists' Strike,' Labour/Le Travailleur 3 (1978): 131–51. See also the Toronto debate in Toronto Trades and Labour Council, Minutes, 2, 16 March; 6, 20 April 1916.

25 Of the 36,267 members of the first contingent of the Canadian Expeditionary Force, fully 42 per cent were English born and another 22 per cent Scottish, Irish, and Welsh born. English Canadians composed 26 per cent and French Canadians about 3 per cent. J.L. Granatstein and J.M. Hitsman, Broken Promises: A History of Conscription in Canada (Toronto 1977), 23. See also Thompson, Harvests, 12–44.

26 Borden to Walters et al., 27 Dec. 1916, as quoted in Granatstein and Hitsman, Broken Promises, 45. See also Martin Robin, Radical Politics and Canadian Labour (Kingston 1968), 120ff, and A. Ross McCormack, Reformers, Rebels and Revolutionaries (Toronto 1977), 134ff.

27 Toronto Trades and Labour Council, Minutes, 4 May 1916, 4 Jan. 1917

28 By far the most perceptive material on this subject has been written by Donald Avery. See, for example, his 'Dangerous Foreigners': European Immigrant Workers and Labour Radicalism in Canada, 1896–1932 (Toronto 1979), especially chapter 3, and his many articles, especially 'The Radical Alien and the Winnipeg General Strike of 1919,' in Carl Berger and Ramsay Cook, eds., The West and the Nation (Toronto 1976), 209–31 and 'Ethnic and Class Tensions in Canada, 1918–1920: Anglo Canadians and the Alien Worker,' in Swyripa and Thompson, eds., Loyalties in Conflict, 79–98. Also of considerable utility is Ian Angus, Canadian Bolsheviks: The Early Years of the Communist Party of Canada (Montreal 1981), esp. 3–86.

29 For a national view of the Red Scare see Theresa Baxter, 'Selected Aspects of Canadian Public Opinion on the Russian Revolution and on Its Impact in Canada, 1917–1919' (MA thesis, University of Western Ontario 1973). Specific to one province is Elliot Samuels, 'The Red Scare in Ontario: The Reactions of the Ontario Press to the Internal and External Threat of Bolshevism, 1917–1918' (MA thesis, Queen's University 1972).

30 Canada's most famous leftist internee was undoubtedly Leon Trotsky, who spent some three weeks interned at Amherst, Nova Scotia, while trying to

return to Russia from New York. See William Rodney, 'Broken Journey: Trotsky in Canada, 1917,' *Queen's Quarterly* 74 (1967): 649–65. For archival records of this event see NA, Department of National Defence, RG 24, vol. 2543, 'Russian Socialists.'

31 PC 332 (14 Feb. 1919)

32 Kirckconnell, 'Kapuskasing,' 273–4

33 Morton, 'Sir William Otter,' 58

34 Costa, 'Alien Enemy,' 161

35 For text see Swyripa and Thompson, eds., *Loyalties in Conflict*, 190–2. 'Publication' included 'any book, newspaper, magazine, periodical, pamphlet, tract, circular, leaflet, handbill, poster or other printed matter.' 'Enemy language' meant 'German, Austrian, Hungarian, Bulgarian, Turkish, Roumanian, Russian, Ukrainian, Finnish, Estonian, Syrian, Croatian, Ruthenian and Livonian.'

36 This list, which is not necessarily definitive, is taken from E.J. Chambers, 'Additions to Revised List of Prohibited Publications of Date August 19th, 1918' (Ottawa, 28 Oct. 1918), NA, RG 18, vol. 2380; 'List of Publications Which Are Prohibited under the Consolidated Orders Respecting Censorship,' [April 1919] RG 18, vol. 2165; and W.H. Routledge to officer commanding, CIB memorandum, no. 115, Regina, 10 Sept. 1919, 'Re: Prohibited Publications,' RG 18, vol. 2380.

37 John Swettenham *Allied Intervention in Russia, 1918–1919, and the Part Played by Canada* (Toronto 1967), and Roy MacLaren, *Canadians in Russia, 1918–1919* (Toronto 1976), are the fullest accounts of this misguided mission. Note especially, MacLaren, *Canadians*, 252–8.

38 The Borden Papers contain many letters and petitions opposing Canadian intervention. In addition, the Canadian armed forces were very concerned about Bolshevik infiltration of the Canadian Expeditionary Force. See, for example, NA, Department of National Defence, RG 24, vol. 2543, file 1, Major Jukes, director of intelligence, Military District 11, to assistant director, Military Intelligence, Ottawa, Victoria, BC, 17 Dec. 1919, which warns of Bolshevik propaganda among the Siberian force. There are many such examples.

39 PC 2521 (15 Oct. 1918); PC 2963 (13 Nov. 1918); PC 702 and 703 (2 April 1919); and PC 2465 (20 Dec. 1919)

40 Routledge to officer commanding, Regina, 10 Sept. 1919, CIB no. 115, RG 18, vol. 2380

41 Henry Trachtenberg, 'The Role of Manitoba's Jews,' 667–80. See also Avery, 'Radical Alien,' 223–6. In his immigration hearing he is described as Solomon Almazoff. For a transcript of his case see NA, RG 18, vol. 3314, folio HV-1, vol. 4.

42 Pilli, *Finnish-Language Press*, 111–17
43 Ibid., 100, 105
44 Ibid., 106. Also see *Canadan Uutiset*, 11 July 1918, article by H.W. Niinimäki, translation by Mauri A. Jalava. All Finnish-language items cited have been translated by Mr Jalava.
45 *Canadan Uutiset*, 5 Dec. 1918
46 Pilli, *Finnish-Language Press*, 113–18
47 Ibid.
48 Ibid., 122–7
49 See, among others, J. Donald Wilson, 'The Finnish Organization of Canada, the "Language Barrier," and the Assimilation Process,' *Canadian Ethnic Studies* 9, 2 (1977): 105–16, for a careful consideration of the negotiations with Cahan. On Cahan and the Public Safety Branch see my 'The Surveillance State: The Origins of Domestic Intelligence and Counter-Subversion in Canada,' *Intelligence and National Security* 7, 3 (1992): 179–210.
50 Pilli, *Finnish-Language Press*, 127–8
51 J.W. Ahlqvist to Trades and Labour Councils and Unions of Canada, Toronto, 8 March 1919, Public Archives of Manitoba, RG 21, Court of King's Bench, Criminal Assizes, *R. v. Ivens et al.*, Exhibits
52 *Canadan Uutiset*, 20 March 1919
53 On the experience of the Ukrainian papers see Peter Krawchuk, *The Ukrainian Socialist Movement in Canada, 1907–1918* (Toronto 1979), 95–9; Martynowych, 'The Ukrainian Socialist Movement in Canada, 1900–1918,' (1976): 27–44; (1977): 26–30; Andrij Makuch, 'Influence of the Ukrainian Revolution on Ukrainians in Canada, 1917–1922,' *Journal of Ukrainian Graduate Studies* 6 (1979): 42–61; and John Kolasky, *The Shattered Illusion: The History of Ukrainian Pro-Communist Organizations in Canada* (Toronto 1979), 1–26. See also Kolasky, *Prophets and Proletarians: Documents on the History of the Rise and Decline of Ukrainian Communism in Canada* (Edmonton 1990), 3–31, and Peter Krawchuk, *Matthew Popovich* (Toronto 1987), 19–46.
54 Pilli, *Finnish-Language Press*, 129–32
55 For the text of PC 2384 see Swyripa and Thompson, eds., *Loyalties in Conflict*, 193–6. The following associations were specifically declared unlawful: 'Industrial Workers of the World; Russian Social Democratic Party; Russian Revolutionary Group; Russian Social Revolutionist; Russian Workers Union; Ukrainian Social Democratic Party; Social Democratic Party; Social Labour Party; Group of Social Democrats of Bolsheviki; Group of Social Democrats of Anarchists; Workers International Industrial Union; Chinese Nationalist League; and Chinese Labour Association.' In addition, the order covered 'any association ... one of whose purposes or professed purposes is to bring

about any governmental, political, social, industrial or economic change within Canada by the use of force, violence, or physical injury to person or property, or by threats of such injury, or which teaches, advocates, advises or defends the use of ...'

56 Edward W. Laine, 'Finnish Canadian Radicalism and Canadian Politics: 'The First Forty Years, 1900–1940,'in Jorgen Dahlie and Tissa Fernando, eds., *Ethnicity, Power and Politics in Canada* (Toronto 1981), 98–9, 107–8. Amended list is in PC 2786. The deletion of the SDP from the list was due to the efforts of Newton Rowell. See Prang, *Rowell*, 267–8.
57 Swyripa and Thompson, eds., *Loyalties in Conflict*, 193–6
58 Particularly useful accounts are given in Avery, *'Dangerous Foreigners,'* 65–89; his 'Radical Alien,' 216–26; and his 'Ethnic and Class Tensions,' 80–7; see also Angus, *Canadian Bolsheviks*, 27–48.
59 For a useful critique see James Conley, 'Frontier Labourers, Crafts in Crisis, and the Western Labour Revolt: The Case of Vancouver, 1900 to 1919,' *Labour/ Le Travail* 23 (1989): 9–37, and James Naylor, 'The New Democracy: Class Conflict in Industrial Ontario, 1914–1925' (PhD dissertation, York University 1988).
60 Major Joseph E. Rogers, superintendent, Ontario Provincial Police, to F.H. Whitton, general manager, Stelco, 24 Feb. 1919, AO, Ontario Provincial Police Papers, RG 23, E 30, file 1.6. On Rogers's career see D.D. Higley, OPP (Toronto to 1984).
61 Rogers to Whitton, as in note 60 above
62 W.H. Routledge to officer commanding, Regina, 16 Aug. 1919, CIB 104, 'Bolsheviki Propaganda – List of Parties Prosecuted in connection with.' NA, RG 18, vol. 2380
63 To sample randomly, I took one name off each of the first ten pages of the list.
64 An example of military pressures can be found in Major-General Gwatkin, chief of the General Staff, 'Memorandum on Censorship,' nd [1918], Hamilton Papers, NA, MG 30, D 84, vol. 2, which cites the IWW threat as a rationale for tougher censorship. Cahan was endearingly described by the British high commissioner in Ottawa a few years later as 'generally accepted as the mouthpiece of the Holt, Gundy and other big business interests of Montreal.' Sir William H. Clark to the Rt Hon. L.S. Avery, 17 May 1929, PRO, DO 35/68
65 This argument is frequently made. See, for example, Howard Palmer, *Patterns of Prejudice: A History of Nativism in Alberta* (Toronto 1982), 47–56.
66 C.H. Cahan to Sir Robert Borden, Montreal, 28 May 1919, NA, Borden Papers, MG 26, H, vol. 113, part 1, file OC564 (1) (A), 61631–2. For a fine example of Cahan's anti-red propaganda see his 'A Pernicious Propaganda'

in *Empire Club of Canada, Addresses, 1919* (Toronto 1920), 191–215. See also Kealey, 'The Surveillance State.'

67 See Kealey, '1919,' and Kerr and Holdsworth, eds., *Historical Atlas of Canada*, vol. 3, plate 39, for statistical evidence on the strike wave of that year.

68 Sergeant B.H. James to A.J. Cawdron, IWW Branch, Dominion Police, Ottawa, 24 March 1919, NA, RG 13, vol. 235, file 1013

69 F.H. Whitton to Joseph E. Rogers, 9 April 1919, with enclosure of agent's report of 27–31 March and 1 April 1919; Joseph E. Rogers to F.H. Whitton, 10 April 1919; Joseph E. Rogers to Albert J. Cawdron, acting chief commissioner of police, 10 April 1919; Albert J. Cawdron to Joseph E. Rogers, 12 April 1919, AO, OPP Papers, RG 23, E 30, file 1.6

70 NA, RG 13, A 2, vol. 233, file 455, and vol. 237, files 1517 and 1537

71 One hastens to add 'more readily available' only for a time. Deposited in the early 1960s under various restrictions, these 1919 RNWMP files were consulted by a number of historians but were then removed from the archives by the RCMP Security Services. For the complex history of these records see Gregory S. Kealey, 'The Royal Canadian Mounted Police, the Canadian Security Intelligence Service, the Public Archives of Canada, and the Access to Information Act: A Curious Tale,' *Labour/Le Travail* 21 (1988): 199–226.

The 'western radicalism' hypothesis has come under attack from many quarters of late. For a useful and considered discussion see Gerald Friesen, *The Canadian Prairies: A History* (Toronto 1984), 287–300, 355–65, and also Conley, 'Frontier Labourers,' and Naylor, 'The New Democracy.' For an unapologetic reassertion see Bercuson, *Confrontation*, 196–205.

72 The most satisfactory account we have of the genesis of the RCMP and particularly its security responsibilities is Horrall, 'The Royal North-West Mounted Police and Labour Unrest.' While a thorough rendering of the force's bureaucratic development, it should be read as a partial apologia for the force written by the head of the RCMP's historical section. See also Betke and Horrall, *Canada's Security Service.*

73 Tom Traves, *The State and Enterprise: Canadian Manufacturers and the Federal Government, 1917–1931* (Toronto 1979). See also Myer Siemiatycki, 'Labour Contained: The Defeat of a Rank and File Workers' Movement in Canada, 1914–1921' (PhD dissertation, York University 1987), and Naylor, 'The New Democracy.'

74 A good discussion of these issues is found in Barbara Roberts, *Whence They Came: Deportation from Canada, 1900–1935* (Ottawa 1988).

75 For a sketchy but useful overview see Sawatsky, *Men in the Shadows.*

76 NA, Communist Party of Canada Papers, MG 28 IV 4, vol. 40, file 40–28. Chief Press Censor, Supplementary Report to RNWMP, 13 Jan. 1920

77 See G.S. Kealey and R. Whitaker, eds., *RCMP Security Bulletins: The Early Years, 1919–1929* (St John's 1992).

78 Naylor, 'The New Democracy,' provides the most detailed account of labourism as a political strategy in these years.

79 Larry Peterson, 'Revolutionary Socialism and Industrial Unrest in the Era of the Winnipeg General Strike: The Origins of Communist Labour Unionism in Europe and North America,' *Labour/Le Travail* 13 (1984): 115–31

'The line must be drawn somewhere': Canada and Jewish Refugees, 1933–1939

IRVING ABELLA AND HAROLD TROPER

On 15 May 1939 907 desperate German Jews set sail from Hamburg on the luxury liner *St. Louis*. Like many who had sailed on this ship before, these passengers were – or at least had been – the cream of German society: distinguished, well-off, educated, cultured. Most had contributed much to their native land. All were now penniless. They had been stripped of their possessions, hounded out of their homes and businesses and now their country. Their most prized possession was the entrance visa to Cuba each carried on board.

For the Jews of Germany life had become impossible. Countless thousands had been brutalized, murdered, or sent off to concentration camps. The Nazis were anxious to empty Germany of its Jews – but where could they go? Initially neighbouring countries such as Holland, France, and later Great Britain had accepted some, but soon the nations of the world had clanged shut their gates before these helpless men, women, and children. Germany was determined to throw their Jews out; everyone else seemed just as determined not to let them in.

A poignant joke at the time says it all. A Jew wishing to travel goes to a Berlin travel agent who places a globe in from of him, whirls it, and says: 'Choose.' After studying the globe for a short time the Jew looks up with a pained expression and asks: 'Do you have anything else?'

The Jews on the *St. Louis* considered themselves lucky. They were leaving. When they reached Havana on 30 May, however, their luck had run out. The Cuban government refused to recognize the entrance visas; none of these wretched people were allowed to disembark, even when they threatened mass suicide.[1] The search for a haven now began in earnest. Argentina, Uruguay, Paraguay, and Panama were approached, in vain, by various Jewish organizations. Within two days all the countries of Latin America had rejected entreaties to allow these Jew to land. On 2 June the *St. Louis* was forced to leave Havana harbour. The last hope seemed to be either Canada or the United States.

The latter did not even bother sending a reply. Instead it sent a gunboat to shadow the *St. Louis* as it made its way north. The American coast guard had been ordered to make certain that the *St. Louis* stayed far enough off shore so that it could not be run aground nor could any of its frantic passengers attempt to swim ashore.[2] Now only Canada remained uncommitted.

The plight of the *St. Louis* had touched some influential Canadians. On 7 June several of these led by the eminent historian George Wrong, and including B.K. Sandwell of *Saturday Night*, Robert Falconer, past president of the University of Toronto, and Ellsworth Flavelle, a wealthy businessman, sent a telegram to prime minister Mackenzie King begging that he show 'true Christian charity' and offer the homeless exiles sanctuary in Canada.[3]

Jewish refugees were far from the prime minister's mind at this time. He was in Washington accompanying the Royal family on the final leg of its triumphant tour of North America. The *St. Louis*, he felt, was not a Canadian problem. Nonetheless, he asked O.D. Skelton, the undersecretary of state for external affairs, to consult the acting prime minister, Ernest Lapointe, and the director of immigration, F.C. Blair, for their advice.[4] Both these men were known for their staunch opposition to Jewish immigration to Canada. They did not disappoint King. Lapointe stated that he was 'emphatically opposed' to the admission of the *St. Louis* passengers, while Blair, the bureaucrat, claimed that these refugees did not qualify under immigration laws for admission and that, in any case, Canada had already done too much for the Jews.[5] Why should Canada 'go out of her way,' he asked Skelton, to allow in people who would likely 'smuggle themselves' across the border to the United States? Blair's great fear, however, was that if these Jews were to find a home they would 'likely be followed by other shiploads.' No country, he added, could 'open its doors wide enough to take in the hundreds of thousands of Jewish people who want to leave Europe: *the line must be drawn somewhere.*[6]

Their last flickering hopes crushed, the despairing passengers of the *St. Louis* headed back for Europe (where the governments of Britain, Belgium, and Holland finally offered temporary shelter). There, many would die in the gas chambers and crematoria of the Third Reich.

In 1933, when Adolf Hitler became chancellor, Jews constituted approximately 1 per cent of the German population; to reduce, and eventually eliminate that percentage became one of Hitler's major objectives. Over the next few years legislation was passed stripping Jews of their citizenship, barring them from schools, from government positions, and from access to the courts, subjecting them to arbitrary arrests and detention, confiscating their property and businesses, and imposing on them enormous collective fines. In addition, acts of violence against Jews and their property were officially sanctioned and even encouraged. In large part, these measures were designed specifically to force Jews to emigrate. And many who could, did. Yet, at the same time, to compound the problems of prospective emigrants, Jews were forbidden to carry German passports and were stripped of all their assets. Without capital Jews became even less attractive as immigrants. Thousands were randomly rounded up and pushed into the no-man's land beyond German borders.

As German frontiers expanded into the Rhineland and, by 1938, into Austria and Czechoslovakia, so did the number of Jews under German rule. Hundreds of thousands were leaving for Poland, France, Britain, Holland, Belgium, and Switzerland. Hundreds of thousands more would have had these nations allowed them in. None of these countries were pleased with the influx of these unexpected – and unwanted – guests. They provided only a temporary haven and insisted that these refugees look for a permanent home somewhere else, anywhere else. Indeed, some countries – especially in Eastern Europe, where antisemitism was a way of life – began making noises about following the German precedent and forcing out unwanted Jews.[7] An acute refugee problem was fast becoming explosive.

International refugee organizations could not begin to cope with the problem. The League of Nations had created the Commission for German Refugees but its accomplishments were pathetic. Most member states chose to ignore or belittle the plight of refugees, in the hope perhaps that the problem would either disappear or solve itself. Most nations argued that if there was a solution it must be on the basis of an accommodation between Germany and her non-Aryan population. No countries came forward either to accept those refugees left in Germany or those living temporarily in the countries surrounding her. As Chaim Weizman, then a leading Zionist and later first president of the State of Israel put it: 'The world seemed to be divided into two parts – those places where the Jew could not live, and those where they could not enter.'[8] Canada fell into the latter category.

Of the more than 800,000 Jews seeking refuge from the Third Reich in the years from 1933 to 1939, Canada found room within her borders for approximately 4000.[9] In a world which was decidedly inhospitable to refugees, Canada was no exception. Yet, even by the standard of the time, Canada stood virtually alone in the niggardliness of her contribution. Argentina, for example, admitted 22,000; Australia, 10,000, and was preparing to receive 15,000 more when war broke out; Brazil, 20,000; China, 15,000; Great Britain, 85,000; Palestine, 100,000; the United States, 140,000; and even penurious Mexico and Colombia had each accepted about 20,000.[10]

That Jews were not welcome in Canada during the 1930s is not surprising; no one else was either. With a third of its people out of work Canada was understandably not receptive to the notion of accepting more job-hungry immigrants. That the economic consequences of the depression throttled immigration cannot be denied. What should be stressed, however, is that the depression also afforded the dramatic opportunity for Canadian officials to complete a process of restriction begun in the boom years of the 1920s.

Canadian immigration policy had always been as ethnically selective as it was economically self-serving. When economic necessity dictated the admission of non-British and non-American immigrants it was always in descending order of ethnic preference. Following British and American immigrants, preference was given northern Europeans and then central Europeans. At the bottom were the Jews, Orientals, and blacks.[11] Those 'non-preferred immigrants' were acceptable as long as they were out of sight, risking life and limb in the mines and smelters of the West and North, holed up in lumber camps deep in the forest, or farming the more marginal areas of the western wheat frontier. Those who escaped this life for perhaps the even worse one in Canada's urban centres to compete for jobs with native or British-born artisans were less acceptable. And to immigration officials the worst culprits were the Jews. Jews, according to Blair, were 'city people.' To almost every request to admit Jewish farmers or agricultural workers, Blair had the same response: it was impossible to keep them on the farm or in the bush. Every attempt to do so had failed. Jewish workers, he claimed, could not 'eat Gentile food' and so took the 'earliest opportunity' to leave for the city 'which is about the only place [they] can find [their] fellow countrymen.'[12]

With the disposition of less desirable immigrants to drift towards cities and the gradual decline in demand for unskilled labour, by the mid-1920s the Canadian government began to restrict the immigration of those on the bottom rungs of the ethnic preference ladder. When, in 1928, the deputy minister of immigration, W.J. Egan, ordered that the admission of Eastern European immigrants be cut back by two-thirds, he explained that though the economy was doing well, these 'non-preferred country immigrants had drifted into non-agricultural work almost immediately upon arrival ... [were] filling positions that might have been filled by immigrants from the Mother Country.'[13]

The onset of the depression gave the government the opportunity to complete drawing the restrictionist circle around Canada. In 1930 an order-in-council (PC 1957) was introduced allowing in only those immigrants with enough capital to establish and maintain themselves on farms. In the following year another order-in-council (PC 659) effectively banned all non-agricultural immigrants who were of non-British or non-American stock. For all intents and purposes, just at the time when she was most needed, Canada shut herself off from the rest of the world. And for the remainder of the decade – and indeed beyond – a determined Canadian government fought every attempt by the wretched European refugees to breach this protective wall of orders-in-council.

The person entrusted with the task of ensuring that there was no breach was Frederick Charles Blair. As director of the Immigration Branch of the Department of Mines and Resources during these years Blair made almost all of the decisions – no matter how small – concerning who got into Canada. And from the point of view of European Jewry this was most unfortunate. Just when they most needed a friend at the gate, they had an enemy; instead of the philo-Semite they required, they had an anti-Semite; instead of the humanitarian, they got a narrow-minded bureaucrat. According to those who knew him, Blair was a tough administrator who 'stuck to the rules' – which is not so surprising since he drafted most of them himself.[14]

Born in Carlisle, Ontario, in 1874, of Scottish parents, Blair joined the

Department of Agriculture in 1901, and two years later became an immigration officer. In 1924 he was appointed the assistant deputy minister of immigration and in 1936 he became director of the branch with full deputy-minister status. He was a religious man, an elder of the Baptist church, and a dedicated civil servant. Indeed, so devoted was he to his job that when he finally retired in 1944, four years beyond normal retirement age, he had accumulated about two years' worth of sick leave.[15]

As the man responsible for Canadian immigration policy, Blair had some seemingly peculiar ideas. According to one observer he 'took the stand that people should be kept out of Canada instead of being let in.'[16] Yet these notions hardly seemed to bother the Canadian government which kept him in his sensitive position as long as it could. He was, as James Gibson, an external affairs official, recalls, 'the single most difficult individual I had to deal with the whole time I was a public servant. He was a holy terror!'[17] Perhaps this was why he stayed in his job for so long; he was precisely the man the King government wanted in this position. His inflexibility, fetish for regulations, and unchallenged control over immigration matters were a convenience to an administration which had no intention of allowing in Jewish refugees but wished to avoid the calumny of not doing so. Though ostensibly Thomas Crerar was the minister responsible for immigration, in fact Blair made policy and implemented it. Crerar knew little of the workings of the immigration branch, and cared even less. He relied almost totally on its director for advice.[18]

To Blair the term refugee was a code word for Jew. Unless 'safeguards' were adopted, he warned Crerar, Canada was in danger of being 'flooded with Jewish people.'[19] His task, as he saw it, was to make sure that the 'safeguards' did not fail. Indeed, he was inordinately proud of his success in keeping out Jews. As he put it: 'Pressure on the part of Jewish people to get into Canada has never been greater than it is now and I am glad to be able to add, after 35 years experience here, that it was never so well controlled.'[20] Blair expressed a strong personal distaste for Jews and especially for 'certain of their habits.' He saw them as unassimilable, as people apart 'who can organize [their] affairs better than other people' and therefore accomplish more.[21] He complained bitterly that Jews were 'utterly selfish in their attempts to force through a permit for the admission of relatives or friends.' 'They do not believe,' he added, that 'No' means more than 'Perhaps ...'[22] Furthermore, Jews, he lamented, 'make any kind of promise to get the door open but ... never cease their agitation until they get in the whole lot.' Behind these

Jewish attempts to somehow get their co-religionists into the country, Blair saw a conspiracy 'to bring immigration regulations into disrepute and create an atmosphere favourable to those who cannot comply with the law.' As he commiserated to the traffic manager of the Canadian Pacific Railway: 'If there is any surer way to close the door in their own face, I do not know of it.'[23]

It seems that Blair's contempt for the Jews was boundless. Only a short time after the outbreak of hostilities in Europe in 1939 Blair confided to his immigration commissioner in London: 'Someone has facetiously said that numbers of our Jewish refugees lustfully sing "Onward Christian Soldiers" but are very content to stay here and grab up all opportunities.'[24] In a revealing letter to a strong opponent of Jewish immigration Blair wrote:

I suggested recently to three Jewish gentlemen with whom I am well acquainted, that it might be a very good thing if they would call a conference and have a day of humiliation and prayer which might profitably be extended for a week or more where they would honestly try to answer the question of why they are so unpopular almost everywhere ... I often think that instead of persecution it would be far better if we more often told them frankly why many of them are unpopular. If they would divest themselves of certain of their habits I am sure they could be just as popular in Canada as our Scandinavians ... Just because Jewish people would not understand the frank kind of statements I have made in this letter to you, I have marked it confidential.[25]

Though it was Blair who gave the final interpretation of government regulations and who acted as the de facto judge and jury on individual requests for admission, to blame him alone for Canada's response to the refugee crisis would be both overly simplistic and incorrect; after all, he was only a civil servant, albeit a powerful one. As a functionary he simply reflected the wishes of his superiors; it was they who were ultimately responsible for government policy. Not to accept refugees was a political decision, not a bureaucratic one. It was Mackenzie King and his cabinet which, in the final analysis, must shoulder the responsibility.

Once Canadian Jews realized that attempting to deal with immigration officials was hopeless, they began flexing their political muscle. Only when it was too late did they discover how flabby it was. Taking charge of the pressure campaign was the organization that was generally recognized as the representative voice of the community on social and political matters, the Canadian Jewish Congress. Founded in 1919, by the mid-1930s the congress was a weak and disorganized body. It was underfinanced – wealthy Jews saw it as a tool of more recent and less-monied immigrants, and unrepresentative – both the far left and the conservative elements of the community remained outside. Only in the latter part of 1938, when the wealthy industrialist Samuel Bronfman became active – he was elected president in January 1939 – did the congress become a credible and weighty vehicle for Jewish interests. Indeed, until then it was the Jewish Immigrant Aid Society [JIAS], an organization founded by the congress in June 1920, which acted as the voice of the community on matters affecting immigration and which did much to help individual immigrants.[26]

By default, therefore, the task of putting forth the Jewish position fell on the shoulders of Jewish members of parliament. In the Liberal sweep in the 1935 election three Jews had won seats: two Liberals, Sam Jacobs from Montreal, the congress president, and Sam Factor from Toronto, and one CCFer, A.A. Heaps from Winnipeg. The Jewish community saw the 1935 Liberal victory as a harbinger of better things. After all, it was the Bennett government which had introduced the restrictive orders-in-council and which snubbed various Jewish delegations attempting to have these orders moderated.[27]

These hopes, however, were dashed almost immediately following the elections. In a meeting with Crerar, Jacobs and Benjamin Robinson, president of JIAS, were told that there would be no exception made for German Jews. Unless they met the requirements necessary for immigration – that is, unless they had sufficient capital to establish a successful farm – they would not be allowed in under any circumstances.[28] And Crerar kept his promise. For the next two years almost no Jewish refugees arrived in Canada. And those few who did manage to come entered under specific orders-in-council, exempting them from the usual immigration requirements. Most of these were relatives of Canadian Jews. Some orders-in-council, however, were granted as 'favours' to prominent government supporters – including Sam Jacobs – to distribute to a fortunate few in the Jewish community.[29] It was a cynical activity, but it worked. For the most part Canadian Jews, though restive, remained loyal to the Liberal government. They had little choice. Making up just over 1 per cent of the population, Canadian Jews knew they did not have the power to change government policy. And until they did, they would accept what crumbs were thrown their way. After all, saving a few lives was better than saving none.

The congress did establish a refugee committee in 1937, but its main function was to work with railway colonization officials, to help in the settlement of the handful of Jewish farmers able to break through into Canada. However, even this activity was short-lived for in April 1938, at the behest of Blair who did not believe that Jews could be farmers, railway colonization agents in Europe were told to allow in as few Jewish 'agriculturalists' as possible.[30] Thus, when a German Jew, Hans Heinemann, applied to enter Canada as a farmer he was told by an overenthusiastic agent of the Canadian Pacific Railway in Hamburg that Jews were no longer being allowed into Canada.[31] It seemed, therefore, that by 1938 the Canadian government was taking steps to close the loopholes through which some Jews were still entering Canada. As the general secretary of the Canadian Jewish Congress, H.M. Caiserman, grimly informed Rabbi Stephen Wise of the American Jewish Congress, 'the possibilities of an increased Jewish immigration to Canada at present are nil.'[32]

In March 1938, just when Canada was further restricting Jewish immigration, Hitler marched into Austria and several hundred thousand more Jews became refugees – some, those who had escaped from Germany, for the second time. As a response to this, and to quiet the storm of protest raised by more liberal elements in the United States, President Franklin Roosevelt took the bold step of issuing an invitation to most of the nations of the world to meet together to discuss possible solutions to the refugee problem. What no one at the time knew – but some suspected – was that the real purpose of the conference was, according to the author of the plan, secretary of state Cordell Hull, to give the United States the initiative 'to get out in front and attempt to guide the pressure, primarily with a view toward forestalling attempts to have immigration laws liberalized.'[33]

Had Canadian officials been aware of the Americans' real motives, they would have been relieved. They were not, however, and thus when the formal invitation to attend this conference arrived in late March, they were decidedly uncomfortable. Even though the Americans had assured Canada that no country would be expected to 'receive a greater number of emigrants than is permitted by its existing legislation' and that private organizations would be expected to fund this emigration,[34] the Canadians felt Roosevelt was baiting a trap. Once committed to attending the conference, the Canadians would be expected to do something to alleviate the refugee problem. And this, King dreaded, meant 'admitting numbers of Jews.'[35] His fears were reinforced by Skelton who warned that the publicity generated by the conference would likely result in strong 'domestic pressure' in Canada to do something for the Jews.'[36]

The prime minister of Canada was obsessed with the notion that the admission of Jewish refugees might destroy his country. As he confided to his diary: 'We must ... seek to keep this part of the Continent free from unrest and from too great an intermixture of foreign strains of blood ...' Nothing was to be gained, he believed, 'by creating an internal problem in an effort to meet an international one.' Allowing Jewish refugees into Canada, he told his cabinet, might cause riots and would surely exacerbate relations between the federal government and the provinces. In effect, any action permitting an appreciable number of Jews to settle in Canada would, in King's mind, undermine the unity of the nation. This was no time for Canada to act on 'humanitarian grounds.' Rather, said the prime minister, Canada must be guided by 'realities' and political considerations.[37]

The realities King had in mind were the attitudes towards refugees in general and Jews in particular within Quebec. He was absolutely convinced that that province would react violently to the admission of Jewish refugees. And with reason. Almost every French-language newspaper had warned the government against opening Canada's doors to European Jews. As *Le Devoir* put it: 'Why allow in Jewish refugees? ... The Jewish shopkeeper on St. Lawrence Boulevard does nothing to increase our national resources.'[38] And this statement was mild compared with vicious anti-Semitic utterances appearing regularly in such papers as *La Nation, L'Action Catholique,* and *L'Action Nationale.* As well, many French-Canadian politicians spoke out – both within and without the confines of parliament – against Jewish immigration. These Liberal members, in particular Wilfrid Lacroix, C.H. Leclerc, and H.E. Brunelle, led the anti-refugee onslaught. Indeed, in a speech in the Commons several months later, Brunelle denounced Jews as having caused 'great difficulties' wherever they lived.[39] In addition, both the prime minister and the Immigration Branch received many letters from such Quebec organizations as the St Jean Baptiste Society, the councils of various counties, several *caisses populaires,* and the provincial Knights of Columbus protesting against any possible government backsliding on the refugee issue.[40] In fact, not long afterwards Lacroix delivered to the House of Commons a petition signed by nearly 128,000 members of the St Jean Baptiste Society opposing 'all immigration and especially Jewish immigration.'[41]

The prime minister, but more especially his Quebec lieutenant, Ernest

Lapointe, were also aware of the grievous situation in which the province's Liberal party found itself. Thrown out of office in 1936 by the Union Nationale under Maurice Duplessis, the Quebec Liberal party was badly split and in a state of disarray. Anything which might further weaken it, King and Lapointe felt, would have to be avoided – no matter the cost. Thus, on Lapointe's recommendation the federal cabinet swallowed hard and refused to disallow the heinous Padlock Act. To do otherwise would, according to Lapointe, have been 'disastrous' for the Quebec Liberal party.[42] Allowing in Jewish refugees would also, at least in Lapointe's mind, play into the hands of Duplessis' nationalist forces and further weaken Liberalism in Quebec. Whatever Lapointe's personal feelings were on this matter – and there is no evidence that he favoured Jewish immigration – for political reasons alone he felt justified in taking a hard line against allowing in refugees. And King believed that 'if the Liberal party was to remain a national party' he had no alternative but to accept the view of Lapointe and his French-Canadian colleagues in the House.[43] The prime minister sincerely believed that illiberal policies were acceptable so long as the basic Liberal objective – national unity – was maintained.[44]

Largely because of this hostility in Quebec, King was reluctant to attend the conference on refugees. For the better part of the next month, while almost all the nations of the world were replying positively to Roosevelt's invitation, and despite the anxious inquiries of the Americans, Canada did not respond. No one in government circles was enthusiastic about attending, least of all the prime minister. Who knew what evil would emanate from this conference? A country – and a prime minister – wedded to the doctrine of no commitments would hardly relish the thought of a conference in which some sort of Canadian commitment would be expected.

As King and his cabinet dallied, Blair was increasingly active. At the behest of Skelton he drafted a response rejecting the invitation. Attending this meeting, Blair said, might involve 'the admission to Canada of many who by training and manner of life are not fitted for the development of any of our primary industries, but would add to the congestion and competition of our cities.'[45] More to the point, it was not 'feasible,' he said, 'to encourage the influx of immigrants of one race and not of others.' He privately told Skelton that it was unfair 'to let down the immigration barriers for the benefit of any particular race of class.'[46] Personally, Blair did not feel that the problem was all that serious. As he put it: 'No problem exists except for the Jewish people,' and the refugee situation, he added, was much worse immediately following the Great War.[47] He warned that the government's first priority must now be to decide 'whether Canada can afford to open the door to more Jewish people than we are now receiving' since 'there is going to be a general Jewish drive for admissions to other countries.' Little good for Canada, he predicted, would come out of attendance at the conference. Canadian policy, he stated, should be not to change its restrictive immigration practice, but simply to announce at the meeting that the government would 'show sympathetic consideration where possible to prospective refugee immigrants.'[48]

What apparently most disturbed Blair was the possibility of a successful conference. 'If the nations now asked to cooperate to save the Jews of Germany and Austria, manage by sacrifice to accomplish this purpose it will please the Germans who want to get rid of this group ... and it will encourage other nations to do likewise and this is probably the greatest danger. Can immigration countries afford to encourage such an eventuality? It is akin in a sense to the paying of ransom to Chinese bandits.'[49] Clearly the real threat to Blair was that the Eastern European countries such as Poland, Hungary, and Roumania would learn from the German precedent and attempt to deport their unwanted Jews.

In addition, Blair had just been advised that the German government had officially announced that it would no longer allow Jewish emigrants from Germany back into the country. At once Blair informed Skelton that Canada has no alternative but 'to refuse the admission of German nationals without presentation of passports endorsed as valid for return to Germany.' His argument was as ingenious as it was cold-blooded: 'If we accept people from Germany on one-way travel documents, we have no excuse for refusing a like class from other countries, and we will soon reach the place where the only persons we can deport will be British subjects and U.S. citizens ... I wish the immigration countries would take united action in refusing to admit nationals of countries who will not allow return by deportation.'[50]

It was not until the latter part of April that King finally made his decision. In fact, Canada probably had no choice. As Skelton warned the prime minister: 'It would not look too well to be the only country, except Fascist Italy, declining even to sit on a Committee.'[51] On 26 April the Canadian government officially announced that it would attend the conference which was to be held in the small French resort town of Evian on the Swiss border. (Switzerland had already rejected the honour of holding the meeting on her territory.) At the same time King informed the Americans that he thought it wrong to encourage countries such as Germany which were trying 'to throw upon other countries the task of solving their internal difficulties.'[52]

The news of the Evian Conference activated the leadership of Canadian Jewry. They felt the time was opportune for some serious, though necessarily secret, lobbying. The Jewish community was in an apprehensive mood. Yet the congress executive felt that discussions with government officials were 'a matter of extreme delicacy.' As Caiserman warned Congress officers in Western Canada: 'I have in mind that we refrain from mass meetings, publicity and noise, because such methods would nullify what we have in mind.'[53] What congress officials feared most of all was that demonstrations might both alienate the government and create an anti-semitic backlash throughout the country. As Caiserman stated: 'Experience concerning the refugee situation has convinced us that too much publicity has always proven detrimental to any request for the widening of the doors for the entry of our co-religionists to Canada ... In Quebec any public agitation for the entry of Jews would bring with it ... a flood of counter agitation.'[54] The congress role was not to mobilize Jewish opinion but to monitor it – to guard against any outburst, spontaneous or otherwise, which might rebound against the community at large. Again it was the Jewish MPs who were the most active. They lobbied unceasingly to get the government to go to Evian. They met with Crerar in a vain attempt to have the immigration regulations modified. Finally, with their colleagues J.S. Woodsworth and Colonel A. Vien they met with King and argued vigorously for a more sympathetic approach to the refugee question.[55] King offered his sympathy but little else. He agreed, however, to set up a special committee of cabinet to look at the problem. This proved to be a hollow gesture since, of the five ministers appointed, two, Lapointe and Fernand Rinfret, were openly hostile to Jewish immigration.[56] Indeed, when this committee met with the Jewish MPs, Lapointe pointedly refused to attend. Jacobs, Factor, and Heaps met privately with the two French-Canadian cabinet ministers and vainly pleaded with them to be less inflexible. Even promises by the Jewish MPs that no Jewish refugees would be permitted to settle in Quebec failed to budge them. Rinfret, and more significantly Lapointe, were unyielding in their determination not to allow Jewish refugees into Canada.[57] The cabinet committee met several more times, achieved nothing, and disbanded.

Congress leaders felt betrayed. They had kept the lid on the Jewish community, had been discreet in their negotiations with the government, and had, for their pains, received nothing in return.[58] And their demands had been minimal. As the president of JIAS informed his counterparts in Europe: 'Our negotiations are directed for the admission of a limited number of refugees over a period of four years.'[59] The congress was asking for the admission of a few hundred families for whom it would accept full financial responsibility. Yet even this proved to be too much for the Jewish MPs to pry out of the government. Though it had not yet lost all hope that Ottawa would come through with some concessions, the congress now began thinking seriously of alternative forms of action.

Meanwhile, without much enthusiasm, the Canadian government began preparing for the Evian Conference. As Canada's representatives, King appointed the Canadian delegate to the League of Nations, Hume Wrong, and the commissioner of immigration in London, William R. Little. Wrong's instructions were succinct: listen, make notes, say as little as possible, and under no circumstances make any promises or commitments.[60] Canada was participating at the conference, the prime minister added, only for 'information,' and for no other reason. In any case, King reminded Wrong that since the League of Nations was shortly to discuss the universal problem of refugees, 'it would be neither practical nor just to discriminate in favour of refugees from Austria or Germany.'

Similarly, in his instructions to Little, Blair suggested that he go on the offensive and point out to the other delegates that Canada had done much more than was required to help solve the Jewish refugee problem. Fully 25 per cent of all special orders-in-council had been given to the Jews, he said. In an attempt to halt the Jewish exodus from Germany in its entirety, Blair suggested that since Jews were being robbed of both their assets and their citizenship, 'the two essentials of immigration,' Little should approach the other delegates to persuade their governments to take a united stand against accepting the immigrants 'without either capital or recognized citizenship.' And in case Little missed the point, in a personal letter two days later, Blair emphasized that there was 'not much enthusiasm in many quarters here for any increase in our Jewish immigration.'[61]

To make certain that whatever concession which might be forced on Canada at Evian was kept at a minimum, the creative director of immigration found a method which was simple and clever. He delayed the admission of the handful of Jewish refugees with substantial amounts of capital whose applications had already be approved by his department but whose names had not yet been forwarded to cabinet for the necessary order-in-council. If Canada were forced to make a gesture, only then would the names to be sent forward. Until them, however, these helpless Jews would have to wait.[62]

As delegates to the conference began arriving, Wrong smelled a rat. The meeting, he predicted, was 'going to be a most unpleasant affair' and his participation in it was 'unwelcome duty.' The proceedings, he feared, 'look very amateurish,' and the entire concept clearly was 'not the product of any well though-out scheme' but simply 'one of Mr. Roosevelt's sudden generous impulses.' If the Americans were seriously concerned with helping refugees, he wondered, why would they send as their delegates Myron Taylor, 'a steel tycoon,' and two minor foreign service officers, one of whom was 'a capable authority on the adminis-tration of the quota law.' Though he realized that there was not much support for the admission of refugees into Canada, he begged the prime minister not to make his instructions 'entirely negative.'[63]

King ignored Wrong's plea. Rather, in a strongly worded letter he reminded the Canadian delegate that Canada was at Evian only to 'exchange information.' Furthermore, Wrong was put on notice that if the Americans made concrete proposals to solve the refugee problem he should oppose them while trying neither to 'lead in this opposition' nor to be 'obstructionist.'[64] And to forestall any American action, King force-fully informed Washington that Canada would neither support nor be a member of any committee which would formulate and carry out a long-range programme to solve the refugee crisis. Canada, he reminded the Americans, could make no commitments to accept any refugees as this would 'raise real difficulties from the point of view of the Canadian Immigration Service.'[65] Though King was concerned with the plight of Germany Jewry, he seemed even more concerned over the administra-tive problems of Canadian Immigration officers.

The prime minister had already been informed by Blair that from the point of view of the Immigration Branch accepting German Jews would only exacerbate the situation. As Blair told Skelton: 'The Jews of Canada will not be satisfied unless the door is kept open in some way to all the Jews from other countries.' Canadian Jews, he added, were largely from Eastern Europe and would apply unremitting pressure to admit fellow Jews from this area.[66] As well, he reminded Crerar that in 1923 Jews had tricked immigration authorities into allowing into Canada more Rouma-nian Jews than had been agreed to. 'Running true to form,' he added, they would now likely use every loophole to bring in their co-religionists from Poland, Roumania, Russia, and Hungary. 'We will not,' he warned, 'satisfy Canadian Jewry by a special effort limited to the Jews of Germany and Austria.'[67]

As soon as the conference began, Wrong realized that Canadian worries had been groundless. The American delegate, Myron Taylor, was the first speaker. Instead of the magnanimous gesture all the representatives expected – and feared – the contribution of the United States government to solving the refugee crisis, Taylor announced, would be to fill its entire German-Austrian quota of 27,730. The delegates sat stunned following Taylor's speech The nations of the world had been mobilized for this? The collective sigh of relief from the assembled representatives was almost audible as Taylor sat down. For the Jews of Europe, Taylor's speech was a cruel letdown; for everyone else at Evian it was a godsend. It was clear that the Americans saw Evian as an exercise in public relations; they had no concrete proposals to solve – or even alleviate – the crisis. If the Americans were going to do nothing, it was hardly likely that anyone else would do anything either.

Sure enough, for the next few days delegate after delegate arose and announced that their respective nations were doing all they could to solve the crisis and that stringent immigration laws prohibited them from doing more.[68] In a short speech Wrong echoed these sentiments, announced that Canada had much sympathy for the impossible situation in which the refugees found themselves but that it could do no more than it was already doing – which was a great deal. 'Certain classes of agriculturalists,' he said, were welcome; everyone else was out of luck.[69]

For ten days, from 6 to 15 July, the thirty-two nations represented at Evian went through the motions of trying to solve the refugee problem without one – with the exception of the Dominican Republic – committing itself to accept more than a mere handful. Thus the conference concluded with a unanimous resolution that the nations of the world were 'not willing to undertake any obligations toward financing involuntary immigration.' Almost as an afterthought the delegates also approved the creation of an Intergovernmental Committee on Refugees to further study the problem.

Evian had clearly shown that no one wanted Jews. The world had been offered them and had declined with thanks. The Jews were now solely Germany's problem and, having turned their backs, the nations of the world could hardly in conscience object to the solution. In the eyes of the Nazis, the world had given them carte blanche to solve their Jewish problem – their way. As a Nazi newspaper put it: 'The Evian Conference serves to justify Germany's policy against Jewry.'[70] So, as the Jew suspected but never really believed until Evian, he was on his own.

The tragic failure of Evian exposed the impotence of world Jewry in general and Canadian Jewry in particular. Not only did the latter have no input in its own government's policy, it was not even told what this policy was. Indeed, only days before the conference began, a JIAS official in Montreal complained to his colleagues in Paris: 'It is quite possible that more will be found about the intentions of our Government in France than we learn on this side.'[71] Canadian Jews had not expected much from their government, but even they were disappointed in how little they received. As the president of JIAS lamented: 'It is quite obvious that the most that can be expected of Canada is to be more lenient in its application of the present regulations.'[72] But even this was a false hope.

Just one month after Evian, on 26 August, Crerar met with Blair and other ranking immigration authorities to review the government's position on refugees. Clearly Crerar had been moved by the tales of horror emanating from Germany and was anxious to do something to aid the refugees. The minister told his officials that, while he thought 'great care should be taken, we probably should admit more of these unfortunate people on humanitarian grounds.'[73] The well-meaning but naïve Crerar was no match for Blair and his 'experts.' By the time the meeting was over the thoroughly confused Crerar had agreed in fact to tighten restrictions even further. Apparently unaware of the regulations, Crerar agreed to raise the necessary capital requirement of prospective Jewish immigrants from $10,000 to $15,000. Canada's official response to Evian, then, was to make it almost impossible for any Jew to immigrate; there were not many refugees with $15,000.

What was perhaps most appalling about Blair's machinations was his admission to an Anglican clergyman not long afterwards that for some time he had been convinced that the destruction of European Jewry was at hand. In an all-too-prophetic letter to Canon W.W. Judd of Toronto, Blair stated that he feared that Jews were facing virtual 'extinction' in Europe. Allowing more of them into Canada, he informed Judd, would not solve the problem.[74]

For A.A. Heaps, who had for some time counselled Canadian Jewry to remain silent and to trust its leaders, the government's response to Evian was the last straw. Screwing up his courage, he wrote a passionate, bitter letter to his friend Mackenzie King stating that he had been betrayed by a duplicitous government whose 'oft-repeated promise' of allowing a reasonable number of refugees to come to Canada had proved to be a hoax. Though Evian had been traumatic for Heaps, he felt that one last desperate appeal to King, pointing out the iniquitous behaviour of his government, might shame the prime minister into some action. As he put it: 'The existing regulations are probably the most stringent to be found anywhere in the whole world. If refugees have no money they are barred because they are poor, and if they have fairly substantial sums, they are often refused admittance on the most flimsy pretext. All I say of existing regulations is that they are inhuman and anti-Christian ... Practically every nation in the world is allowing a limited number to enter their countries ... The lack of action by the Canadian government is leaving an unfortunate impression ... I regret to state that the sentiment is gaining ground that anti-Semitic influences are responsible for the government's refusal to allow refugees to come to Canada ...' King shunted the letter off to Crerar and Blair for their consideration. Heaps did not get a reply.[75] His was the last serious attempt by a Jewish MP to influence the government. Seriously weakened by the death of Sam Jacobs in late September, the contingent of Jewish MPs was no longer a factor in the battle for the admission of refugees. As the executive director of JIAS sadly informed Jewish officials in France: 'The remaining two Jewish members of Parliament were finally compelled to give up their efforts ... [as] they find themselves unable to be of any material assistance.'[76]

Embittered and frustrated, Jewish community leaders began giving serious consideration to organizing a nondenominational, anti-Nazi group which might more effectively lobby on behalf of the refugees. Perhaps a wider coalition of forces in which Jews would be less conspicuous though no less active, and for whom refugees would be seen as a humanitarian rather than a Jewish cause, might succeed where Jewish groups had not. At its annual convention in October the congress endorsed the creation of a nonsectarian body which could 'approach the Government and appeal to them directly for favourable consideration on purely humanitarian ground.'[77] Fortuitously, at exactly this moment, a respected non-sectarian organization had decided, on its own, to undertake precisely this course of action.

For some time the Canadian League of Nations Society had been in a state of despondency and had become almost moribund. As the world seemed hell-bent on another war, the organization had seemingly become as irrelevant as the league itself. Most of its membership were deeply disturbed by the apparent inhumanity of the Canadian government's refugee policy. In a sense, the Jewish refugee issue proved to be a boon to the society; it gave it new life, and new sources of membership and funds. It seemed to be the last great moral crusade of a dismal decade. In early October the society announced that it would 'place the strength of [its] entire organization behind a move to aid the Jewish refugees ... by requesting the Canadian government to take immediate action.' The society's president, the indefatigable Senator Cairine Wilson, a close friend and political ally of the prime minister, stated that the organization was already beginning to mobilize for such an effort. As part of that effort the Canadian Jewish Congress covertly promised to finance the campaign, but fearful that the society might be tarred as a 'Jewish front,' it was agreed that 'Jewish representation should be small.'[78]

Within a few weeks it hardly seemed to matter. Time had run out for German Jewry. On 9 and 10 November occurred the worst pogrom in modern world history to that time. *Kristallnacht* (literally crystal night, because of the broken glass from Jewish homes and businesses that littered the streets in every city, town, and village in Germany and Austria) was incited by the government to terrorize the Jews. Countless synagogues, Jewish stores and homes were plundered and razed. Men, women, and children were wrenched from their homes, beaten, shot, or dragged off to concentration camps. Scores were killed, hundreds injured, thousands arrested.

These tragic events finally touched the prime minister of Canada. 'The sorrows which the Jews have to bear at this time,' he wrote in his diary, 'are almost beyond comprehension.' 'Something,' he added, 'will have to be done by our country ...'[79] Coincidentally, on the following day, he personally shared in Jewish grief as he attended the funeral of Mrs Heaps. Again, he was overwhelmed by the breadth of the tragedy which was about to envelop the Jews. Writing in his diary that night he noted that it would be 'difficult politically,' and his cabinet might oppose him, but he was going to 'fight' for the admission of some Jewish refugees since it was 'right and just, and Christian.'[80]

The following week while he was in Washington for talks with Roosevelt concerning the upcoming visit of the Royal family, the conversation turned to the ghastly lot of Jewish refugees. While the president, Myron Taylor, and Cordell Hull discussed what could be done, King remained silent. In his own words, he 'just listened.' Yet during the conversation he 'felt more than ever' that since countries with 'more crowded areas,' such as Great Britain and the United States, were accepting refugees, Canada must open her doors. On his return to Ottawa he told the governor general, Lord Tweedsmuir, that on human-itarian grounds alone Canada should allow in some refugees and warned that 'if we tried to keep our country to ourselves, we would lose it altogether some day.' It seemed at long last that Canada was prepared to do something for the desperate Jews of Germany.[81]

It was precisely at this time that the Jews of Canada mobilized for one last dramatic effort to help save Germany Jewry. *Kristallnacht* had driven the community into a state of frenzied activity. On 14 November, at a special emergency meeting, the executive council of the Canadian Jew-ish Congress decided to proclaim Sunday, 20 November, 'a day of mourning' at which memorial meetings would be held across the coun-try. It instructed its local organizations to ensure that these meetings were 'non-sectarian,' that non-Jewish community leaders play a 'promi-nent role,' and that most of the speakers be Gentile. These meetings were to 'capitalize on the sympathy' felt towards the helpless victims of Nazi brutality and to 'impress' the government that public opinion was in favour of admitting some of them to Canada. In addition, each com-munity was sent a draft of a protest resolution which should be adopted at these meetings and forwarded to Ottawa.[82]

Surprisingly, with only five days to organize, the congress achieved dramatic results. Across Canada from Glace Bay, Nova Scotia, to Victo-ria, British Columbia, mass meetings were held and resolutions passed pleading with the government to open its heart and, more especially, its gate. And at almost every one of these meetings the featured speaker was a non-Jew. Mayors, judges, MPs, and businessmen took their place on the platform in support of the refugees. Twenty thousand partici-pated in Toronto, four thousand in Winnipeg, six hundred in Quebec City, two hundred in Vegreville, Alberta, eight hundred in Niagara Falls, twelve hundred in Kingston, three hundred in Humboldt, Saskatch-ewan. Telegrams, resolutions, petitions, and letters poured into the offices of the prime minister and various members of parliament. The demonstrations were, in the words of the Toronto *Globe and Mail*, an example of the 'brotherhood of man asserting itself.' Scores of news-papers across the nation, with the singular exception of the French press in Quebec, called for a more generous policy towards refugees.[83] To capitalize on this vast outpouring of public support, a high-powered delegation of Canadian Jews arrived in Ottawa on 22 November to meet with the prime minister to plead the case for Jewish refugees.

Unfortunately, it seemed they had come too late, for on the day they arrived in Ottawa the cabinet took up the refugee question. Despite King's urging to make some 'provision' for refugees, the Quebec ministers, led by Lapointe, were solidly opposed. Rather than press the issue and risk alienating Quebec, King announced to the press that the whole question needed further study.[84] This decision prompted the first serious signs of dissension within the Jewish community. The *Hebrew Journal* of Toronto castigated the congress leadership for being too.timid for too long. It called for more militant action against a government which had humiliated the Jewish community by 'shamelessly' making decisions concerning refugees the day before a delegation of Jewish leaders was to meet with the prime minister to make its representation.[85]

It was a shaken group of Jews who were ushered into King's office on 23 November. It included both Jewish MPs and the leaders of all the important community organizations, including the congress, JIAS, and the Zionist Organization of Canada. They pleaded with King and Crerar to open up Canada's doors by a crack and to admit 10,000 refugees whom the community would guarantee would not become public charges. They were politely rebuffed. King pointed out that unemployment in Canada was still high and that his first duty was 'the avoidance of strife ... maintaining the unity of the country,' and fighting 'the forces of separatism.' He sympathized with the refugees, he said, but he had 'to consider the constituencies and the views of those supporting the Government.' Crerar added that there were great administrative problems involved and in any case Canada had already accepted three hundred refugees over the past year. With that the delegation was excused.[86]

On the following day King again met his cabinet and, as he recorded in his diary, he once more asked them to adopt a 'liberal attitude,' to act as the 'conscience of the nation' even though it might not be 'politically most expedient,' and offer some aid to Jewish refugees. There was no response to his appeal. The cabinet, according to the prime minister, feared 'the political consequences of any help to the Jews.' What it was prepared to do, after some discussion, was to help find a home for these Jews 'in some [other] land.' King then dropped the issue as he 'did not wish to press the matter any further.'[87]

For Canadian Jews the cabinet decision was a shock; to their leaders it was devastating. Following a week of mass organization, demonstration, and protest, a week in which almost every English-language newspaper in the nation had condemned the government for its timidity, a week in which thousands had signed petitions demanding a more generous policy towards the refugees, it was generally assumed that the cabinet response would be positive. Especially mortified were Jewish leaders who had come to the prime minister with what they considered a minimal package that would cost the government nothing – allowing in a mere 10,000 refugees over a five-year period who the Jewish community would guarantee would never become 'burdens on Canadian society.' The prime minister had rejected every proposal and had told the Jews that if they wanted a change in government policy they should go out and 'arouse public opinion.' This the congress set out to do at once.[88]

Immediately following the fruitless confrontation with King, congress leaders met with Senator Cairine Wilson of the League of Nations Society of Canada. Together they began planning a vast lobbying and educational campaign to be undertaken by the society's newly created Canadian National Committee on Refugees [CNCR] to point out to Canadians the advantages to be gained by accepting Jewish refugees. These activities would be largely funded by the Canadian Jewish Congress.[89]

On 1 December, it seemed as if the Jewish community had won over its most important convert. On that day during a cabinet meeting Thomas Crerar, obviously troubled by his government's behaviour, announced to his stunned colleagues that he was prepared to recommend the admission of 10,000 refugees. The cabinet would not budge. Disassociating himself from the hapless immigration minister, whose proposal he thought was made 'without consideration' of the problems involved, King found a convenient solution. He suggested to his colleagues that they make use of the BNA Act to justify their inaction. He would publicly announce that nothing could be done for German Jews until the provinces were consulted, since immigration legislation was concurrent. At the same time he chided Crerar, told him to do his homework, and to prepare a statement which the cabinet would discuss.[90]

Crerar's defection clearly troubled King. Even more bothersome, however, was the announcement on the same day by the Australian government that it was now prepared to admit 15,000 refugees over the next three years. At once Crerar warned the prime minister that Canada would be put under 'a good deal of pressure' to follow suit.[91] As well, King received a trenchant letter from A.A. Heaps that the Australian decision had made him 'ashamed' as a Canadian and that the government's policy was 'inhumane' and 'lacking principle.'[92]

On 13 December, the cabinet took up the refugee issue once again. Aware that he had no support either from his cabinet colleagues or his departmental officials, Crerar read a statement, drafted by Blair, which said nothing about the admission of 10,000 refugees but which simply recommended the easing, ever so slightly, of the present immigration regulations.[93] After straying somewhat, Crerar had again been brought back into line. A relieved cabinet accepted the new position not to change the regulations but to interpret them 'as liberally as possible.' What this meant in practice, according to the prime minister, was that Jews already landed in Canada as tourists would be allowed to remain. However, no more Jewish refugees would be admitted to Canada 'lest it might foment an anti-Semitic problem ... and [create] a new problem.'[94] Thus, after months of wrestling with the question of Jewish refugees, the cabinet had at long last found an answer: keep them out.

Ironically, at the same meeting at which it was decided not to allow in Jews, the cabinet agreed to permit the entry of Czechs and Sudeten Germans since they were underwritten by a $500,000 gift from the British, French, and Czechoslovakian governments and since, in King's words, they 'had been sacrificed for the sake of the world's peace of which [Canadians] were beneficiaries.'[95]

There were, however, several additional reasons for the choice of Czech over Jew. The British government was applying heavy pressure on the dominions to admit Sudeten refugees. Indeed, immediately following the Munich agreement, Malcolm MacDonald, the dominions and colonial secretary, called together all the high commissioners and informed them that 'all those concerned with the recent settlement in Czechoslovakia had a greater responsibility in the matter than fell upon them, for example, in respect of the Jewish refugees in Germany and Austria.'[96] As well, the Canadian high commissioner in London was using what influence he had to make sure that restrictions on Jews entering Canada remained.

For Jewish refugees anxious to come to Canada it was unfortunate that the Canadian representative in London was, to say the least, no partisan of Jewish immigration. Vincent Massey, the prominent scion of the wealthy Massey family, had in fact become a fringe member of the aristocratic, largely pro-German and anti-Semitic Cliveden set centred around Lord and Lady Astor.[97] Though he was much too 'Anglophilic' to have the confidence or even the trust of Mackenzie King – indeed, the prime minister had once told Massey to his face that he was 'quite wrong on his views of most things' – his recommendations still had weight with the government, especially when they were in line with policies being considered by cabinet.[98] And on the question of Jewish refugees, their positions coincided.

Massey was enthusiastic about the anti-Nazi Sudetens, most of whom were Social Democrats or Catholics. Many of them, he told the prime minister, were skilled craftsmen, professionals, and farmers – exactly the type of settlers Canada craved. And perhaps even better, only a small percentage of them were Jews. He immediately saw an opportunity to score some public relations points for Canada at minimal cost. Would it not be a wonderful tactic, he suggested to King, to accept 'as many as possible Aryan Sudeten Germans.' These, he stated, were surely 'more desirable' than other refugees. But more to the point: 'If we could take a substantial number of them it would put us in a much stronger position in relation to later appeals from and on behalf of non-Aryans.' He also pleaded that the government consider Sudeten Germans 'quite separately from other refugees ... as they include ... many persons who would be much more desirable as Canadian settlers and much more likely to succeed in our country than certain other types of refugees.'[99] And in case the prime minister missed the point, Massey emphasized that 'these refugees are of a superior type to certain other categories of refugees who are engaging our attention.'[100]

Such cynicism was clearly not unappreciated in Ottawa and Skelton was quick to assure Massey that his suggestions were 'in line' with proposals already before cabinet.[101] It was not long after the high commissioner's recommendations arrived that the government decided to keep out the Jews and let in the Sudeten Germans. Massey was delighted with this decision. He congratulated King and at the same time informed him that there were now a large number of Central Europeans 'of means and education' who would enrich Canada 'in both the material sense and otherwise' who were finding Canadian immigration laws 'too wooden.' Canada was missing a golden opportunity, he told King, if it did not accept these people. Naturally, he added, he did not have in mind Jews, but rather 'the numerous non-Jewish people who find life quite intolerable under the Nazi regime.' In addition, he urged the prime minister to publicly announce that Canada was prepared to admit an unspecified number of non-Jewish German political refugees from the Sudeten.[102]

By the onset of 1939 an unofficial unholy triumvirate had been forged in the Immigration Service, the cabinet, and, to a much lesser degree, the Department of External Affairs against refugees in general and Jewish refugees in particular. In Immigration the intransigent and morally obtuse Blair gave vent to his anti-Semitism by placing every possible bureaucratic encumbrance in the path of refugees. In cabinet Ernest

Lapointe scuttled any cabinet backsliding – including that of the prime minister – on the refugee issue. In External Affairs Vincent Massey flirted with the aristocratic crowd in London, while doing what he could to keep Jews out of Canada. Individually, each had significant power; collectively, they seemed beyond challenge. Each had his own sphere of influence but on the refugee issue these spheres overlapped. Though there is no evidence that they consulted on this issue – and they likely did not – what united them was a common conviction: Canada did not need more Jews.

   Though the prime minister was not a prisoner of this anti-Jewish coterie, he could not help but be influenced by it. When the foremost immigration authority, the leading French-Canadian politician in the country, and the nation's senior foreign diplomat spoke, he listened, especially since they were all saying the same thing. King himself vacillated. At times his humanitarian and religious instincts led him to argue the refugee case; yet always his political instincts overcame these arguments. His sympathy for the refugees was genuine. He sincerely wanted to find them a home – anywhere but in Canada. Thus the barriers would remain. Only a vast public outcry, he told a delegation from the CNCR, could overturn them. He urged the delegates to go out to the nation and provide it with a 'proper education on this question.'[103] Just how much public support would have to be generated before the government would change its policy, King did not indicate. He did not have to. The combined forces of Jews and the CNCR, he knew, could hardly overcome government policy.

   Nor did he particularly want them to. Above all else, King was committed to keeping Canada united. Allowing in Jews, he feared, would disrupt that unity, and not only in Quebec.[104] Anti-Semitism, perhaps most overt in that province, was prevalent throughout English-speaking Canada as well. Jewish quotas existed in various professions, universities, medical schools, and industries. Jews were restricted from buying property in some areas, from holidaying at some resorts, from joining many private clubs or using their recreational facilities, and even from sitting on the boards of various charitable, educational, financial, and business organizations.[105] Anti-Jewish sentiments were being voiced regularly, and with impunity, throughout these years by many respectable newspapers, politicians, businessmen, and churchmen, and by leading officials of such groups as the Canadian Corps Association, the Orange Order, the Knights of Columbus, and prominent farm and business organizations.[106] There was even some violence as Jew and anti-

Semite confronted one another on the streets of Toronto, Winnipeg, or other Canadian cities.[107] Indeed, so grave did this problem appear that at its founding convention the CNCR resolved that one of its major priorities must be to combat the anti-Semitism that seemed so rife in Canada.[108]

If it is possible to overemphasize the extent of anti-Semitism in Canada at this time, it is not possible to ignore it. It existed and King was well aware that it did. Any move to admit Jewish refugees, he feared, might cost him political support. Although some organizations and some high-placed members of some religious groups such as the Anglican and United churches actively campaigned on behalf of Jewish refugees, most Canadians seemed indifferent to the suffering of German Jews and hostile to admitting some of them to Canada. Indeed, in March of 1939, the Rev. Claris Silcox, the general secretary of the Social Service Council of Canada and a leading pro-refugee advocate, delivered what he called a 'post-mortem' on Canada's refugee policy to a large audience at the University of Toronto. He listed a series of reasons for Canada's failure to respond to the crisis. These ranged from timid leadership and a bad economic situation to the success of Nazi propagandists and the xenophobia in Quebec. But the most important reason, he claimed, was 'the existence throughout Canada ... of a latent anti-Semitism.'[109] It was this anti-Semitism, he charged, which had prevented Canada from carrying out its duty as a Christian nation and which allowed her government to close Canada's doors to Jewish refugees.

Nevertheless, despite all the obstacles, Jewish leaders persevered; they had no choice. In December 1938 all the disparate refugee activities of the Jewish community were united into a single organization, the Canadian Committee for Jewish Refugees [CCJR] headed by the congress president, Samuel Bronfman. Though it was understaffed and underfunded, it co-operated with various local refugee committees in organizing a series of 'educational' campaigns. In January 1939, for instance, Silcox was sent out on a speaking tour of Western Canada. Officially travelling under the banner of the CNCR to address community groups and service clubs, he was actually funded out of Toronto by the CCJR. A gifted public speaker, Silcox attracted both wide media coverage and editorial support for his cause. He also made himself available to local Jewish groups and helped organize refugee committees throughout the West. In addition, the local committees worked with the CNCR to publicize the successful business ventures begun by refugee industrialists in Britain and the United States and pointed out the opportunities which Canada was missing by keeping these people out. Similar arguments were also made respecting the potential wealth of scholarly and scientific manpower that could now be Canada's for the asking.[110]

Buoyed by numerous supporting editorials and a gratifying response to public speakers, Jewish leaders were again in Ottawa in late February. Convinced that there was now a groundswell of popular support in English Canada, they fully expected 'a definite and favourable decision.' As delegates would later report to their communities: 'It was felt that by now opinion has been crystallized and the government is in a position to tell the Jews of Canada what it intends to do.'[111] And indeed it was. Though polite and sympathetic, it was unyielding. Crerar and Blair congratulated the Jewish delegates on their success in coalescing so much national support in so short a time but offered them nothing. Indeed, a disingenuous Blair told them that with respect to the Sudeten refugees, there would be no discrimination against Jews, 'a number of whom would be included in the allotment.'[112] Two weeks later Crerar announced in parliament that after a careful study of every family, he could assure the House that 'probably 95 percent of these people are Roman Catholics.'[113] Quebec could hardly complain; nor could Vincent Massey.

The meeting with Crerar and Blair finally disabused Jewish leaders of any notion they still cherished that the government would change its policy. King saw no need for any shift. He felt that whatever popular support there was for refugees in English Canada was ephemeral. As well, with an election in the offing, could he dare alienate his base in Quebec? As he explained to George Wrong, who had written of his agony and frustration over Canada's shameful behaviour towards the refugees, the issue was 'the most baffling of our international problems.' He promised to make a 'contribution to its solution' but feared that by doing so he might create a 'condition which it may be more difficult to meet than the one it is intended to cure.' Allowing in Jewish refugees, he dreaded, would undermine the Canadian unity he had fought so hard to maintain.[114]

It was now almost too much for Canadian Jews to bear. There was no longer any hope of convincing the King administration to change its mind. Yet with newspapers full of horror stories of German Jews being whipped through the streets, thrown off roofs, and dehumanized in every possible way, Canadian Jewry could not possibly admit defeat. Failure was unthinkable even as the unthinkable was beginning to happen in Europe. Thus a newly revamped Jewish refugee committee was formed in March 1939 under the leadership of an energetic young Montreal lawyer, Saul Hayes.[115] The creation of yet another committee was too much for one prominent Jew. Mirroring the rancour that was now pervading the community, S.M. Shapiro, the publisher of the *Hebrew Journal*, complained bitterly: 'The policy of secret diplomacy pursued until now has not brought results. The public was duly impressed by the arguments advanced that any undue publicity was likely to do harm to the cause ... For two years the leaders of the Congress sought to assuage any misgivings on the part of the Jewish public by assuring it that they were negotiating with the authorities in Ottawa. The impression was conveyed that they were given some secret commitment by the government. Yet ... it is becoming apparent that the secret negotiations accomplished nothing and that our leaders had no more promises from the Ottawa government than if they had done nothing at all in the matter.'[116]

Though his judgment was harsh, Shapiro was undoubtedly correct. Jewish leadership had been led down a garden path by the King administration. And yet they were still anxious to have another go at the government, this time with the revitalized refugee committee. That Hayes and his committee would have succeeded where others had failed is doubtful. They did not even get the chance; events in Europe were moving too quickly. As the committee was making preparations to go to Ottawa, Hitler was making preparations to go to Warsaw.

Hitler struck first. On 1 September Germany marched into Poland. The fate of European Jewry was sealed. Blair, Lapointe, Massey, and King had stood fast just long enough. The Canadian Jewish community would soon turn its attention to saving the remnants of Auschwitz.

The Canadian government's success in withstanding pressure from pro-refugee groups, both Jewish and non-Jewish, was virtually complete. The Depression, the general apathy in English Canada, the outright hostility of French Canada, the unyielding opposition of certain key officials, the prime minister's concern for votes, and the overlay of anti-Semitism that dominated official Ottawa thinking on the question combined to ensure that no more than a mere handful of Jewish refugees would find a haven in Canada. And even the outbreak of hostilities held its own irony for the refugees. Ever watchful lest Jews might slip past him, Blair did not see the beginning of the war as an excuse to let down his guard. With thousands of Jewish refugees desperately scrambling to escape still unoccupied Europe, Blair confidently advised Skelton that there was no need to worry. The Jews would not get into Canada. After all, most of these refugees were German nationals and, therefore, enemy aliens. Enemy aliens were expressly forbidden admission into Canada.[117] The line had been drawn. It was not about to move.

NOTES

This article is from *Canadian Historical Review* 60 (2) (1979). Reprinted with permission of University of Toronto Press Incorporated.

The authors are indebted to Robert F. Harney of the Multicultural History Society of Ontario, David Rome of the Canadian Jewish Archives, and Lawrence Tapper of the Canadian Ethnic Archives for their encouragement and assistance.

1 G. Thomas and M.M. Witts, *The Voyage of the Damned* (New York 1974), 135–217
2 *New York Times*, 3–5 June 1939
3 Public Archives of Canada [PAC], King Papers, Wrong et al. to King, 7 June 1939, 238579
4 PAC, King Diary, 8 June 1939, King Papers, King to Skelton, 8 June 1939, 237087
5 King Papers, Skelton to King, 9 June 1939, 237095–6
6 PAC, Department of Immigration Records [IR], Blair to Skelton, 8 June 1939; 16 June 1939, file 644452 (our italics)
7 J. Hope Simpson, *The Refugee Problem: Report of Survey* (London 1939), 49–66
8 Quoted in A.J. Sherman, *Island Refuge: Britain and Refugees from the Third Reich 1933–9* (London 1973), 112
9 It is impossible to specify the exact number of refugees of all classes, or Jewish refugees in particular, admitted into Canada in the prewar years. In reply to a letter in 1940 from an MP requesting these statistics, the director of immigration conceded: 'We have no refugee classification in our immigration statistics as the term is a temporary variable one and we try to keep statistics by race [ethnicity], nationality, occupation and destination.' Nevertheless, it is possible to systematically approximate the total number of Jewish refugees. In these years government statistics reveal that, of a total immigration of some 100,000, only 6000 were Jews. By allowing for those Jews who entered Canada from countries such as the United States and the United Kingdom, beyond the shadow of the Nazi threat, or who emigrated before Nazi expansion made flight imperative, we can assume

that about 4000 entered as refugees. This latter figure is given added weight when considered in the light of the findings of Michael Proudfoot. In his important study of world refugee movements, Proudfoot employs international statistics to estimate that in the period between 1933 and the outbreak of war, Canada admitted 6000 refugees of all classes of whom 1500 were Sudeten Germans. It is not unreasonable then to assume approximately 4000 of the remaining refugees were Jews. IR, Blair to J.F. Pouliot, 16 July 1940, file 673931/1; *Canada Year Book, 1940*, 152; *1941*, 114; Louis Rosenberg, *The Jewish Population of Canada*, Canadian Jewish Population Studies no 2 (Montreal 1947); Michael J. Proudfoot, *European Refugees, 1939–52* (London 1952), 27

10 Proudfoot, *European Refugees*; Simpson, *The Refugee Problem*, 54–63; A. Tartakower and K.R. Grossman, *The Jewish Refugee* (New York 1944), 263–4, 318–27
11 See, for example, *Canada Year Book, 1939*, 158
12 IR, Blair to Mrs I. Grenovsky, 5 Dec. 1938, file 644452; PAC, Manion Papers, Blair to R.A. Bell, private secretary to Manion, 29 Feb. 1938
13 *Canadian Annual Review*, 1928–9, 153–9
14 PAC, Historical Personnel Files, vol. 420, file on F.C. Blair
15 Ibid.
16 Ibid.; Austin Cross in *The Family Herald and Weekly Star*, 16 June 1943
17 Interview with James Gibson, Vineland, Ontario, 26 June 1978
18 See Gerald Dirks, *Canadian's Refugee Policy: Indifference or Opportunism?* (Montreal 1977), 44–97; Robert Domanski, 'While Six Million Cried: Canada and the Refugee Question 1938–41' (unpublished thesis, Institute of Canadian Studies, Carleton University, 1975), 14–16.
19 IR, Blair to Crerar, 12 Oct. 1938, file 54782/5
20 IR, Blair to F.N. Sclanders, commissioner of Saint John Board of Trade, 13 Sept. 1938, file 54782/5
21 IR, Blair to Crerar, 28 March 1938, file 54781/5
22 IR, Blair to H.R.L. Henry, 30 Jan. 1939, file 644452
23 IR, Blair to W. Baird, 4 May 1938, file 54782/5
24 IR, Blair to W.A. Little, 24 Oct. 1939, file 54782/6
25 IR, Blair to Sclanders, 13 Sept. 1938, file 54782/5
26 Simon Belkin, *Through Narrow Gates: A Review of Jewish Immigration, Colonization and Immigrant Aid in Canada* (Montreal 1966), 169–70; Joseph Kage, *With Faith and Thanksgiving* (Montreal 1962), 66–9
27 Belkin, *Through Narrow Gates*, 170–3
28 IR, Memorandum for file, Blair, 20 Jan. 1936, file 54782/4
29 YIVO Institute, New York, Jewish Historical Collection, Hebrew Immigrant

Aid Society [HICEM], files, Report of JIAS Montreal, 18 Feb. 1937; interview, Saul Hayes, Montreal, 20 June 1978. See also Leo Heaps, *The Rebel in the House: The Life and Times of A.A. Heaps, M.P.* (London 1970), 155

30 IR, Memorandum for file, Blair, 19 April 1938, file 54782/5
31 Canadian Jewish Congress [CJC], CPR, Hamburg, to H. Heinemann, Breslau, 8 May 1938. Heinemann sent a copy of this telegram to the congress with a plea for the congress to help him save his family from the Nazis.
32 CJC, Caiserman to Wise, 4 Feb. 1938
33 National Archives, Washington, State Department Records, Memorandum on Refugees, 1938, files 900–1/2; 840–8
34 John Munro, ed., *Documents on Canadian External Relations*. VI: *1936–39* (Ottawa 1972) [DCER VI], Memorandum from the United States Delegation, 25 March 1938, 790–1
35 King Diary, 29 March 1938
36 King Papers, Skelton to King, 25 March 1938, C122621
37 King Diary, 29 March 1938
38 Quoted in David Rome, 'A History of Anti-Semitism in Canada,' unpublished manuscript, Montreal 1978, unpaginated
39 See, for example, Brunelle's speech in House, Canada, House of Commons, *Debates*, 1939, I, 305.
40 See, for example, IR, file 165172.
41 *Debates*, 1939, I, 428. For a survey of anti-Semitism in Quebec, see David Rome, *Clouds in the Thirties: On Anti-Semitism in Canada, 1929–1939*, 3 vols. (Montreal 1977); Lita Rose Betcherman, *The Swastika and the Maple Leaf* (Toronto 1975); W.D. Kernaghan, 'Freedom of Religion in the Province of Quebec' (PhD thesis, Duke University, 1966).
42 King Diary, 5 and 6 July 1938
43 H. Blair Neatby, *William Lyon Mackenzie King. III: The Prism of Unity* (Toronto 1976), 268. Canadian Jewish leaders were not unaware of the position of cabinet ministers from Quebec. Following the provincial Liberal party's defeat in Quebec, the president of the Jewish Immigrant Aid Society in Montreal reported to his board 'that he had it on good authority that the French Canadian element in the Federal Cabinet is strongly opposed to the admission of Jews to Canada.' JIAS, Eastern Region (Montreal), Minutes of the Board of Directors, 9 Dec. 1936
44 King Diary, 6 July 1938
45 IR, Blair draft, 19 April 1938, file 644452
46 King Papers, Blair to Skelton, 14 April 1938, C122627
47 IR, Memorandum for file, Blair, 19 April 1938, file 644452

48 IR, Blair to Crerar, 28 March 1938, file 644452

49 IR, Memorandum for file, Blair, 19 April 1938, file 644452

50 IR, Blair to Skelton, 8 April 1938, file 644452

51 King Papers, Skelton to King, 21 April 1938, C122124

52 DCER VI, King to Simmons, 26 April 1938, 793–4

53 PAC, Western Canadian Jewish Historical Society Papers [WCJH], Caiserman to M.A. Averbach, 15 April 1938, vol. 101

54 CJC, Caiserman to O.B. Roger, 25 April 1938

55 CJC, Heaps to N.A. Gray, 25 May 1938; Benjamin Robinson (president of JIAS) to O.B. Roger, 23 May 1938

56 King Papers, Cabinet Memorandum, 18 May 1938, 214192

57 King Papers, Pickering to King, 2 June 1938, 214193; CJC, Heaps to Caiserman, 23 May 1938

58 CJC, N.A. Gray to Caiserman, 26 May 1938

59 CJC, B. Robinson to HICEM, Paris, 2 June 1938

60 DCER VI, King to Wrong, 11 June 1938, 801–5

61 IR, Blair to Little, 4 and 6 June 1938, file 644452

62 IR, Blair to Jollife, 13 June 1938, file 644452

63 DCER VI, Wrong to Skelton, 21 June 1938, 806–7

64 King Papers, King to Wrong, 30 June 1938, 223086

65 DCER VI, King to Simmons, 28 June 1938, 807–10

66 IR, Blair to Skelton, 13 June 1938; Blair memorandum, 13 June 1938, file 644452

67 IR, Blair to Crerar, 14 June 1938, file 644452

68 D.A. Wyman, *Paper Walls; America and the Refugee Crisis, 1938–1941* (Boston 1968), 43–51. See also H.L. Feingold, *The Politics of Rescue: The Roosevelt Administration and the Holocaust, 1938–1945* (New Brunswick, NJ, 1970).

69 PAC, External Affairs Records [EA], Wrong Speech to Evian Conference, box 1870, file 327–1

70 *Danzinger Vorposter*, quoted in Peggy Mann, 'When the World Passed by the Other Side,' *The Guardian*, 7 May 1978, 18

71 CJC, M.A. Salkin to HICEM, Paris, 23 June 1938

72 CJC, Robinson to Oscar Cohen, 14 July 1938

73 IR, Blair memorandum on meeting with Crerar, 26 Aug. 1938, file 54782/5

74 IR, Blair to W.W. Judd, Oct. 1938, file 54782/5

75 King Papers, Heaps to King, 9 Sept. 1938, 214195; H.R.L. Henry to Heaps, 15 Sept. 1938, 214197

76 CJC, Salkin to James Bernstein, Paris, 3 Oct. 1938

77 CJC, Proceedings of 1938 Convention

78 PAC, League of Nations Society of Canada Papers, Executive Minutes,

15 Oct. 1938; interview, Constance Haywood, Toronto, 8 May 1978; *Western Jewish News*, Winnipeg, 6 Oct. 1938; WCJH, Oscar Cohen to B. Sheps, 30 Oct. 1938

79 King Diary, 12 Nov. 1938

80 Ibid., 13 Nov. 1938

81 Ibid., 17 and 20 Nov. 1938

82 CJC, Memorandum from H. Caiserman, 15 Nov. 1938

83 CJC, Regional reports on 20 Nov. meetings; clipping file, Nov. 1938, with excerpts from thirty-five newspapers and weeklies; Toronto *Globe and Mail*, 22 Nov. 1938

84 King Diary, 22 Nov. 1938; *Toronto Star*, 23 Nov. 1938

85 *Hebrew Journal* (Yiddish), 23 Nov. 1938

86 King Diary, 23 Nov. 1938; King Papers, A.J. Freiman (president of the Zionist Organization of Canada) to King, 23 Nov. 1938, 213348

87 King Diary, 24 Nov. 1938

88 CJC, Caiserman to Sheps, 28 Nov. 1938; *Toronto Star*, 25 Nov. 1938

89 CJC, Oscar Cohen to Sheps, 29 Nov. 1938

90 King Diary, 1 Dec. 1938

91 King Papers, Crerar to King, 2 Dec. 1938, C122661

92 Ibid., Heaps to King, 2 Dec. 1938, 214198

93 IR, Draft Statement ... regarding Refugees, 12 Dec. 1938; King Papers, Pickersgill to King, 13 Dec. 1938, file 644452

94 King Diary, 21 Dec. 1938

95 Ibid. For details see IR, file 916207, and B.A. Gow, 'A Home for Free Germans in the Wilderness of Canada: The Sudeten Settlers of Tupper Creek, British Columbia,' *Canadian Ethnic Studies*, X, 1978, 62–74.

96 Quoted in Sherman, *Island Refuge*, 141. See also DCER VI, Massey to King, 18 Oct. 1938, 828.

97 Interview with James Gibson. See also Vincent Massey, *What's Past Is Prologue* (Toronto 1963), 114–15; Christopher Sykes, *The Life of Lady Astor* (London 1972), 364–411; D.C. Watt, *Personalities and Policies* (London 1965), 26, 119, 161.

98 J.L. Granatstein and R. Bothwell, 'A Self-Evident National Duty: Canadian Foreign Policy 1935–9,' *Journal of Imperial and Commonwealth History*, III, 1975, 214; King Diary, 5 Oct. 1935; Lester B. Pearson, *Mike: The Memoirs of the Right Honourable Lester B. Pearson*, I: *1897–1948* (Toronto 1972), 105–6

99 DCER VI, Massey to King, 29 Nov. 1938; Massey to Skelton, 1 Dec. 1938, 837, 844–5

100 EA, Massey to King, 2 Dec. 1938, box 1870, file 327–II

101 Ibid., Skelton to Massey, 2 Dec. 1938

102 Ibid., Massey to King, 13 Jan. 1939, box 1870, file 327–III; King Papers, Massey to King, 3 Feb. 1939, 231607–10
103 PAC, Cairine Wilson Papers, Minutes of CNCR Founding Convention, 6 Dec. 1938, 4
104 Neatby, *King*, III, 304–5
105 CJC, Files on Anti-Semitism in Canada 1930–40. These contain reports to the congress from Jews throughout Canada on anti-Jewish attitudes and behaviour in their localities.
106 CJC, Files on Anti-Semitism; Betcherman, *The Swastika and the Maple Leaf*, 99–137; Howard Palmer, 'Nativism and Ethnic Tolerance in Alberta, 1920–1972' (PhD thesis, York University, 1973)
107 See, for example, *Toronto Star*, 17–19 Aug. 1933, for descriptions of the infamous Christie Pits riots.
108 PAC, Cairine Wilson Papers, Minutes, 7
109 United Church Archives, Silcox Papers, Speeches, 'Canadian Post-Mortem on Refugees,' Toronto, 21 March 1939
110 WCJH, Oscar Cohen to Sheps, 30 Dec. 1938; Silcox Papers, Clipping File, Western Canada Tour, Jan. 1939
111 CJC, Report on Interview with T.A. Crerar and F.C. Blair, 24 Feb. 1939, 1
112 Ibid., 4
113 *Toronto Star*, 10 March 1939
114 King Papers, Wrong to King, 17 Feb. 1939; King to Wrong, 25 Feb. 1939, 238576–8
115 CJC, Caiserman to Sheps, 13 March 1939. During the war years Hayes was to prove such an effective advocate for Jewish refugees on the government's refugee board that Blair complained: 'To prevent the more generous scale of assistance to Jewish cases ... I think the best way to do this would be to get rid of Sol [sic] Hayes ...' IR, Blair to Byers, 20 Sept. 1941, file 694687
116 *Hebrew Journal*, 2 May 1939
117 IR, Blair to Skelton, 16 Nov. 1939, file 644452

TOPIC EIGHT
Regulating Minorities in 'Hot' and 'Cold' War Contexts, 1939–1960s

Not only at the time of arrival do immigrants capture the attention of government officials or reform-minded gatekeepers. Dramatic events that fuel concerns about a country's resources and its capacity to mount a united national effort inevitably provoke anxious debate about the disloyalty or 'divided loyalty' of racial-ethnic minorities. The Second World War provides an example of how a wartime context could unleash 'a war within' as state authorities and others sought to regulate the behaviour of immigrants, in part through a massive propaganda campaign designed to rally immigrants to Canada's war, but also through the surveillance and repression of 'undesirables.' The fears and, sometimes, the hysteria unleashed by the Cold War also influenced the responses and activities of officials, reformers, and social 'experts' involved in immigrant reception work. Whether sympathetic, indifferent, or hostile towards the backgrounds and predicaments of the newcomers they treated and serviced, their efforts were part of a larger goal to remake immigrants into model citizens for Canadian democracy.

The readings in this section consider the treatment of minorities in two dramatic contexts: the Second World War and the Cold War. In September 1939 Canadians entered the war against Germany with deep reservations, mindful of the death and destruction that had resulted from the First World War and of the military might of Nazi Germany. Prime Minister Mackenzie King also feared Quebec opposition and other threats to national unity that might be unleased by the decision. Would Canadians in general tolerate the punishing effects of war both on the battlefront and the homefront? As in the First World War, Canadians saw government intervene dramatically in their daily lives, freezing prices and wages, overseeing factory production in munitions industries, and rationing such essential consumer items as food and gasoline. Faced with acute labour shortages at home, a consequence of a boom economy and an atrocious loss of life overseas, the government encouraged women to enter the workforce. By fall 1944, a million women were employed full-time in industry. At war's end, they were told to return to their homes.

Government intervention brought the war into the homes of Canadians, many of whom followed closely the conduct of the war. The early military successes of Germany alarmed Canadians and accentuated the fissures of a multi-ethnic society. The Japanese attack on Pearl Harbor in December 1941 created a state of near-hysteria in British Columbia, with dire consequences for the more than 20,000 Japanese Canadians living there. The response of English and French Canadians to 'ethnic' Canadians, both foreign- and Canadian-born, was the manifestation of long-standing prejudices combined with the stresses and paranoia caused by war. For example, the 1942 evacuation of Japanese Canadians from British Columbia was prompted by the actions of white British Columbians who predicted a Japanese attack from within the province, but it was not really about national security. Rather, Ottawa bowed to pressure from white British Columbians who had long treated Asians with suspicion and scorn.[1]

Similar patterns were evident elsewhere in the country, though with less harmful consequences. Howard Palmer's article suggests that prevailing attitudes towards minority groups in wartime Alberta were rooted in the pre-war status of these groups. For instance, Italians and Germans, because of their high degree of integration into Albertan society, were spared some of the intense animosity suffered by other minorities even though Germany and Italy were enemy nations. Other groups, such as Doukhobors, Mennonites, and Hutterites, pacifists who refused to actively support the war, drew the harshest treatment. Their anti-militarism, in turn, reinforced their pre-war status as 'other.' What was for these men and women a political and moral choice to oppose war was given a racial-ethnic colouring as loyalty to the Canadian state came to be defined in terms of Anglo conformity. To what extent did Canadian policy-makers dance to a tune played by public opinion on the question of ethnic minorities in wartime? Did 'foreigners' pose a legitimate national security risk? Given that Canada was at war with Germany, Italy, and Japan by the end of 1941, why did Ottawa evacuate virtually all Japanese Canadians while interning only a relatively small number of Italian and German Canadians? How did the response of Canadian government and society to its ethnic minorities differ in the two world wars?

In the years after the war, as much of Europe lay in ruins, many North Americans experienced the benefits of economic growth and general prosperity. Partly out of economic self-interest, industrialists and agriculturalists in both Canada and the United States rushed to help their allies and trading partners in Europe and Asia in picking up the pieces of their war-torn economies. The war had also resulted in the dislocation of thousands of ordinary people, many of whom knocked on Canada's door hoping to be allowed in. Many Canadians wanted to keep newcomers out altogether, but the demands of an expanding economy for cheap labour and international pressures to help alleviate an enormous refugee crisis convinced King's Liberal government to admit certain immigrants. These included eastern European political refugees who refused to return to Soviet-occupied lands, and economic emigrants from Britain and Europe in search of employment and upward mobility. The numbers tell the dramatic story of the postwar influx of newcomers. In 1945, just under 23,000 immigrants arrived in Canada; in 1951, close to 200,000 arrived. In the 1950s, no fewer than 100,000 newcomers arrived in Canada each year. In 1957, the wave of immigrants reached its peak at close to 300,000.

The government's adoption of a more open-door immigration policy replaced the highly restrictionist policy of the 1930s. But it did not mark a total break with traditional policy. Responses to new immigrants after the Second World War were still conditioned by strident anti-Communism and an overriding desire to preserve and promote as much as possible the Anglo-Celtic, northern, white 'character' of the Canadian population. Hence the continued preference for British, white American, and northern Europeans. Another continuity that reemerged after the Second World War was the close connection between immigration policy and the economic needs of the country. It was economics more than altruism, for example, that ultimately led to the removal in 1967 of certain longstanding racial barriers that effectively prohibited immigration from 'non-white' sources such as South Asia and the Carribean. One result has been the increasing racial diversification of Canada's peoples. Yet barriers remain. For example, since the 1950s the federal government has recruited Black Caribbean women to work as domestic servants in Canada. But the intention has been to allow only a limited number into Canada as temporary workers, not landed immigrants, in order to meet the demand for cheap domestic labourers, and to maintain good trading relations with the British Caribbean. Once the contracts expire, the Caribbean domestics were (and are) expected to return home.

Beyond the realm of official policy were the hundreds of social agencies that dealt with the postwar newcomers' settlement needs. This task took on some urgency with the onset of the Cold War. Franca Iacovetta's article suggests that these social agencies were self-appointed instruments of Canadianization that tried, though not entirely successfully, to make immigrant families over according to a preconceived conception of the 'model' family. Her analysis of a large Toronto social agency that catered to non-British immigrants suggests that it was against the backdrop of the Cold War anxieties about the future of the family that social workers tried to sell to immigrants their ideal of family, an ideal informed by specific notions of gender, class, and race-ethnicity. What was this ideal of the model family? How did it correspond to the realities of immigrants? Of other Canadians? Indeed, how did the immigrants themselves respond both to official policy and to the efforts of social agencies? Were they merely passive subjects? Or could they manipulate 'the system' for their own ends? Should we distinguish between immigration and refugee policy? Have attitudes toward newcomers changed since, say, the 1960s? Are there still lines of continuity to be drawn from the era of Clifford Sifton? Finally, the readings suggest how the urgency of a 'hot' and 'cold' war can create a pretext for pursuing offensive or questionable objectives. Do you agree or disagree?

NOTES

1 See the works by Adachi, Sunahara, and Ward cited in the bibliography below; others have offered justifications for Ottawa's action (see Granatstein et al., also cited below).

BIBLIOGRAPHY AND SUGGESTED READINGS

Abella, Irving, and Harold Troper. *None Is Too Many: Canada and the Jews of Europe, 1933–1948*. Toronto 1982.
Adachi, Ken. *The Enemy That Never Was: A History of the Japanese Canadians*. Toronto 1976.
Broadfoot, Barry. *Six War Years*. Toronto 1974.
Danys, Milda. *DP: Lithuanian Immigration to Canada after the Second World War*. Toronto 1987.
Dirks, Gerald. *Canada's Refugee Policy: Indifference or Opportunism?* Montreal 1977.

Granatstein, J.L. *Canada's War: The Politics of the Mackenzie King Government*. Toronto, 1975.

Granatstein, J.L., Patricia Roy, Masako Iino, and Hiroko Takamura. *Mutual Hostages: Canadians and Japanese during the Second World War*. Toronto 1990.

Hawkins, Freda. *Canada and Immigration: Public Policy and Public Concern*. Montreal 1972.

Harney, Robert F. '"So Great a Heritage as Ours": Immigration and the Survival of the Canadian Polity.' *Daedalus* 117:4. (Fall 1988),

Hillmer, N., B. Kordan, and L. Luciuk, eds. *On Guard for Thee: Ethnicity and the Canadian State, 1939–1945*. Ottawa 1988.

Iacovetta, Franca. *Such Hardworking People: Italian Immigrants in Postwar Toronto*. Kingston and Montreal 1992.

– 'Remaking Their Lives: Women Immigrants, Survivors and Refugees.' In Joy Parr, ed., *A Diversity of Women: Ontario, 1945–80*. Toronto 1995.

Li, Peter S., and B. Singh, eds. *Racial Minorities in Multicultural Canada*. Toronto 1983.

Whitaker, Reginald. *Double Standard: The Secret History of Canadian Immigration*. Toronto 1987.

Pierson, Ruth Roach. *They're Still Women after All*. Toronto 1986.

Stacey, C.P. *Arms, Men and Governments: The War Policies of Canada, 1939–1945*. Ottawa 1970.

Silvera, Makeda. *Silenced*. Toronto 1988.

Sunahara, Ann. *The Politics of Racism: The Uprooting of Japanese Canadians during the Second World War*. Toronto 1981.

Ward, Peter. *White Canada Forever: Popular Attitudes and Public Policy towards Orientals in British Columbia*. Montreal and Kingston 1978.

Ethnic Relations in Wartime: Nationalism and European Minorities in Alberta during the Second World War

HOWARD PALMER

The impact of national crises such as war on ethnic relations in Canada is a subject which has recently begun to receive scholarly attention. Historians John Thompson and Donald Avery have discussed the upsurge of nativism towards 'enemy aliens' during World War I, and a number of authors have recently examined the impact of World War II on attitudes toward the Japanese. However, the fate of minority ethnic groups other than the Japanese during the Second World War has not been examined.[1]

This article focuses on ethnic relations in Alberta from 1939 to 1945 and attempts to assess the impact of the war on inter-group relations. During this period, attitudes were altered, either negatively or positively, toward many ethnic groups in the province. Wartime hostility was new neither to the Germans (the largest non-British ethnic group in the province), nor to the three small pacifist sects, the Hutterites, Mennonites and Doukhobors. But two small groups in the province who had been on the 'right' side during the First World War – Italians and Japanese[2] – now found themselves associated in the public mind with Axis enemy powers in Europe and the Far East.

Examining attitudes towards these groups entails the examination of some key questions. To what extent did the existing degree of acculturation of individual ethnic groups determine the nature of attitudes toward them during the war? Would the fight against Hitler also become a fight against Hitler's racism?

For the purposes of this essay, racism or racial prejudice has been defined as 'antipathy toward a racial group.' By nationalism, particularly within a wartime context, I mean 'the state of mind in which the individual feels that everyone owes his or her supreme secular loyalty to the nation-state.' The term 'nativism' is used to describe the amalgam of prejudice and nationalism. Thus nativism is defined as 'opposition to an internal minority on the grounds that it poses a threat to Canadian national life.'[3]

Wartime Alberta: The Economic, Social and Political Context

Wartime Alberta was a different place from the Alberta of the depression. Albertans were living in an era of contradictions, of simultaneous harmony and discord; it was a time of economic growth but also of pronounced social strain.

Although the presence of the armed forces generated considerable mobility, the size of Alberta's population during the war was relatively stable. The population increased only slightly, from 769,000 in 1941 to 803,000 in 1946. Fewer than 600 immigrants from abroad arrived in any given year, an even smaller number than during the last years of the Depression. In the period 1941–1946 there was a net emigration of 72,000 people, composed primarily of those who left to serve in the Canadian armed forces as well as those who left to obtain war-industry jobs in other parts of the country. There were no large permanent population shifts from one region to another within the province, although there was a definite trend toward urbanization. The numbers of people living in urban areas increased from 28 percent in 1941 to 34 per cent in 1946, largely as a result of rural people moving to wartime industries and military bases in the major cities. Although agriculture boomed during the war, the percentage of the population living on farms declined from 48 per cent in 1941 to 42 per cent in 1946.

There were, however, no marked shifts in Alberta's ethnic composition. With the cessation of immigration during the depression, the Alberta population had become increasingly 'Canadian.' The proportion of Canadian-born in the population increased from 58% in 1931 to 70% by 1941. The only significant permanent change in ethnic composition during the war was the arrival of 2,600 Japanese who were relocated by the federal government from British Columbia in 1942, allegedly as a wartime security measure. These new arrivals increased by five times the number of Japanese in the province.[4]

War lifted Alberta out of the Depression of the 1930s and this changed economic climate affected ethnic relations. Improved prices for farm products, growth of wartime industries and economic spin-offs from the British Commonwealth Air Training Plan led to an economic boom. Nearly all economic indicators doubled from the late 1930s through the war years. By the end of the war, the province's per capita income of $829 equalled the national annual income, an indicator that Alberta was no longer a poor relation within Confederation. Mixed farming expanded since many farmers diversified into livestock and feed grain production. These years also brought a revitalization of the sugar-beet industry in the irrigated region of southern Alberta in response to the cutting off of imports from the Philippines after the Japanese invasion. And lastly, the economic activity stimulated by the Turner Valley oil industry offered further stimulus to Alberta's wartime growth.

This wartime boom eliminated many of the economic grievances which had kindled nativism in Alberta during the Depression. Competition for jobs between immigrants and the native-born vanished as unemployed youth joined the armed forces. Wartime prosperity also blunted ethnic political radicalism, which had poisoned public attitudes toward central and eastern-European minorities during the interwar years. The government's proscription of several left-wing ethnic organizations at the outset of the war certainly played a part in the decline of ethnic radicalism, but immigrant support for the Communist Party also waned during the war.[5]

The lack of immigrants and the return to prosperity certainly did not mean that Alberta had become a stable society, for the social and political strains of the thirties had merely been replaced by new sources of stress. The routine functioning of social structures and institutions was, as elsewhere in Canada, disrupted during the war years by the breakup of family units, by the imposition of food, housing and fuel rationing and by wage and price controls. A constant state of wartime anxiety was sustained by concern for loved ones in the armed forces, by constant news coverage of the war, by endless victory bond campaigns and by community drives to collect scrap metal, paper and rubber.

Despite social tensions and disruptions caused by massive war-related movements of people, Albertans were united to an unprecedented degree. They began to forget the bitter class and political conflicts which had absorbed them during the Depression – conflicts engendered not only by the rise of the highly successful Social Credit movement but also by the strong support for the Communist party, particularly in the province's coal mining areas. Canadians were encouraged to become a fighting unit at home. This participation in a common cause produced a sense of comradeship and cohesion that had seldom before existed in the province; Albertans now had a strong sense of who they were and what they stood for.[6]

Social Credit remained in power during the forties, but the political and economic conditions which had nourished it had changed. Provincial politics were not as important to Albertans as they had been just a few years before. Political innovation ceased, and the rhetoric of monetary reform had become almost quaint in the transformation to a wartime economy. There were also new actors on the political stage. William Aberhart died suddenly in 1943 and was succeeded by his longtime protegé and fellow lay preacher, Ernest Manning.

Wartime nativism shaped the social history of many ethnic minorities in Alberta; however, many changes in ethnic groups in the province were unrelated to negative wartime attitudes. The war experience played an important role in bringing people of different backgrounds together and thereby facilitating assimilation. War industries and the armed forces marshalled new combinations of people in unaccustomed settings, and the expansive wartime economy opened fresh channels of mobility for ethnic groups in Alberta. The second generation of predominantly rural ethnic groups such as the Estonians, Roumanians, Ukrainians, Poles, and Hungarians, whose previous opportunities had been rigidly proscribed, were now allowed some social mobility. Thus, despite undeniable prejudice towards groups associated with the enemy powers, the war fostered new patterns of assimilation.[7]

The Enemy Within? Attitudes toward Germans and Italians

During the 1930s there had been little concern about the loyalty or assimilability of people of German background, who then comprised ten per cent of the population. Indeed, since they were more culturally assimilated and more dispersed than other large minorities such as Ukrainians, most people of German background had almost regained the position of high esteem which they had held prior to the First World War. Once again they were respected both as frugal farmers and energetic urban workers. But in late 1938 and 1939, when the war appeared increasingly likely, and after German agents circulated among settlers of German origin, a wary spotlight was once again focused on them.[8]

With the outbreak of World War II in September 1939, 'anti-alien' sentiment and anti-German sentiment escalated in Alberta. The *High River Times* south of Calgary editorialized in rather exaggerated prose that the war called attention to an 'alien problem' which had resulted from the open-door immigration policy of the twenties: 'The result is a strange mixture of nationalities drawn from all these explosive centres of Europe.' Undoubtedly they would eventually become 'true Canadians,' but in the meantime, the writer argued, 'military vigilance' was needed. Canadian Legion branches throughout the province passed resolutions expressing their view of how to deal with the 'alien' question. Suggestions included the prohibition of the use of any 'enemy' language in Canada, the internment of all 'enemy aliens' (naturalized or not) and a special tax on 'aliens.' One Legion branch claimed with alarm that the attitude of unnaturalized immigrants, who were ineligible for military service, was 'you fellows go to war, we stay here and make good money.'[9]

While Legion branches were demanding strong measures against 'enemy aliens,' the urban press, initially at least, advocated tolerance toward German-Canadians. Editorials emphasized that the vast majority of German-Canadians were loyal and that the authorities were apprehending and interning the few pro-Nazis. They also pointed out that there were many German-Canadians who wanted to speak out against Hitler, but who were afraid to do so because of reprisals which might be taken against their relatives in Germany.[10]

The anxieties of zealous patriots were partially eased when the federal government announced that it had introduced Defence of Canada Regulations requiring unnaturalized Germans, Austrians and Czechs to register with the police, to carry identification cards, to report monthly to the police, to secure police permission for travel and to surrender firearms. The Defence of Canada Regulations also provided for summary arrest and internment without explanation or publicity. Empowered by these regulations, the police interned about eighty 'enemy aliens' in Calgary and Edmonton.[11]

Reacting to growing suspicion about their loyalty, various ethnic groups in Alberta from 'enemy' countries rushed to proclaim their allegiance. For example, the Barrhead *Leader*, which was published in an area with many people of German origin, noted that contrary to rumours about naturalized Canadians not enlisting, 'it is ... gratifying to note that quite recently there have been enlistments around here from quarters more or less unexpected.' The Crow's Nest Pass division of the National Alliance of Slovaks, Czechs and Carpatho-Russians also proclaimed its loyalty to the British Empire.[12]

Despite German-Canadian reassurances of their loyalty, substantial hostility began to develop toward them. Patriotic groups found it increasingly difficult to restrain their public hostility toward the German state from incorporating the Germans in Canada, especially during the early part of the war when the allied forces suffered repeated defeats. Several Boards of Trade, farm organizations, miners' unions and service clubs demanded the abolition of German language courses which were being taught in high schools and universities. The Castor local of the French-Canadian Association of Alberta demanded that teachers of German and Italian origin, including those who were Canadian-born or naturalized, be prevented from teaching in schools 'in order that pro-German or pro-Italian tendencies will not filter through the teaching to our children,' that all school commissioners of German or Italian origin be removed from their posts and that it be made impossible for them to be re-elected.[13]

The hostile attitudes later described in a postwar context by Jean Burnet towards Germans who had emigrated from Russian to the south-central Alberta town of Hanna were typical of wartime attitudes toward German-Russians in many other parts of the province:

In spite of their lack of sympathy for Germany, German-Russians were identi-fied with the enemy by the rest of the people and made objects of hostility. The principal indications of the hostility were references to the use of the German language, accusations of draft-dodging and the placing of stress on the slight evidence of subversive activity.

Attempts were made in Hanna to have the use of the German lan-guage suppressed, and two rural Lutheran churches near Hanna decided to discontinue the use of German during the war in order to allay suspicions of subversive activity. The German-Russian response to these pressures – denial of their German origins and a strongly expressed desire for assimilation – was re-enacted in other areas of the province.[14]

Anti-alien and anti-German feeling peaked in the late spring and early summer of 1940 both in Alberta and in the rest of Canada. In the anxious climate created by the thrust of German troops into Denmark and Norway, and later France, the Netherlands, Belgium and Luxem-bourg, considerable publicity was given to 'fifth column' activity – aid furnished to the German army by German sympathizers in each of these countries. Many Albertans suspected that Alberta also harboured 'fifth columnists' who might attempt to aid the Nazi cause. The subsequent panic over such potential 'subversives' focused primarily on people of German origin, and to a lesser extent on Communists. Those articulat-ing the scare seldom made distinctions in their sweeping denunciations between people of German background, immigrants from Germany and German-speaking immigrants from other countries, or between natural-ized and unnaturalized immigrants. The term 'enemy alien' was applied indiscriminately to all of these groups. The entry of Italy into the War on June 10, 1940 further emphasized the perilous position of the allied armed forces and elevated patriotic anxiety to feverish levels.

Calgary, which had the largest urban concentration of people of German origin in the province, proved to be a focal point of Albertan anxiety about Germans. With the *Calgary Herald* advocating that home defence units be organized to deal with 'German sympathizers,' spokes-men for the police and the veterans met with City Council in May, 1940, to discuss measures for guarding against 'fifth column' activities. A few days later, forty Calgary service clubs sponsored a mass meeting attended by 7,000 Calgarians to discuss the need for taking 'more vigorous action' against enemy aliens. World War One veterans, unable to fight in Europe but wanting to contribute their share to the war effort, proclaimed that they were 'willing and eager' to deal with enemy aliens. Some who spoke at the mass meeting argued that no distinction could be made between naturalized and unnaturalized Germans and that both should be interned. Others urged that the government outlaw the employment of Germans. There was also debate about whether German church services should be allowed. Shortly after the meeting, three Lutheran churches in Calgary prudently announced that they were discontinuing German language services. Their explanation, that 'Canadian Lutherans gladly obey their government and work for the welfare of their country because of the bounteous blessings of religious liberty ...' appears strikingly ironic.[15]

Pressure intensified on federal authorities to take more vigorous steps against 'aliens.' Calgary's Mayor Andy Davison, who had led a campaign to deport unemployed immigrants during the depression, spearheaded the Alberta crusade against 'fifth columnists.' He admonished Prime Minister Mackenzie King that unless more strenuous action were taken by the federal government against enemy aliens, the people of Alberta might take the law into their own hands. The Alberta command of the Canadian Legion and the town council of Forestburg, which had a large German-Catholic population, wired the Prime Minister their approval of the position taken by Mayor Davison and repeated his warning that 'independent protective action' against the 'western alien' menace was 'imminent.' Davison then organized an early June conference of representatives from eighteen towns and cities across the province. They met to discuss the war effort and the 'problem' of 'enemy aliens' and 'fifth columnists,' and passed resolutions demanding the registration 'of all those of foreign birth.' Afterwards, Davison once again turned his attention to Calgary and along with the City Commissioners, recommended to City Council that all city employees who had been born in an enemy country, and whether naturalized or not, be fired. City Council readily agreed, but soon discovered that there were no German-born city employees. There were, however, twenty-four Italian-born city maintenance workers who were duly dismissed.[16]

Late May and early June of 1940 saw nearly identical enemy-alien scares in the cities of Edmonton, Lethbridge and Medicine Hat and in the rural areas surrounding them. Similar interest groups demanded similar action from the government, as World War One veterans offered to do their part to fight 'fifth columnists' and city councils fretted in anxious debates about the danger of an Alberta 'fifth column.' In Edmonton, the Married Ex-Servicemen's Association demanded the internment of *all* 'alien enemies.' The Canadian Legion held an emotion-charged mass meeting in which 'more than 1,000 ex-servicemen' jammed an Edmonton ballroom and amidst 'shouts for quick action' urged the federal government to form a volunteer home defence force to combat potential fifth columnists. The Chairman of the meeting, George Gleave, warned that it was not the enemy aliens who were dangerous to Canadian security since these people were known to Canadian authorities, but the naturalized Canadians of German birth. He claimed that 'naturalization has been granted to thousands of persons since the war began ... thousands of persons who never should have been allowed in the country in the first place.' According to Gleave, there were not enough aliens in internment camps and many of those in the camps would have been released had it not been for the protests of veterans' organizations. Clearly warming to his subject, Gleave alerted his audience to the danger of 'the invasion of Canada through the United States of Germans in the guise of tourists.' Veterans continually interrupted the meeting with shouts and cheers, demands for action by authorities and offers of volunteer action against local Nazis.[17]

A conference of German Lutherans held in Edmonton shortly after the Legion's rally praised Canada and pledged its loyalty to the King; but this did little to allay the city's mounting fears. The next week at yet another emotional meeting sponsored by the Chamber of Commerce there were in attendance 2,000 veterans from Edmonton and environs. This patriotic mass meeting made even more sweeping demands than had been made in the previous veterans' rally.[18] Edmonton City Council was quick to respond to the public furor. The reporter for the *Edmonton Bulletin* aptly began his account of Council's discussion – 'Visions of fifth columners danced before the eyes of Edmonton's city fathers.' After a prolonged debate, which included suggestions that all naturalization granted to enemy aliens since 1920 be cancelled and that 'all contracts given out by the city require that no aliens be employed on such work,' Council settled for a recommendation that all contractors be prohibited from hiring 'enemy aliens.'[19]

Not everyone was infected by the public hysteria over aliens and fifth columnists. Some newspaper editors and ministers counselled against a growing tendency toward witch-hunting. The Mounted Police also reassured the public that they had the situation under control and that the police should be entrusted with the job of ferret-ing out potential enemies.[20] The R.C.M.P. reported with some exaspera-tion that they had been 'inundated with complaints of the activities of alleged enemy aliens, causing our work to increase out of all pro-portion to the results obtained.' For the most part, police and federal government authorities ignored the most extreme proposals of over-zealous patriots.[21]

The federal government was not, however, totally unresponsive to public concerns over aliens and 'fifth columnists.' In early June, 1940, it outlawed a number of pro-fascist and pro-communist organizations, including three allegedly pro-fascist German organizations and several left-wing ethnic clubs: the Ukrainian Labour-Farmer Temple Associa-tion, the Canadian Ukrainian Youth Federation, the Finnish Organiza-tion of Canada, the Russian Workers and Farmers Club and the Polish Peoples Association. Whether this governmental action simply con-firmed nativists' fears or reassured them that the government had the situation well in hand, is impossible to say.[22]

Eventually, despite the intensity of these suspicions of subversion, improving war fortunes and failure to uncover any evidence of fifth-column activities in Alberta led to a decline in anti-German sentiment. Britain's heroic defence during the Battle of Britain and the entries of the Soviet Union and the United States into the war in 1941 removed the fear of an immediate German victory. The large numbers of German-Canadians from Alberta who enlisted in the Canadian Armed Forces must also have had a positive effect on attitudes toward people of Ger-man origin.

Yet another brief flurry of anti-German fervor followed the results of balloting in the conscription referendum on April 27, 1942 in which the government asked to be released from its pledge not to introduce con-scription during the war. When some newspaper editors discovered that there was a substantial 'no' vote in the heavily German-speaking Riverside-Bridgeland residential district of Calgary and in the predomi-nantly German-speaking rural area north of Medicine Hat, they con-cluded that all those who voted 'No' were voting for Hitler.[23] Ultimately, however, more moderate voices prevailed and public fears about German fifth columnists gradually dissipated. Some of the long-term demographic and social factors which had been at work during the late thirties – growing assimilation of those of German background and the emergence of a Canadian-born generation – slowly but inexorably undermined hostility toward people of German background.

If, in assessing attitudes toward Germans in Alberta during the Second World War, one has in mind comparisons with the treatment they received during the First World War or with the treatment of Japanese-Canadians during the Second World War, the anti-German sentiment of 1939 and 1940 seems relatively benign. Despite the various manifestations of anti-German feeling, public hostility was not nearly as intense as it had been during the First World War. There was neither as great an outpouring of vituperation in the press, nor were there anti-German riots. Losing one's job because of one's German origin was also the exception rather than the rule, as it had been in the World War One era.[24]

Several factors account for the difference between attitudes during the first and second World Wars. First, German-Canadian organizational life was not as active by the time of the Second World War as it had once been. Also, the absence during the late thirties of highly organized and visible pro-Nazi sympathy in Alberta, such as there was in Winnipeg or in Saskatchewan, meant that once the war broke out, agonizing reappraisals and recriminations were uncommon. The Nazis had made efforts to attract sympathizers in the province through German-Canadian newspapers and propaganda and through the efforts of German consular officials and railway and steamship agents. But since only a small minority of people of German origin in Alberta were from Germany itself, and since a large number had lived in the province for decades, most people of German background were sufficiently acculturated or at least sufficiently removed from German life to remain indifferent to the appeal of National Socialism, even if they were deeply proud of their German background. The *Deutscher Bund*, a pro-Nazi organization masquerading as a German cultural club, was only able to attract eighty members in the entire province. Writing in 1937 to explain the lack of attachment to Germany of the Russian, Polish and American-born Germans, Elizabeth Gerwin suggests 'their group consciousness is not nationalistic but cultural in character and they are to a great extent immune from the effect of pro-German or anti-German sentiment.' It is significant that in 1941, only seven per cent (5,592) of the almost 78,000 people of German origin in Alberta had been born in Germany, while 69 per cent were Canadian-born, and the rest had come from eastern Europe or the United States. Relatively high rates of naturalization and of intermarriage with Canadians among German-origin people also helped to explain why there was less hostility toward Germans in Alberta during the Second World War than there had been during World War One.[25]

Yet, Albertans were not always ready to acknowledge differences among the various distinct groups of German background people, or to distinguish between the vast majority of German-Canadians and the tiny handful of pro-Nazi German sympathizers. Their tolerance of German people had definite limits: German-Canadians in the cities felt compelled to close their ethnic clubs for the duration of the war; and, when hostility toward Germans in general abated, the longer tradition of hostility towards two German-speaking pacifist sects – Mennonites and Hutterites – persisted.[26]

Italians in Alberta experienced the war from a very different position in Alberta's social and economic life than that occupied by the Germans. First, Italians were a much smaller group than those of German origin – there were only 4,872 people of Italian origin in Alberta in 1941. The German 'community' as such really did not exist, but was, rather, composed of many different communities centered primarily around a particular religious group in a rural area of the province. By contrast to people of German background, the Italians formed a genuine community. Most of the Italians were from northern Italy and shared a common religion and a common working-class experience. While the settlements of Germans scattered across the province were scarcely aware of the existence of other German-speaking communities, except to the degree that religious or family ties brought them to one another's attention, Italians had a number of inter-community links. Seasonal migration of single males between coal mining towns and the cities connected a number of Italian communities and most centres of Italian population were also united by a common mutual aid society, *Fior d'Italia* (The Flower of Italy), which provided much needed sick and death benefits in an era that predated medicare and social welfare. By contrast to people of German origin in the province who were primarily farmers, less than one-fourth of the Italians in Alberta were farmers. Instead, they were concentrated in small coal-mining communities and in the province's four main cities as miners, labourers and service workers.[27]

Italy entered the war in June 1940, when Hitler's forces were achieving their most notable victories in Europe and when the anti-alien panic reached its peak in Alberta. There was, however, no strong public outcry against people of Italian origin; worry about Italians was overshadowed by the larger concern about 'fifth columnists,' who were assumed to be either Germans or Communists. The numbers of Italians were therefore too small to attract much attention. Registration of all Italians naturalized after 1922 and the internment of a few who were suspected of sympathizing with the enemy reassured the public. Aside from the aforementioned incident of firing Italian city employees in Calgary, economic reprisals against them were uncommon. The dismissal of Calgary's Italian city employees also proved to be short-lived; man-power shortages and their almost irreplaceable knowledge of the city's water and sewage system soon made it imperative to rehire them.[28]

There were several reasons (aside from their small numbers) for the lack of hostility toward Italian-Canadians. Like people of German origin, the Italians had been in the province long enough to become established and accepted in the communities where they lived. A new generation, born and raised in Alberta, had reached maturity; in fact, 57 per cent of those of Italian origin in 1941 were Canadian-born. Another factor was the Italian concentration in coal mining, which was a crucial wartime industry; Italian miners who had experienced great difficulty finding enough work during the Depression now found their services very much in demand. The Crow's Nest Pass newspaper, the *Coleman Journal*, reminded its readers that Italians had been in the community for thirty years 'and to all intents and purposes are Canadians.' Also, very few Italians had expressed support for Mussolini. Some Italians thought that Mussolini might win respect for them in the New World, but the only fascist organizations in Alberta had been in Calgary and Edmonton, and they were small and short lived. These fascist clubs had not attracted the large numbers of Italian sympathizers that they had in Toronto and Montreal, where the consuls played a role in eliciting support.[29]

It should not, however, be implied that there was no animosity toward Italians during the war. Had they been completely accepted, Coleman's Italian-born Mayor, John d'Appolonia, and one town councillor would not have felt compelled to resign their offices as gestures of 'good faith,' and Italian-Canadian social and mutual benefit clubs would not have felt it necessary to suspend their activities for the duration of the war. Certainly the second generation and many of the first did not want to be associated with organizations which were being indiscriminately labeled as fascist. But it is not clear to what extent the closing of some clubs would have occurred naturally in a community whose second generation was losing interest in ethnic activities.[30]

In general, Albertans of Italian origin do not remember the wartime experience as a traumatic one. Indeed, they are more likely to perceive the war as a time when increased wages and improved prices for wheat made possible a modicum of economic security which they had not had

during the Depression. Perhaps the strongest resentment was felt by
Canadian-raised Italian Canadians who were indiscriminately treated as
Italian nationals, regardless of their youthfulness when they came to
Canada. The absurdity of government regulations is clearly revealed by
the story of a young farm wife in the Carmangay area of southern
Alberta. Norrie Legare Macmillan had come to Canada from Italy in
1913 at the age of four with her widowed mother and three other children, had grown up in Calgary, attended normal school, taken out
Canadian citizenship and had taught in a small country school before
marrying a Scots immigrant farmer. But when Italy entered the war, this
farm-wife, who was busy raising her own family and helping to run the
farm, had to travel to the nearest R.C.M.P. offices, be fingerprinted and
then report monthly to government authorities. Her bitterness at this
treatment by the Canadian government lingered for many years.[31]

Other intangible factors may have limited further hostility toward
people of German and Italian background. The strong ideological component of the war – the emphasis on fighting fascism and fascist leaders
as opposed to fighting the German and the Italian people – certainly had
some impact on checking hostility toward people of German and Italian
background in Alberta. But Italians were never considered as potentially
dangerous as the Germans in Canada. Paradoxically, the stereotype of
Italians as indifferent fighters probably contributed to the lack of anti-
Italian sentiment. By December 1942, the Canadian federal government,
influenced by United States policy, began making it possible for Italian
nationals to be exempted from enemy alien regulations, though no such
provision was allowed for German nationals.[32]

The Un-Canadian Pacifists: Attitudes toward Mennonites, Hutterites and Doukhobors

Once again, the war served to meld the Hutterites, Mennonites and
Doukhobors in the public mind. While opposition to these three groups
was not universal, the consensus about their undesirability which had
surfaced publicly at the end of World War I and in the late 1920s resur-
faced during the early years of the war. Attitudes toward each group
developed in a slightly different context because of differences in numbers, settlement patterns and degrees of isolation. However, the three
groups had been linked in the public's perception since the First World
War by their isolationist tendencies, their 'alienness' and their pacifism.
The Hutterites and Mennonites had the additional handicap of being

primarily German-speaking, and thus vaguely associated with the enemy. The Doukhobors of Alberta bore the equally heavy burden of having to live down the reputation of the Sons of Freedom Doukhobor sect in Saskatchewan and British Columbia. Though together these three religious groups composed only 1.6 per cent (13,000) of Alberta's 1941 population, concern about them and hostility toward them long out-lived the anti-German 'fifth column' scare of 1940. Actual numbers were much less important than their 'visibility' in determining attitudes towards these minorities during wartime.

Concern about people of German origin largely abated after the summer of 1940, but anxieties about Hutteries and, to a lesser extent, Mennonites, remained throughout the war. Since all three groups were more visible than the majority of German-speaking farmers, and since hostility toward them was more deeply rooted, they were convenient targets and scapegoats for the frustrations and anxieties engendered by war. Although pacifism had gained some prestige in the 1920s as a legitimate reaction to the events of World War I, and was espoused by such groups as the United Church affiliated Fellowship for a Christian Social Order, most Canadians still believed it was incompatible with 'true Canadian citizenship.' Hostility toward Hutterites and Mennonites was as intense during the 1940s as it had ever been, and wartime nationalism was the main catalyst for this heightening of ethnic tension.[33]

Widespread concern about Doukhobors, Hutterites and Mennonites first emerged in the summer of 1940. Lethbridge City Council passed a resolution claiming that 'within this province certain groups of foreign extraction, for example Doukhobors, Hutterites and Mennonites and others are given special privileges with respect to education of their children which tend to prevent such groups from becoming true Canadians,' and urged the end of instruction in languages other than English or French. The council also resolved 'that the immigration of further members of such groups be absolutely prohibited under any special privileges of the Immigration Act.' An editorial in the *Pincher Creek Echo*, serving the only area in the province in which members of all three religious sects resided, was titled 'Unassimilable Sects Not Wanted,' and demanded that the government cancel the military exemptions of all three groups. One citizen of nearby Cowley, where the province's largest concentration of Doukhobors resided, expressed his feelings in a letter to the editor: 'Why should these people be privileged above all others, to ignore the laws of the country? Why should they have any concessions that every Canadian-born or British could not have?' He then demanded the cancellation of military exemption and the introduction of measures to assimilate these three groups.[34]

Ironically, Mennonites, who had argued during the late twenties that they deserved special consideration as immigrants since they were among the 'preferred' Germans, now had to attempt to disassociate themselves from the Germans. This was not easy, since during the 1930s a few Mennonites had been sympathetic to Nazism, partly because of their German cultural ties, but primarily because, like many other Canadians, they admired Hitler's anti-Communism. But by 1940 Mennonite leaders were trying to allay public fears about their politics. They pointed out that the use of the German language did not indicate support for Nazi political institutions, but resulted simply from the difficulties immigrants had in acquiring a new language.[35]

Despite these reassurances, resentment against the approximately 8,000 Mennonites in the province continued to grow. Under pressure from various patriotic groups, Mennonites closed their German-language Bible and Saturday schools and German libraries. In the southern Alberta town of Vauxhall, opposition to the use of German in church services swelled to such proportions during June 1940 that two Mennonite churches were burned. Their right to own land was also questioned. In Pincher Creek, the Loyalist League, a patriotic organization, urged that farm lands held by the Mennonites be purchased by the Government and then resold. When in 1942 a bill was introduced in the Legislature to prohibit Hutterite land expansion, the Taber branch of the Canadian Legion argued that Mennonites as well as Hutterites posed a threat to farm life and should also be prohibited from expanding their holdings.[36]

Mennonites responded in a variety of ways to these pressures. To keep a low profile, Mennonites in many communities kept the number of their religious services to a minimum. In their anxiety to refute charges of pro-Germanism, nearly half of the eligible Mennonite young men joined the armed forces. This inevitably led to considerable soul-searching and generational conflict within Mennonite communities. Mennonites also participated in war bond drives and established their own war relief programs. Those who registered as conscientious objectors were sent to work in government supervised camps, national parks, forest experiment stations, or (with growing labour shortages in 1943) were placed by the government's alternative service system on farms and in factories.[37]

Although the Mennonites hardly enjoyed friendly acceptance by the majority of Albertans, they did not encounter the same degree of hostility as the more isolationist Hutterites because of their increasing assimilation and their willingness to cooperate in a limited way in the war effort. In a series of thirteen articles on Mennonites, Hutterites and Doukhobors, which was published in the *Calgary Herald* in the summer of 1942, columnist Richard Needham concluded that 'The Mennonites are not patriotic people, but they are not subversive either.' He pointed out that many Mennonites had joined the services, that Mennonite youth were becoming assimilated and that 'the Mennonites are really playing a much fuller part in the war than the isolationist Hutterites or the stubborn Doukhobors.' Demographic and social factors which Needham did not mention also played a part. The Mennonites, although twice as numerous, could not be seen as a homogeneous bloc like the Hutterites; they were scattered in rural pockets in almost every area of the province and there were six different Mennonite sects who had little or no contact with each other. That many Mennonites were of Swiss-German origin, had come to Alberta by way of the United States and were no longer German-speaking also helped to diffuse the negative image of Mennonites. Thus, it was not the Mennonites, but the Hutterites with their colonies and distinctive dress who were destined to be one of the two primary foci of Albertans' nativist anxieties during the war.[38]

Throughout the 1930s the Hutterites, who had first arrived in Alberta in 1918, had expanded in southern Alberta, establishing new colonies to accommodate their large families, which averaged ten children. By the early 1940s the original ten colonies in the province had grown to thirty-four and the number of Hutterites to approximately 4,000, or about 120 in each colony, with the average colony occupying 5,000 acres of land. During the twenties and thirties most of the expansion had been in the area south of Lethbridge: by 1942 twenty-five of the thirty-four Hutterite colonies in the province and seventy-five per cent of the province's Hutterites lived within a sixty-mile radius of Lethbridge. Given this rapid expansion and regional clustering, opposition to the Hutterites and agitation to restrict their expansion was predictable. But wartime nationalism endowed anti-Hutterite agitation with a legitimacy that was politically irresistible.[39]

The apparent acceptance which the Hutterites had found during the 1930s when they were considered an economic asset did not survive past the outbreak of the war. Many patriotic groups, which mushroomed during the war as expressions of intensified nationalism, objected to the Hutterites' being allowed alternative service. They did so on the grounds that it enabled them to fulfill their 'obligations' too easily and freed them to 'gobble up more land,' while non-Hutterite young men were off fighting and local people were sacrificing through food-rationing and the curtailment of home building and business expansion. Local resentment also flared when some came to the erroneous conclusion that the Hutterites were not willing to donate to 'Victory Bond' drives.

Perhaps some of the opposition to the Hutterites stemmed from populist sentiments which were strongly rooted in rural southern Alberta. While the populist slogan 'Equal Rights to All, Special Privileges to None' had been used by rural Albertans to criticize the CPR and eastern banks, it could also do service when it came to the issue of pacifist exemption from military service in the case of the Hutterites.

Paradoxically, anti-Hutterite sentiment also stemmed from the prevailing belief in individualism and 'democracy.' Some people believed that individual Hutterites were denied freedom of choice by their theocratic and communal system. Wartime opposition to German totalitarianism stimulated concern about Hutterite authoritarianism and regimentation. In his series of articles in the *Calgary Herald* in 1942, Richard Needham described the Hutterite colony as 'the dream world of the clerical fascist.' According to Needham, the colonies provided economic security 'for anyone who is willing to surrender his individuality in return.'[40]

Many misconceptions about the Hutterites flourished because of their isolation, and they had few public defenders. Nor did farm groups feel the need to promote telerance toward Hutterites as they did toward other groups, since the Hutterites did not join these organizations. The people of Alberta who were most sympathetic to the Hutterites were the Mennonites, and their own status was too insecure to enable them to defend the Hutterites publicly.[41]

Farm, municipal and patriotic groups – the same array of organizations which had led the opposition to Hutterites upon their arrival in Alberta in 1918 – advocated 'solutions' to the 'Hutterite problem' ranging from expulsion, to conscription, to restriction of land expansion. The Imperial Order of the Daughters of the Empire passed a resolution at their 1942 Provincial meeting asking the federal government to repeal the act which granted the Hutterites exemption from military duty:

There are known to be in our midst organizations and religious sects of direct enemy origin ... who, while claiming exemption from military service on religious grounds ... at the same time are using their language as a means of spreading propaganda among their youth, subversive to the Defense of Canada regulations.

Similarly, the United Farmers of Alberta, an economic organization and pressure group, passed resolutions urging that the provincial Social Credit government prevent the expansion of Hutterite Colonies, withdraw the exemption from military duties, and 'cause the Hutterite people to conform to Canadian ways' by 'compelling their children to take the same educational training as Canadian children of surrounding districts.' Citizens at a mass meeting held in Raymond in March 1942, which was also convened to protest the anticipated arrival of Japanese from British Columbia, passed resolutions recommending that the government 'should serve notice on them (the Hutterites) that at some future date to be set, title of land should no longer be issued to them unless they are willing to accept the responsibility of Canadian citizenship.'[42]

Anti-Hutterite agitation was widespread throughout southern Alberta, but was centred in Raymond, a predominantly Mormon town approximately twenty miles south of Lethbridge. The Raymond area had the greatest concentration of Hutterite colonies in the province – by 1942 there were thirteen colonies within a twenty-five mile radius of the town. Solon Low, a prominent Mormon whose home was near Raymond, was the Provincial Treasurer. He became the main government spokesman in the introduction of legislation restricting Hutterite expansion. Rulon Dahl, another prominent Mormon from Raymond, was the chairman of the Southern Alberta Citizens Association, an organization created primarily to pressure the government to restrict Hutterite expansion. Agitation was not, of course, limited to Raymond, but included citizen and veterans groups from all four southwestern Alberta counties and municipal districts in which the Hutterites resided.[43]

Although it was not suprising that this degree of concentration would produce tension between the Hutterites and their neighbours, it was nevertheless paradoxical that Mormons were responsible for leading the agitation against Hutterite expansion during the war. Mormons in the same census area outnumbered Hutterites by more than three to one; they had a long history as a persecuted minority (including opposition to them when they had first come to the province in the late 1880's) and their own religion taught the superiority of a quasi-communitarian ideal (the 'United Order'), even if they no longer practised this ideal form of society. The wartime attitudes of many southern-Alberta Mormons thus make sense only when placed within the context of two groups competing economically and demographically in an area settled originally by Mormons.

The Mormons clearly thought of southwestern Alberta as 'Mormon country.' They had been the pioneers who had opened up much of the area. Approximately two-thirds of all Mormons in the province lived there and some resented what seemed to be a rapid Hutterite takeover of the territory. They prided themselves on their large families and good farming ability, but they were no demographic match for the Hutterites. While the number of Mormons in the census division had only increased from 7,900 in 1921 to 10,055 in 1941, an increase of 27 per cent, the number of Hutterites had almost quadrupled to 3,000. Many of the children of Mormon pioneers had left for the cities in the United States as well as in Canada, but all of the Hutterite offspring remained in the area. Now wartime prosperity was making further Hutterite expansion possible while many Mormon young men were off fighting in Europe. During the war, over 100 young Mormon men from southern Alberta were killed fighting for the allied cause.[44] Mormons had thus become almost fully acculturated to Alberta and to Canada, so for them it did not seem incongruous to be leading the drive to restrict Hutterite expansion.

On March 17, 1942 Solon Low introduced a bill in the Alberta Legislature, the Land Sales Prohibition Act, which prohibited all land sales to enemy aliens and Hutterites. In introducing the measure, Low claimed that the bill was 'not a persecuting measure, but one to meet a situation which has developed since the war started.' Low stated that Hutterites were 'good people generally' and had purchased war bonds, but that public opinion demanded action against them, and he defended his bill as a means of preventing already threatened violence against the Hutterite colonies. The bill received strong support, not only from the party in power, but also from the opposition Independents, who were led by James Walker, another prominent Mormon from Raymond.[45]

In March 1943, the Legislature amended the statute to include a prohibition on the leasing of the land, since it was widely claimed that Hutterites were evading the act by leasing new lands and taking possession of land through agents. On April 7 of that year, however, the federal government disallowed the bill because it included enemy aliens, and under the Defence of Canada regulations, enemy aliens were solely within the jurisdiction of the federal government. Southern Albertans were incensed by the disallowance. Regional animosity was aroused, reopening the wounds made by the earlier disallowance of Social Credit monetary reforms. Various patriotic groups pressed for the enactment of federal legislation to replace the provincial statute or for revised provincial legislation. Chairman Dahl of the Southern Alberta Citizens' Committee wrote to Premier Manning to express the prevailing sentiment in southern Alberta. Reporting that the Hutterites had refused to stop purchasing land during the war despite entreaties from neighbours and government officials, the letter concluded:

... these Hutterites have no sense or feeling of British justice. They ignore the wishes of the people of this district who have given them every courtesy in time of Peace, in spite of the unfair disadvantage under which we as citizens have been forced to compete with them in the field of agriculture. When with the present serious conditions that confront us under our War effort, they not only refuse to support our Government, but seek to expand their holding, while our boys are defending our country.[46]

Public anxiety was finally allayed, however, by the passage of another provincial bill in March 1944, a revised version of the Land Sales Prohibition Act. This time the bill applied only to Hutterites and prohibited the sale or lease of land to them. The Act was to terminate at the end of the war, but it was later extended to 1947 when the whole issue was reopened. The only question which was raised by the opposition Independents concerning this legislation was why Mennonites and Doukhobors had not been included in the bill along with the Hutterites. Social Crediters replied that neither the Mennonites nor the Doukhobors were a problem in Alberta. In 1947, after public hearings by a legislative committee, during which Hutterites were repeatedly denounced by farm, municipal and patriotic groups, the Alberta Government introduced the Communal Property Act which restricted the amount of land Hutterite colonies could own and designated the areas of the province in which they could expand. This act remained in force until 1972.[47]

Wartime controversy over Mennonites and Hutterites also inevitably raised the question of the merits of the Doukhobors, since the three groups were so firmly connected in the public mind. Throughout the 1930s, nude parades, bombings and burnings by the Sons of Freedom Doukhobors in British Columbia kept the sect in the news, but relatively little of this adverse publicity reflected directly and immediately on Alberta Doukhobors because of the virtual absence of Sons of Freedom activity in the province. Some attention had been given during the 1930s to the breakup of the communal Doukhobor settlements in Alberta and to the burning of one school and a flour mill in the Lundbreck and Cowley area in the southwestern corner of the province; but the Alberta Doukhobors did not command much public attention in the Depression era, with its abundance of more immediate issues. This is not to say, however, that the plethora of newspaper articles on Doukhobor activities in British Columbia during the 1930s had no effect on attitudes in Alberta; for many this publicity merely confirmed long-standing assumptions that the government's decision to open Canada's doors to the allegedly wild and unfathomable Doukhobors had been a mistake.[48]

Although Doukhobors were not a major issue of public concern in Alberta during the 1930s, attitudes toward them had changed little, and with the outbreak of the Second World War attention was again focused on them. As previously indicated, they were grouped with the Mennonites and Hutterites in veterans' resolutions attacking pacifist groups, and the Hutterite controversy led to some public debate as to whether or not restrictions should also be placed on Doukhobor farmers. But three factors combined to prevent the Doukhobors from facing the level of hostility encountered by Mennonites and Hutterites. First, they were not German-speaking and thus could not be directly associated with the enemy; second, their numbers in the province were very small (the census reported 822 in 1941); and third, there was a decine in Doukhobor publicity from British Columbia during the war as conflict between the Sons of Freedom and the Orthodox Doukhobors subsided.[49]

Although in 1940, hostility toward Doukhobors, Hutterites and Mennonites was relatively uniform, the contrasting position of each group in Alberta society and their differing responses to the war eventually affected public opinion, and attitudes toward each of them took a slightly different course. Perhaps the most significant factor in determining the attitudinal differences was the group's willingness to compromise with the larger society. This is clearly illustrated by a comparison between the rapid fluctuation of hostility toward Mennonites and the stubborn persistence of opposition to Hutterites. Many Mennonites responded to pressure from the larger society by closing a number of German language institutions and many Mennonite young men joined the armed forces. On the other hand, Hutterites, already more isolated than Mennonites from the surrounding society, made no compromises. The war years were a turning point for the Mennonites; many chose accommodation and assimilation and their societal reward was gradual acceptance. The Hutterites continued with uncompromising pacifism and a communal lifestyle, and their societal legacy was enduring hostility.

Walking a Fine Line: Ukrainians and the War

In contrast to their experience in World War I, when most Ukrainians were regarded as enemy aliens and were subject to a variety of oppressive measures, including restrictions on their involvement in the war, they now had the opportunity to join in the war effort on an equal footing with other Canadians. Unlike the Mennonites, Hutterites and Doukhobors whose pacifism reawakened only partially dormant fears about them, the war helped remove Ukrainians from the public's list of troublesome groups. The first months of the war saw some concern expressed about potential 'fifth column' proclivities of Ukrainian Communists and about possible pro-Nazi sympathies among Ukrainian nationalists, but these worries were largely overshadowed by anxiety about people of German origin and by the desire for national unity and solidarity in the face of war. Since Ukrainians were the second largest non-British group in the province (after those of German origin), numbering 72,000 in 1941, it is not surprising that government authorities would make a special effort to ensure full Ukrainian support of the war effort.

At first Ukrainians found themselves in a somewhat precarious position. Prior to the war, some Ukrainian nationalists had been inclined to be pro-German because of Hitler's anti-communism and because they thought he might be sympathetic to the establishment of an independent Ukrainian nation. But Hitler's seizure of Czechoslovakia, his non-aggression pact with the Soviet Union and Ukrainians' growing awareness that Hitler regarded the Slavs as an inferior people caused most of them to reconsider whatever pro-Hitler sympathies they had. When the war with Germany was finally declared, many Ukrainian nationalists expressed support for the allies, partly to allay fears about their loyalty, but also because they hoped that the war might enable the Ukraine to recover its independence.[50]

The federal government was sufficiently concerned about Ukrainian involvement in the war effort to play an active role in encouraging their participation. Military authorities made use of local Ukrainian elites to promote recruitment drives and the National Film Board circulated propaganda in the Ukrainian districts supporting the war. The most decisive step was taken in 1940. After prolonged negotiations, the Department of National War Service, working through two English-Canadian academics – George Simpson of the University of Saskatchewan and Watson Kirkconnell of McMaster University – persuaded all non-Communist Ukrainian organizations to unite; they formed the Ukrainian-Canadian Committee whose principal task was to mobilize support for the war effort. That enlistment of Ukrainian volunteers was eventually higher than the national average may have been due as much to unemployment among young Ukrainians as to patriotic sentiment or governmental prodding. Nevertheless, their involvement served to reassure those in the government and elsewhere who doubted Ukrainian loyalty.[51]

Despite the efforts of the government and the Ukrainian-Canadian Committee, some Ukrainian nationalists remained ambivalent toward the war effort since Poland and later the Soviet Union, were not completely agreeable allies. The predominantly 'No' vote (57 per cent) in the largely Ukrainian Vegreville constituency in the 1942 plebiscite on conscription probably reflected this ambivalence as well as a long standing opposition to conscription and a feeling that this was someone else's war. The results of the plebiscite occasioned an expression of great disgust in the Vegreville paper and some comment in other western newspapers. The *Vegreville Observer* and the local Ukrainian business and political elite had done their best to elicit enthusiasm for a 'Yes' vote; former United Farmer of Alberta member of parliament, Michael Luchkovich, and Social Credit M.P. Anthony Hlynka had both publicly expressed their support for a 'Yes' vote in the plebiscite. The plebiscite was being billed by the newspapers not as a referendum on releasing King from a political promise, but rather as a vote for or against Hitler. It had been proclaimed by the local Vegreville paper as a test of loyalty to Canada, not only of Ukrainians in the Vegreville district, but of non-Anglo-Saxons in all of Canada. So it was with considerable feeling that the *Vegreville Observer* headlined its post-referendum article with the caption, 'Vegreville Constituency Disgraces Alberta,' and editorialized that 'in Vegreville Electoral district Herr Hitler must have friends for the result in this district was almost incredible.' Significantly, however, the plebiscite results did not become fodder for any concerted public attack on Ukrainians. Given earlier attitudes of the *Observer* and other newspapers, what is perhaps most striking about the reaction to the referendum results was the absence of any sustained commentary.[52]

The major public concern with regard to Ukrainians was not about Ukrainian nationalists; rather, it was focused on Ukrainian communists.

With the onset of war, the Ukrainian communists had followed the example of the Communist Party of Canada which denounced the war as a stage in capitalist economic development and urged the 'masses' to use the opportunity for a revolutionary overthrow of the Canadian government. Because of the Communists' opposition to the war effort, in June 1940, under the Defence of Canada Regulations, the Canadian Government outlawed the Ukrainian Labour Farmer Temple Association and its press, interned its leading members, including those in Alberta, and confiscated its halls, literature and documents. However, when Hitler attacked the Soviet Union in June 1941, the attitude of Ukrainian-Canadian communists rapidly reversed and they began advocating complete support of the war. Despite this recantation, the group was still regarded with suspicion by government authorities and influential academics such as Watson Kirkconnell who publicly denounced the ULFTA as 'poison on the pantry shelf,' and, although the ban on the organization was lifted in October 1943, its community halls were not returned until 1945.[53]

In spite of continuing concern about the loyalty of both Ukrainian nationalists and communists, the war's general effect was to increase the acceptability of Ukrainians and to alleviate many fears about their loyalty and assimilability. The press reported the recruitment drives among Ukrainians in Alberta and stressed their positive response. With approximately 35,000 men of Ukrainian origin in the Canadian Armed Forces out of a total Ukrainian-Canadian population of 306,000 any charges of disloyalty to Canada could easily be dismissed.[54]

Indeed, the war was in many ways a significant turning point with regard to the position of Ukrainians in Canadian society. Although suspicions lingered that they were over-prone to factionalism, that they were too concerned with old world politics – in short, that they were 'hyphenated Canadians' – Ukrainians could no longer be treated as second class citizens. World War Two veterans of Ukrainian background commanded respect, support for the left was on the wane in Ukrainian communities and, perhaps most important, the socio-economic status of Ukrainians was changing by the end of the war. Even by 1941, nearly seventy per cent of people of Ukrainian background in Alberta were native-born. They were no longer a rural immigrant peasant group and they were led increasingly by a Canadian-born generation who had been educated in the province's schools. There was a strong emphasis on education in Ukrainian homes, so their educational levels had risen significantly and a substantial Ukrainian business and professional class had emerged in the predominantly Ukrainian towns and in Edmonton. There was growing prosperity among Ukrainian farmers. All of these changes now made it impossible to regard Ukrainians in Alberta as an 'unassimilated,' 'radical,' 'lower-class' or 'alien' group.

Conclusion

Public attitudes toward the Hutterites, Mennonites and Doukhobors during the war reflected the features of wartime nativism. National loyalty and conformity to a particular idea of Anglo-Canadian society were seen as synonymous. Only groups which accepted 'Canadian' ways of living, including individual economic enterprise and military service, were regarded as *bona fide* citizens entitled to the full privileges of Canadian citizenship. The greater resentment toward Doukhobors, Hutterites, and Mennonites than toward other people of German origin or Italians and Ukrainians can only be understood in the larger perspective of the interplay of traditional attitudes toward the three groups, their visibility during a period of social stress and prevailing conceptions of Canadian citizenship and national unity. The hostility toward Germans and Italians could not be sustained because of their relative lack of visibility, their greater degree of integration into Alberta society, and their decision to maintain a low public profile for the duration of the war. Despite the difference between the treatment of Germans, Italians and the religious sects, they were all spared the excesses of hostility toward Japanese Canadians in western Canada and the full weight of government violations of their civil rights.[55] It was more difficult to see the European minorities as the agents of an enemy power and there were fewer racial myths and stereotypes clouding public perceptions of them.

The war period served, then, to heighten hostility toward a number of different European minorities for varying periods of time. Part of this hostility stemmed from the need for scapegoating during a period of stress, and part of the hostility stemmed from the heightened nationalism of wartime. The negative side of the wartime *esprit de corps* which emerged in Alberta was that visible minorities such as the Hutterites and Japanese, who were viewed as 'alien' and 'un-Canadian,' encountered increased levels of hostility. The idea that isolationist religious groups like the Hutterites could not be considered true Canadians was not new. But the wartime milieu of nationalist fervor and patriotic sentiment proved conducive to the elevation of these assumptions from the level of popular prejudices to actualization as public policy.

NOTES

This article is from *Canadian Ethnic Studies* 14 (3) (1982). Reprinted with permission.

1 John Thompson, *The Harvests of War: The Prairie West, 1914–1918* (Toronto: McClelland & Stewart, 1977), Chapter 4; Donald Avery, *Dangerous Foreigners: European Immigrant Workers and Labour Radicalism in Canada, 1896–1932* (Toronto: McClelland & Stewart, 1979), Chapter 3; W.P. Ward, *White Canada Forever* (Montreal: McGill-Queen's University Press, 1978), Chapter 8; Ken Adachi, *The Enemy That Never Was* (Toronto: McClelland & Stewart, 1976); Ann Sunahara, *The Politics of Racism* (Toronto: James Lorimer, 1981).
2 H. Palmer, 'Patterns of Racism: Attitudes toward Chinese and Japanese in Alberta, 1920–1950,' *Social History* 8 (25) 1980, p. 137–160.
3 For a more detailed explanation of these terms and their usage in the Alberta context, see H. Palmer, *Patterns of Prejudice: A History of Nativism in Alberta* (Toronto: McClelland & Stewart, 1982) p. 6. For the definition of nationalism see 'Nationalism' *Encyclopedia Britannica*, 15th edition, Vol. 12, p. 851.
4 Figures on population from Alberta Bureau of Statistics, *Graphs of Growth* (Edmonton, 1954) and *Census of Canada*, 1941.
5 For discussion of ethnic relations during the depression, see H. Palmer, *Patterns of Prejudice: A History of Nativism in Alberta*, Chapter 4; Ivan Avakumovic, *The Communist Party in Canada* (Toronto: McClelland & Stewart, 1975), Chapter 5.
6 The best single source to give insight into Canada on the home front during the war is Barry Broadfoot, *Six War Years* (Toronto: Doubleday, 1974). My characterization of Alberta during the war years is based on a score of interviews.
7 *Census of Canada*, 1931, Table 23 and 24; *Census of Alberta*, 1946, Table 10.
8 *Calgary Herald* (hereinafter referred to as *C.H.*), December 19, 1939; *Calgary Albertan* (hereinafter referred to as *C.A.*), April 13, 14, 1939.
9 Quoted in the *Wetaskiwin Times*, September 7, 1939; *C.H.*, September 16, 1939.
10 *Edmonton Journal* (hereinafter referred to as *E.J.*), September 11, 14, 20, 1939; *C.H.*, September 28, 20, October 11, 1939; *People's Weekly* quoted in *Stettler Independent*, September 18, 1939.
11 Ramsay Cook, 'Canadian Liberalism in Wartime' (M.A. thesis, Queen's University, 1955), p. 84; Public Archives of Canada (PAC), RG 76, Immigration Department Papers, Box 49, No. 675985.
12 Barrhead *Leader*, October 5, 1929; *C.H.*, September 15, 1939; *C.H.* September 12, 1939; *E.J.* September 13, 1939.

13 George Thielman, 'The Canadian Mennonites, A Study of an Ethnic Group in Relation to the State and Community' (Ph.D. thesis, Western Reserve University, 1955), pp. 249, 258; Alberta Provincial Archives (APA), Premier's Papers, Francis Jabeuf to Minister of Education, July 27, 1940.
14 Jean Burnet, *Next Year Country* (Toronto: University of Toronto Press, 1951), pp. 47, 49.
15 *C.H.*, May 20, 24, June 3, 1940. For letters to the editor demanding action against aliens see *C.A.* June 24, 1940, *C.H.*, June 15, 20, 22, 26, 1940.
16 *C.H.*, May 22, 1940; *Edmonton Bulletin* (hereinafter referred to as *E.B.*), June 7, 1940; *C.H.*, June 12, 14, 1940. See also Glenbow Alberta Archives (GAA), City of Calgary, Commissioners Report, June 7, 1940: Minutes of Meeting of Representatives of Alberta Urban Municipalities, June 8, 1940.
17 *E.J.*, May 16, 18, 22, 25, 1940; also *E.B.*, May 18, 1940. For details of meetings, resolutions and editorials concerning Medicine Hat, see *Medicine Hat News*, May 2, 9, 15, 21, June 8, 1940.
18 *E.B.*, May 23, 1940.
19 *E.B.*, June 11, 1940; *E.J.*, May 23, 1940.
20 *E.B.*, May 28, 29, 1940.
21 *E.B.*, June 6, 7, 1940; *C.H.*, June 12, 19, 24, 26, 1940, *C.A.* June 19, 1940; RCMP, *Annual Report* (Ottawa, 1941), p. 13.
22 *E.B.*, June 5, 1940; Avakumovic, *The Communist Party in Canada*, pp. 139–142. Left-wing organizations were banned because of the Communist Party's denunciation of the war as 'imperialist' and their demand that Canada remain out of the war.
23 Editorial in *Lethbridge Herald (L.H.)*, May 5, 1942.
24 Several oral history accounts of people of German origin who experienced both wars indicate that prejudice was stronger during World War One. See APA, Oral History Tapes, 73.297, Emil Janke, Edmonton, 1973; 73.295, Frederick Miller, Edmonton, 1973; 73.298, Gertrude Dahl, Edmonton, 1973; 73.303, Theodore Block, Edmonton, 1973.
25 For a general discussion of pro-Nazi activities in Canada see Jonathan Wagner, 'The Deutscher Bund Canada, 1934–9,' *Canadian Historical Review*, June (1977), pp. 176–200; 'The Deutscher Bund Canada in Saskatchewan,' *Saskatchewan History*, Spring (1978), p. 41–60; Lita Rose Betcherman, *The Swastika and the Maple Leaf* (Don Mills, Ontario: Fitzhenry and Whiteside, 1975), pp. 73: Watson Kirkconnell, *Canada, Europe and Hitler* (Toronto: Oxford University Press, 1939), p. 122. Description of *Bund* activities in Alberta and quote from Elizabeth Gerwin, 'A Survey of the German-Speaking Population in the Province of Alberta' (M.A. thesis, University of Alberta, 1938), p. 108. See also p. 120, 121, 125. On demographic variables see Burton Hurd, *Ethnic*

Origin and Nativity of the Canadian People (Ottawa, 1941), Chapters 7 & 8. Information on leaders of Nazi organizations in Alberta contained in transcripts of hearings in internment camps. PAC, RG 13, Cl, Department of Justice, Vol. 966–971.

26 APA, Oral History Tapes, 73.294, Fred Kabitz, Edmonton, 1973; 73.298, and Gertrude Dahl, Edmonton, 1973, discuss the closing of German-Canadian clubs.

27 Elizabeth Gerwin, 'A Survey,' p. 106; 78 per cent of those of German origin lived in rural areas as compared to 61 per cent of the general population and 52 per cent of those of Italian origin. Compared to the general population where 51 per cent of the male population was engaged in agriculture, 74 per cent of those of German origin were farming, while only 24 per cent of males of Italian origin were farmers. While less than 3 per cent of Alberta males and only 1.5 per cent of German origin males were involved in mining, 35 per cent of Italian males in the Province were miners. *Census of Canada,* 1941, Vol. VII, Table 12, pp. 416–423.

28 *C.H.,* June 1940, passim.

29 *Coleman Journal,* June 18, 1940. RCMP Report, *Law and Order in Canadian Democracy* (Ottawa, 1952); APA, Oral History Tapes, 74.106/5, Henry Butti, Edmonton, Alberta, 1973; 74.106/10, Victor Losa, Edmonton, 1973; Interview, Mario Grassi, Calgary, 1978. For discussion of pro-fascist sympathies in eastern Canada see Robert Harney, 'The Italian Community in Toronto,' in Jean Elliott, ed., *Two Nations, Many Cultures* (Scarborough, Ontario: Prentice Hall, 1979), pp. 227–229; A. Spada, *The Italians in Canada* (Montreal: Riveria Printers, 1969), p. 125; Betcherman, *The Swastika and the Maple Leaf,* p. 83, 85, 135, 141.

30 *C.H.,* June 12, 22, 1940; APA, Oral History Tapes, 74.106/8, Joe Fabbri, Taber, 1974; Interview, Mario Grassi.

31 APA, Oral History tapes, Joe Fabbri, ibid., 74.106/2, Mrs. Gisella Biollo, Edmonton, 1974; Interview, Mrs. Norrie MacMillan, Calgary, 1979.

32 Richard Polenberg, *War and Society: The United States, 1941–1945* (Philadelphia, 1972), pp. 42–43 discusses the relative lack of hostility toward Germans and Italians in the U.S. during the war and develops the ideological argument to help explain it. For Canadian policy toward Italians and Canadians of Italian origin see PAC, RG 2, 18, Privy Council Office, Vol. 45, File D-15.2.

33 On pacifism in the United Church see Jack Granatstein, *Canada's War: The Politics of the Mackenzie King Government* (Toronto: University of Toronto Press, 1975), p. 22; John W. Grant, *The Church in the Canadian Era* (Toronto: McGraw Hill Ryerson, 1972), p. 149–150.

480   Howard Palmer

34 For a record of the Lethbridge City Council's proceedings, see GAA, City of Calgary Papers, Office of the City Clerk, Lethbridge to Calgary City Clerk, June 18, 1940; *Pincher Creek Echo*, August 15, 1940.
35 Frank Epp, 'An Analysis of Germanism and National Socialism in the Immigrant newspapers of a Canadian Minority Group in the 1930's' (Ph.D. thesis, University of Minnesota, 1965); Aron Sawatzsky, 'The Mennonites of Alberta and Their Assimilation' (M.A. thesis, University of Alberta, 1964), Chapter 5; *L.H.*, June 1, 1940.
36 Sawatzksy, 'The Mennonites of Alberta and their Assimilation,' p. 175–77; *L.H.*, June 18, 24, 1940, March 17, 24, 1942. However, Taber's Social Credit MLA defended the Mennonites.
37 Rudy Wiebe, *Peace Shall Destroy Many*, paperback ed. (Toronto: McClelland & Stewart, 1972). See also Sawatzsky, 'The Mennonites,' p. 175–188; Hildegaard Martens, 'Accommodation and Withdrawal: The Response of Mennonites in Canada to World War II,' *Social History*, 14 (1974), p. 307–327; John Toews, *With Courage to Spare: The Life of B.B. Janz* (Winnipeg, 1978), Chapter 10.
38 See *Census of Canada*, 1941; also H. Palmer, *Land of the Second Chance* (Lethbridge, 1972) Chapter 7; Article by Needham in *C.H.*, June 26, 1942; Sawatzsky, op. cit., pp. 10, 134, 135.
39 Figures on colonies calculated from Simon Evans, 'The Dispersal of Hutterite Colonies in Alberta, 1918–1971; the Saptial Expression of Cultural Identity' (M.A. thesis, University of Calgary, 1973), Chapter 1. Figures on size of Hutterite holdings from Raymond Recorder, January 30, 1947.
40 *C.H.*, June 29, 1942.
41 C.F. Steele, 'Canada's Hutterite Settlements,' *Canadian Geographic Journal* (June 1941), pp. 309–314.
42 *L.H.* Letter File, 1942; See also *C.H.*, June 10, 1941 for a report of the provincial command of the Canadian Legion passing of a resolution that would refuse 'special privileges' (i.e. military exemption) for Hutterites and Doukhobors; GAA, United Farmers of Alberta Papers, n.d.; *L.H.*, March 10, 1942; *C.H.*, January 9, November 10, 1943.
43 Hutterites comprised approximately 10 per cent of the population in southwestern Alberta, Census Division No. 2. There were approximately 3,000 Hutterites in a rural population of 30,000. *Census of Canada*, 1941, Vol. 1, Table 32, pp. 481, 482.
44 *Census of Canada*, 1941, Vol. 2, Table 37: *Irrigation Builders* (Lethbridge, 1974), pp. 308–309; *A History of the Mormon Church in Canada* (Lethbridge Herald, 1968), p. 149. Interviews, Lethbridge, Raymond, Cardston, Spring 1979.
45 *L.H.*, March 17, 1942; *E.B.*, March 17, 1942; *E.J.*, March 17, 1942.
46 *L.H.*, Letter File, Rulon Dahl, Chairman, Southern Alberta Citizens Associa-

tion to Senator Buchanan, April 1943; APA, Premier's Papers, Southern Alberta Citizens' Committee to Manning, February 15, 1944.

47 *C.H.*, March 1, 1944.

48 *C.H.*, August 6, 7, September 11, 1931; June 25, 1932; February 12, June 30, 1934; May 20, 1935, September 1938; *E.B.*, November 8, 1943.

49 George Woodcock and Ivan Avakumovic, *The Doukhobors* (Toronto: Oxford University Press, 1968), pp. 319–320; *Census of Canada*, 1941; *C.H.*, January 11, 1941; *Gleichen Call*, August 28, 1940; *Pincher Creek Echo*, August 15, 1940; *C.H.*, July 1942; *C.H.*, July 7, 1942; Doukhobor War Resisters,' *MIR*, 3, 1 (1975), pp. 14–15; Interview, Mike Verigin, Cowley, Alberta, July, 1980.

50 J.M. Deverell, 'The Ukrainian Teacher as an Agent of Assimilation' (M.A. thesis, University of Toronto, 1941); Vic Stecyk, 'Saskatchewan and the Conscription Plebiscite, April 27, 1942,' unpublished seminar paper, York University, 1971; Watson Kirkconnell, *Canada, Europe and Hitler*, p. 137–149; Michael Marunchak, *The Ukrainian Canadians: A History* (Winnipeg; Ukrainian Free Academy of Sciences, 1970), p. 557; *E.J.*, March 27, 1939, Nov. 25, 1940; *E.B.*, Feb. 9, 1942; A. Hlynka, *Debates*, House of Commons, Nov. 25, 1940, pp. 380–381; Myrna Kostash, *All of Baba's Children* (Edmonton: Hurtig, 1977), Chap. 13.

51 Marunchak, *Ukrainian Canadians*, p. 550.

52 Stecyk, ' Conscription'; *Vegreville Observer*, April 15, 22, 29, May 6, 1942. Of course, not all of the 'no' vote came from Ukrainian nationalists.

53 Paul Yuzyk, *Ukrainians in Manitoba*, p. 109; Ivan Avakumovic, *The Communist Party in Canada* (Toronto: McClelland & Stewart, 1977), p. 142; Helen Potrebenko, *No Streets of Gold* (Vancouver: New Star Books, 1977), pp. 267–269; PC No. 8022, October 14, 1943; *E.J*, Nov. 4, 1945; Watson Kirkconnell, *Our Ukrainian Loyalists* (Winnipeg: Ukrainian Canadian Committee, 1943), p. 18.

54 Numbers of enlisted Ukrainians taken from Watson Kirkconnell, *Our Ukrainian Loyalists*, p. 27.

55 W. Peter Ward, *White Canada Forever*, Chapter 8; Ken Adachi, *The Enemy That Never Was*, Chapter 9; Ann Sunahara, *The Politics of Racism*; 'Patterns of Racism,' p. 148–158; David Iwaasa, 'Canadian Japanese in Southern Alberta' (unpublished research paper, University of Lethbridge, 1972); Chris Liebich, 'The Coming of the Japanese Canadians to Alberta, 1942–1949: A Study in Public Policy and Public Attitude' (Honors essay, University of Alberta, 1976).

Making 'New Canadians': Social Workers, Women, and the Reshaping of Immigrant Families

FRANCA IACOVETTA

In the spring of 1958 Mrs Gabura, a Hungarian refugee, entered the office of the International Institute of Metropolitan Toronto, a social agency offering aid to the city's non-British immigrants. With her husband employed out of town, Gabura came to the institute hoping to find a job and locate a daycare for her two small children. The Hungarian-speaking counsellor assigned to the case promptly placed her client in private service and the children in a Catholic nursery. It soon became clear, however, that a seemingly straightforward case of job placement masked a turbulent history of marital cruelty.

Staff workers first learned of Gabura's unhappy home life when she returned to the institute in mid-summer and recounted the following story. Earlier that week, two men claiming to be government inspectors had come to her flat demanding 'to investigate her private life.' While searching her place, they claimed to be looking for 'evidence of immorality' as her husband wished 'to get a divorce and take the children.' The next night they returned, this time admitting they were private detectives hired by the husband to discredit her reputation.

It was not until weeks later, after Gabura had been served a divorce writ and the agency had found her a lawyer, that the counsellors discovered the full extent of the woman's problems. According to a pretrial statement, the husband for years had been abusive, 'very often' committing 'physical violents' (sic) on his wife and children and flaunting his adulterous affairs. The couple had actually separated in the fall of 1956, when the Hungarian revolution broke out and the husband fled to a refugee camp. But he later convinced his wife to join him and, a few months later, the family arrived in Toronto. Domestic life did not improve, however. Soon after they arrived in the city, an ugly scene transpired when Gabura's husband, accusing his wife of flirting with a neighbour, slapped and kicked her until she fled and found refuge in the home of some Hungarian friends. By the winter of 1957 the couple was legally separated and the husband, now working out of town, was obliged to pay her child support, which he did irregularly. Thus it was that when Gabura first came to the institute, she was especially eager to secure work.

Following her encounter with the private detectives, Gabura had moved in with a Hungarian woman. But this arrangement proved to be disastrous, and when she returned to the agency in the winter of 1958 she was distraught. According to the notes taken by the professional social worker who now took on her case: 'She was very upset ... she told me ... [the roommate] is often drunk and she and her boyfriend are rough ... and asked several times for money, which [Gabura] cannot give ... [Gabura] was afraid [the roommate] would be a witness against her in the divorce proceedings.'

Although aware of her plight, none of the institute staff could have guessed that Gabura, terrified of losing her children, would attempt suicide by swallowing poison. The attempt failed, however, and in hospital she agreed to undergo psychiatric evaluation and to place her children with the Catholic Children's Aid Society until her situation improved. At the time of her release in January 1959, the children were still living with Gabura's roommate. Gabura now became determined to get her children into a temporary foster home so that she could return to work and thus eventually provide a better home for them. This strategy would also offer her a defence against her husband's allegations that she was an unfit mother. For days, she phoned the institute repeatedly, asking for help in finding a home for her children. As the case comes to an end in the spring of 1959, she has learned that the placement process was being stalled by her husband's interventions. In response, Gabura, having just landed a job, defiantly takes matters into her own hands and registers her children in an orphanage located outside the city.[1]

Mrs Gabura's file is especially bulky and relates an unusually complicated tale, but it is one of hundreds of case histories contained in the confidential records of the Department of Individual Services of the International Institute. The professional and volunteer counsellors who staffed this department sought to play an interventionist role in the lives of their immigrant clients so as to ensure the newcomers' 'integration' into postwar Canadian society. In the immediate post-1945 era, as the world entered the nuclear age and the Cold War, there was much anxiety about the crisis facing Canadian families as well as considerable discussion regarding the need to ensure the social and political integration of the postwar European arrivals. There was also much agreement among the nation's middle-class professionals that, after two decades of depression and war, Canadians be encouraged to return to the privacy and comparative calm of a 'normal' family life.

The construction of the family that underlined the dominant rhetoric assumed a gendered arrangement in which husbands supported a wage-dependent wife and children, and women took on the task of running an efficient household and cultivating a moral environment for their children. The response of institute counsellors to Mrs Gabura and the other clients we shall encounter in this paper reflected a desire to preserve family life and, moreover, to reshape 'foreign' or otherwise deviant families according to a North American, middle-class model that combined patriarchal ideals of family and motherhood with the notion of a modern, companionate marriage. This aim was in keeping with the larger goal of assimilation. Notwithstanding the social workers' respect for the folkloric traditions of the European immigrants, many of the professionals saw their institutions primarily as instruments of 'Canadianization,' a view reinforced by the Cold War. That the institute counsellors were not usually successful in reshaping their clients' lives reflects in large part both the limited contact caseworkers had with their clients and the selective and pragmatic approach many clients adopted towards the agency.

This article is a preliminary look at the complex nexus of class, racial, and gender relations that characterized the encounter between social workers and their immigrant clients during the 1950s and early 1960s. The case files deal with those immigrants who actually sought assistance from sources beyond their family and kin networks, and thus they are more likely than other kinds of historical sources to highlight personal tragedies and conflicts. Because they were drawn up by counsellors trained in social work techniques, the records are themselves constructions reflecting the biases of a group of middle-class professionals and volunteers. And yet, even while the files are obviously biased texts, we can find in them significant clues that tell us something about the strategies and responses of the clients themselves.

While the case files of the International Institute hardly offer a complete portrait of the varied lives of immigrant and refugee women, they do provide a useful starting point for developing an approach that avoids the dichotomy of immigrant victims/immigrant heroes. The case files point to a wide range of situations experienced by minority women and reveal the relationships that women forged, or eschewed, both within and outside the family or ethnic colony. As such, they provide a window on those complicated and, at times, even contradictory, aspects of women's lives.

From the Point of View of Integration

When the International Institute opened its new downtown Toronto office in October 1956, the staff were aware of the formidable task they faced. The declared aim of the agency was 'to foster and promote the integration of "New Canadians."' Its staff workers found themselves in a city where tens of thousands of immigrants had settled. They came from a wide variety of backgrounds but, overwhelmingly, in the period before 1965, the immigrants were British or European. 'From the point of view of integration,' explained a staff supervisor, 'the purpose of the Institute is to serve as a bridge between the old world and the new.[2] In seeking to be such a bridge, the institute was not an isolated agency. Rather, it was part of the complex and sometimes bewildering amalgam of public and private support services that existed at the national and local level.

In contrast to their predecessors a half-century before, the immigrants who came after 1945 potentially had access to a fairly wide network of services associated with the postwar welfare state. Notwithstanding their shortcomings, the immigrants benefited from a national system of unemployment insurance, mothers' allowances, and improvements in health, welfare, and workers' compensation schemes. They could also tap the more traditional forms of aid offered by charitable agencies, churches, and volunteer groups that had long served immigrant and working-class families. In Toronto, middle-class women's organizations, such as the Young Women's Christian Association (YWCA), the Women's Christian Temperance Union (WCTU), and the Toronto Junior League, organized clothing and food drives and baby clinics, hosted child-rearing lectures, and dispatched volunteers to meet women arriving by train at Union Station. Both nationally and locally, the Imperial Order Daughters of the Empire (IODE) was involved in citizenship work, educating immigrants in Canadian government and encouraging them to become naturalized citizens. Many local branches regularly 'adopted' needy families, who were then supplied with emergency funds and had their house bills paid. Toronto's settlement houses acted as job placement centres and offered English classes and recreational activities. So, too, did Catholic, Jewish, and Protestant organizations. In addition to long-standing ethnic organizations, some new ones also emerged at this time. Through their referral services, all of these groups were in frequent contact with government departments, including the local offices of the National Employment Service (NES), the Immigration Branch, and the provincial Department of Public Welfare. Clients were also referred to hospitals, family court, and a host of family and child-protection agencies that, as in the case of the Children's Aid Society, were semi-autonomous but nevertheless an integral part of the apparatus of the welfare state.

The International Institute, which received charitable moneys through the city's United Appeal fund as well as private donations, belonged to this elaborate network of services. The agency was itself an amalgam of several organizations that had been involved in immigrant aid work since 1952. At that time, St Andrew's Presbyterian Church and the Toronto Welfare Council (later the Social Planning Council) agreed to run the church's old St Andrew's Memorial House as a friendship house, serving immigrants with the help of funds obtained through the Community Chest. Soon afterwards, a group of well-to-do Torontonians established within the house a counselling and orientation service for immigrants. Called the New Canadians Services Association, this organization became in the fall of 1954 a fund-raising project of the Junior League of Toronto. Initially, its only full-time and professional staff member was Mrs W.E. (Nell) West, a social worker who had served as assistant deputy minister of public welfare in Ontario during the Depression and as a senior official with the United Nations Relief and Rehabilitation Administration (UNRRA) after the war. In 1956 their service officially amalgamated with St Andrew's House to form a multifaceted immigrant aid society.[3]

The International Institute differed from many of the city's agencies in that its clientele was exclusively immigrant. More specifically, it served non-British newcomers, which, in these years, meant predominantly European-born arrivals, including Displaced Persons from central and Eastern Europe and, later, Hungarian refugees, Germans, and Mediterranean groups like the Italians, Greeks, and Portuguese. It was not until the late 1960s that the institute attracted many immigrants of colour. While an awareness within the agency of the need to combat racism against people of colour was evident as early as 1963, when the institute joined forces with the Ontario Human Rights Commission to launch an anti-racism campaign,[4] the institute before 1965 worked mainly among white Catholic, Protestant, and Jewish Europeans.

Considering itself a 'specialized, non-political and non-sectarian agency,'[5] the institute sought to answer the needs of the newcomers it attracted by performing three major services. The mostly volunteer staff of the Department of Group Services ran the institute's reception centre and conducted community advocacy work. At the reception centre, staff workers organized a variety of cultural, educational, and recreational activities. These ranged from movies, afternoon teas, and Saturday night dances, to English instruction, bridge classes, and, for married women, lessons in nutrition, child-rearing, and the operation of domestic appliances. Amateur Nights showcasing talented immigrant musicians were designed to offer newcomers an opportunity not only to learn about Canada or to meet one another but also to mingle with the Anglo-Celtic Torontonians whom the institute staff sought to attract to these events. In this way it was hoped that, as one staff worker put it, 'the newcomers may be encouraged to become adjusted to the new culture and add to it by meeting, observing, and understanding their Canadian friends.'[6]

Although staff members frequently noted their failure in attracting more married women to the reception centre, they considered the reception programme, which drew both fee-paying members and casual attenders, a success. Writing years later, a former institute president recalled the events held at the reception centre with obvious fondness: 'Hundreds of people came virtually every evening ... They made music, played games, danced, talked with one another, or just enjoyed sitting in a decent surrounding instead of the sad and shabby rooms in which newcomers live ... That did not exclude that during the day they were counselled and referred, and what not.'[7] His view mirrored the sentiments of the supervisor of group services, David H. Stewart, who, a decade earlier, had described the program in these terms: 'Every activity ... is designed to foster and promote the integration of Old and New Canadian.' 'It is interesting to observe,' he added, 'that historical conflicts are resolved in this setting, within the special groups and in the general activities, as they could not be resolved elsewhere. The atmosphere ... is such that all members, through fellowship, avoid the expression of prejudice in pursuit of their common goal as Canadian citizen. Deliberately we cultivate freedom of expression and try to show that this personal freedom can thrive only in mutual self-respect. This general philosophy we foster as the groundwork for the Institute member when he eventually drops his membership to integrate into the community at large.'[8]

Second, while the institute staff adopted a model of cultural pluralism that assumed respect for some of the cultural traditions of immigrants, they hoped, ultimately, to Canadianize them. Amid the Cold War, staff workers, like many other Canadians, associated the willingness of newcomers to adapt to a Canadian life-style and adopt Canadian citizenship as a victory in the struggle against the Soviet Union and as proof of the moral superiority of Western democracies like Canada. Such an orientation fit neatly with the broad program of the Canadian government during the early years of the Cold War. Immigration officials welcomed applicants likely to be anti-communist because of their European experiences and established screening processes to block the entry of 'Communists.' And, in 1950, the Liberal government set up the Citizenship Branch within the new Department of Citizenship and Immigration. Building on earlier practices of the wartime Nationalities Branch, the Citizenship Branch monitored Canada's ethnic communities and supplied organizations with materials depicting the Soviets negatively and Western democracies positively. Many of the movies, lectures, and other educational materials presented by the institute were designed to celebrate Canadian traditions and to reveal the horrors of communism.[9]

This interest in remaking immigrants into Canadians also explains why the institute staff viewed ethnic organizations with suspicion even while they cooperated with them. It was assumed that while such organizations gave immigrants 'a feeling of belonginess,' they retarded the process of assimilation. As one institute supervisor advised: 'The ethnic halls and clubs do good work in the sense that they help preserve the cultural heritage, but they do bad work in that they, unwittingly, I am sure, create national ghettoes and thus slow the integration, the Canadianization ..., of the newcomers.' By contrast, he maintained, 'the Institute produces a mix of groups, of oldtimers and natives. In that respect, it is comparably more beneficial than any ethnic organization.'[10]

The third major service offered by the institute was undertaken by a specialized staff of professional social workers and trained volunteers who, under the guidance of a supervisor, ran the Department of Individual Services. It was their responsibility to provide information, a referral service, and counselling, when this was deemed appropriate. Although it is difficult to pinpoint precisely the number of counsellors employed at the institute in these years, the evidence suggests that at any given time there were between eight and ten, divided more or less evenly between men and women and between professional social workers and volunteers. While the supervisor held a master's degree in social work, most of the professionally trained personnel had obtained a bachelor of social work. All the professional social workers were men, whereas the volunteers, with one exception, were women. Most of these women appear to have been married. They also represented an ethnically diverse group; about one-half were Canadian-born while the remainder were either the Canadian-raised children of immigrants or themselves recent immigrants. In the latter case, all were Eastern Europeans from families with professional backgrounds. The one male volunteer, a refugee from Eastern Europe, was similarly a professional. Altogether, the staff could offer counselling in nineteen different languages.[11]

If the caseworkers belonged to the middle class, the clients generally belonged to the ranks of the economically disadvantaged, the working class, and even the poor. The vast majority of the clients in our sample (and virtually every southern European) came from a peasant or rural artisanal family background but had now joined the ranks of the urban working class. A small number of clients, approximately 15 per cent, were skilled factory workers who now found themselves underemployed or out of work. A tiny minority (6 per cent), most of them Eastern Europeans, were either professionals or married to professionals. In each case, they were facing difficulties in obtaining a Canadian licence or establishing a local practice, and were thus experiencing downward mobility. The clients came to the institute from various sources: while some were referred to the service from government departments, the courts, other agencies, or even the institute's own Group Services section, others came on their own, having heard of the institute by 'word-of-mouth,' usually from kin or neighbours.[12]

The Ordinary Family in Extraordinary Times

The institute's counsellors differed from each other in training or specialization, but they shared a basic commitment to the case-work approach that by the 1950s was a widely used social work technique.[13] When it came to considering how best to address their immigrant client's needs, they also shared a family orientation that placed much emphasis on the promotion of a stable familial environment, one in which, ideally, working husbands kept family finances relatively secure and housekeeping mothers maintained a loving and moral home. In an address to a local IODE chapter, Dr Robert Kreem, a social worker and West's successor as institute director in 1965, argued that along with 'financial success,' a 'happy family life' was an essential ingredient in the successful adjustment of immigrants. He added that as family tensions and discord' had 'a hampering effect on adjustment,' the institute staff had been committed to resolving intra-familial conflict and supporting struggling families, as well as attacking other barriers, like unemployment, that impeded the immigrants' successful adjustment. In making a case for the value of his agency, he used the metaphor of the family, calling it a 'home-away-from-home,' where the immigrants 'can discuss all their problems or share their joy.'[14]

In showing concern about the nuclear family and for the preservation of family life, Dr Kreem and his colleagues were scarcely alone. Indeed, their views reflected a family ideology that pervaded not only the social work profession in this period but most elements of society. In the immediate postwar years there was much hand-wringing about the challenges facing Canadian families. An educational specialist voiced the concerns of many when, in an address to the Toronto Local Council of Women in 1952, he declared: 'Children are growing up in an anxious age, where there is a threat of war. Homes are broken or both parents work. Modern life stresses specialization and scientific advancement has outrun comprehension.'[15] There was also considerable debate about how best to preserve, indeed, strengthen the family in a rapidly changing, modern world.

It was generally acknowledged that following two decades of suffering and devastation owing to the Great Depression and the Second World War, many Canadians were eager to resume their private lives, to marry, and seek happiness in a 'normal' family life. The plight of Displaced Persons, especially the children, was held up as a reminder of the havoc that war wreaked on family life and the misery experienced by those without families. Contemporary observers and social experts also pointed to the alarming evidence that families in Canada, as elsewhere, were facing extraordinary pressures. Rising rates of divorce and juvenile delinquency, an increase of married women in the paid workforce, the lack of affordable housing for newly married couples and young families, and the new fears unleashed by the threat of nuclear war were all viewed as indicators that the family was in need of bolstering.[16]

In an address entitled 'The Ordinary Family in Extraordinary Times,' a casework supervisor with the Family Welfare Association of Montreal provided a gendered analysis of her times:

[F]amily life has been taking a beating during the past 20 years ... [T]he great depression ... [meant the] postponement of marriage for many young people because of lack of jobs, which was extremely serious, both biologically and psychologically ... Many husbands and fathers appeared to be failing in their role as breadwinner and consequently in the eyes of their children to be total failures ... Then came the war ... Couples were flung apart to have widely different experiences. When the war was over, they had to begin all over again, but the situation was not the same ... For men there was the difficulty of settling down to a hum-drum life. For women too, who during the war had to rally and do many things that they had never done before, there was a letdown ... A very special hazard to family life has been the extreme housing shortage [so that] young people have been unable to find a place of their own ... Overcrowding ... in the homes of rela-tives does not offer a natural opportunity for family life to grow and has contrib-uted greatly to the development of strained and broken family relationships and subsequently less useful citizens.'[17]

As these comments suggest, the postwar discourse among middle-class observers and experts regarding family life was predicated on a model of the family that posited a strict gender-based division of tasks. The claim that men and women had different but complementary roles to play could also be accommodated to the ideal of a companionate mar-riage. Ideally, wives were perceived to be happy homemakers fulfilling their destiny to create a loving and stable home for a hardworking husband and children. In the words of the Reverend Dr W.J. Gallagher of the Canada Council of Churches, 'homelife, social standards and moral behaviour are the responsibility of women.'[18] Marriages were expected to be loving partnerships. It was nonetheless clear, as Ruth Pierson has recently shown, that the dominant rhetoric, and, indeed, the welfare policies of the day, assigned economic primacy and final authority to the man on the grounds that he supported a household of dependants.[19]

Such socially conservative assumptions were evident in the argu-ments of even progressive social workers who called for greater state intervention on behalf of the unemployed and poor. In a 1954 article that appeared in the *Social Worker*, official organ of the Canadian Association of Social Workers, three female community workers argued that male unemployment remained a serious threat to family life. Like many of their colleagues, the authors saw unemployment as essentially a crisis in masculinity and thus ignored the growing numbers of wage-earning w.ves who were keeping family finances afloat. In their discussion of the 'evil effects' of unemployment, wives are portrayed unsympatheti-cally: 'the growing and persistent feeling of inadequacy of the man ... unable to supply his family's needs, the tensions arising between hus-band and wife, and the nagging that even the most understanding wife occasionally indulged in ...'[20]

In positing a return to a 'normal' family life, Canada's family and medical experts, like the American and British colleagues whose viewpoints they shared, were simultaneously expounding a familiar, middle-class ideal of womanhood that reaffirmed women's domestic orientation. Women, it was argued, possessed the moral capacity to provide their families with an emotional haven in an uncertain world, and it was precisely through their selfless contributions to home and family that they found true happiness and fulfilment. Both popular commentators and social scientists of the day affirmed the view that women were primarily responsible for creating a happy marriage as well as for child care and parenting. The ideal portrait of the married woman, then, was of a cheerful wife and good mother who accepted her social responsibility and reaped the benefits in the form of a contented husband and well-adjusted children. There was, however, a darker side to the argument for, as Veronica Strong-Boag has observed, those women who deviated from or defied such conventions were blamed for producing society's 'misfits,' be they deserting husbands, homosexual sons, juvenile delinquents, or the mentally unstable.[21]

As the contributions of community and agency workers to the *Social Worker* document, Canada's postwar volunteer and professional social workers sought to reform the behaviour of their troubled clients by encouraging them to conform to the prevailing notions of 'normal' family life and 'healthy' gender relations. Thus, for example, while family agency workers counselled against pressuring unmarried mothers to give up their babies, they applauded when the desired outcome occurred. As one caseworker observed, through adoption the illegitimate child was given a two-parent family and 'economic and emotional security,' while the young woman was freed to form 'an attachment to another man leading to marriage.'[22]

Social workers who served an immigrant clientele similarly saw the process of assisting their clients' 'adjustment' as primarily a process of reshaping 'deviant' families according to the prevailing, North American model that combined patriarchal ideals of family with the notion of a companionate marriage. Arguing the merits of a 'socio-cultural approach' to social work that recognized the role of cultural background in explaining certain behaviourial traits among people, Benjamin Schlesinger, a lecturer at the University of Toronto School of Social Work, explained the objectives of his profession in relation to the postwar immigrants: 'Public agencies are asked to investigate deviations and social workers are faced with interpreting community standards to the "New Canadian."' Such community standards, as the remainder of his article made clear, included a more 'egalitarian' view of the family that placed limitations on the husband's domineering attitude towards his wife, including his right to beat her, and a more indulgent form of child rearing.

In making his case, Schlesinger was expressing the view of many Canadians, including the institute counsellors, that the newly arrived families from Eastern and southern Europe lagged behind the more modern North American family. But in seeking to reshape the immigrants' lives, they were not so concerned to eliminate the patriarchal organization of 'traditional' European families – many of which were peasant or rural artisanal families that had long combined traditions of masculine authority with a cooperative work ethos – as to alter its character and give it a more modern or North American basis. While immigrant men thus were expected to acquire sole responsibility for the economic support of their family, and be companionable partners to their wives, married women were expected to adapt to Canadian standards of domestic life in everything from cooking to child-rearing methods, and thereby provide a 'well-adjusted' home for their husband and children. Social workers saw themselves as gate-keepers of a modern, socially progressive society, with a right to intervene in the lives of their needy or unruly immigrant clients. As Schlesinger explained, the newcomers had come to a country that sanctioned 'the community's right to protect children, to regulate family disorganization, and to interfere in difficult family relations.'[23]

The case records of Toronto's International Institute provide a fine opportunity to consider how these approaches and ideals were translated into daily practice. Did the counsellors stick rigidly to prevailing notions of women and femininity and, for that matter, men and masculinity? To what extent did the clients themselves frustrate the aims of their counsellors? Did the demands and behaviour of the clients force their caseworkers to reconsider their objectives or at least to tolerate some deviance from the hegemonic ideal?

Tending to the Battered and Deserted Wife

Even while they made up only a small percentage of the institute's heavy caseload, the plight of women like Mrs Gabura and the other battered and deserted wives reinforced in the minds of the counsellors the association of minority women with victimization by men who came from cultures that sanctioned the harsh treatment for women and children. Their perceptions of how best to tend to the needs of such women was correspondingly influenced by their adherence to prevailing North American notions of gender and family.

We can see these factors at play in the Gabura case. In responding to Mrs Gabura's call for help, the caseworkers were initially most con- cerned to bring about a reconciliation between husband and wife. When Gabura first reported the incident involving the private detectives, the staff were genuinely alarmed. They also acted promptly, alerting the police to the situation and sending a stern letter to the husband. Con- vinced that the marriage could eventually be mended and the family reunited, however, the staff also encouraged the man to return home and seek therapy. 'If you have family problems,' read the letter sent to him, 'there are community agencies from whom you may get advice and counsel. We will be glad to help you make contact with them.'

Thus, Gabura's definition of her own problem – to be rid of an abu- sive husband and to raise the children on her own – became redefined by institute workers as a family problem. But in seeking to preserve her family, the caseworkers had not been interested merely to bring the hus- band back into the household. Rather, they had also hoped to reform him and thus reshape the dynamics of this deviant family along a more companionate model. It was only when caseworkers were completely convinced that there was no chance of reconciliation – the point being made painfully clear when her husband's continuing harassment drove Gabura to attempt suicide – that they abandoned the idea of reuniting the family and began to think of Gabura as a single mother. The sympa- thy they showered on her also reflected their conviction that she was indeed 'a good mother,' as one caseworker described her, and thus a worthy client.

Gabura's file stands out from most of the other cases involving vio- lence against women in the considerable length of time that the institute counsellors were involved in her affairs. For a period, the woman devel- oped a trusting relationship with the female volunteer who became her chief caseworker. Even this case, however, ends abruptly when Gabura ceased relations with the agency apparently because she no longer found it useful to herself and her children. Indeed, while they might have hoped to play a more profound role in all their clients' lives, the institute counsellors often found themselves confined to providing their women clients with material aid – donating food and clothing vouchers or referring them to the local Welfare or immigration office for emer- gency handouts. At the same time, institute caseworkers, like their col- leagues elsewhere, sought to avoid encouraging a family to develop a permanent dependency on state and community services. Thus, their desire to help a truly needy client was tempered by the belief that, in the long run, families ought to be economically independent. Such a conviction, as Linda Gordon has documented for the United States, has pervaded the profession of social work since the turn of the century. In the 1950s, social workers discovered the 'multi-problem family' that could not escape the vicious cycle of dependency. Such families absorbed a disproportionate amount of attention and financial assistance. It was thus all the more important, the professionals argued, that they be discriminating.[24] How, then, did these competing demands affect the institute caseworkers' response to the problems confronted by the battered or deserted wife?

Before venturing an answer to these questions, let us consider a few more illustrations. The following four case histories involving abused and/or deserted women offer different variations on a similar theme.

The client in our first example, Bella Schiff, was a young Jewish woman from Eastern Europe who came to the institute in the spring of 1959. The caseworker's initially guarded response to Schiff can be attributed largely to the fact that she had been referred to the agency by her probation officer. However, as the woman's story unfolded, the caseworker, yet another of the female volunteers on staff, became more sympathetic. On arriving in Canada two years previously, Schiff, it turned out, had entered into a common-law marriage with a man whom she had met on the voyage over. For much of the time she had been supporting him, until she was laid off from her factory job in October 1958. Though she had reported regularly to the local office of the Immigration Branch, she had repeatedly rejected the jobs assigned to her until the placement officers, convinced she was not serious about finding work, stopped the small handouts normally offered to immigrants who did not qualify for unemployment insurance. The resulting financial difficulties left the couple in considerable debt, prompting them to orchestrate a forgery scam in which they tried to cheat a friend out of his savings. The effort failed and landed both of them in jail for a few months. When she was released on probation, Schiff became determined to leave her partner, who, she now disclosed, had been abusive towards her 'most of the time.' Although she had tried to leave him on several occasions, each time he had forced his way back into her home. 'She is frightened,' wrote the caseworker after hearing the woman's story, 'and wants to separate from him.' In responding to Schiff's predicament, the caseworker agreed to cooperate with the woman's probation officer, who had already made arrangements for her to acquire a legal separation from her common-law husband. The institute counsellor also set about trying to find her client a job and convinced her to register in English classes. She also referred Schiff to the Jewish Family Agency for additional counselling, where it was hoped the woman might benefit from talking with a social worker who would better understand her racial background.

As promised, Schiff returned to the institute several days later, informing the caseworker that the Jewish Family Agency had helped her to qualify for welfare benefits (amounting to $17.00 each month) and to move her into a new flat. She declared that she was now ready to look for a job. As the following file entry suggests, the caseworker was pleased with the woman's progress but remained sceptical that the client, having already shown herself to be a poor judge of men and a woman of low morals, might easily be seduced into another relationship with a man she barely knew. 'She talked to me clearly and sensibly,' the entry reads, 'and I had the impression that she was really glad about the separation. It could be also possible that she will cling to another [man] because of loneliness.'

Over the course of the next month, as Schiff was fired from one job after another, her caseworker's attitude towards her reverted to one of suspicion. Typically, the caseworker had found her client domestic service work. Within a week of obtaining her first job, the employer who had hired Schiff as her cleaning lady let her go. 'I heard,' the caseworker recorded in her file, accepting the employer's explanation of matters, 'that she was not interested to work and took it too easy. Smoked cigarets all the time and was slow.' When Schiff was fired again, this time from a hotel where she had been employed as a chamber maid for three weeks, a frustrated caseworker barked: 'It seems to me that she cannot hold any employment.' To make matters worse, the woman, by this time, had done the expected and taken up with another man. While the caseworker tried a few more times to place the woman in jobs, Schiff moved in with her new lover and subsequently disappeared.[25]

If the caseworker's perception of Schiff was clouded by the woman's less than sterling reputation, the converse could be equally true. As we saw in Gabura's case, the women who appeared as virtuous wives in no way responsible for their unfortunate predicament elicited a far more sympathetic response. Another Jewish woman, Mrs Karlinsky, for example, had been referred to the institute from family court, where her husband was in the process of obtaining a divorce. In the interim, however, he was making life miserable for her and she wanted to get out of the house as soon as possible. A pertinent case entry reads: 'He is treating her badly ... [T]hey are living together but everyday he tells her to get out of the place. [She] wants to find work to earn some money because the husband refuses to give her any ... [She] was in tears ... said that she has to find work to be on her own and not to ask for every penny from her husband.' Her eagerness to get on with her life was further evident in her eagerness to accept the domestic placement her caseworker secured for her in a nursing home. Two years later, when the caseworker reopened the file to find out what had become of her client, she found that, to her obvious delight, the woman was still employed at the same place.[26]

The counsellor's readiness to accept Karlinsky's version of events – that her husband was unredeemable and the marriage definitely over – was linked to the fact that a colleague on staff had acted as the court interpreter during the divorce proceedings and could confirm the client's claim that the husband was an unrepentant brute and the woman was better off without him.

In two cases taken from the early 1960s and involving Italian women, the institute staff were similarly convinced that there was little possibility of reuniting a wife with a husband who deserted the family. In the first instance, Mrs Caruso, a forty-two-year-old mother of five young children, came to the agency after she found herself abandoned by a husband to whom she had been married for fifteen years. The husband, who had a history of mental illness, had also been abusive towards his wife. Caruso had been referred to the institute by a social worker employed with a local community agency, the Neighbourhood Workers Association, in the hopes that the Italian-speaking volunteers might establish 'a friendly relationship' with her and enlist her into the reception centre's program. At the institute, the professional social worker assigned to the case agreed with his colleague's assessment, noting that the woman ought to be encouraged to break out of the isolation of her home and become more involved in her wider community. The pertinent file entry reads: '[She] is culturally isolated and is not involved with either the English or Italian community ... She seems to be interested in learning English but is hindered because she has three children at home. The three eldest children are attending [an elementary school].' Over the next few years, the institute acted much as a surrogate family, dispatching Italian volunteers to visit the woman, encouraging her to register her children in summer day camps, and even enlisting her in English and 'kitchen' classes while volunteers watched her children.[27]

The institute caseworkers apparently did not consider the possibility that Caruso might enter the workforce. She had neither experience in the labour force nor relatives with whom she might leave her young children, and as an older woman she was not an attractive prospect to employers. The caseworkers seemed resigned to the fact that, at least until her children grew up, she would remain dependent on government welfare benefits and other social services. This situation contrasts sharply, however, with the second Italian case in which the deserted wife had been a working woman with considerable experience in the workforce. Thus, when this woman, the mother of four teenage boys, found herself abandoned by her husband shortly after she experienced a workplace injury, the thrust of the caseworker's response was to secure the woman compensation payments until she could return once again to the workforce.[28]

As these cases suggest, the institute counsellors often found themselves having to recommend or accept remedies to a particular situation that they considered less than ideal. While they might have preferred that a woman compelled by circumstance to abandon a marriage might one day remarry and resume a 'normal' two-parent family arrangement, their daily experience also taught them that the chances of this happening were slim. They recognized there had to be some alternative for these female-headed households lest they become seduced into dependency. A single mother's entry into the workforce, especially when it might help to keep her family from either poverty or dependency, was considered far the lesser of two evils.

In seeking to find appropriate solutions to their clients' predicament, the institute caseworkers did not always respond in a consistent fashion. While a model of the ideal family influenced their assessments, other factors, such as the fear of fueling a racist backlash, were at times equally compelling. Thus when in the spring of 1958 a Hungarian woman who had been raped by a compatriot living in the same boarding house came to the institute wanting to lay assault charges against the man, the counsellors persuaded her and her husband to keep the matter quiet. A statement, filed some days after the event, reveals the caseworkers' motives: 'Acting on the premise that the more publicity given to such cases, the more difficult would be our general job, we decided to try to settle this out of court.' In the end, they convinced the woman to drop the charges on the condition that the institute find the couple 'better accommodation.' The case ends with a familiar, class-specific explanation of male aggression. 'As with so many cases,' the entry reads, the incident 'had arisen out of the frustration of poor lodgings, lack of employment for the men, and the general insecurity.'[29]

Although they required a great deal of attention, the cases of abandoned wives, as noted earlier, made up a small proportion of a counsellor's workload. More typically, when the institute intervened in the life of a family whose husband was absent, the man had been only temporarily removed on account of illness or injury. In these instances, as the following case involving Mrs De Rosa demonstrates, it was quite common for the institute staff to see themselves as stepping in temporarily until the husband could resume his position as the head of the household and family breadwinner. De Rosa was a Portuguese woman whose husband contracted tuberculosis and was hospitalized in the Ontario Sanitorium in 1958. He husband's illness left De Rosa, a young mother who had recently given birth, facing outstanding mortgage payments on a house the couple had recently purchased.

During the course of the next two years, the institute staff kept tabs on the woman, referring her to a lawyer who helped her to sell the house (though at a substantial financial loss to the couple), dispatching volunteers for home visits and English lessons, filling out application forms for welfare benefits, as well as helping her to move to a location nearer the hospital so she might visit her husband regularly. When it became clear that her welfare benefits were insufficient for her family's needs, her institute caseworker, a professional social worker, and the staff supervisor also recommended her to a local chapter of the IODE, which agreed to pay the woman's grocery and outstanding gas and heating bills. By offering De Rosa regular support, the institute staff were in effect helping her to continue to fulfil her domestic responsibilities and to maintain close relations with her husband. As the file comes to an end, it seems clear that her caseworker expects the husband will soon be on his feet and the family reunited.[30]

The priority that prevailing notions about family gave to women's domesticity were amply illustrated by those cases where illness or injury took the wife, rather than the husband, away from the household. Consider, for example, how caseworkers responded to the problem posed by an Italian family when, in the fall of 1959, the mother was hospitalized for 'nervous exhaustion.' She was a forty-year-old woman who, since her arrival in Toronto three years previously, had been combining full-time factory work with raising a family. Convinced that the father could not adequately care for the children, his counsellor advised that the children, some of whom had become disruptive at school, be temporarily placed in a Catholic orphanage until his wife recovered. Such a response not only reflected prevailing notions about women's proper role but also the assumption that men alone could not be responsible for parenting.[31]

Men, Women and Parental Responsibilities

Women, of course, were not the only sex to whom particular gender roles had been assigned. While men were generally given far greater rein than women, they, too, were expected to meet carefully delineated family roles as hard-working husbands and authoritative but fair-minded fathers. Typically, as we have seen, the men who defied the rules did not make themselves available to social agencies, nor did they show much interest in reforming their behaviour and reintegrating themselves into their families. This makes the few occasions when husbands did receive such counselling particularly significant.

Only one case could be found in the current sample where institute caseworkers considered themselves successful at saving a marriage and reuniting a family by reforming the husband's behaviour. More typically, when clients were suspected of being irresponsible, uninformed, or neglectful parents, the women took much of the blame. When, for example, institute caseworkers suspected one family of taking a disproportionate share of the agency's weekly food voucher and clothing handouts, they decided to visit the family to determine the root of the problem. This visitor was an experienced female volunteer who conducted many of the agency's home visits in these years. Reporting on the sorry state of the household, she filed the following report:

The family has two rooms, kitchen and bathroom. When visiting them I found only Sonya (16 years) with the rest of the children. Helena [8] is suffering from chickenpox. Sonya mentioned the doctor and the medicine costs lot (sic) of money. The place was depressing, the rooms untidy, though furniture is new it looks like old because it is very badly kept. The floor was dirty. It was morning and the courtains (sic) were still in the same position as were during the night. On account of the untidiness the girl (Sonya) was very embarrassed and she didn't know where she could have an interview. In the children's room was a bed where the sick Helena sleeps together with Sonya. The boy [11] has another bed and Melissa [3] sleeps in the crib. We couldn't have an interview in the kitchen either because the floor was to[o] dirty and many unwashed dishes laying around. Finally we went into parents['] bedroom. Even though the bed was covered it was still [noticeable] the dirty bedding.

While the visitor's preoccupation with dirty bedding and unwashed dishes smacks of middle-class prejudice, her report was generally sympathetic and confirmed the client's story that her family was in a tight financial spot, a situation made worse by medical bills and the outstanding debts owed to a furniture company. In the end, however, she concluded that the mother needed 'help for budgetting,' thereby laying a large part of the problem on the woman's supposedly inefficient running of the household. In positing a recommendation that reaffirmed women's domestic role, the caseworker also engaged in some victim blaming.[32]

In contrast to the twelve deserting or abusive husbands in our sample, only three files expose an unfaithful wife and one case an abusive mother. Not surprisingly, the caseworkers were particularly nasty in their evaluation of women who left husbands, took up lovers, or had illegitimate children. While caseworkers might attribute the physical abuse of children by fathers to their cultural background, immigrant mothers were exempt from such explanations, presumably because motherly love was thought to be a universal attribute all women, regardless of race or class, ought to possess. While this general assumption smacked of sexism, the brutality of the abusive mother documented here goes some way towards explaining why the institute caseworkers were so condemnatory.

In discussing the case of the abusive mother, it should be noted that much of the evidence gathered against the woman came in the form of accusations from her estranged husband while the couple was going through a messy divorce and child custody battle. He had enlisted the help of the institute to try to get the child placed in a temporary foster home until after the legal battle. Many of his accusations, however, were later confirmed by neighbours and even one of the woman's former lovers. The husband's account of his wife's abusive behaviour towards their young daughter included engaging in sexual intercourse with men in front of the child, and sexually 'touching' the child. Although the wife denied the charges when institute staff workers approached her in family court, they were unmoved, largely because they had read a letter she had written to her husband in which she apparently revealed some damning evidence about herself. The case files do not contain the letter, but the response it evoked from one caseworker suggests the nature of its contents: 'It was terrible – disgusting the language she used. I hardly could believe that a woman was writing such things.' The caseworkers' general contempt for the woman might explain why, after the father absconded with the child in the middle of the divorce proceedings, there were no disparaging comments made about him in the file. The case ends with a lengthy letter that the husband sent to the local police department. 'I am not willing to leave the child with the mother,' he concludes, 'I tried to persuade my wife to educate the child in a normal way but it was useless. I will teach my daughter Canadian morals and not the morals of her mother.'[33]

Housekeeping Mothers and Married Women Workers

The case files often reveal a good deal more about the caseworker's approach or attitude towards the client than they do about the client. By contrast, only rarely are we treated to the unmediated voice of the client, usually in the form of a written note left for the counsellor. Even such evidence, of course, does not preclude the possibility that the client might be acting in a manipulative fashion or constructing herself as a deserving client. Most of the time we are compelled to read the version of the client's story as filtered through the caseworker's 'professional' eyes. But just as we tease from these files evidence regarding the ideological and methodological inclinations of the counsellor, so, too, can we glean valuable information about the clients themselves, even if we cannot always determine their emotional or psychological state. At times, even the silences and absences in the files speak volumes. A consideration of the files reveals, for example, that while the counsellors' professional biases might have led them to depict many of their female clients as victims lacking the wherewithal or resources to tackle their difficulties, the women cannot simply be dismissed as either passive victims or passive recipients of the welfare apparatus. Even Mrs Gabura of our opening story, though obviously the victim of a cruel husband and materially disadvantaged as a single mother, cannot simply be labelled a passive victim who allowed herself to be processed by a team of specialists. While she benefited from the support she received from the institute staff, she chose, in the end, to take matters into her own hands, a decision that appeared to correspond with a new-found sense of confidence following her recovery from her suicide attempt.

If caseworkers might have found it difficult to see Gabura and the other battered and abandoned women they encountered in their office as protagonists, the same cannot be said for their response to the far more numerous women who came to them in search of work or other forms of short-term, practical aid. Hundreds of immigrant housewives, most of them mothers of young children, showed up at the institute in these years, ready to collect clothing donations, food vouchers, and other handouts. Mothers with newborns picked up baby layettes; others attended the institute's free picnics and Easter and Christmas parties so they could collect the food baskets and presents for the children. Often, the woman had been directed to the agency by relatives or neighbours who had themselves benefited from the services the institute offered. For many of these families, the institute was not a substitute for support from family and kin; rather, it was an additional form of support.

Apart from trying to weed out fraudulent requests for aid – a preoccupation that might lead them to conduct home visits – the institute staff found little difficulty in processing these cases. When they did express concern for these clients and their families, it was one born of a frustration that they were not more successful in recruiting immigrant housewives into their English classes, civics lectures, and other programs offered through the reception centre. As late as 1967, for example, staff workers identified as a primary goal 'a need to meet the house-bound wife, with small children.'[34] The interest they showed in immigrant housewives reflected a genuine interest in providing a forum in which non-English-speaking women living in the isolation of their homes might make some contact with the wider society. This, in turn, was linked to their larger commitment to encourage immigrant mothers to convert to Canadian ways. In these aims, however, they were thwarted by the clients themselves, many of whom adopted a pragmatic approach to the agency. Most of the housewives in our sample, for example, declined to become members of the institute or to enrol in any of the programs offered through its reception centre. No doubt, heavy domestic duties and cultural differences partially explain why these women did not participate. But their behaviour more accurately reflected the selective ways in which many of these women made use of available services.

In seeking such forms of aid, the immigrant housewives did not, of course, pose a challenge to prevailing notions about woman's domesticity. By contrast, however, the image of the married woman worker did not conform to the hegemonic ideal of womanhood. By far the most common reason prompting married women to approach the institute was to secure help in finding a job so that they could contribute to their family's limited finances. Married women who were living in two-parent households, most of them with children, made up a majority of the female job placement cases. Fully 70 per cent of our sample deal with women seeking paid work, of whom close to two-thirds were married. The vast majority of the placements, or 95 per cent, involved domestic service placements and factory work, where many immigrant women were already employed. Indeed, immigrant women accounted for a significant share of the growing numbers of married women who entered the Canadian workforce in the two decades after the Second World War. By 1961, European-born women represented more than one-third of Toronto's total female labour force.[35]

The high proportion of married immigrant women in the workforce or seeking paid work reflected, above all, economic need related to the inability of the husband to earn a wage sufficient to support a wife and children. As scholars have observed for earlier periods, women's role as the family's secondary wage earner was a dramatic illustration of the great gap between the ideology of family breadwinner and reality: most working-class (and some middle-class) men could not earn a wage sufficient to support their families. The immediate post–Second World War era was no exception, particularly as it pertained to immigrant wage earners. But whereas in an earlier era the family's additional wage earner might more commonly have been a son and/or daughter, the general youthfulness of immigrant families in these years, coupled with more stringent schooling laws and plentiful job opportunities for low-skilled women in cities like Toronto, largely explains the higher number of immigrant wives who took up the slack.[36]

That so many married women came to the institute seeking jobs further attests to this fact. As the case files indicate, married women's work was prompted by economic need and their movement in and out of the workforce was largely determined by the demands of their family. Some women sought jobs to augment the income being earned by husbands in low-skilled jobs. It was just such a predicament that prompted the wife of a Hungarian factory worker to come to the institute looking for work in the summer of 1959. Her caseworker, an East-European professional recently recruited onto the institute's volunteer staff, evidently considered it unfortunate that a young mother should be compelled to enter the workforce, but he nonetheless obliged. His response was based on a recognition that the woman's pay cheque could prevent the family from falling into serious debt: 'Husband earnings $0.80 per hour in a small factory. Can hardly live on his earnings. Needs urgently some work to help out. Very shy, helpless looking but pleasant personality.' She was placed as a domestic.[37] In other cases, the sudden injury or seasonal lay-off of a husband prompted nonworking wives like Mrs Dos Santos to seek temporary jobs to keep family finances afloat. She was a Portuguese woman and mother of two children whose husband had been laid off from his construction job in November 1960 and received $36.00 per month on unemployment benefits. She landed a factory job earning $8.00 per day. Three months later, when the husband was again employed, she informed her caseworker that she was quitting work, saying that someone had to watch the young children. The following winter, however, when the husband once again found himself out of work, she returned to the agency and accepted a placement as a cleaning lady in a private home.[38] Similar scenarios appear again and again in the files, and they suggest the selective way in which many women made use of the institute.

Given the ideological predilection of the institute counsellors, one might have expected them to have expressed considerable anxiety, if not hostility, about the remarkably high numbers of married women they encountered wanting a paid job. And yet, just as the files involving single mothers described earlier indicate, their responses revealed a less rigid adherence to prevailing gender assumptions than we might expect.

To be sure, in their responses to working women, the institute counsellors did distinguish between single and married women. Unless it concerned some unrelated factor pertaining to the woman's apparently disagreeable personality or her allegedly poor work habits, none of the cases in our sample involving single women seeking paid employment were cause for comment. This tacit approval of the single woman worker is not surprising given that unmarried immigrant women were expected to seek paid employment. Large numbers of single immigrant women, after all, had been recruited by immigration officials precisely to fill labour shortages, especially in domestic service.[39]

By contrast, the case records of married women workers suggest that caseworkers preferred that married women remain in the household. They shared the commonly expressed view that the working wife might threaten the delicate gender balance that defined relations between husband and wife. When, for example, a mother of two children enlisted the help of the institute to get a hospital job, her counsellor, a volunteer female caseworker, advised her client to stay at home with the children at least until they were old enough to begin school, 'as they need her to adjust to the new environment.'[40]

But this file also reveals a significant degree of tolerance for the working mother, for the woman's caseworker also advised her client that, while her sons were preschoolers, she learn English and thus improve her chances for a better paying job in the near future. Often, the tolerance they showed such clients was linked to the caseworker's perception that a wife's entry into the labour force was intended as a temporary (and in many cases, seasonal) intervention – to keep her family from falling over the brink of poverty or to enable her family to accumulate some savings and purchase a home. It was generally assumed that once a husband had established himself, the wife would return to the household. And if the home to which she returned was no longer the multiple-family dwelling so characteristic of the housing arrangements of recent immigrants, so much the better. At least in the short-term, however, the overall needs of the immigrant family – whatever was needed to ensure a more smooth economic adjustment – took temporary precedence over the concern that men and women be encouraged to fulfil their prescribed roles.

The following two case histories, each one of them depicting scenarios in which the wife had become the family's sole breadwinner, nicely capture this complex dynamic. In each case, the counsellor faced the task of advising the unemployed husband, who saw his breadwinner wife as a sign of his failure as a husband and father. The first involved a Hungarian couple who, in 1956, came to the institute looking to find the husband a job. While his wife had for months been employed in an office, he had been completely unsuccessful on the job market ever since their arrival in the country. In the absence of his wife, the husband explained that he had 'lost his confidence' and 'felt depressed' about having to depend on his wife's earnings. In responding to his client, the caseworker was sympathetic. However, rather than try to place the man in a job, the caseworker suggested to him that since his wife apparently did not mind working, he should consider registering in the centre's English classes to improve his chances of securing a better-paying job. Although the man agreed, he never returned.[41]

The same caseworker had more success one year later with a Yugoslavian man who was similarly upset after being laid off from his factory job. In complaining about his predicament, the client claimed he opposed his wife's working since he would 'lose prestige with his friends.' In response, the caseworker advised the client, who had been a university graduate back home, to ignore his friends and consider pursuing a trade degree while his wife supported him and their young son.

In this way, he could, on graduation, land a well-paying job and support his family on his own. The man returned to school and, three years later, the final entry of the case history indicates that the expected had in fact occurred.[42]

The institute caseworkers, in their daily encounter with female clients, showed a far less rigid adherence to the dominant rhetoric regarding the inappropriateness of working wives than was evident in the writings and legislation of family and welfare experts of the period.[43] In explaining this pattern, economic factors clearly loom large. First-hand experience with hundreds of clients had taught the staff members of the institute's Department of Individual Services (and, for that matter, their colleagues elsewhere) the critical economic role that many women within immigrant and working-class families played as the family's secondary wage earner. Indeed, one might also argue that, notwithstanding the dominant rhetoric of the day, staff workers were well aware that the married woman worker was in these years becoming an increasingly familiar figure. While the immigrant working wife did not correspond to the hegemonic ideal of womanhood, she nevertheless did conform to an emerging alternative pattern of married womanhood in the post-Second World War era. It might also be worth recalling that a good proportion of the caseworkers were not only themselves working married women but also refugees and immigrants. Despite differences in class (or wealth) between them and their women clients, the European women volunteer counsellors might also have felt some empathy for their compatriots who came to them for help in getting work.

Conclusion

While a preliminary consideration of a few hundred case files belonging to one immigrant aid society cannot offer an exhaustive analysis of the busy and sometimes chaotic world of the social worker's office, the confidential case records of the International Institute of Metropolitan Toronto provide us with an opportunity to begin an exploration of the complex relations that developed between the economically disadvantaged non-British immigrants who entered postwar Canada and the middle-class professionals and volunteers who sought to intervene in and even regulate the lives of their ethnic clients. Strongly committed to the process of guiding the integration of the postwar immigrants into Canadian life, the men and women who staffed the institute's Individual Services operated within a decidedly gendered notion of what constituted the ideal family, and they also saw themselves as having the right to intervene in the lives of deviants. At the same time, however, they were concerned that the 'disorganized families' they encountered (to return to Schlesinger's phrase) did not in the long run become a dependent or 'multi-problem family.'

As the frustration they expressed over their inability to exert a more permanent influence over some of their clients suggests, the institute counsellors were not dealing with passive recipients who could easily be remoulded. To a considerable degree, their success or failure in a particular case was contingent upon many factors, including the client's willingness to cooperate with her caseworker. In this regard, the case files hint at the diversity of relationships forged between caseworker and woman client, ranging from brief or hostile encounters to extended counselling sessions. This calls into question the easy generalization of immigration historians who have assumed that the relations between newcomers and the host society's 'caretakers' were necessarily and irrevocably hostile. A battered wife might well prefer the company of her female counsellor to her husband. Nevertheless, as Gordon has astutely observed, the relationship between caseworker and client was always one between unequal players. The assistance of even sympathetic counsellors was offered in the hope that they might eventually be successful in imposing a North American and middle-class model of the family.[44] Far from exhibiting any inclination to adopt or mimic Canadian customs, many of the institute's women clients responded in a pragmatic fashion to the institute, taking advantage of its services to meet their own needs as they defined them. And on more than one occasion, the institute counsellors, in turn, were compelled by their clients to agree to assist them in ways that they, as the experts, did not necessarily condone.

NOTES

This abbreviated article is from *Gender Conflicts: New Essays in Women's History,* ed. Franca Iacovetta and Mariana Valverde. Toronto: University of Toronto Press, 1992. Reprinted with permission.

1 Archives of Ontario (AO), International Institute of Metropolitan Toronto (IIMT), Confidential Case Files, Series F-3, case 89. In order to protect the anonymity of clients and caseworkers alike, and to meet the terms under which I was permitted access to the records, I have used fictitious names

and, in recounting case histories, have either eliminated or modified bio-graphical detail. I have quoted verbatim from the files; unless otherwise stated, where a client is quoted, I have relied on the words recorded by the caseworker. In referencing the 320 case files that make up the data base for the paper, I have assigned each case a number from 1 to 320. My coding system bears no resemblance to that used by the institute. For a valuable discussion of methodological issues concerning the historian's use of social-work files see Linda Gordon, *Heroes of Their Own Lifes: The Politics and History of Family Violence* (New York: Penguin 1980).

2 Both quotations are David A. Stewart and are cited in AO, IIMT, MU6444, File: Group Services, *Annual Report* 1958–9.

3 MU6474, File: Immigrant Assistance 1957–61, Memorandum, 'History of the Institute'; MU6447, File: Individual Services Department 1961–4, Report on First Year 1956–7

4 MU6444, File: Human Rights, A. Sandberg to W.E. West, 18 April 1963; West to Sandberg, 18 April 1963; Minutes of Meeting with Human Rights Commission, 26 April 1963

5 MU6390, File: Personnel 1964–73, Personnel Code

6 MU6474, File: Reception Centre 1960, Progress Report, nd (c. 1960). See also ibid., D. Stewart to W.E. West, 19 Jan. 1958; AO, Local Council of Women (LCW) Collection, Local Council of Women of Toronto, *Minute Books*, Minutes of Meeting, 15 Nov. 1949, 25 Jan. 1954

7 MU6390, J. Gellner to C. Bourquet, 19 Oct. 1973 File: Board of Directors, Executive Minutes

8 MU6444, File: Group Services, *Annual Report* 1958–9

9 On the institute see, for example, MU6474 File: Reception Centre 1960, Minutes of the Meeting of the Executive, 5 Dec. 1960; MU6444, File: Group Services General 1956–64, File on Students' Cultural Nights; File: Current Programme 1955–63 Memorandum, nd. See also LCW *Minute Books*, Minutes of Meetings, 28 Jan. and 15 Nov. 1949, 17 Oct. 1950, 20 Nov. 1951, and 25 Jan. 1954; Woman's Christian Temperance Union, *Annual Report*, Minutes of Provincial Annual Meeting, May 1953; National Archives of Canada (NA), Imperial Order Daughters of the Empire, MG 28, file 14, vol. 24, File on IODE Anti-Communist Committee: NA, MG 26, Canadian Citizenship Council, File on Pamphlets and Immigrant Education, Vol. 70. On the Canadian government and immigrants during and immediately after the Second World War see Reginald Whitaker, *Double Standard: The Secret History of Canadian Immigration* (Toronto: Lest & Orpen Dennys 1978); and essays in Norman Hillmer, Bohdan Kordan, and Lubomyr Luciuk, eds., *On Guard for Thee: Ethnicity and the Canadian State*, 1939–45 (Ottawa: Canadian Committee for the

History of the Second World War 1988), especially N.F. Dreisziger, 'The Rise
of a Bureaucracy for Multiculturalism: The Origins of the Nationalities
Branch, 1939–1941.' My thanks to Ramsay Cook for bringing this work to my
attention, and to Fred Dreisziger for fielding my questions regarding his
research. As part of my larger study on postwar immigrants I am investigat-
ing the records of the Citizenship Branch at the National Archives.

10 Gellner to Bourquet, 19 Oct. 1973, as in note 10 above

11 Unfortunately, no complete list of staff and volunteers appears to be available. My observations are largely based on my reading of the case files, but
other materials proved helpful. For example, see MU6474, File: Job Classification, Personnel Memorandum, nd, MU6390, File: Personnel, Memorandum on Policies and Duties of Officers; Minutes of the Meeting of the
Executive, 11 Sept. 1961, 17 May 1965; File Reception Centre 1960, Counselling Service Report, 1 and 4 April 1960; MU6463, File: Individual Services/
Group Services, Reports of Individual Services, 1959–61; MU6446, File: Individual Services Department, Activity Reports 1961–4.

12 MU6384, *Annual Report* 1962, 1964

13 Historical studies of the social work profession in the early post-Second
World War era is scanty. Valuable material can be found in Gordon, *Heroes of
Their Own Lives*; James Leiby, *A History of Social Welfare and Social Work in the
United States* (New York: Columbia University Press 1978); Amitai Etzioni,
ed., *The Semi-Professions and Their Organization: Teachers, Nurses, Social Work-
ers* (New York: Free Press 1969); James Struthers, *'No Fault of Their Own':
Unemployment and the Canadian Welfare State 1914–1941* (Toronto: University
of Toronto Press 1983); his recent 'How Much Is Enough? Creating a Social
Minimum in Ontario, 1930–44,' *Canadian Historical Review* 72, 1 (1991); Caro-
line Andrew, 'Women and the Welfare State,' *Canadian Journal of Political Science* 17, 4 (1984); Allan Moscovitch, *The Welfare State in Canada* (Waterloo:
Wilfrid Laurier Press 1983); Allan Moscovitch and Jim Albert, eds., *The
Benevolent State: The Growth of Welfare in Canada* (Toronto: Garamond Press
1987): Jacquelyn Gale Wills, 'Efficiency, Feminism and Cooperative Democracy: Origins of the Toronto Social Planning Council' (PhD thesis, University
of Toronto 1989).

14 Dr Robert Kreem, Address to the IODE, St George Chapter, Toronto 28 March
1966, MU6474, File: Immigration General 1964–7

15 LCW *Minute Books*, Minutes of Meeting, 20 May 1952

16 Ruth Roach Pierson, *'They're Still Women after All': The Second World War and
Canadian Womanhood* (Toronto: McClelland and Stewart 1986); her '"Home-
Aide": A Solution to Women's Unemployment after World War II,' *Atlantis* 2,
2 (spring 1977); Alison Prentice et al., *Canadian Women: A History* (Toronto:

Harcourt, Brace, Jovanovich 1988), chap. 12: Yvonne Mathews-Klein, 'How
They Saw Us: Images of Women in National Film Board Films of the 1940's
and 1950's,' *Atlantis* 4, 2 (spring 1979); Susan Bland, 'Henrietta the Home-
maker and "Rosie the Riveter": Images of Women in Advertising in
Maclean's Magazine, 1939–50,' *Atlantis* 8 (spring 1983); Linda Ambrose,
'"Youth, Marriage and the Family": The Report of the Canadian Youth Com-
mission's Family Committee, 1943–1948,' paper presented to the Canadian
Historical Association Annual Meeting, Queen's University, June 1991;
Veronica Strong-Boag, '"Getting on with Life": Women and the Suburban
Experience in Canada 1945–1960,' unpublished paper, Feb. 1990. My thanks
to Nikki Strong-Boag for sending me her paper. For contemporary examples
see M.J. Henshaw, 'UNRRA in the role of Foster Parent,' *Social Worker* 15, 1
(Sept. 1946P: 11–15; 'Entry of Displaced Persons to Canada,' *Social Worker* 16,
1 (Sept. 1947): 7–9; William Glen, 'Social Workers New Unity of Purpose,'
Social Worker 18, 5 (June 1950): 22–5; Josie Svanhuit, 'Multi-Problem Family
or Multi-Agency Problem?' *Social Worker* 31, 4 (Oct. 1963): 14–16.
17 Elinor G. Barstead, 'The Ordinary Family in Extraordinary Times,' *Social
Worker* 16, 2 (Dec. 1947): 1–9
18 LCW *Minute Book*, Minutes of Meeting, 19 Feb. 1952
19 Ruth Roach Pierson, 'Gender and the Unemployment Debates in Canada,
1934–1940,' *Labour/Le Travail* 25 (spring 1990): her '"The Married Woman
Worker" and Canadian Unemployment Insurance Policy, 1934–1950,' paper
presented to the Berkshire Conference on the History of Women, Rutgers
University, June 1990; Prentice et al., *Canadian Women*, 311–14; Susan Prentice, 'Workers, Mothers, Reds: Toronto's Postwar Daycare Fight,' paper presented to the Canadian Studies Conference, University of Edinburgh, May
1990. See also Denise Riley, 'Some Peculiarities in Social Policy Concerning
Women in Wartime and Postwar Britain,' in Margaret Randolph Higonnet et
al., eds., *Behind the Lines: Gender and the Two World Wars* (New Haven: Yale
University Press 1987).
20 Eva Kenyon, Eileen Titus, Alice Hall, 'The Perpetual Crisis,' *Social Worker* 22,
4 (April 1954): 3–3
21 Strong-Boag, 'Getting On With Life': references in note 22. See also Shirley
Tillotson, 'Government and the Privacy of Leisure: A Gender Analysis of
Public/Private Dualisms in Ontario's Recreation Movement, 1945–1955,'
paper presented to the Canadian Historical Association Annual Meeting,
Queen's University, June 1991.
22 See the discussion in Betty K. Isserman, 'The Casework Relationship in Work
with Unmarried Mothers,' *Social Worker* 17, 1 (June 1951): 12–17.
23 Benjamin Schlesinger, 'Socio-Cultural Elements in Casework – The Cana-

dian Scene,' ibid., 30, 1 (Jan. 1962); 40–7. See also J. Kage, 'From "Bohunk"
to "New Canadian,"' ibid. 29, 4 (Oct. 1961); his 'The Jewish Immigrant Aid
Society of Canada (JIAS) Social Services for Immigrants,' ibid. 18, 3 (Feb.
1960): 21–5; Brigitta L. Ball, 'With a Hungarian Accent,' ibid. 26, 1 (Oct.
1957): 30–43. On Canada's earlier medical experts see Eleoussa Polyzoi,
'Psychologists' Perceptions of the Canadian Immigrant Before World War
II,' *Canadian Ethnic Studies* 18, 1 (1968): Barbara Roberts, 'Doctors and
Deports: The Role of the Medical Profession in Canadian Deportation,
1900–20,' ibid. 3 (1986).
24 Gordon, *Heroes*, chap. 3: Leiby, *Social Welfare and Social Work*, 283–5; Svanhuit,
'Multi-Problem Family'
25 Case 121
26 Case 54
27 Case 311
28 Case 173
29 Report on case, MU6505, File: Case Histories (not restricted)
30 Case 143
31 Case 283
32 Case 17
33 Case 41
34 MU6339, File: K. Brown Staff Meetings 1966–7, Staff Minutes, 6 Jan. 1967. See
also Edith Ferguson, *Newcomers in Transition* (A Project of the International
Institute of Metropolitan Toronto, 1962–4).
35 As detailed in S.J. Wilson, *Women, the Family and the Economy* (Toronto:
McGraw-Hill Ryerson 1972), 19, the percentage of married women in the
Canadian female labour force grew from 4.5 per cent in 1941, to 11.2 per cent
in 1951, and to 22 per cent in 1961. According to the unpublished census data
for Metropolitan Toronto, in 1961 the total number of women employed in
the labour force stood at 260,633. European-born women numbered 96,941.
(The data does not provide marital status.) Dominion Bureau of Statistics,
Unpublished Tables, 1961.
36 For the pre-1930 era see, for example, Michele Barrett and Mary McIntosh,
'"The Family Wage": Some Problems for Socialists and Feminists,' *Capital and
Class* 11 (1980): 51–72; Martha May, 'Bread before Roses: American Working-
men, Labor Unions and the Family Wage,' in Ruth Milkman, ed., *Women,
Work and Protest: A Century of U.S. Women's Labor History* (London: Routledge
and Kegan Paul 1985). On the postwar period see Patricia Connelly, 'Female
Labour Force Participation: Choice or Necessity? *Atlantis* 3, 2 (spring 1978);
Pat Armstrong and Hugh Armstrong, *The Double Ghetto: Canadian Women and
Their Segregated Work*, rev. ed. (Toronto: McClelland and Stewart 1984). For an

immigrant example, see my calculation regarding male and female incomes within Italian families in *Such Hardworking People*, chaps. 3 and 4.

37 Case 72

38 Case 167

39 For the immediate postwar years see, for example, Milda Danys, *DP: Lithuanian Immigration to Canada after the Second World War* (Toronto: Multicultural History Society of Ontario 1986), especially her discussion of the domestic schemes. Several studies, including Makeda Silvera, *Silenced* (Toronto: Williams Wallace 1988), deal with a later period and document the racist aspects of the domestic schemes as they were applied to West Indian women and other immigrant women of colour.

40 Case 28

41 Case 14

42 Case 109

43 See, for example, Pierson, 'Gender and the Unemployment Debates,' and her 'The Married Woman Worker.'

44 Gordon, *Heroes*, chap. 3